Snow Drop

**Volume Seven
by Choi Kyung-ah**

**English Adaptation
by Sarah Dyer**

TOKYOPOP®

HAMBURG // LONDON // LOS ANGELES // TOKYO

Snow Drop Vol. 7

created by Choi Kyung-ah

Translation - Jennifer Hahm
English Adaptation - Sarah Dyer
Associate Editor - Suzanne Waldman
Retouch and Lettering - Benchcomix
Production Artist - Jose Macasocol, Jr.
Cover Artist - Anna Kernbaum

Editor - Julie Taylor
Digital Imaging Manager - Chris Buford
Pre-Press Manager - Antonio DePietro
Production Managers - Jennifer Miller and Mutsumi Miyazaki
Art Director - Matt Alford
Managing Editor - Jill Freshney
Editor-in-Chief - Mike Kiley
VP of Production - Ron Klamert
President and C.O.O. - John Parker
Publisher and C.E.O. - Stuart Levy

A  Manga

TOKYOPOP Inc.
5900 Wilshire Blvd. Suite 2000
Los Angeles, CA 90036

E-mail: info@TOKYOPOP.com
Come visit us online at www.TOKYOPOP.com

ISBN: 1-59532-043-1

First TOKYOPOP printing: January 2005
10 9 8 7 6 5 4 3 2 1
Printed in the USA

Previously in

Snow Drop

On their trip together, the scheming
Hwi-Rim and Sun-Mi attempt to
split up So-Na and Hae-Gi. Hwi-Rim
has his mind set on one thing: the
tender love of So-Na. The excitement
goes into full bloom with a
shocking wedding and an even more
scandalous revelation about Ha-Da!

C·O·N·T·E·N·T·S

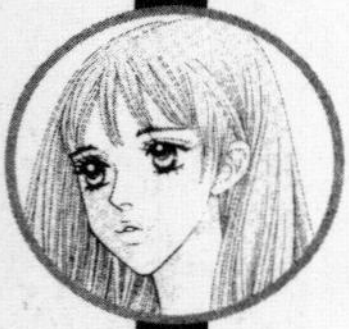

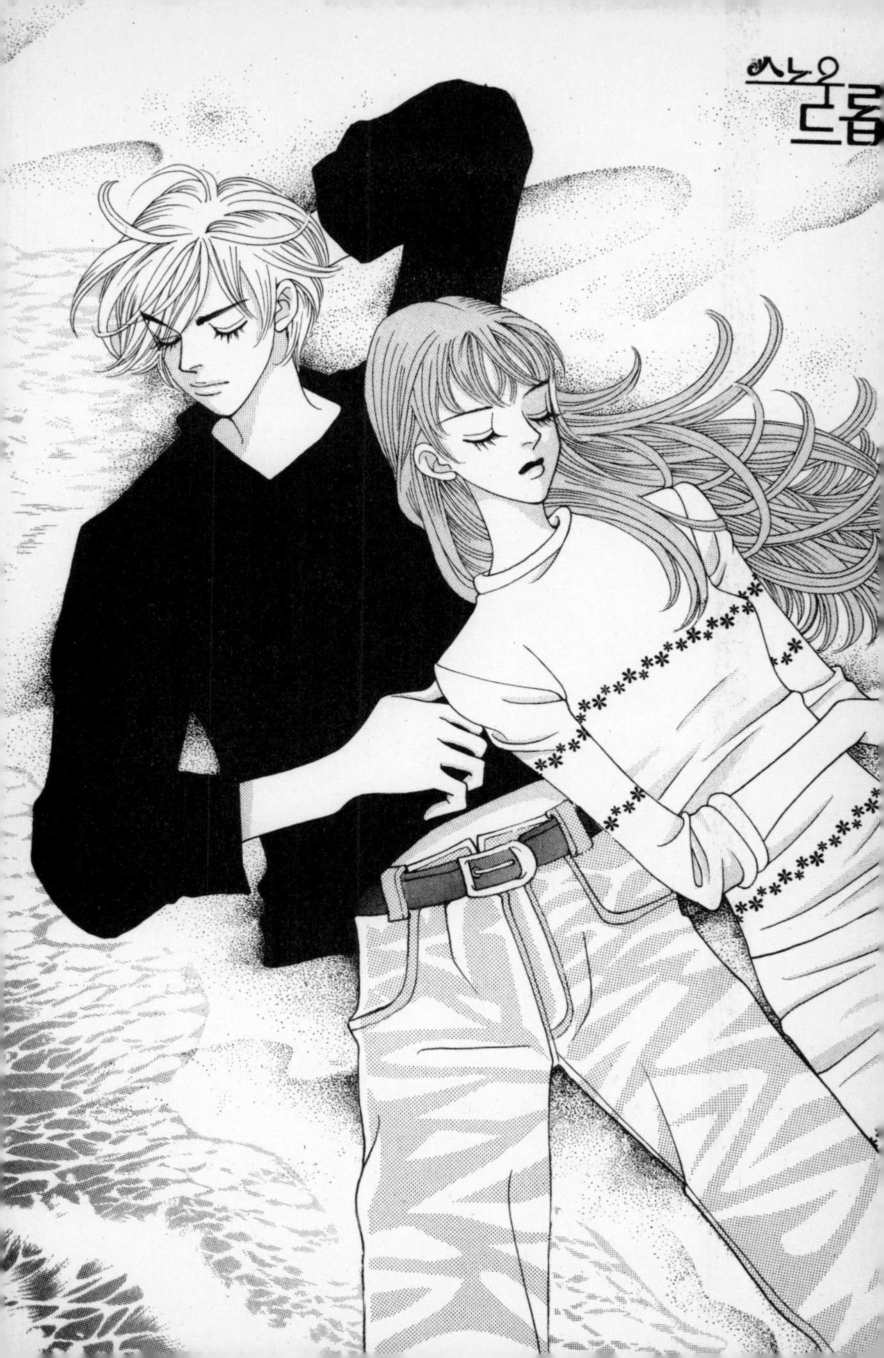
스노우 드롭

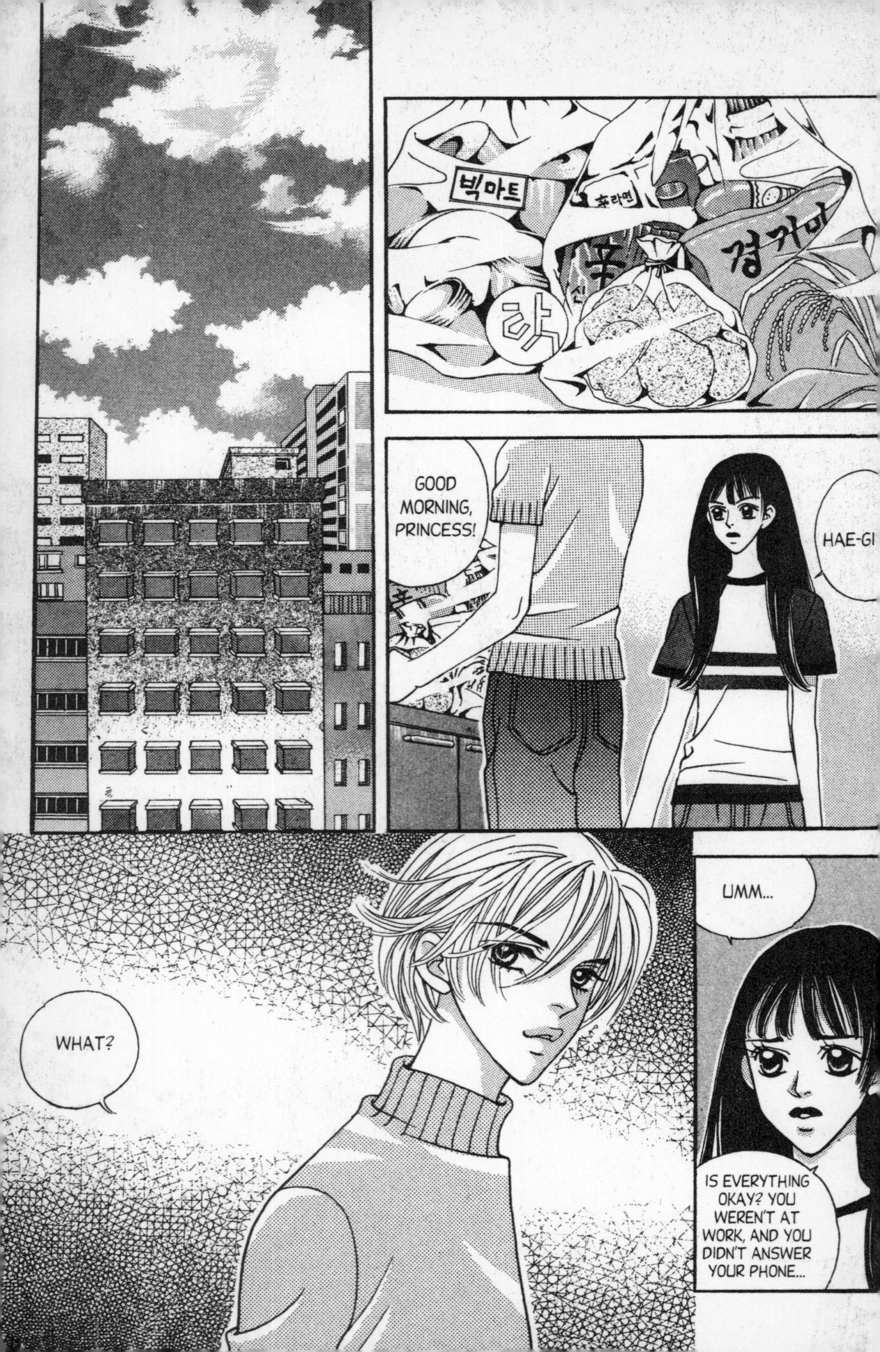
빅마트
경기미
GOOD MORNING, PRINCESS!
HAE-GI
WHAT?
UMM...
IS EVERYTHING OKAY? YOU WEREN'T AT WORK, AND YOU DIDN'T ANSWER YOUR PHONE...

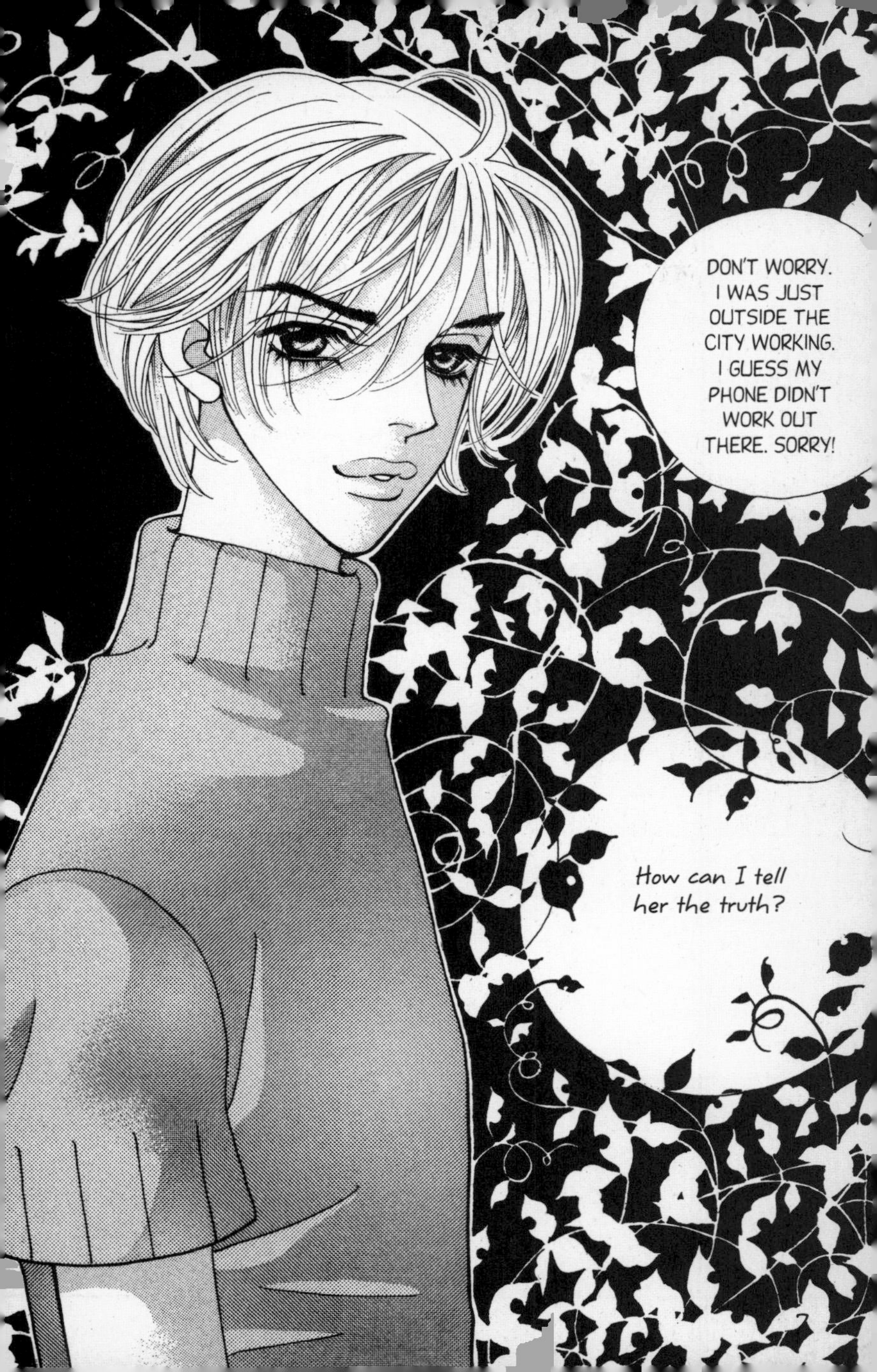
DON'T WORRY. I WAS JUST OUTSIDE THE CITY WORKING. I GUESS MY PHONE DIDN'T WORK OUT THERE. SORRY!
How can I tell her the truth?

YOU MUST BE HUNGRY, RIGHT? I EVEN GOT RICE, SO LET'S MAKE SOMETHING QUICK.

YOU CAN COOK TOO? LET'S MAKE SOMETHING TOGETHER.

The truth—that the people who watch over her attacked and threatened me.

They left my face and arms untouched...as if they knew that I was a model and they didn't want anyone to know...

OF COURSE I CAN COOK. HOW DO YOU THINK WE ATE THE WHOLE TIME MY MOM WAS IN THE HOSPITAL?

WELL, WHAT DO YOU WANT TO MAKE?

HMMM, LET'S SEE...

They even took me to the hospital and sent me home— and paid for everything.

8

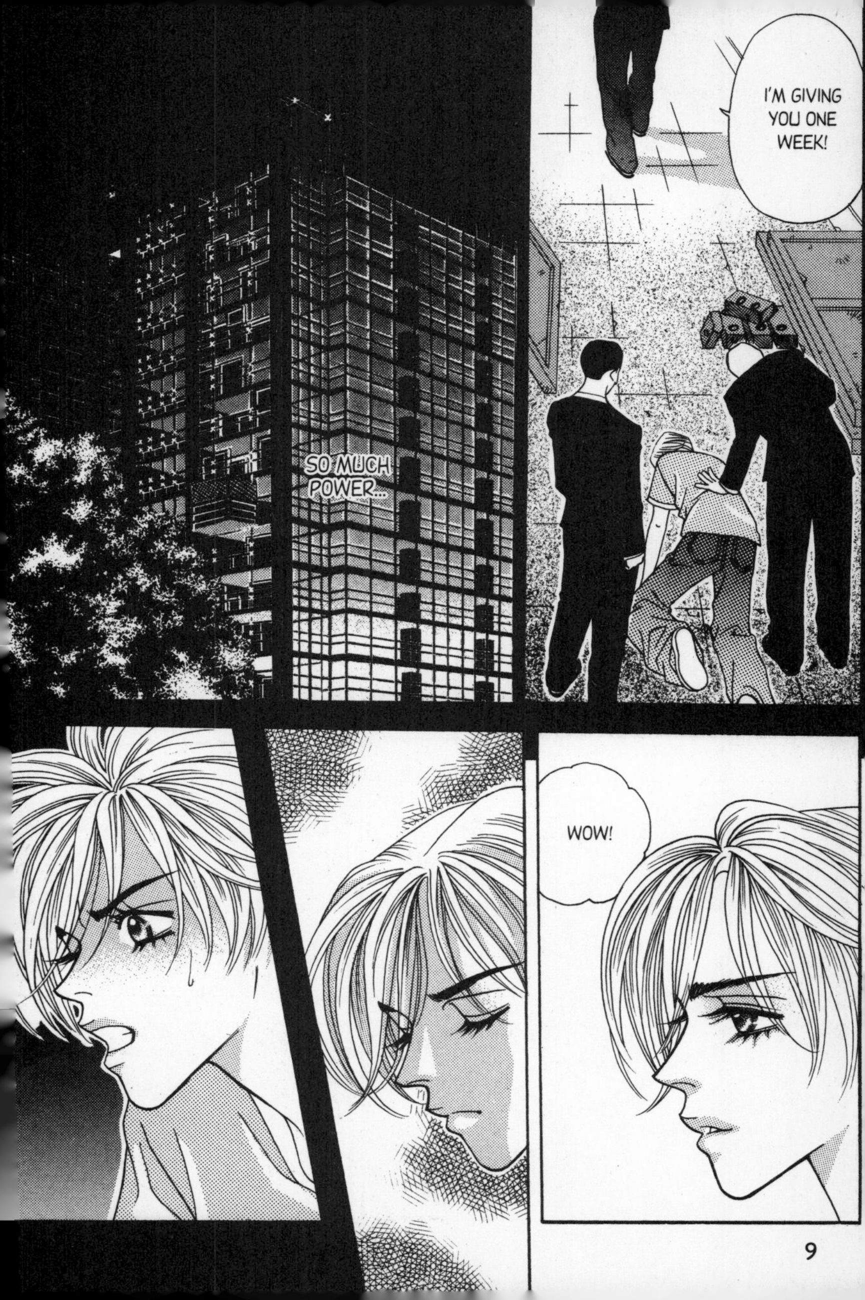
SO MUCH POWER...
I'M GIVING YOU ONE WEEK!
WOW!

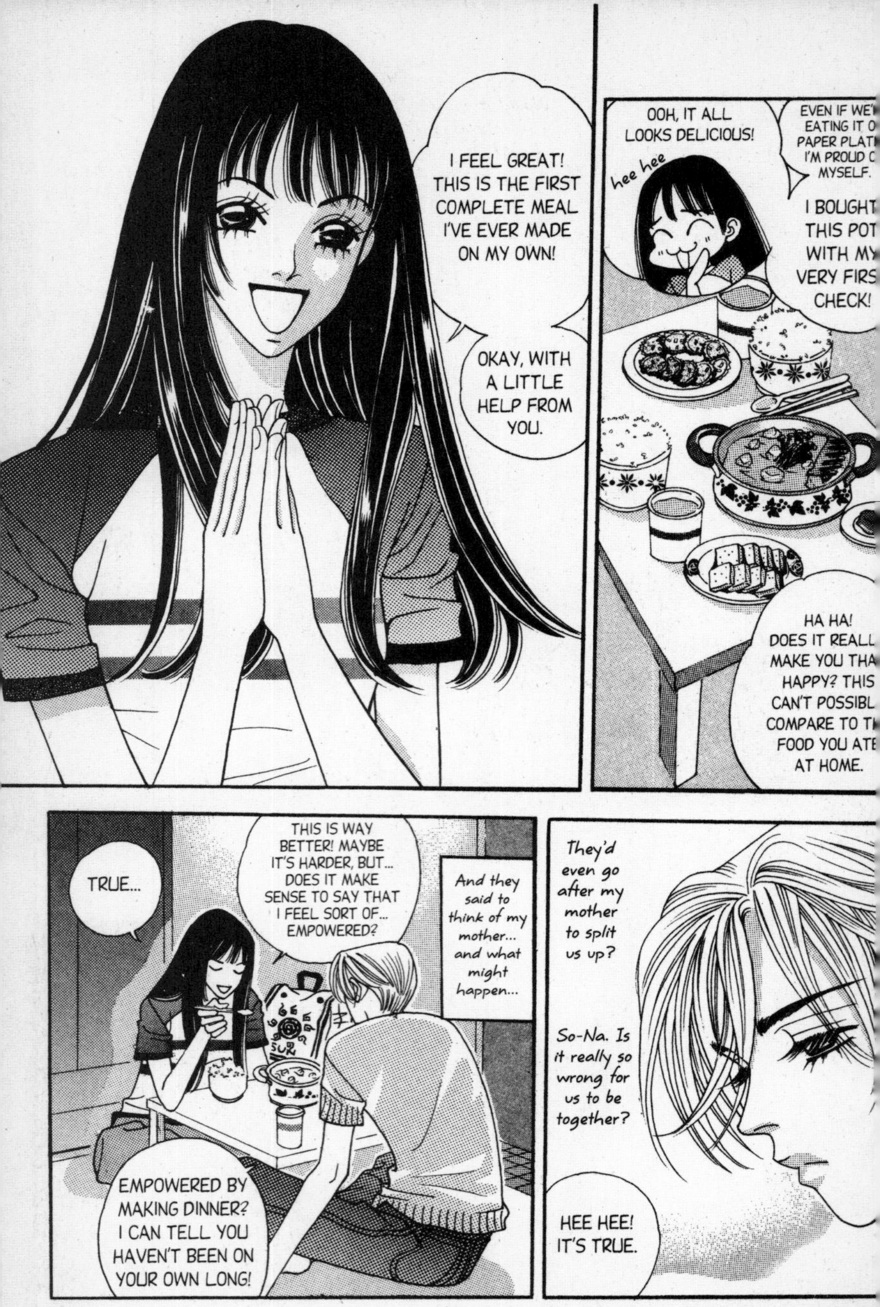
I FEEL GREAT! THIS IS THE FIRST COMPLETE MEAL I'VE EVER MADE ON MY OWN!
OKAY, WITH A LITTLE HELP FROM YOU.
OOH, IT ALL LOOKS DELICIOUS!
hee hee
EVEN IF WE' EATING IT O PAPER PLAT I'M PROUD C MYSELF.
I BOUGHT THIS POT WITH MY VERY FIRS CHECK!
HA HA! DOES IT REALL MAKE YOU THA HAPPY? THIS CAN'T POSSIBL COMPARE TO T FOOD YOU ATE AT HOME.
TRUE...
THIS IS WAY BETTER! MAYBE IT'S HARDER, BUT... DOES IT MAKE SENSE TO SAY THAT I FEEL SORT OF... EMPOWERED?
And they said to think of my mother... and what might happen...
EMPOWERED BY MAKING DINNER? I CAN TELL YOU HAVEN'T BEEN ON YOUR OWN LONG!
They'd even go after my mother to split us up?
So-Na. Is it really so wrong for us to be together?
HEE HEE! IT'S TRUE.

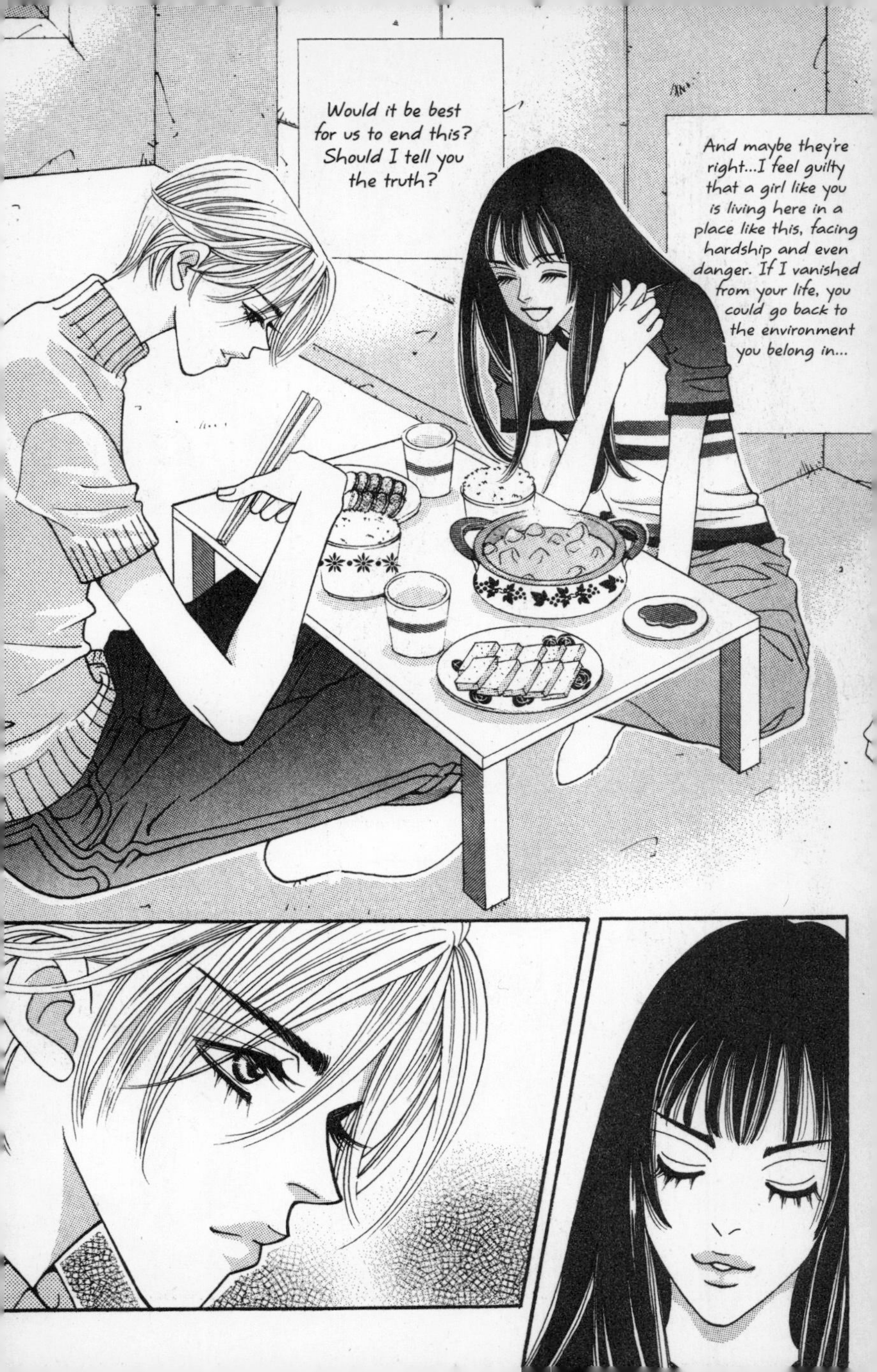
Would it be best for us to end this? Should I tell you the truth?
And maybe they're right...I feel guilty that a girl like you is living here in a place like this, facing hardship and even danger. If I vanished from your life, you could go back to the environment you belong in...

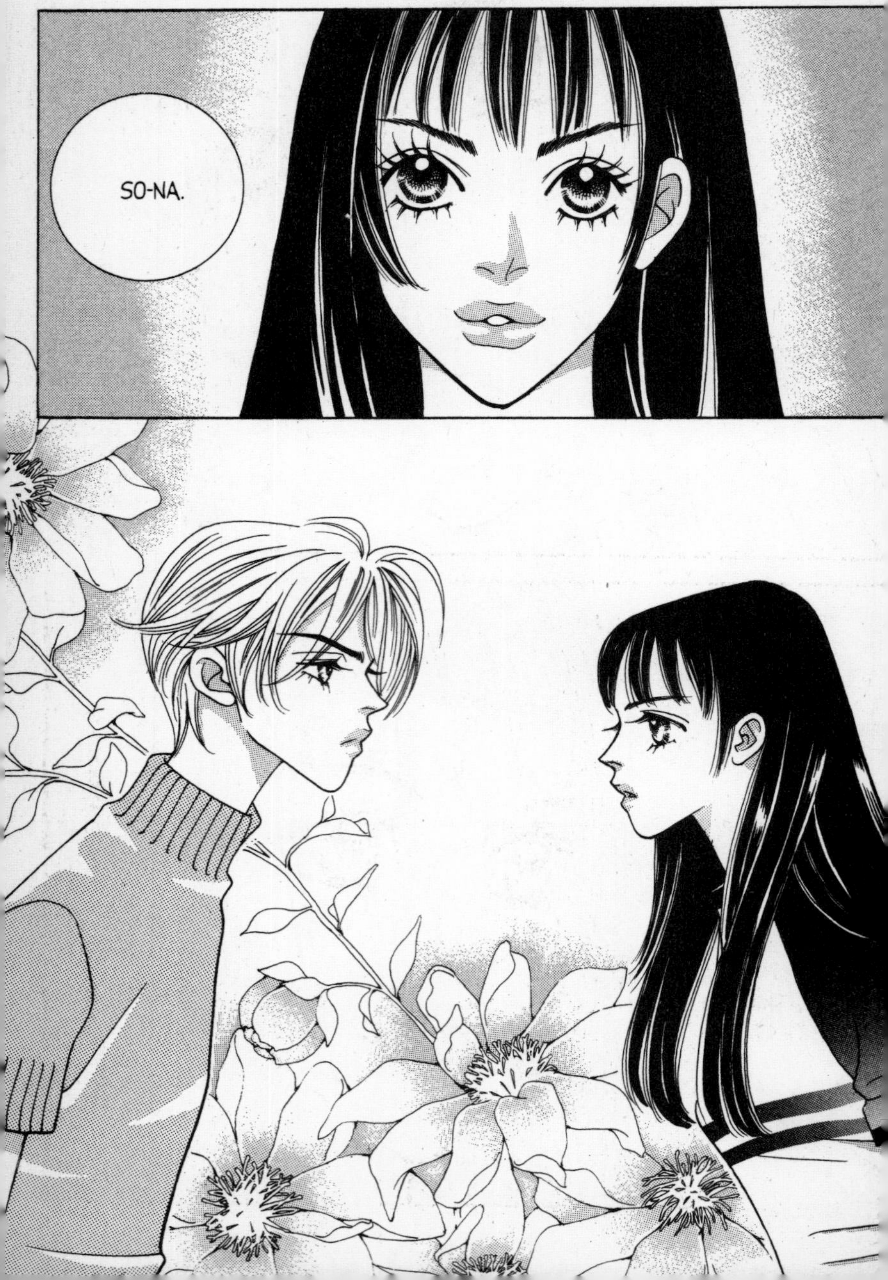
SO-NA.

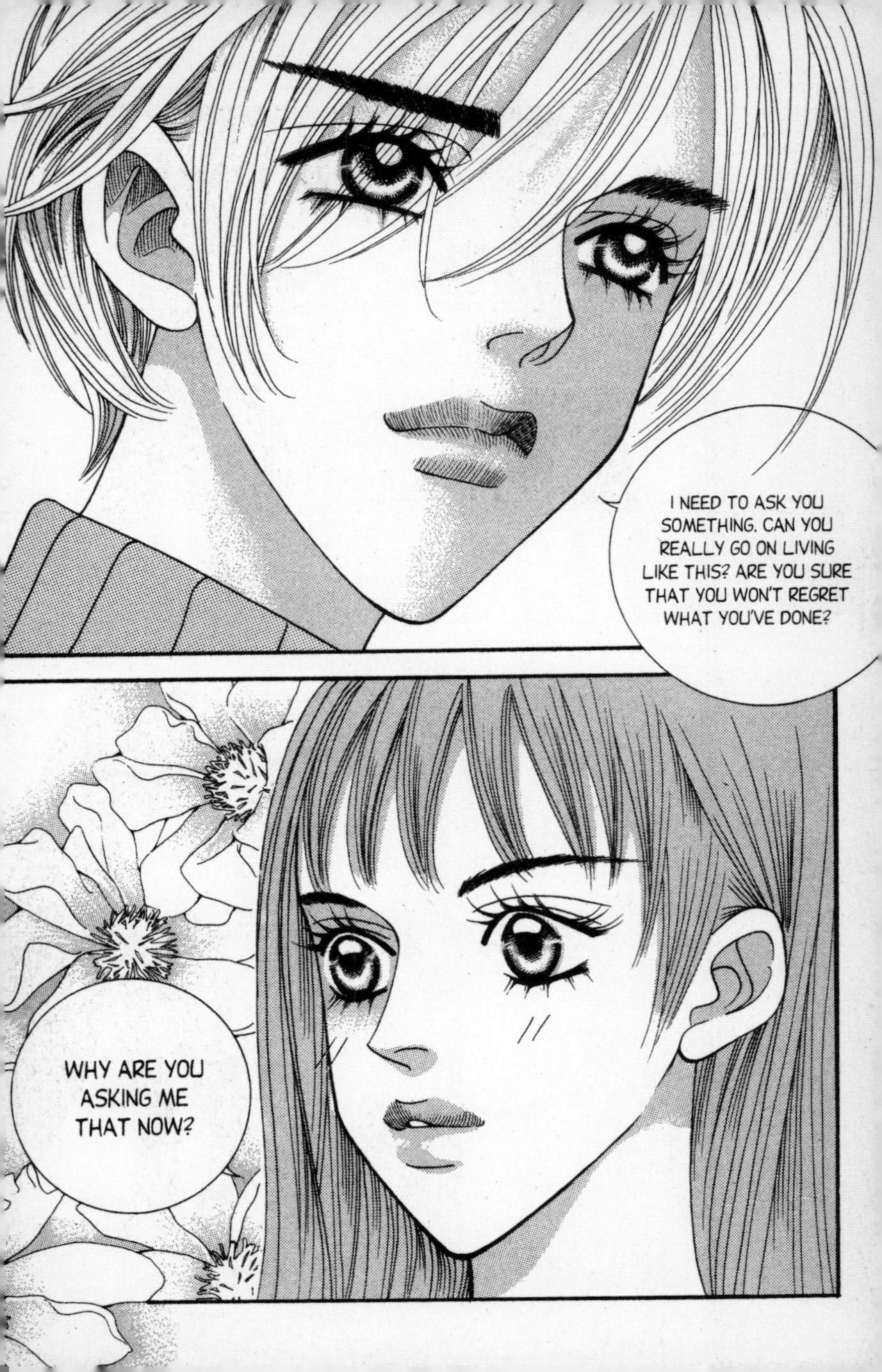
I NEED TO ASK YOU SOMETHING. CAN YOU REALLY GO ON LIVING LIKE THIS? ARE YOU SURE THAT YOU WON'T REGRET WHAT YOU'VE DONE?
WHY ARE YOU ASKING ME THAT NOW?

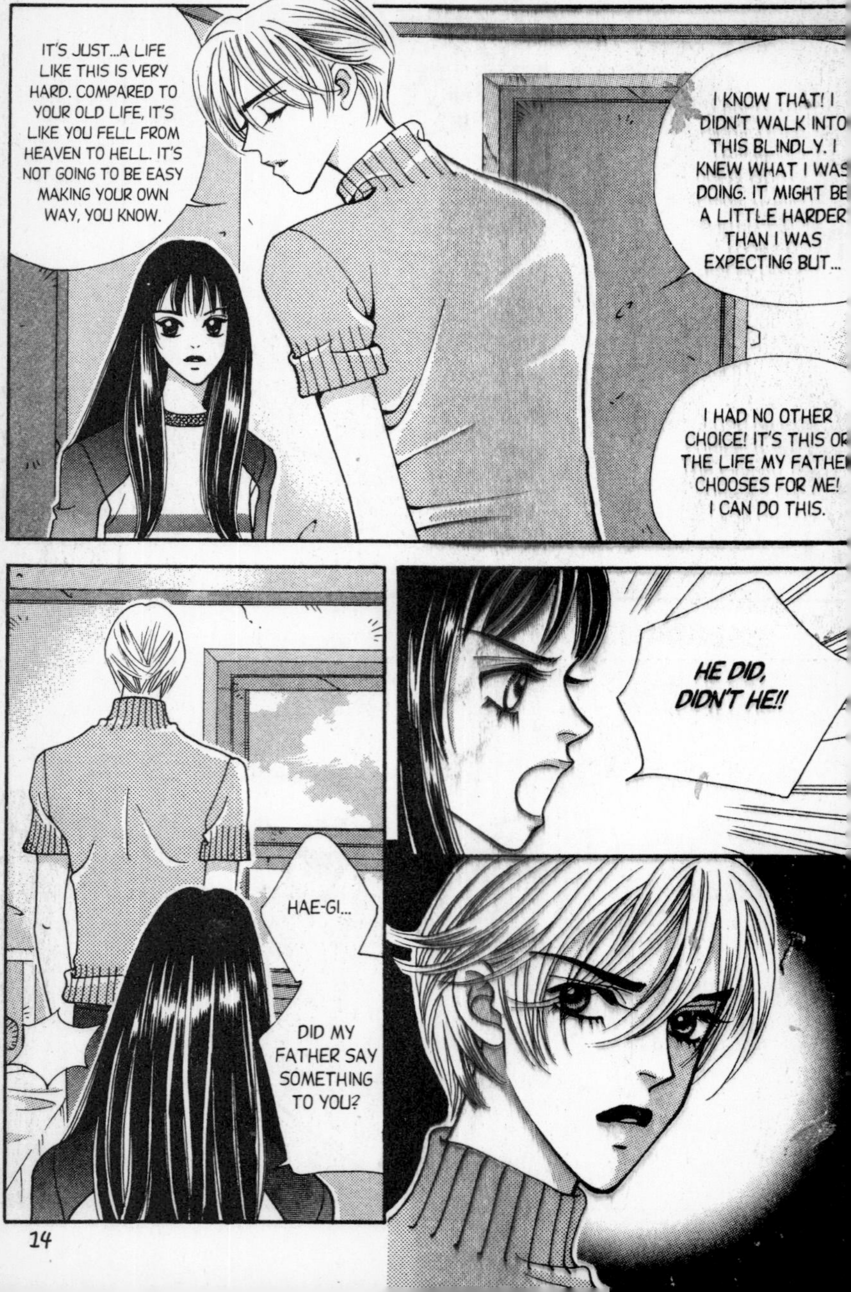
IT'S JUST...A LIFE LIKE THIS IS VERY HARD. COMPARED TO YOUR OLD LIFE, IT'S LIKE YOU FELL FROM HEAVEN TO HELL. IT'S NOT GOING TO BE EASY MAKING YOUR OWN WAY, YOU KNOW.
I KNOW THAT! I DIDN'T WALK INTO THIS BLINDLY. I KNEW WHAT I WA DOING. IT MIGHT BE A LITTLE HARDER THAN I WAS EXPECTING BUT...
I HAD NO OTHER CHOICE! IT'S THIS O THE LIFE MY FATHE CHOOSES FOR ME! I CAN DO THIS.
HAE-GI...
DID MY FATHER SAY SOMETHING TO YOU?
HE DID, DIDN'T HE!!

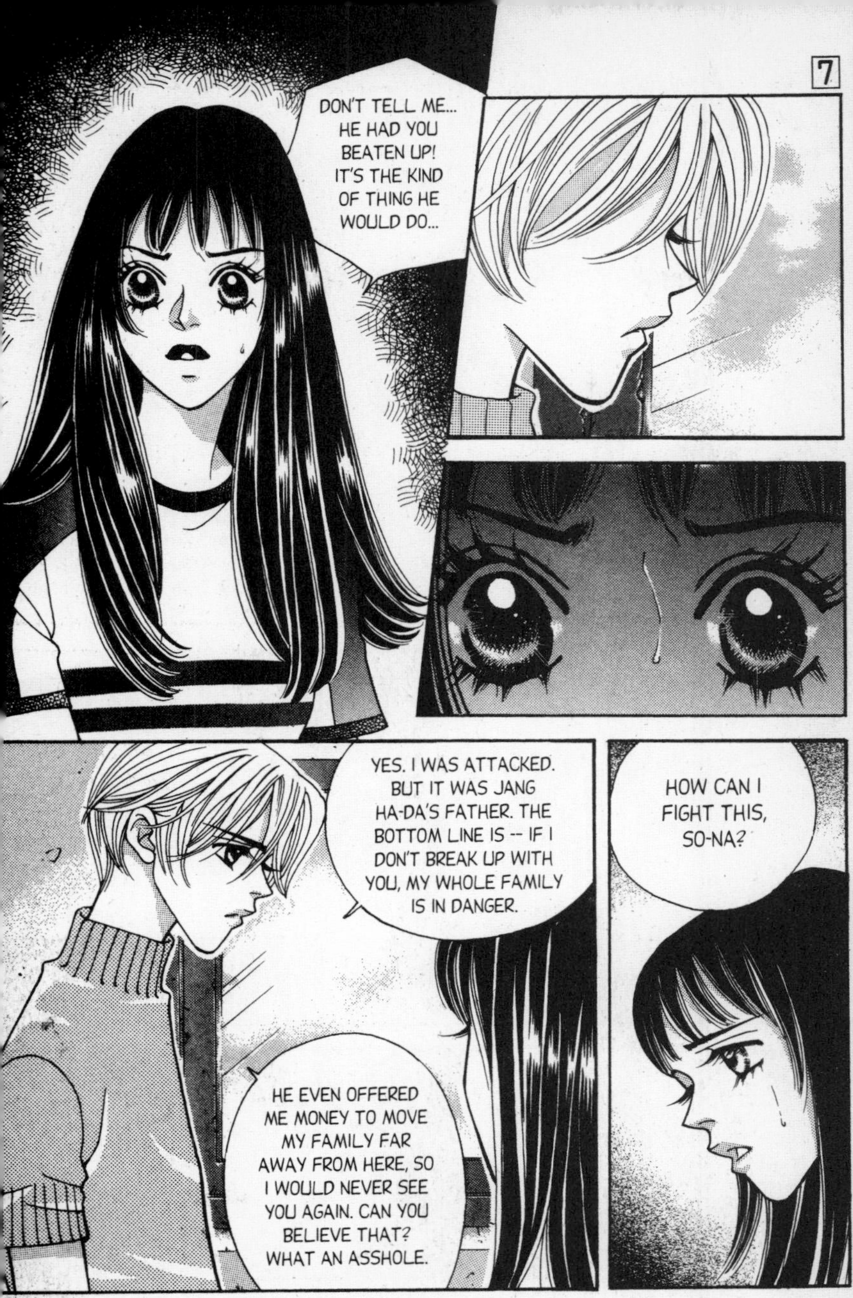
7
DON'T TELL ME... HE HAD YOU BEATEN UP! IT'S THE KIND OF THING HE WOULD DO...
YES. I WAS ATTACKED. BUT IT WAS JANG HA-DA'S FATHER. THE BOTTOM LINE IS -- IF I DON'T BREAK UP WITH YOU, MY WHOLE FAMILY IS IN DANGER.
HE EVEN OFFERED ME MONEY TO MOVE MY FAMILY FAR AWAY FROM HERE, SO I WOULD NEVER SEE YOU AGAIN. CAN YOU BELIEVE THAT? WHAT AN ASSHOLE.
HOW CAN I FIGHT THIS, SO-NA?

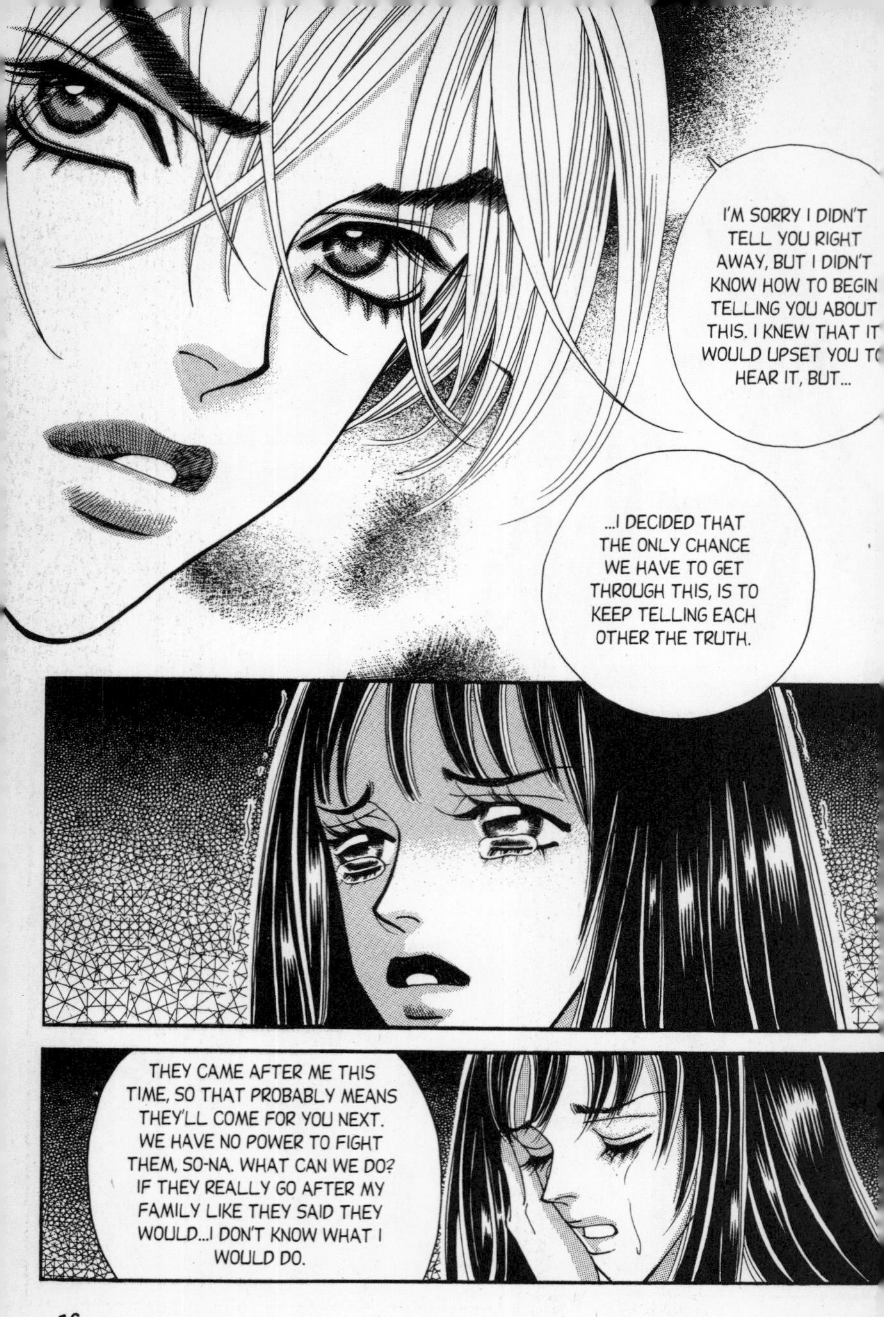
I'M SORRY I DIDN'T TELL YOU RIGHT AWAY, BUT I DIDN'T KNOW HOW TO BEGIN TELLING YOU ABOUT THIS. I KNEW THAT IT WOULD UPSET YOU TO HEAR IT, BUT...
...I DECIDED THAT THE ONLY CHANCE WE HAVE TO GET THROUGH THIS, IS TO KEEP TELLING EACH OTHER THE TRUTH.
THEY CAME AFTER ME THIS TIME, SO THAT PROBABLY MEANS THEY'LL COME FOR YOU NEXT. WE HAVE NO POWER TO FIGHT THEM, SO-NA. WHAT CAN WE DO? IF THEY REALLY GO AFTER MY FAMILY LIKE THEY SAID THEY WOULD...I DON'T KNOW WHAT I WOULD DO.

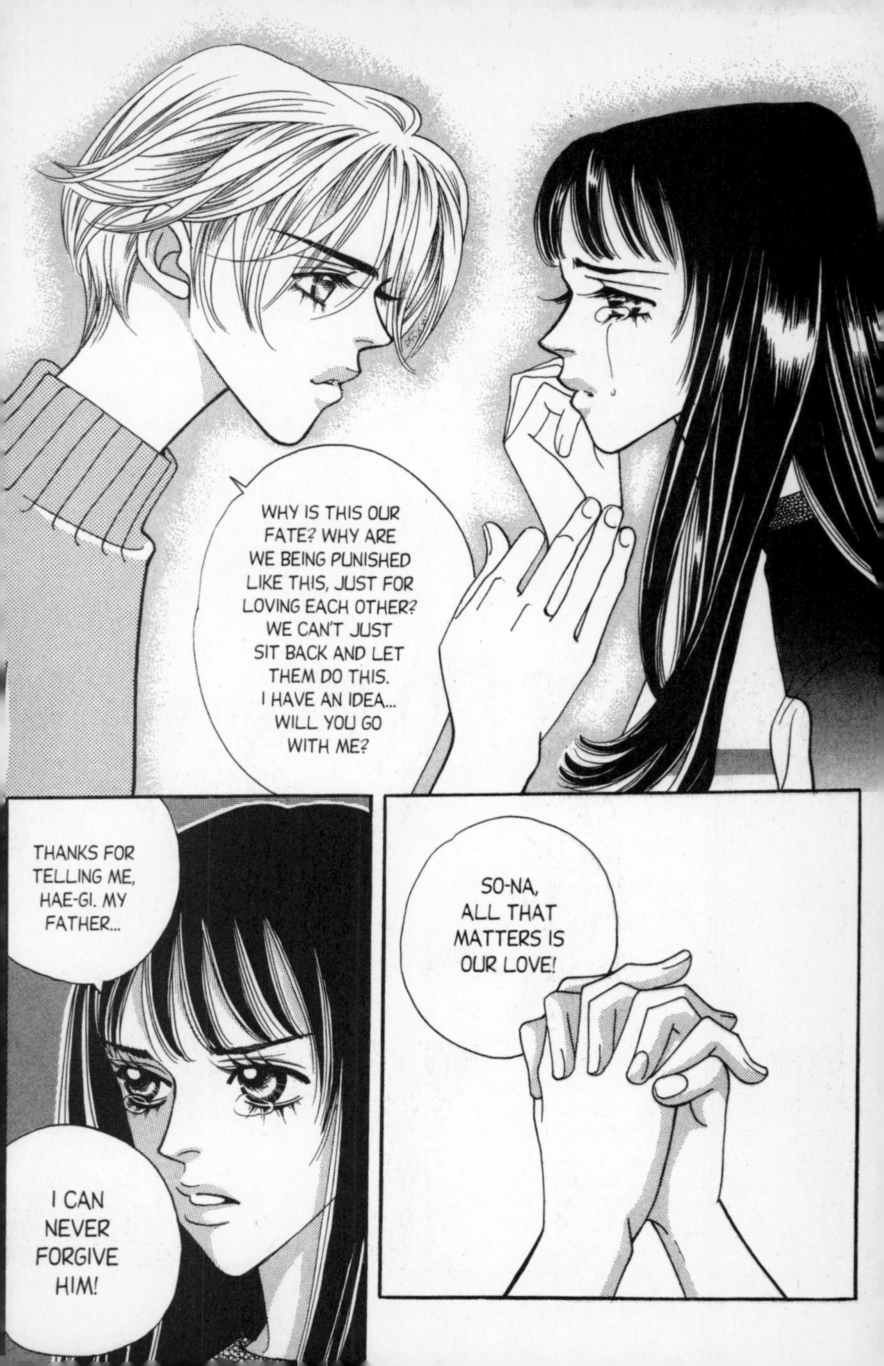
WHY IS THIS OUR FATE? WHY ARE WE BEING PUNISHED LIKE THIS, JUST FOR LOVING EACH OTHER? WE CAN'T JUST SIT BACK AND LET THEM DO THIS. I HAVE AN IDEA... WILL YOU GO WITH ME?
THANKS FOR TELLING ME, HAE-GI. MY FATHER...
I CAN NEVER FORGIVE HIM!
SO-NA, ALL THAT MATTERS IS OUR LOVE!

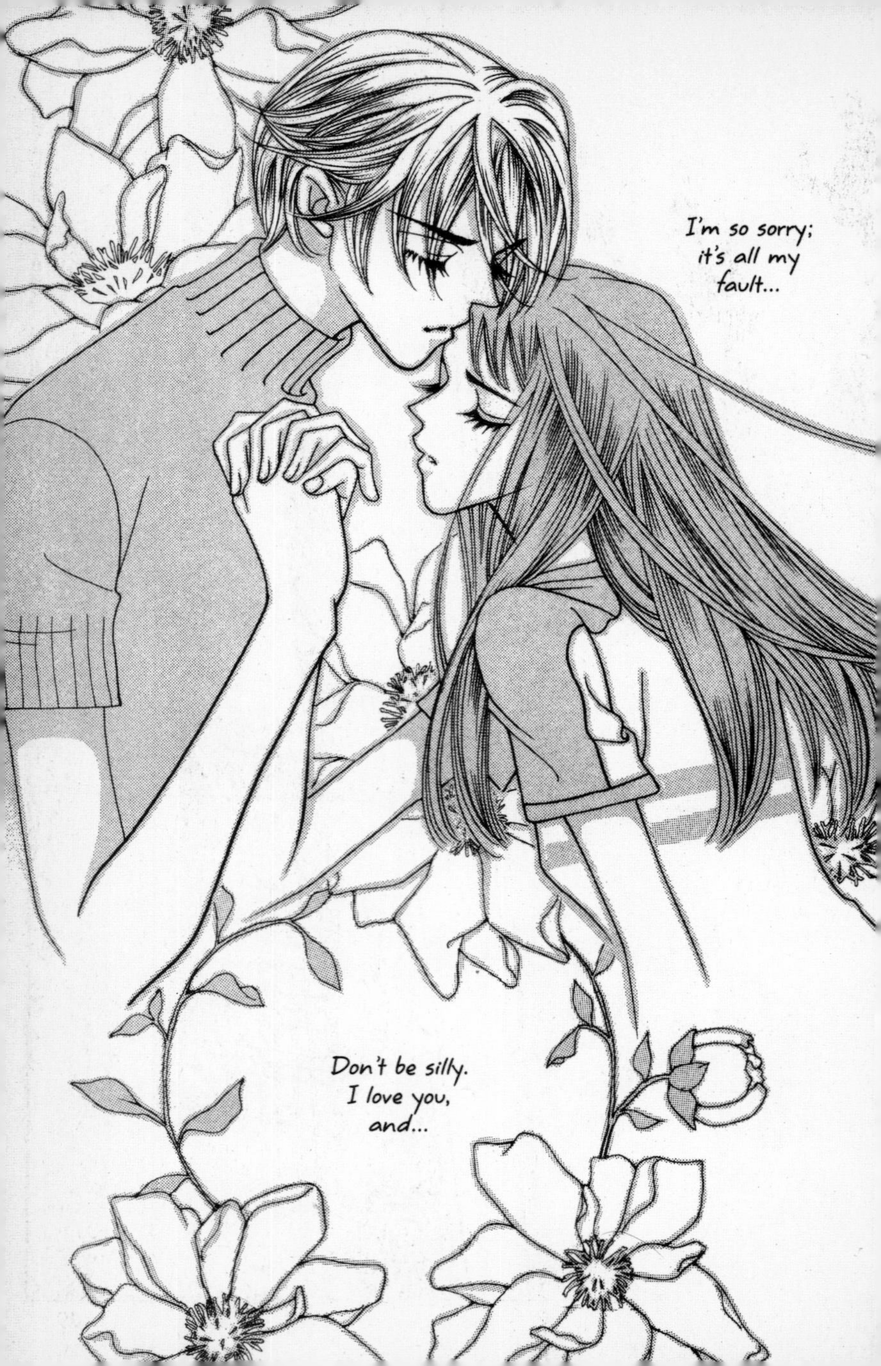
I'm so sorry; it's all my fault...
Don't be silly. I love you, and...

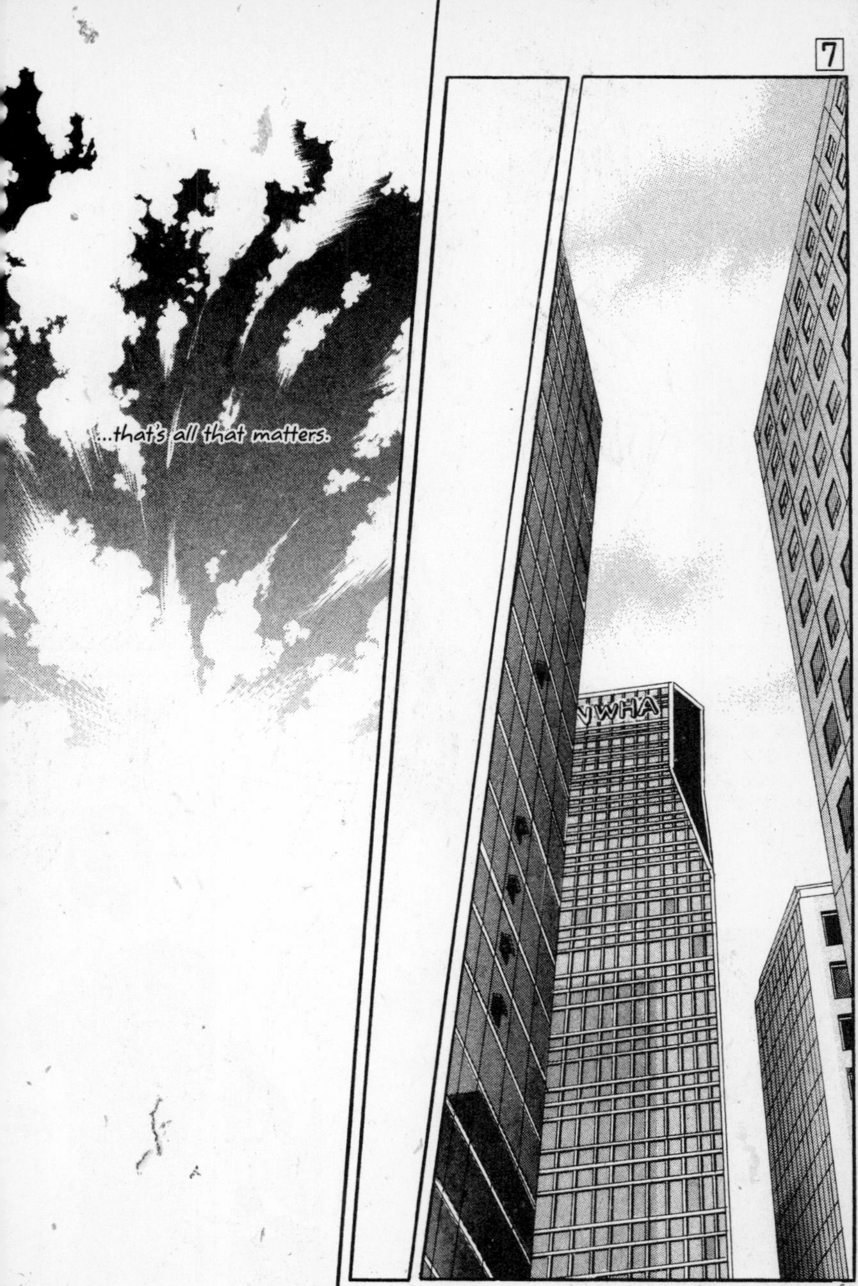
...that's all that matters.
7

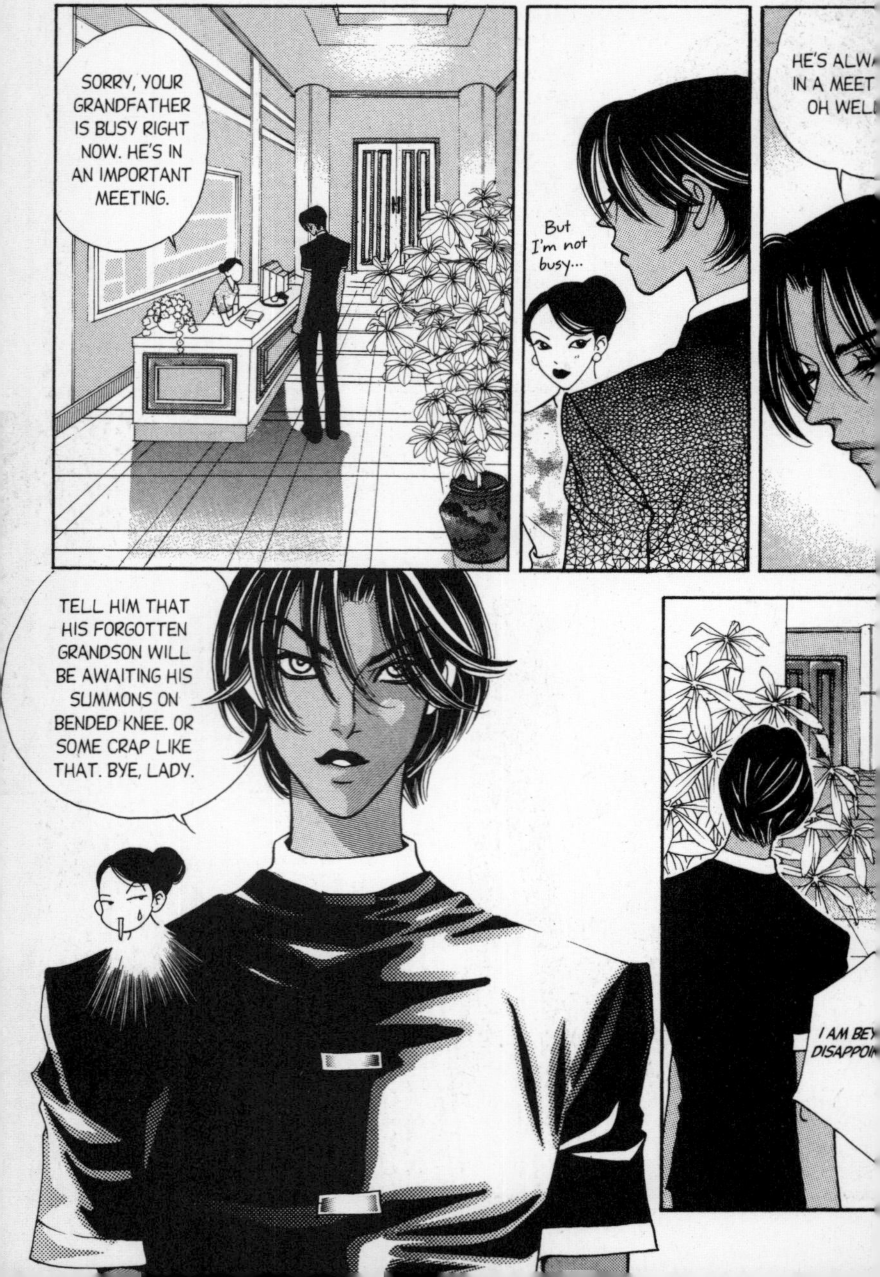
SORRY, YOUR GRANDFATHER IS BUSY RIGHT NOW. HE'S IN AN IMPORTANT MEETING.
But I'm not busy...
HE'S ALW
IN A MEET
OH WEL
TELL HIM THAT HIS FORGOTTEN GRANDSON WILL BE AWAITING HIS SUMMONS ON BENDED KNEE. OR SOME CRAP LIKE THAT. BYE, LADY.
I AM BE
DISAPPOI

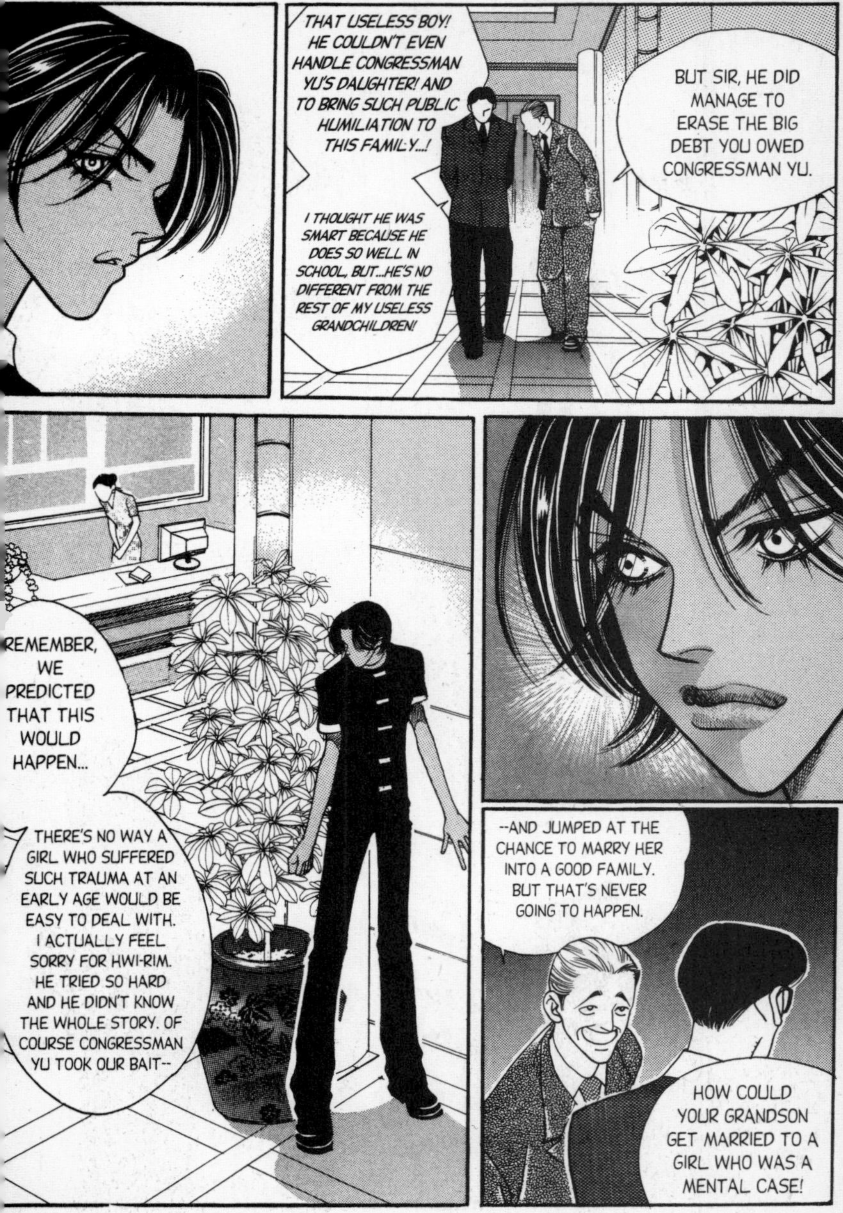

THAT USELESS BOY! HE COULDN'T EVEN HANDLE CONGRESSMAN YU'S DAUGHTER! AND TO BRING SUCH PUBLIC HUMILIATION TO THIS FAMILY...!
I THOUGHT HE WAS SMART BECAUSE HE DOES SO WELL IN SCHOOL, BUT...HE'S NO DIFFERENT FROM THE REST OF MY USELESS GRANDCHILDREN!
BUT SIR, HE DID MANAGE TO ERASE THE BIG DEBT YOU OWED CONGRESSMAN YU.
REMEMBER, WE PREDICTED THAT THIS WOULD HAPPEN...
THERE'S NO WAY A GIRL WHO SUFFERED SUCH TRAUMA AT AN EARLY AGE WOULD BE EASY TO DEAL WITH. I ACTUALLY FEEL SORRY FOR HWI-RIM. HE TRIED SO HARD AND HE DIDN'T KNOW THE WHOLE STORY. OF COURSE CONGRESSMAN YU TOOK OUR BAIT--
--AND JUMPED AT THE CHANCE TO MARRY HER INTO A GOOD FAMILY. BUT THAT'S NEVER GOING TO HAPPEN.
HOW COULD YOUR GRANDSON GET MARRIED TO A GIRL WHO WAS A MENTAL CASE!

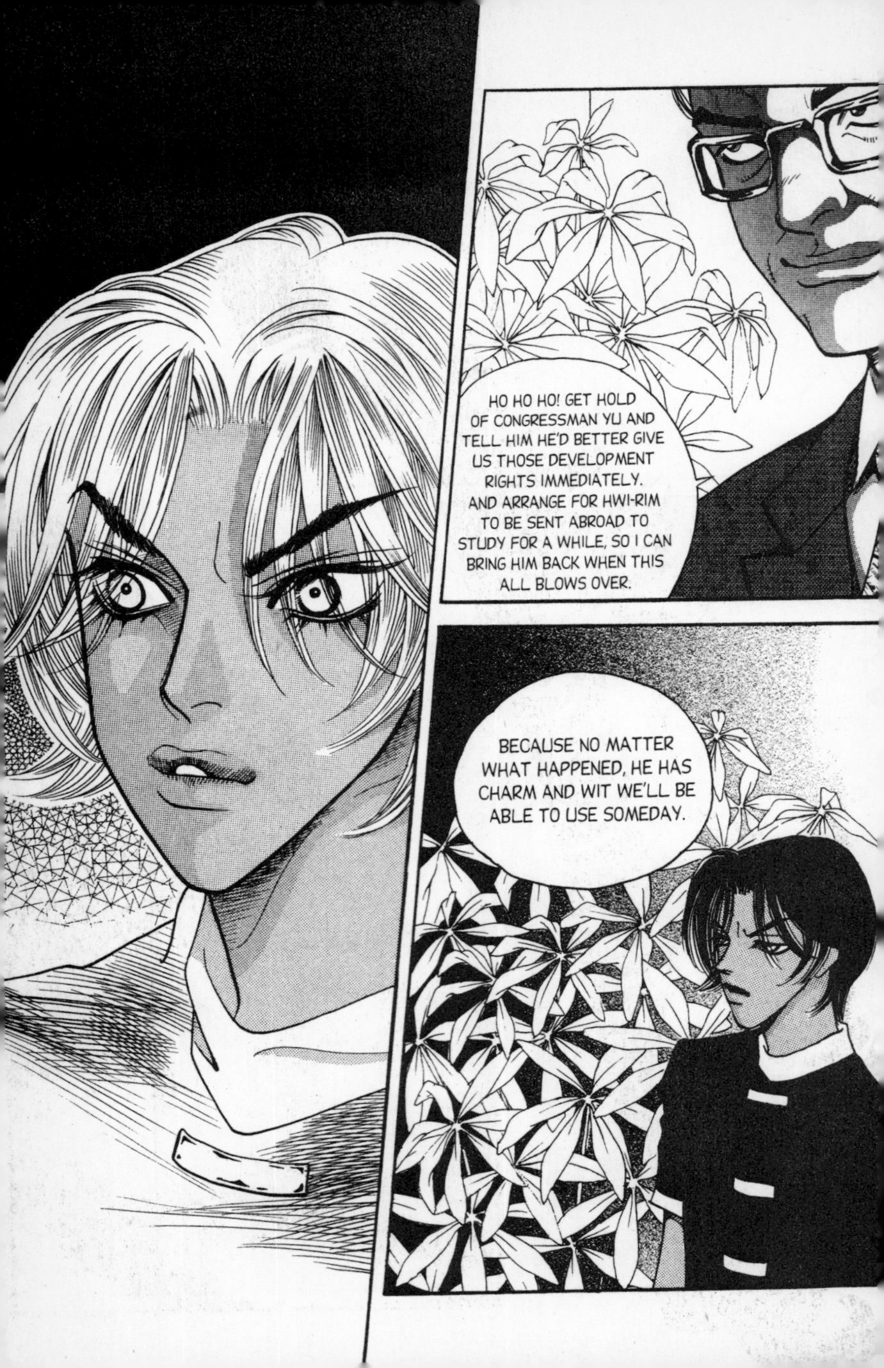
HO HO HO! GET HOLD OF CONGRESSMAN YU AND TELL HIM HE'D BETTER GIVE US THOSE DEVELOPMENT RIGHTS IMMEDIATELY. AND ARRANGE FOR HWI-RIM TO BE SENT ABROAD TO STUDY FOR A WHILE, SO I CAN BRING HIM BACK WHEN THIS ALL BLOWS OVER.
BECAUSE NO MATTER WHAT HAPPENED, HE HAS CHARM AND WIT WE'LL BE ABLE TO USE SOMEDAY.

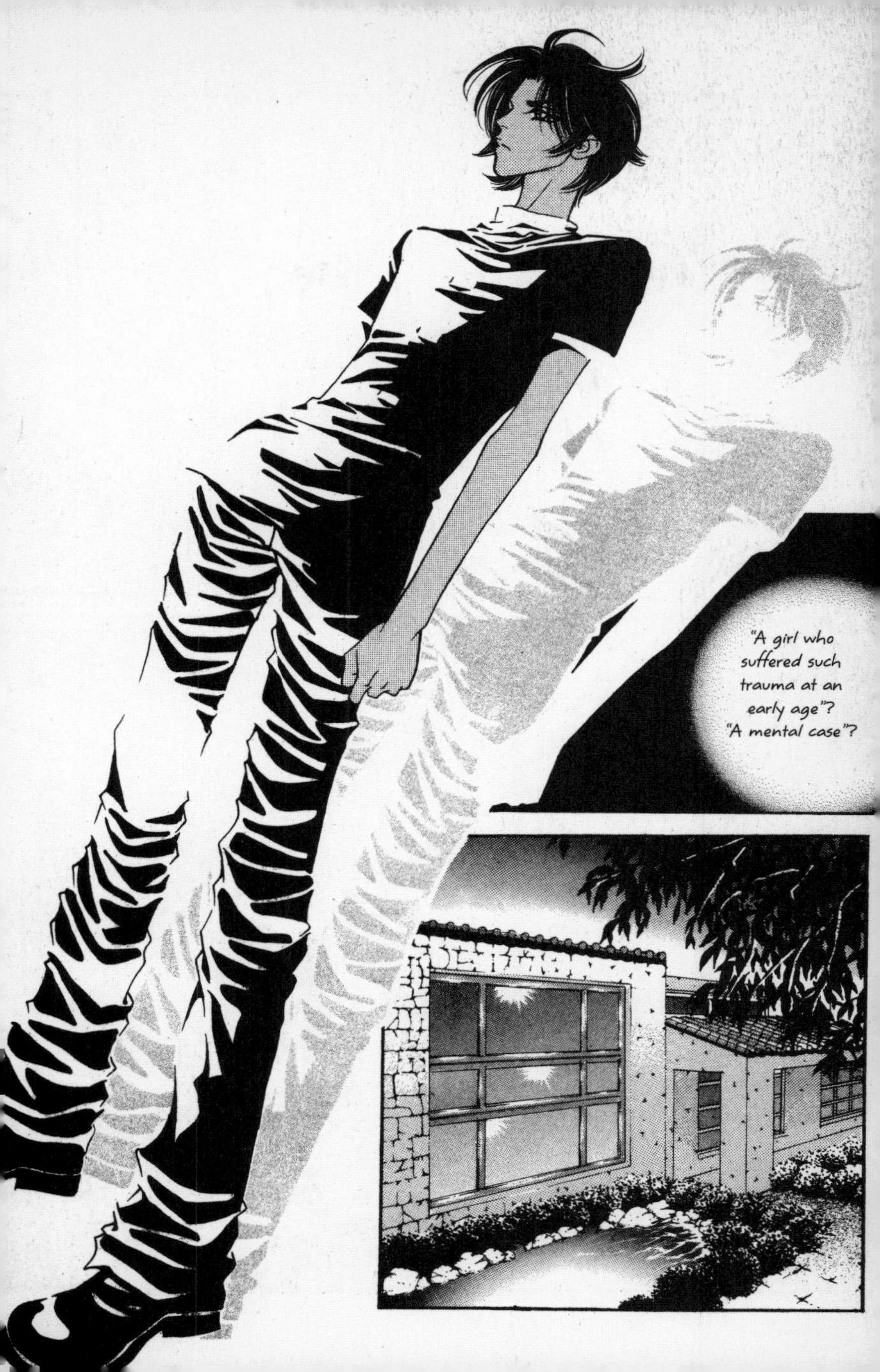
"A girl who suffered such trauma at an early age"? "A mental case"?

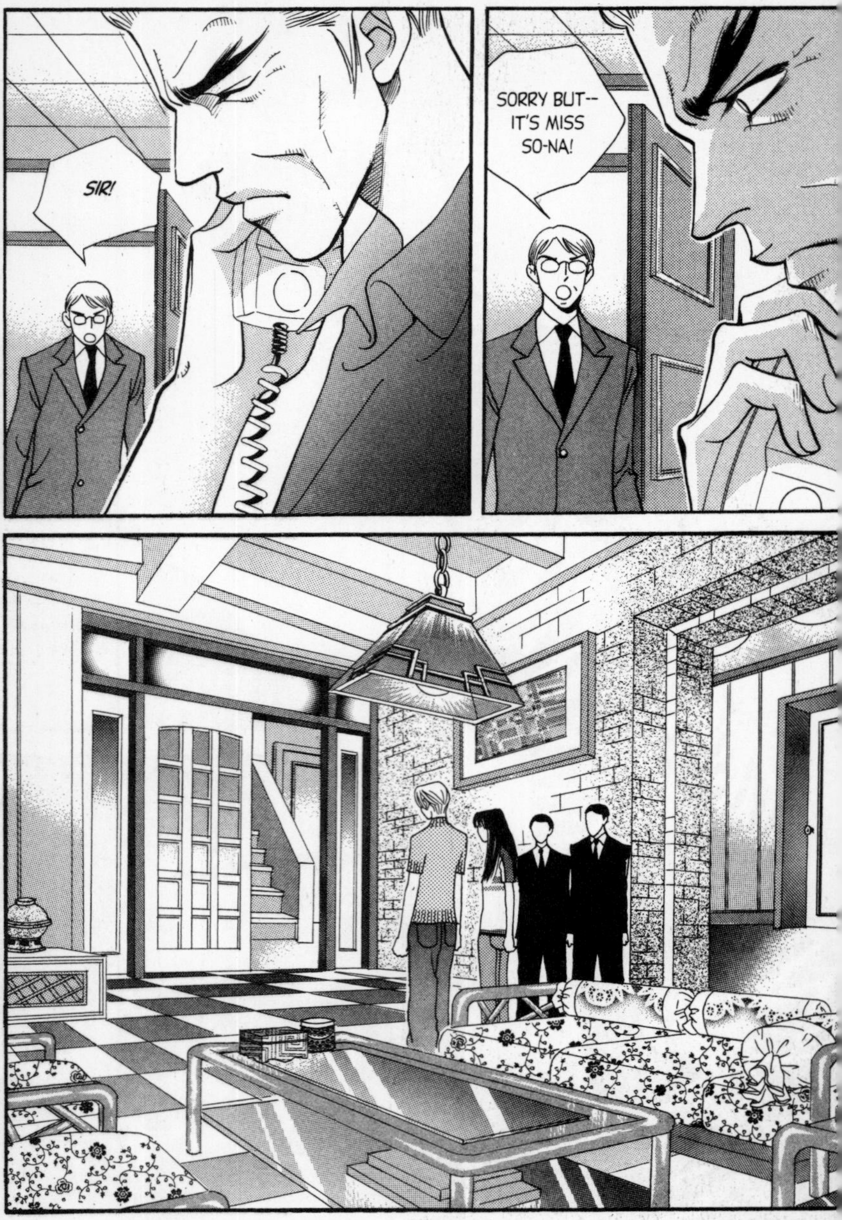
SIR!
SORRY BUT--
IT'S MISS
SO-NA!

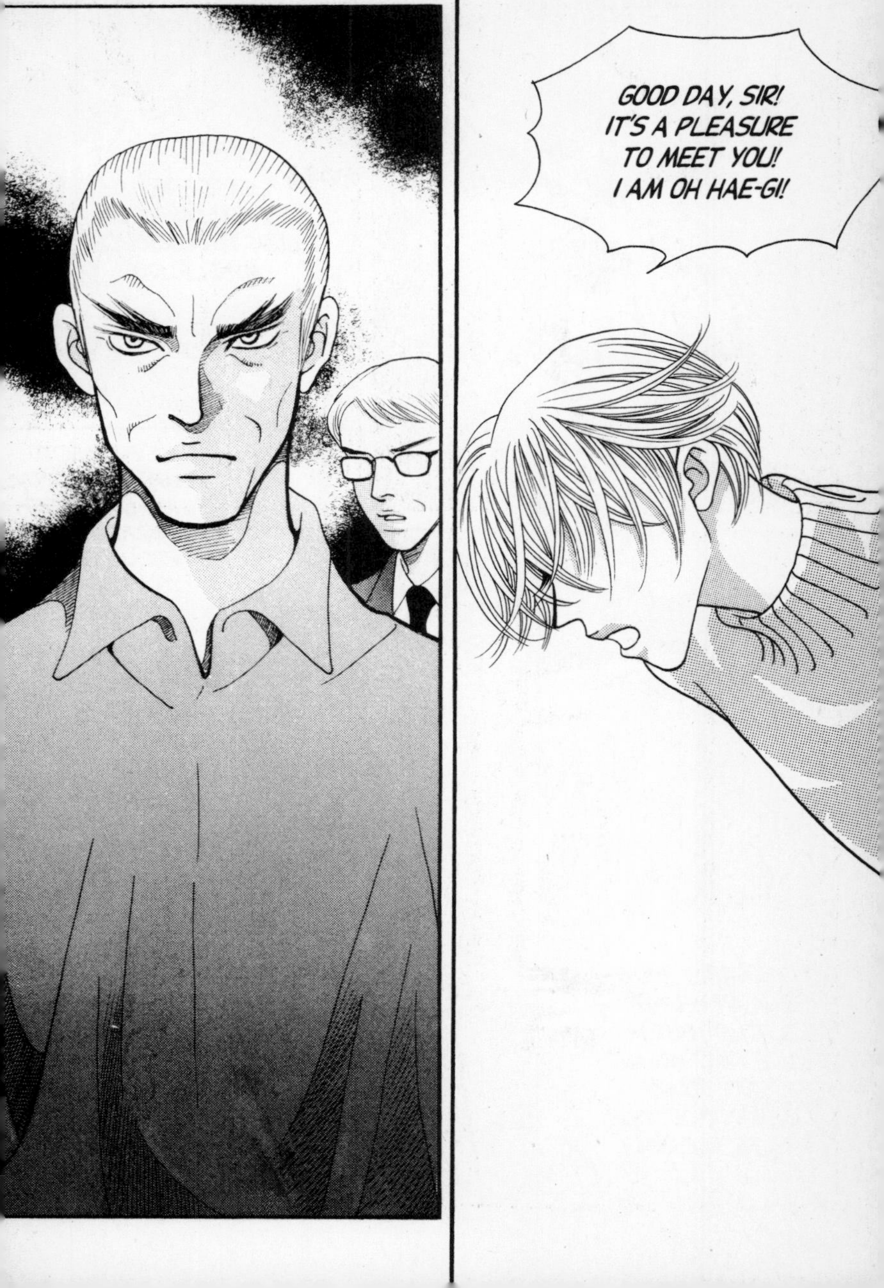
GOOD DAY, SIR! IT'S A PLEASURE TO MEET YOU! I AM OH HAE-GI!

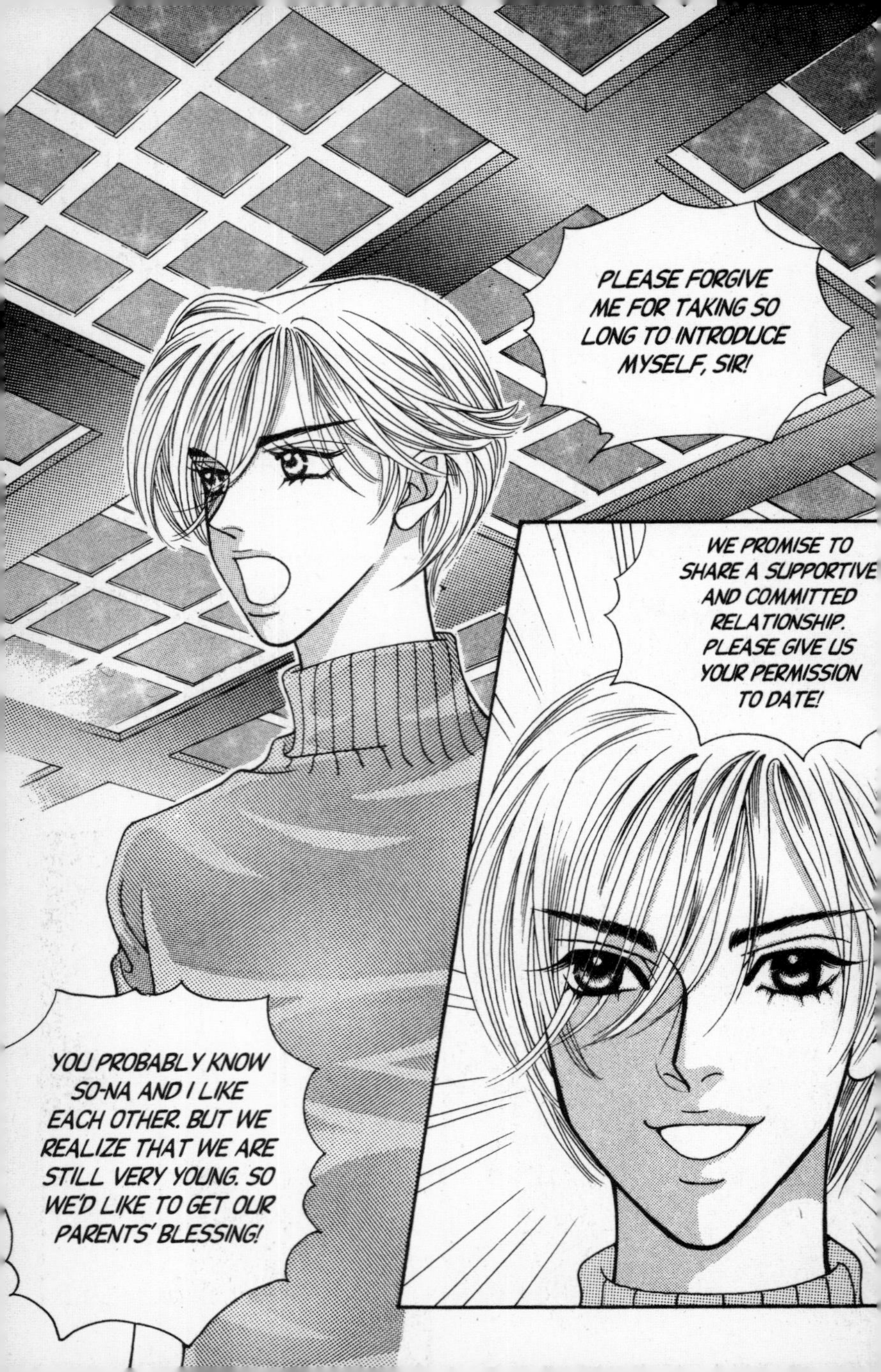
PLEASE FORGIVE ME FOR TAKING SO LONG TO INTRODUCE MYSELF, SIR!
YOU PROBABLY KNOW SO-NA AND I LIKE EACH OTHER. BUT WE REALIZE THAT WE ARE STILL VERY YOUNG. SO WE'D LIKE TO GET OUR PARENTS' BLESSING!
WE PROMISE TO SHARE A SUPPORTIVE AND COMMITTED RELATIONSHIP. PLEASE GIVE US YOUR PERMISSION TO DATE!

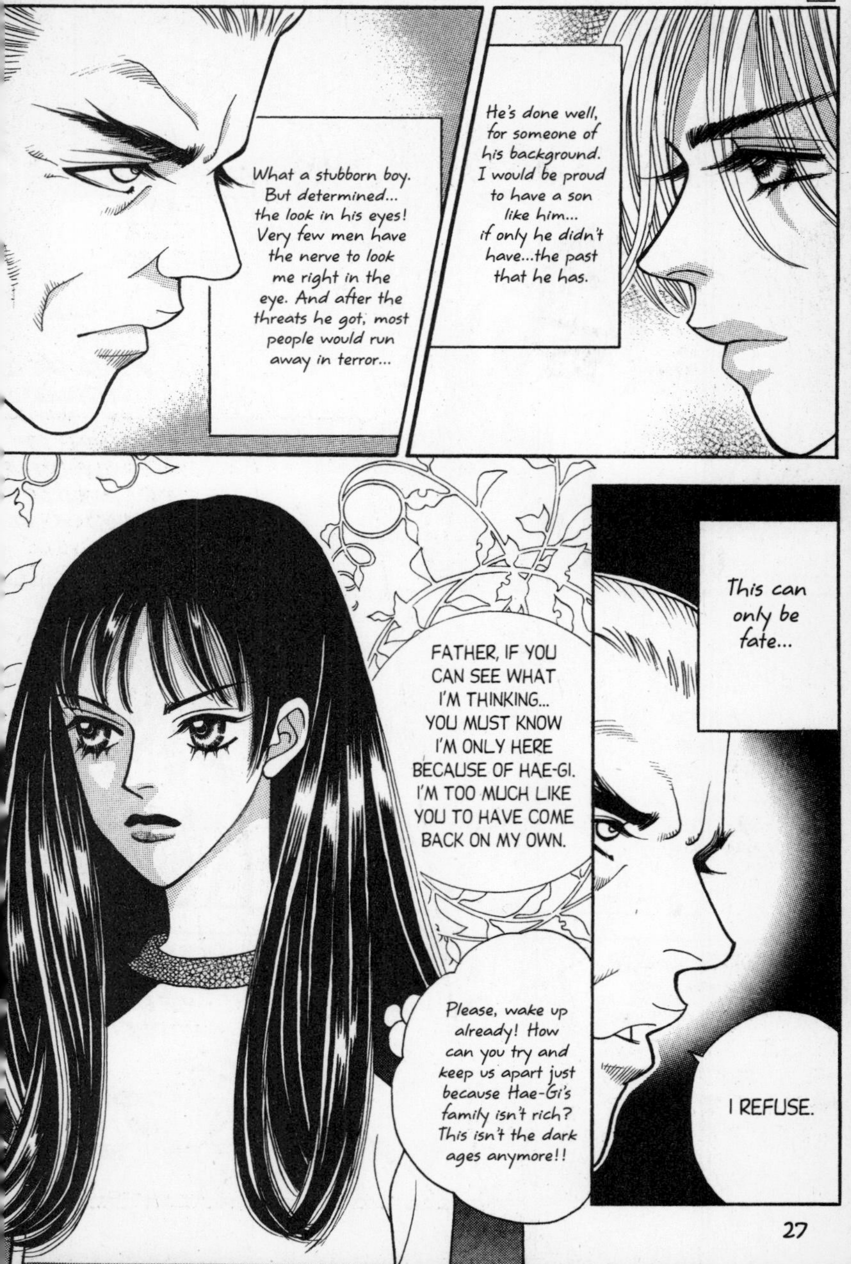
What a stubborn boy. But determined... the look in his eyes! Very few men have the nerve to look me right in the eye. And after the threats he got, most people would run away in terror...
He's done well, for someone of his background. I would be proud to have a son like him... if only he didn't have...the past that he has.
FATHER, IF YOU CAN SEE WHAT I'M THINKING... YOU MUST KNOW I'M ONLY HERE BECAUSE OF HAE-GI. I'M TOO MUCH LIKE YOU TO HAVE COME BACK ON MY OWN.
Please, wake up already! How can you try and keep us apart just because Hae-Gi's family isn't rich? This isn't the dark ages anymore!!
This can only be fate...
I REFUSE.

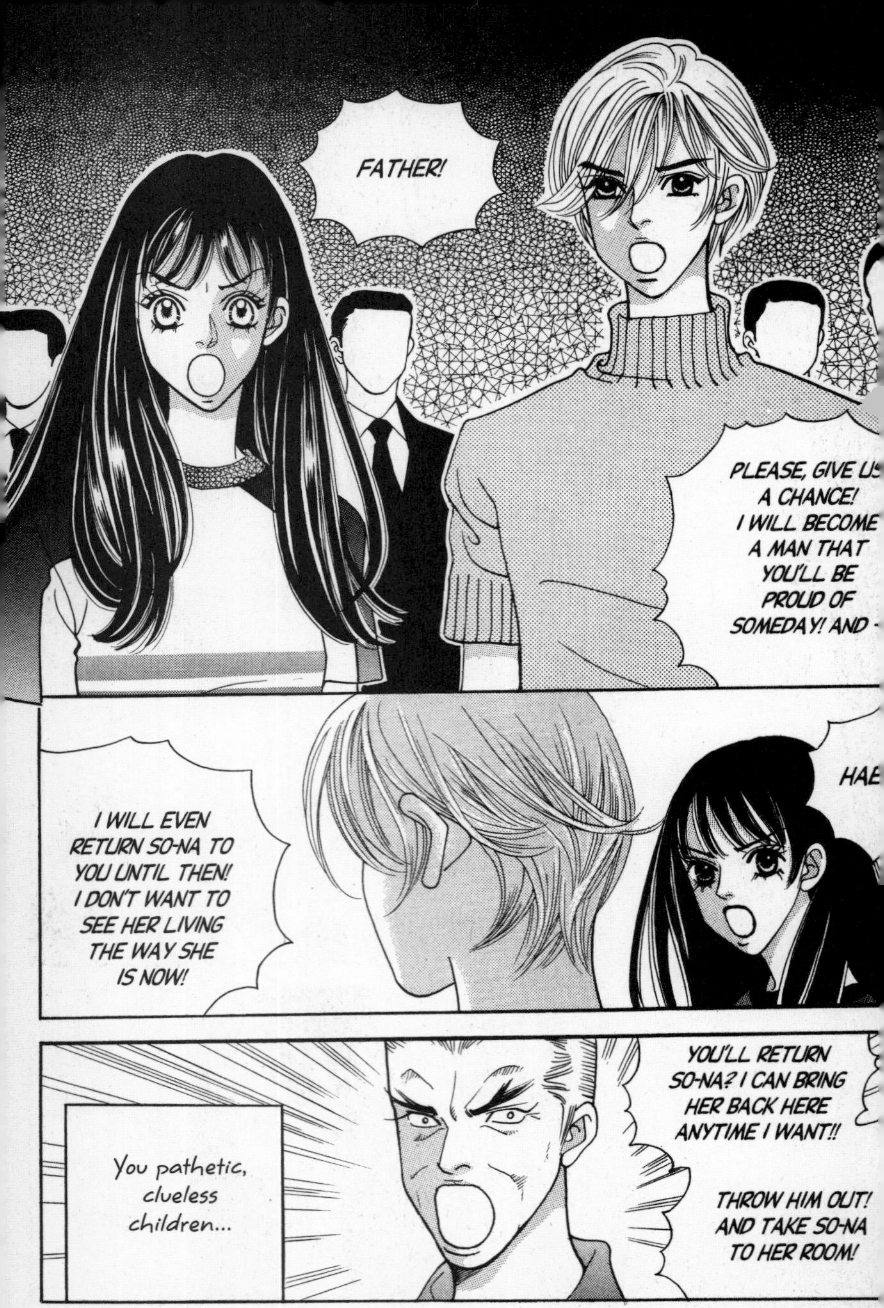
FATHER!
PLEASE, GIVE US A CHANCE! I WILL BECOME A MAN THAT YOU'LL BE PROUD OF SOMEDAY! AND -
I WILL EVEN RETURN SO-NA TO YOU UNTIL THEN! I DON'T WANT TO SEE HER LIVING THE WAY SHE IS NOW!
HAE
You pathetic, clueless children...
YOU'LL RETURN SO-NA? I CAN BRING HER BACK HERE ANYTIME I WANT!!
THROW HIM OUT! AND TAKE SO-NA TO HER ROOM!

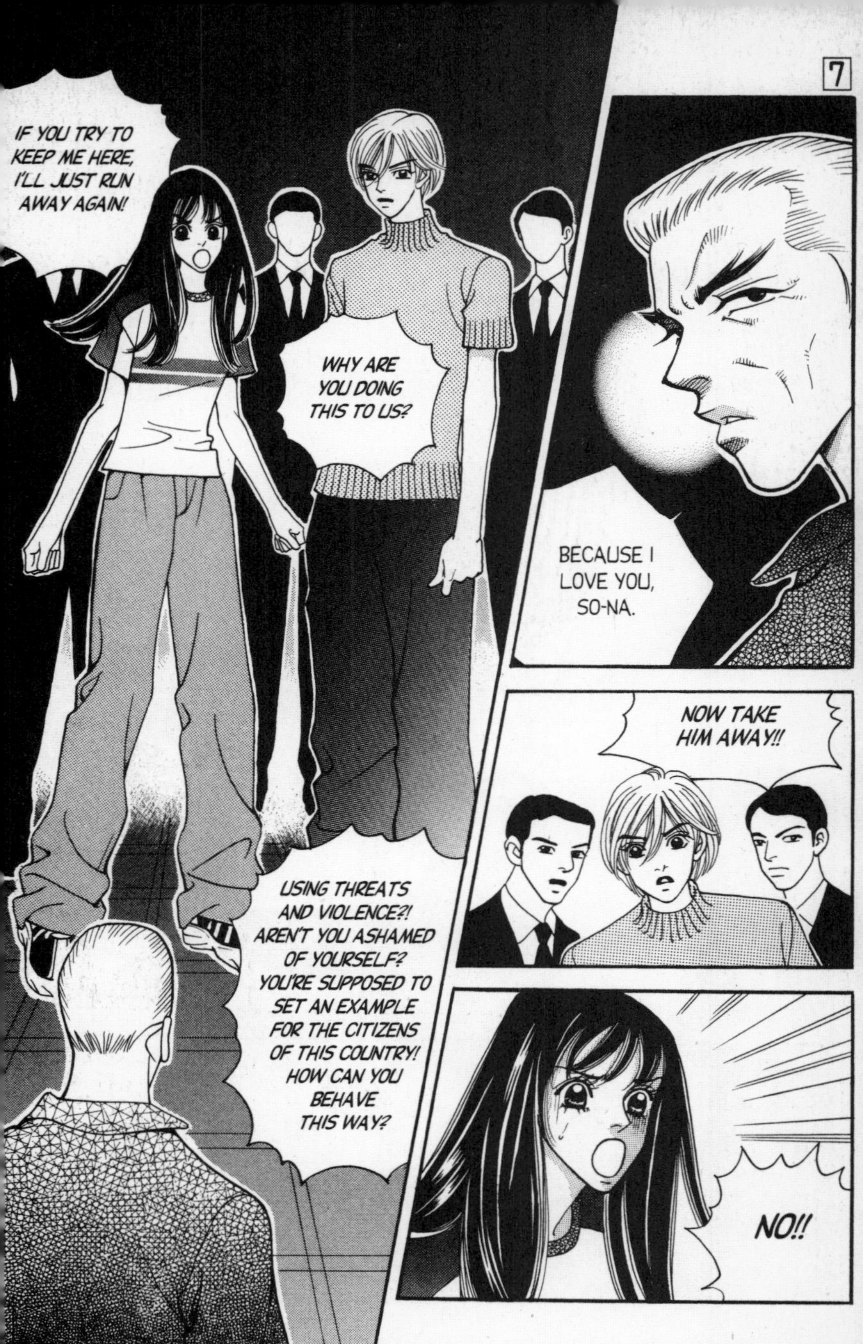
IF YOU TRY TO KEEP ME HERE, I'LL JUST RUN AWAY AGAIN!
WHY ARE YOU DOING THIS TO US?
USING THREATS AND VIOLENCE?! AREN'T YOU ASHAMED OF YOURSELF? YOU'RE SUPPOSED TO SET AN EXAMPLE FOR THE CITIZENS OF THIS COUNTRY! HOW CAN YOU BEHAVE THIS WAY?
BECAUSE I LOVE YOU, SO-NA.
NOW TAKE HIM AWAY!!
NO!!

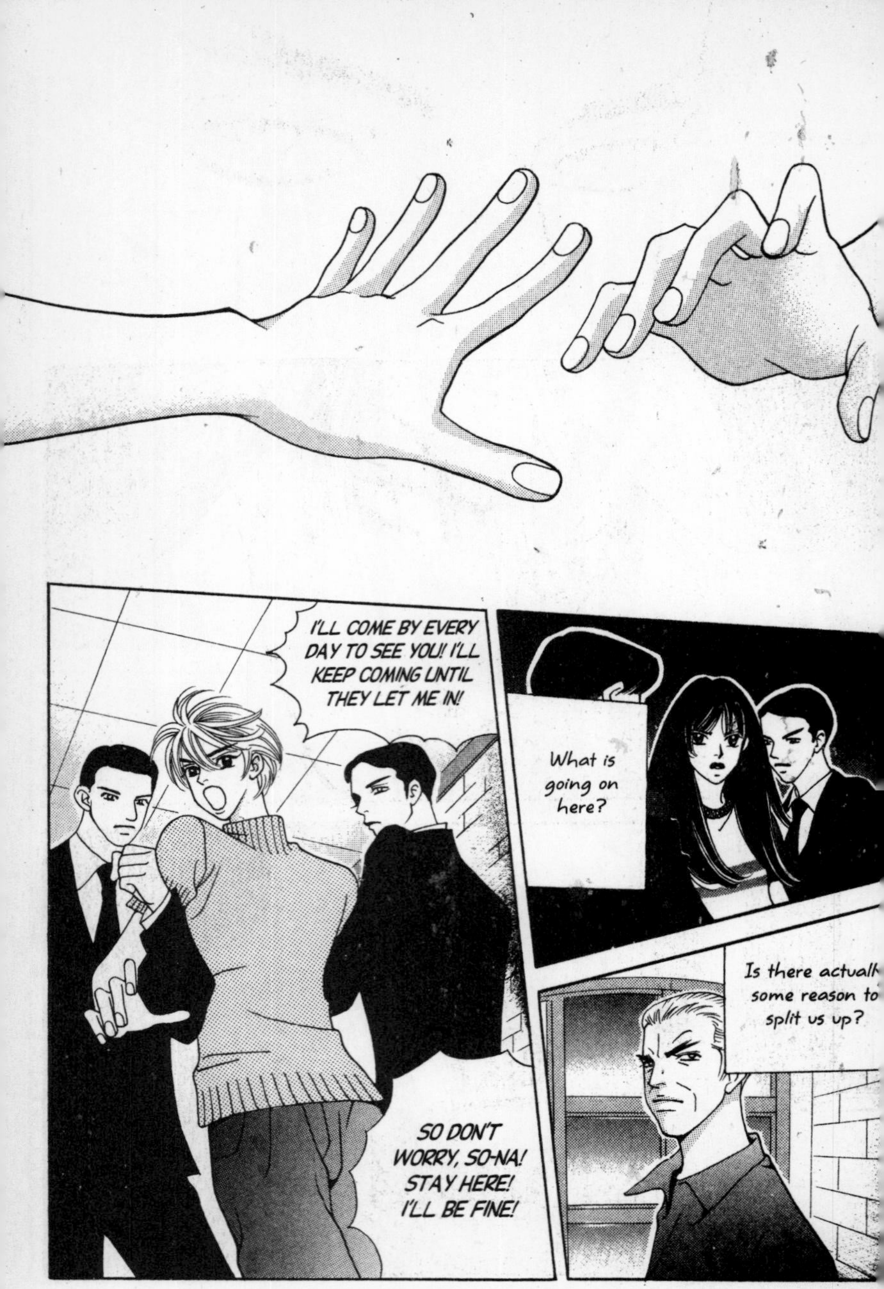
I'LL COME BY EVERY DAY TO SEE YOU! I'LL KEEP COMING UNTIL THEY LET ME IN!
SO DON'T WORRY, SO-NA! STAY HERE! I'LL BE FINE!
What is going on here?
Is there actuall some reason to split us up?

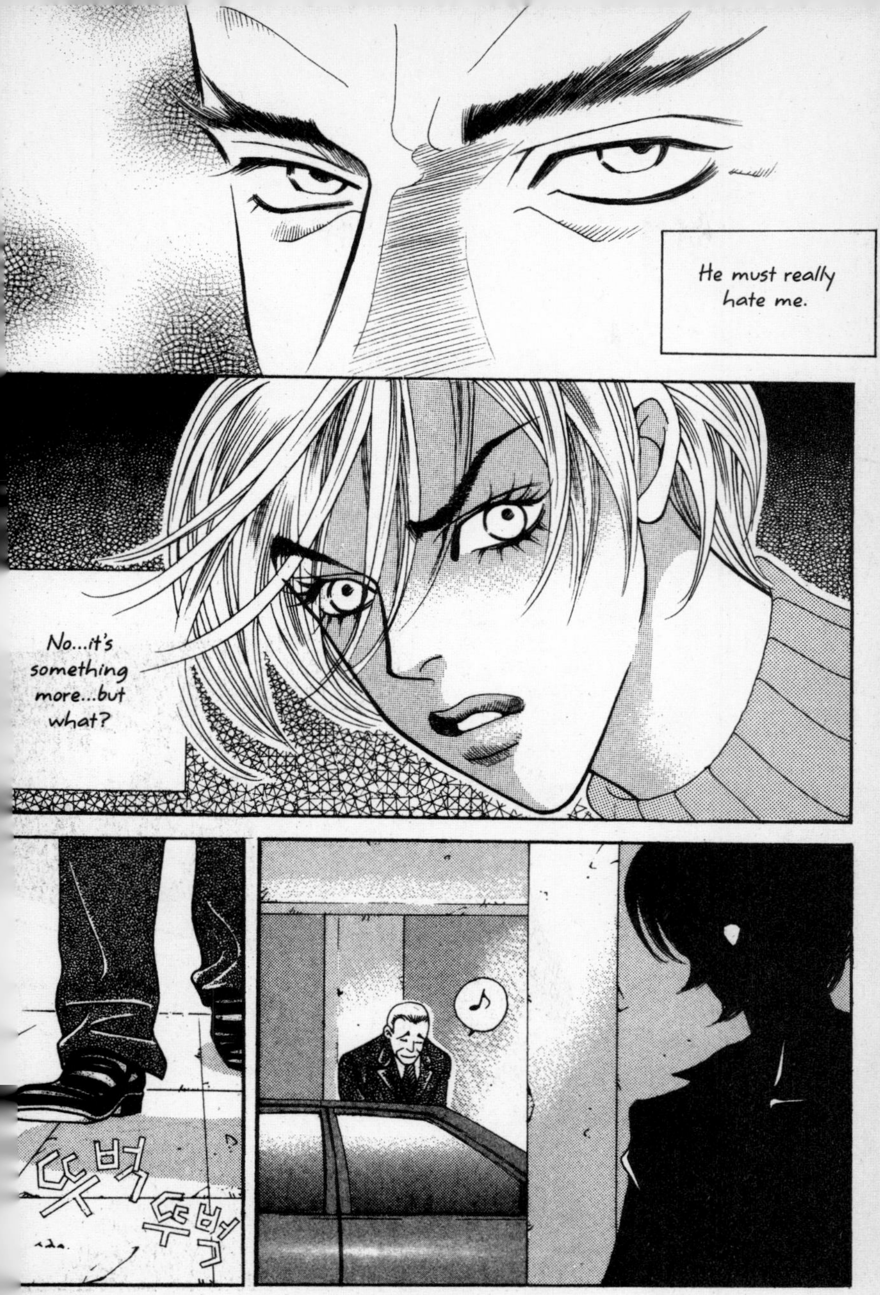
He must really hate me.
No...it's something more...but what?

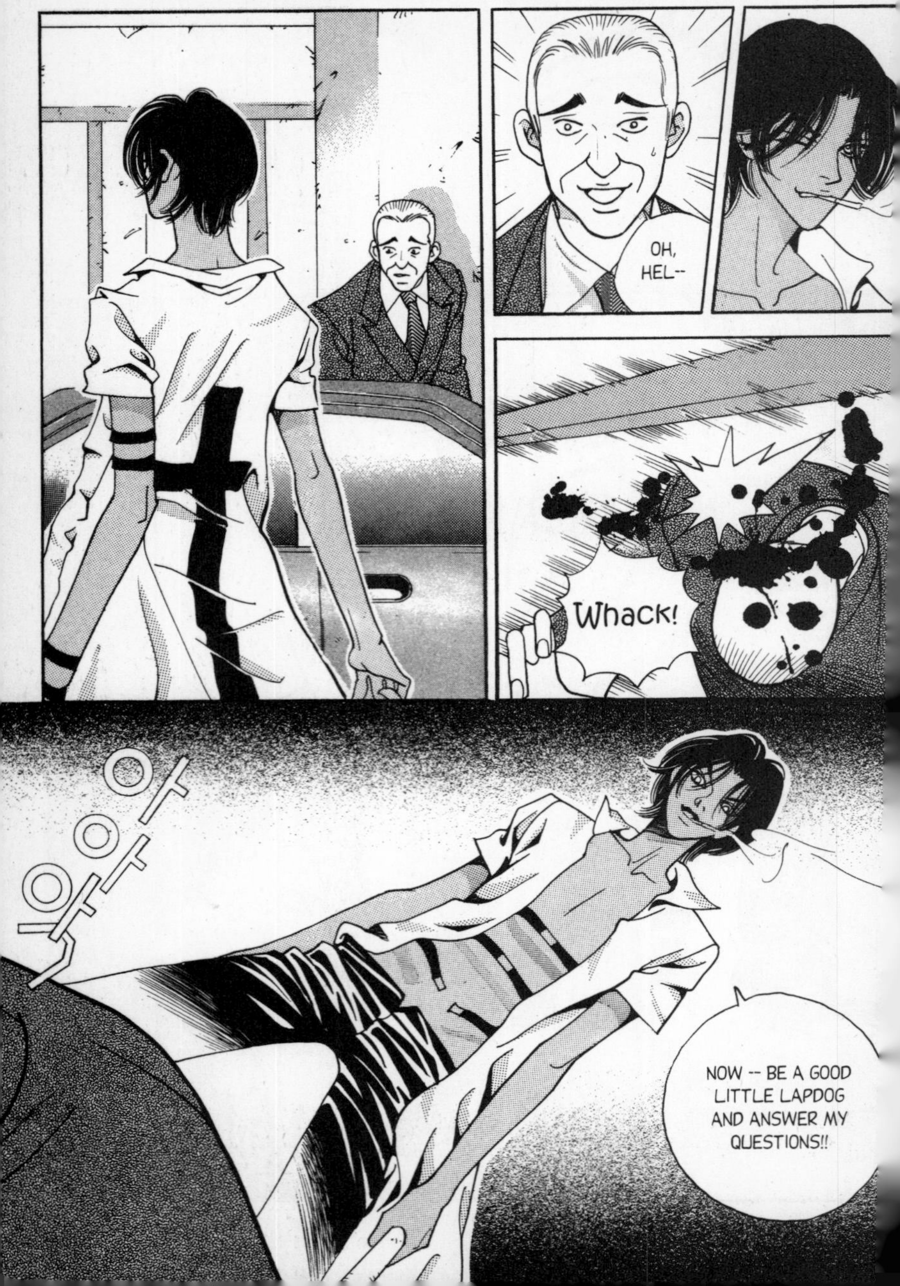
OH, HEL--
Whack!
NOW -- BE A GOOD LITTLE LAPDOG AND ANSWER MY QUESTIONS!!

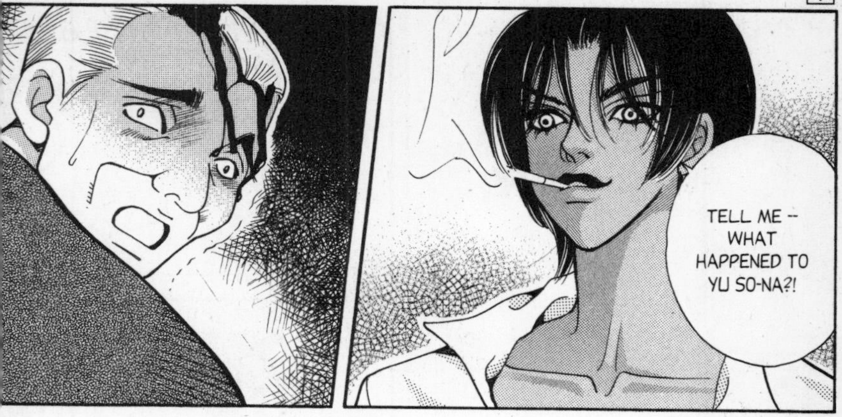
TELL ME -- WHAT HAPPENED TO YU SO-NA?!

Part 25: Truth

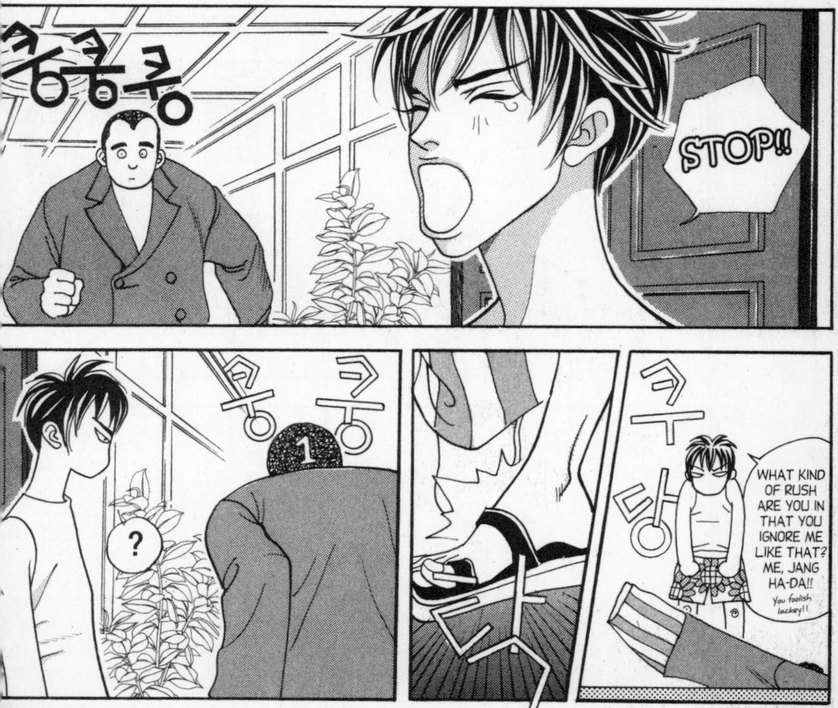
STOP!!
?
WHAT KIND OF RUSH ARE YOU IN THAT YOU IGNORE ME LIKE THAT? ME, JANG HA-DA!!
You foolish lackey!!

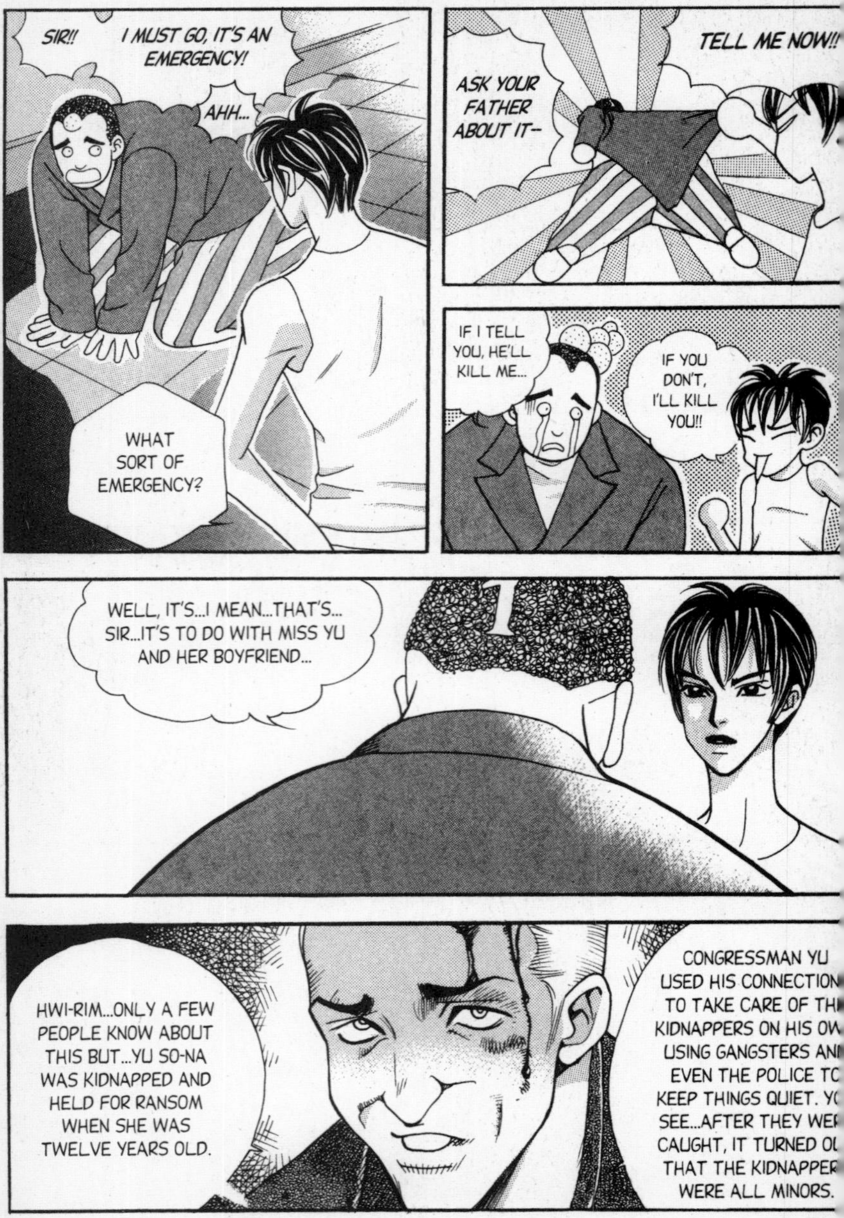
SIR!!
I MUST GO, IT'S AN EMERGENCY!
AHH...
WHAT SORT OF EMERGENCY?
ASK YOUR FATHER ABOUT IT–
TELL ME NOW!!
IF I TELL YOU, HE'LL KILL ME...
IF YOU DON'T, I'LL KILL YOU!!
WELL, IT'S...I MEAN...THAT'S... SIR...IT'S TO DO WITH MISS YU AND HER BOYFRIEND...
HWI-RIM...ONLY A FEW PEOPLE KNOW ABOUT THIS BUT...YU SO-NA WAS KIDNAPPED AND HELD FOR RANSOM WHEN SHE WAS TWELVE YEARS OLD.
CONGRESSMAN YU USED HIS CONNECTION TO TAKE CARE OF TH KIDNAPPERS ON HIS OW USING GANGSTERS AN EVEN THE POLICE T KEEP THINGS QUIET. Y SEE...AFTER THEY WE CAUGHT, IT TURNED O THAT THE KIDNAPPER WERE ALL MINORS.

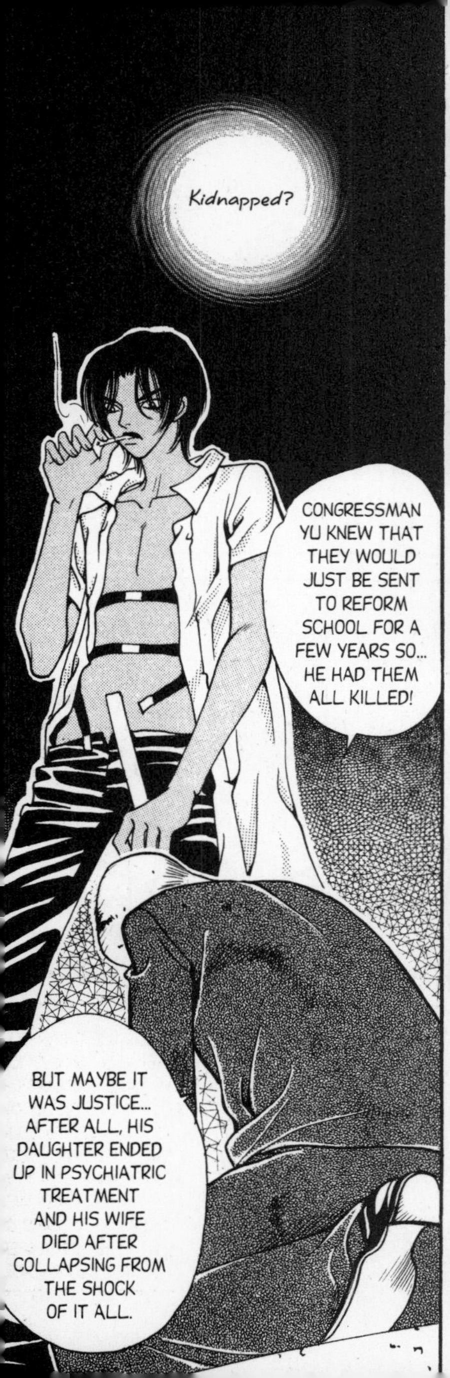
Kidnapped?
CONGRESSMAN YU KNEW THAT THEY WOULD JUST BE SENT TO REFORM SCHOOL FOR A FEW YEARS SO... HE HAD THEM ALL KILLED!
BUT MAYBE IT WAS JUSTICE... AFTER ALL, HIS DAUGHTER ENDED UP IN PSYCHIATRIC TREATMENT AND HIS WIFE DIED AFTER COLLAPSING FROM THE SHOCK OF IT ALL.

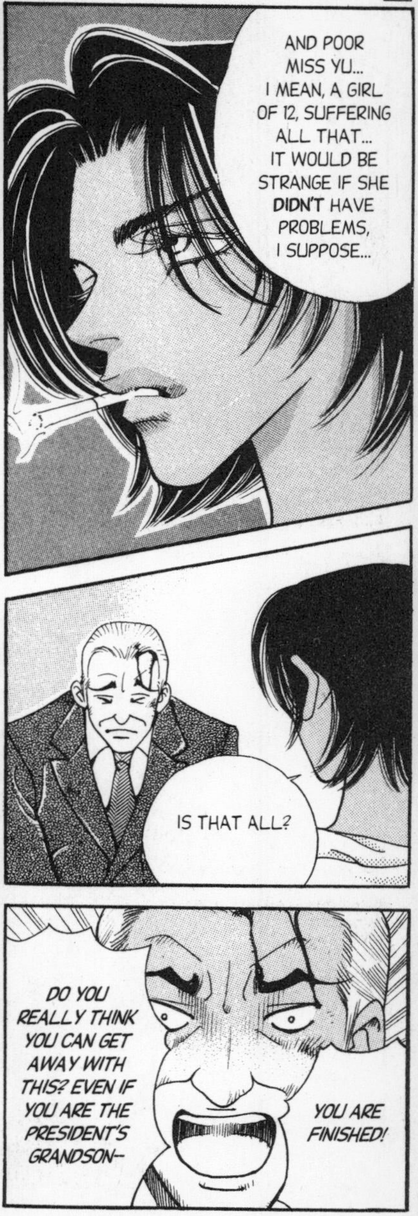
AND POOR MISS YU... I MEAN, A GIRL OF 12, SUFFERING ALL THAT... IT WOULD BE STRANGE IF SHE DIDN'T HAVE PROBLEMS, I SUPPOSE...
IS THAT ALL?
DO YOU REALLY THINK YOU CAN GET AWAY WITH THIS? EVEN IF YOU ARE THE PRESIDENT'S GRANDSON–
YOU ARE FINISHED!

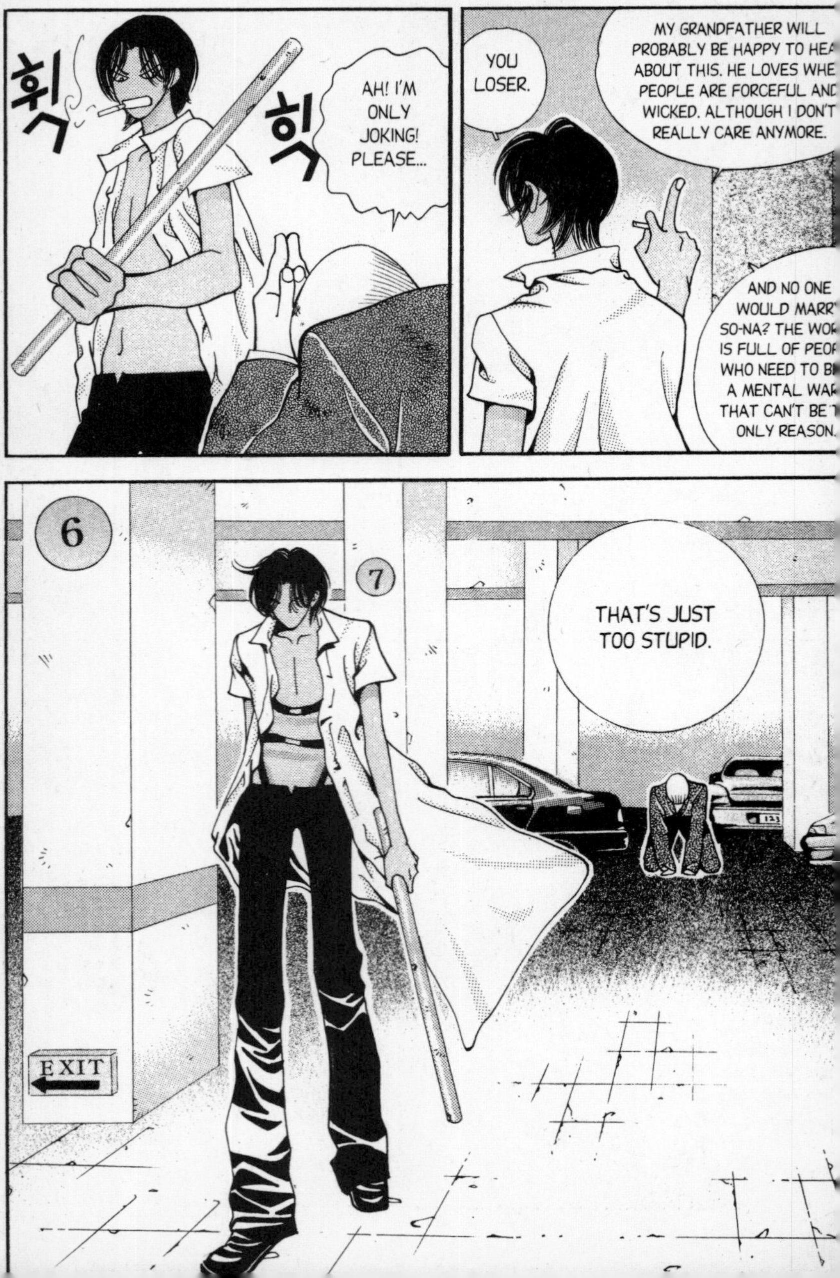
휙
힉
AH! I'M ONLY JOKING! PLEASE...
YOU LOSER.
MY GRANDFATHER WILL PROBABLY BE HAPPY TO HEA ABOUT THIS. HE LOVES WHE PEOPLE ARE FORCEFUL AND WICKED. ALTHOUGH I DON'T REALLY CARE ANYMORE.
AND NO ONE WOULD MARR SO-NA? THE WOR IS FULL OF PEOP WHO NEED TO B A MENTAL WAR THAT CAN'T BE T ONLY REASON.
6
7
THAT'S JUST TOO STUPID.
EXIT

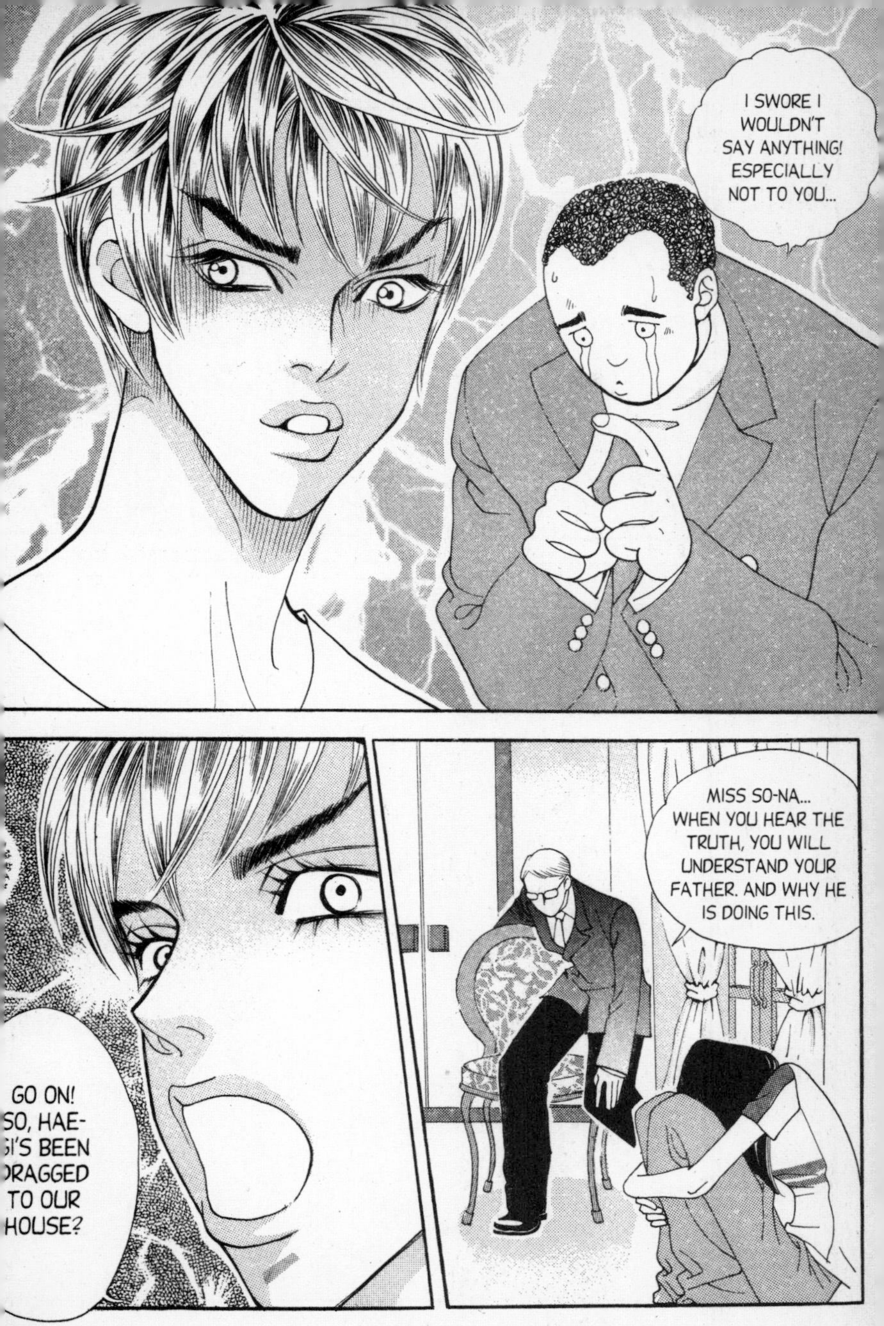
I SWORE I WOULDN'T SAY ANYTHING! ESPECIALLY NOT TO YOU...
GO ON! SO, HAE-GI'S BEEN DRAGGED TO OUR HOUSE?
MISS SO-NA... WHEN YOU HEAR THE TRUTH, YOU WILL UNDERSTAND YOUR FATHER. AND WHY HE IS DOING THIS.

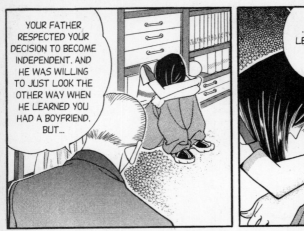

YOUR FATHER RESPECTED YOUR DECISION TO BECOME INDEPENDENT. AND HE WAS WILLING TO JUST LOOK THE OTHER WAY WHEN HE LEARNED YOU HAD A BOYFRIEND. BUT...

...THEN HE LEARNED HIS NAME.

I'M SURE YOU DON'T LIKE TO THINK ABOUT IT BUT...IT'S CONNECTED TO YOUR PAST...

DON'T YOU REMEMBER? ONE OF YOUR KIDNAPPERS WAS NAMED OH GAE-RI.

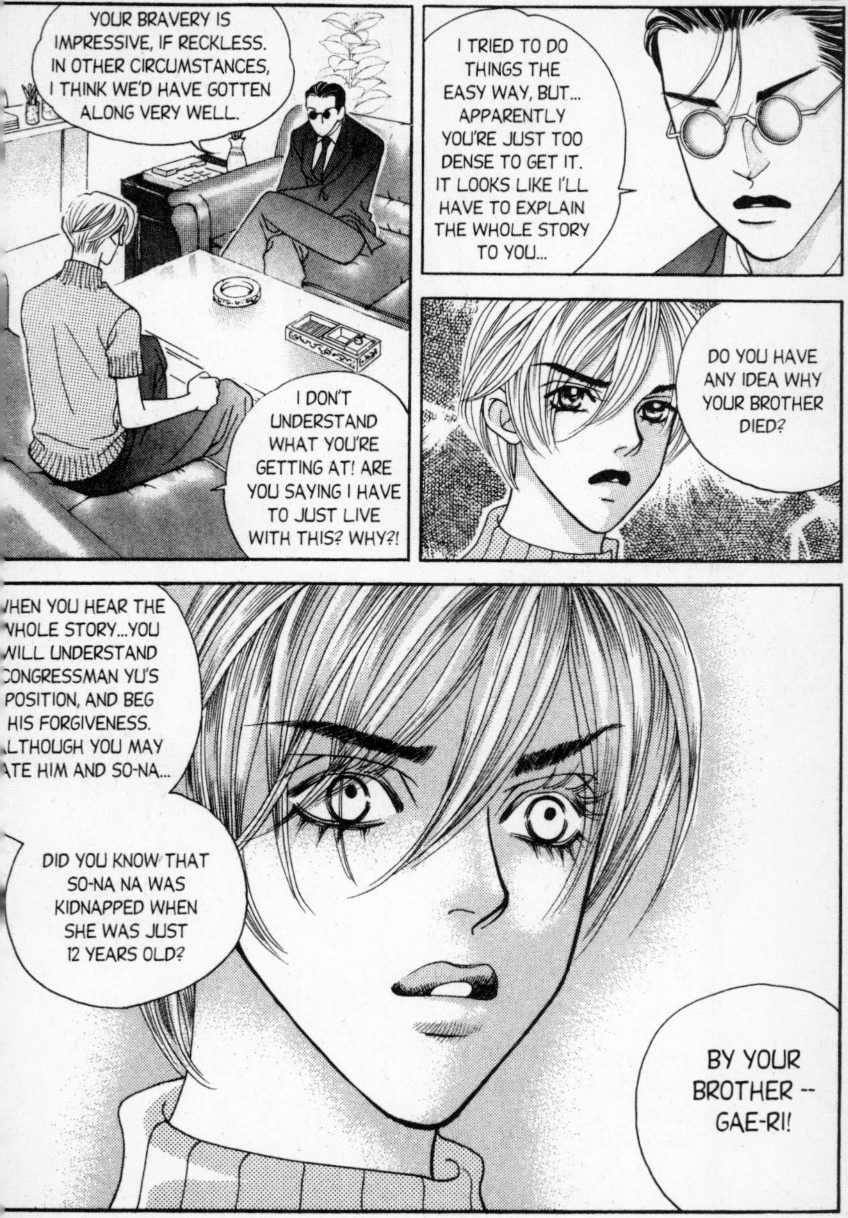
YOUR BRAVERY IS IMPRESSIVE, IF RECKLESS. IN OTHER CIRCUMSTANCES, I THINK WE'D HAVE GOTTEN ALONG VERY WELL.
I DON'T UNDERSTAND WHAT YOU'RE GETTING AT! ARE YOU SAYING I HAVE TO JUST LIVE WITH THIS? WHY?!
I TRIED TO DO THINGS THE EASY WAY, BUT... APPARENTLY YOU'RE JUST TOO DENSE TO GET IT. IT LOOKS LIKE I'LL HAVE TO EXPLAIN THE WHOLE STORY TO YOU...
DO YOU HAVE ANY IDEA WHY YOUR BROTHER DIED?
HEN YOU HEAR THE HOLE STORY...YOU ILL UNDERSTAND ONGRESSMAN YU'S POSITION, AND BEG HIS FORGIVENESS. LTHOUGH YOU MAY ATE HIM AND SO-NA...
DID YOU KNOW THAT SO-NA NA WAS KIDNAPPED WHEN SHE WAS JUST 12 YEARS OLD?
BY YOUR BROTHER -- GAE-RI!

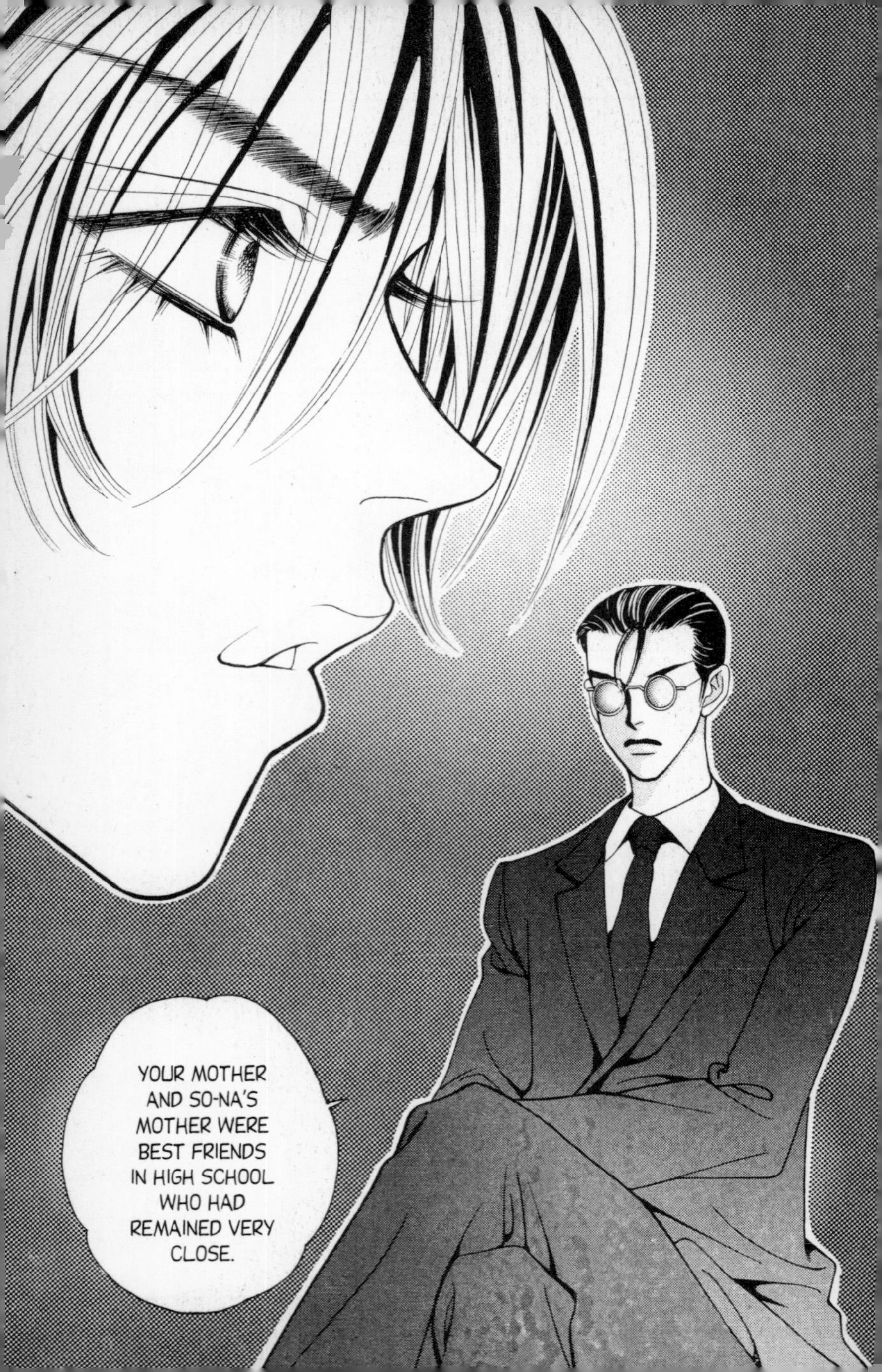
YOUR MOTHER AND SO-NA'S MOTHER WERE BEST FRIENDS IN HIGH SCHOOL WHO HAD REMAINED VERY CLOSE.

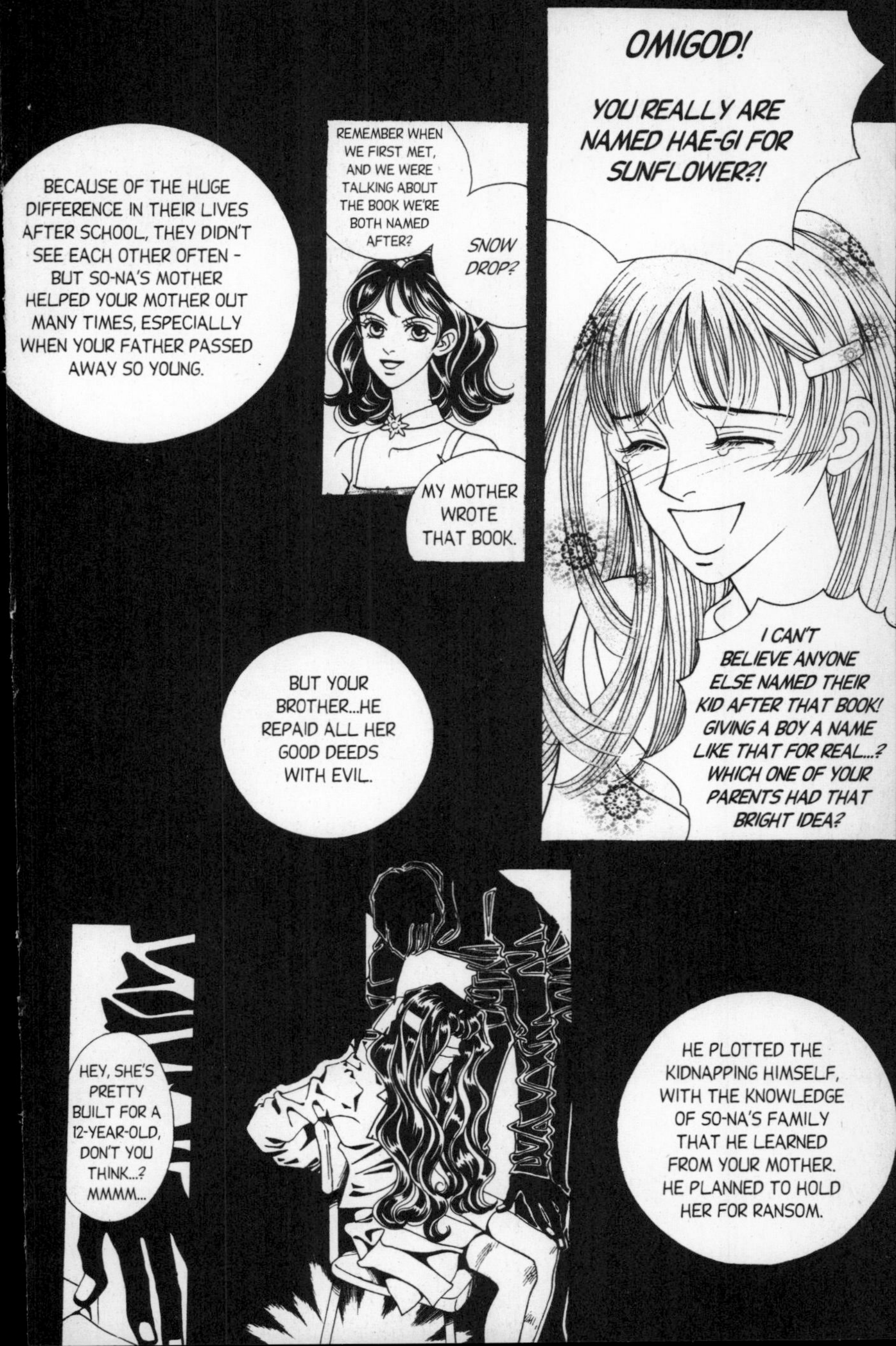
BECAUSE OF THE HUGE DIFFERENCE IN THEIR LIVES AFTER SCHOOL, THEY DIDN'T SEE EACH OTHER OFTEN - BUT SO-NA'S MOTHER HELPED YOUR MOTHER OUT MANY TIMES, ESPECIALLY WHEN YOUR FATHER PASSED AWAY SO YOUNG.
REMEMBER WHEN WE FIRST MET, AND WE WERE TALKING ABOUT THE BOOK WE'RE BOTH NAMED AFTER?
SNOW DROP?
MY MOTHER WROTE THAT BOOK.
OMIGOD!
YOU REALLY ARE NAMED HAE-GI FOR SUNFLOWER?!
I CAN'T BELIEVE ANYONE ELSE NAMED THEIR KID AFTER THAT BOOK! GIVING A BOY A NAME LIKE THAT FOR REAL...? WHICH ONE OF YOUR PARENTS HAD THAT BRIGHT IDEA?
BUT YOUR BROTHER...HE REPAID ALL HER GOOD DEEDS WITH EVIL.
HEY, SHE'S PRETTY BUILT FOR A 12-YEAR-OLD, DON'T YOU THINK...? MMMM...
HE PLOTTED THE KIDNAPPING HIMSELF, WITH THE KNOWLEDGE OF SO-NA'S FAMILY THAT HE LEARNED FROM YOUR MOTHER. HE PLANNED TO HOLD HER FOR RANSOM.

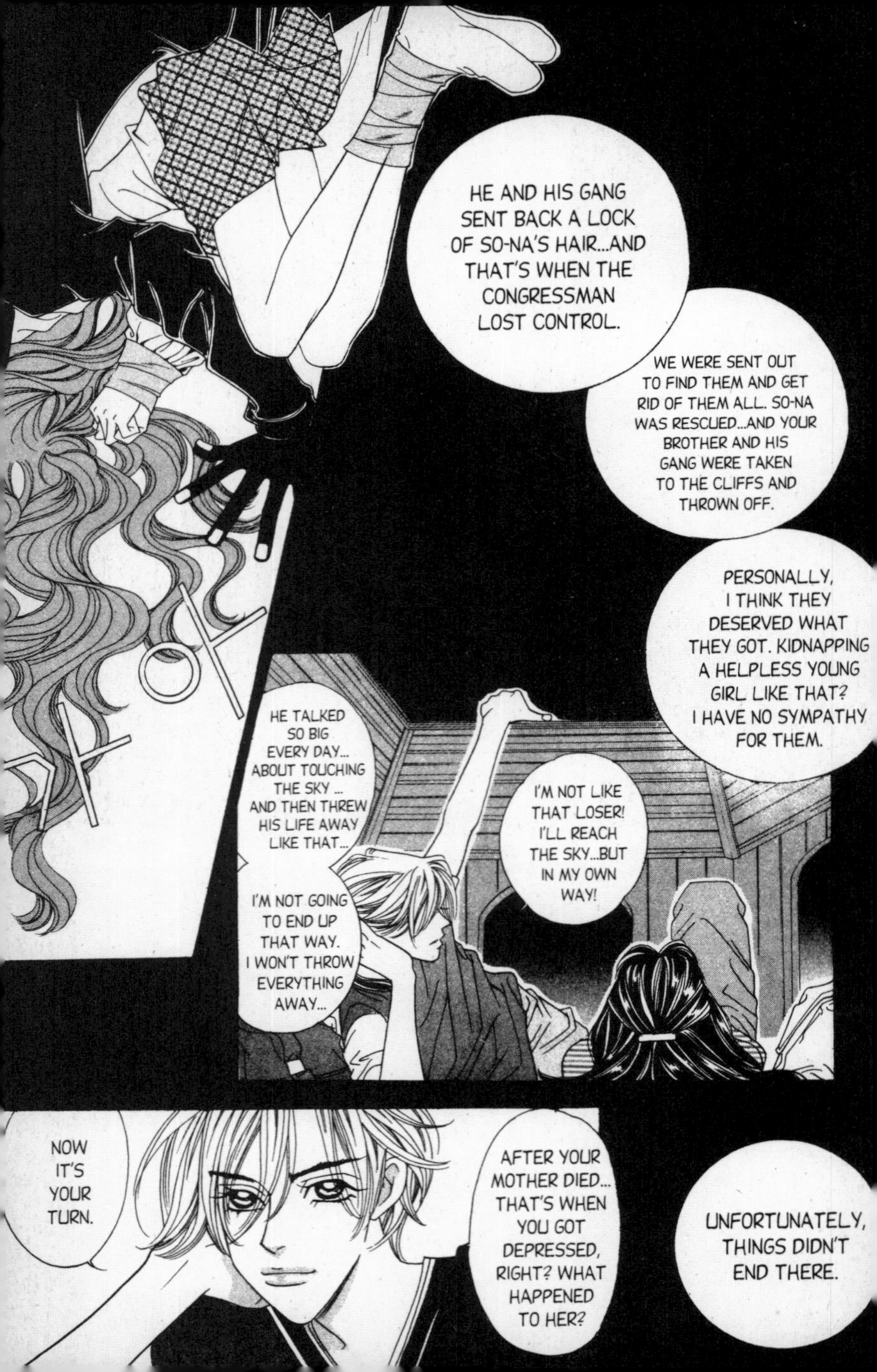
HE AND HIS GANG SENT BACK A LOCK OF SO-NA'S HAIR...AND THAT'S WHEN THE CONGRESSMAN LOST CONTROL.
WE WERE SENT OUT TO FIND THEM AND GET RID OF THEM ALL. SO-NA WAS RESCUED...AND YOUR BROTHER AND HIS GANG WERE TAKEN TO THE CLIFFS AND THROWN OFF.
PERSONALLY, I THINK THEY DESERVED WHAT THEY GOT. KIDNAPPING A HELPLESS YOUNG GIRL LIKE THAT? I HAVE NO SYMPATHY FOR THEM.
HE TALKED SO BIG EVERY DAY... ABOUT TOUCHING THE SKY ... AND THEN THREW HIS LIFE AWAY LIKE THAT...
I'M NOT GOING TO END UP THAT WAY. I WON'T THROW EVERYTHING AWAY...
I'M NOT LIKE THAT LOSER! I'LL REACH THE SKY...BUT IN MY OWN WAY!
NOW IT'S YOUR TURN.
AFTER YOUR MOTHER DIED... THAT'S WHEN YOU GOT DEPRESSED, RIGHT? WHAT HAPPENED TO HER?
UNFORTUNATELY, THINGS DIDN'T END THERE.

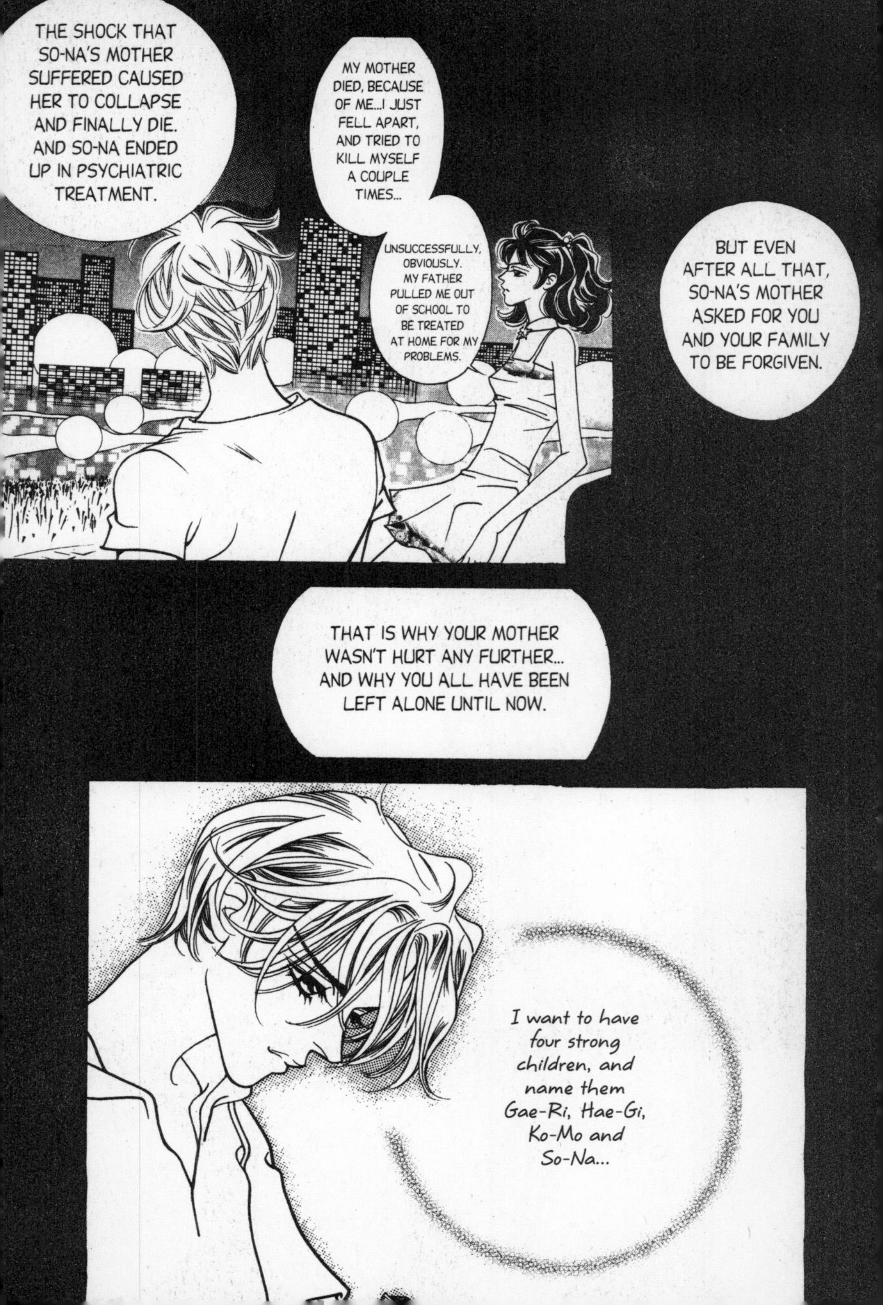
THE SHOCK THAT SO-NA'S MOTHER SUFFERED CAUSED HER TO COLLAPSE AND FINALLY DIE. AND SO-NA ENDED UP IN PSYCHIATRIC TREATMENT.
MY MOTHER DIED, BECAUSE OF ME...I JUST FELL APART, AND TRIED TO KILL MYSELF A COUPLE TIMES...
UNSUCCESSFULLY, OBVIOUSLY. MY FATHER PULLED ME OUT OF SCHOOL TO BE TREATED AT HOME FOR MY PROBLEMS.
BUT EVEN AFTER ALL THAT, SO-NA'S MOTHER ASKED FOR YOU AND YOUR FAMILY TO BE FORGIVEN.
THAT IS WHY YOUR MOTHER WASN'T HURT ANY FURTHER... AND WHY YOU ALL HAVE BEEN LEFT ALONE UNTIL NOW.
I want to have four strong children, and name them Gae-Ri, Hae-Gi, Ko-Mo and So-Na...

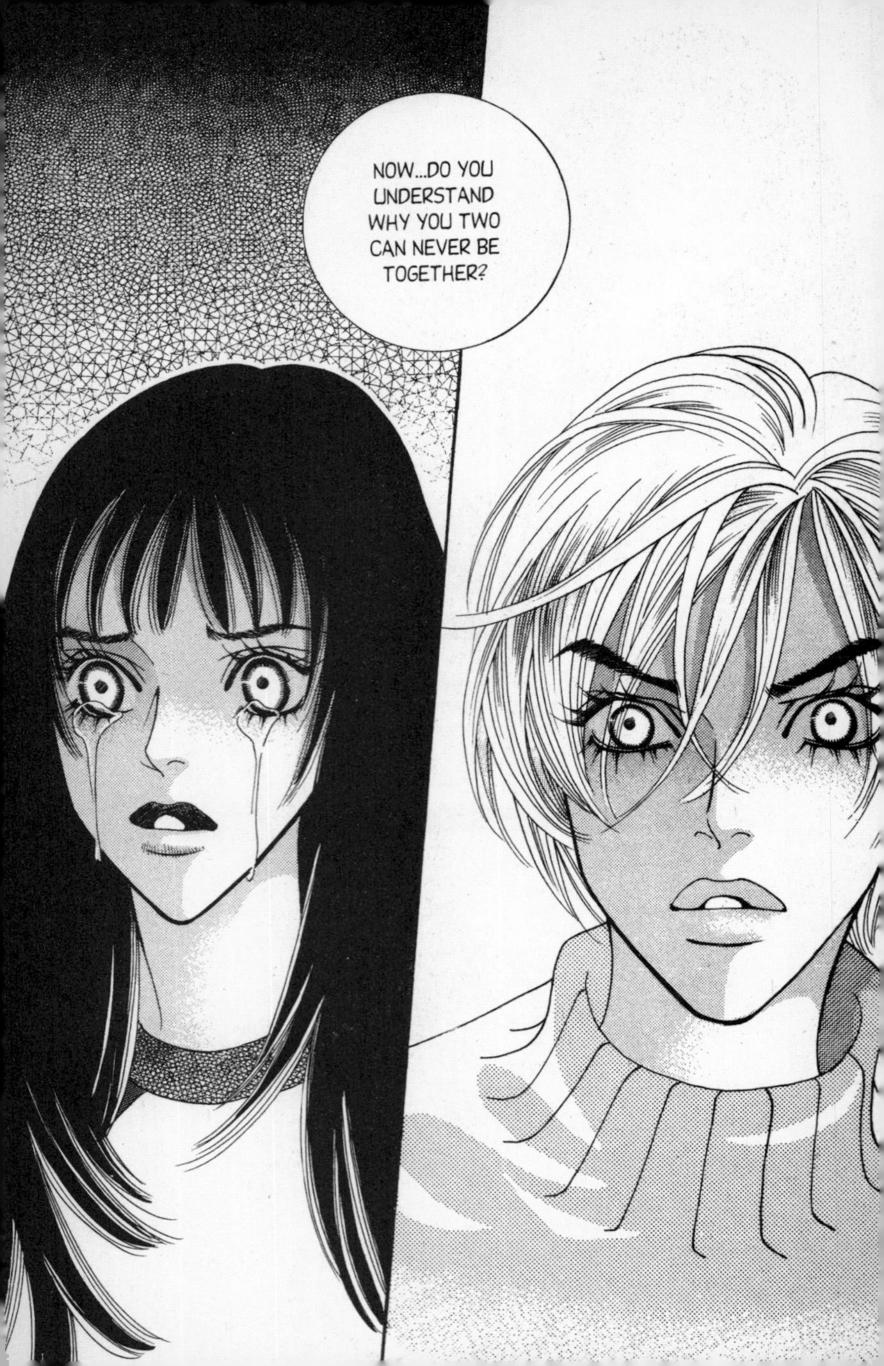
NOW...DO YOU UNDERSTAND WHY YOU TWO CAN NEVER BE TOGETHER?

스노우 드롭

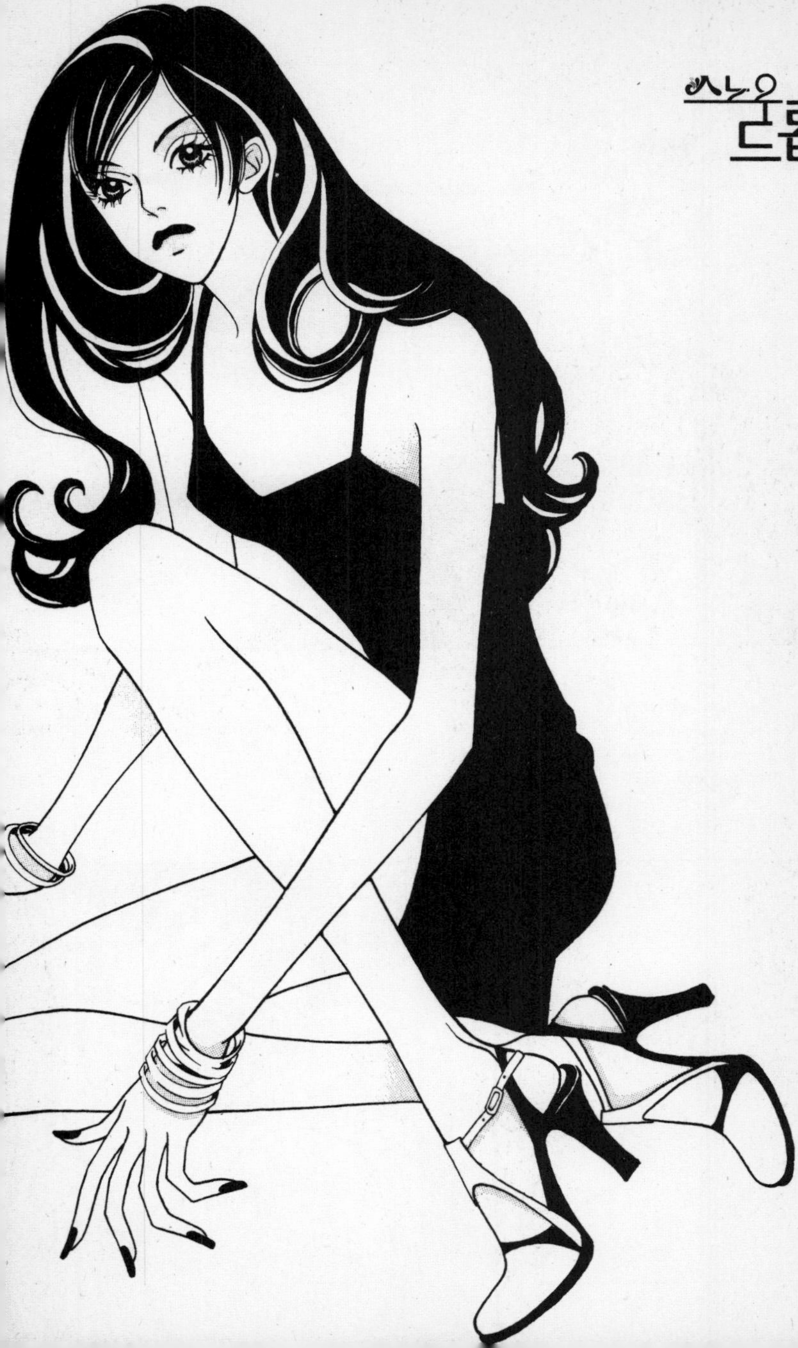

Can you really go on seeing each other under these circumstances?

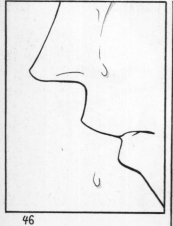

YOU WANT ME TO BELIEVE THAT ONE OF MY KIDNAPPERS WAS HAE-GI'S BROTHER?

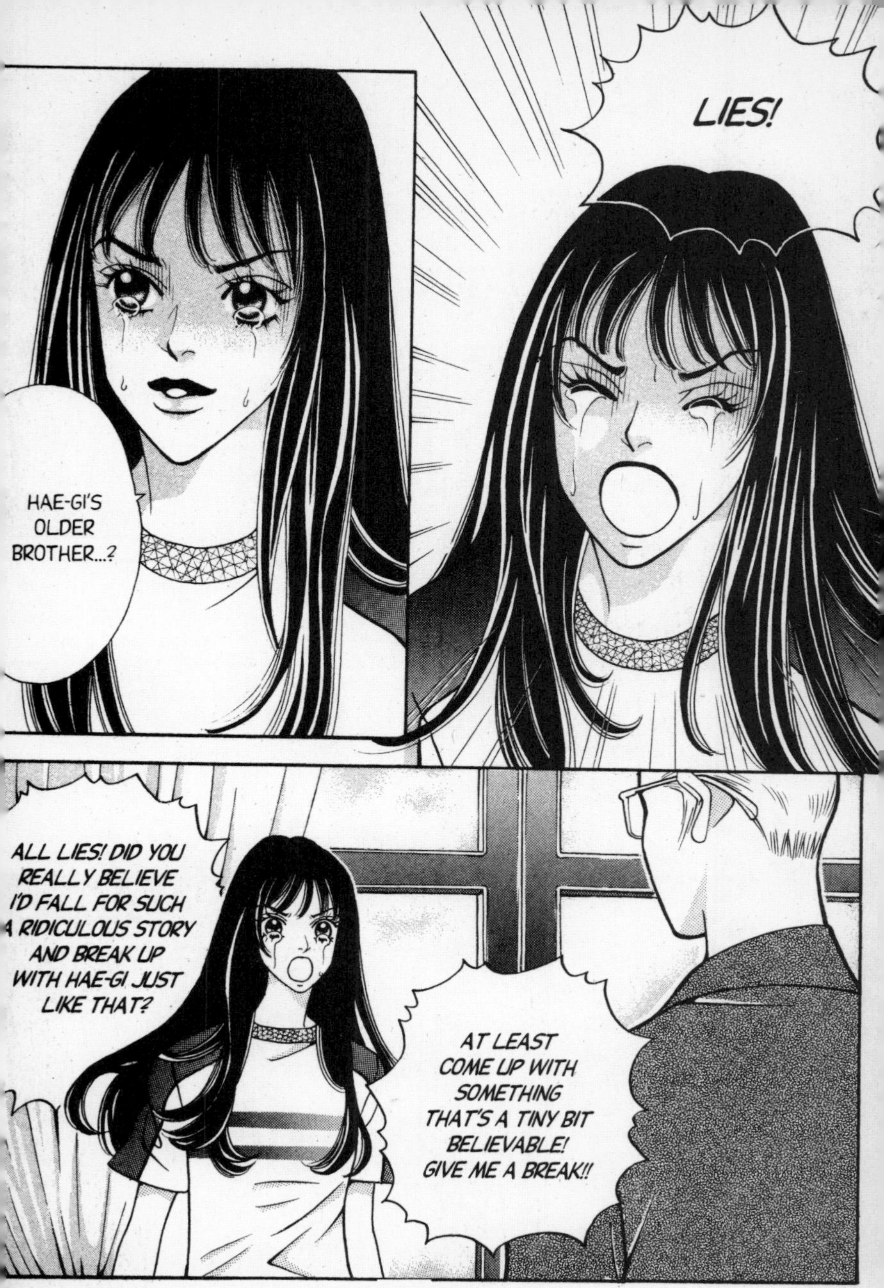
HAE-GI'S OLDER BROTHER...?
LIES!
ALL LIES! DID YOU REALLY BELIEVE I'D FALL FOR SUCH A RIDICULOUS STORY AND BREAK UP WITH HAE-GI JUST LIKE THAT?
AT LEAST COME UP WITH SOMETHING THAT'S A TINY BIT BELIEVABLE! GIVE ME A BREAK!!

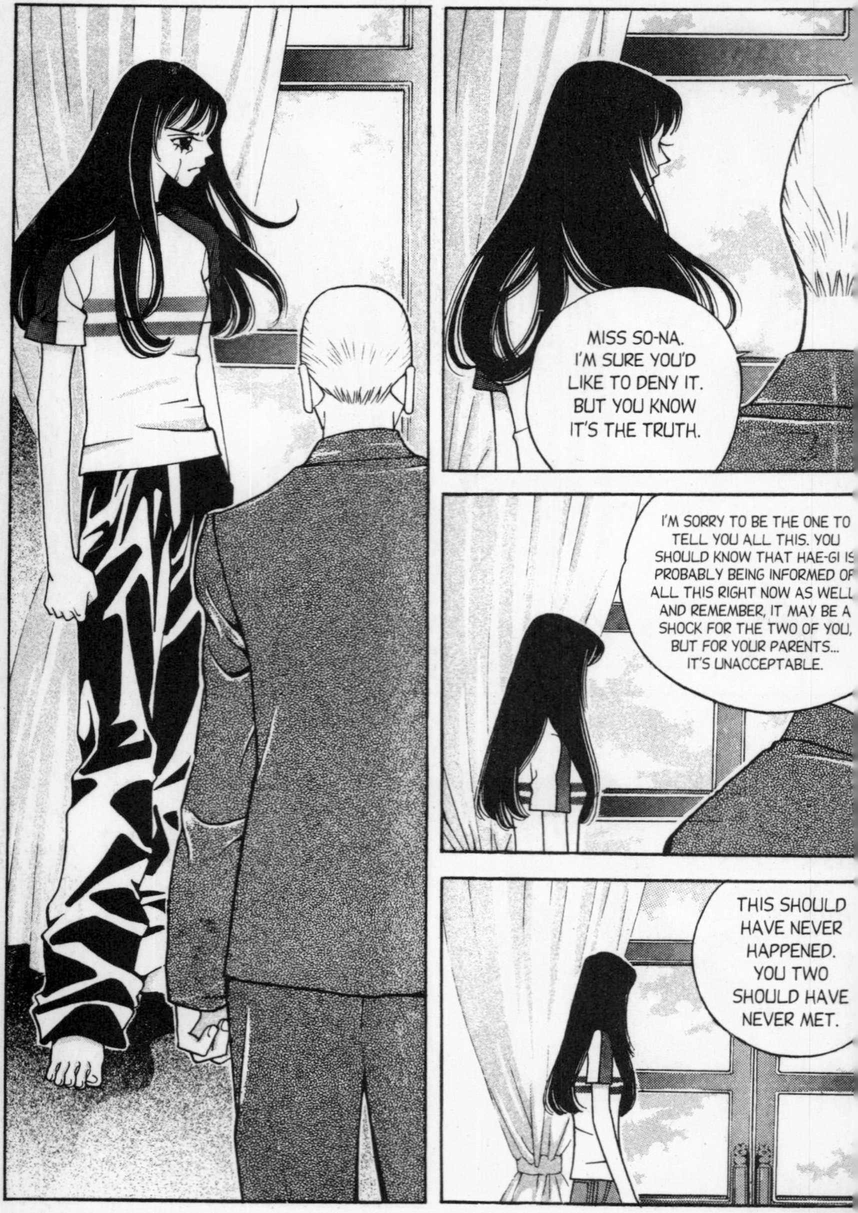
MISS SO-NA. I'M SURE YOU'D LIKE TO DENY IT. BUT YOU KNOW IT'S THE TRUTH.
I'M SORRY TO BE THE ONE TO TELL YOU ALL THIS. YOU SHOULD KNOW THAT HAE-GI IS PROBABLY BEING INFORMED OF ALL THIS RIGHT NOW AS WELL AND REMEMBER, IT MAY BE A SHOCK FOR THE TWO OF YOU, BUT FOR YOUR PARENTS... IT'S UNACCEPTABLE.
THIS SHOULD HAVE NEVER HAPPENED. YOU TWO SHOULD HAVE NEVER MET.

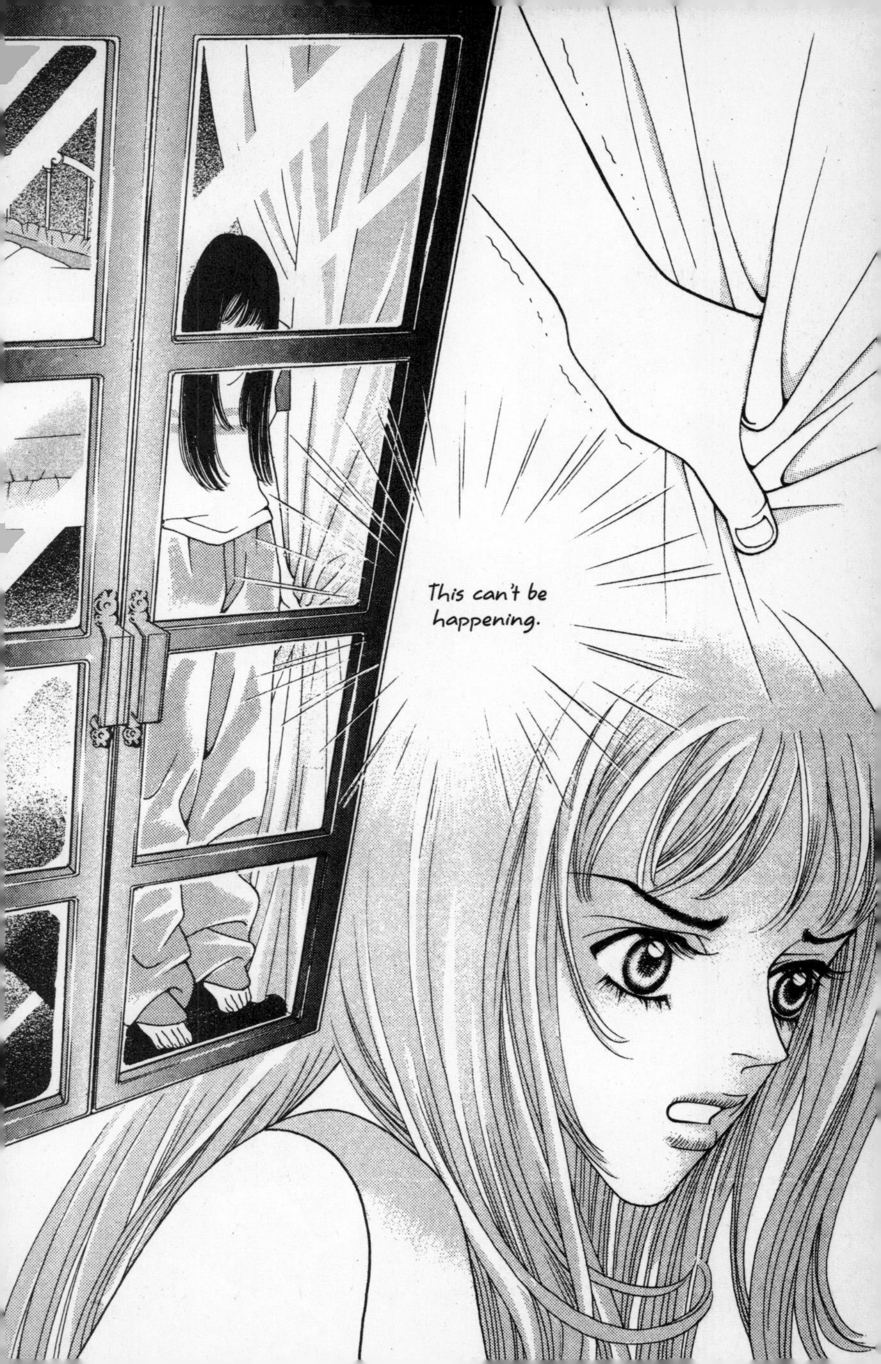
This can't be happening.

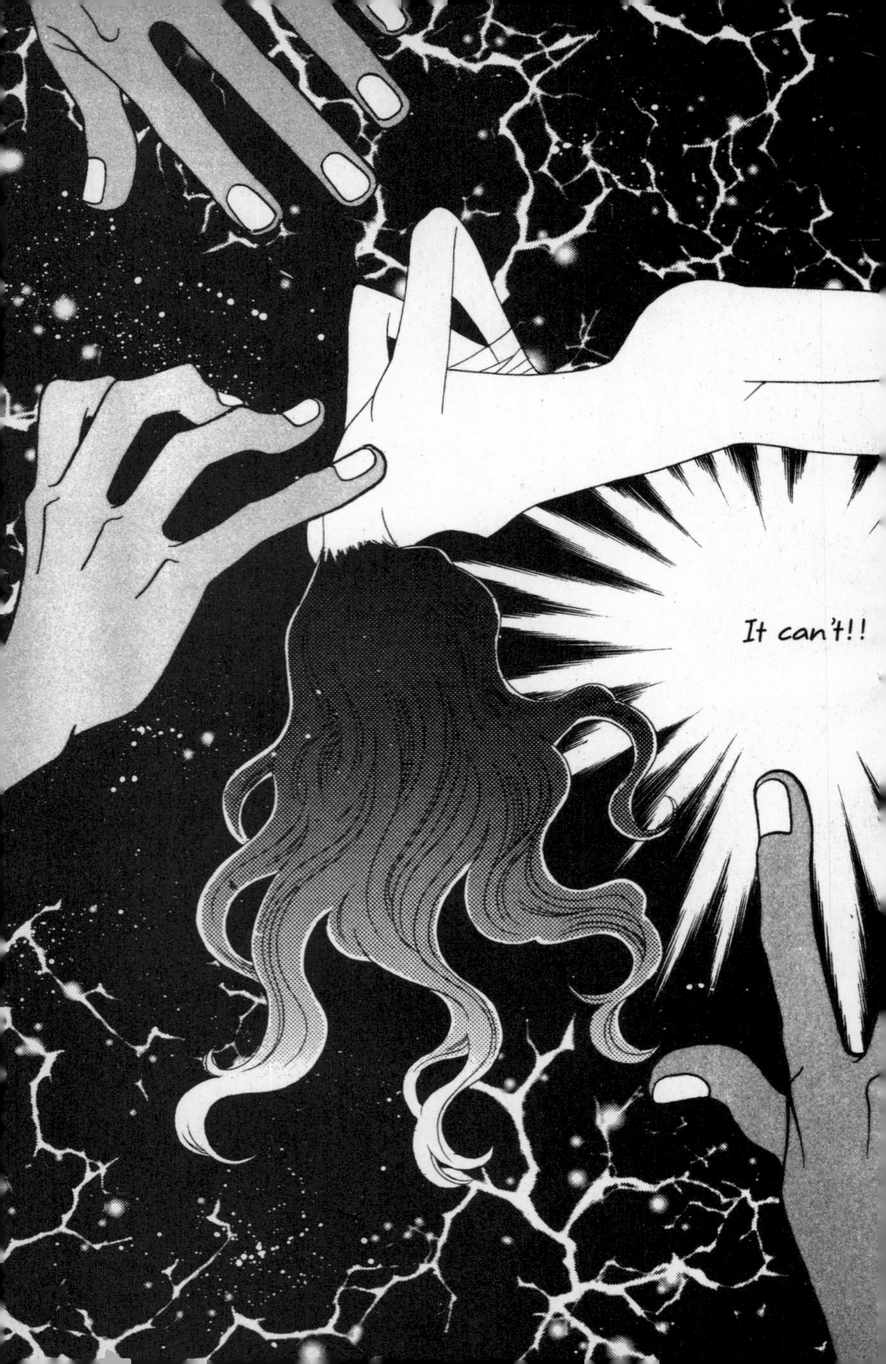
It can't!!

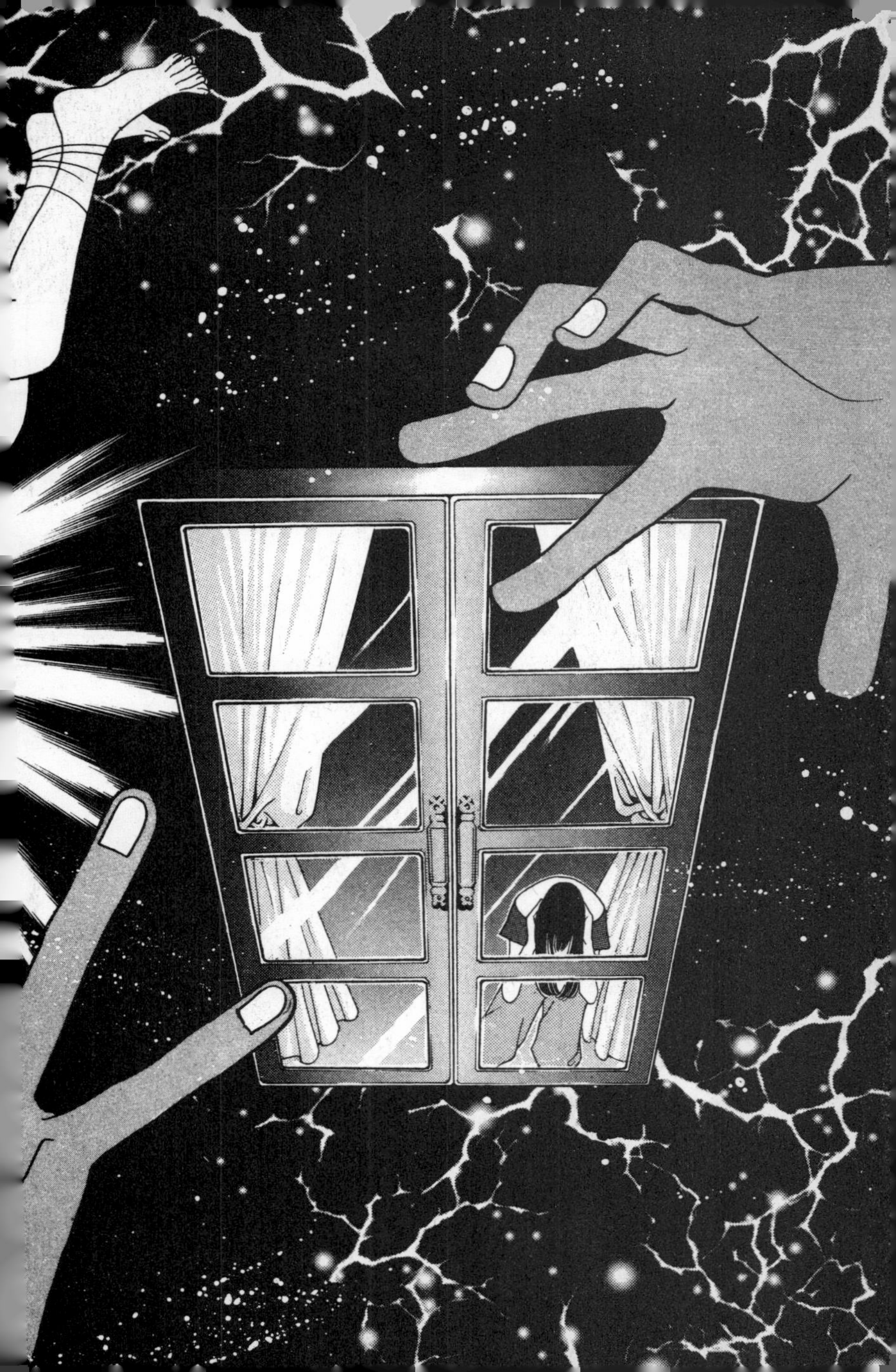

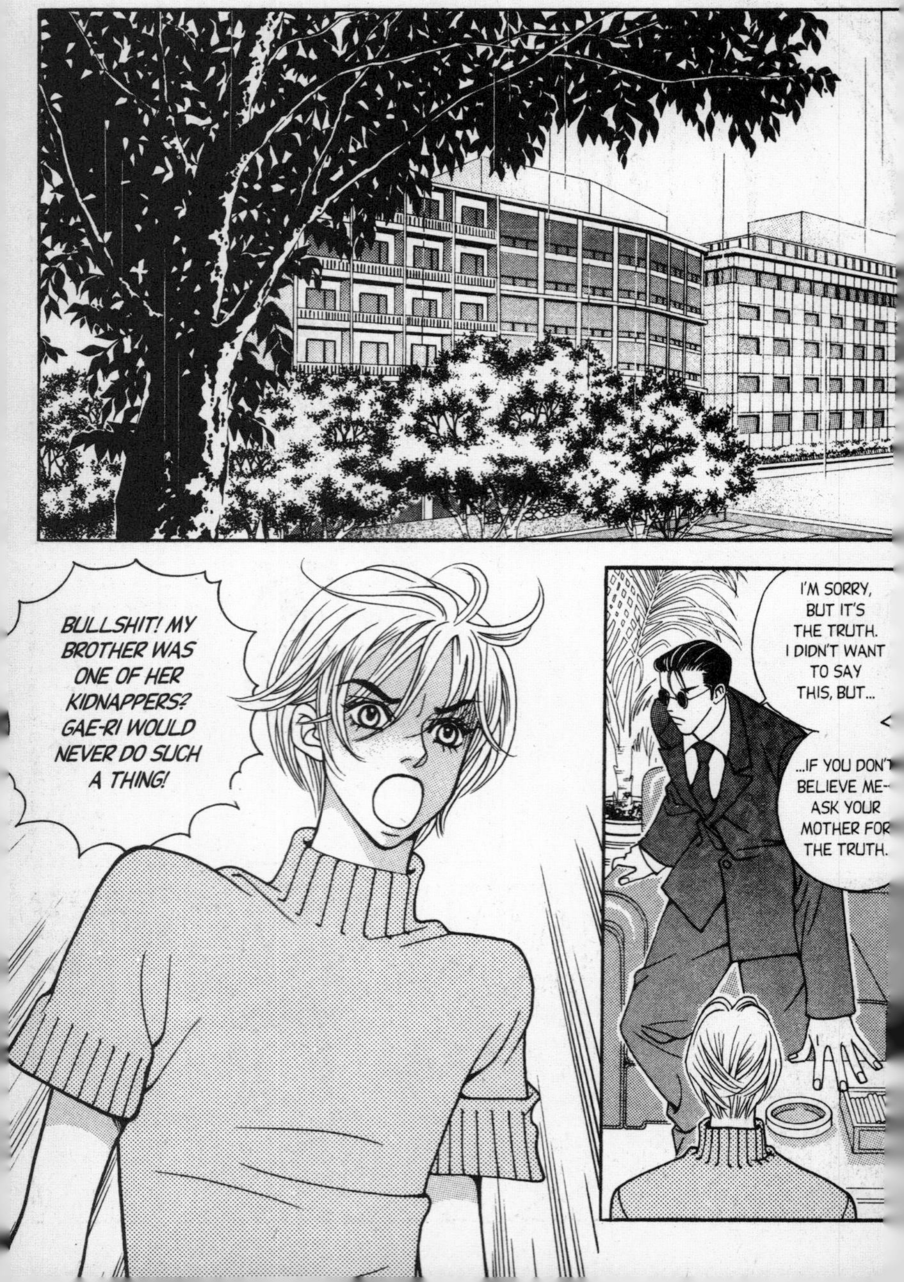
BULLSHIT! MY BROTHER WAS ONE OF HER KIDNAPPERS? GAE-RI WOULD NEVER DO SUCH A THING!
I'M SORRY, BUT IT'S THE TRUTH. I DIDN'T WANT TO SAY THIS, BUT...
...IF YOU DON'T BELIEVE ME-- ASK YOUR MOTHER FOR THE TRUTH.

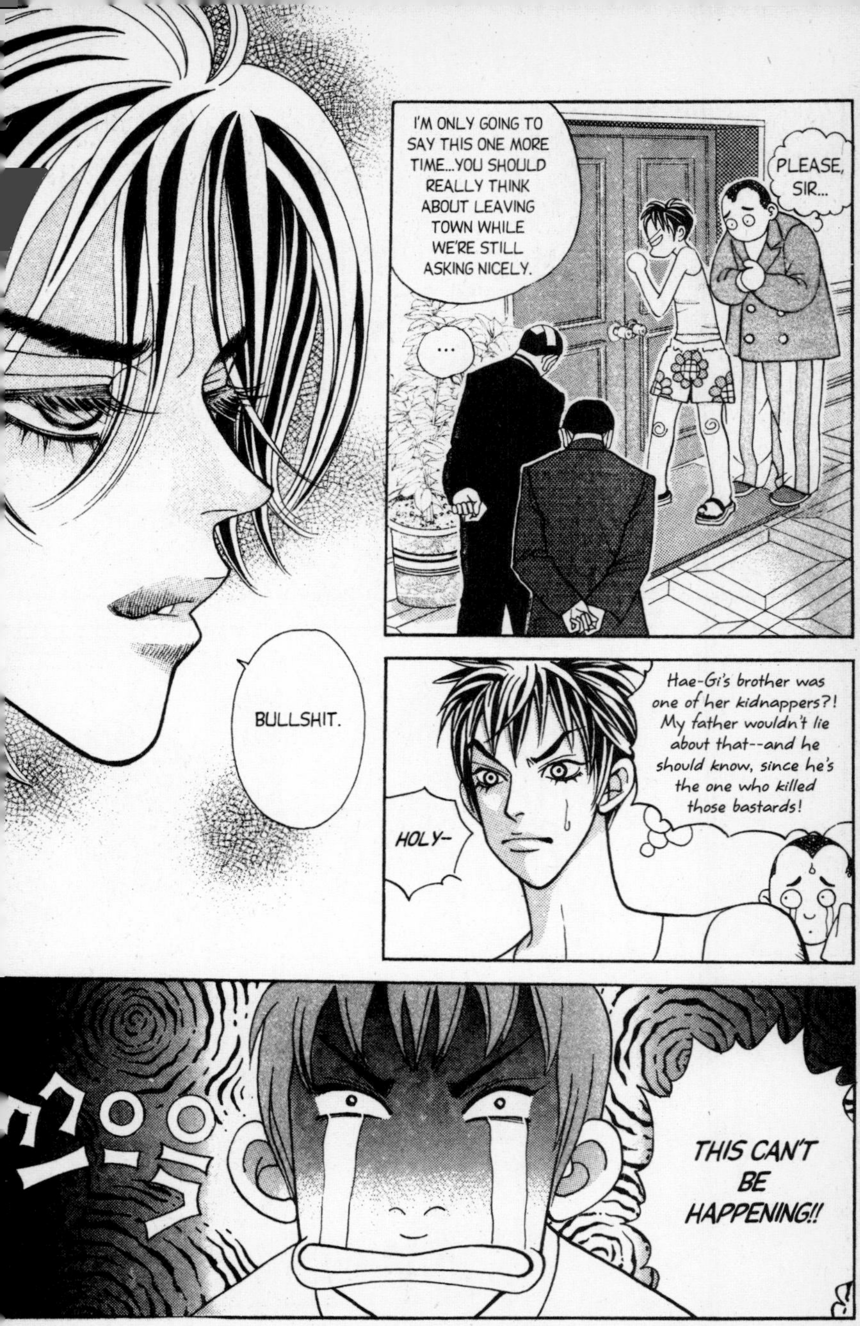
BULLSHIT.
I'M ONLY GOING TO SAY THIS ONE MORE TIME...YOU SHOULD REALLY THINK ABOUT LEAVING TOWN WHILE WE'RE STILL ASKING NICELY.
PLEASE, SIR...
...
HOLY--
Hae-Gi's brother was one of her kidnappers?! My father wouldn't lie about that--and he should know, since he's the one who killed those bastards!
THIS CAN'T BE HAPPENING!!

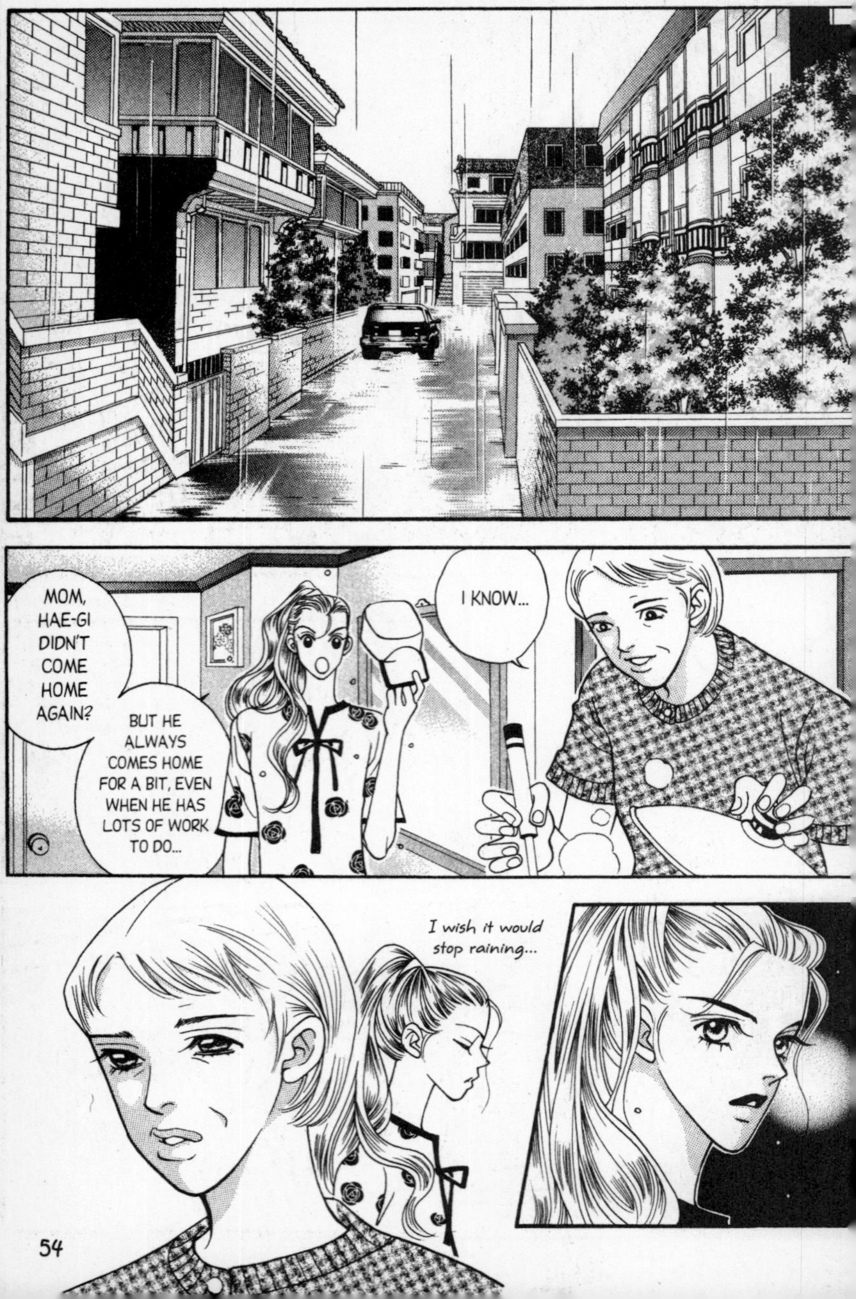
MOM, HAE-GI DIDN'T COME HOME AGAIN?
BUT HE ALWAYS COMES HOME FOR A BIT, EVEN WHEN HE HAS LOTS OF WORK TO DO...
I KNOW...
I wish it would stop raining...

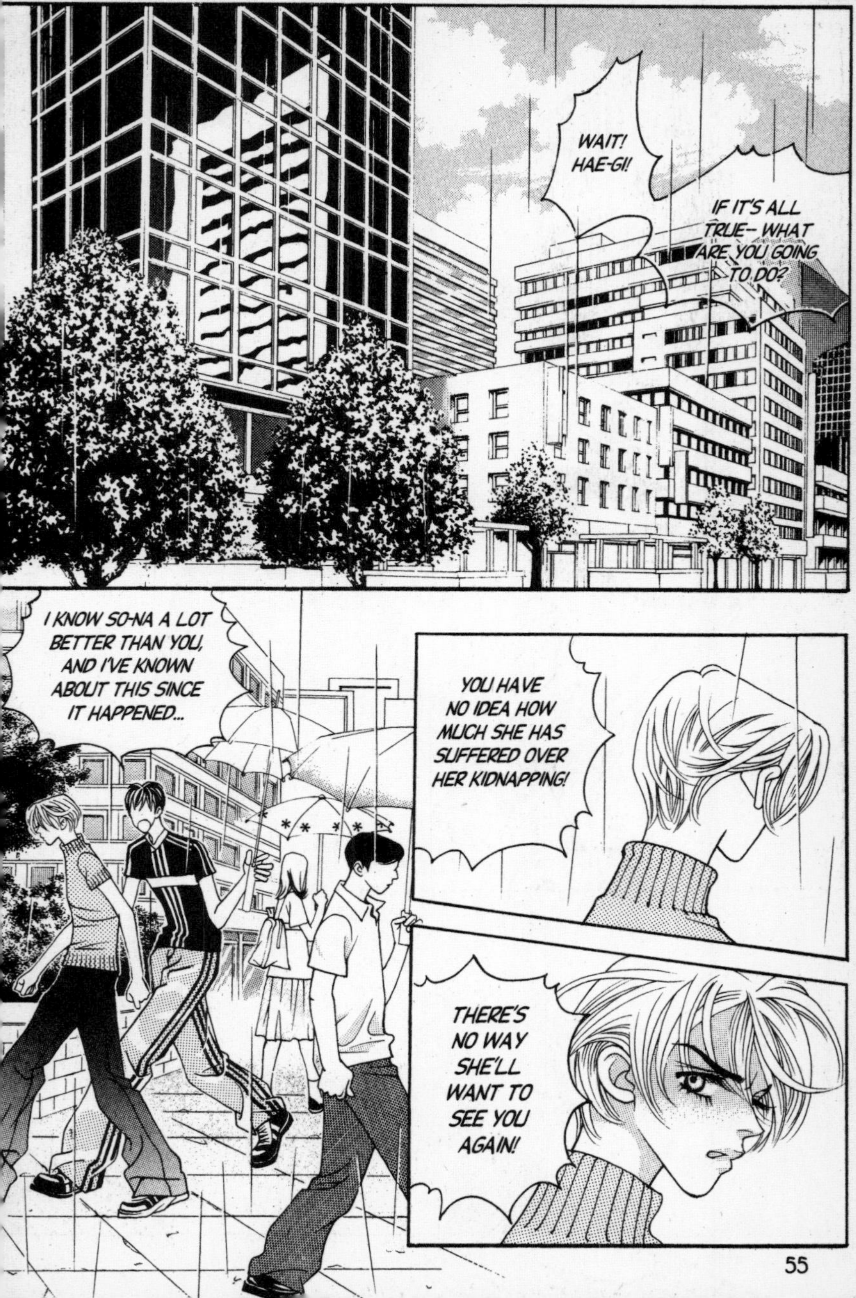
WAIT! HAE-GI!
IF IT'S ALL TRUE-- WHAT ARE YOU GOING TO DO?
I KNOW SO-NA A LOT BETTER THAN YOU, AND I'VE KNOWN ABOUT THIS SINCE IT HAPPENED...
YOU HAVE NO IDEA HOW MUCH SHE HAS SUFFERED OVER HER KIDNAPPING!
THERE'S NO WAY SHE'LL WANT TO SEE YOU AGAIN!

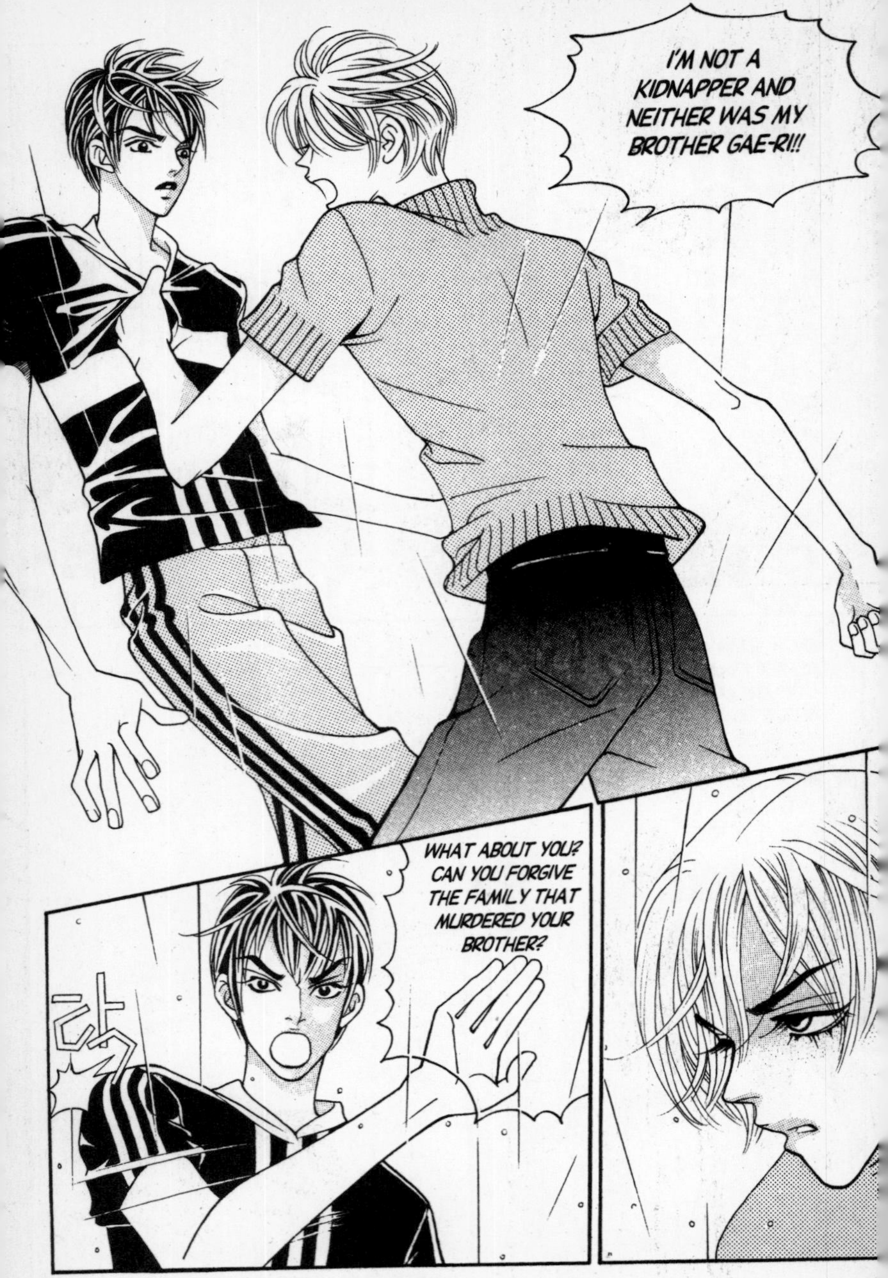
I'M NOT A KIDNAPPER AND NEITHER WAS MY BROTHER GAE-RI!!!
WHAT ABOUT YOU? CAN YOU FORGIVE THE FAMILY THAT MURDERED YOUR BROTHER?

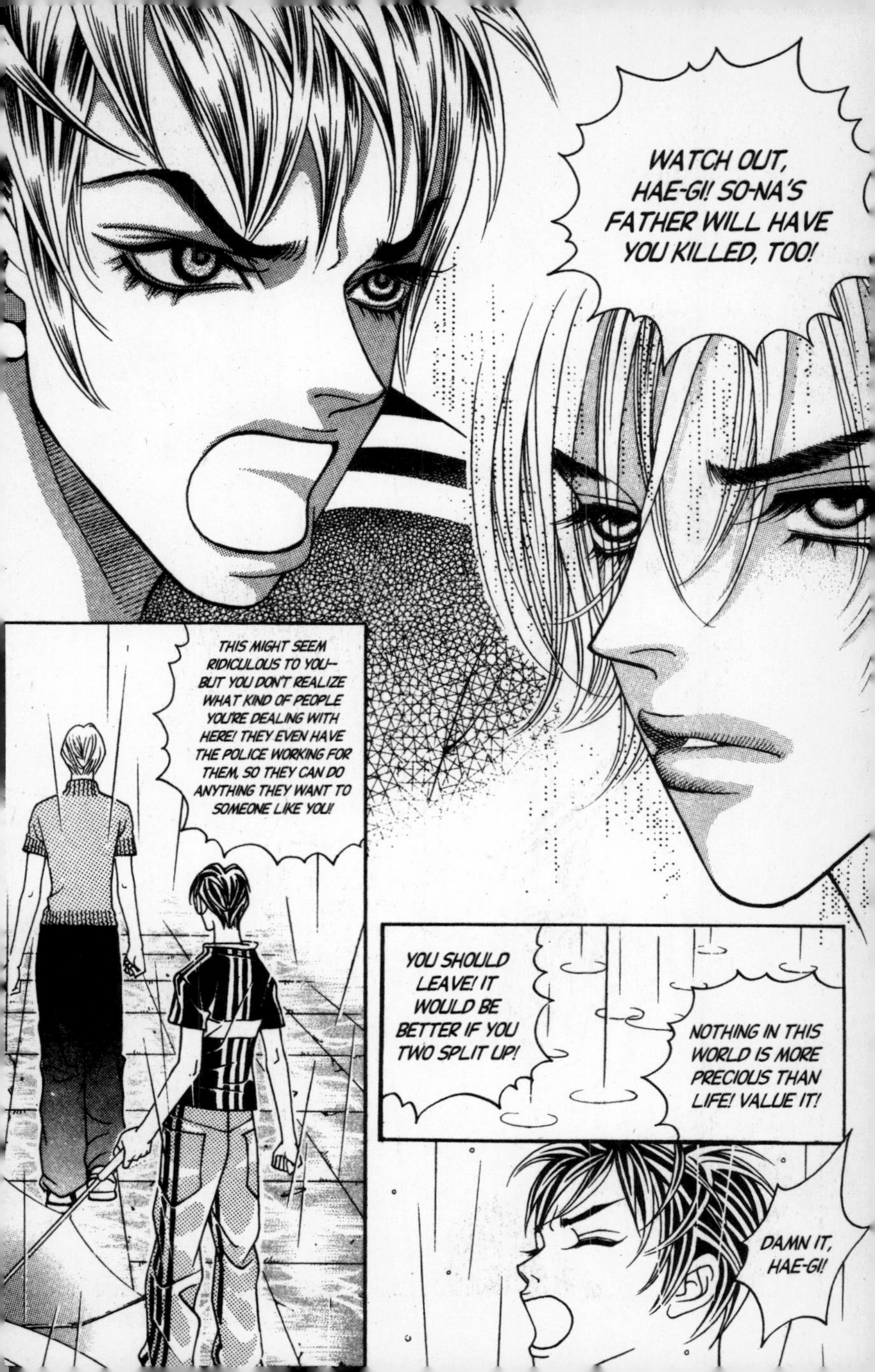
WATCH OUT, HAE-GI! SO-NA'S FATHER WILL HAVE YOU KILLED, TOO!
THIS MIGHT SEEM RIDICULOUS TO YOU-- BUT YOU DON'T REALIZE WHAT KIND OF PEOPLE YOU'RE DEALING WITH HERE! THEY EVEN HAVE THE POLICE WORKING FOR THEM, SO THEY CAN DO ANYTHING THEY WANT TO SOMEONE LIKE YOU!
YOU SHOULD LEAVE! IT WOULD BE BETTER IF YOU TWO SPLIT UP!
NOTHING IN THIS WORLD IS MORE PRECIOUS THAN LIFE! VALUE IT!
DAMN IT, HAE-GI!

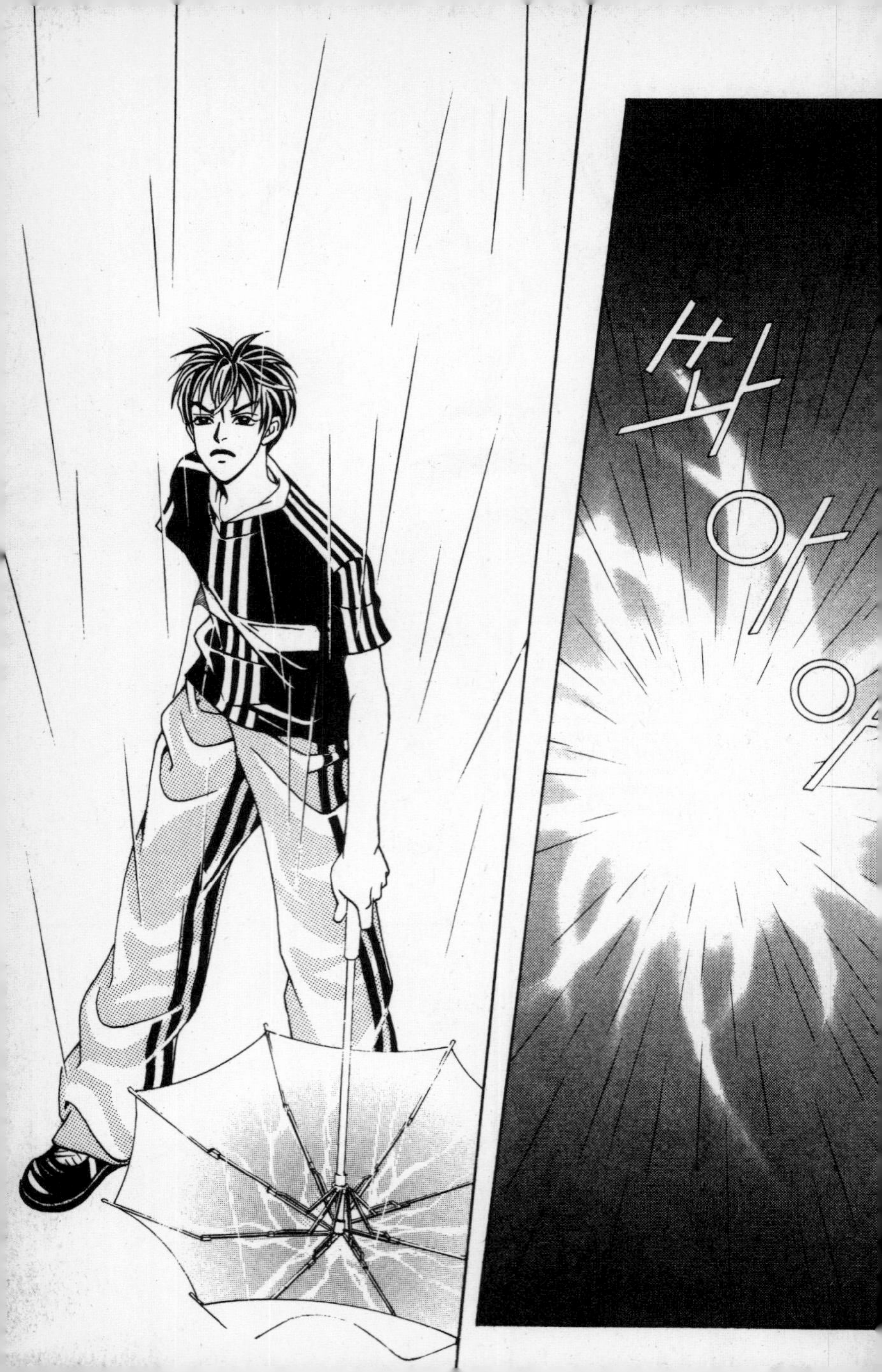
쏴아아

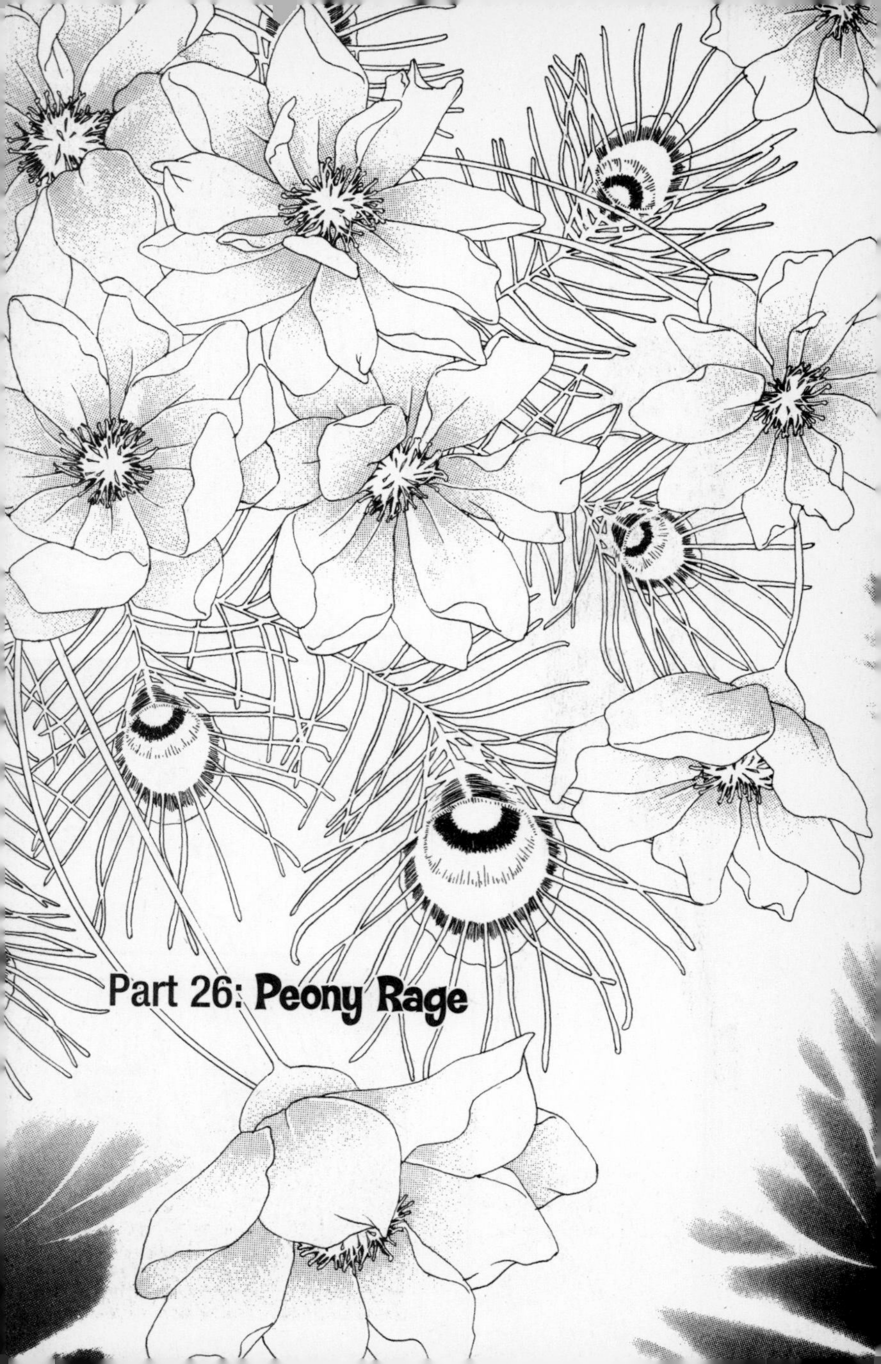
Part 26: Peony Rage

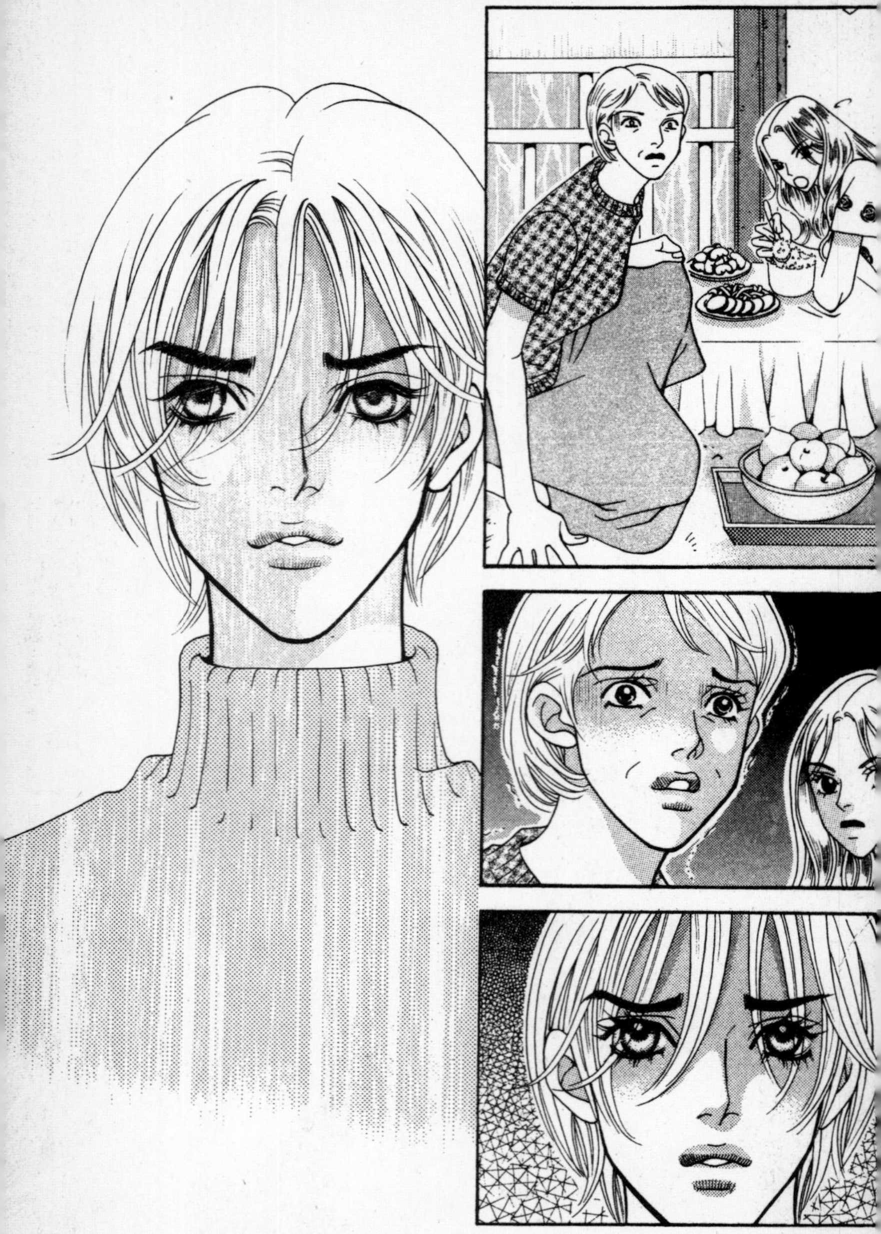

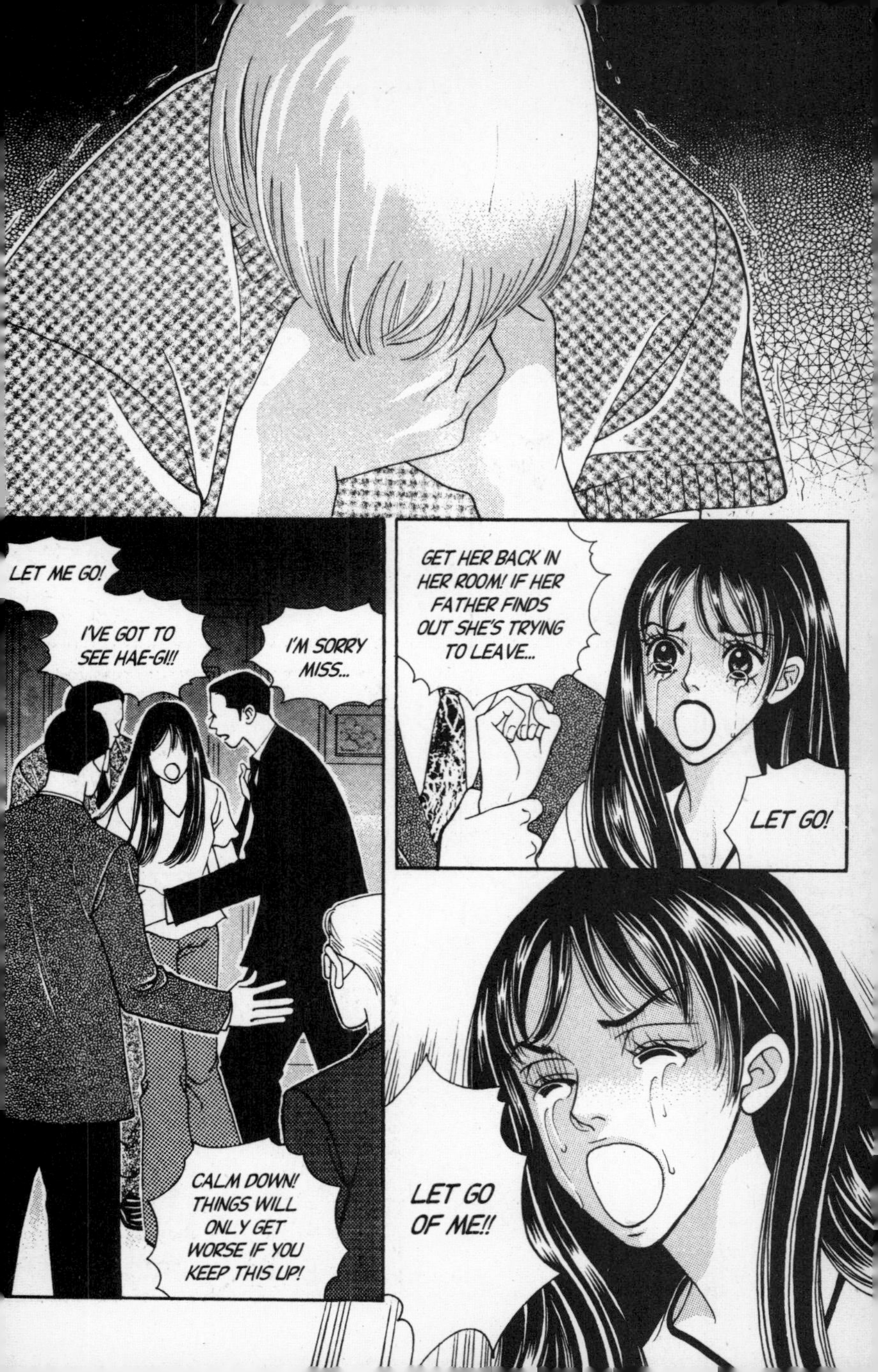
LET ME GO!
I'VE GOT TO SEE HAE-GI!!
I'M SORRY MISS...
CALM DOWN! THINGS WILL ONLY GET WORSE IF YOU KEEP THIS UP!
GET HER BACK IN HER ROOM! IF HER FATHER FINDS OUT SHE'S TRYING TO LEAVE...
LET GO!
LET GO OF ME!!

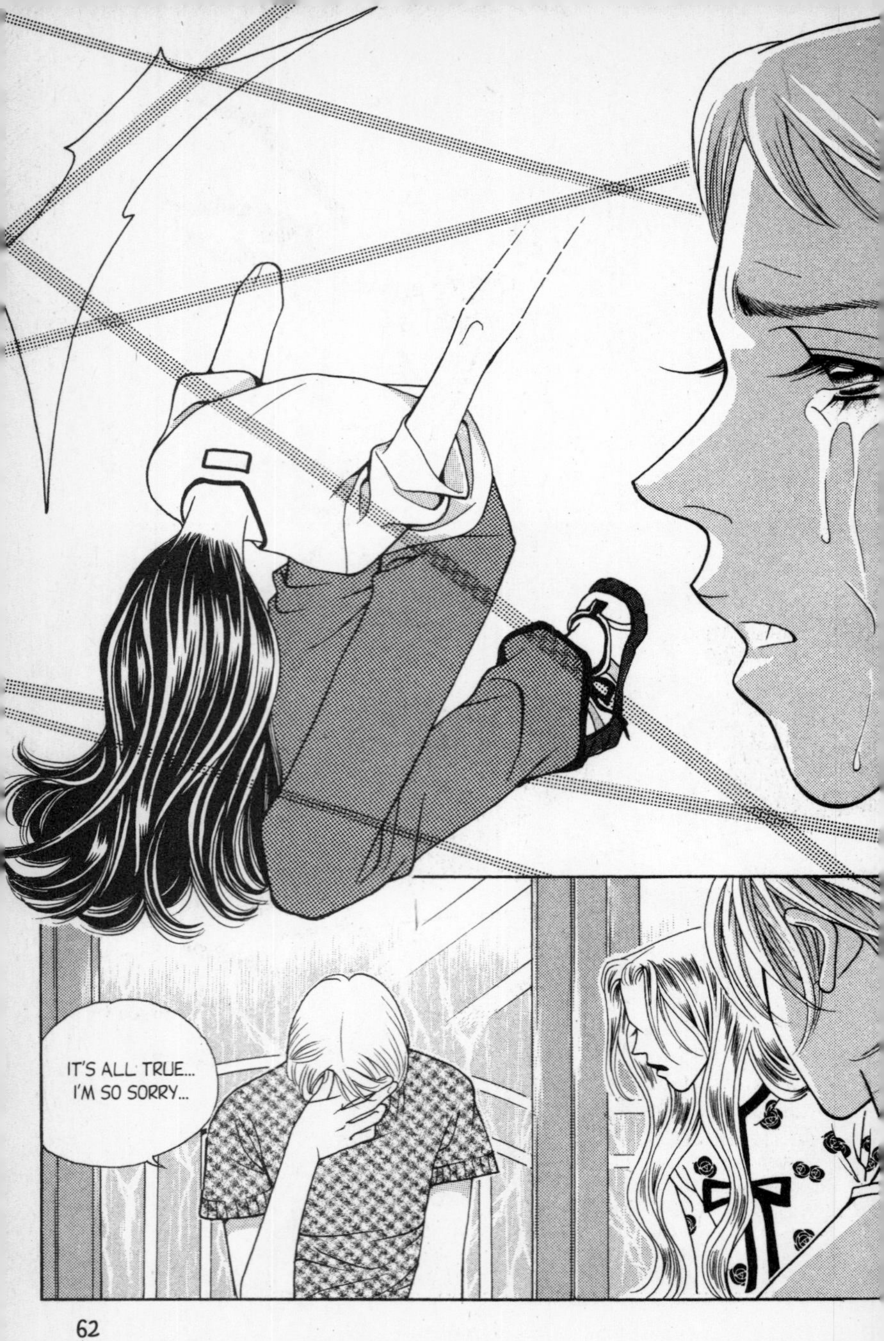
IT'S ALL TRUE...
I'M SO SORRY...

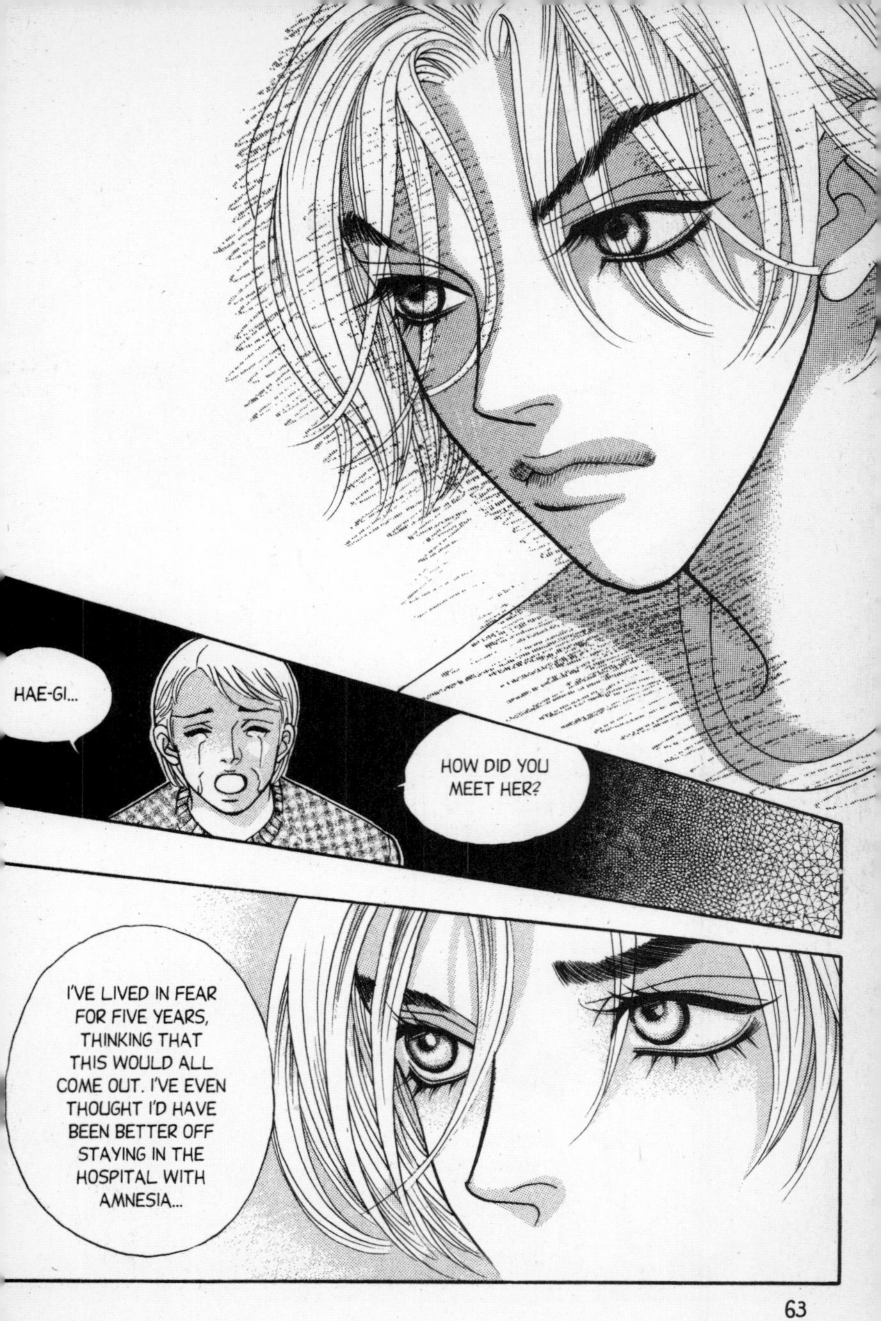
HAE-GI...
HOW DID YOU MEET HER?
I'VE LIVED IN FEAR FOR FIVE YEARS, THINKING THAT THIS WOULD ALL COME OUT. I'VE EVEN THOUGHT I'D HAVE BEEN BETTER OFF STAYING IN THE HOSPITAL WITH AMNESIA...

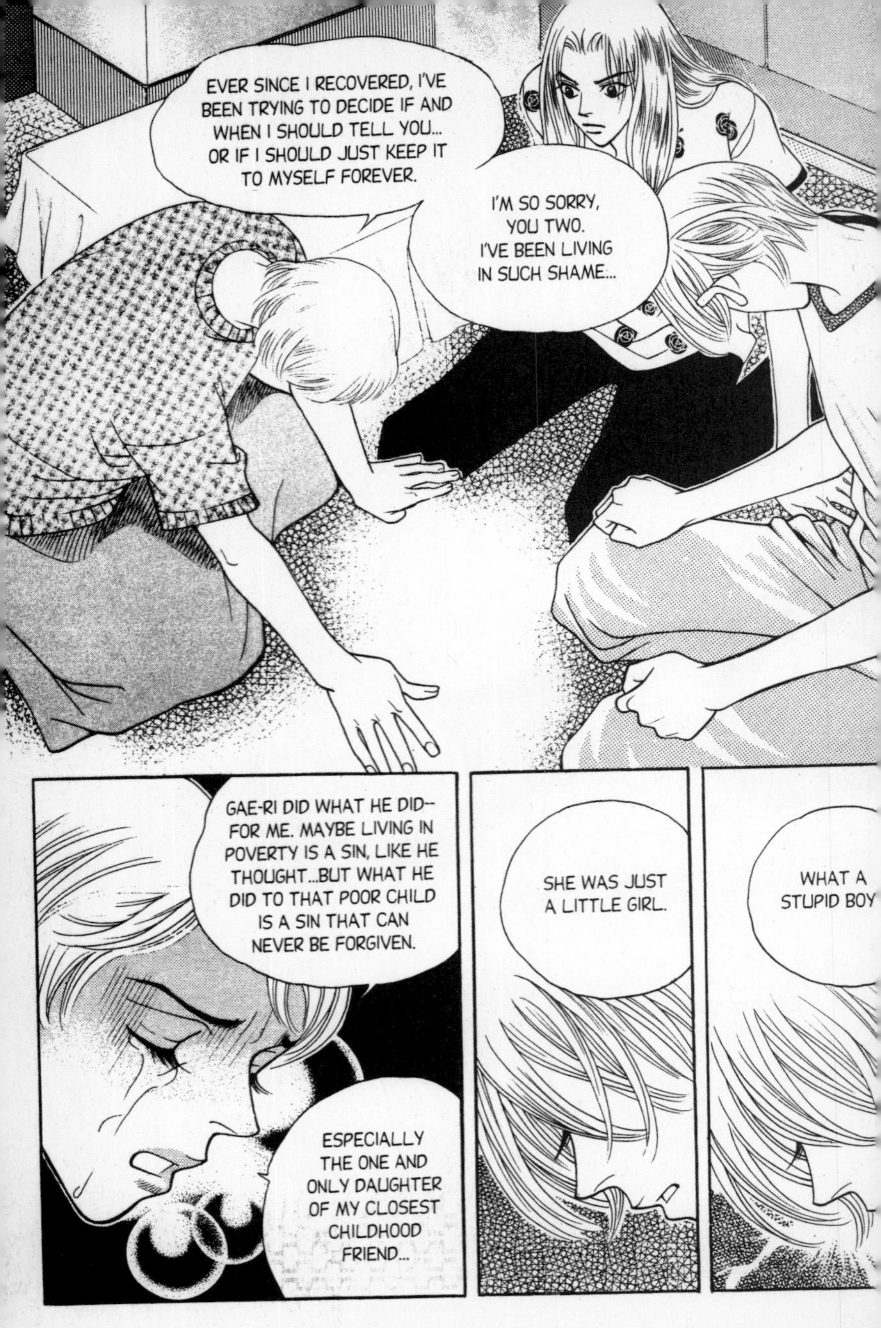
EVER SINCE I RECOVERED, I'VE BEEN TRYING TO DECIDE IF AND WHEN I SHOULD TELL YOU... OR IF I SHOULD JUST KEEP IT TO MYSELF FOREVER.
I'M SO SORRY, YOU TWO. I'VE BEEN LIVING IN SUCH SHAME...
GAE-RI DID WHAT HE DID-- FOR ME. MAYBE LIVING IN POVERTY IS A SIN, LIKE HE THOUGHT...BUT WHAT HE DID TO THAT POOR CHILD IS A SIN THAT CAN NEVER BE FORGIVEN.
ESPECIALLY THE ONE AND ONLY DAUGHTER OF MY CLOSEST CHILDHOOD FRIEND...
SHE WAS JUST A LITTLE GIRL.
WHAT A STUPID BOY

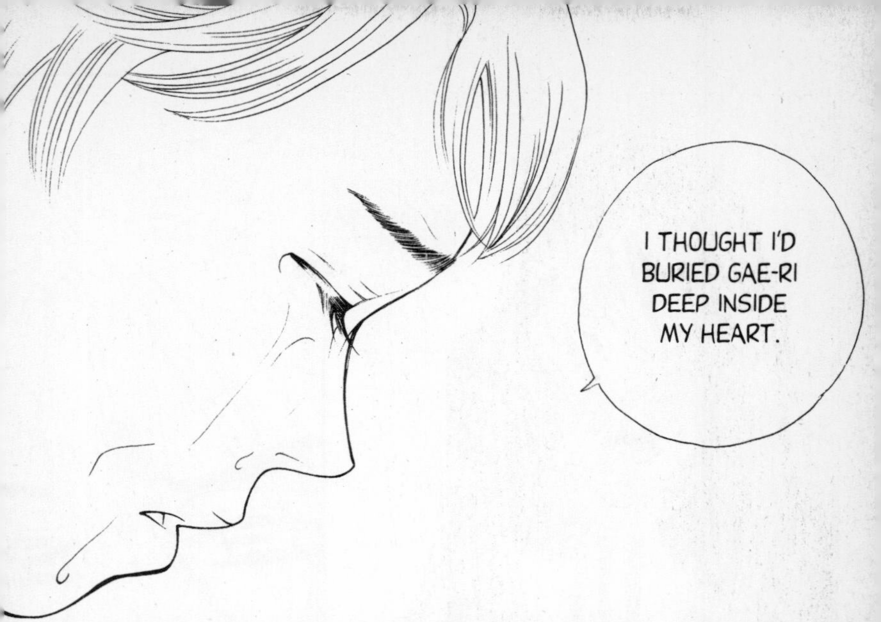
I THOUGHT I'D BURIED GAE-RI DEEP INSIDE MY HEART.

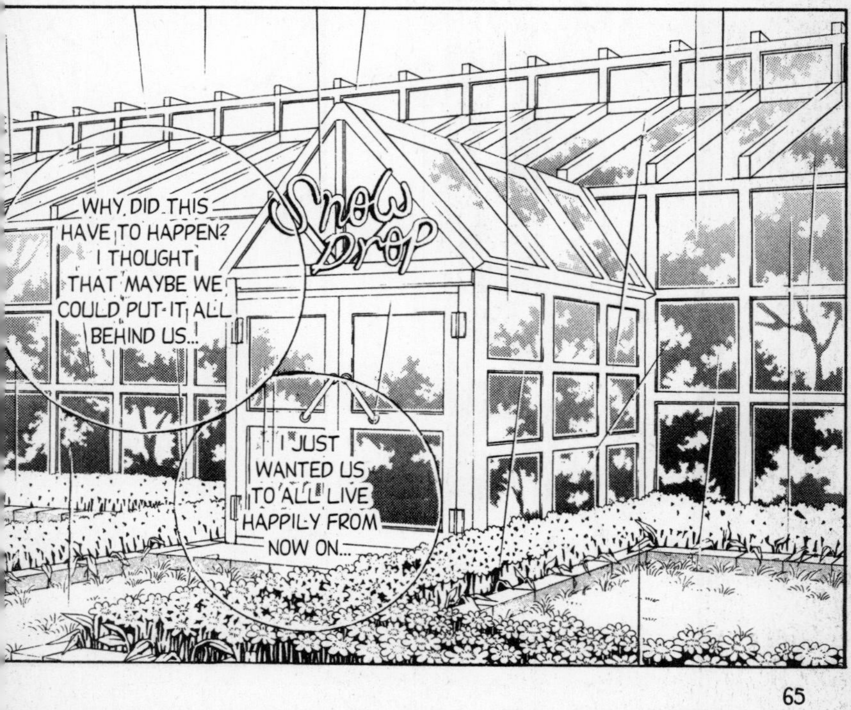
Snow Drop
WHY DID THIS HAVE TO HAPPEN? I THOUGHT THAT MAYBE WE COULD PUT IT ALL BEHIND US...
I JUST WANTED US TO ALL LIVE HAPPILY FROM NOW ON...

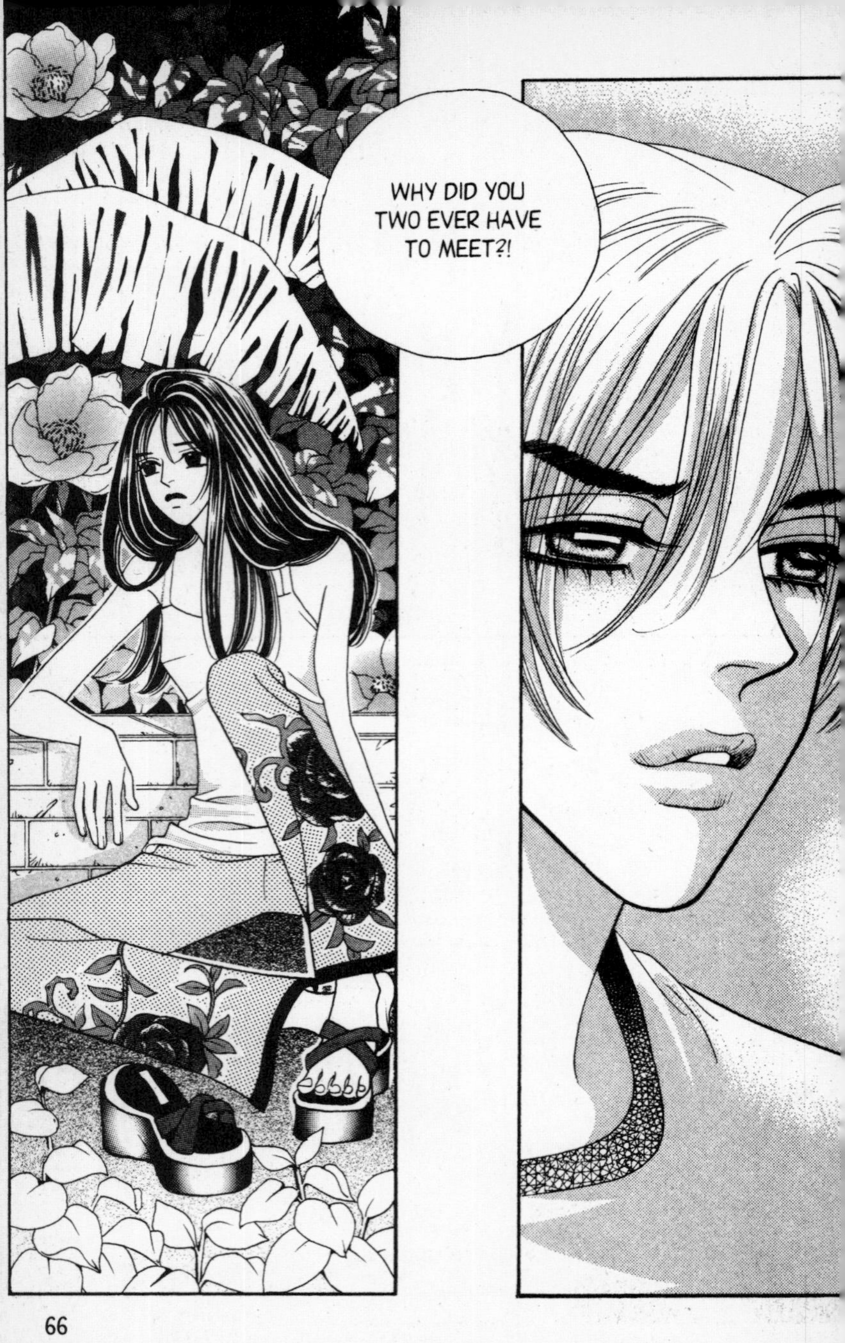
WHY DID YOU TWO EVER HAVE TO MEET?!

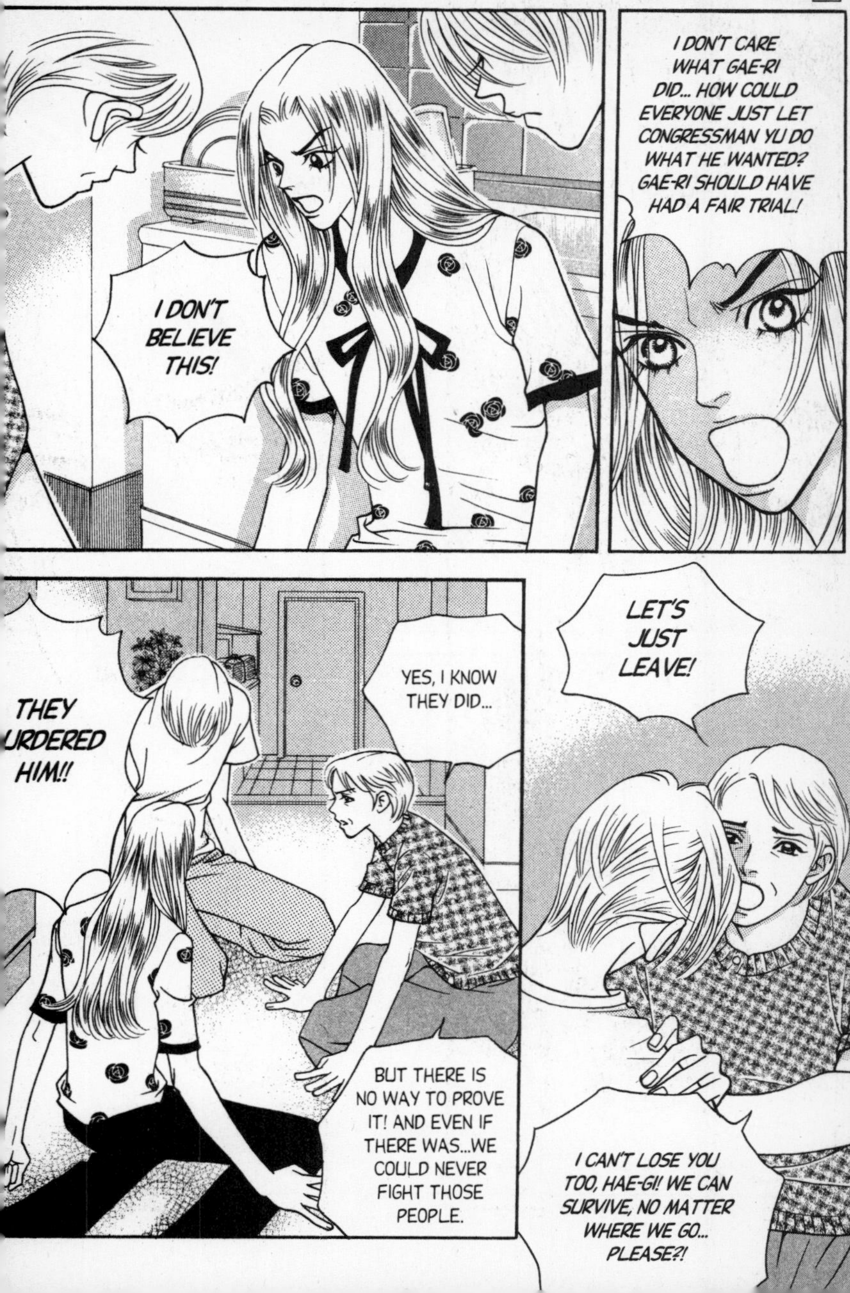
I DON'T BELIEVE THIS!
I DON'T CARE WHAT GAE-RI DID... HOW COULD EVERYONE JUST LET CONGRESSMAN YU DO WHAT HE WANTED? GAE-RI SHOULD HAVE HAD A FAIR TRIAL!
THEY URDERED HIM!!
YES, I KNOW THEY DID...
BUT THERE IS NO WAY TO PROVE IT! AND EVEN IF THERE WAS...WE COULD NEVER FIGHT THOSE PEOPLE.
LET'S JUST LEAVE!
I CAN'T LOSE YOU TOO, HAE-GI! WE CAN SURVIVE, NO MATTER WHERE WE GO... PLEASE?!

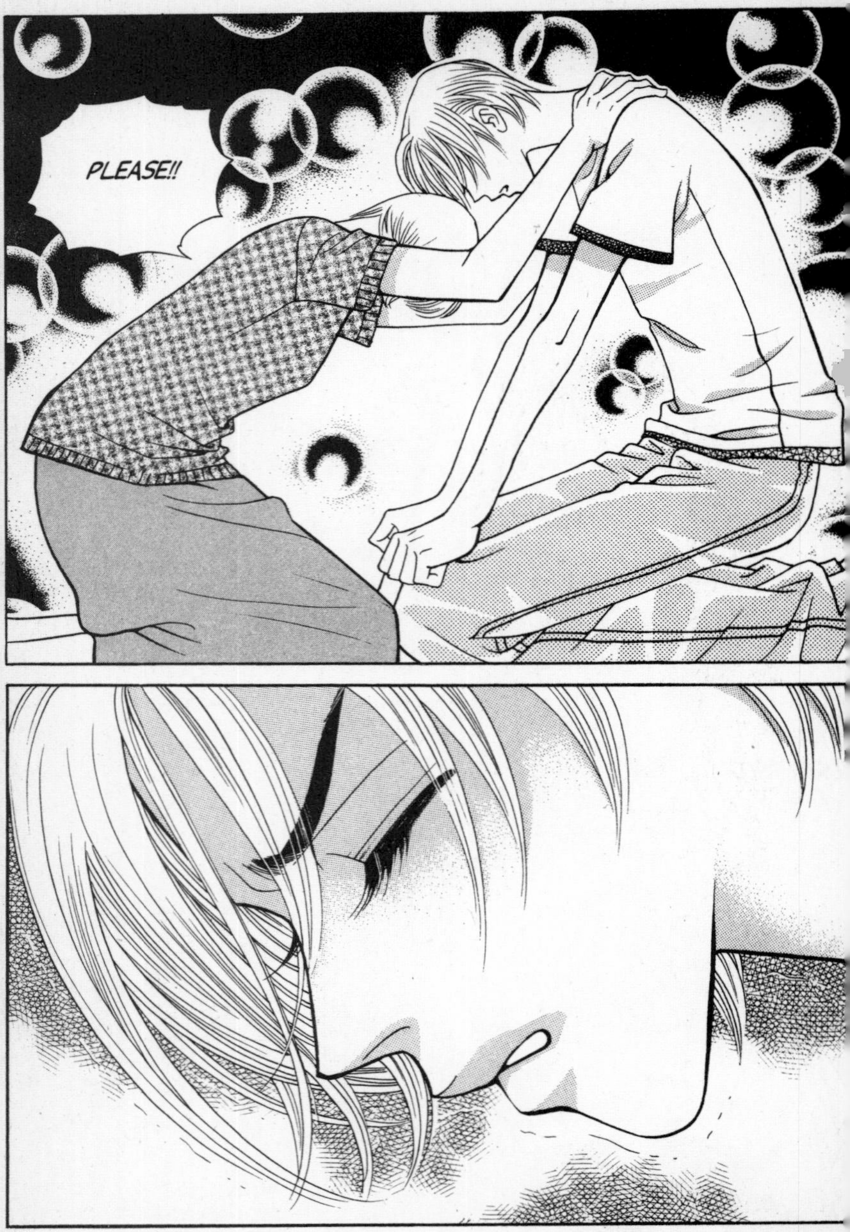
PLEASE!!

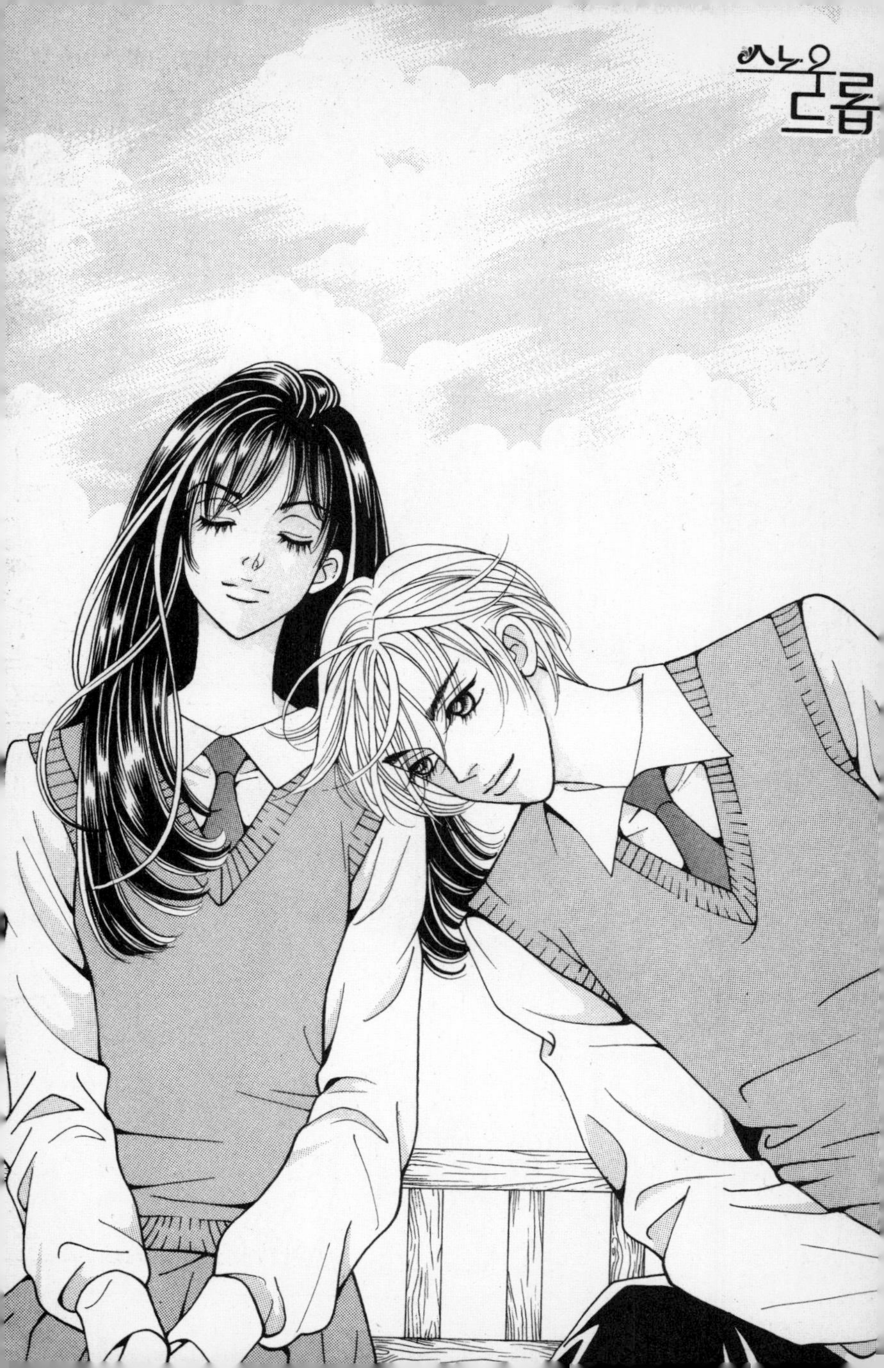
스노우
드롭

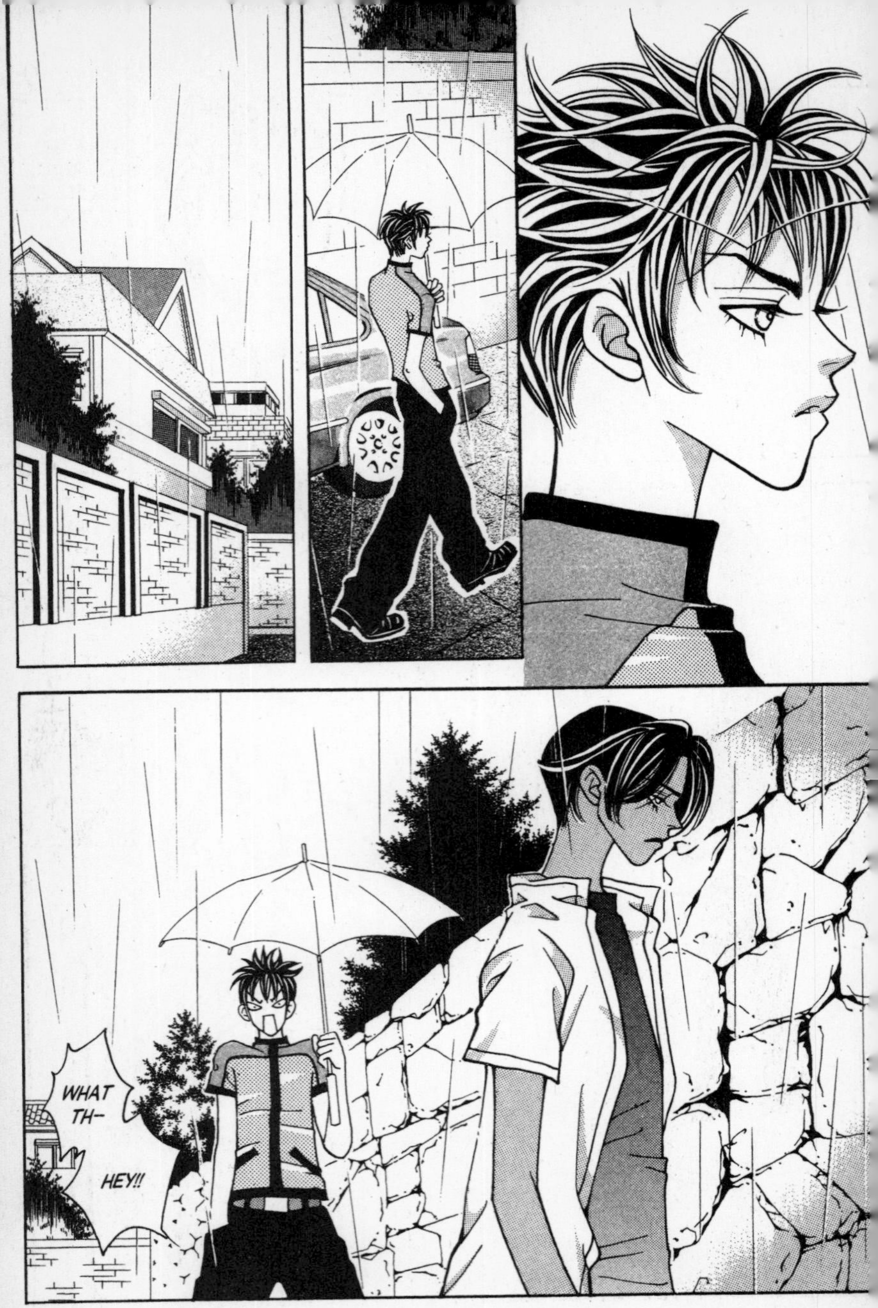
WHAT TH–
HEY!!

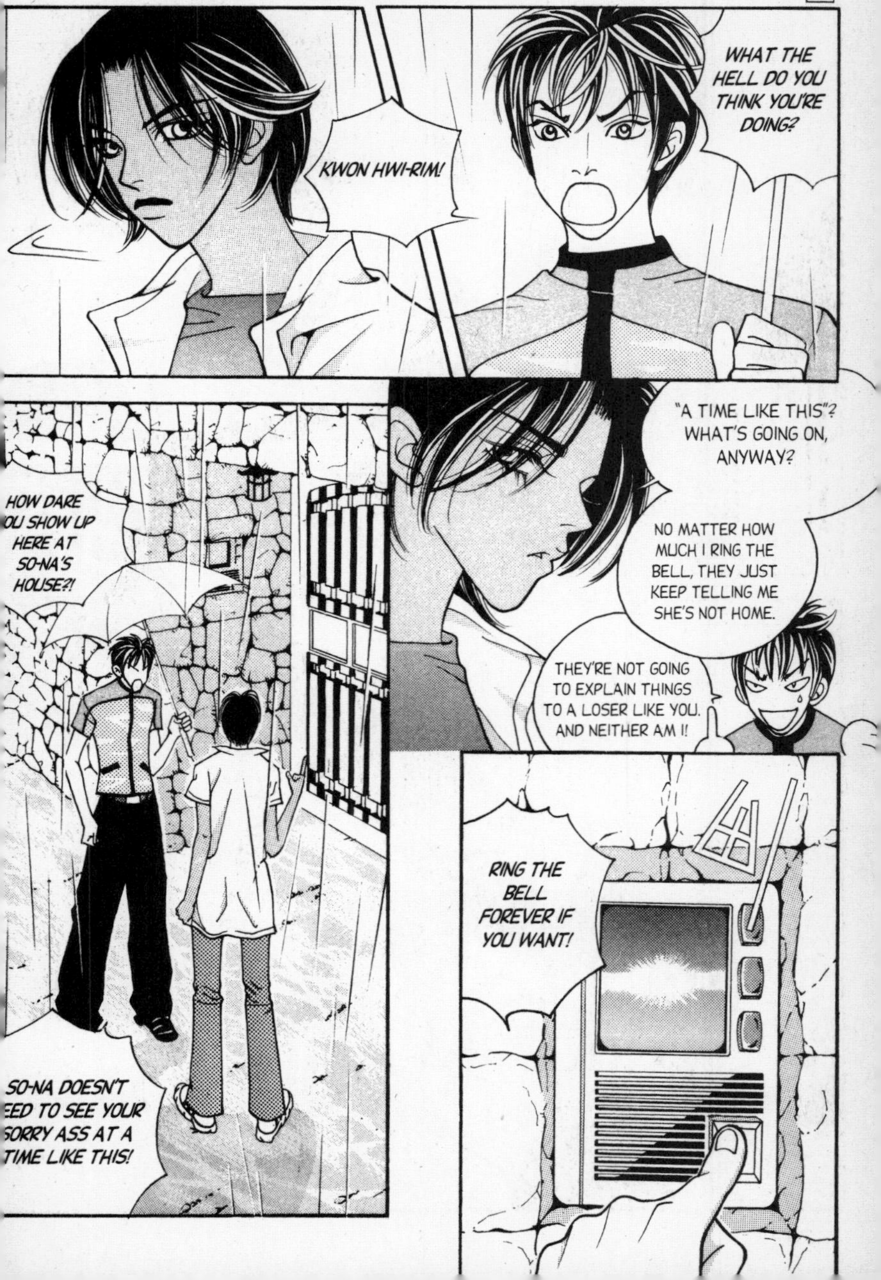
KWON HWI-RIM!
WHAT THE HELL DO YOU THINK YOU'RE DOING?
HOW DARE OU SHOW UP HERE AT SO-NA'S HOUSE?!
SO-NA DOESN'T EED TO SEE YOUR SORRY ASS AT A TIME LIKE THIS!
"A TIME LIKE THIS"? WHAT'S GOING ON, ANYWAY?
NO MATTER HOW MUCH I RING THE BELL, THEY JUST KEEP TELLING ME SHE'S NOT HOME.
THEY'RE NOT GOING TO EXPLAIN THINGS TO A LOSER LIKE YOU. AND NEITHER AM I!
RING THE BELL FOREVER IF YOU WANT!

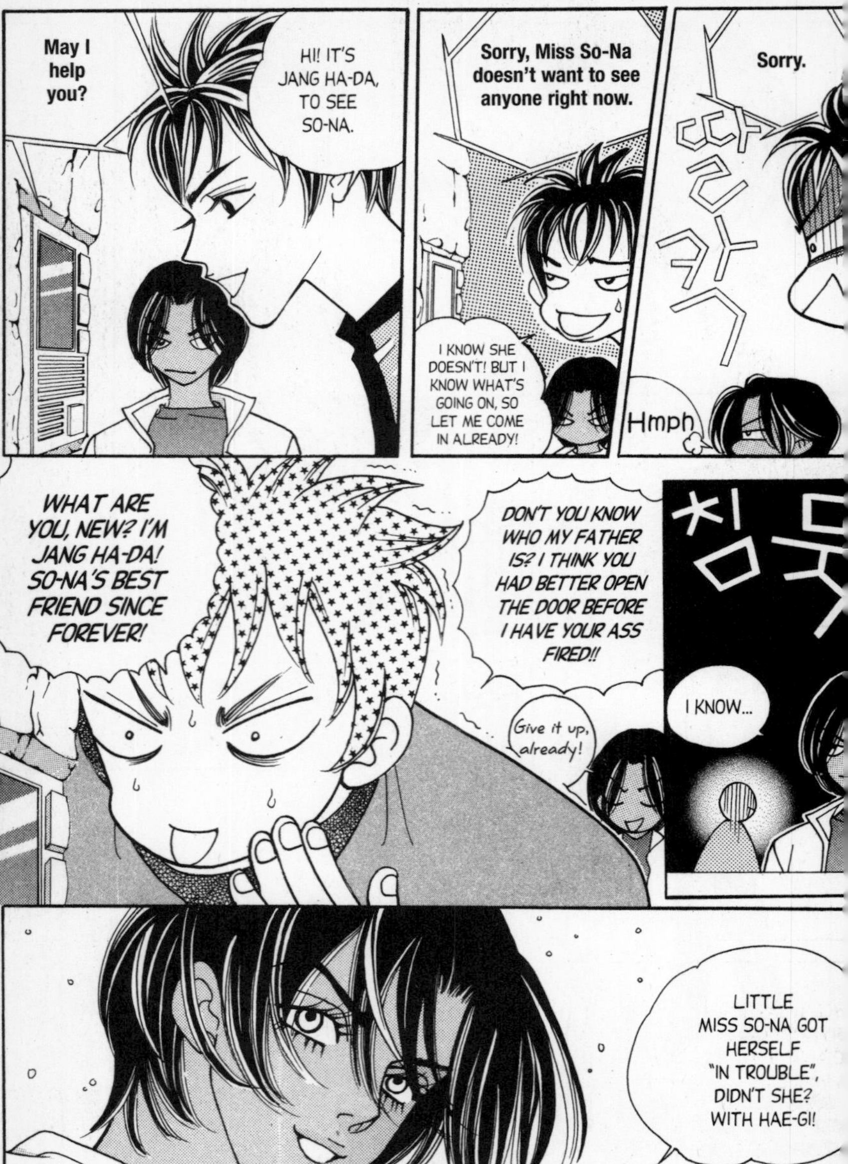
May I help you?
HI! IT'S JANG HA-DA, TO SEE SO-NA.
Sorry, Miss So-Na doesn't want to see anyone right now.
I KNOW SHE DOESN'T! BUT I KNOW WHAT'S GOING ON, SO LET ME COME IN ALREADY!
Sorry.
Hmph
WHAT ARE YOU, NEW? I'M JANG HA-DA! SO-NA'S BEST FRIEND SINCE FOREVER!
DON'T YOU KNOW WHO MY FATHER IS? I THINK YOU HAD BETTER OPEN THE DOOR BEFORE I HAVE YOUR ASS FIRED!!
Give it up, already!
I KNOW...
LITTLE MISS SO-NA GOT HERSELF "IN TROUBLE", DIDN'T SHE? WITH HAE-GI!

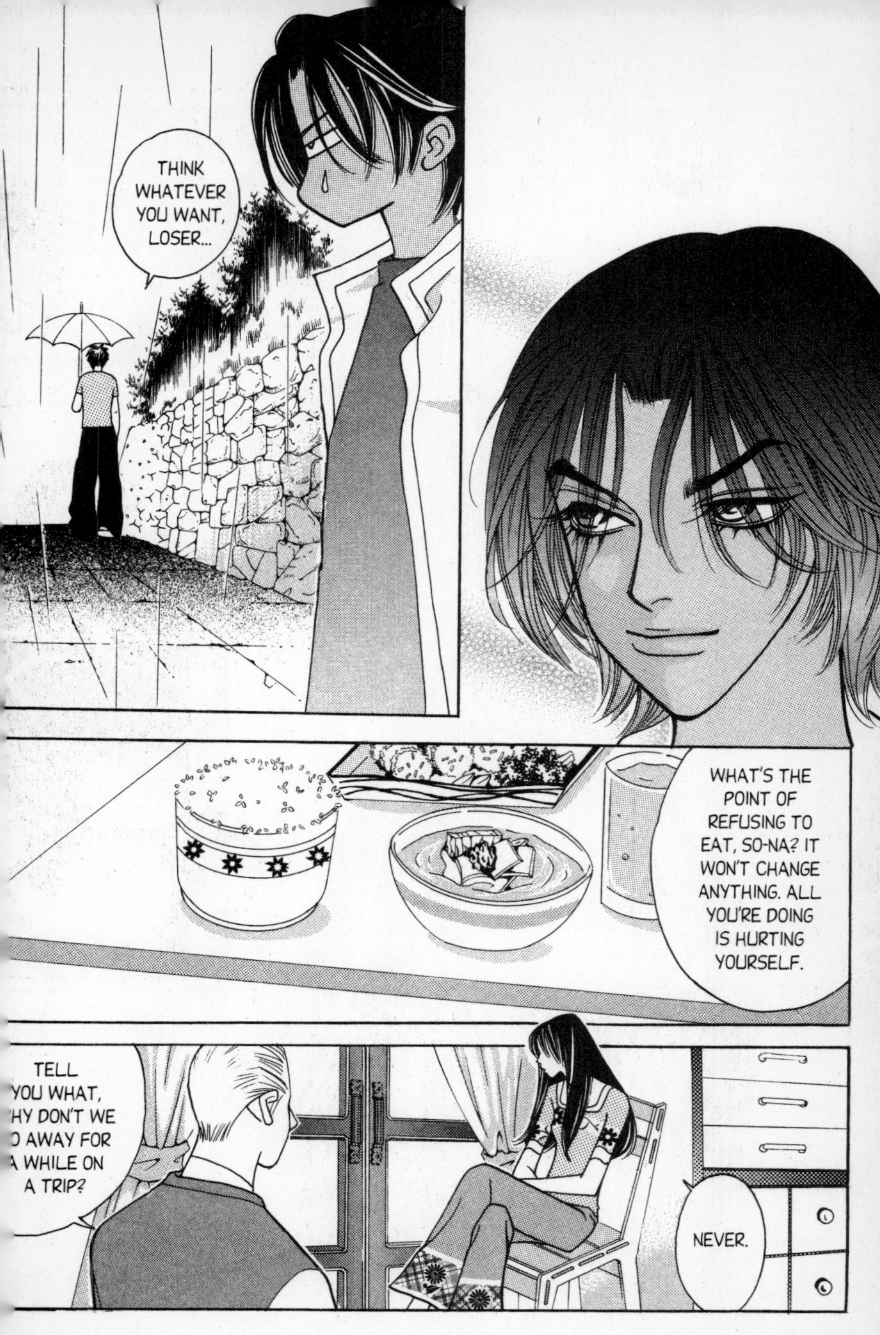

THINK WHATEVER YOU WANT, LOSER...
WHAT'S THE POINT OF REFUSING TO EAT, SO-NA? IT WON'T CHANGE ANYTHING. ALL YOU'RE DOING IS HURTING YOURSELF.
TELL YOU WHAT, HY DON'T WE O AWAY FOR A WHILE ON A TRIP?
NEVER.

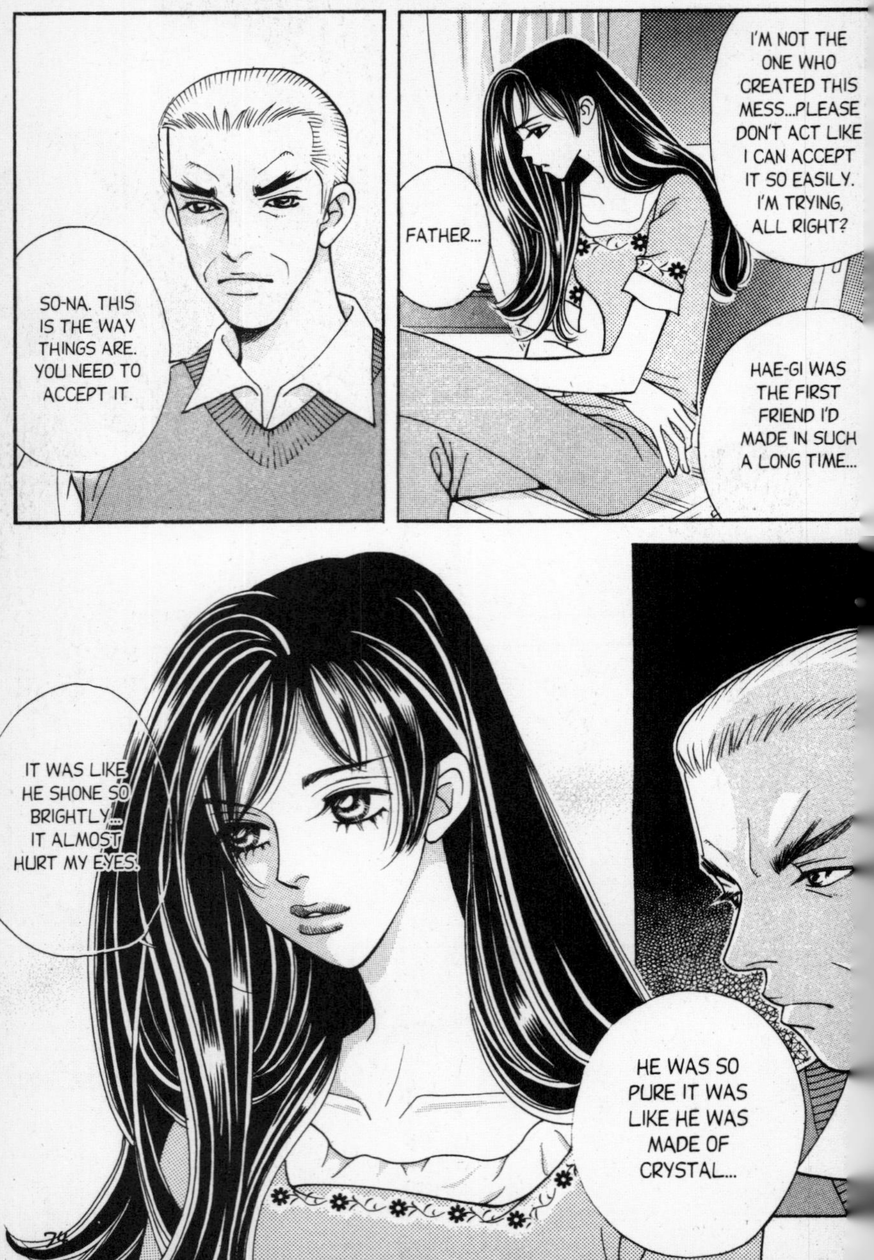

SO-NA. THIS IS THE WAY THINGS ARE. YOU NEED TO ACCEPT IT.
FATHER...
I'M NOT THE ONE WHO CREATED THIS MESS...PLEASE DON'T ACT LIKE I CAN ACCEPT IT SO EASILY. I'M TRYING, ALL RIGHT?
HAE-GI WAS THE FIRST FRIEND I'D MADE IN SUCH A LONG TIME...
IT WAS LIKE HE SHONE SO BRIGHTLY... IT ALMOST HURT MY EYES.
HE WAS SO PURE IT WAS LIKE HE WAS MADE OF CRYSTAL...

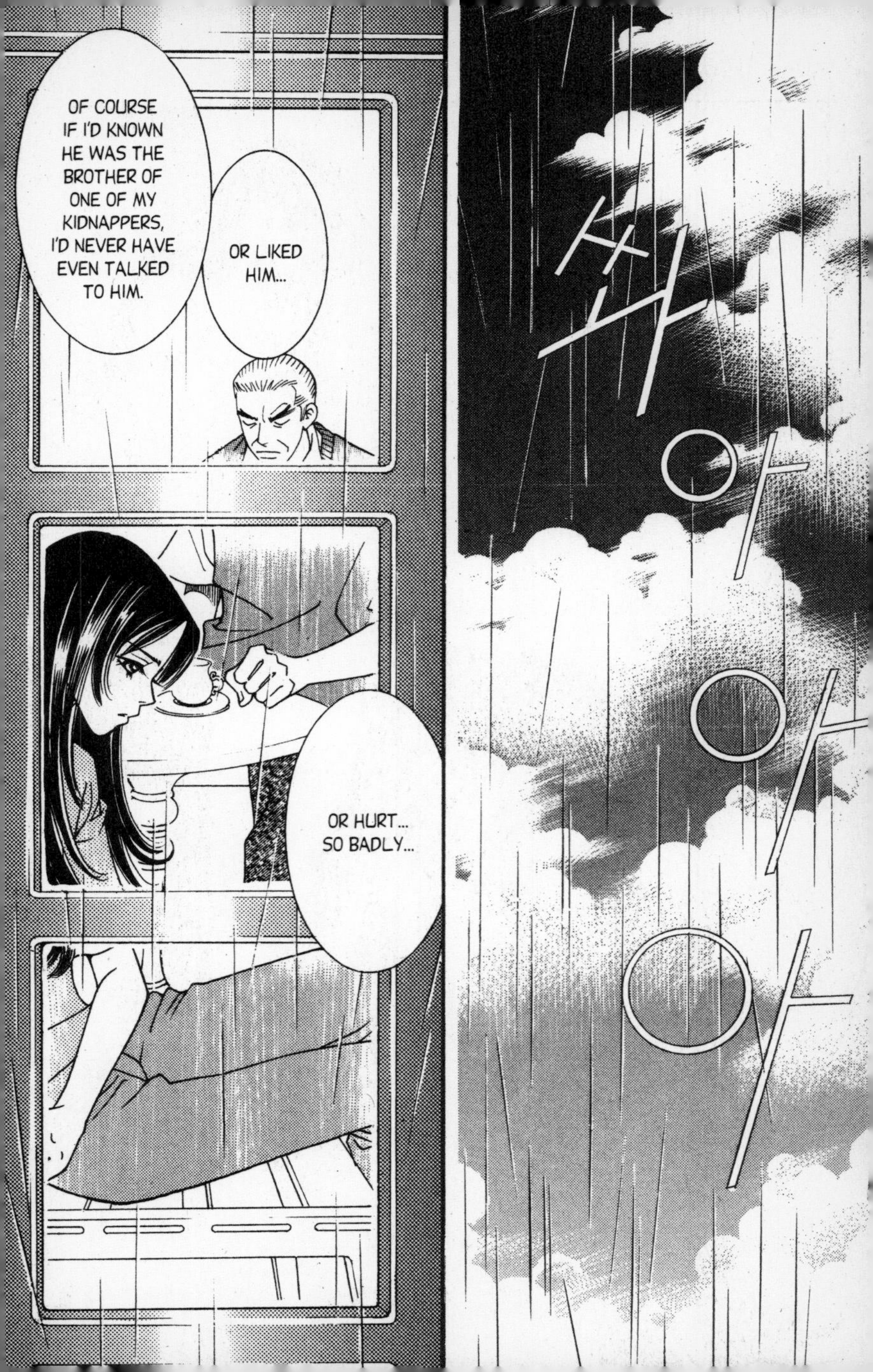
OF COURSE IF I'D KNOWN HE WAS THE BROTHER OF ONE OF MY KIDNAPPERS, I'D NEVER HAVE EVEN TALKED TO HIM.
OR LIKED HIM...
OR HURT... SO BADLY...
쏴아아아

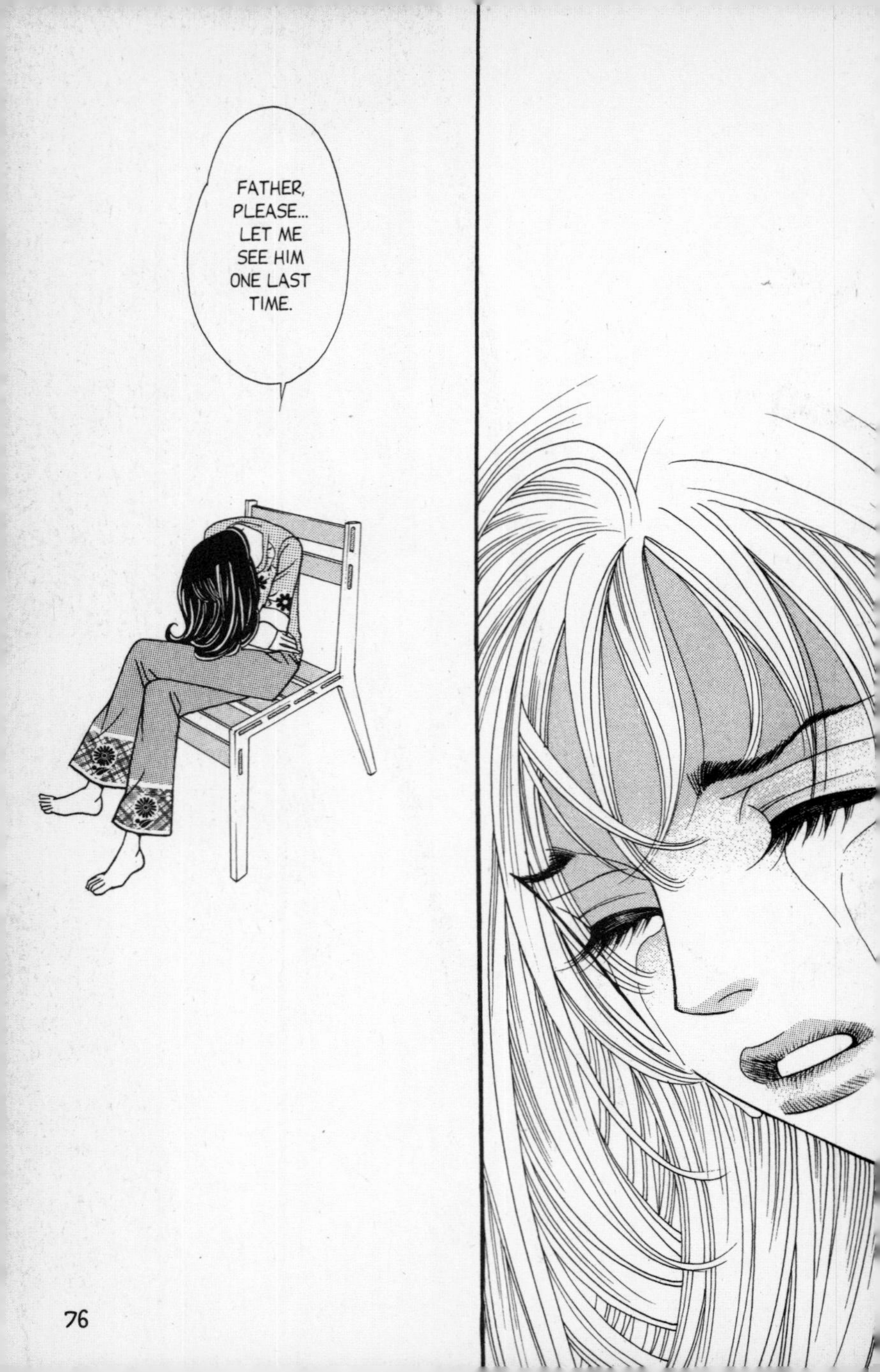
FATHER, PLEASE... LET ME SEE HIM ONE LAST TIME.

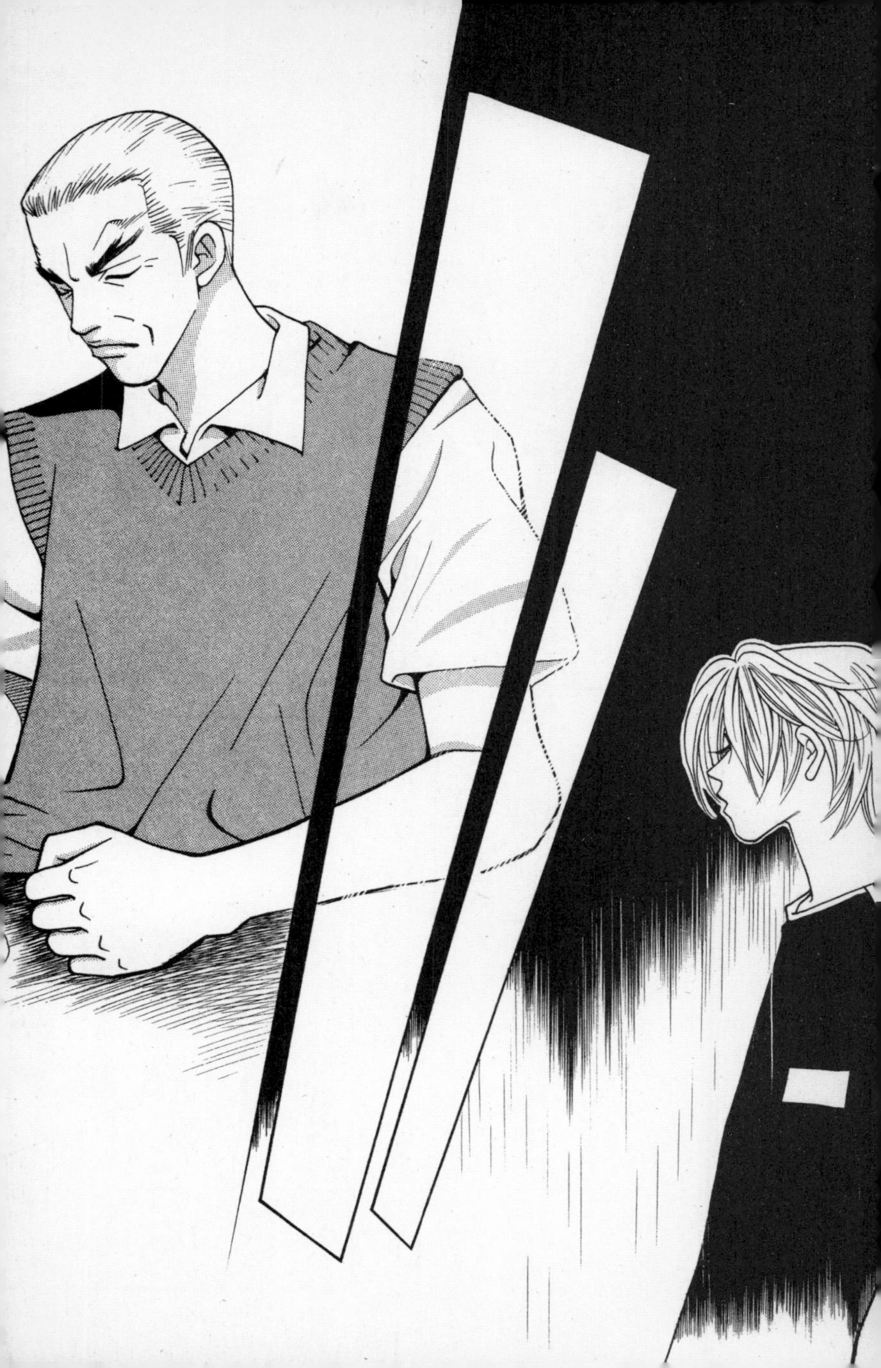

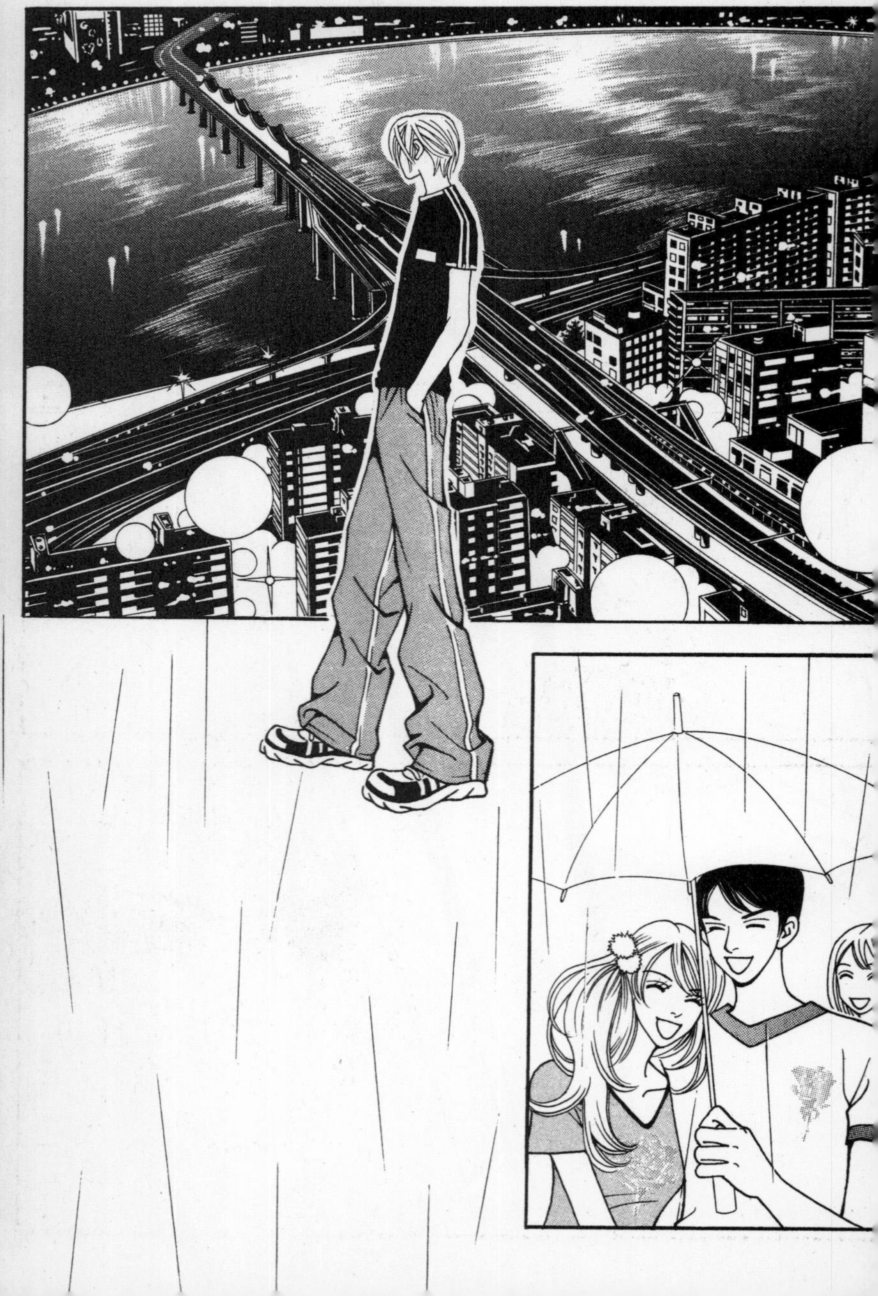

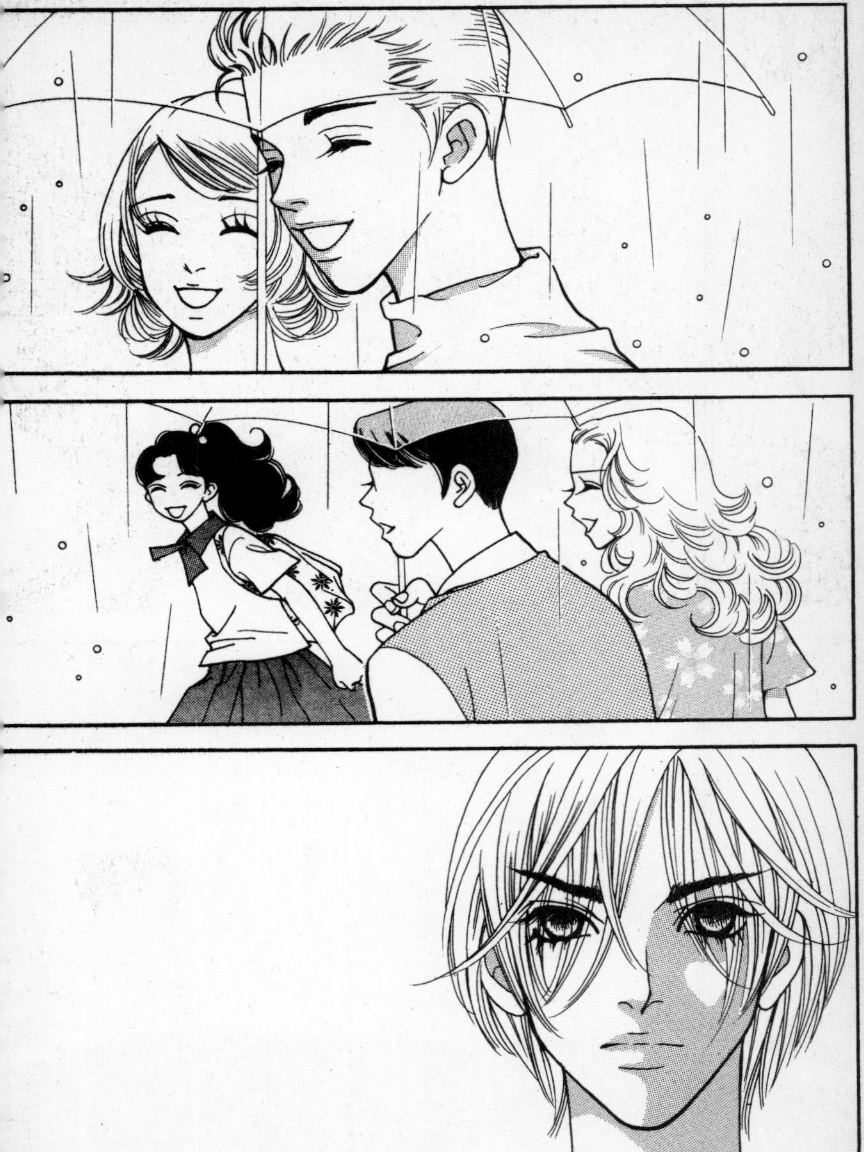

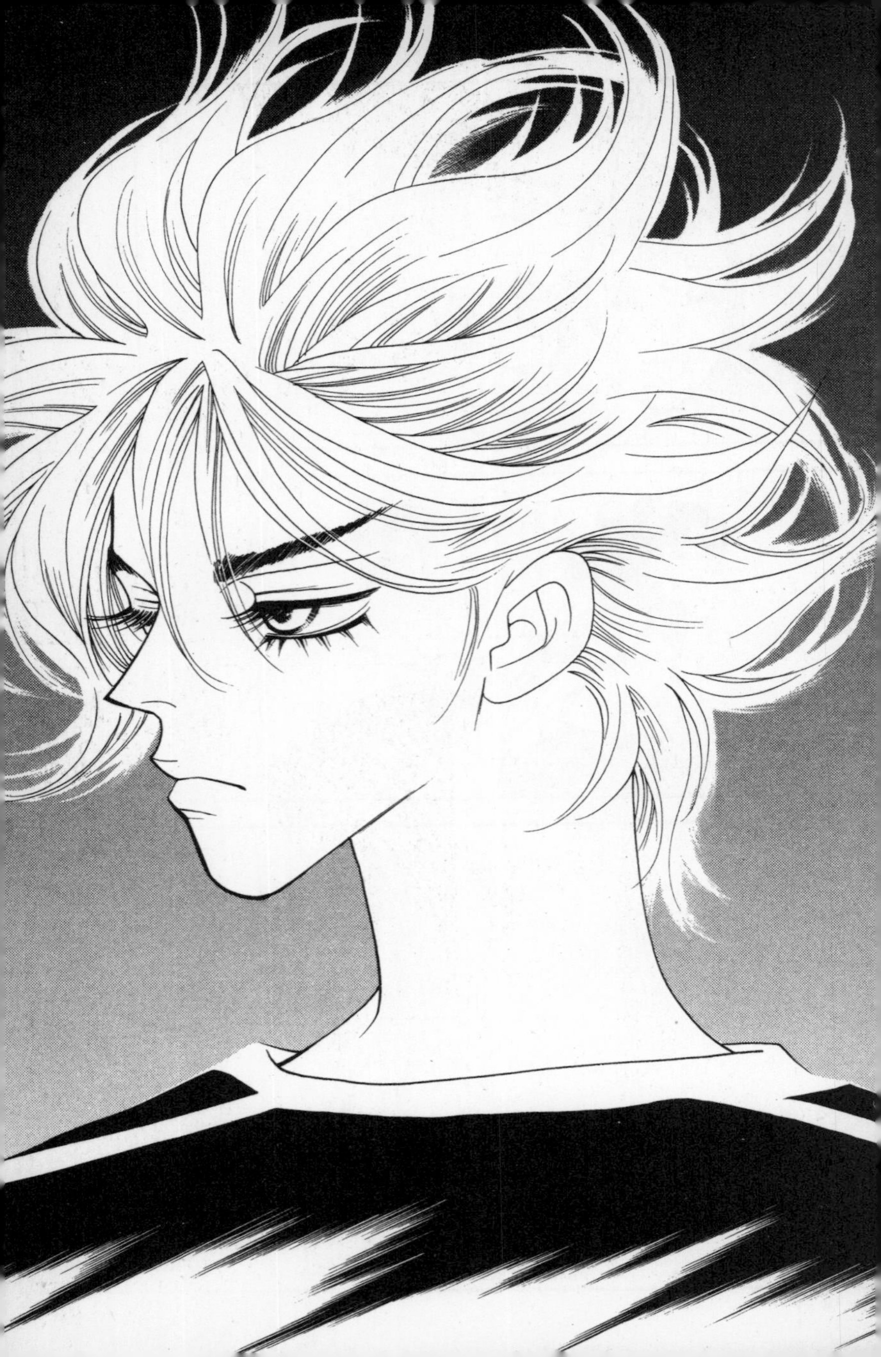

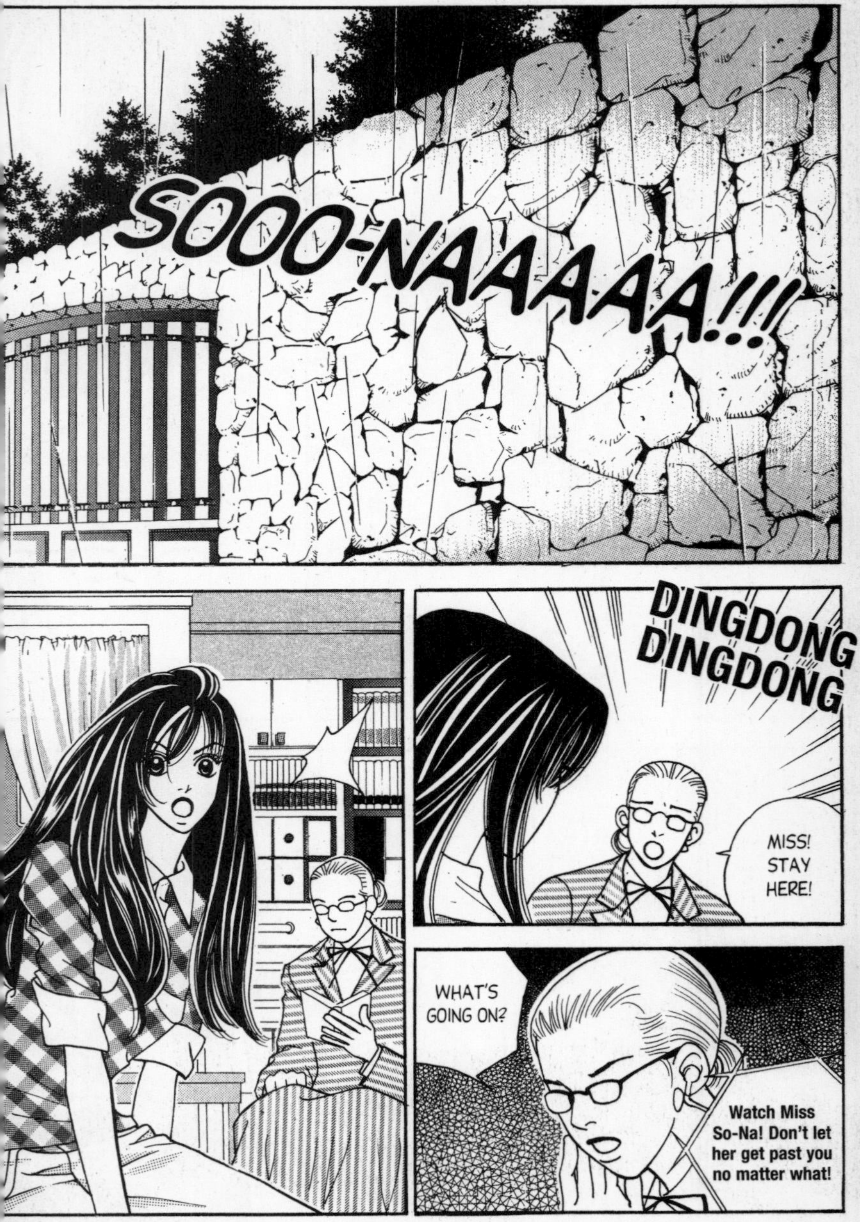
SOOO-NAAAAAA!!!
DINGDONG DINGDONG DINGDONG
MISS! STAY HERE!
WHAT'S GOING ON?
Watch Miss So-Na! Don't let her get past you no matter what!

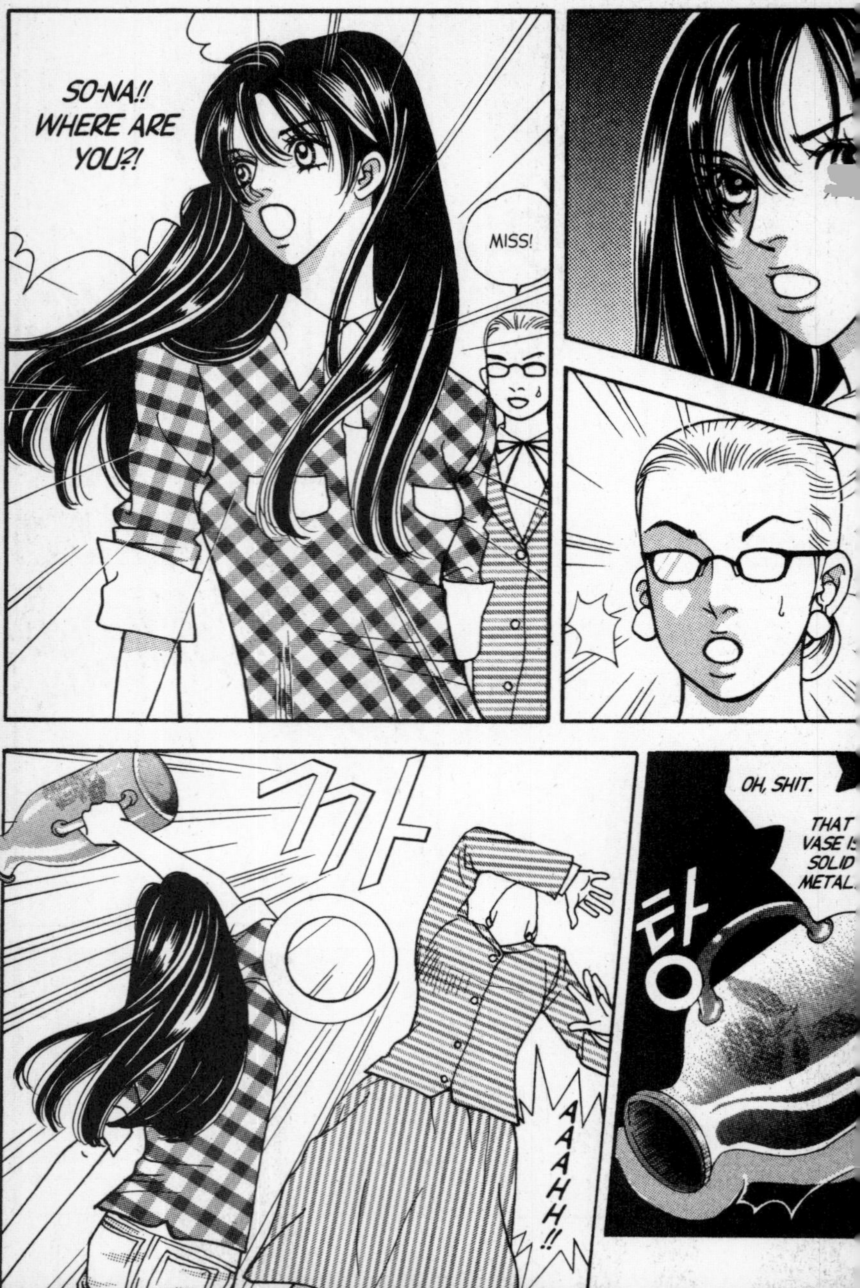
SO-NA!! WHERE ARE YOU?!
MISS!
꺄
AAAHH!!
OH, SHIT.
THAT VASE IS SOLID METAL.
탕

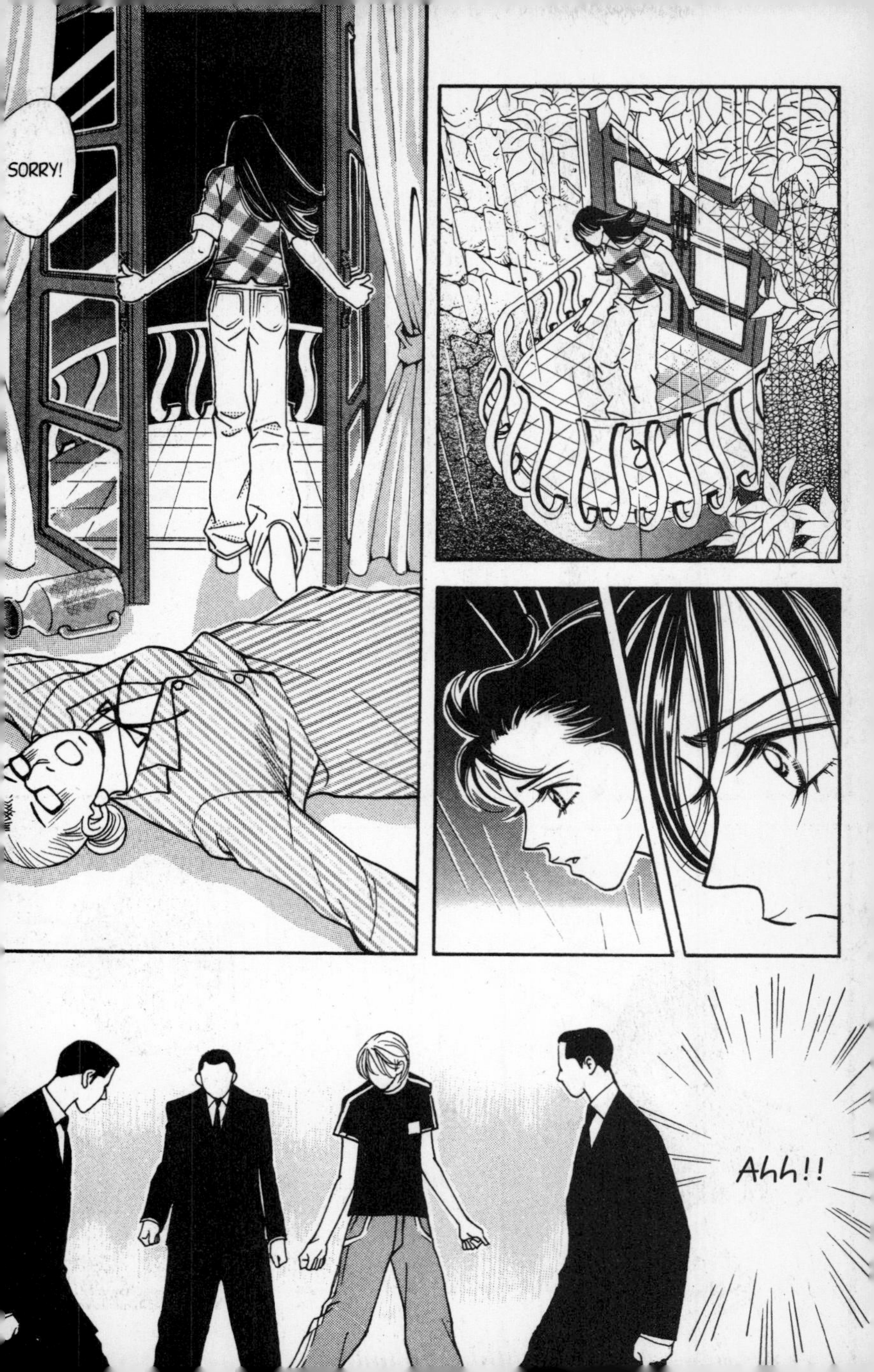
SORRY!
Ahh!!

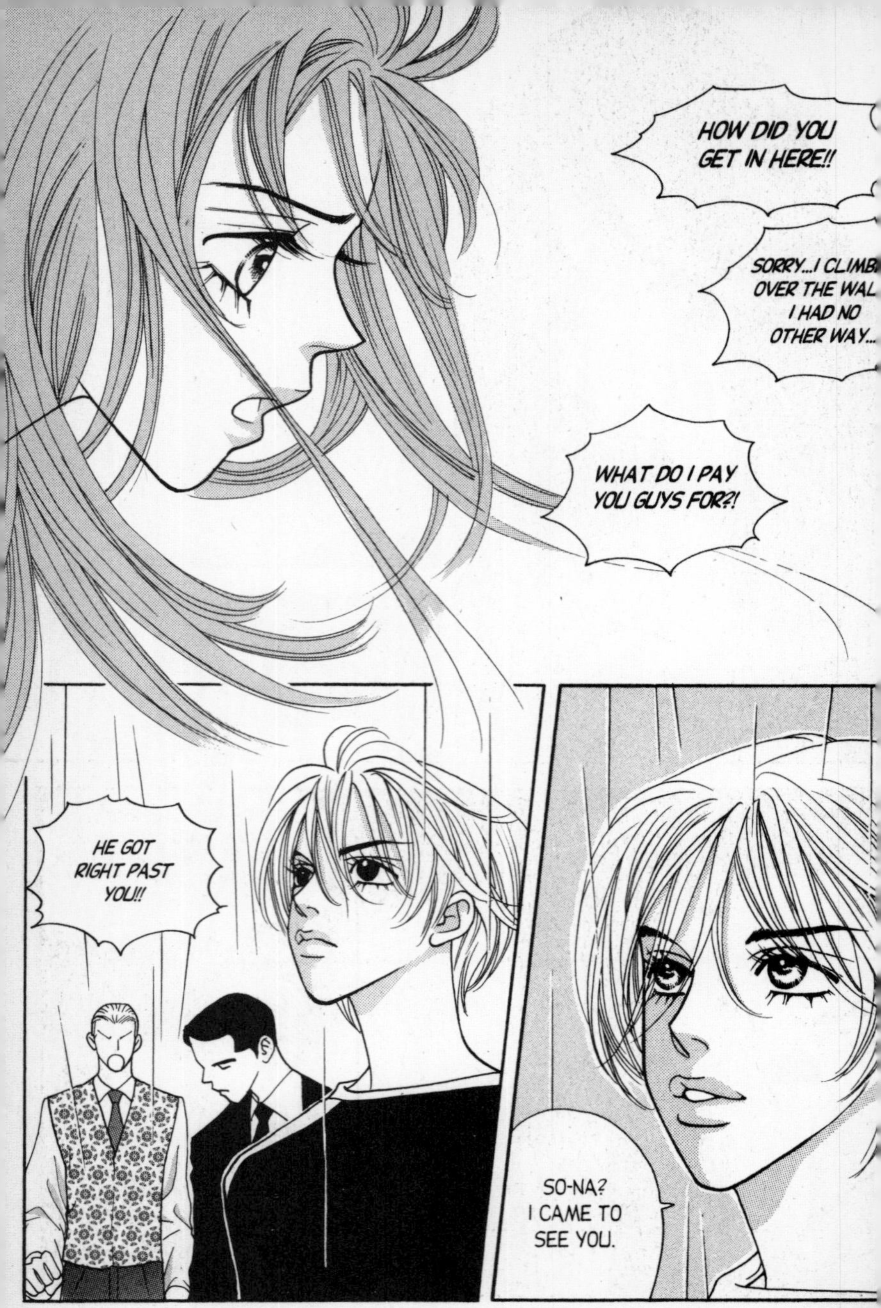
HOW DID YOU GET IN HERE!!
SORRY...I CLIMB OVER THE WAL I HAD NO OTHER WAY...
WHAT DO I PAY YOU GUYS FOR?!
HE GOT RIGHT PAST YOU!!
SO-NA? I CAME TO SEE YOU.

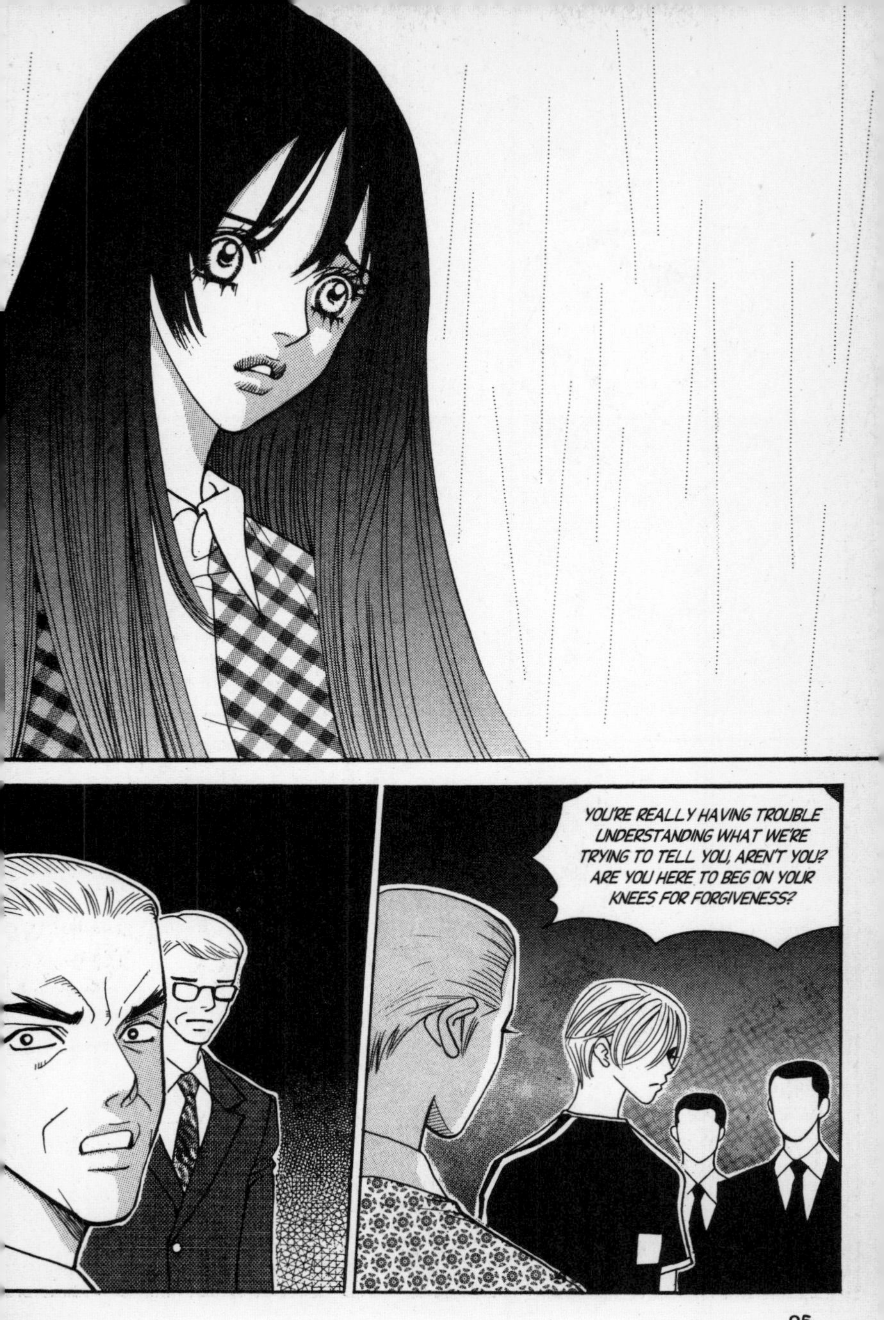
YOU'RE REALLY HAVING TROUBLE UNDERSTANDING WHAT WE'RE TRYING TO TELL YOU, AREN'T YOU? ARE YOU HERE TO BEG ON YOUR KNEES FOR FORGIVENESS?

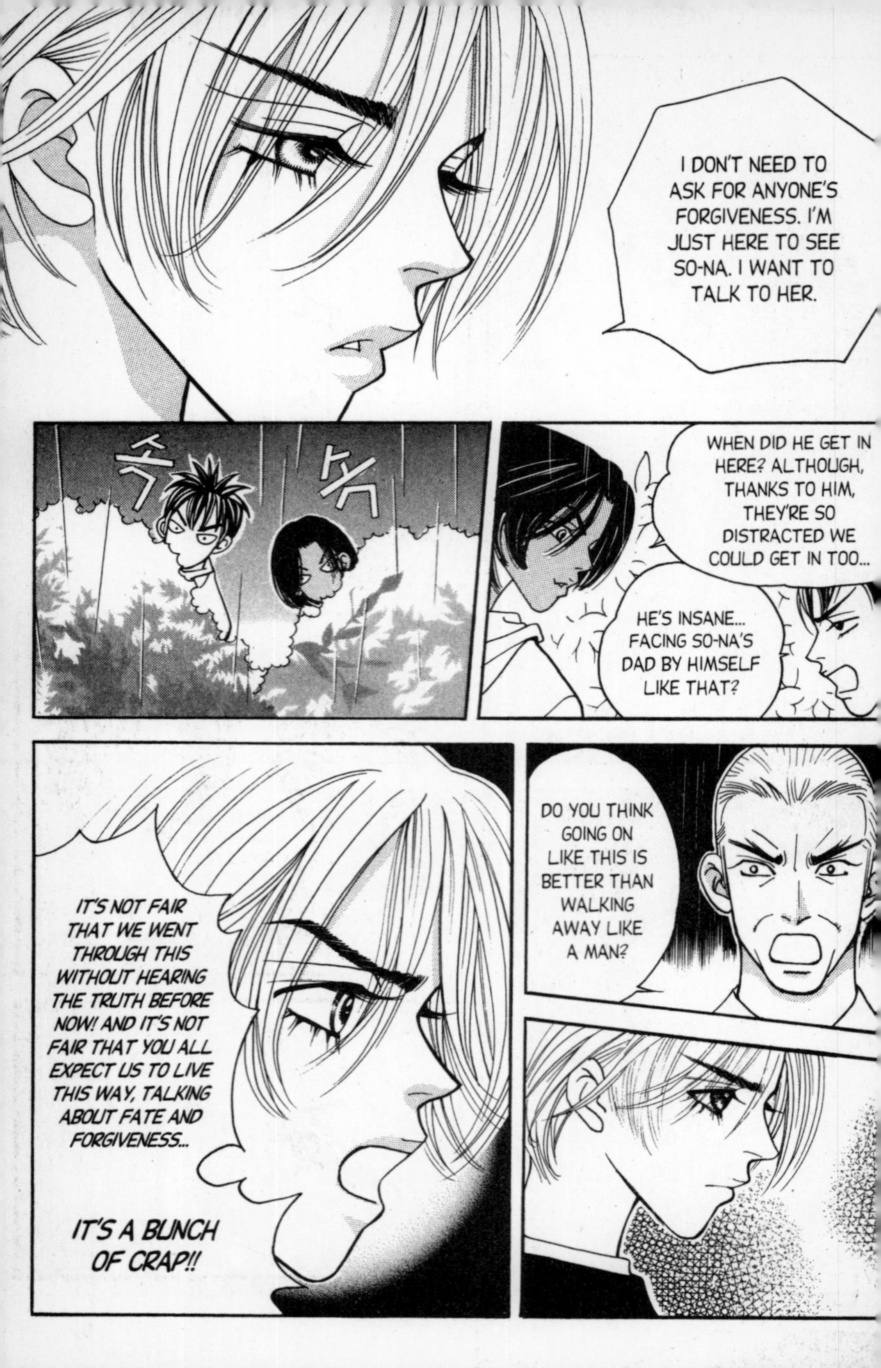
I DON'T NEED TO ASK FOR ANYONE'S FORGIVENESS. I'M JUST HERE TO SEE SO-NA. I WANT TO TALK TO HER.
WHEN DID HE GET IN HERE? ALTHOUGH, THANKS TO HIM, THEY'RE SO DISTRACTED WE COULD GET IN TOO...
HE'S INSANE... FACING SO-NA'S DAD BY HIMSELF LIKE THAT?
IT'S NOT FAIR THAT WE WENT THROUGH THIS WITHOUT HEARING THE TRUTH BEFORE NOW! AND IT'S NOT FAIR THAT YOU ALL EXPECT US TO LIVE THIS WAY, TALKING ABOUT FATE AND FORGIVENESS...
IT'S A BUNCH OF CRAP!!
DO YOU THINK GOING ON LIKE THIS IS BETTER THAN WALKING AWAY LIKE A MAN?

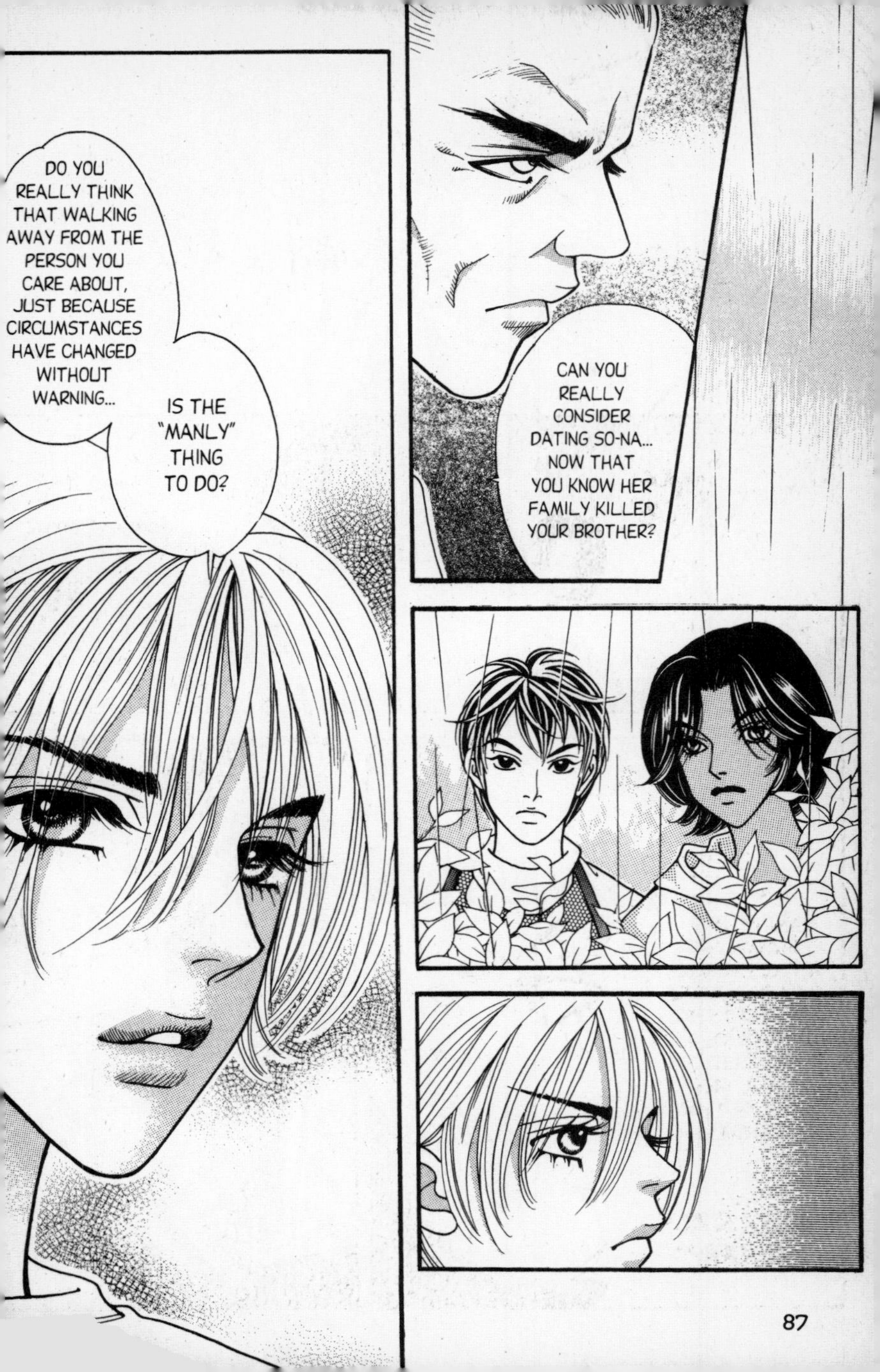
DO YOU REALLY THINK THAT WALKING AWAY FROM THE PERSON YOU CARE ABOUT, JUST BECAUSE CIRCUMSTANCES HAVE CHANGED WITHOUT WARNING...
IS THE "MANLY" THING TO DO?
CAN YOU REALLY CONSIDER DATING SO-NA... NOW THAT YOU KNOW HER FAMILY KILLED YOUR BROTHER?

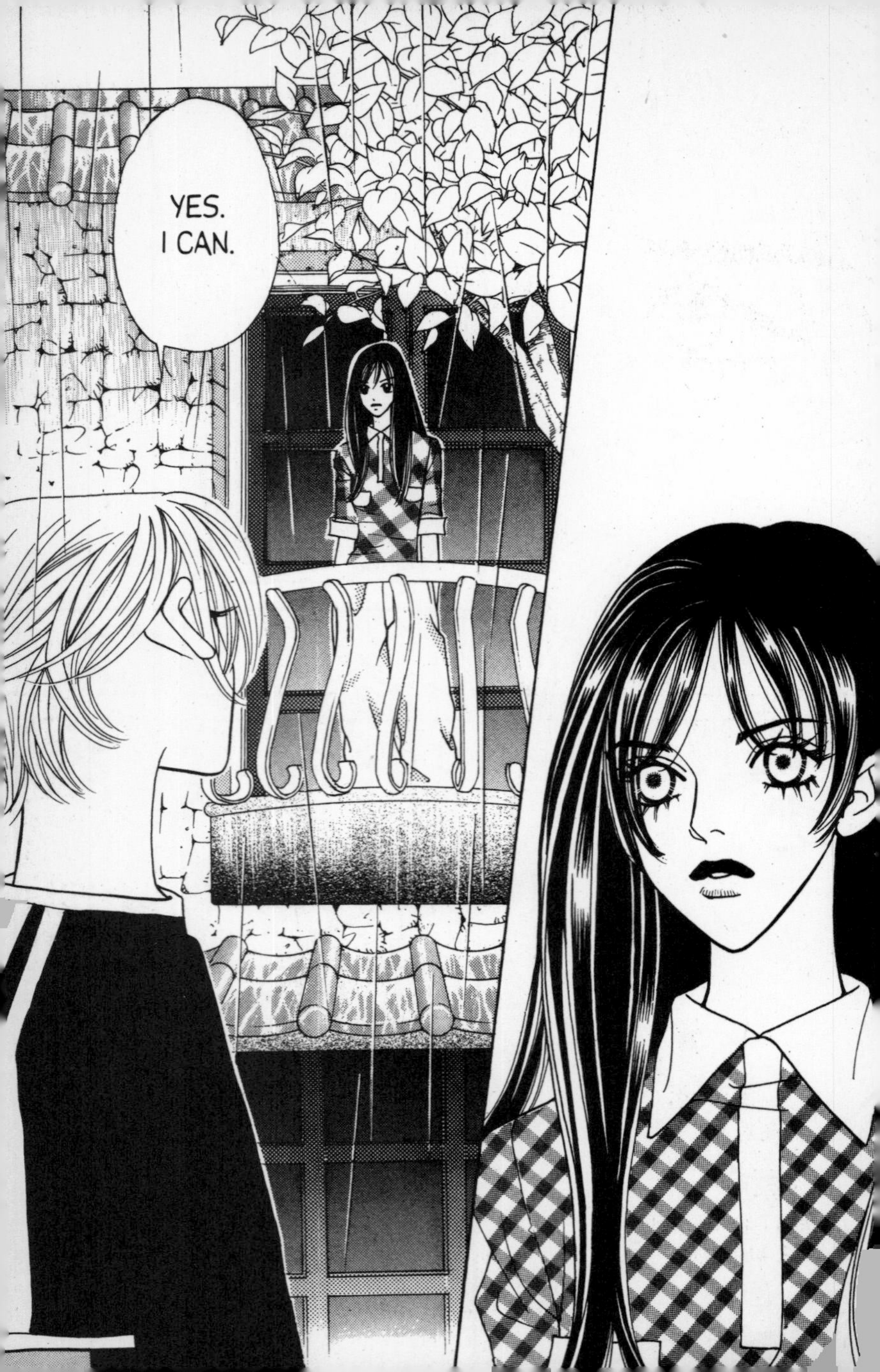
YES.
I CAN.

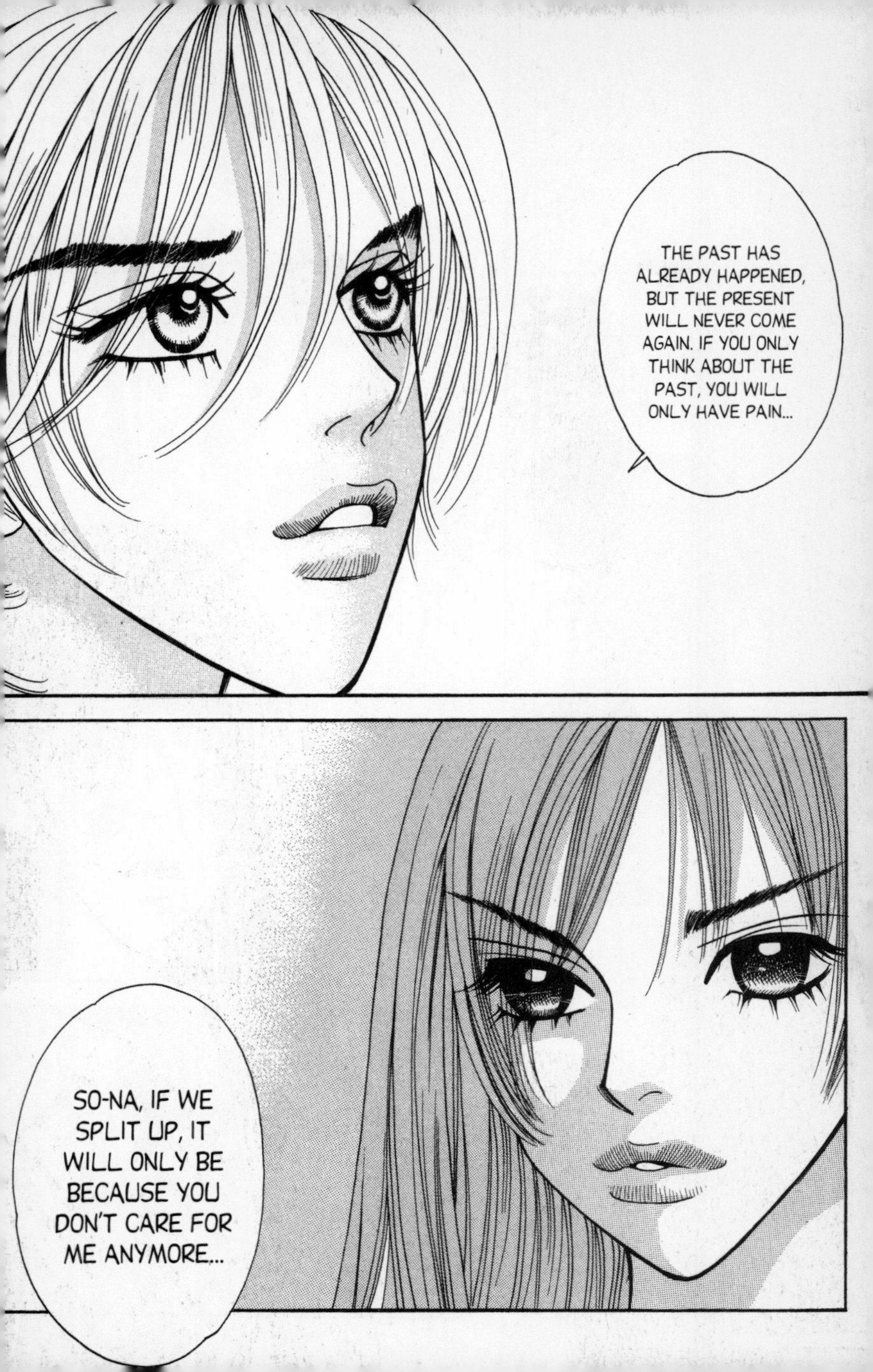
THE PAST HAS ALREADY HAPPENED, BUT THE PRESENT WILL NEVER COME AGAIN. IF YOU ONLY THINK ABOUT THE PAST, YOU WILL ONLY HAVE PAIN...
SO-NA, IF WE SPLIT UP, IT WILL ONLY BE BECAUSE YOU DON'T CARE FOR ME ANYMORE...

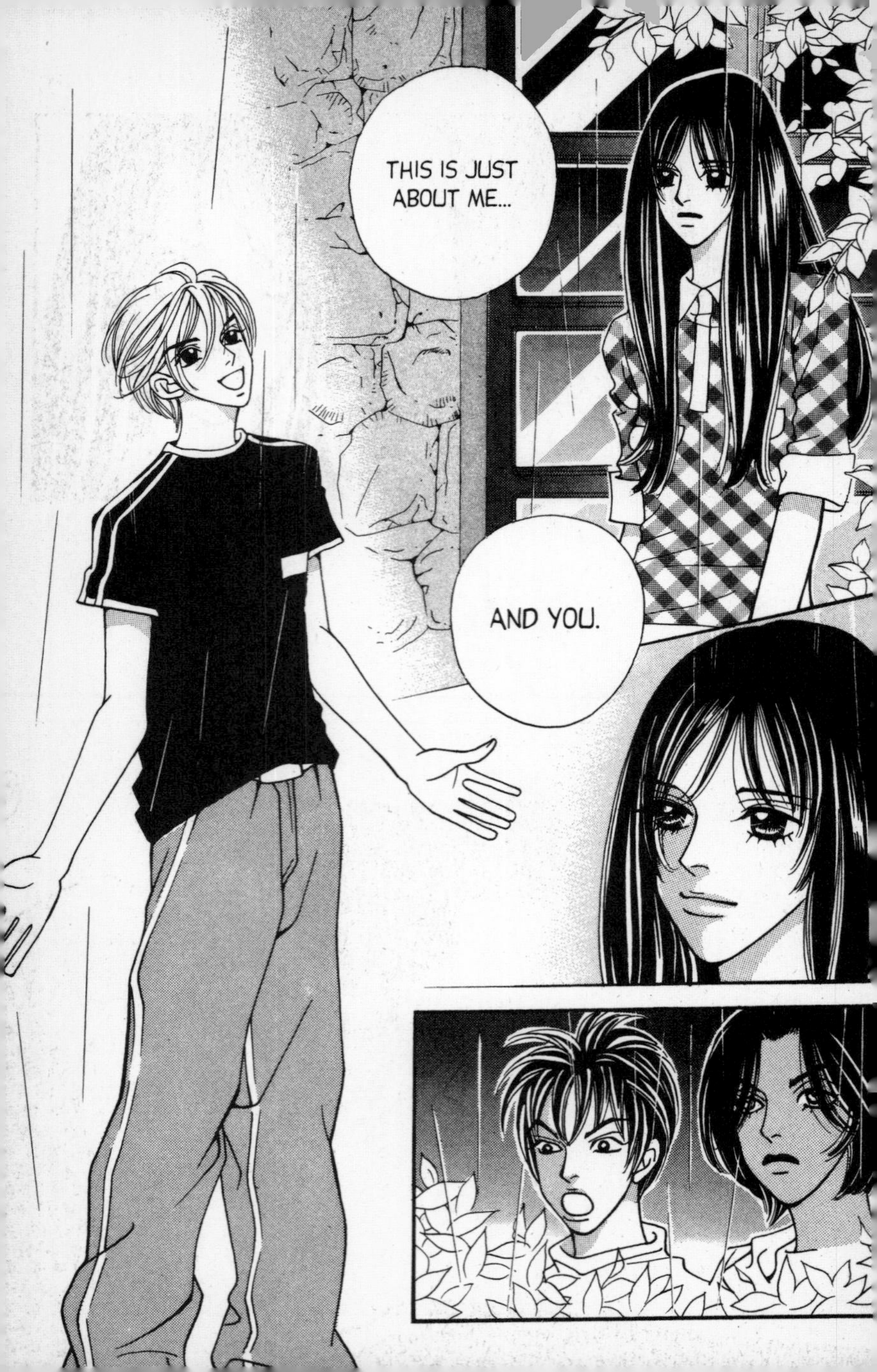
THIS IS JUST ABOUT ME...
AND YOU.

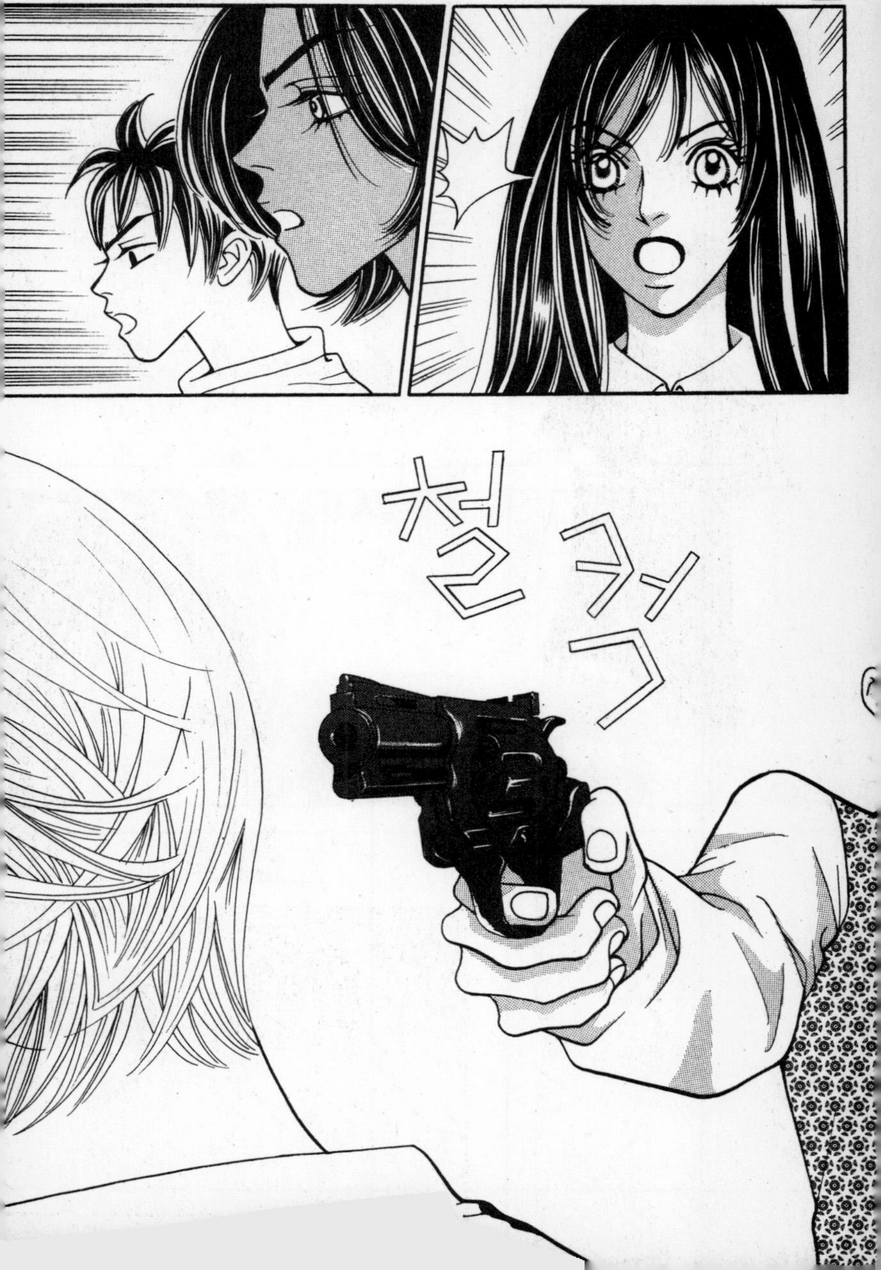
철컥

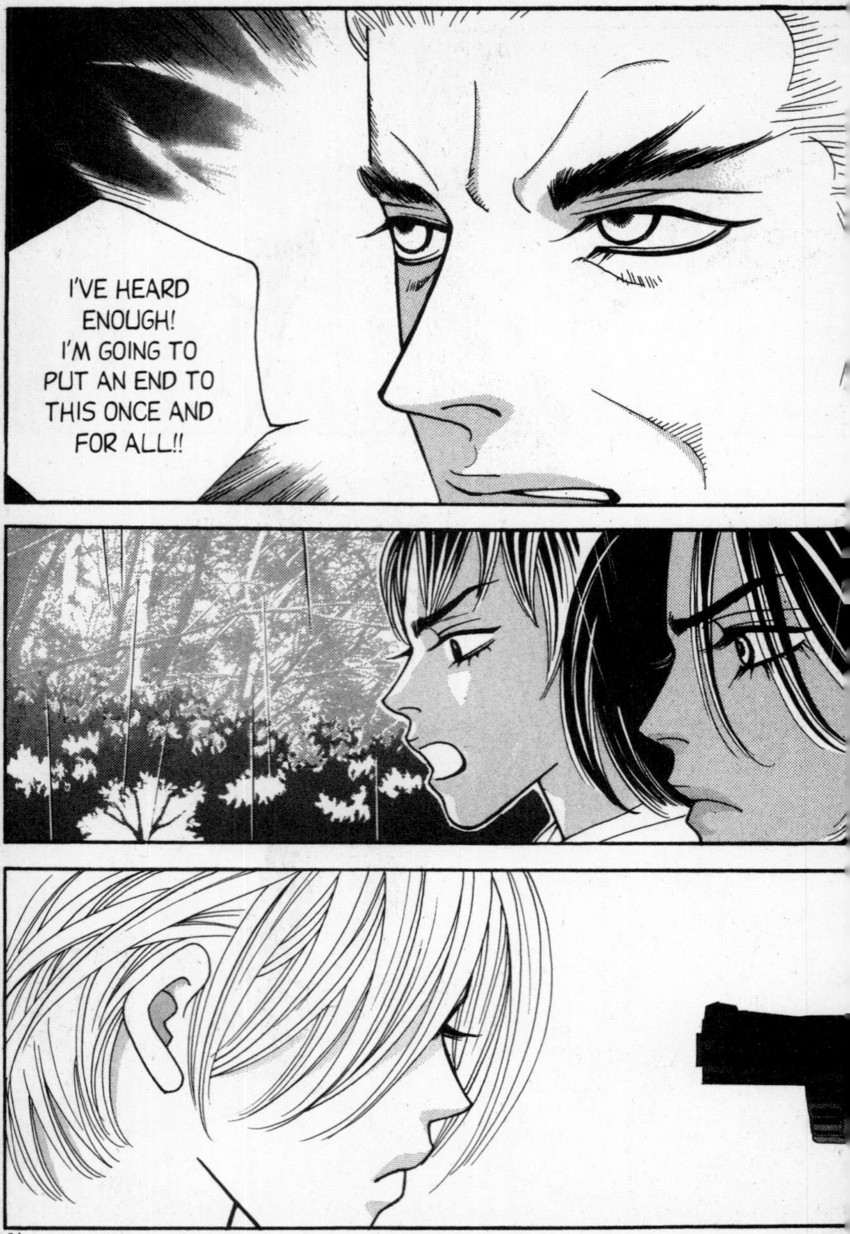
I'VE HEARD ENOUGH! I'M GOING TO PUT AN END TO THIS ONCE AND FOR ALL!!

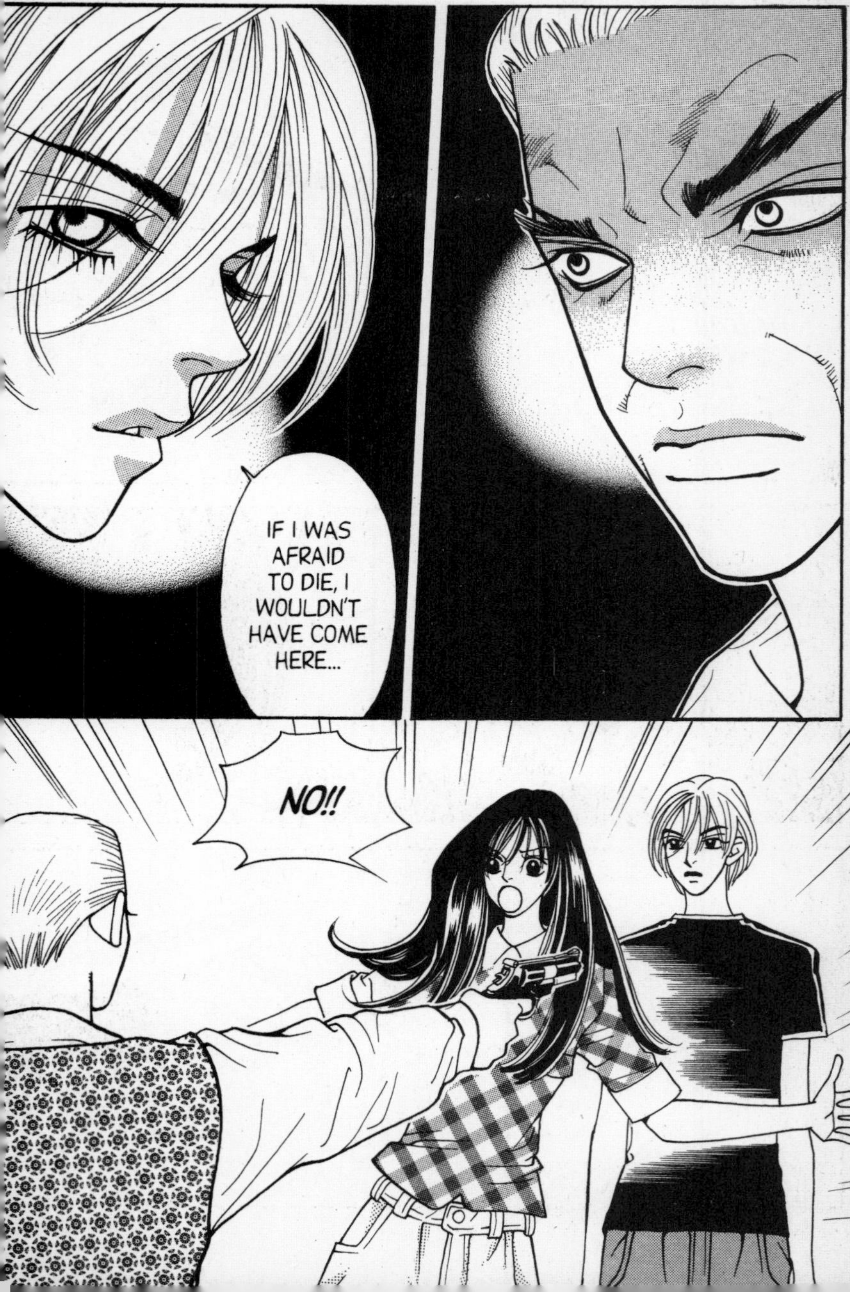
IF I WAS AFRAID TO DIE, I WOULDN'T HAVE COME HERE...
NO!!

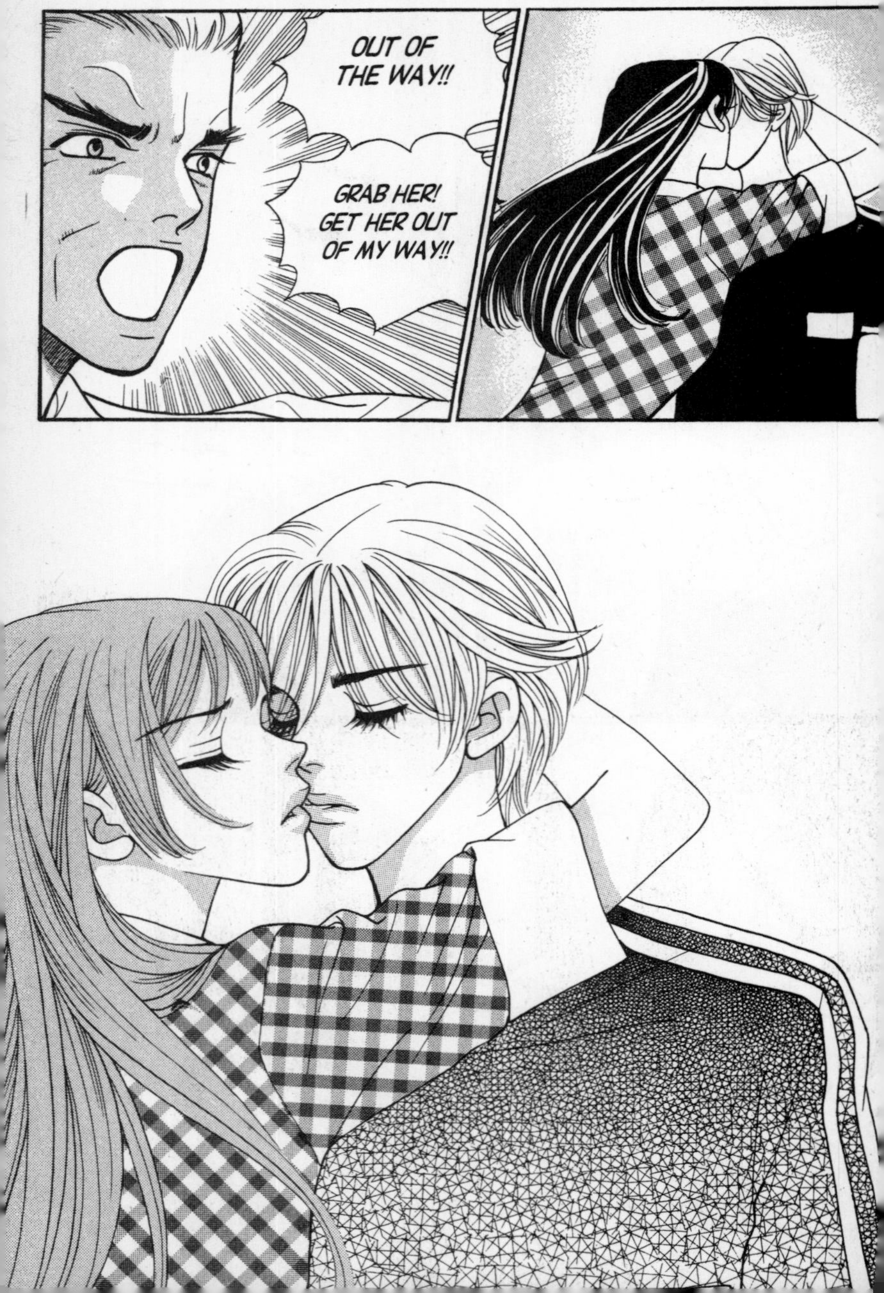

OUT OF THE WAY!!
GRAB HER! GET HER OUT OF MY WAY!!

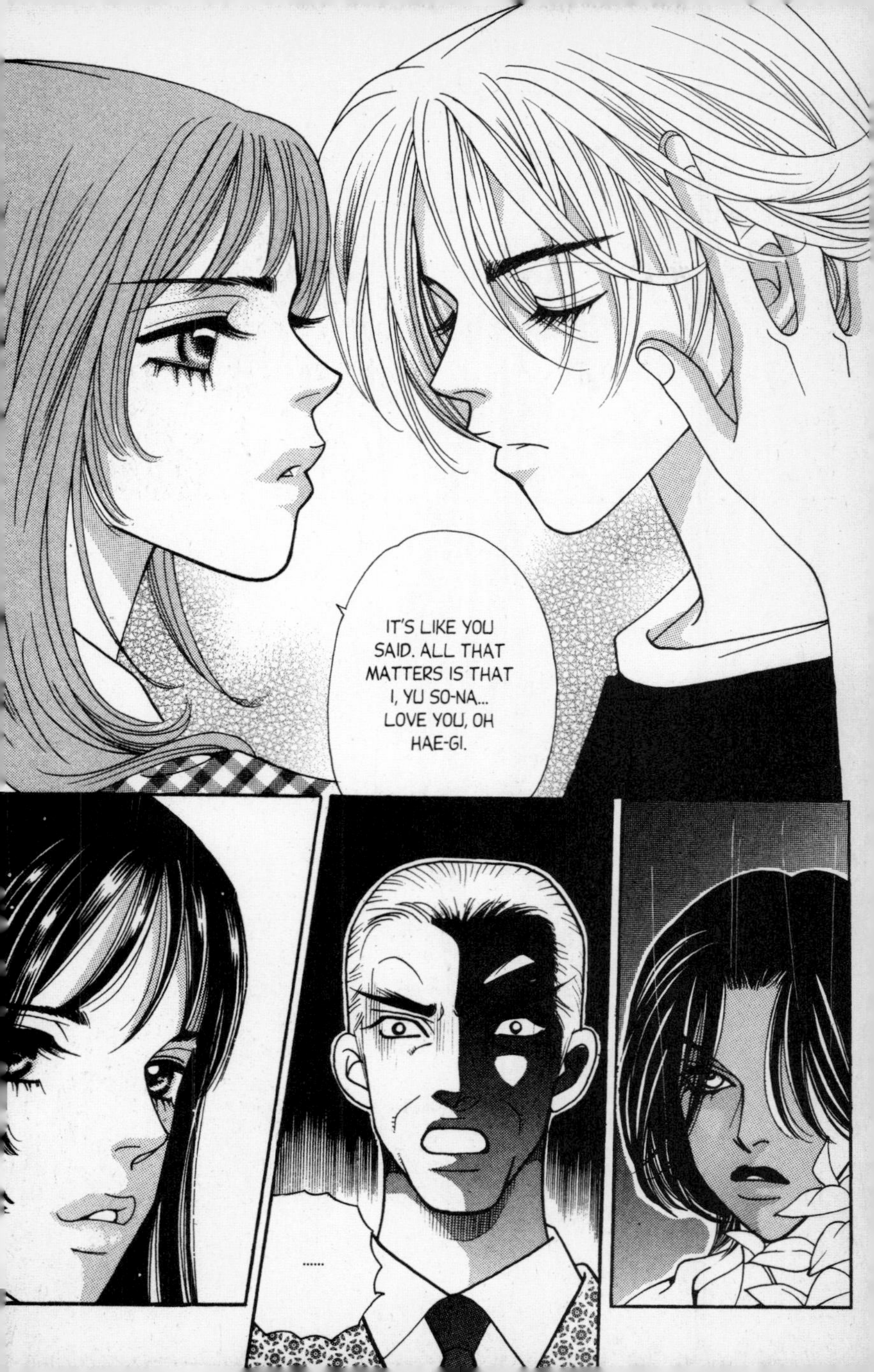
IT'S LIKE YOU SAID. ALL THAT MATTERS IS THAT I, YU SO-NA... LOVE YOU, OH HAE-GI.
......

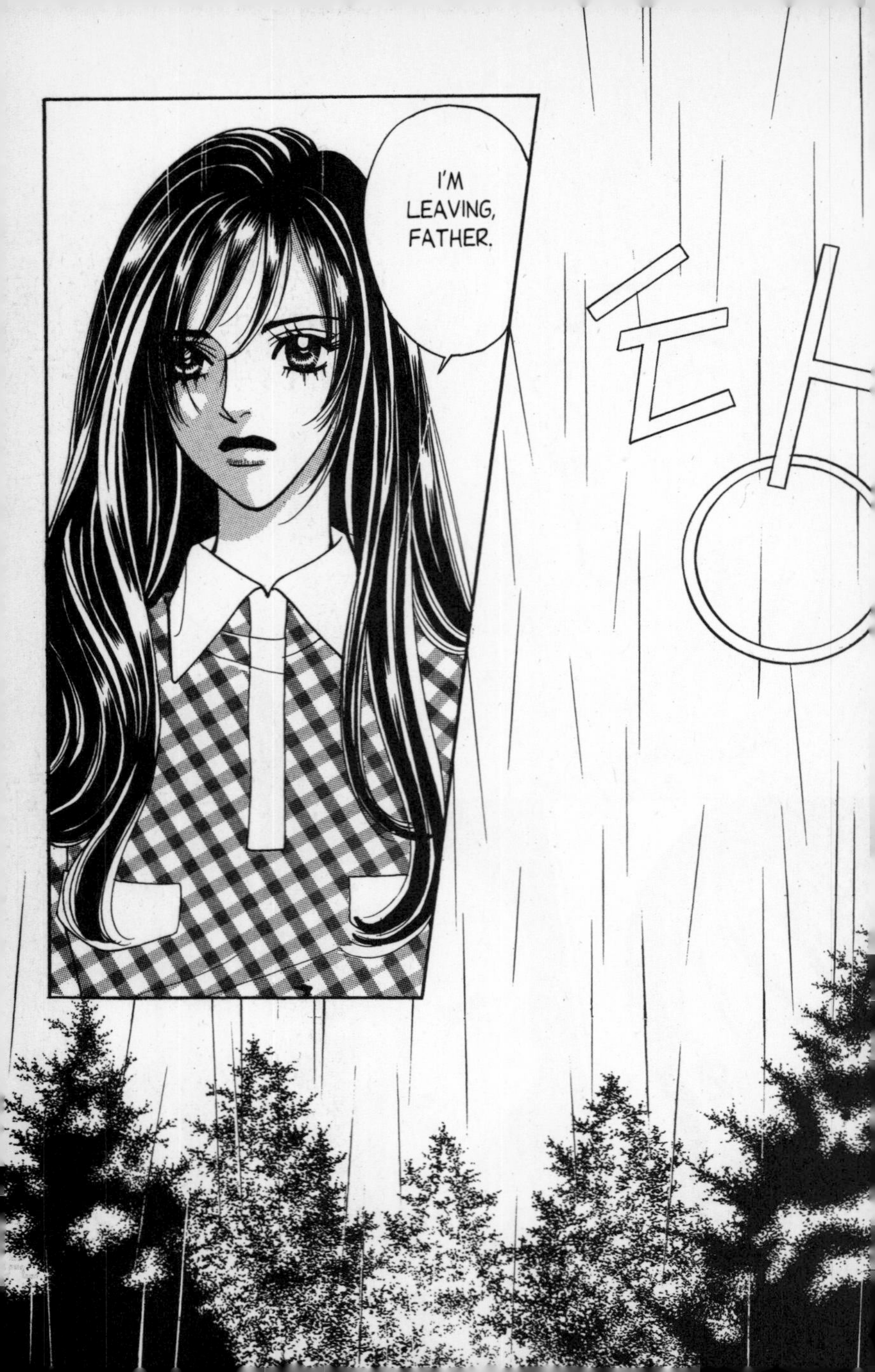
I'M LEAVING, FATHER.

스노우 드롭

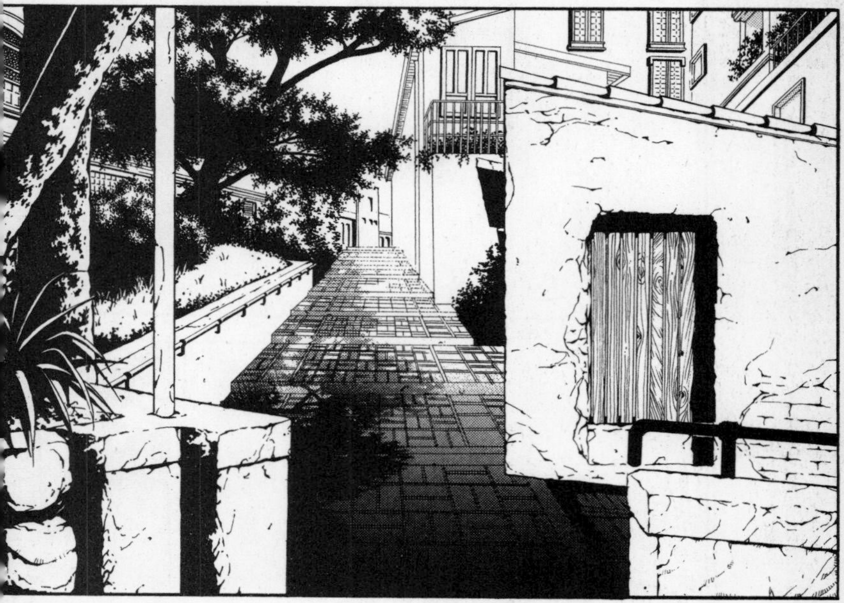

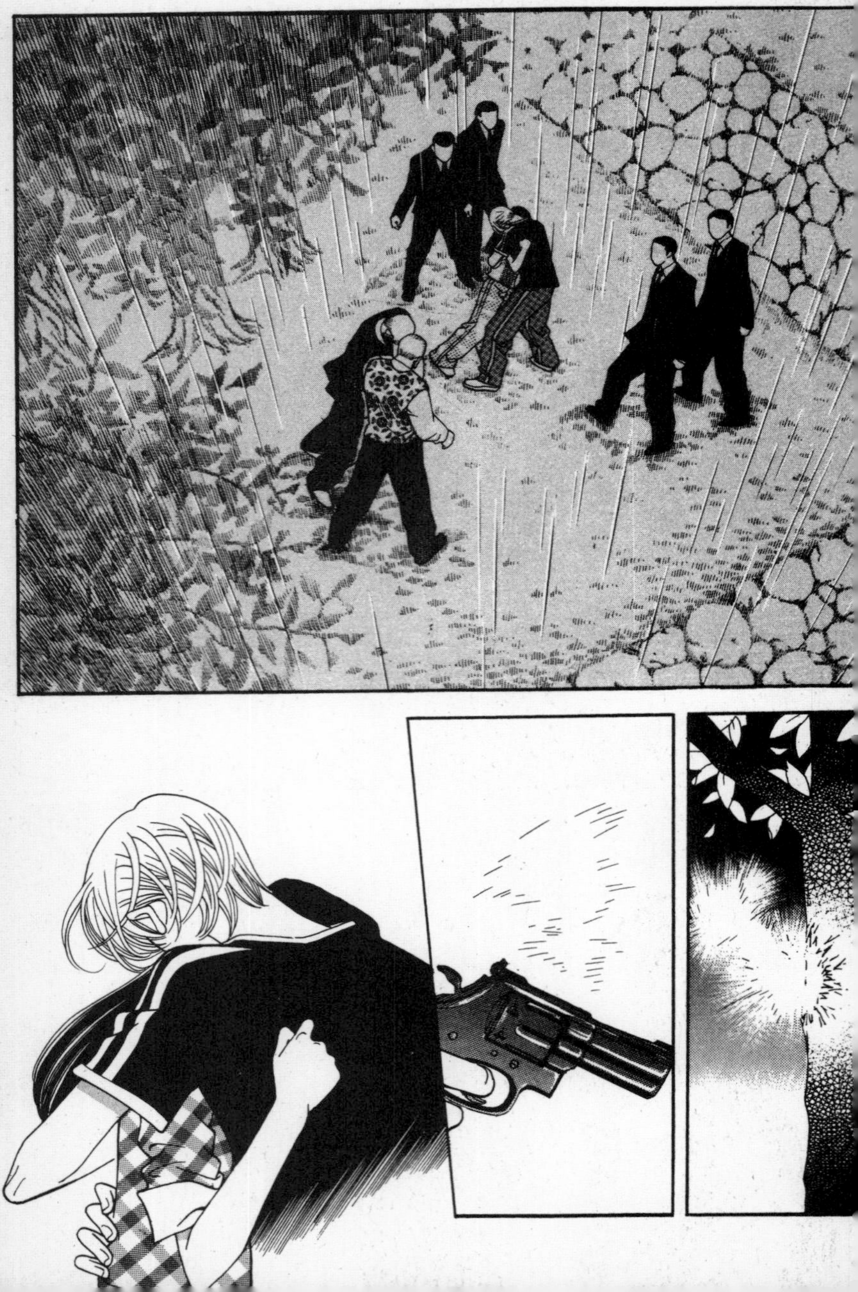

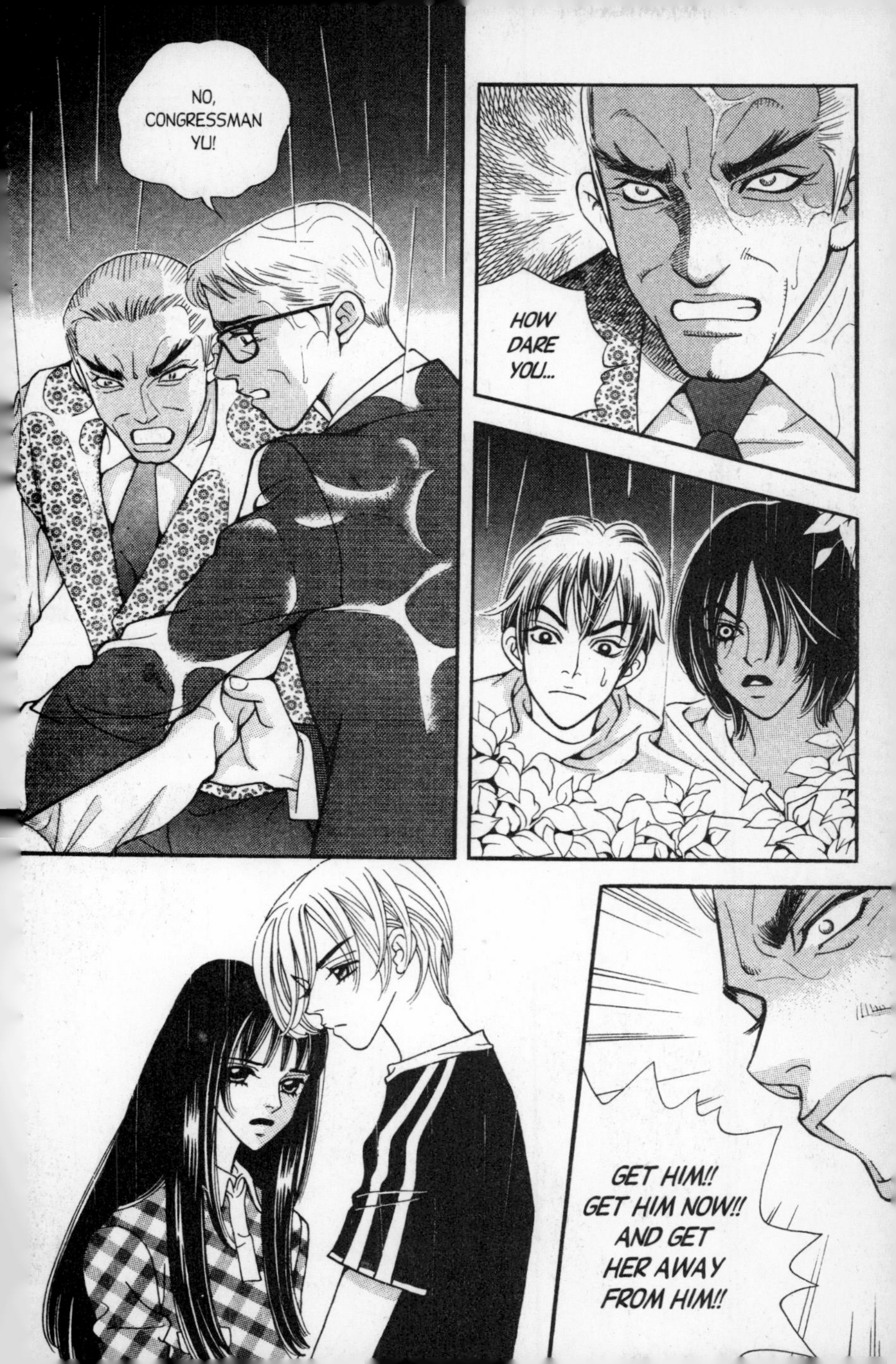
NO, CONGRESSMAN YU!
HOW DARE YOU...
GET HIM!! GET HIM NOW!! AND GET HER AWAY FROM HIM!!

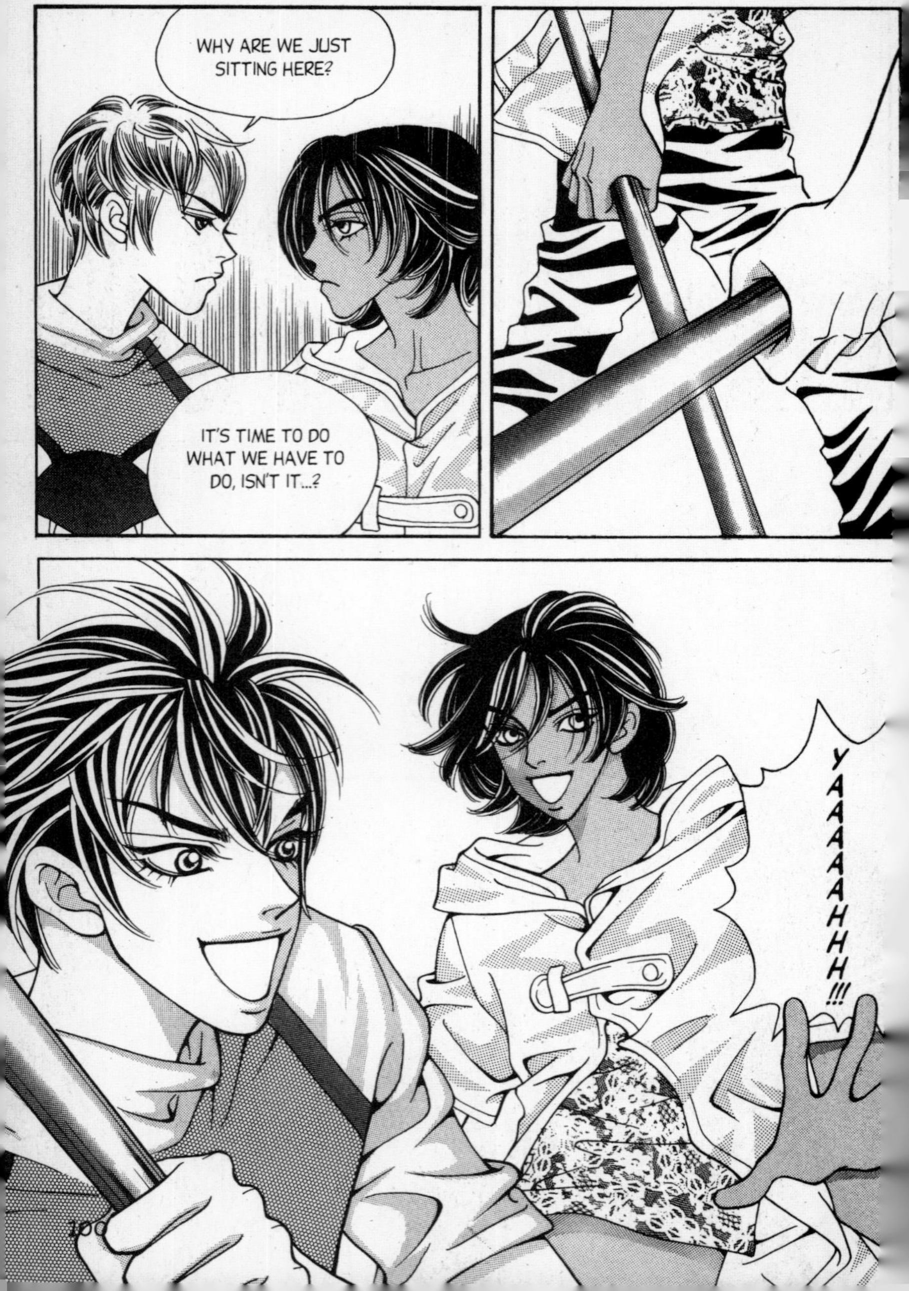
WHY ARE WE JUST SITTING HERE?
IT'S TIME TO DO WHAT WE HAVE TO DO, ISN'T IT...?
YAAAAAHHH!!!

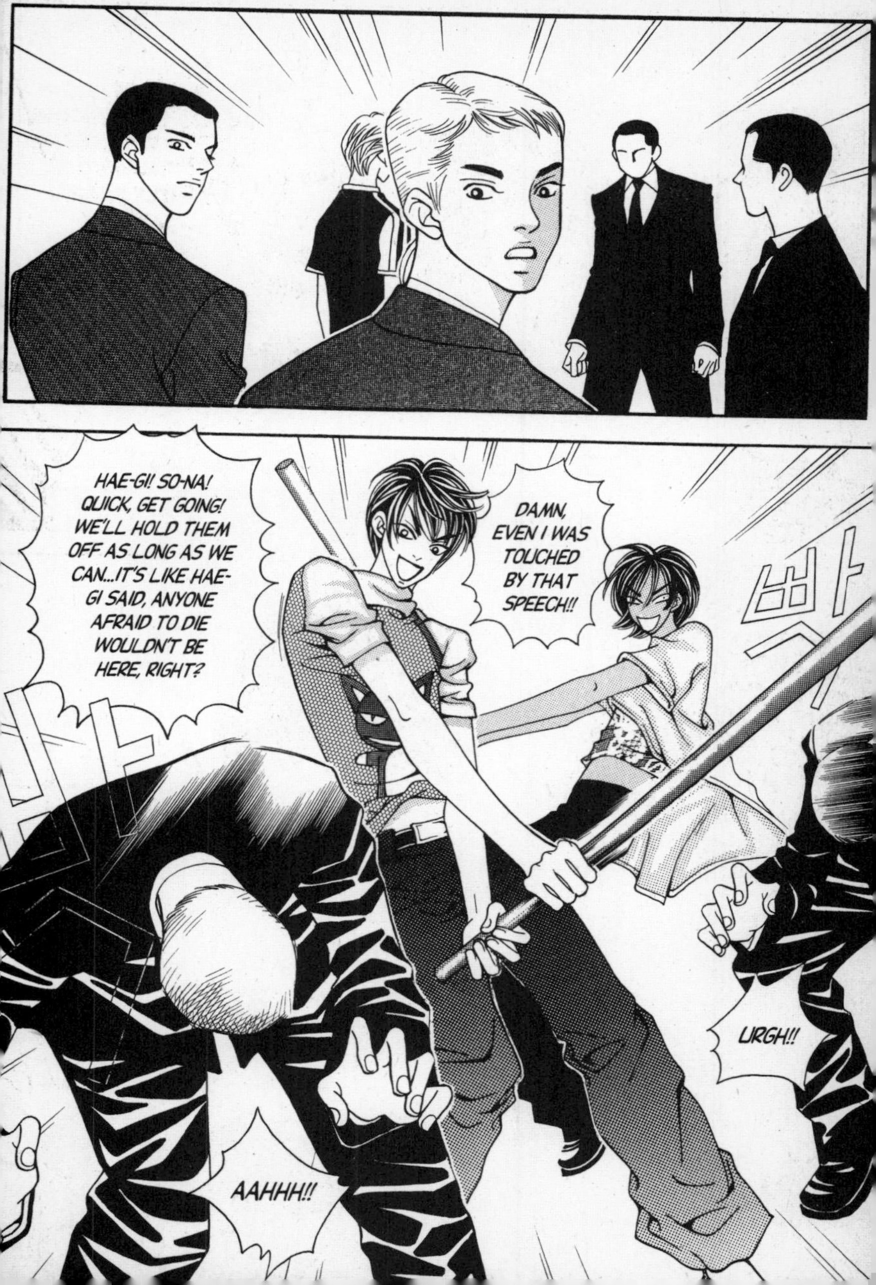
HAE-GI! SO-NA! QUICK, GET GOING! WE'LL HOLD THEM OFF AS LONG AS WE CAN...IT'S LIKE HAE-GI SAID, ANYONE AFRAID TO DIE WOULDN'T BE HERE, RIGHT?
DAMN, EVEN I WAS TOUCHED BY THAT SPEECH!!
URGH!!
AAHHH!!

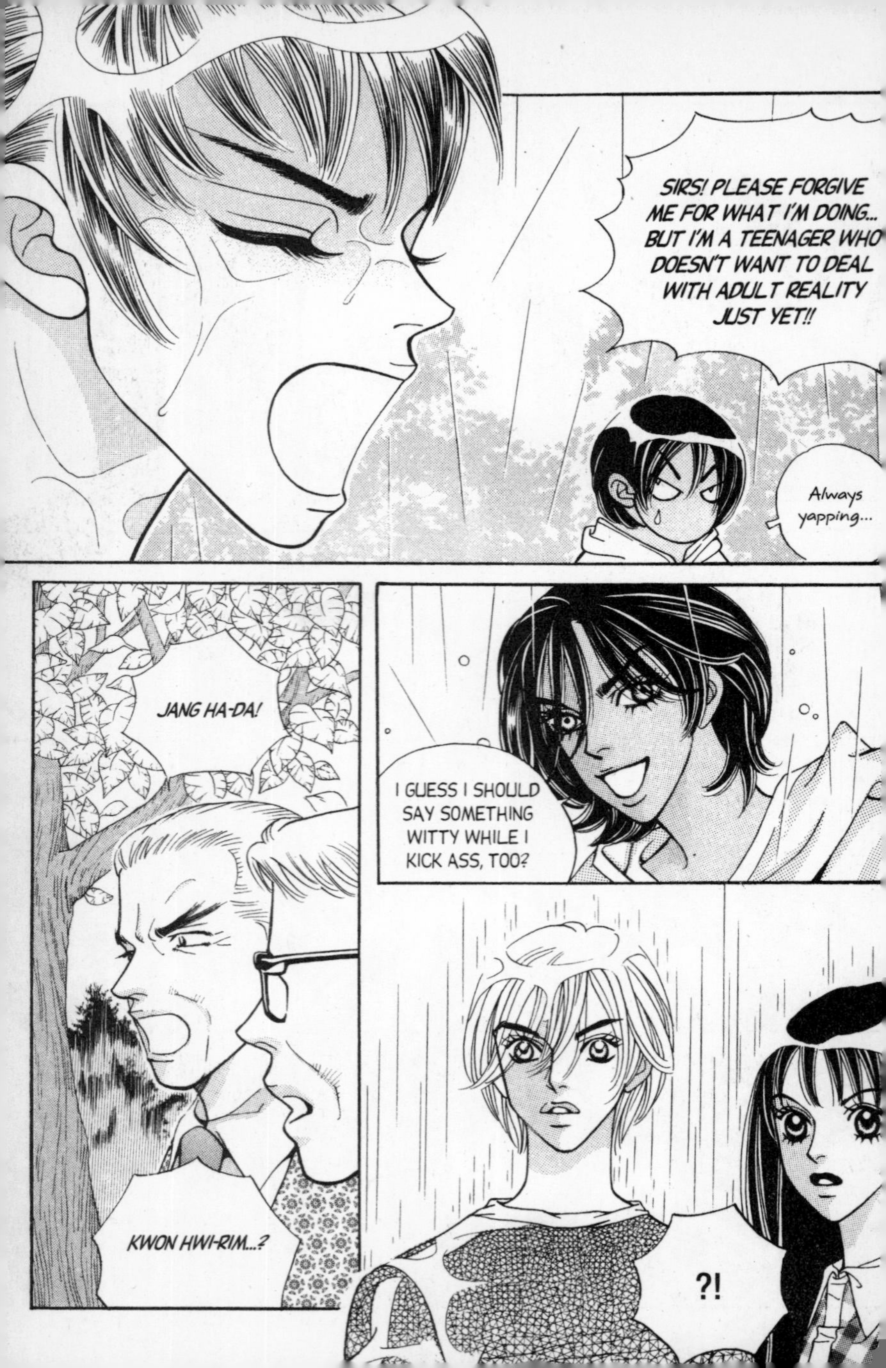
SIRS! PLEASE FORGIVE ME FOR WHAT I'M DOING... BUT I'M A TEENAGER WHO DOESN'T WANT TO DEAL WITH ADULT REALITY JUST YET!!
Always yapping...
JANG HA-DA!
KWON HWI-RIM...?
I GUESS I SHOULD SAY SOMETHING WITTY WHILE I KICK ASS, TOO?
?!

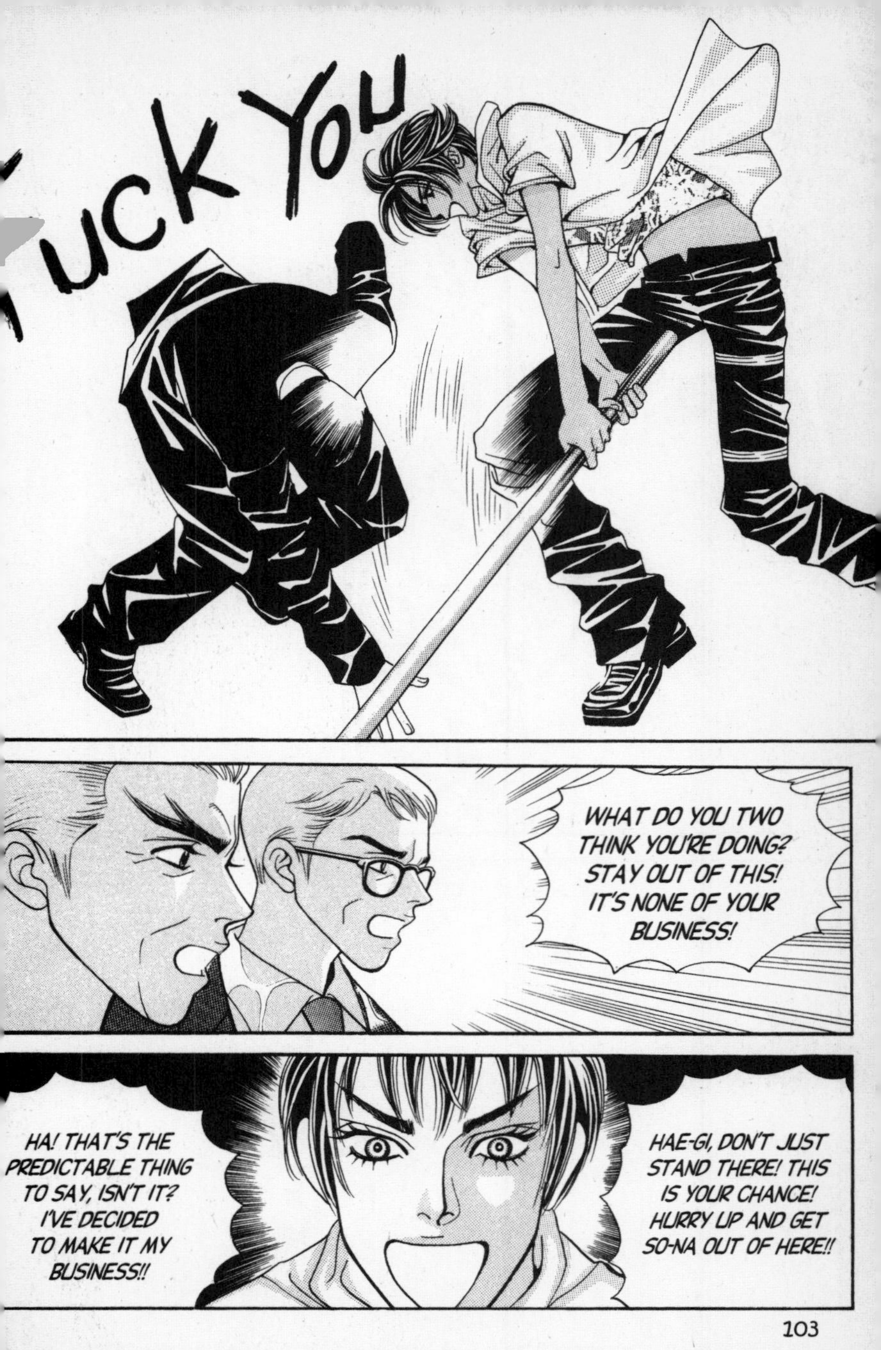
FUCK YOU
WHAT DO YOU TWO THINK YOU'RE DOING? STAY OUT OF THIS! IT'S NONE OF YOUR BUSINESS!
HA! THAT'S THE PREDICTABLE THING TO SAY, ISN'T IT? I'VE DECIDED TO MAKE IT MY BUSINESS!!
HAE-GI, DON'T JUST STAND THERE! THIS IS YOUR CHANCE! HURRY UP AND GET SO-NA OUT OF HERE!!

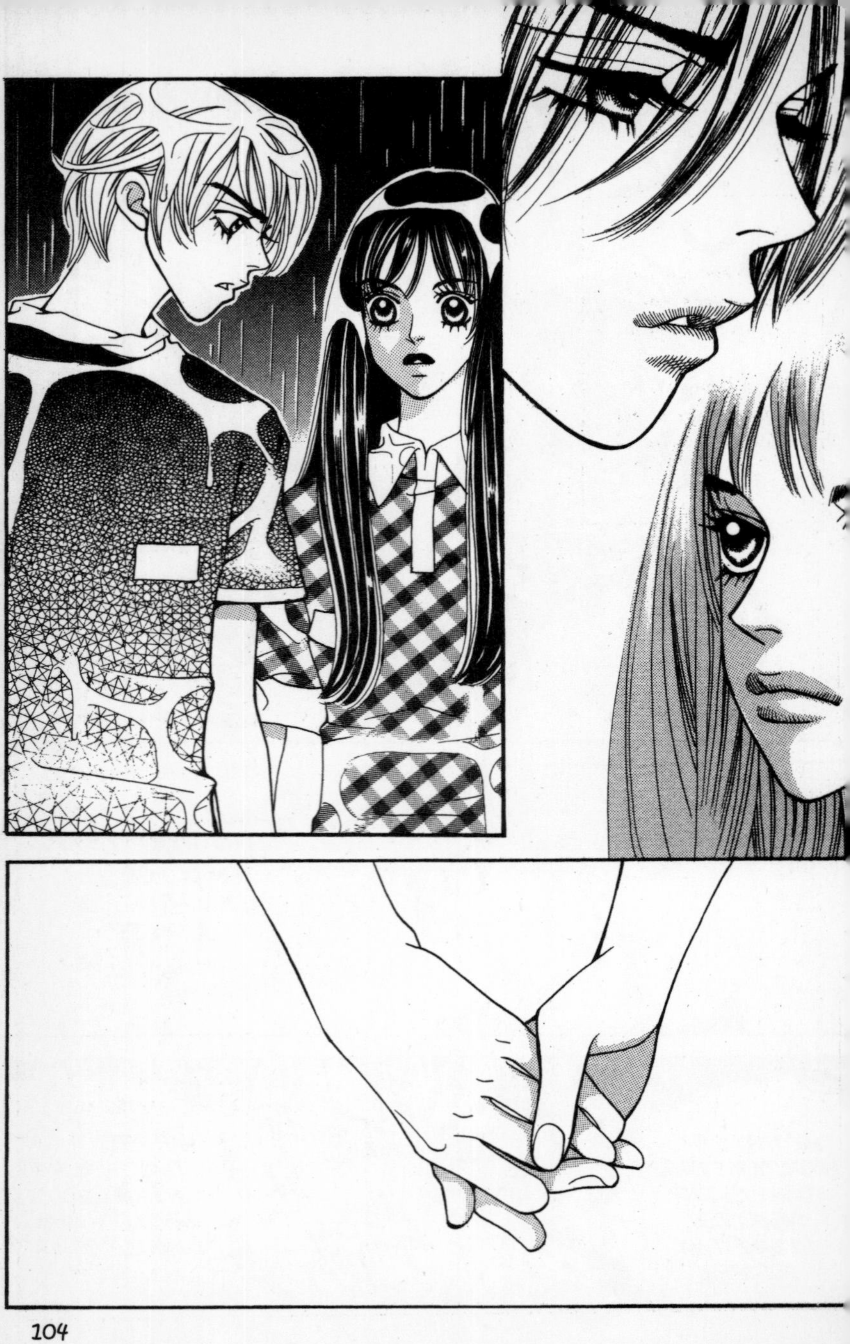

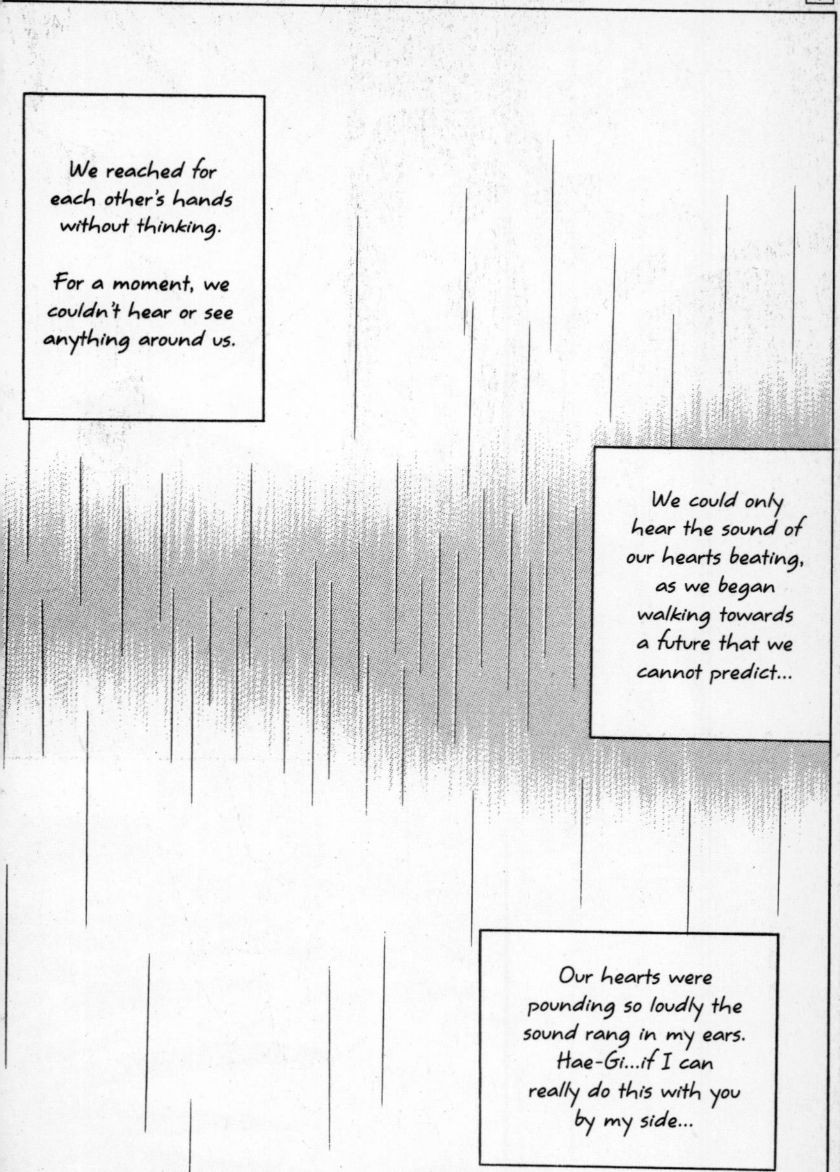
We reached for each other's hands without thinking.
For a moment, we couldn't hear or see anything around us.
We could only hear the sound of our hearts beating, as we began walking towards a future that we cannot predict...
Our hearts were pounding so loudly the sound rang in my ears. Hae-Gi...if I can really do this with you by my side...

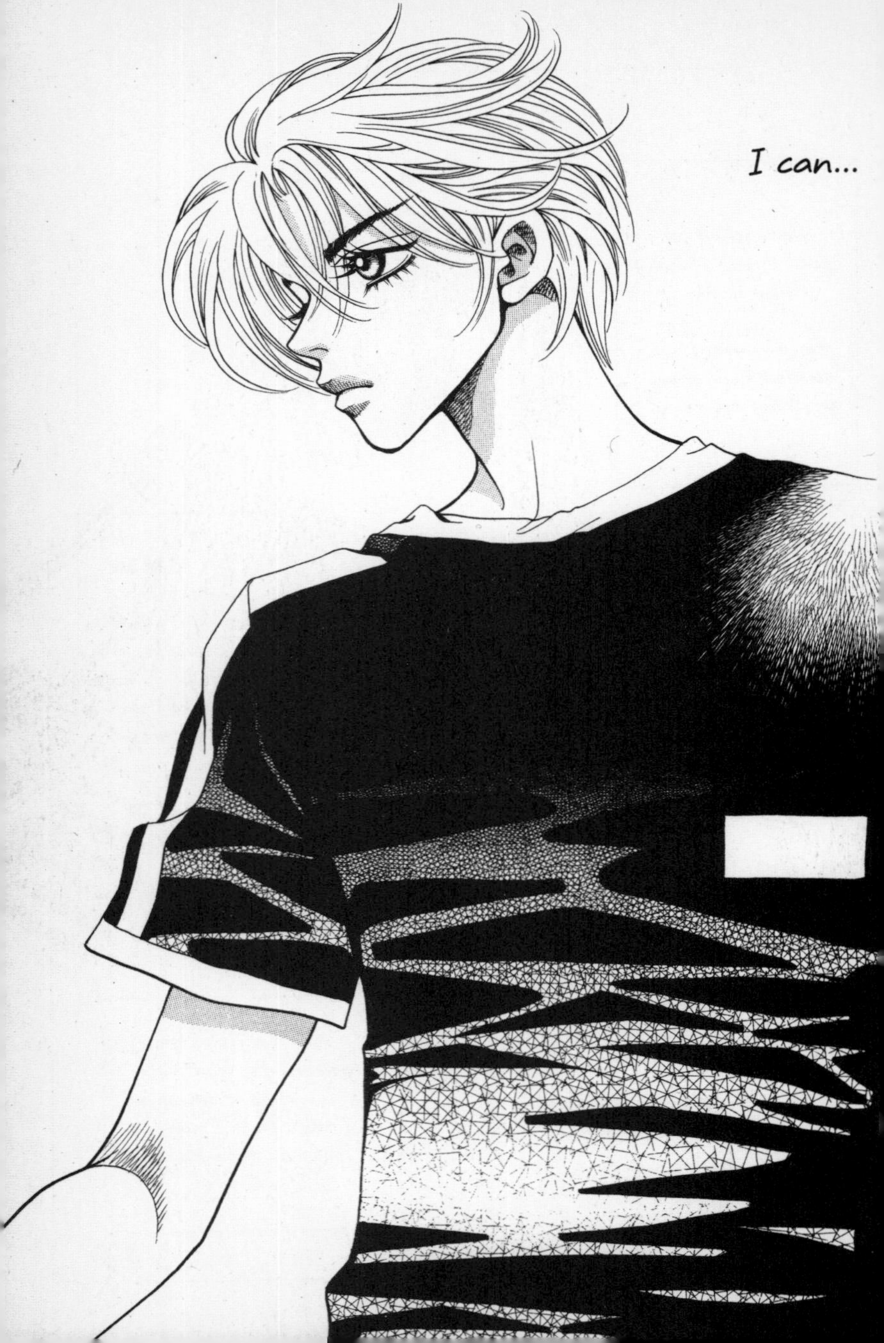
I can...

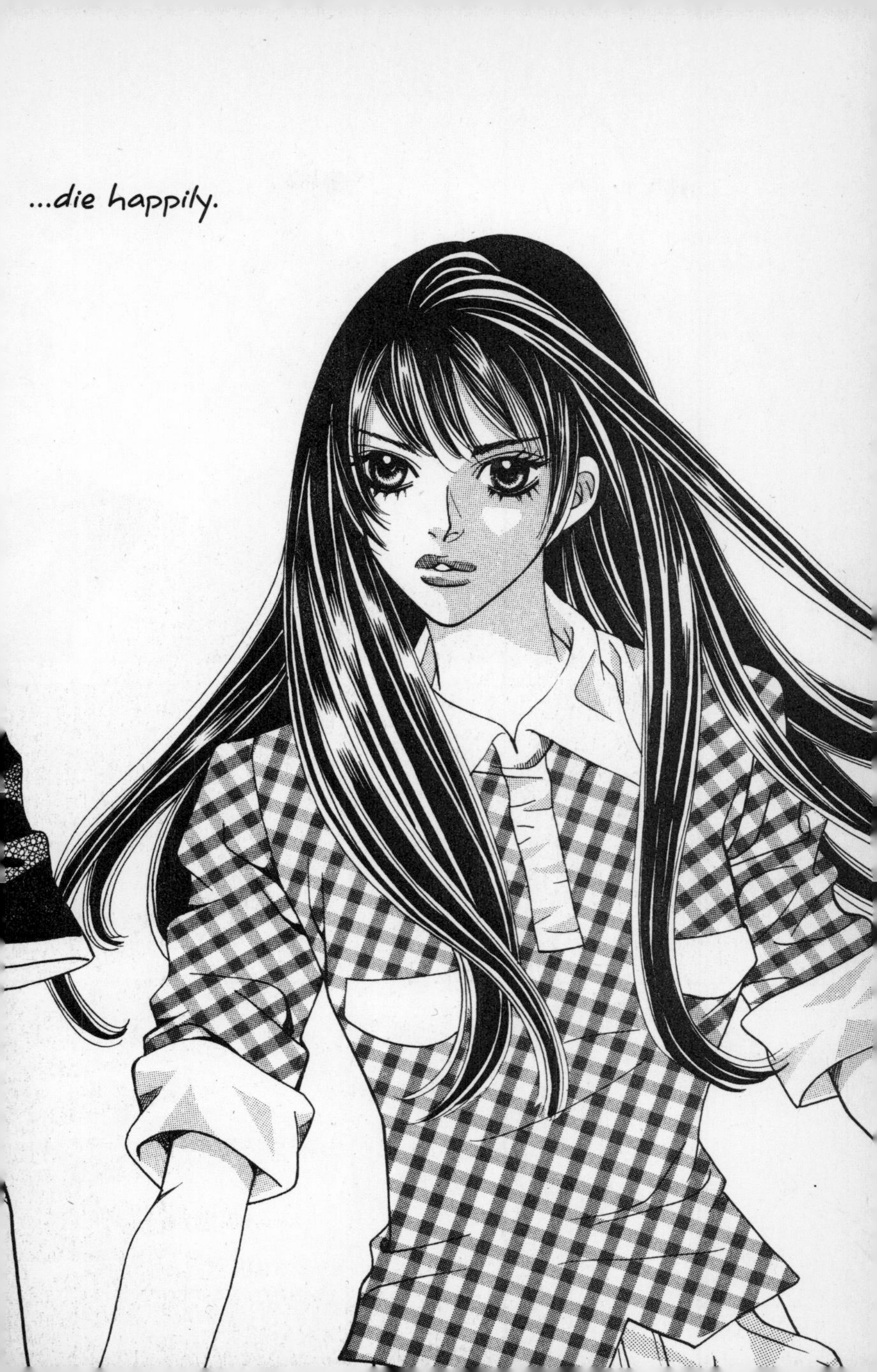
...die happily.

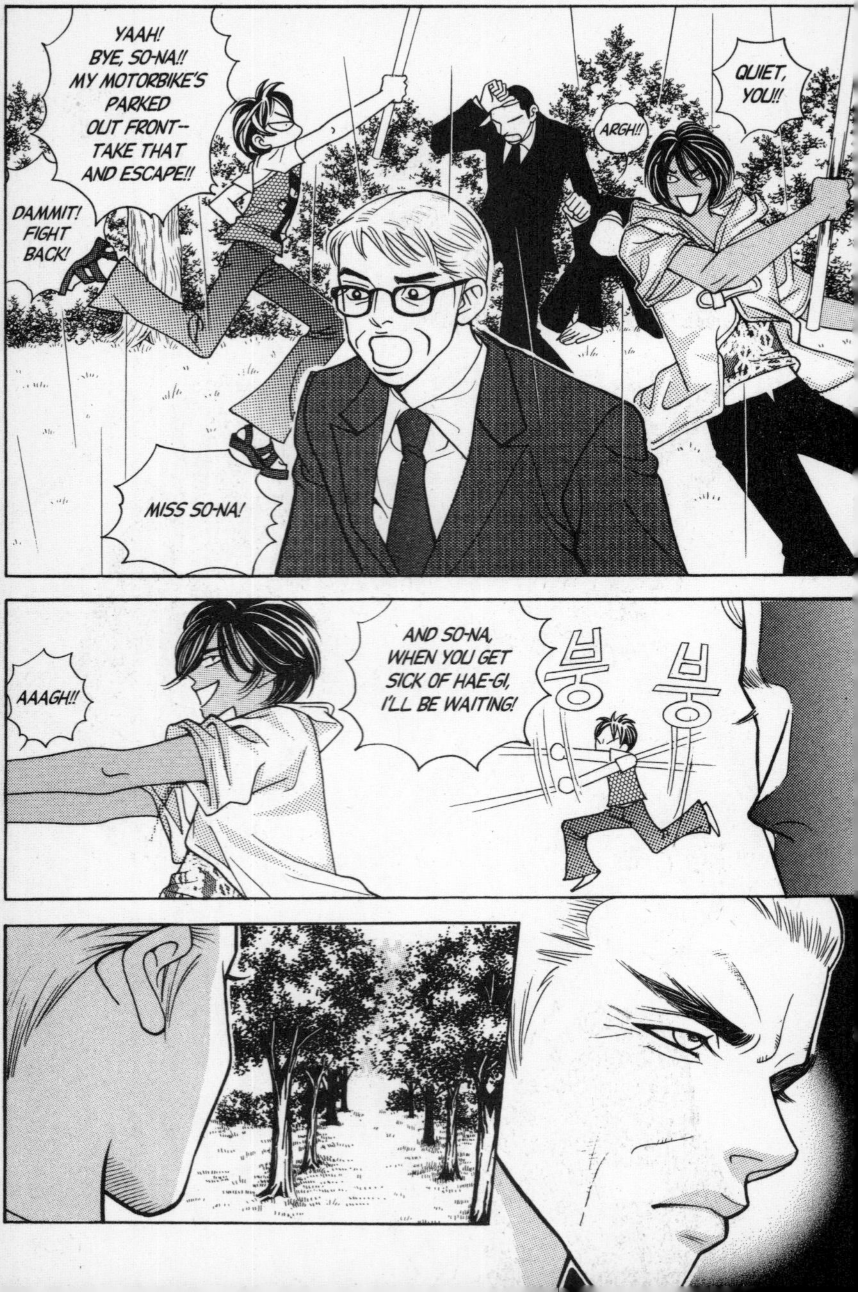
YAAH! BYE, SO-NA!! MY MOTORBIKE'S PARKED OUT FRONT-- TAKE THAT AND ESCAPE!!
DAMMIT! FIGHT BACK!
ARGH!!
QUIET, YOU!!
MISS SO-NA!
AAAGH!!
AND SO-NA, WHEN YOU GET SICK OF HAE-GI, I'LL BE WAITING!
붕 붕

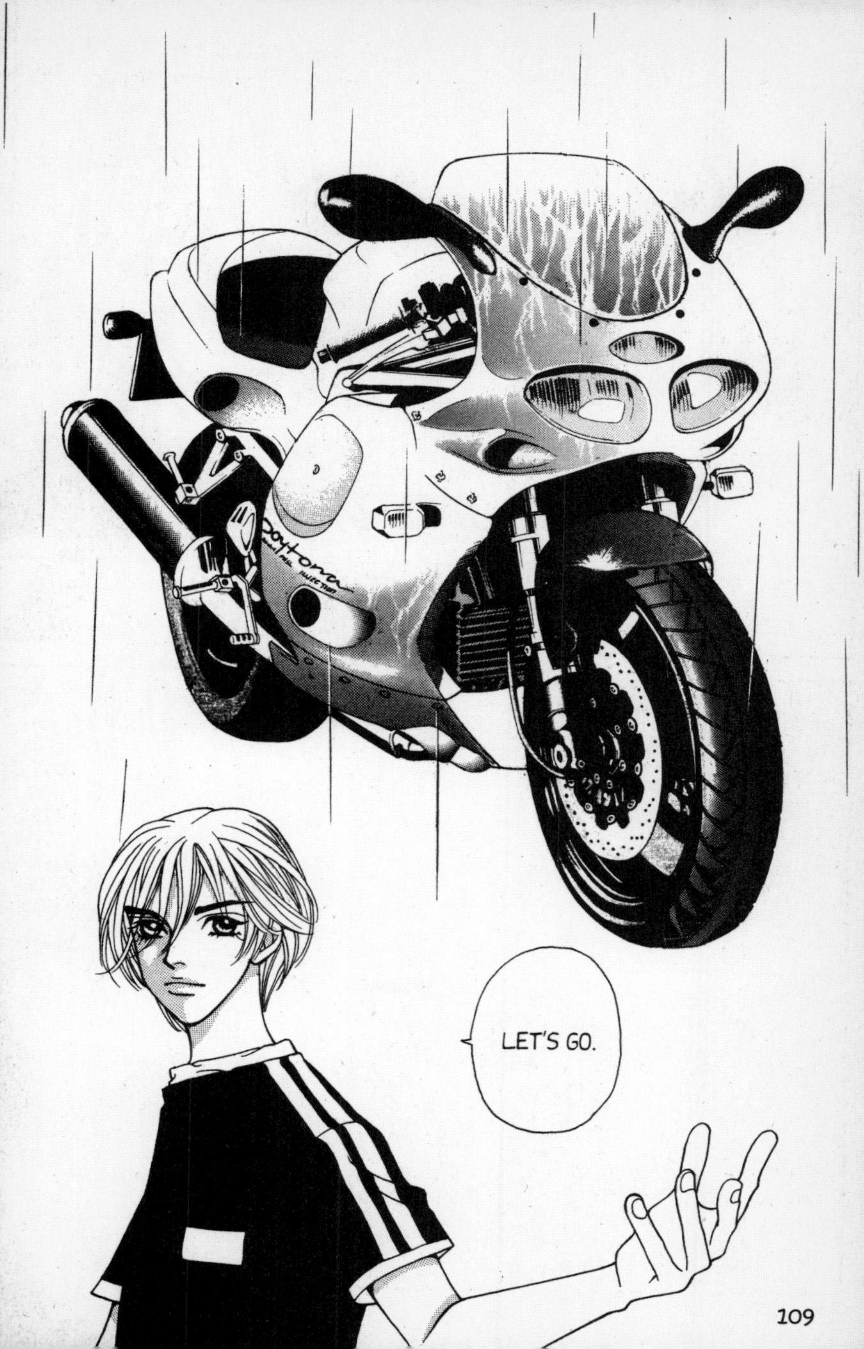
LET'S GO.

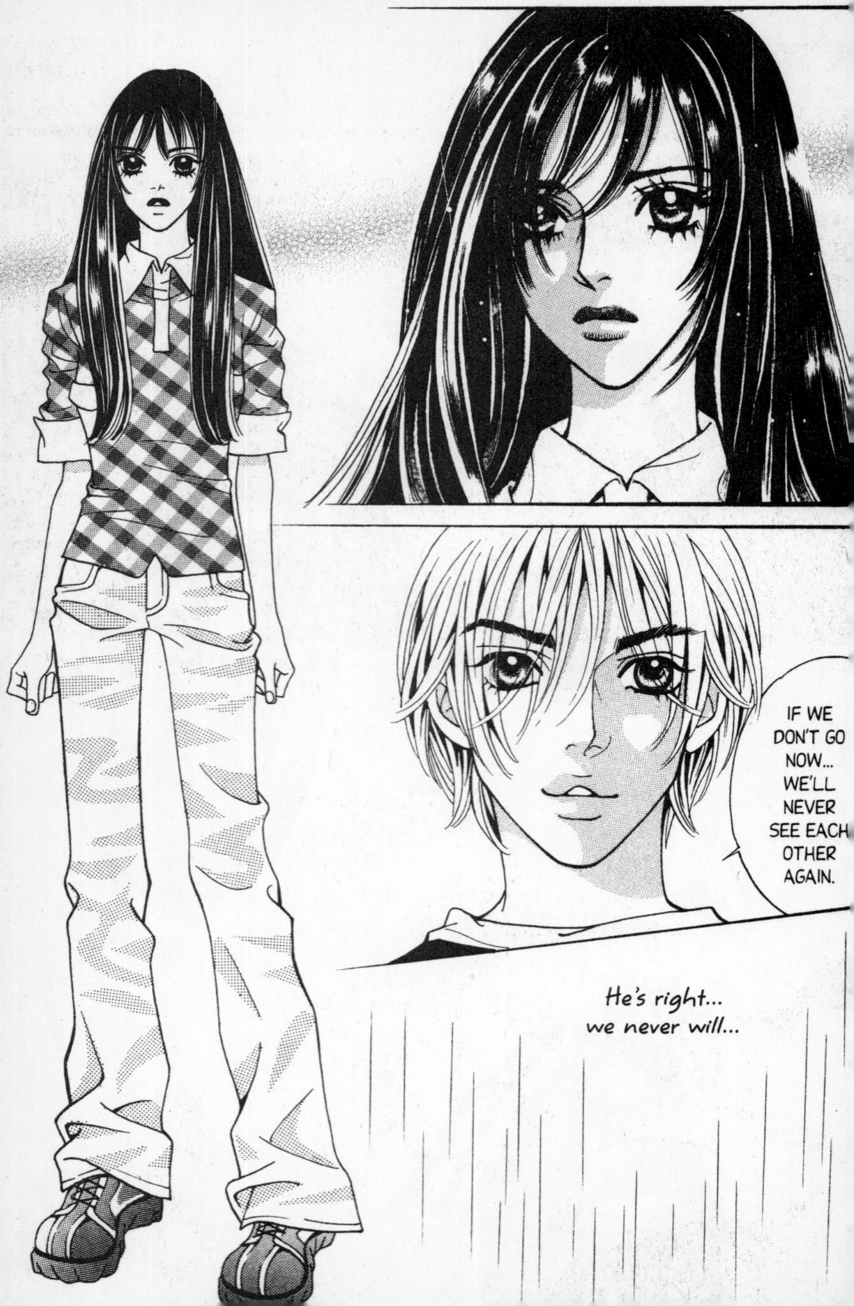
IF WE DON'T GO NOW... WE'LL NEVER SEE EACH OTHER AGAIN.
He's right... we never will...

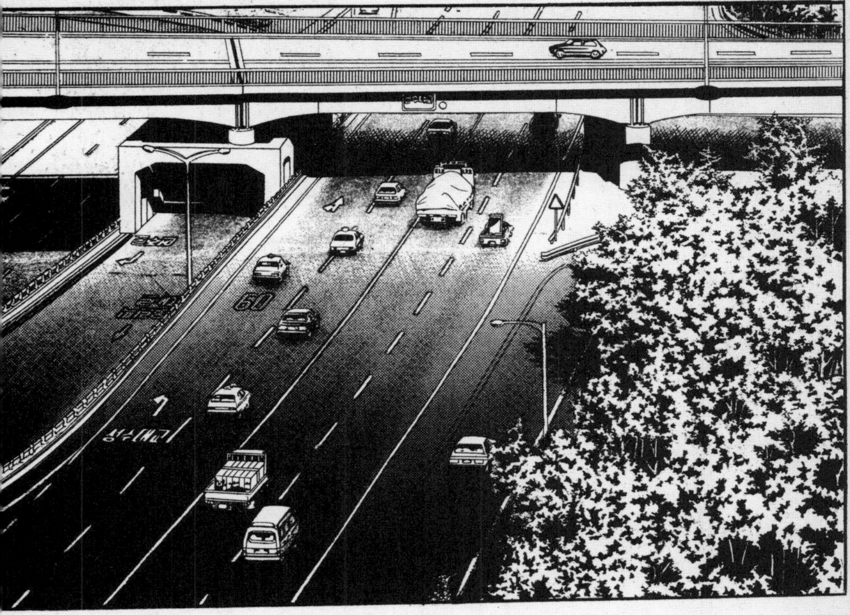

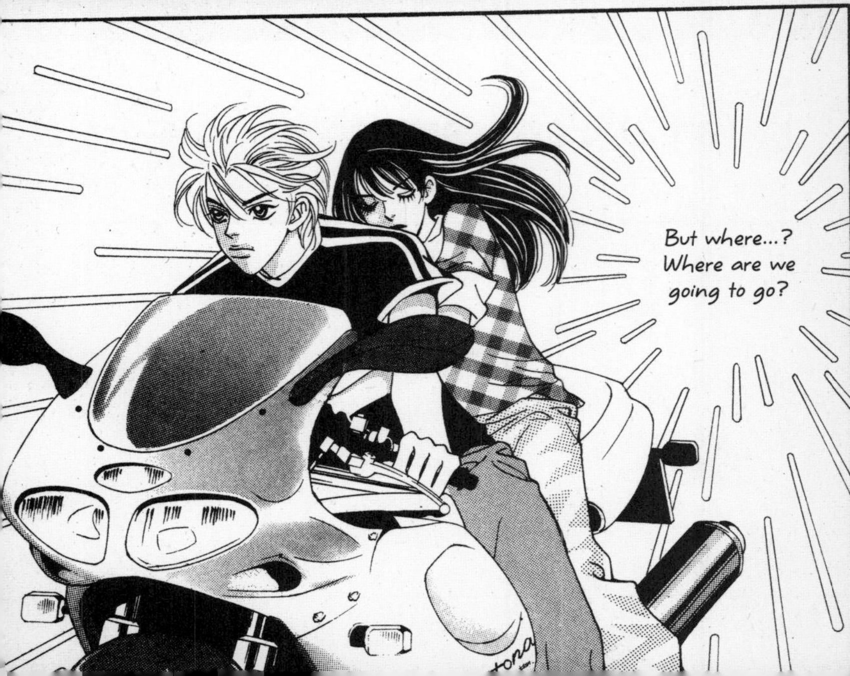
But where...? Where are we going to go?

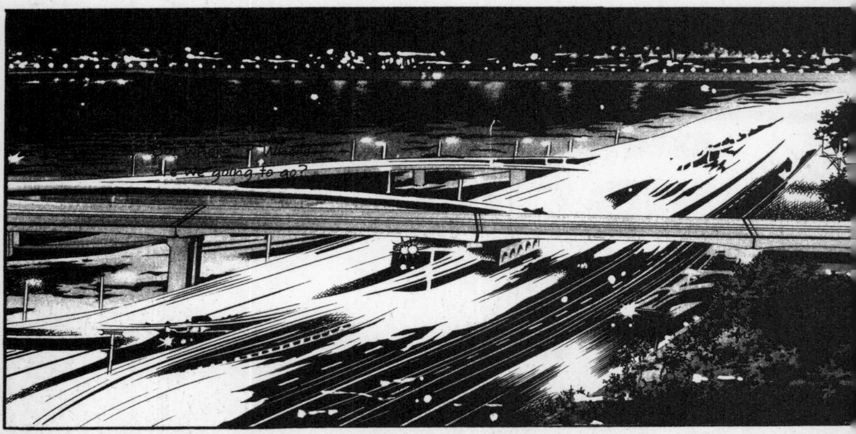
are we going to go?

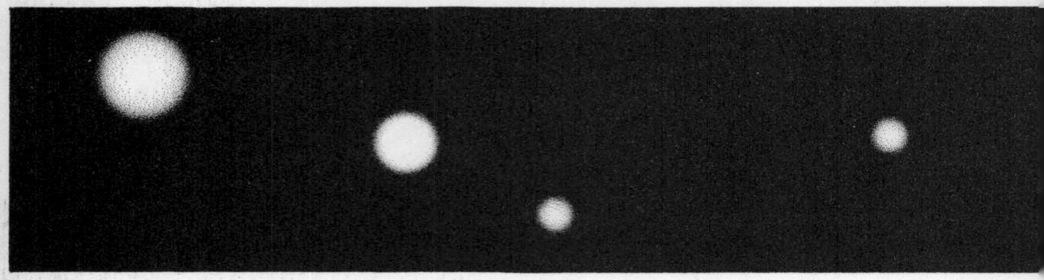

Part 27: Fearlessness

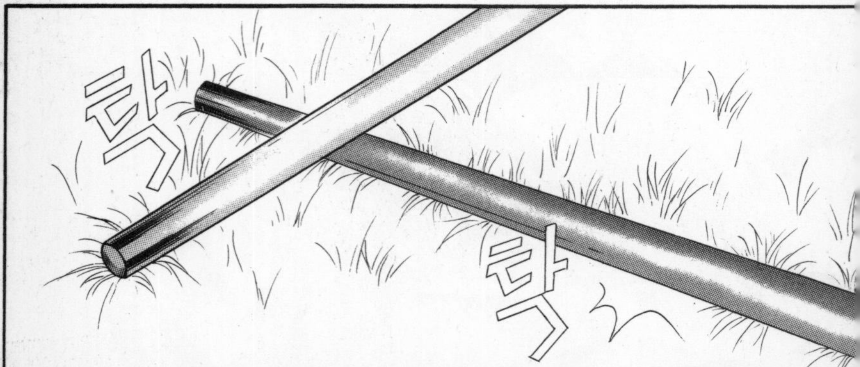
탁
탁

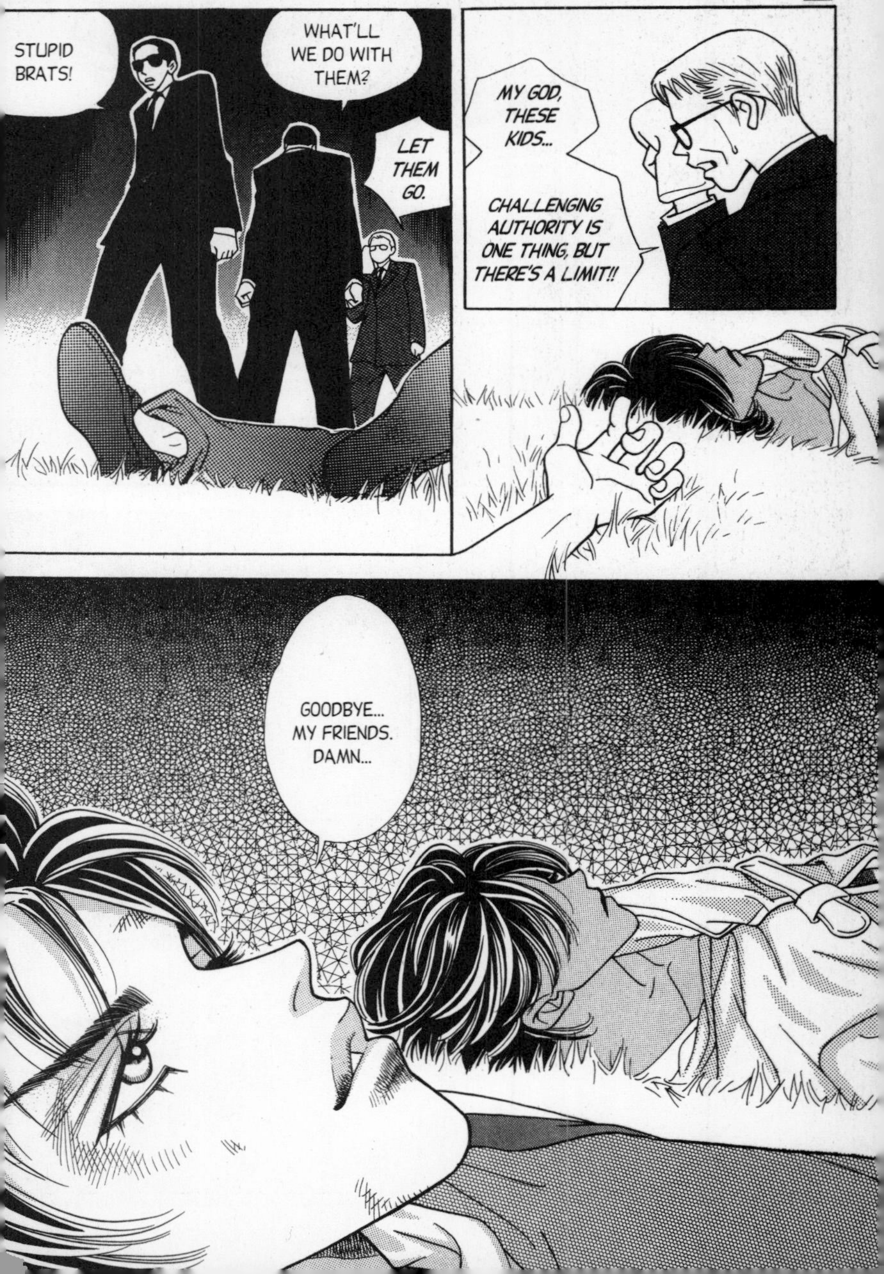
STUPID BRATS!
WHAT'LL WE DO WITH THEM?
LET THEM GO.
MY GOD, THESE KIDS...
CHALLENGING AUTHORITY IS ONE THING, BUT THERE'S A LIMIT!!
GOODBYE... MY FRIENDS. DAMN...

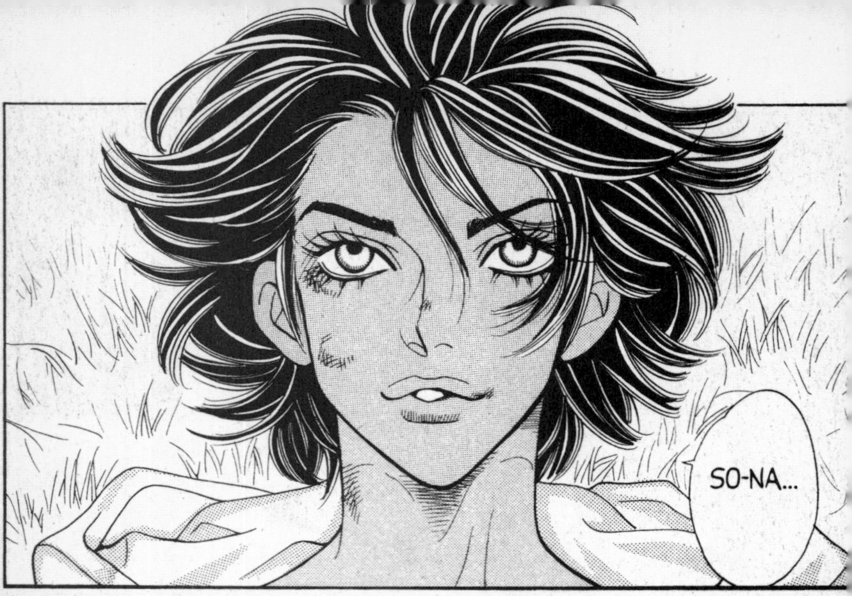
SO-NA...
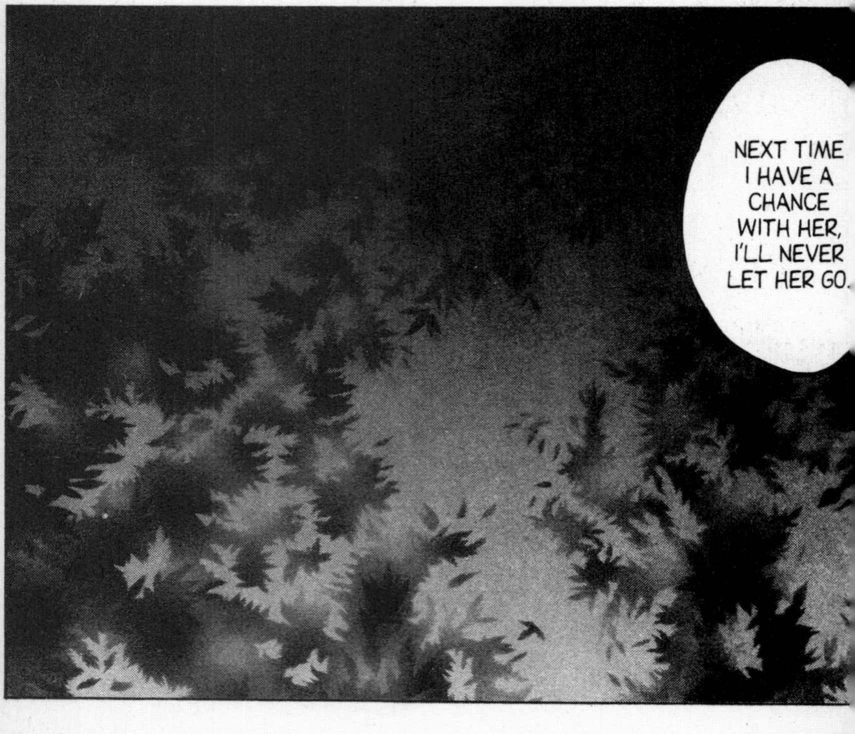
NEXT TIME I HAVE A CHANCE WITH HER, I'LL NEVER LET HER GO.

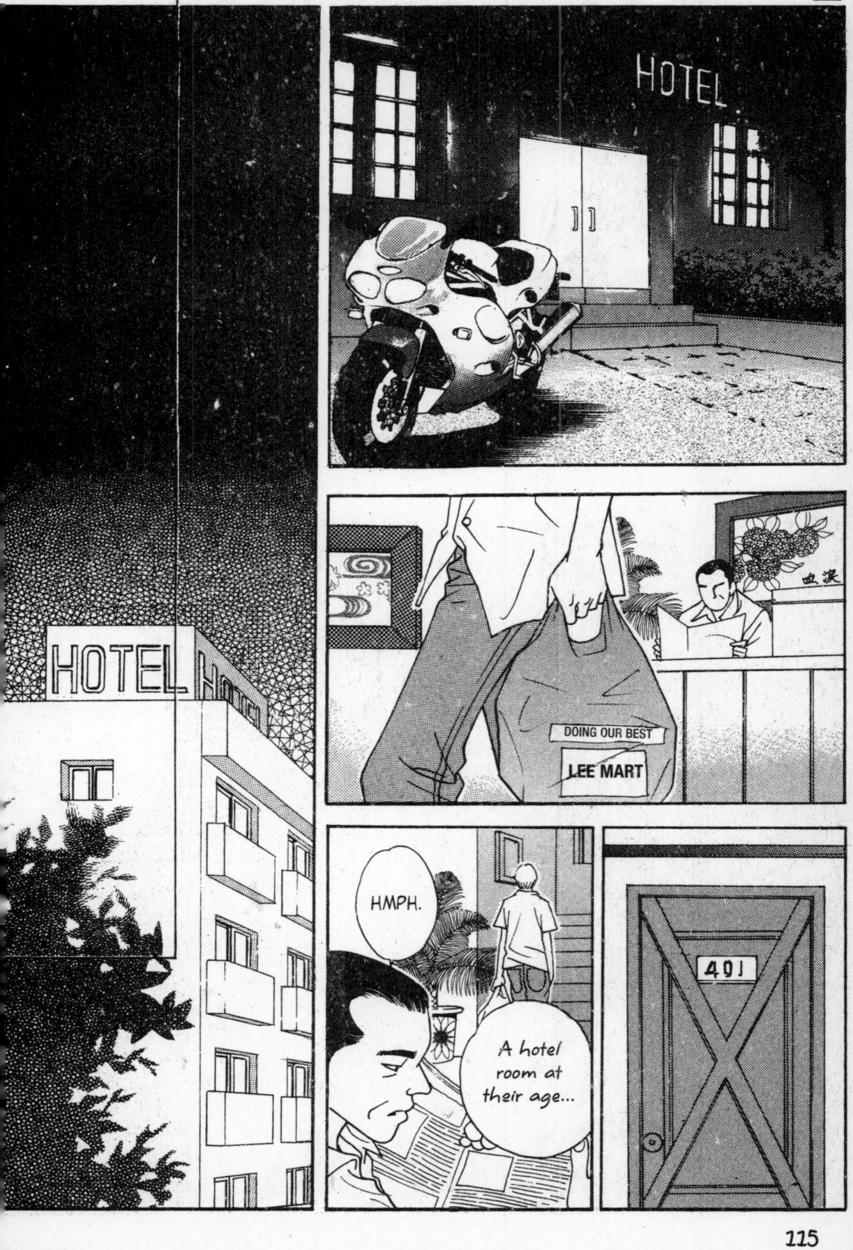
HOTEL
HOTEL
HOTEL
血涙
DOING OUR BEST
LEE MART
HMPH.
A hotel room at their age...
401

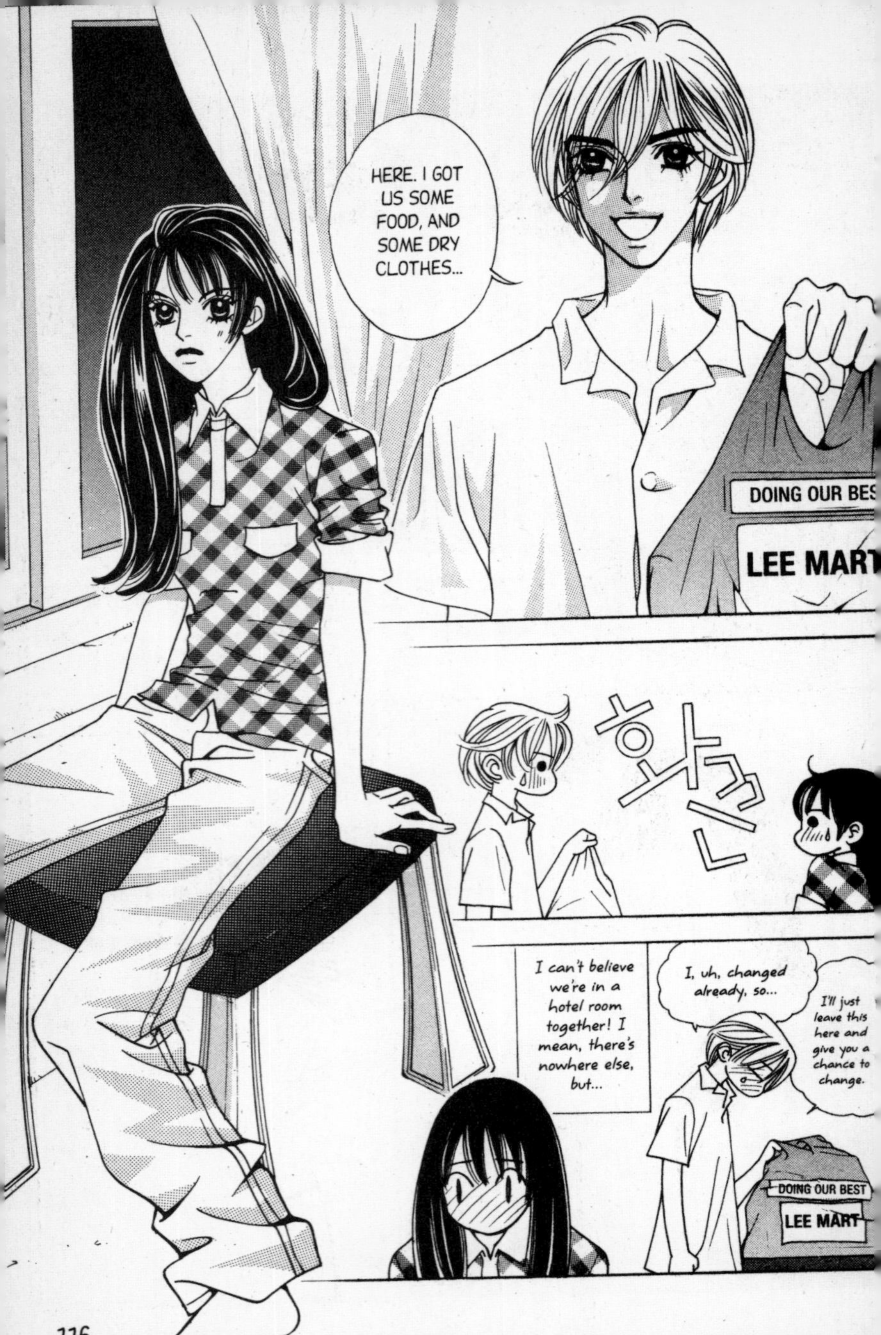
HERE. I GOT US SOME FOOD, AND SOME DRY CLOTHES...
DOING OUR BES
LEE MART
I can't believe we're in a hotel room together! I mean, there's nowhere else, but...
I, uh, changed already, so...
I'll just leave this here and give you a chance to change.
DOING OUR BEST
LEE MART

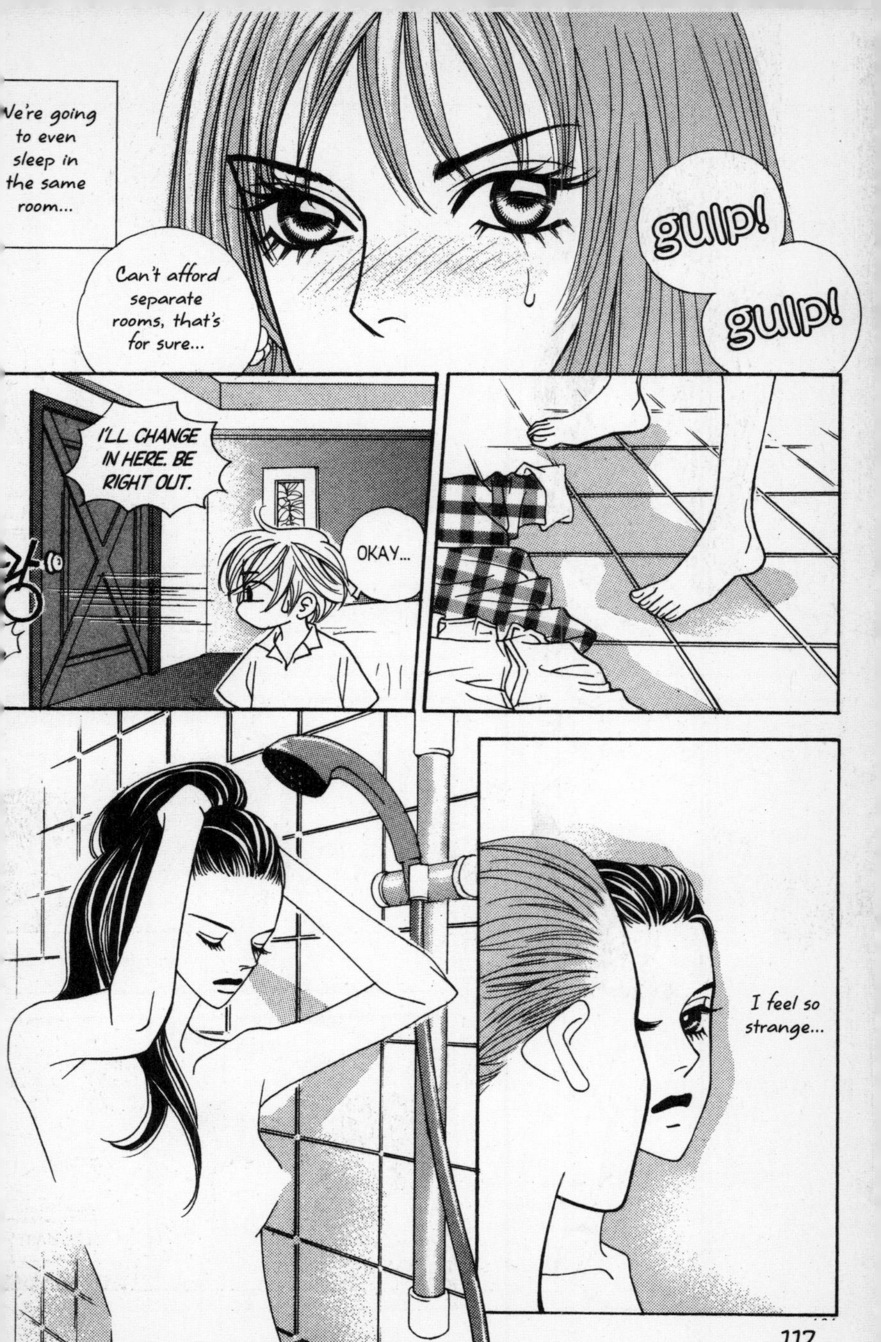

We're going to even sleep in the same room...
Can't afford separate rooms, that's for sure...
gulp!
gulp!
I'LL CHANGE IN HERE. BE RIGHT OUT.
OKAY...
I feel so strange...

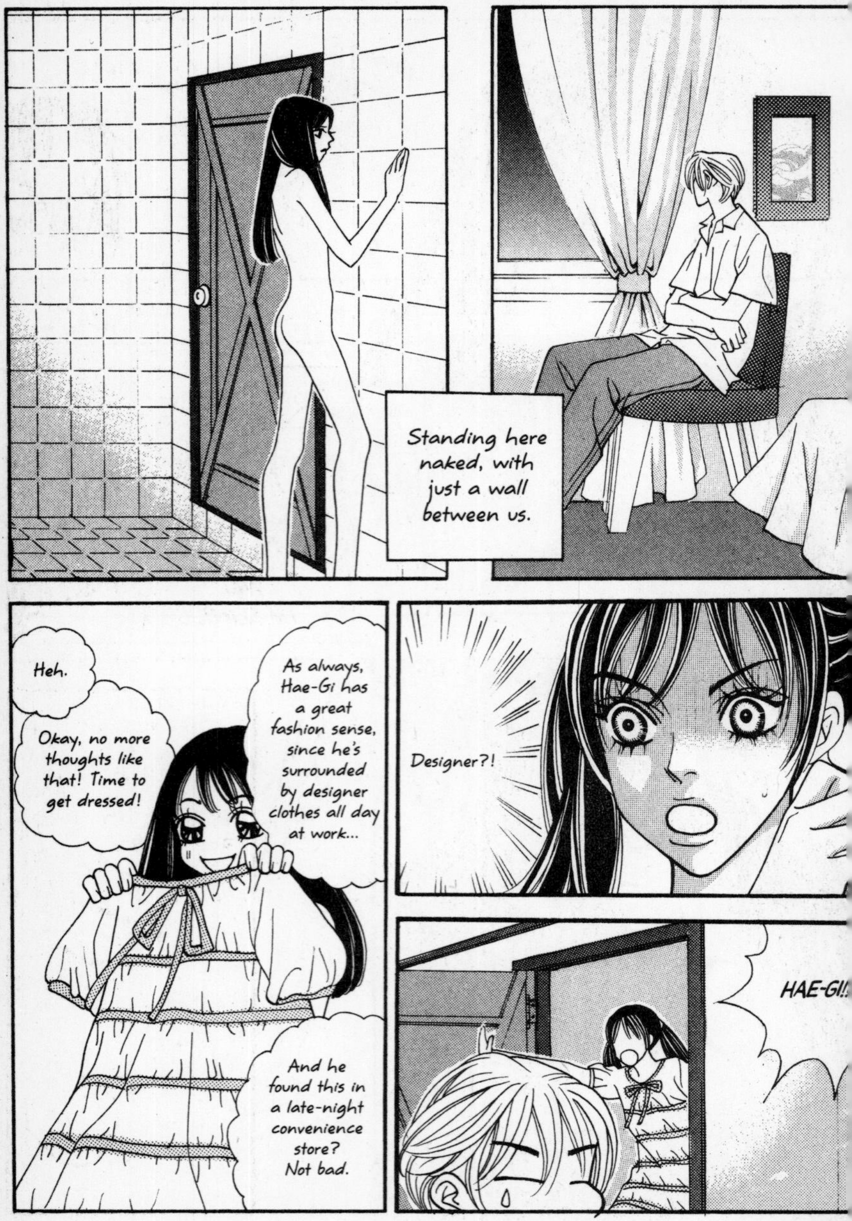
Standing here naked, with just a wall between us.
Heh.
Okay, no more thoughts like that! Time to get dressed!
As always, Hae-Gi has a great fashion sense, since he's surrounded by designer clothes all day at work...
And he found this in a late-night convenience store? Not bad.
Designer?!
HAE-GI!!

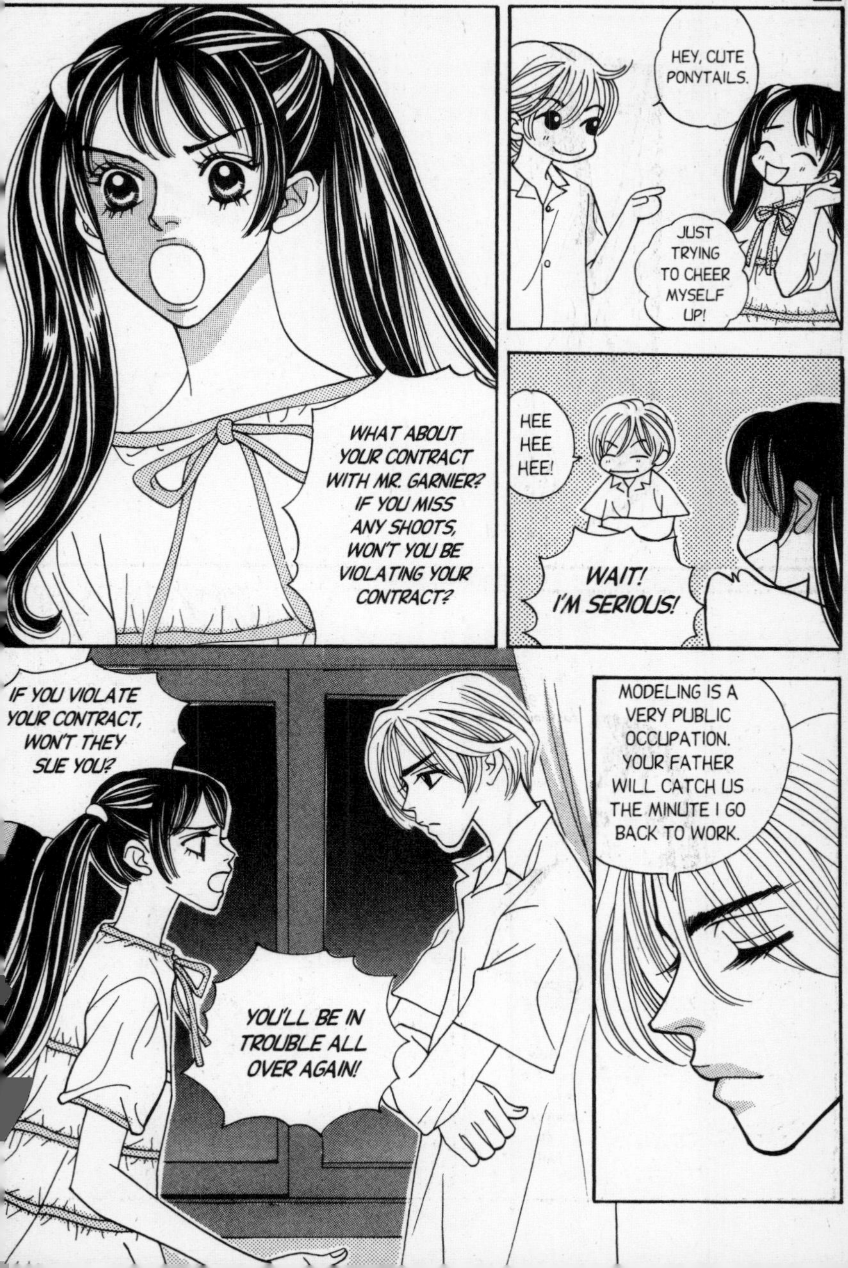
WHAT ABOUT YOUR CONTRACT WITH MR. GARNIER? IF YOU MISS ANY SHOOTS, WON'T YOU BE VIOLATING YOUR CONTRACT?
HEY, CUTE PONYTAILS.
JUST TRYING TO CHEER MYSELF UP!
HEE HEE HEE!
WAIT! I'M SERIOUS!
IF YOU VIOLATE YOUR CONTRACT, WON'T THEY SUE YOU?
YOU'LL BE IN TROUBLE ALL OVER AGAIN!
MODELING IS A VERY PUBLIC OCCUPATION. YOUR FATHER WILL CATCH US THE MINUTE I GO BACK TO WORK.

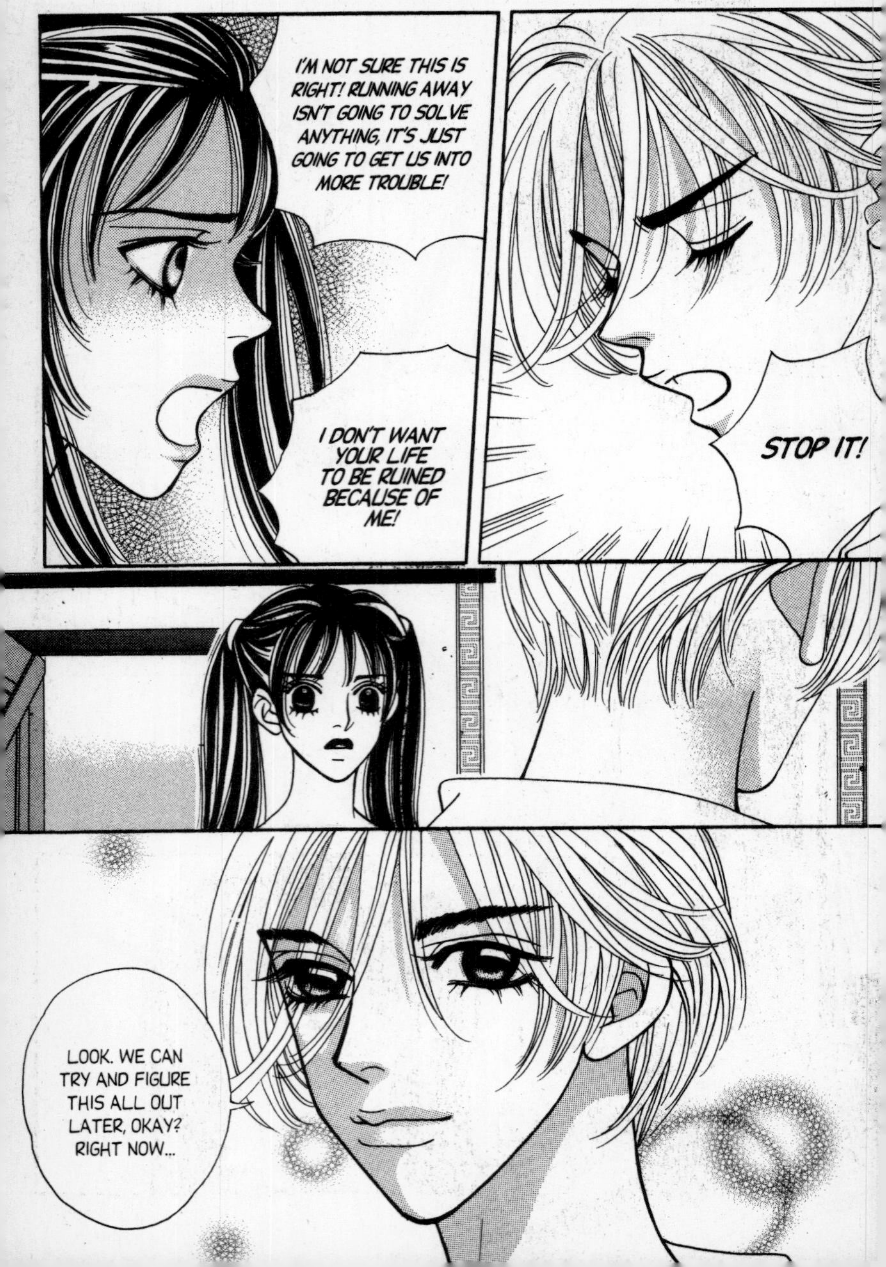
I'M NOT SURE THIS IS RIGHT! RUNNING AWAY ISN'T GOING TO SOLVE ANYTHING, IT'S JUST GOING TO GET US INTO MORE TROUBLE!
I DON'T WANT YOUR LIFE TO BE RUINED BECAUSE OF ME!
STOP IT!
LOOK. WE CAN TRY AND FIGURE THIS ALL OUT LATER, OKAY? RIGHT NOW...

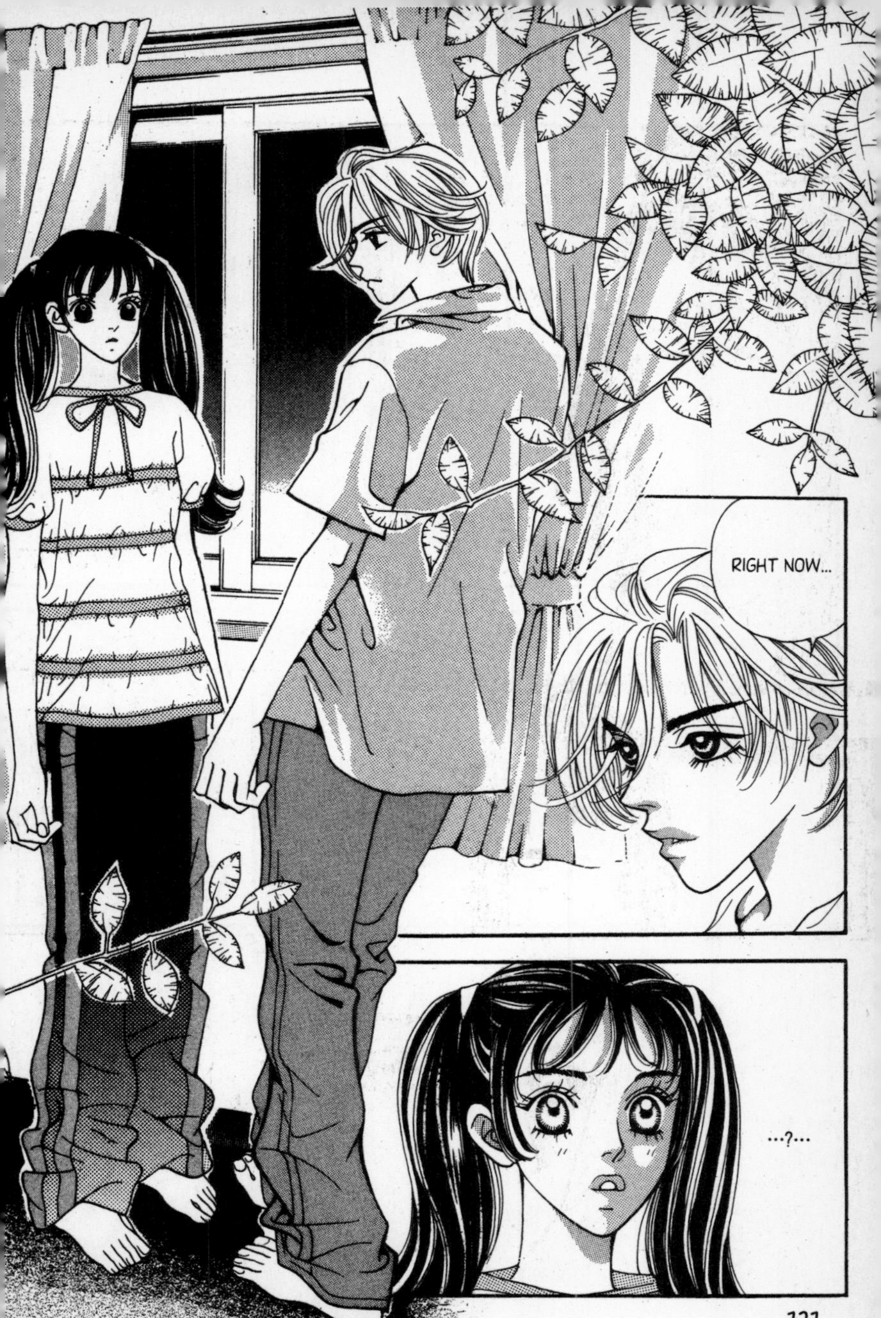
RIGHT NOW...
...?...

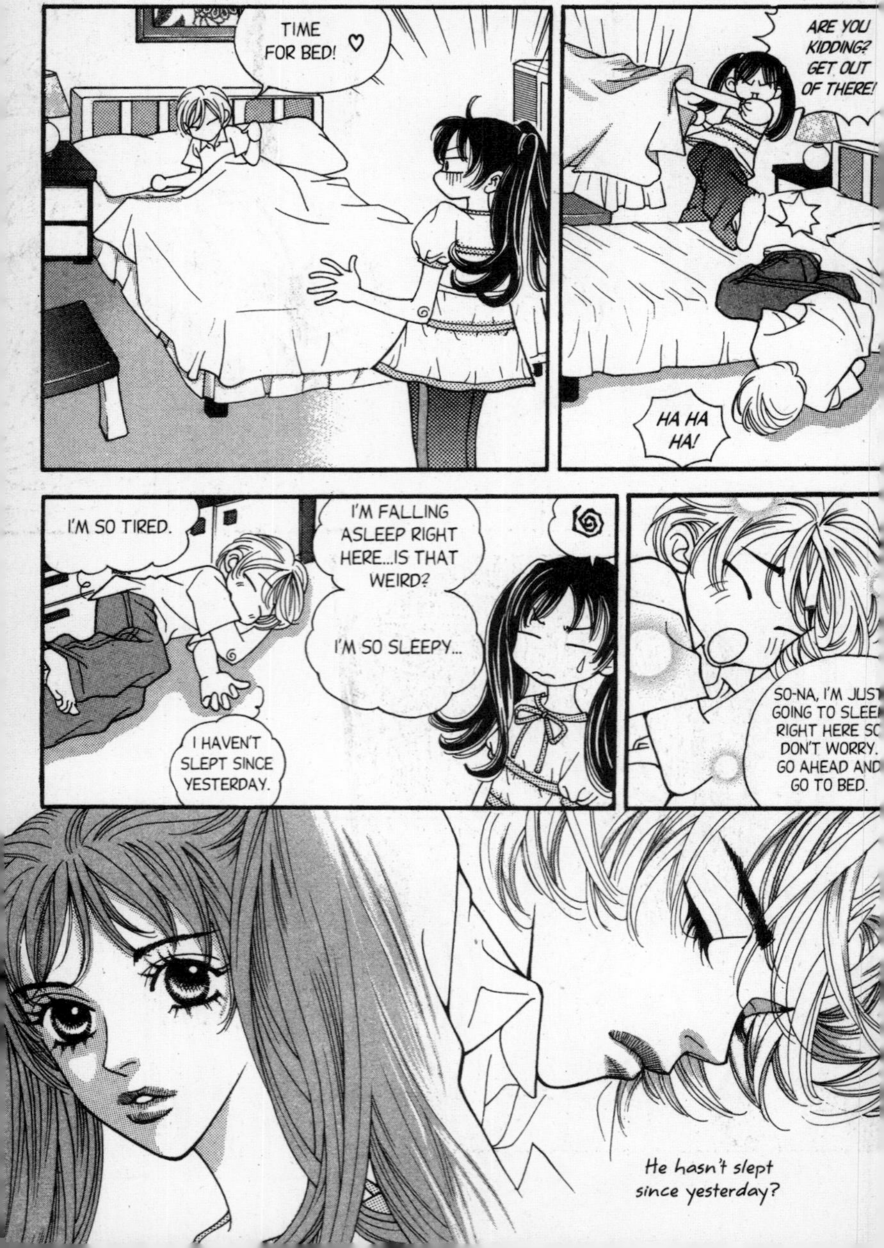
TIME FOR BED! ♡
ARE YOU KIDDING? GET OUT OF THERE!
HA HA HA!
I'M SO TIRED.
I HAVEN'T SLEPT SINCE YESTERDAY.
I'M FALLING ASLEEP RIGHT HERE...IS THAT WEIRD?
I'M SO SLEEPY...
SO-NA, I'M JUST GOING TO SLEEP RIGHT HERE SO DON'T WORRY. GO AHEAD AND GO TO BED.
He hasn't slept since yesterday?

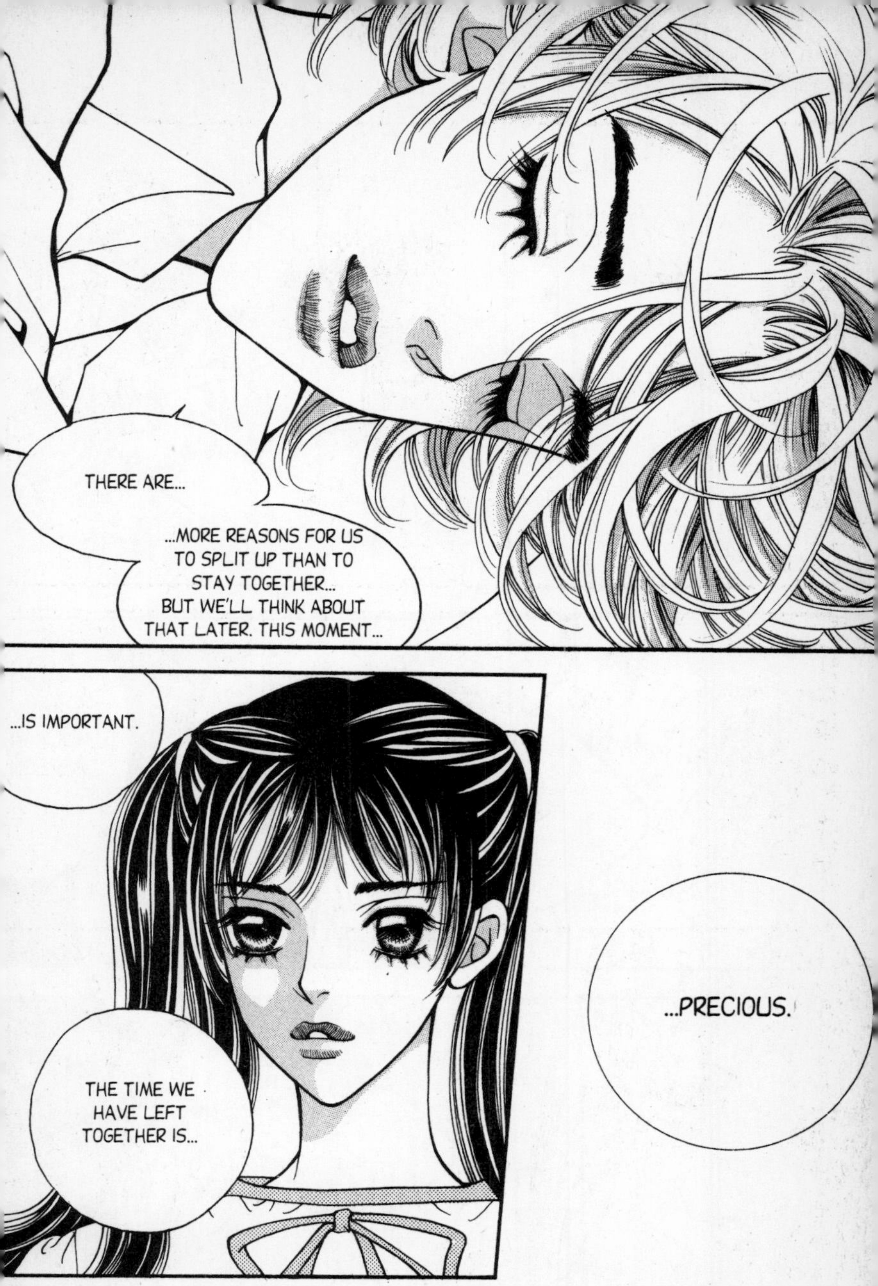
THERE ARE...
...MORE REASONS FOR US TO SPLIT UP THAN TO STAY TOGETHER... BUT WE'LL THINK ABOUT THAT LATER. THIS MOMENT...
...IS IMPORTANT.
THE TIME WE HAVE LEFT TOGETHER IS...
...PRECIOUS.

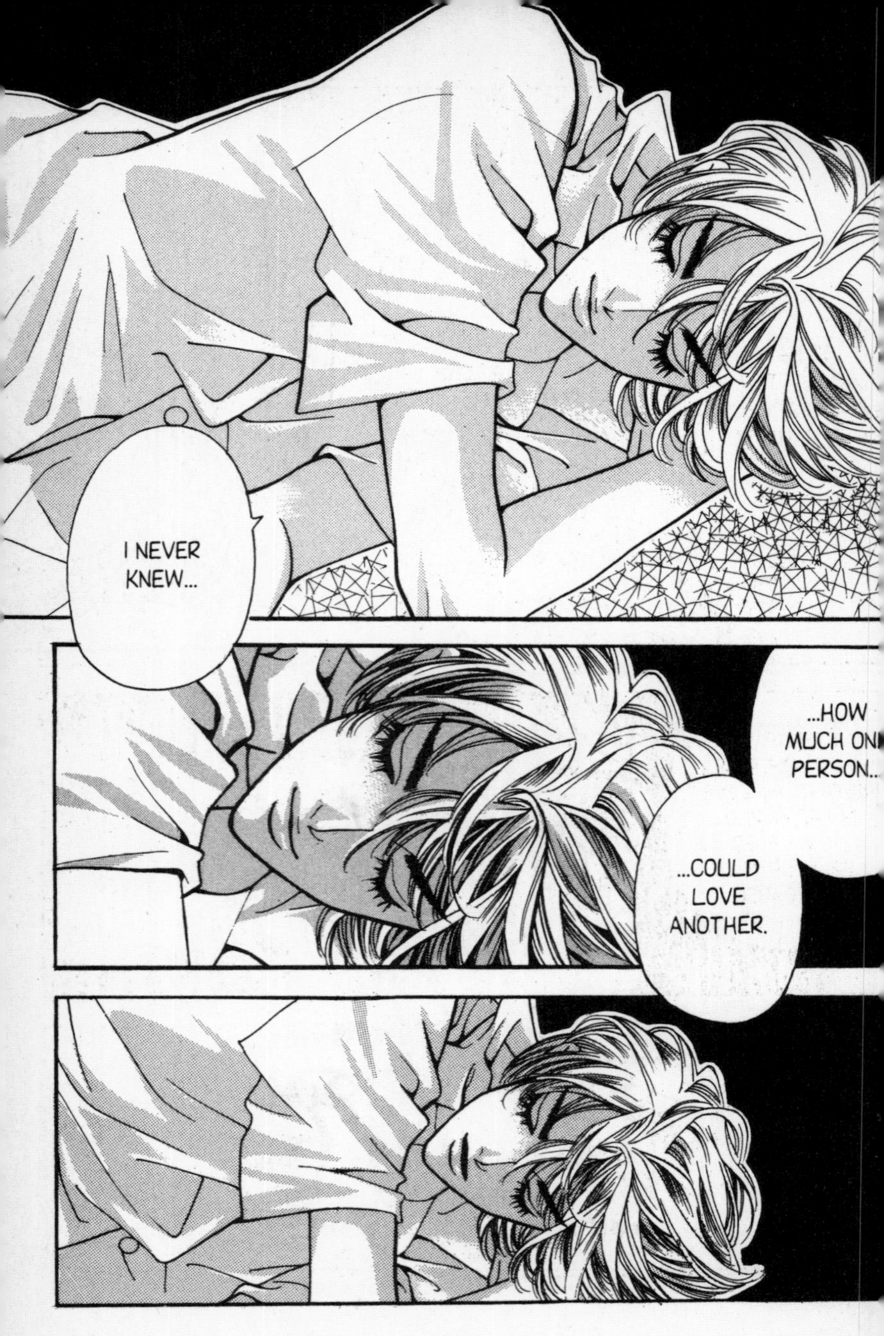
I NEVER KNEW...
...HOW MUCH ONE PERSON...
...COULD LOVE ANOTHER.

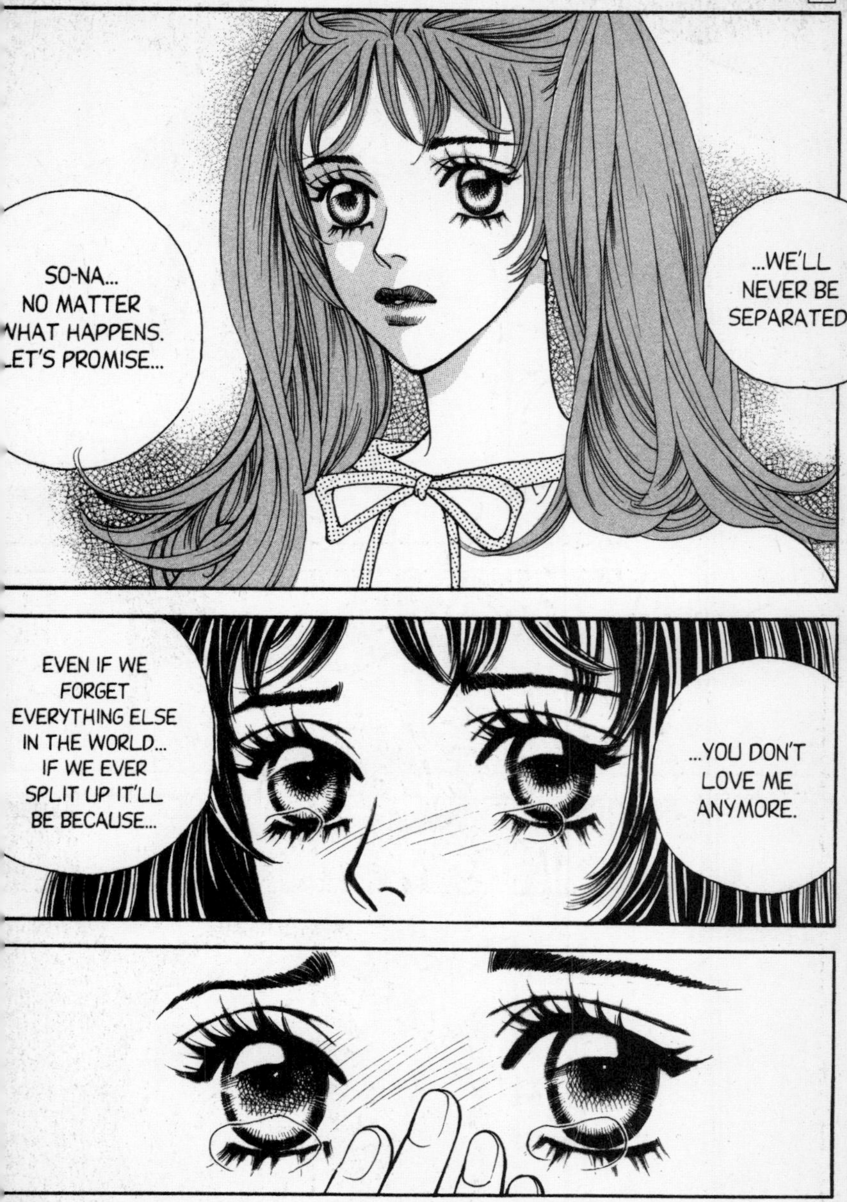
SO-NA...
NO MATTER
WHAT HAPPENS.
LET'S PROMISE...
...WE'LL
NEVER BE
SEPARATED.
EVEN IF WE
FORGET
EVERYTHING ELSE
IN THE WORLD...
IF WE EVER
SPLIT UP IT'LL
BE BECAUSE...
...YOU DON'T
LOVE ME
ANYMORE.

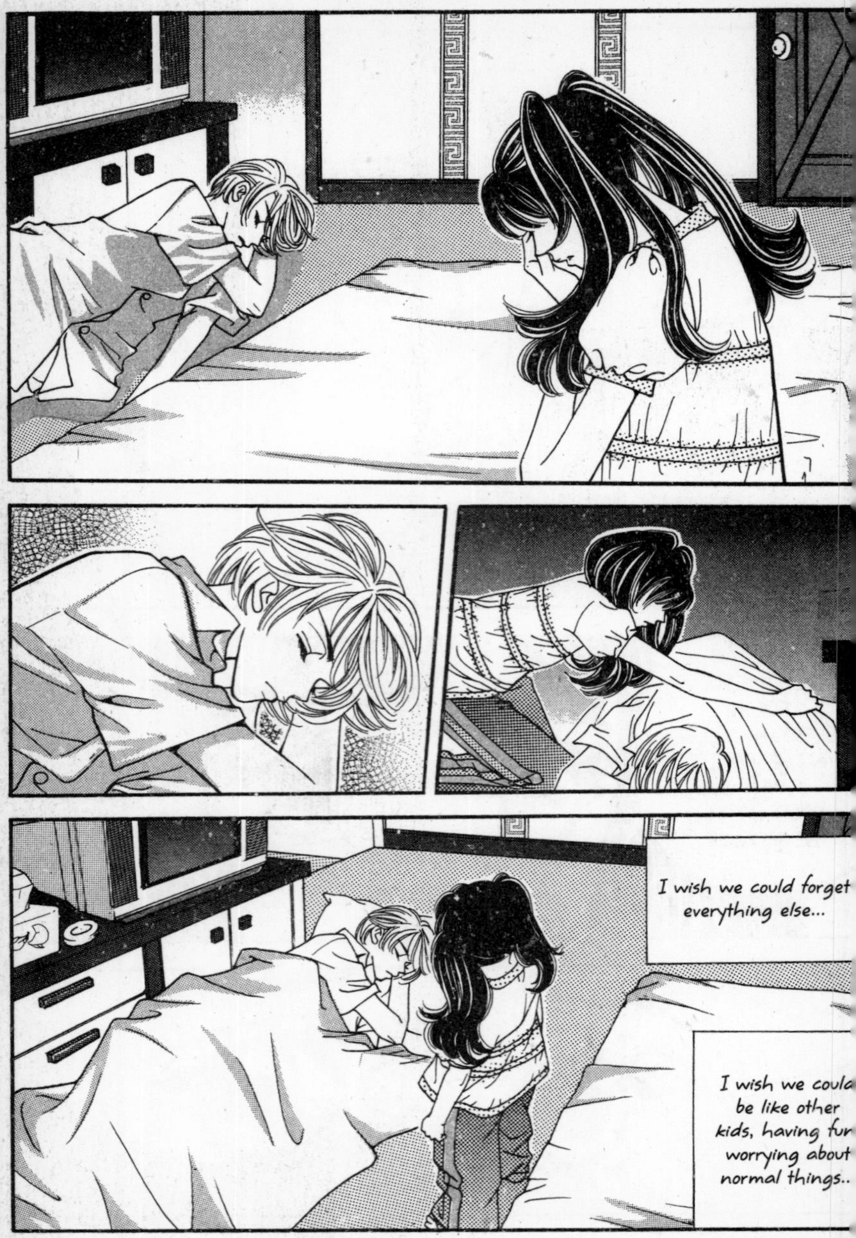
I wish we could forget everything else...
I wish we coul
be like other
kids, having
worrying about
normal things..

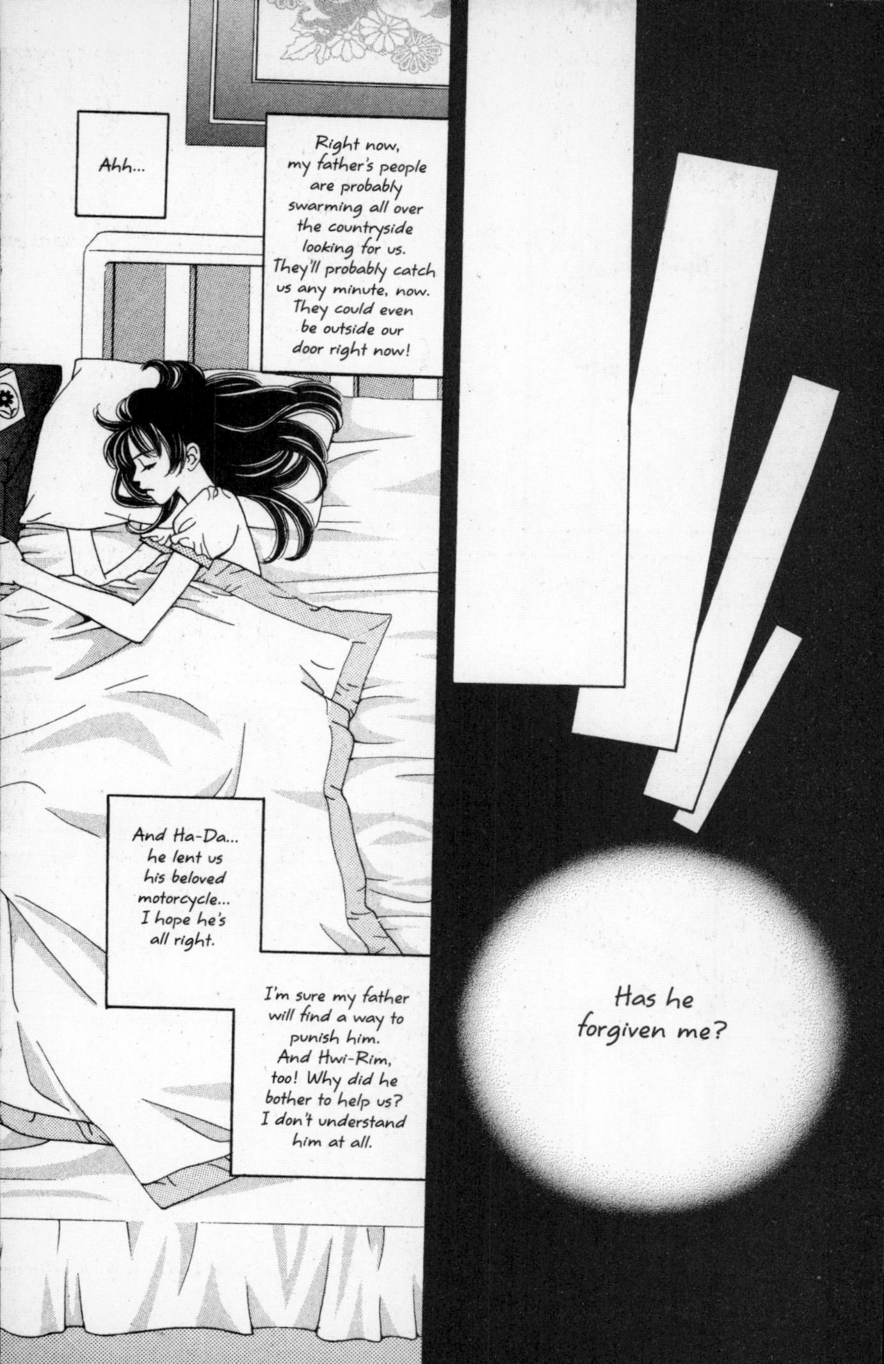
Ahh...
Right now, my father's people are probably swarming all over the countryside looking for us. They'll probably catch us any minute, now. They could even be outside our door right now!
And Ha-Da... he lent us his beloved motorcycle... I hope he's all right.
I'm sure my father will find a way to punish him. And Hwi-Rim, too! Why did he bother to help us? I don't understand him at all.
Has he forgiven me?

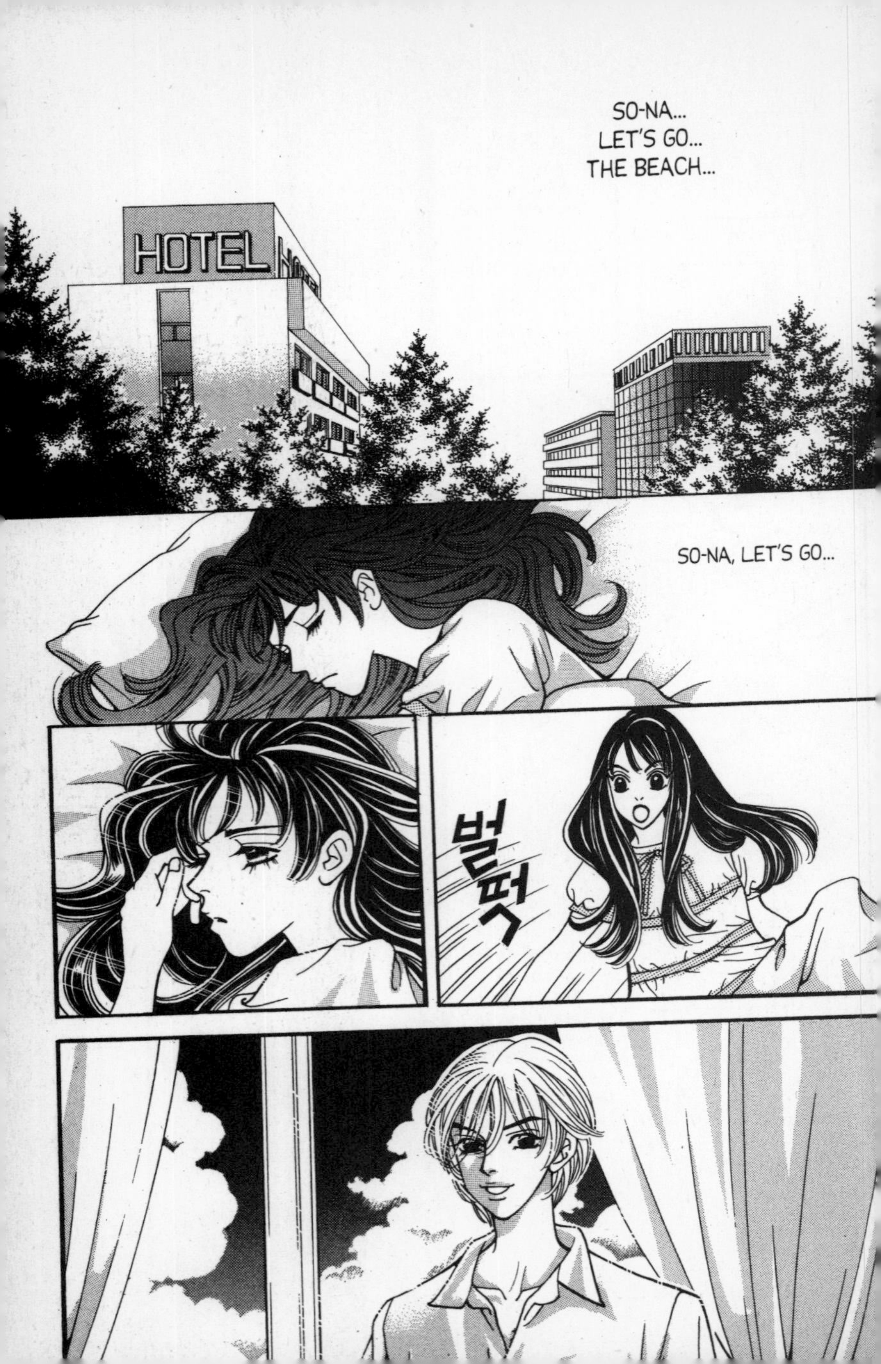
SO-NA...
LET'S GO...
THE BEACH...
HOTEL
SO-NA, LET'S GO...
벌떡

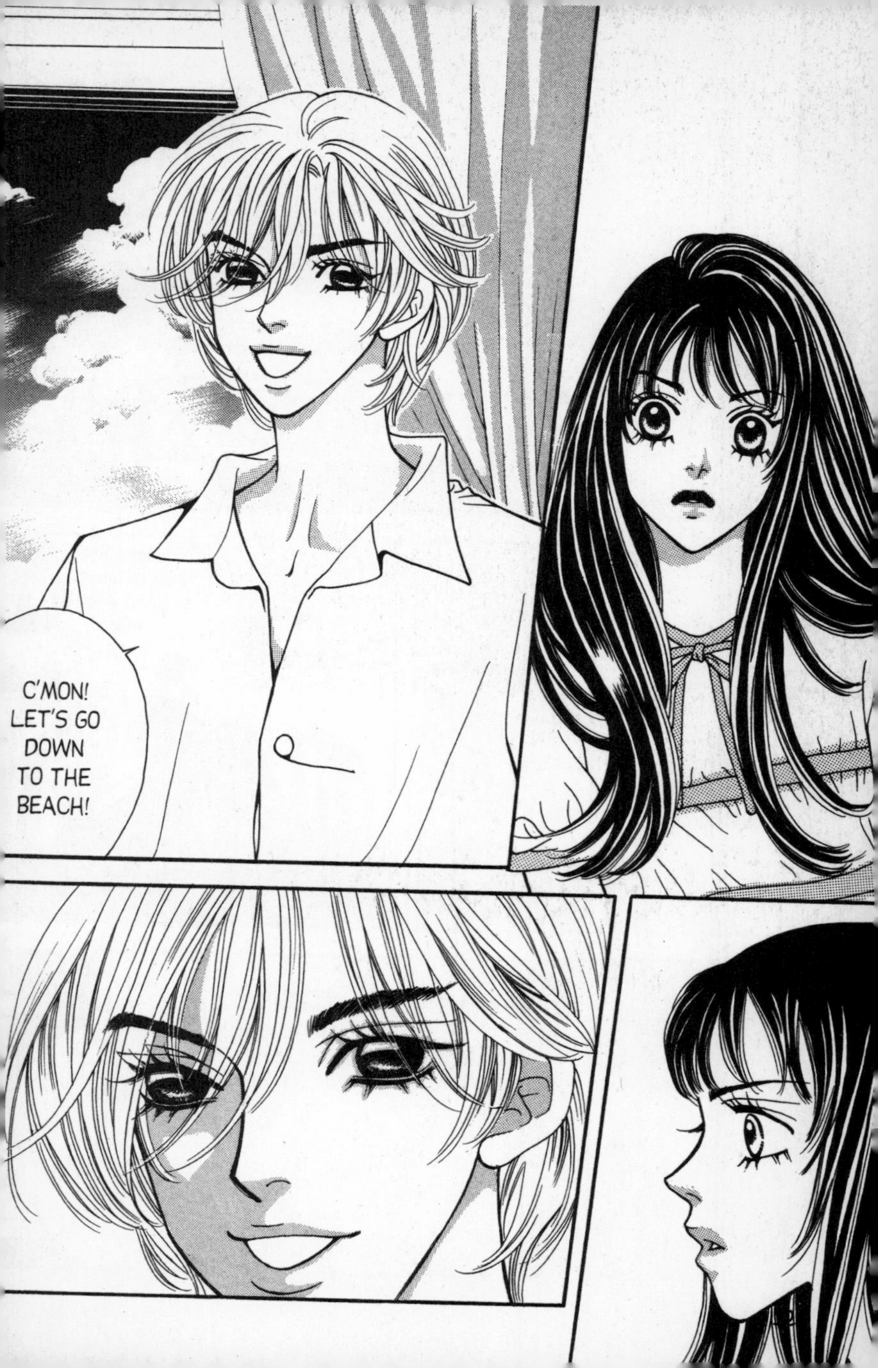
C'MON! LET'S GO DOWN TO THE BEACH!

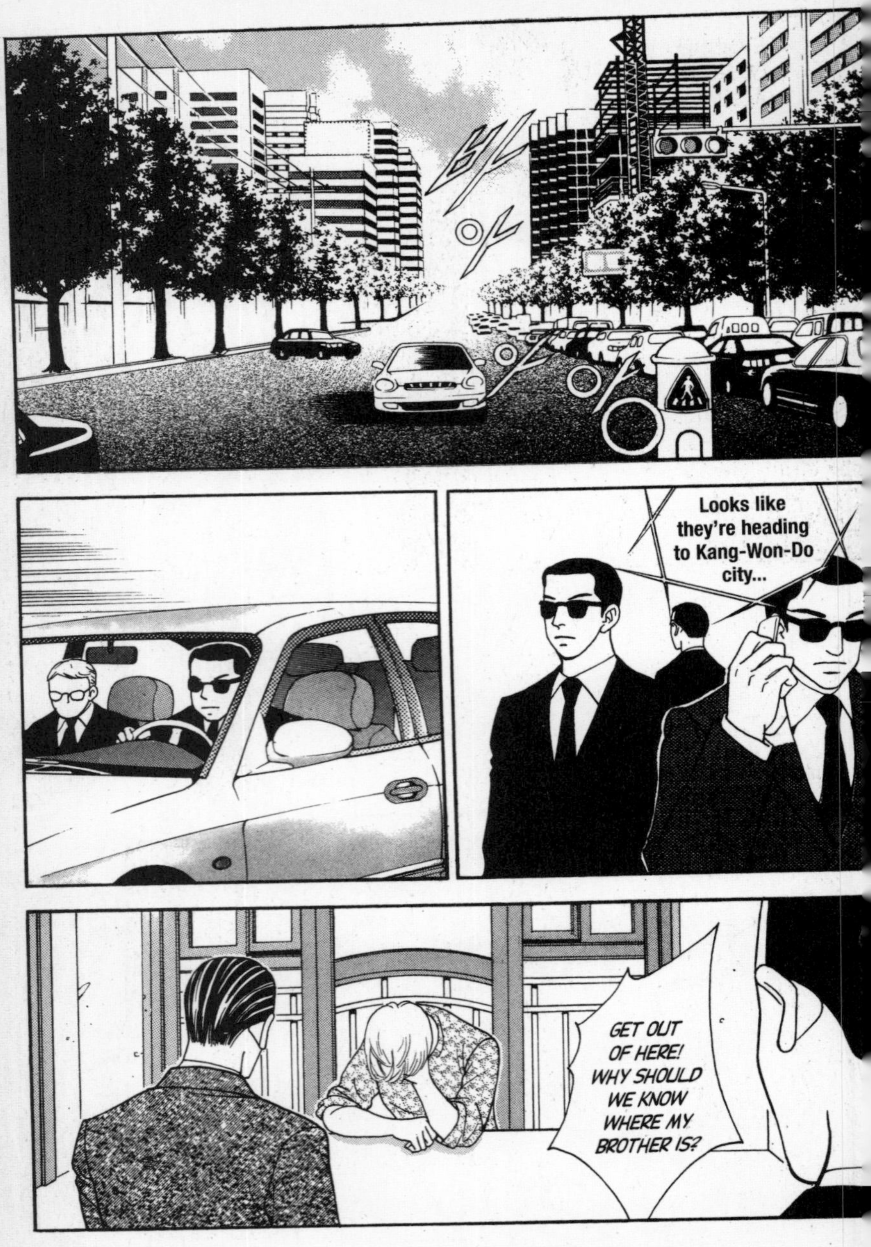
Looks like they're heading to Kang-Won-Do city...
GET OUT OF HERE! WHY SHOULD WE KNOW WHERE MY BROTHER IS?

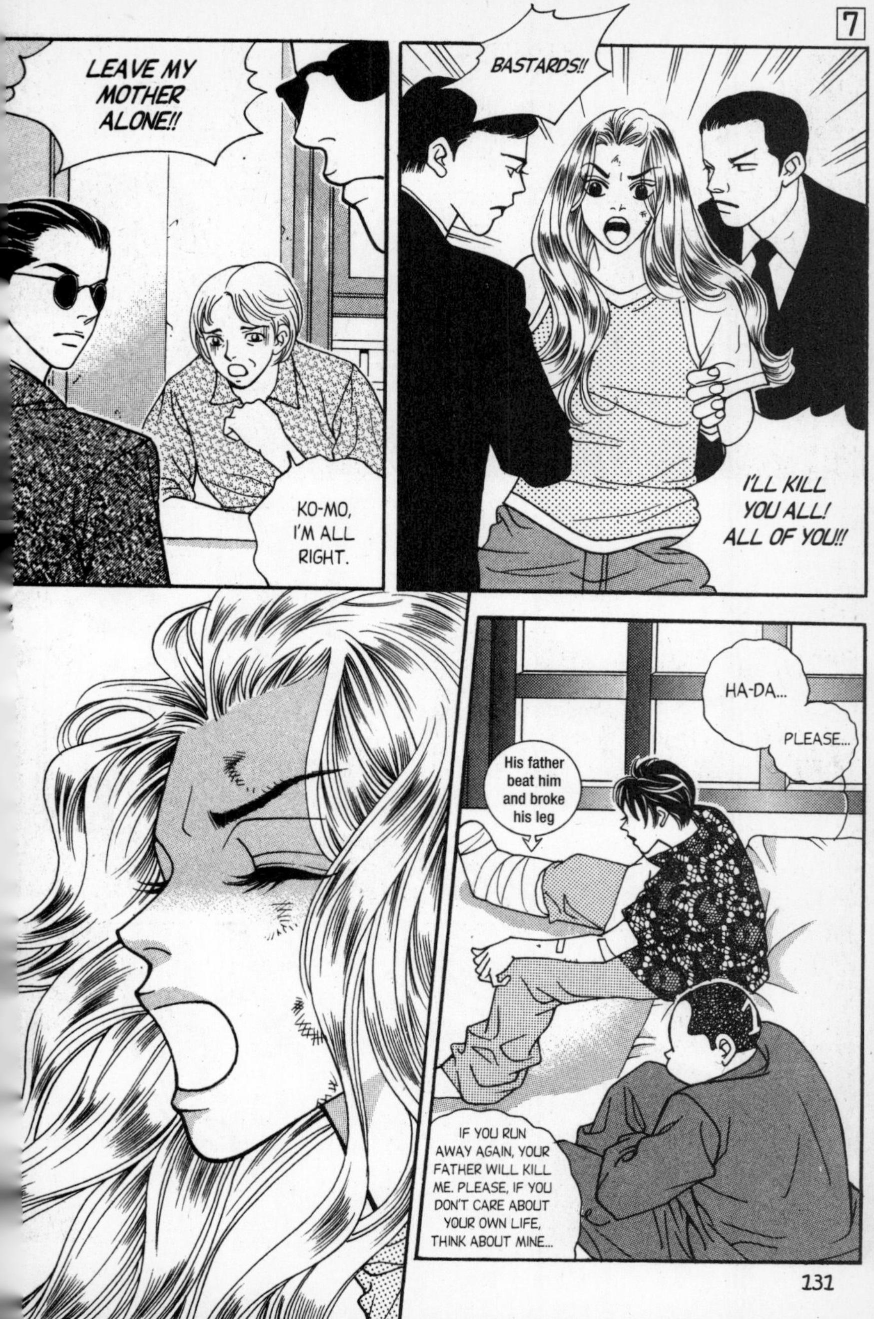
LEAVE MY MOTHER ALONE!!
KO-MO, I'M ALL RIGHT.
BASTARDS!!
I'LL KILL YOU ALL! ALL OF YOU!!
HA-DA...
PLEASE...
His father beat him and broke his leg
IF YOU RUN AWAY AGAIN, YOUR FATHER WILL KILL ME. PLEASE, IF YOU DON'T CARE ABOUT YOUR OWN LIFE, THINK ABOUT MINE...

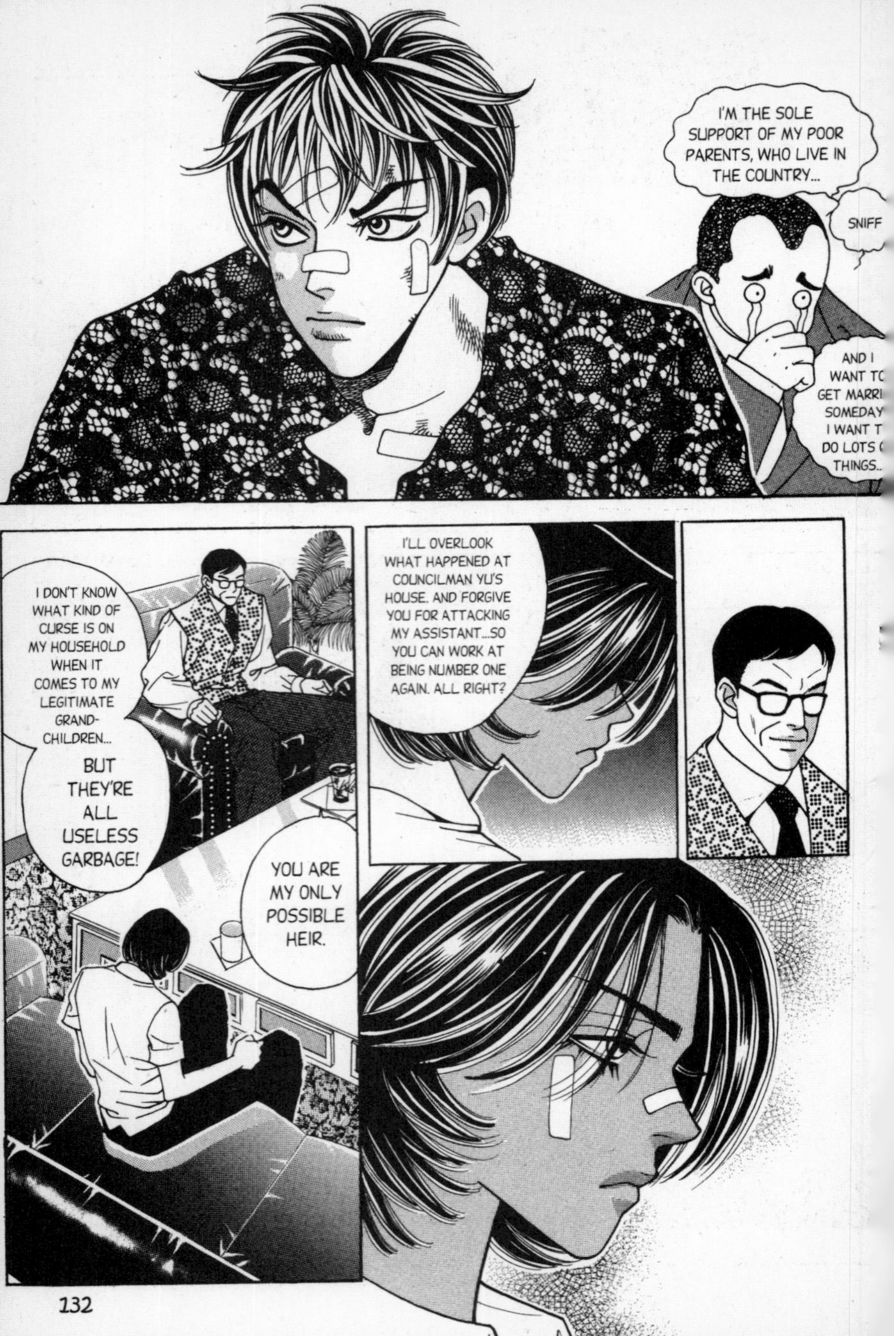
I'M THE SOLE SUPPORT OF MY POOR PARENTS, WHO LIVE IN THE COUNTRY...
SNIFF
AND I WANT T GET MARRI SOMEDAY I WANT T DO LOTS THINGS...
I DON'T KNOW WHAT KIND OF CURSE IS ON MY HOUSEHOLD WHEN IT COMES TO MY LEGITIMATE GRAND-CHILDREN...
BUT THEY'RE ALL USELESS GARBAGE!
YOU ARE MY ONLY POSSIBLE HEIR.
I'LL OVERLOOK WHAT HAPPENED AT COUNCILMAN YU'S HOUSE. AND FORGIVE YOU FOR ATTACKING MY ASSISTANT...SO YOU CAN WORK AT BEING NUMBER ONE AGAIN. ALL RIGHT?

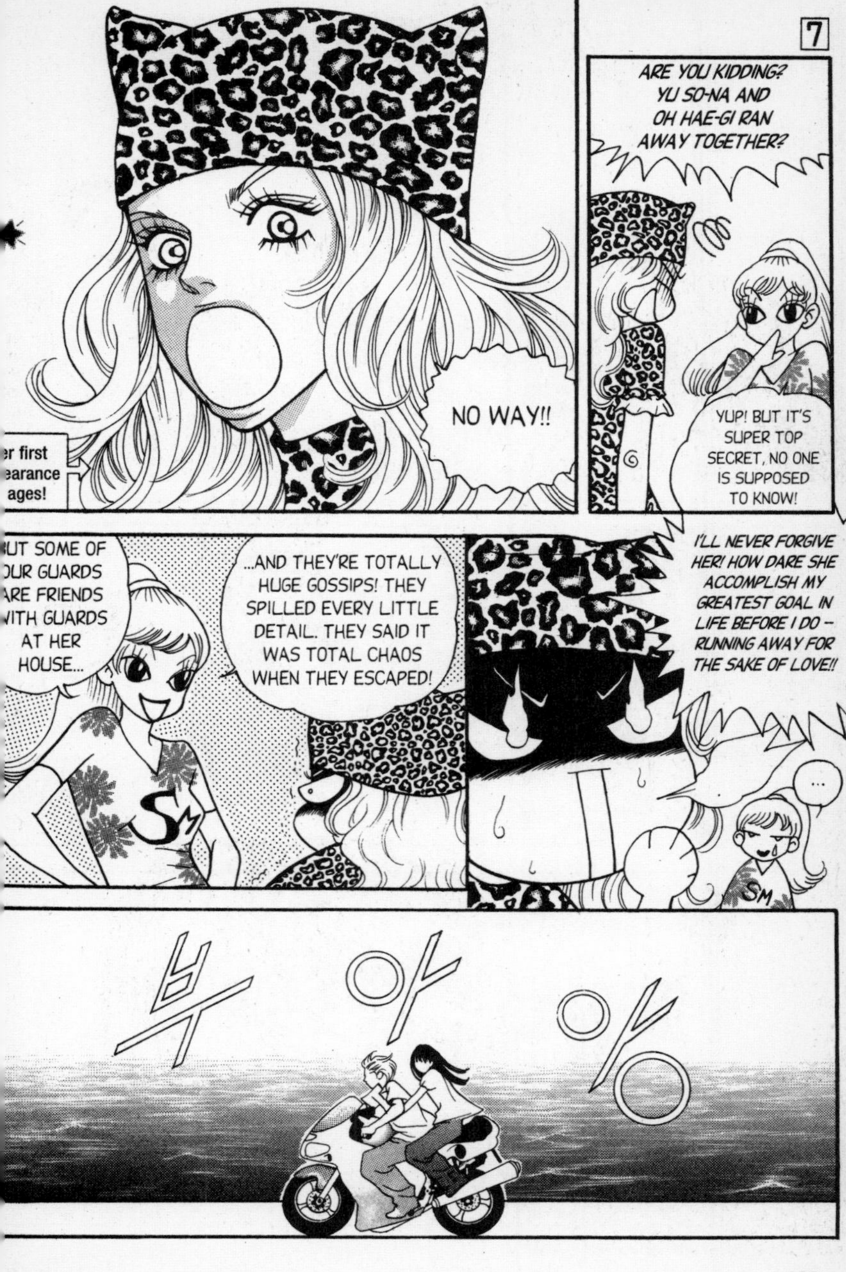
7
NO WAY!!
er first
earance
ages!
ARE YOU KIDDING? YU SO-NA AND OH HAE-GI RAN AWAY TOGETHER?
YUP! BUT IT'S SUPER TOP SECRET, NO ONE IS SUPPOSED TO KNOW!
UT SOME OF OUR GUARDS ARE FRIENDS WITH GUARDS AT HER HOUSE...
...AND THEY'RE TOTALLY HUGE GOSSIPS! THEY SPILLED EVERY LITTLE DETAIL. THEY SAID IT WAS TOTAL CHAOS WHEN THEY ESCAPED!
I'LL NEVER FORGIVE HER! HOW DARE SHE ACCOMPLISH MY GREATEST GOAL IN LIFE BEFORE I DO – RUNNING AWAY FOR THE SAKE OF LOVE!!
...
부아앙

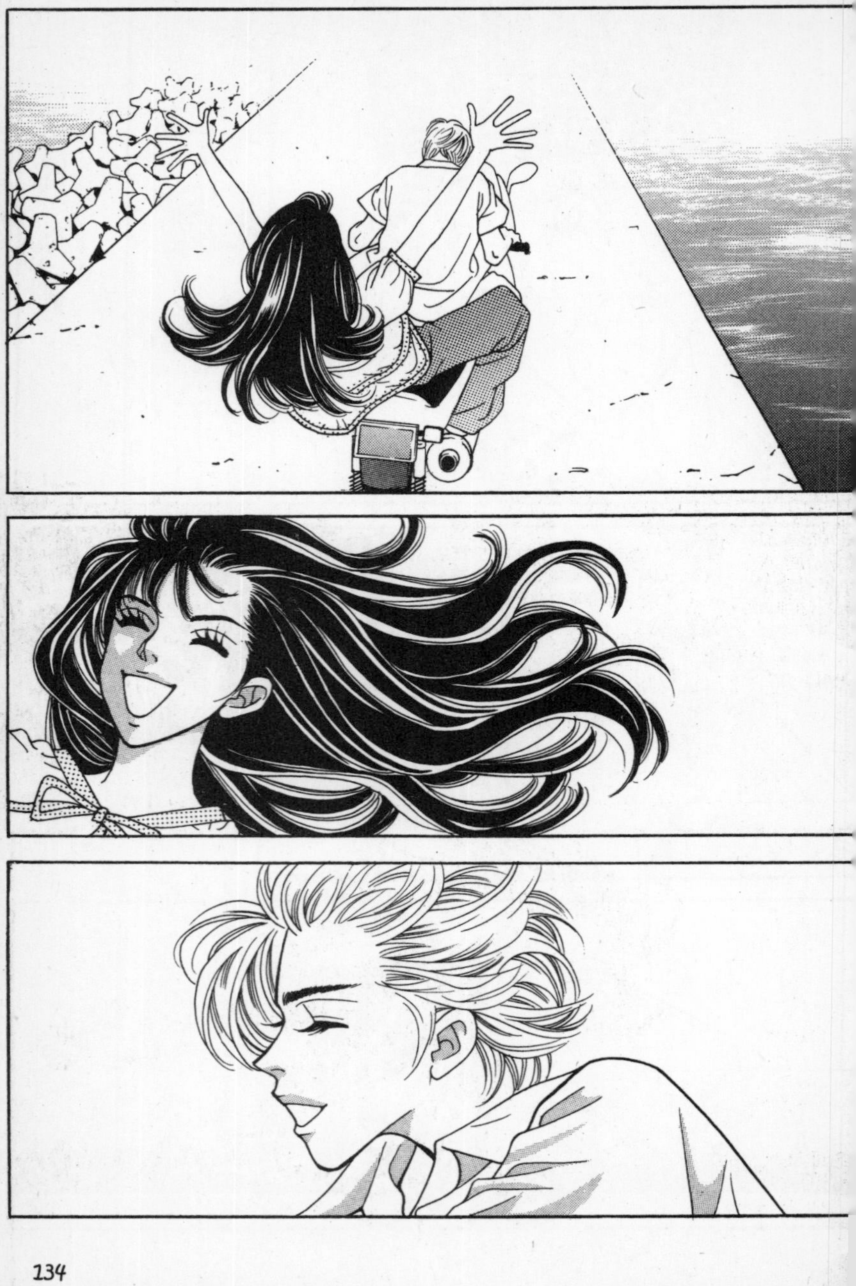

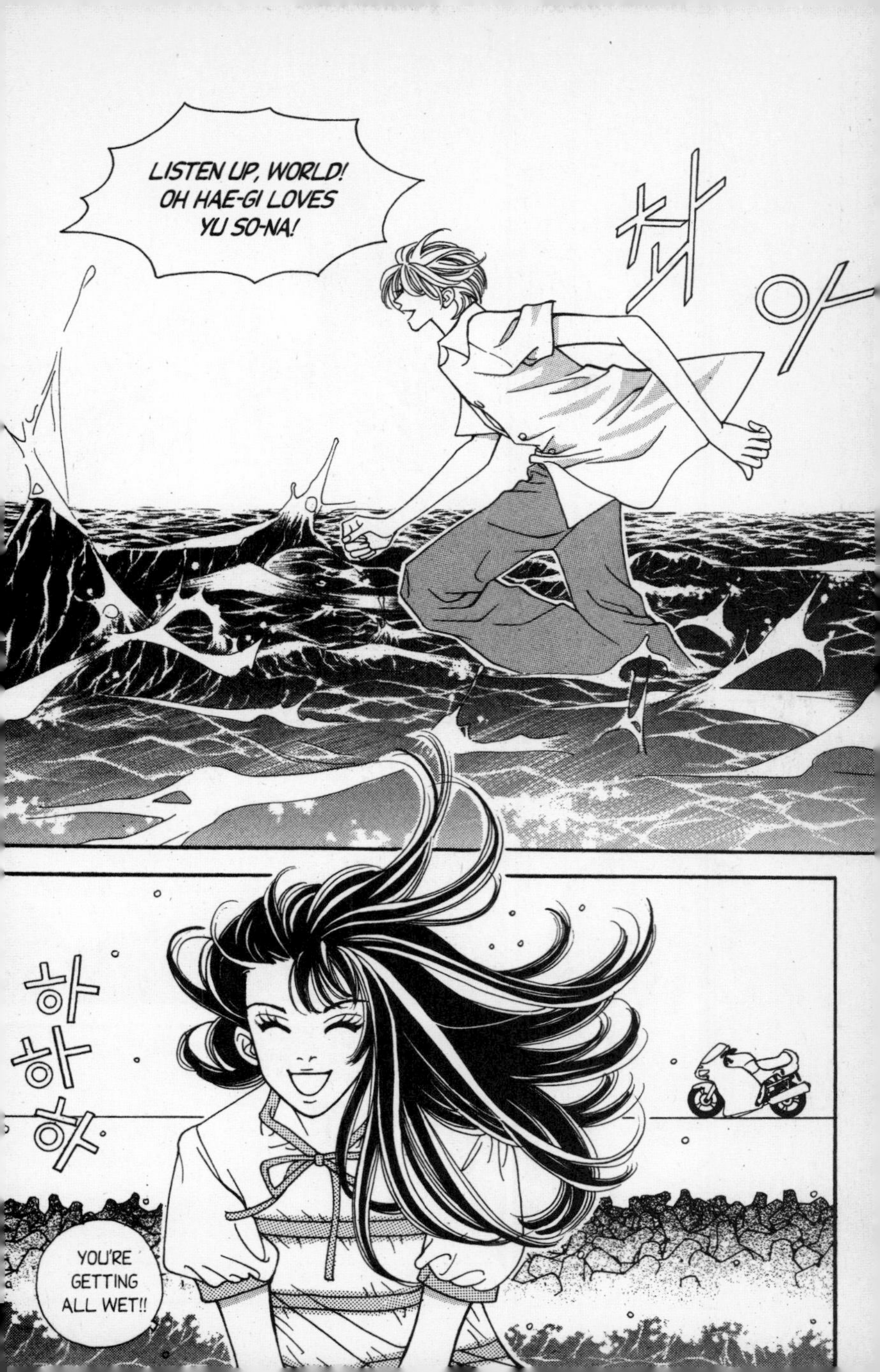
LISTEN UP, WORLD! OH HAE-GI LOVES YU SO-NA!
촤아
하하하
YOU'RE GETTING ALL WET!!

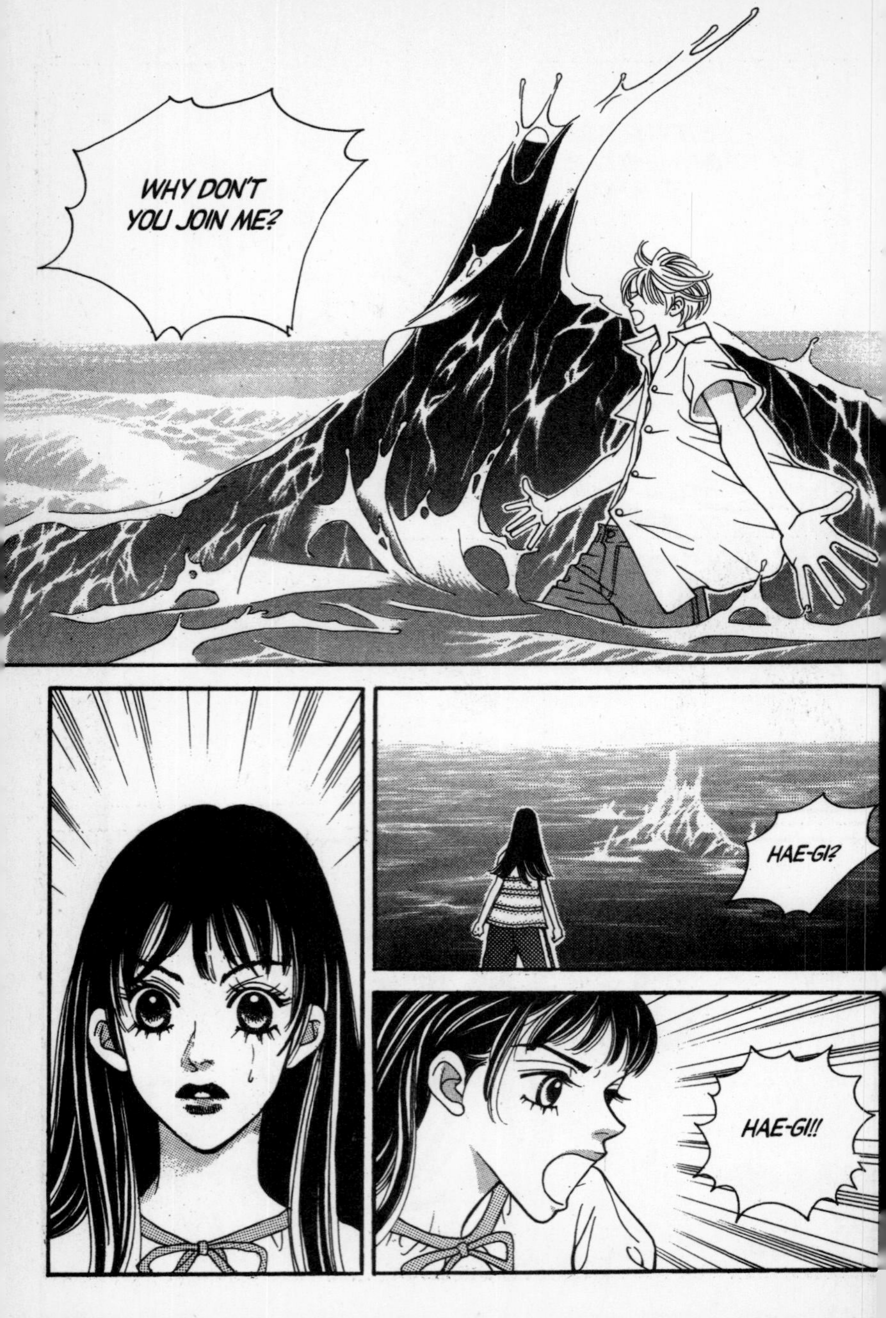
WHY DON'T YOU JOIN ME?
HAE-GI?
HAE-GI!!

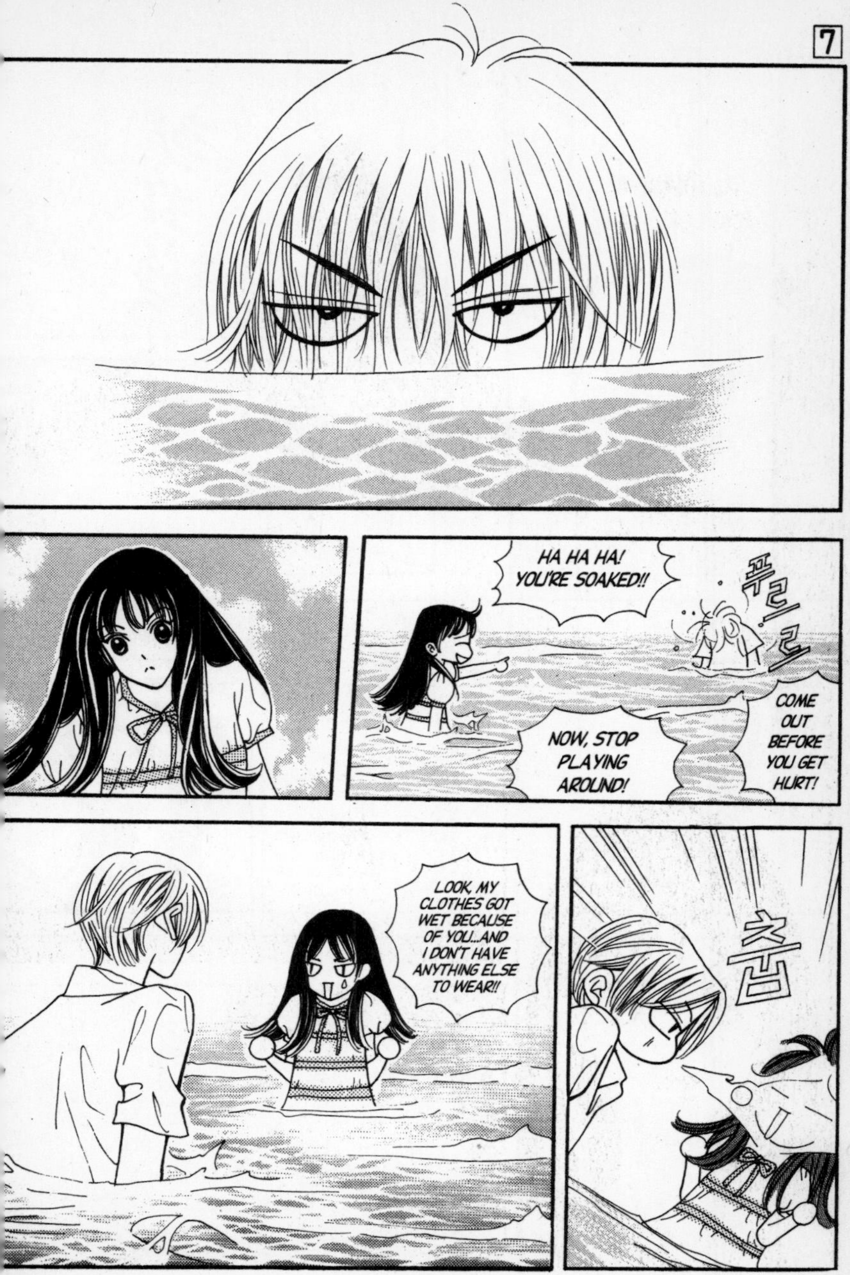
HA HA HA! YOU'RE SOAKED!!
NOW, STOP PLAYING AROUND!
COME OUT BEFORE YOU GET HURT!
LOOK, MY CLOTHES GOT WET BECAUSE OF YOU...AND I DON'T HAVE ANYTHING ELSE TO WEAR!!

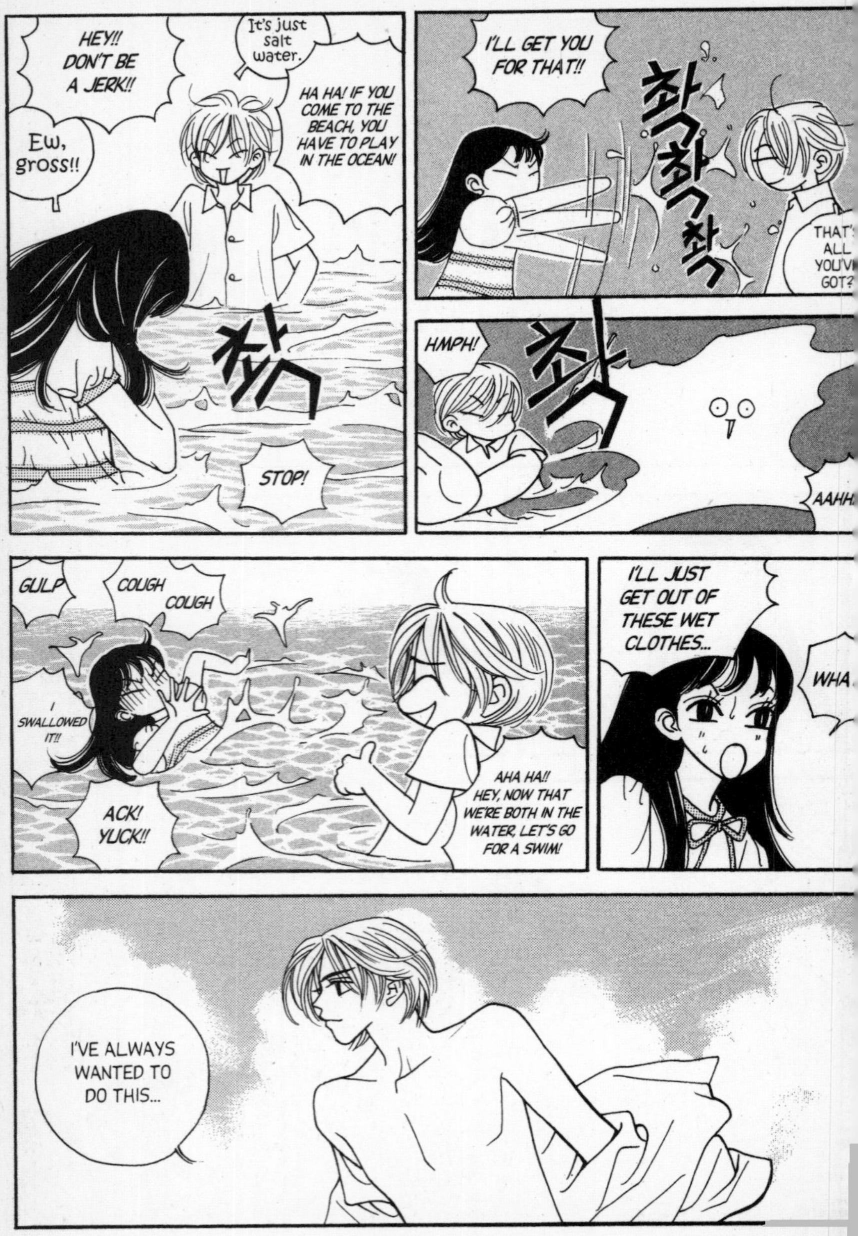
HEY!! DON'T BE A JERK!!
It's just salt water.
HA HA! IF YOU COME TO THE BEACH, YOU HAVE TO PLAY IN THE OCEAN!
Ew, gross!!
촥
STOP!
I'LL GET YOU FOR THAT!!
촥촥촥촥
THAT'S ALL YOU'V GOT?
HMPH!
촥
AAHH
GULP
COUGH COUGH
I SWALLOWED IT!!
ACK! YUCK!!
AHA HA!! HEY, NOW THAT WE'RE BOTH IN THE WATER, LET'S GO FOR A SWIM!
I'LL JUST GET OUT OF THESE WET CLOTHES...
WHA
I'VE ALWAYS WANTED TO DO THIS...

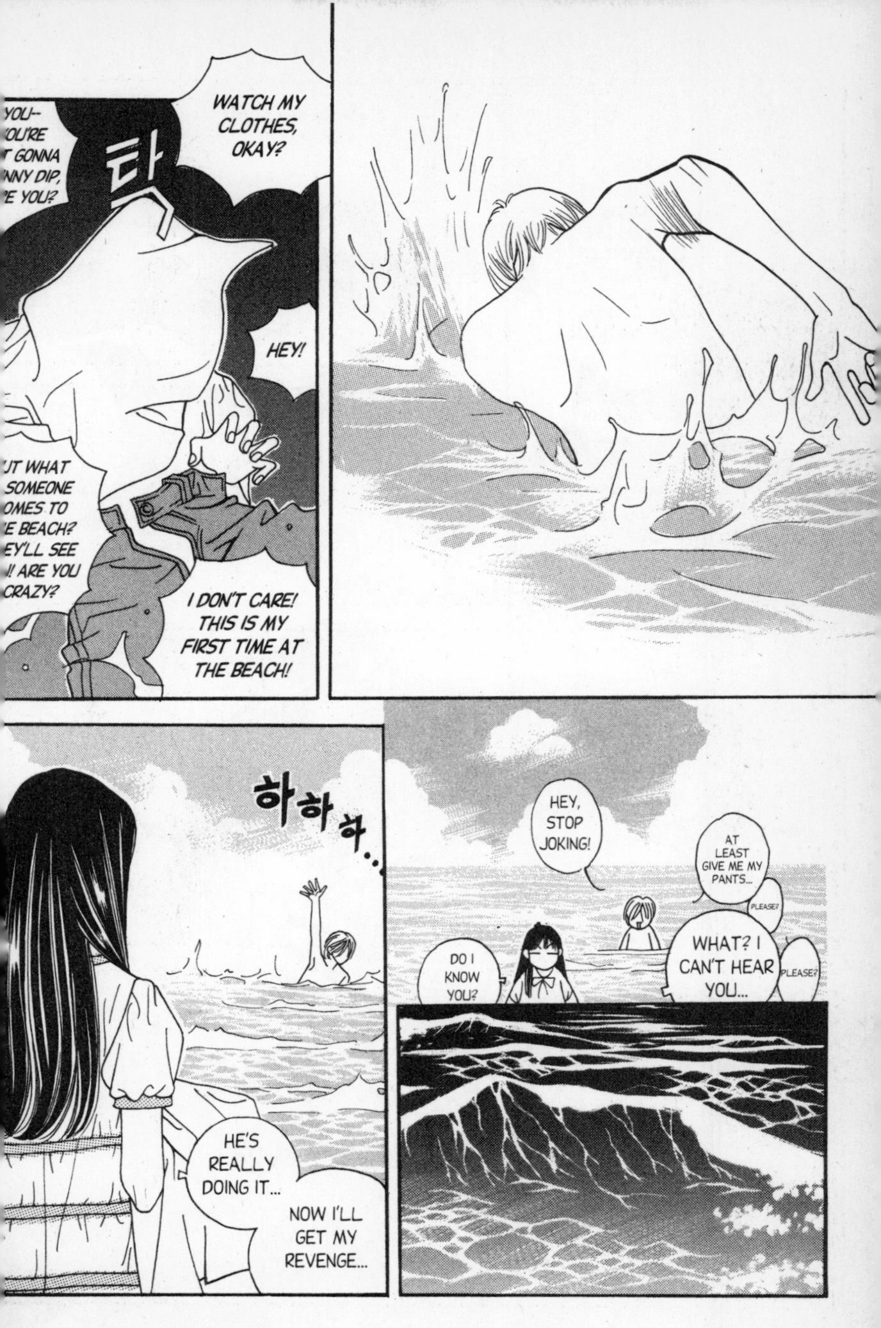
YOU--
OU'RE
T GONNA
NNY DIP,
E YOU?
타
WATCH MY CLOTHES, OKAY?
HEY!
UT WHAT
SOMEONE
OMES TO
E BEACH?
EY'LL SEE
! ARE YOU
CRAZY?
I DON'T CARE! THIS IS MY FIRST TIME AT THE BEACH!
하하하...
HE'S REALLY DOING IT...
NOW I'LL GET MY REVENGE...
HEY, STOP JOKING!
AT LEAST GIVE ME MY PANTS...
PLEASE?
DO I KNOW YOU?
WHAT? I CAN'T HEAR YOU...
PLEASE?

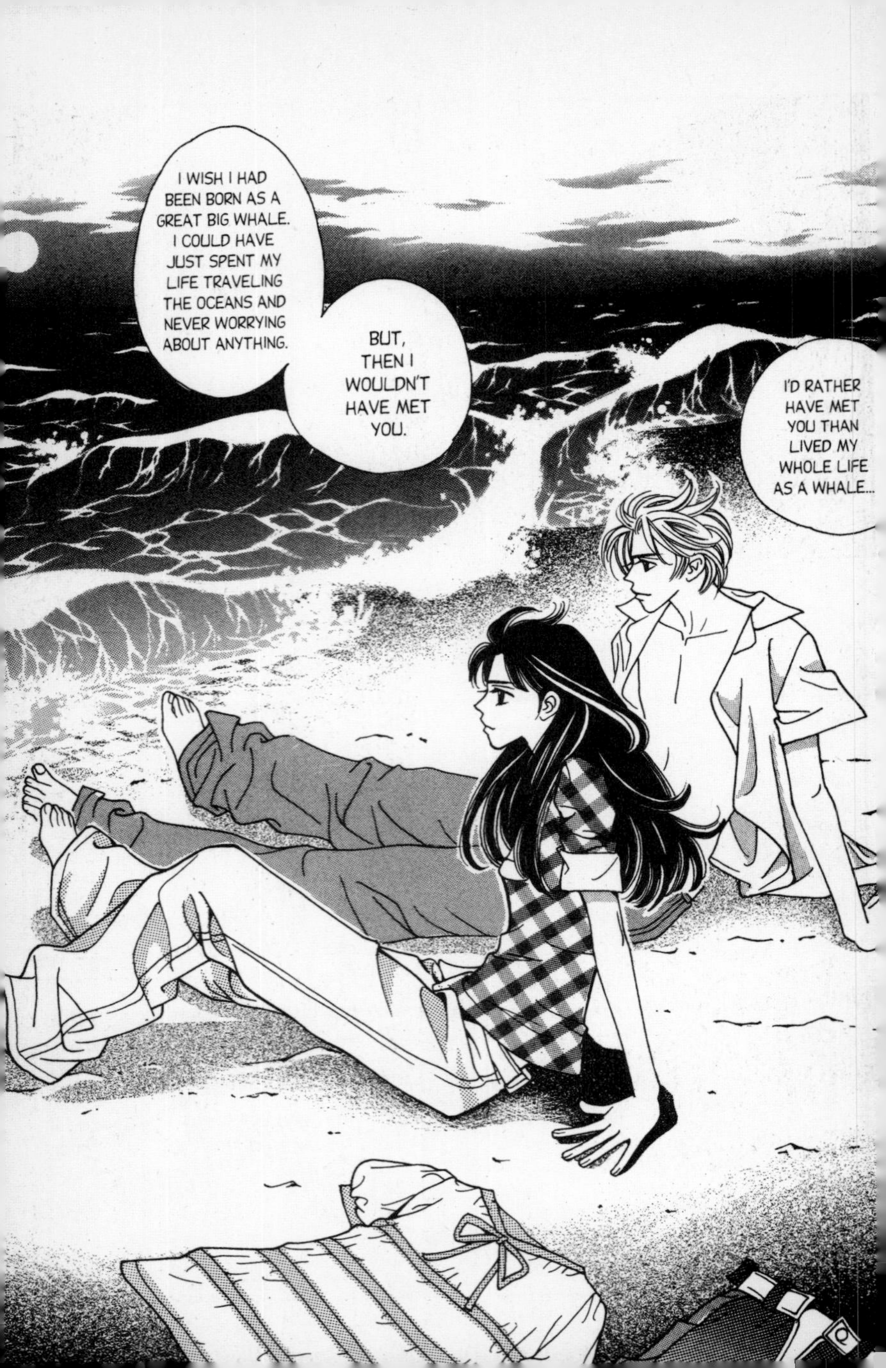
I WISH I HAD BEEN BORN AS A GREAT BIG WHALE. I COULD HAVE JUST SPENT MY LIFE TRAVELING THE OCEANS AND NEVER WORRYING ABOUT ANYTHING.
BUT, THEN I WOULDN'T HAVE MET YOU.
I'D RATHER HAVE MET YOU THAN LIVED MY WHOLE LIFE AS A WHALE...

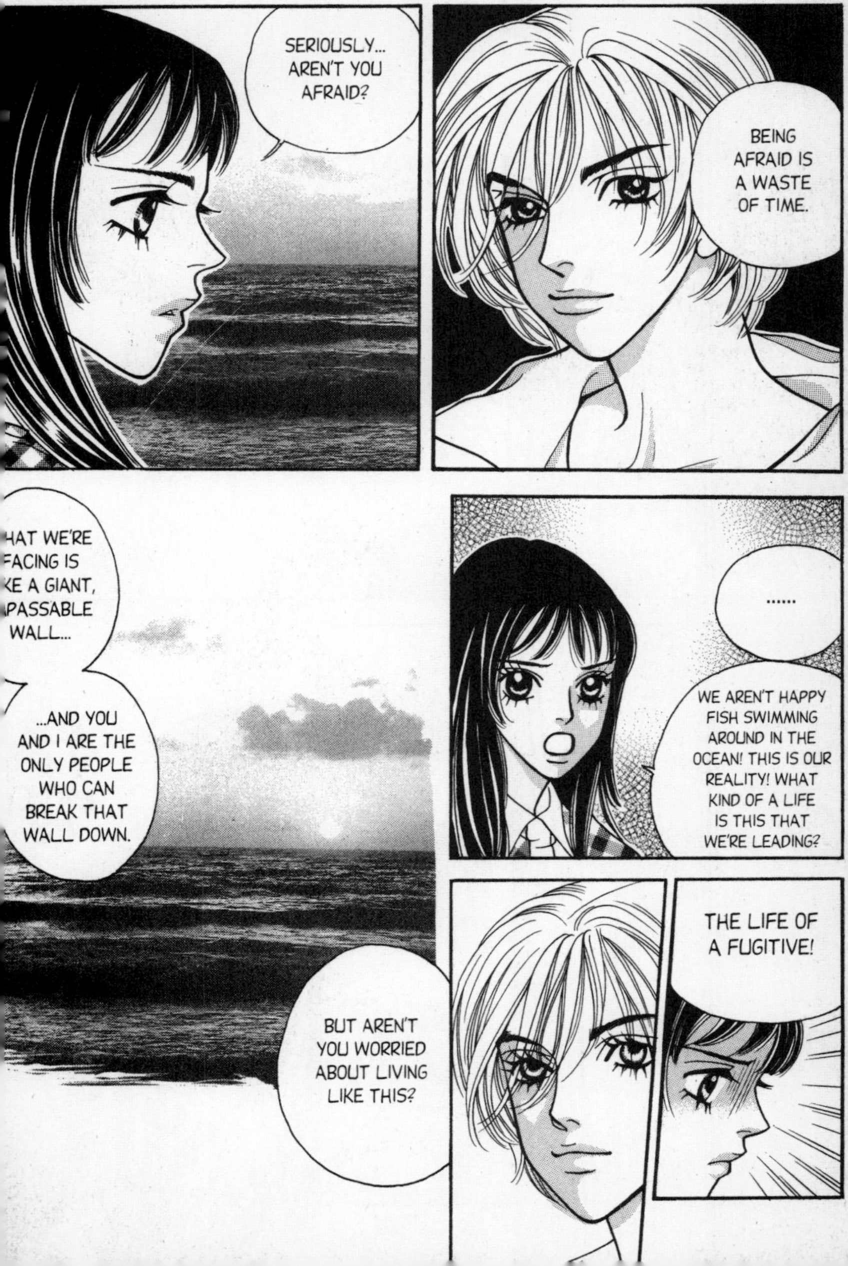
SERIOUSLY... AREN'T YOU AFRAID?
BEING AFRAID IS A WASTE OF TIME.
HAT WE'RE FACING IS KE A GIANT, PASSABLE WALL...
...AND YOU AND I ARE THE ONLY PEOPLE WHO CAN BREAK THAT WALL DOWN.
BUT AREN'T YOU WORRIED ABOUT LIVING LIKE THIS?
......
WE AREN'T HAPPY FISH SWIMMING AROUND IN THE OCEAN! THIS IS OUR REALITY! WHAT KIND OF A LIFE IS THIS THAT WE'RE LEADING?
THE LIFE OF A FUGITIVE!

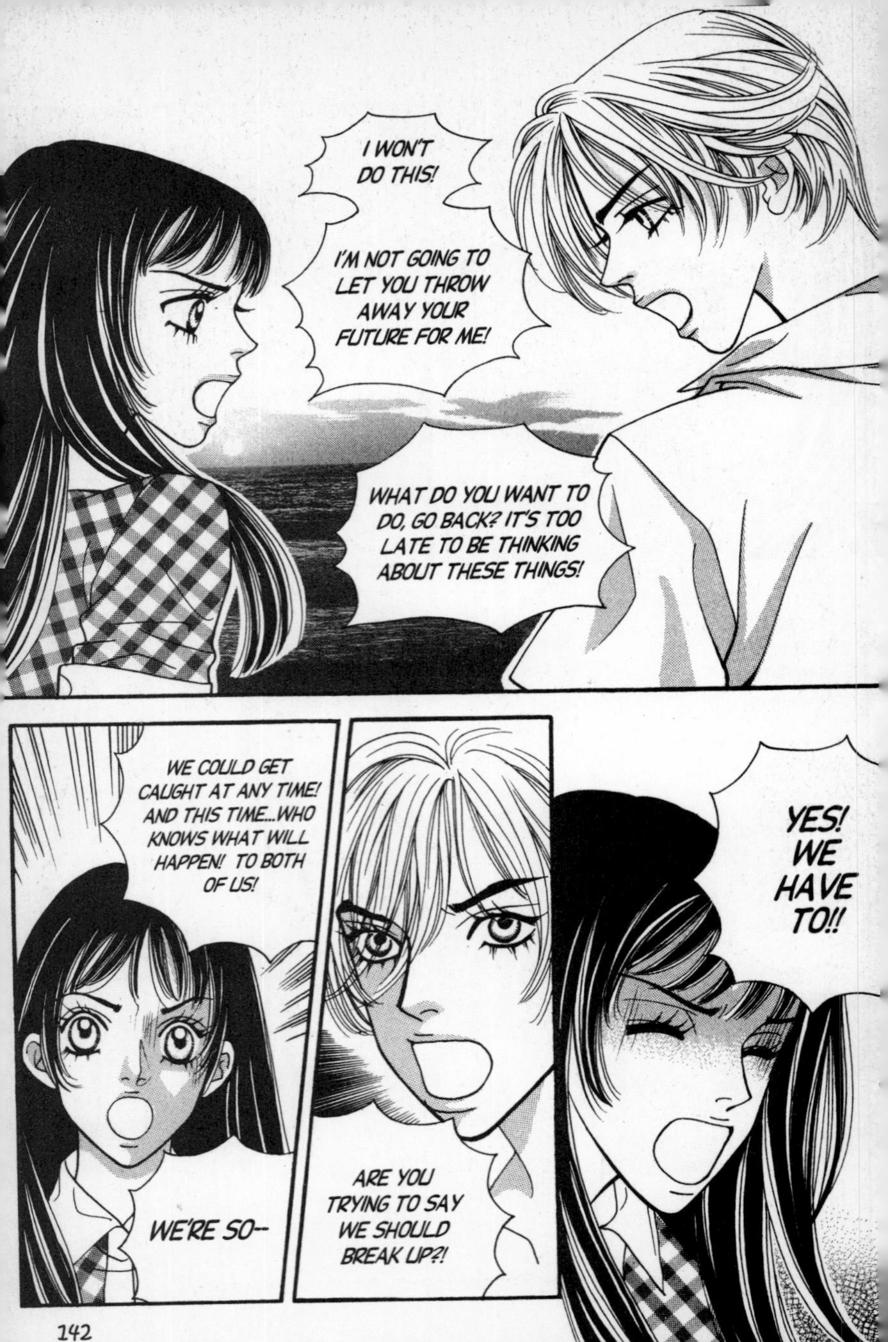
I WON'T DO THIS!
I'M NOT GOING TO LET YOU THROW AWAY YOUR FUTURE FOR ME!
WHAT DO YOU WANT TO DO, GO BACK? IT'S TOO LATE TO BE THINKING ABOUT THESE THINGS!
WE COULD GET CAUGHT AT ANY TIME! AND THIS TIME...WHO KNOWS WHAT WILL HAPPEN! TO BOTH OF US!
WE'RE SO--
ARE YOU TRYING TO SAY WE SHOULD BREAK UP?!
YES! WE HAVE TO!!

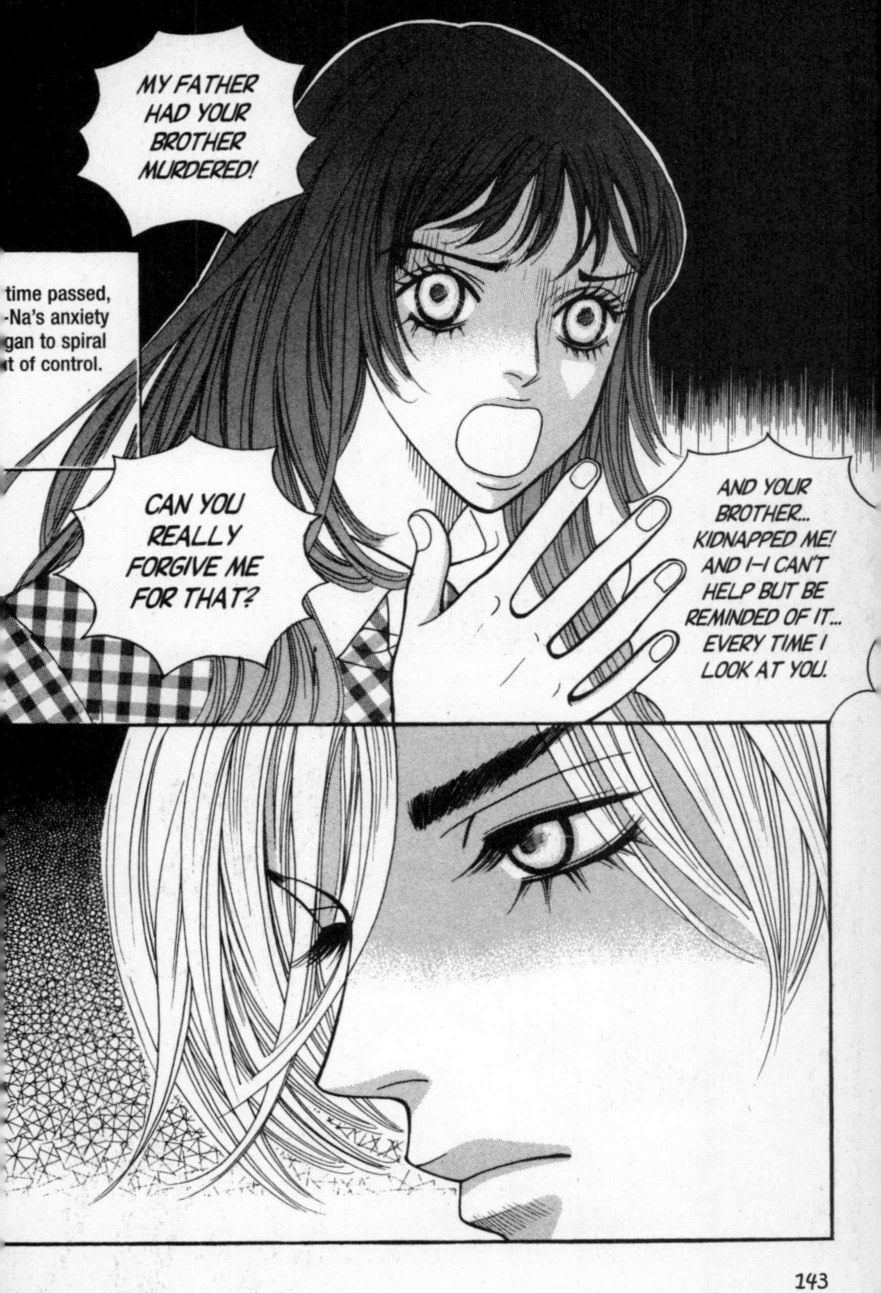
MY FATHER HAD YOUR BROTHER MURDERED!
time passed, -Na's anxiety gan to spiral t of control.
CAN YOU REALLY FORGIVE ME FOR THAT?
AND YOUR BROTHER... KIDNAPPED ME! AND I–I CAN'T HELP BUT BE REMINDED OF IT... EVERY TIME I LOOK AT YOU.

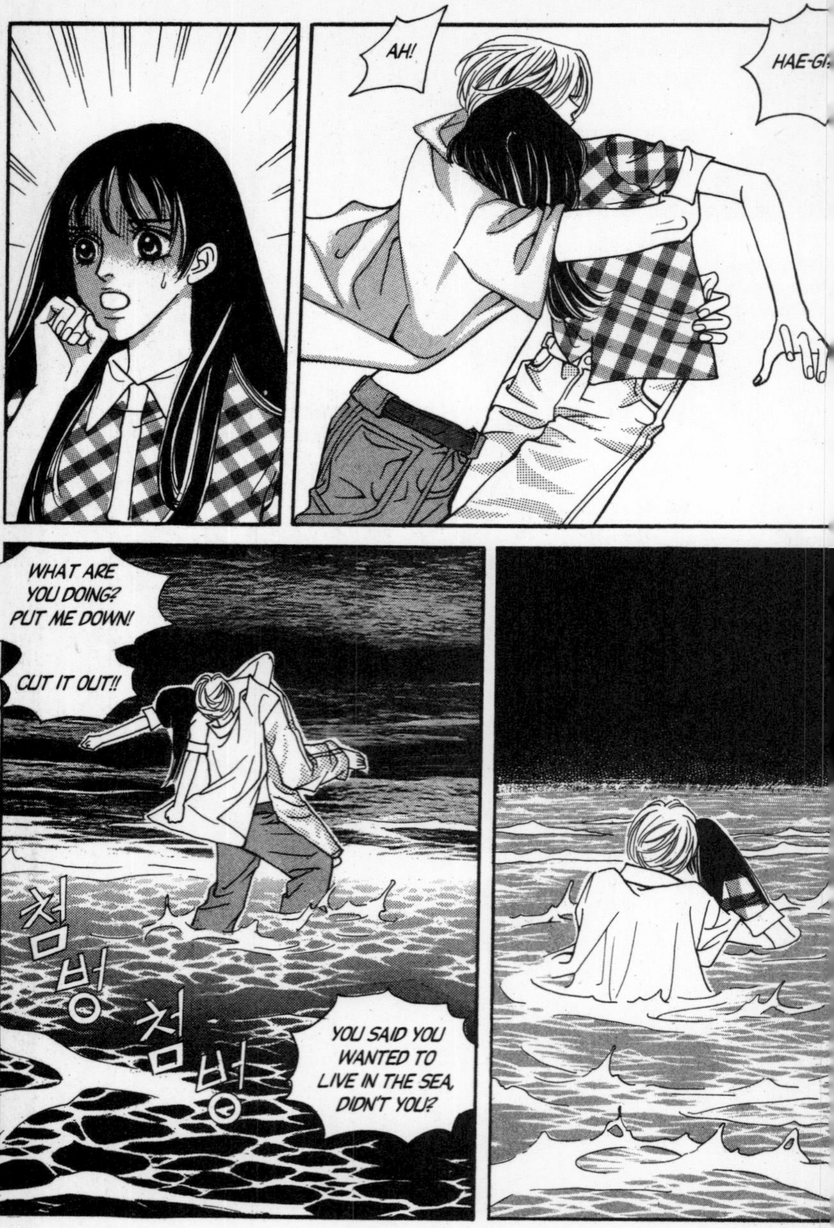
AH!
HAE-GI
WHAT ARE YOU DOING? PUT ME DOWN!
CUT IT OUT!!
첨벙
첨벙
YOU SAID YOU WANTED TO LIVE IN THE SEA, DIDN'T YOU?

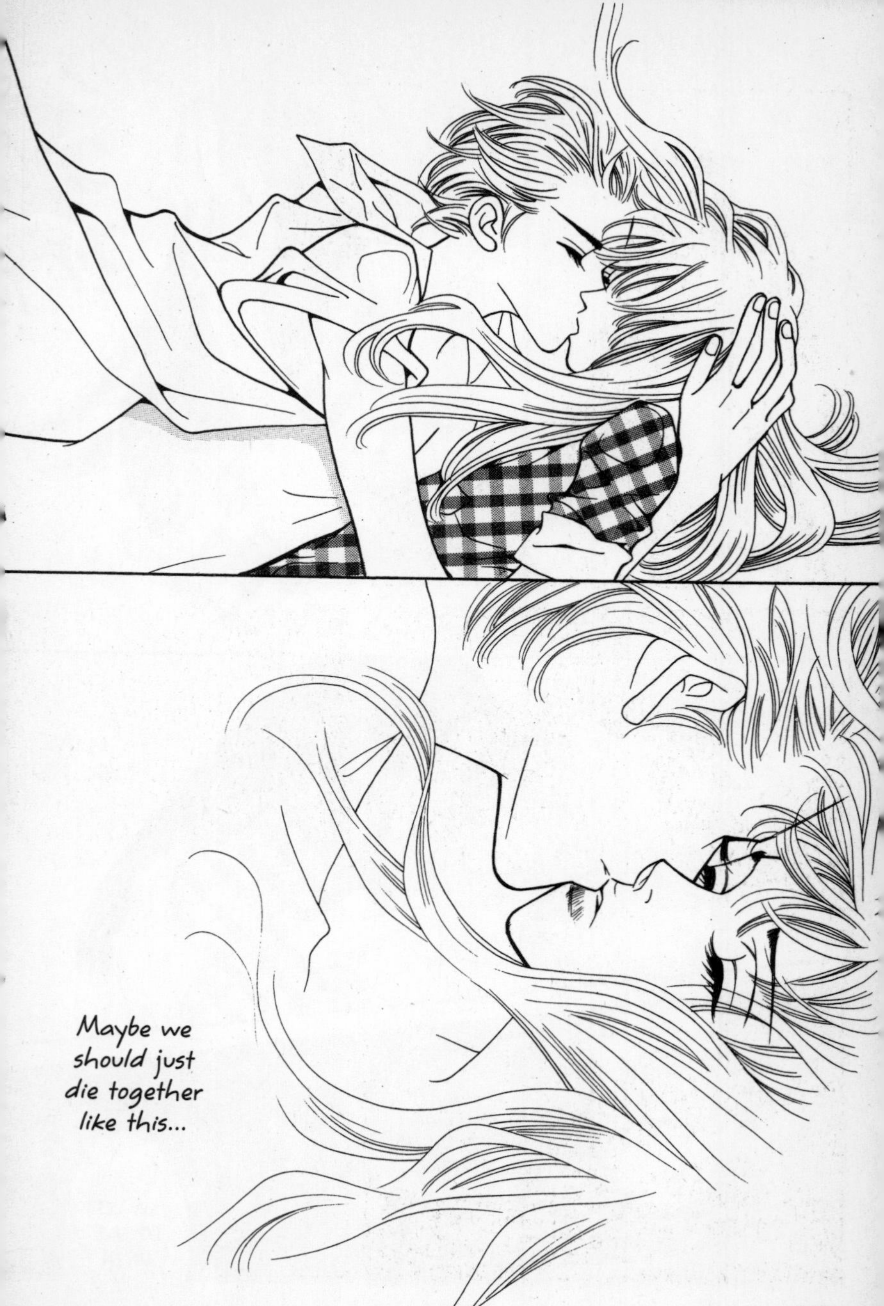
Maybe we should just die together like this...

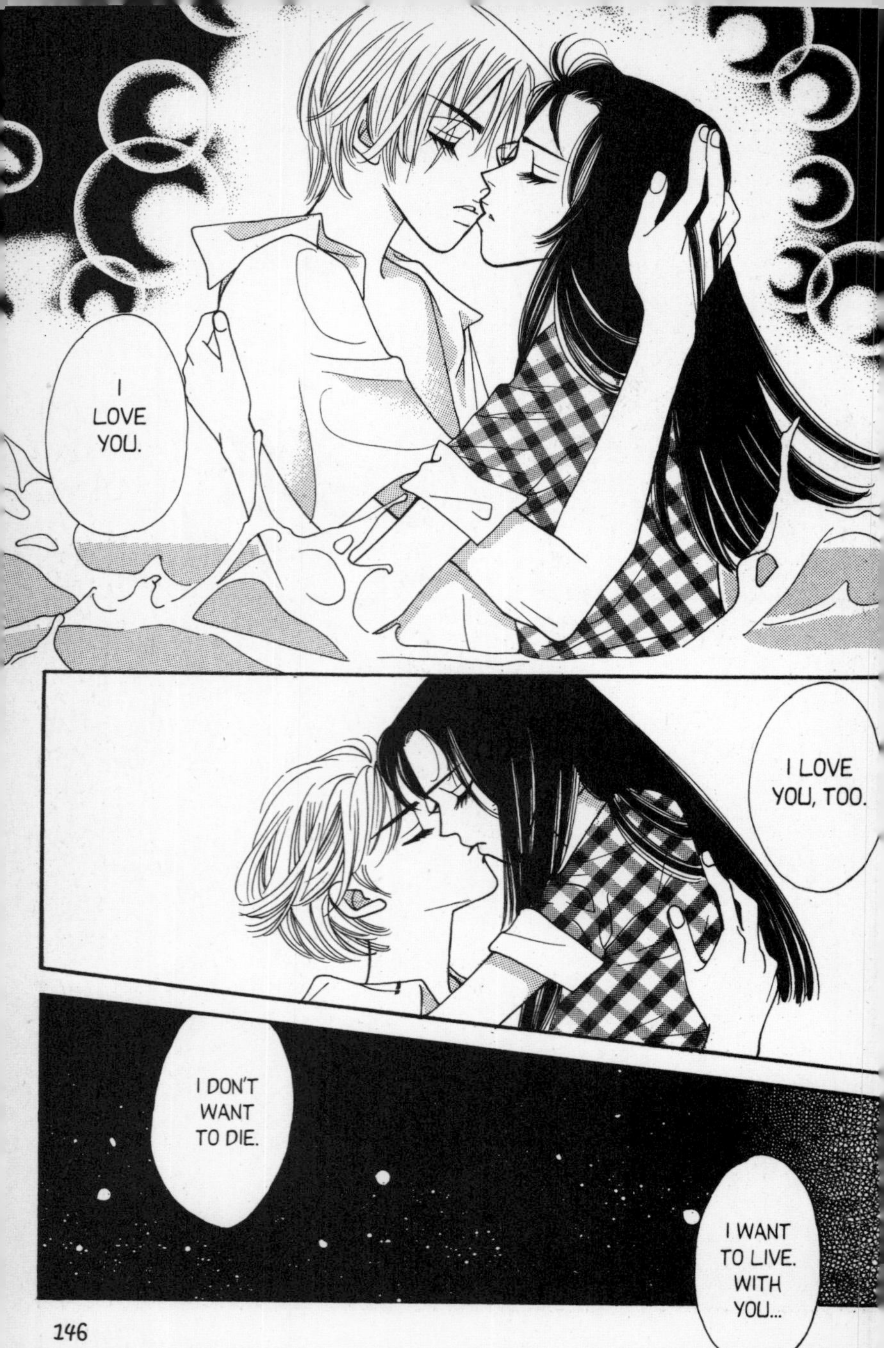
I LOVE YOU.
I LOVE YOU, TOO.
I DON'T WANT TO DIE.
I WANT TO LIVE. WITH YOU...

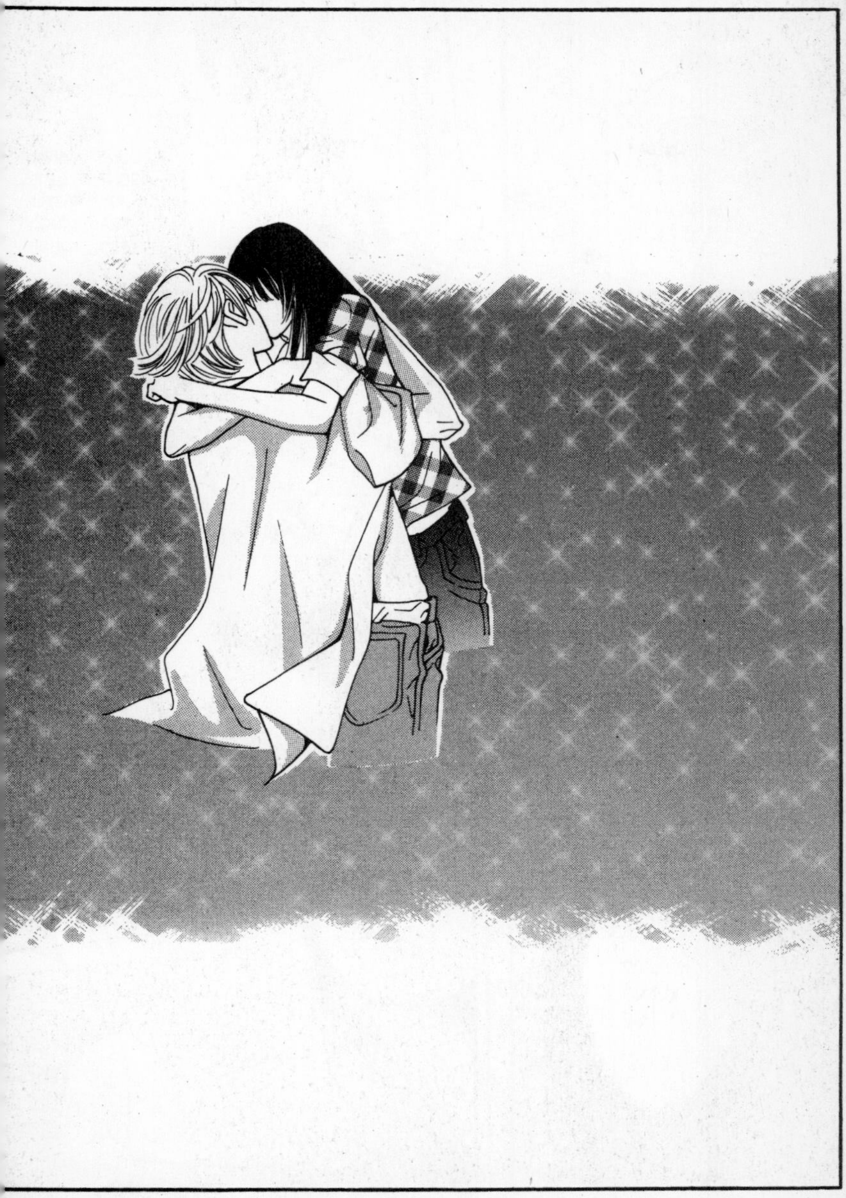

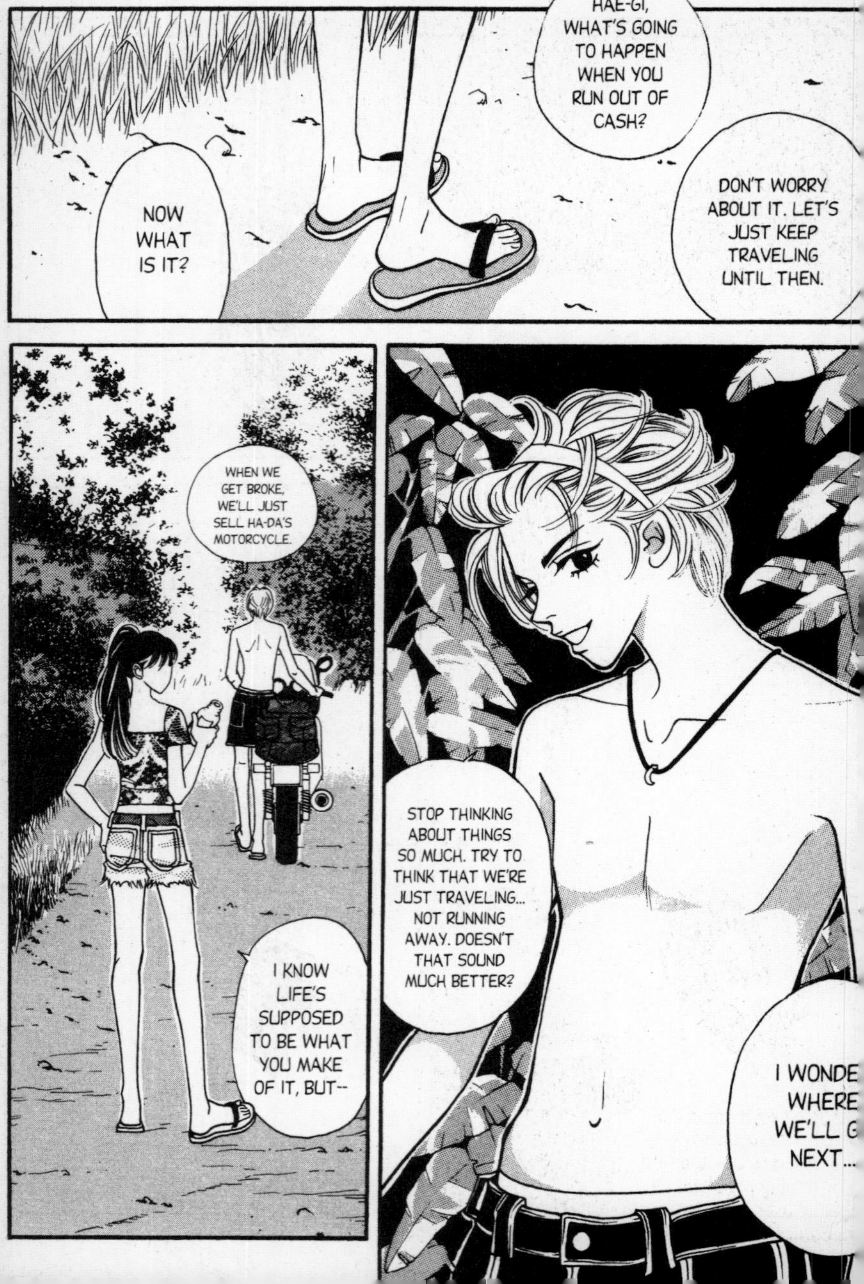
NOW WHAT IS IT?
HAE-GI, WHAT'S GOING TO HAPPEN WHEN YOU RUN OUT OF CASH?
DON'T WORRY ABOUT IT. LET'S JUST KEEP TRAVELING UNTIL THEN.
WHEN WE GET BROKE, WE'LL JUST SELL HA-DA'S MOTORCYCLE.
I KNOW LIFE'S SUPPOSED TO BE WHAT YOU MAKE OF IT, BUT--
STOP THINKING ABOUT THINGS SO MUCH. TRY TO THINK THAT WE'RE JUST TRAVELING... NOT RUNNING AWAY. DOESN'T THAT SOUND MUCH BETTER?
I WONDE WHERE WE'LL G NEXT...

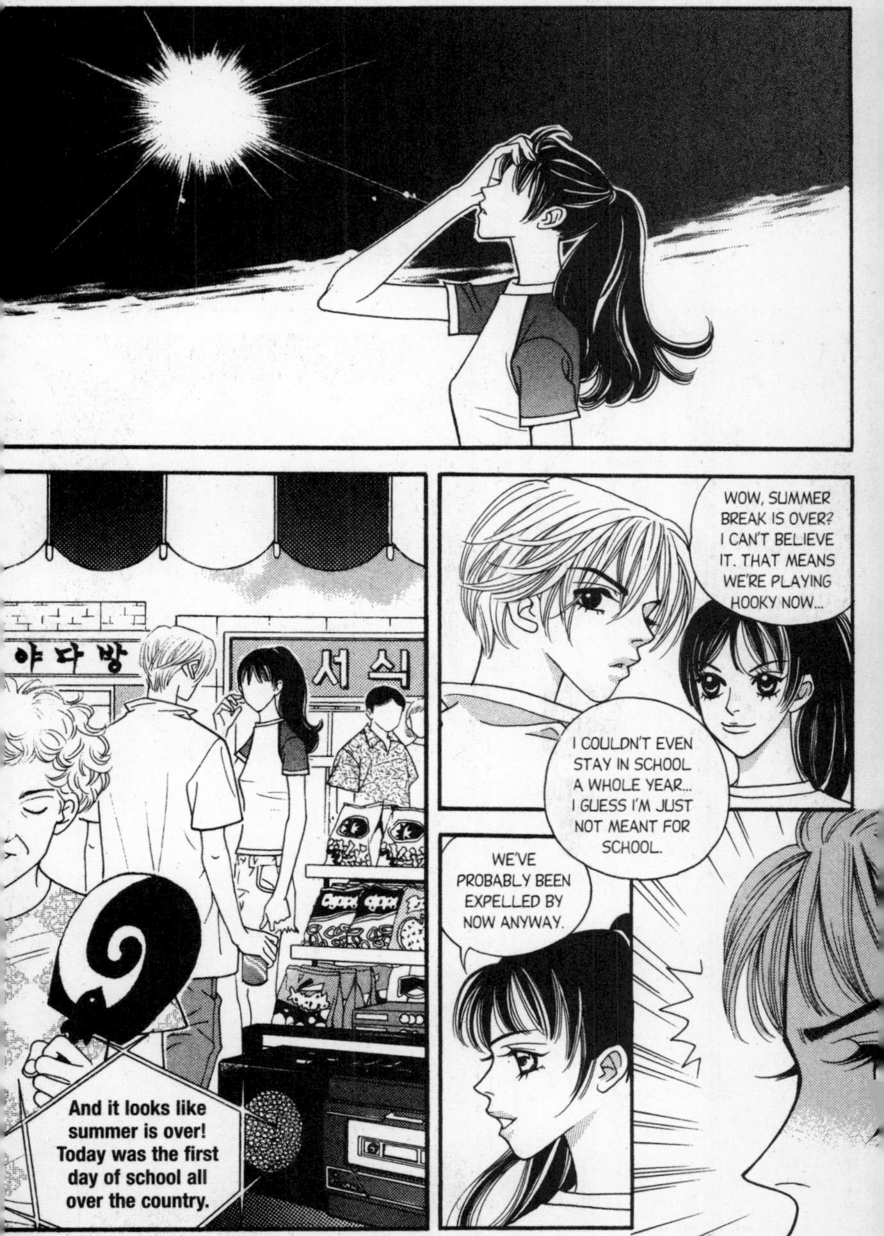
야다방
서식
And it looks like summer is over! Today was the first day of school all over the country.
WOW, SUMMER BREAK IS OVER? I CAN'T BELIEVE IT. THAT MEANS WE'RE PLAYING HOOKY NOW...
I COULDN'T EVEN STAY IN SCHOOL A WHOLE YEAR... I GUESS I'M JUST NOT MEANT FOR SCHOOL.
WE'VE PROBABLY BEEN EXPELLED BY NOW ANYWAY.

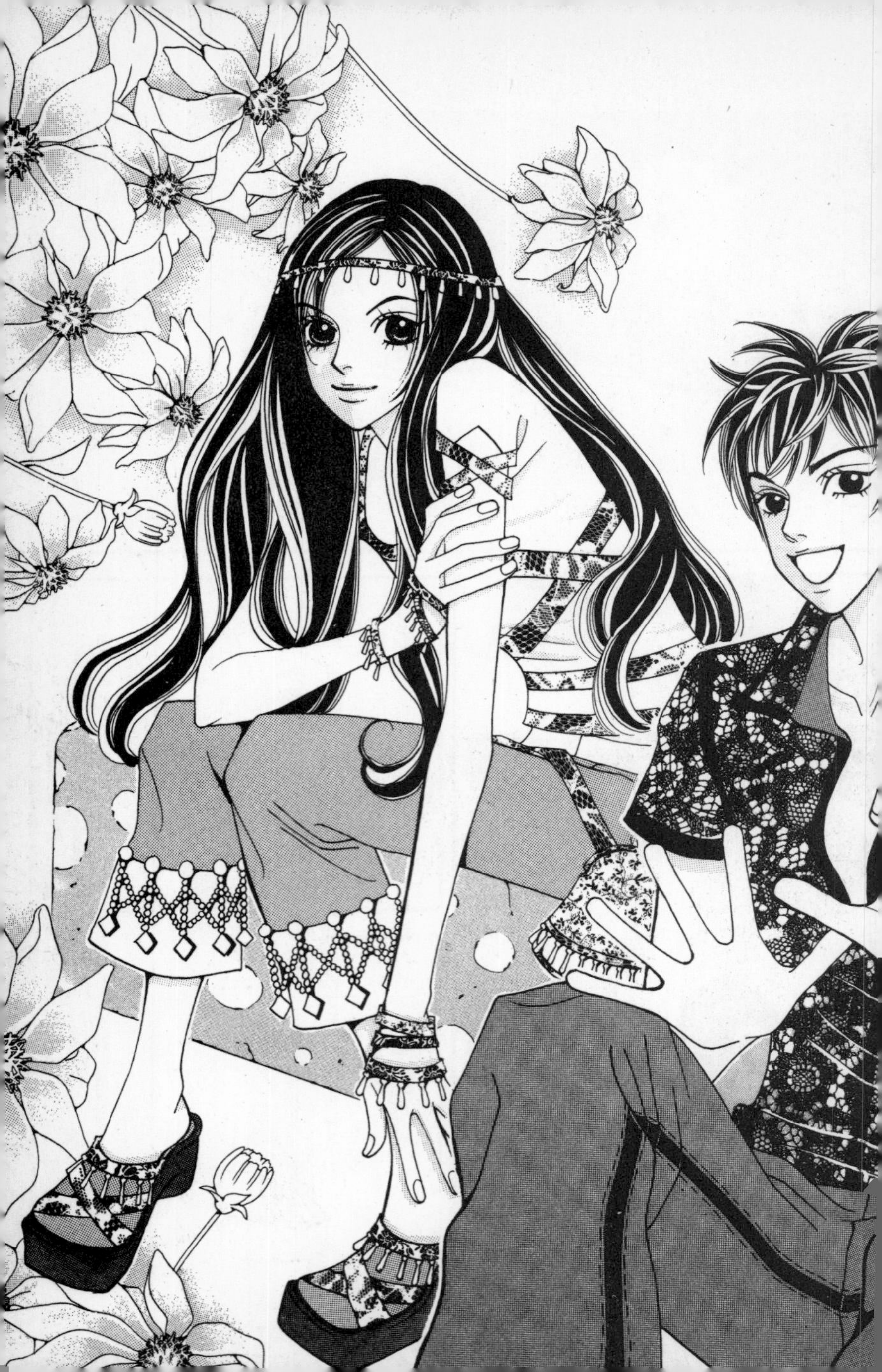

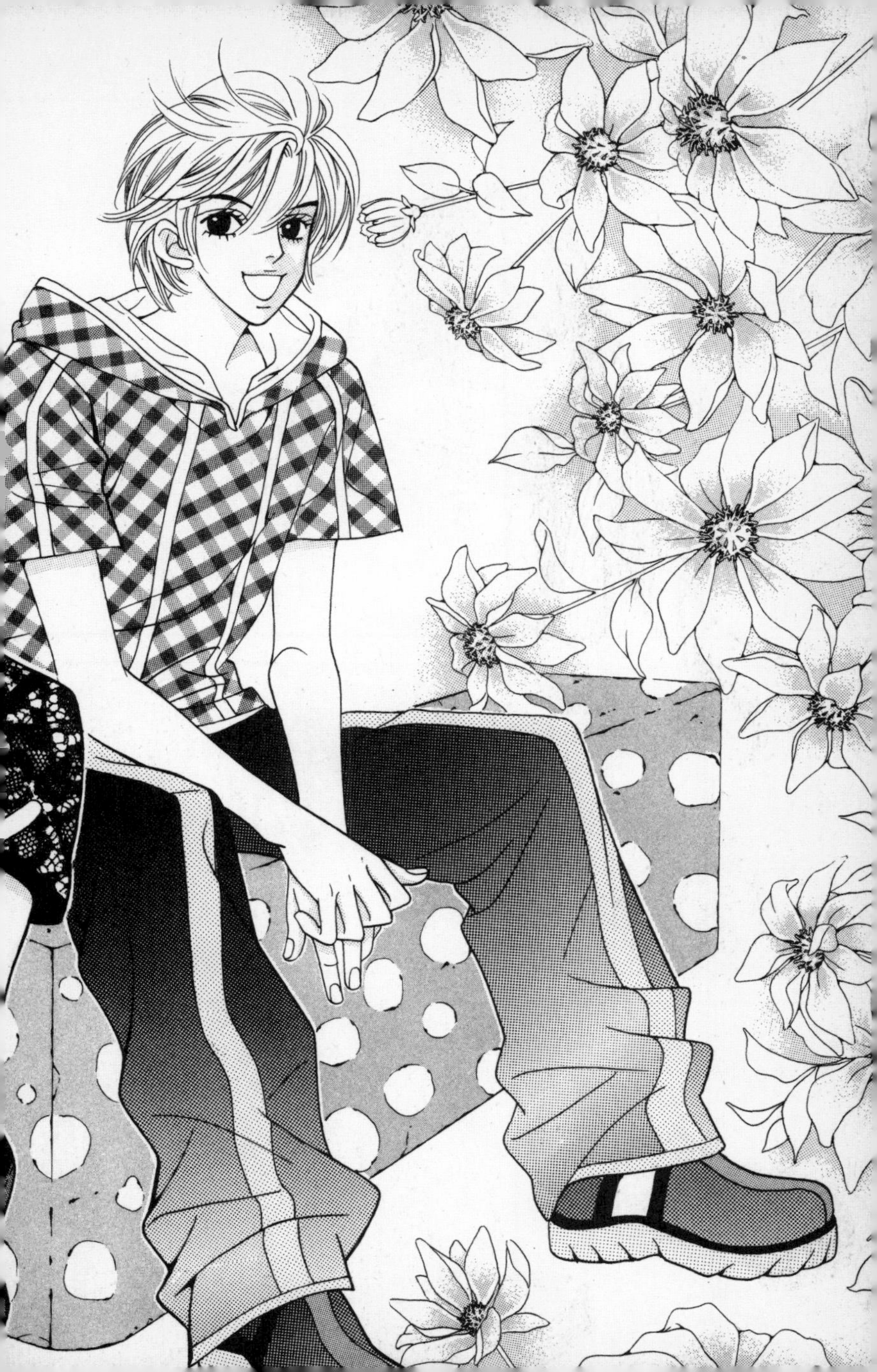

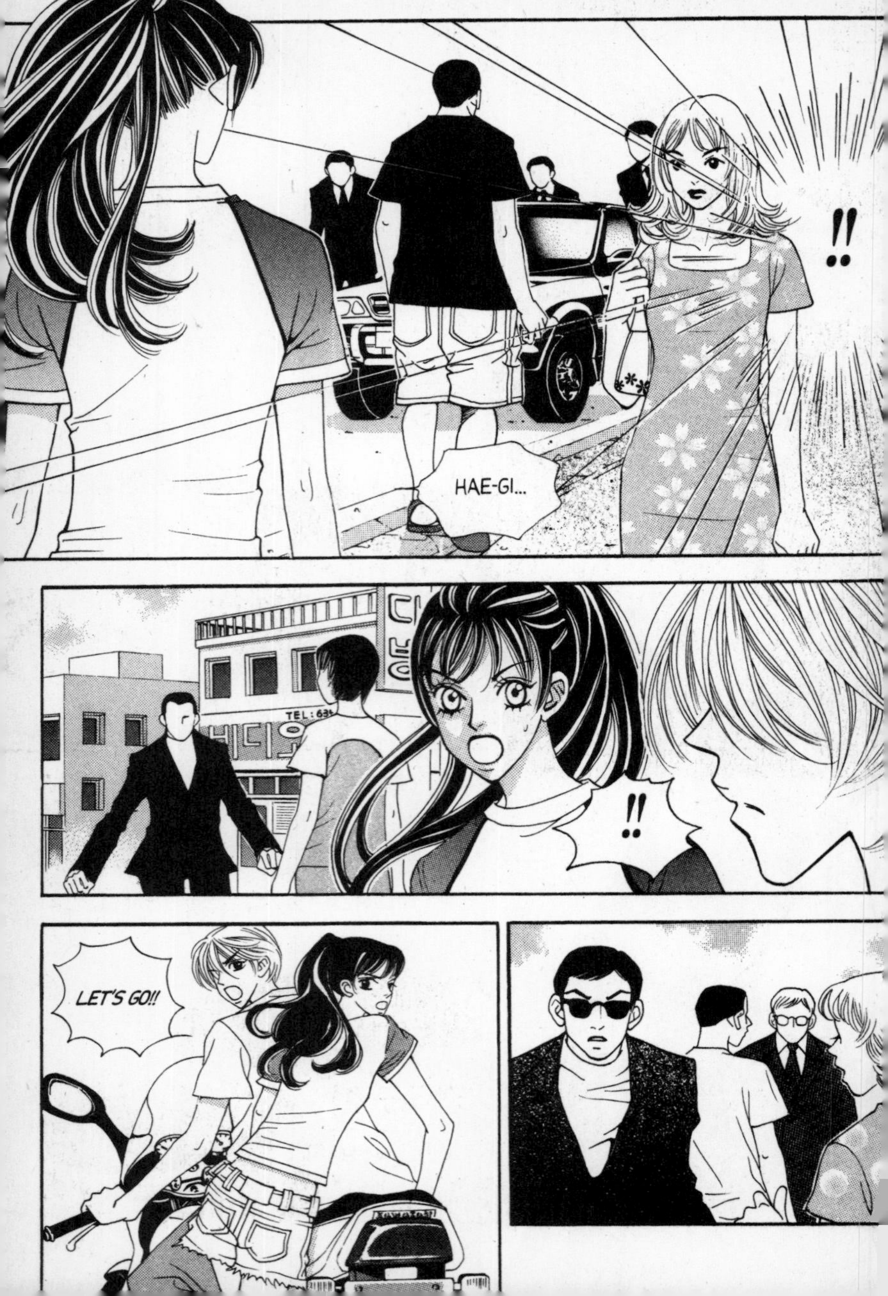
!!
HAE-GI...
!!
LET'S GO!!

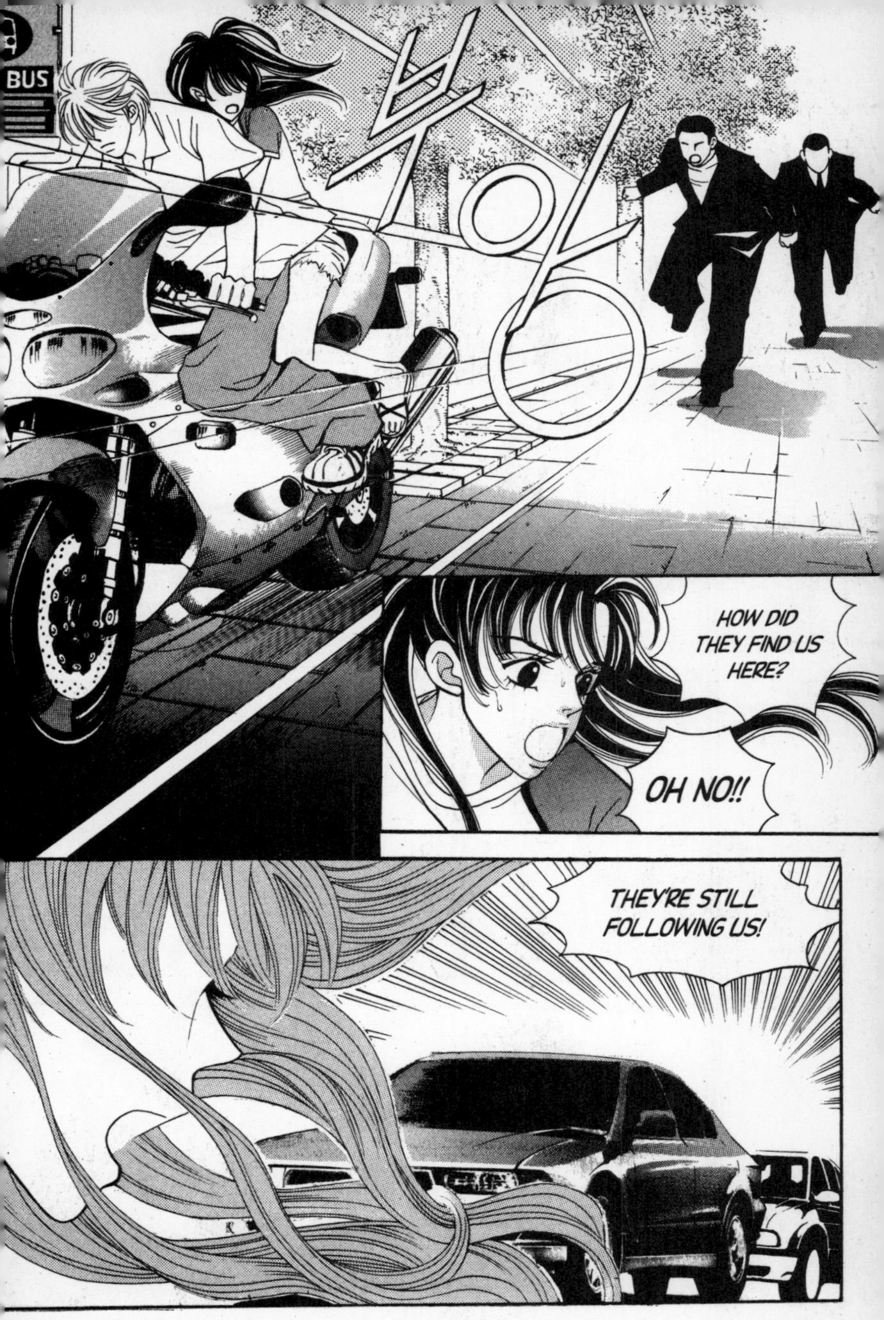
BUS
HOW DID THEY FIND US HERE?
OH NO!!
THEY'RE STILL FOLLOWING US!

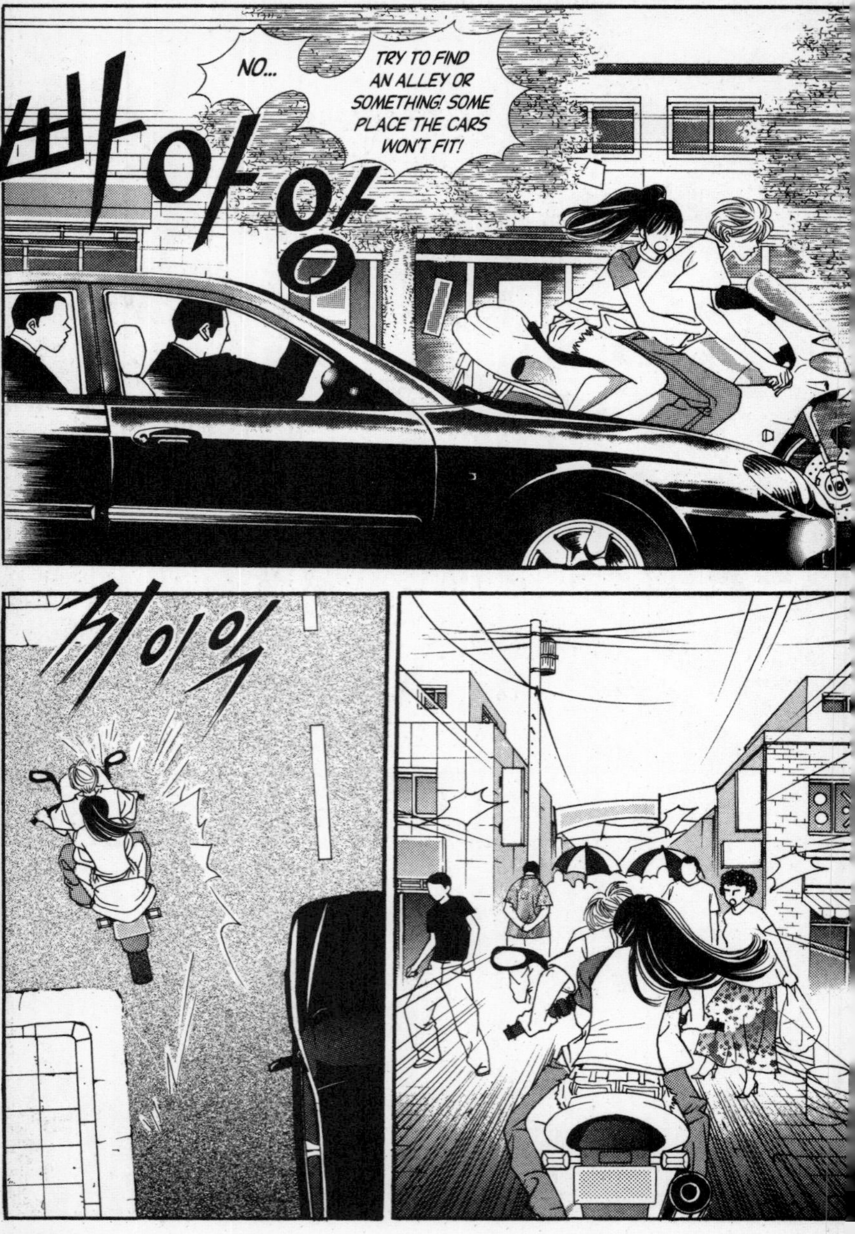
빠아앙
NO...
TRY TO FIND AN ALLEY OR SOMETHING! SOME PLACE THE CARS WON'T FIT!
치이익

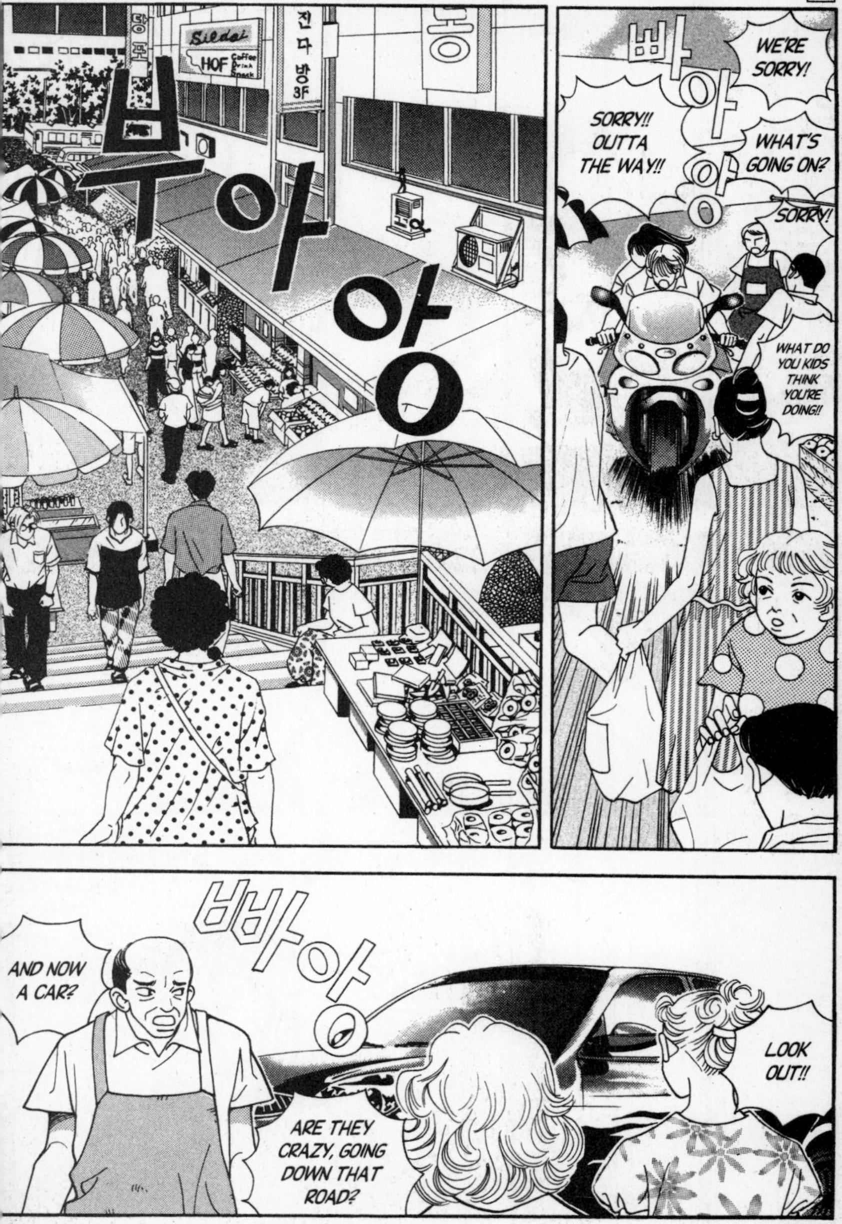
부아앙
HOF
빠아앙
SORRY!! OUTTA THE WAY!!
WE'RE SORRY!
WHAT'S GOING ON?
SORRY!
WHAT DO YOU KIDS THINK YOU'RE DOING!!
빠아앙
AND NOW A CAR?
ARE THEY CRAZY, GOING DOWN THAT ROAD?
LOOK OUT!!

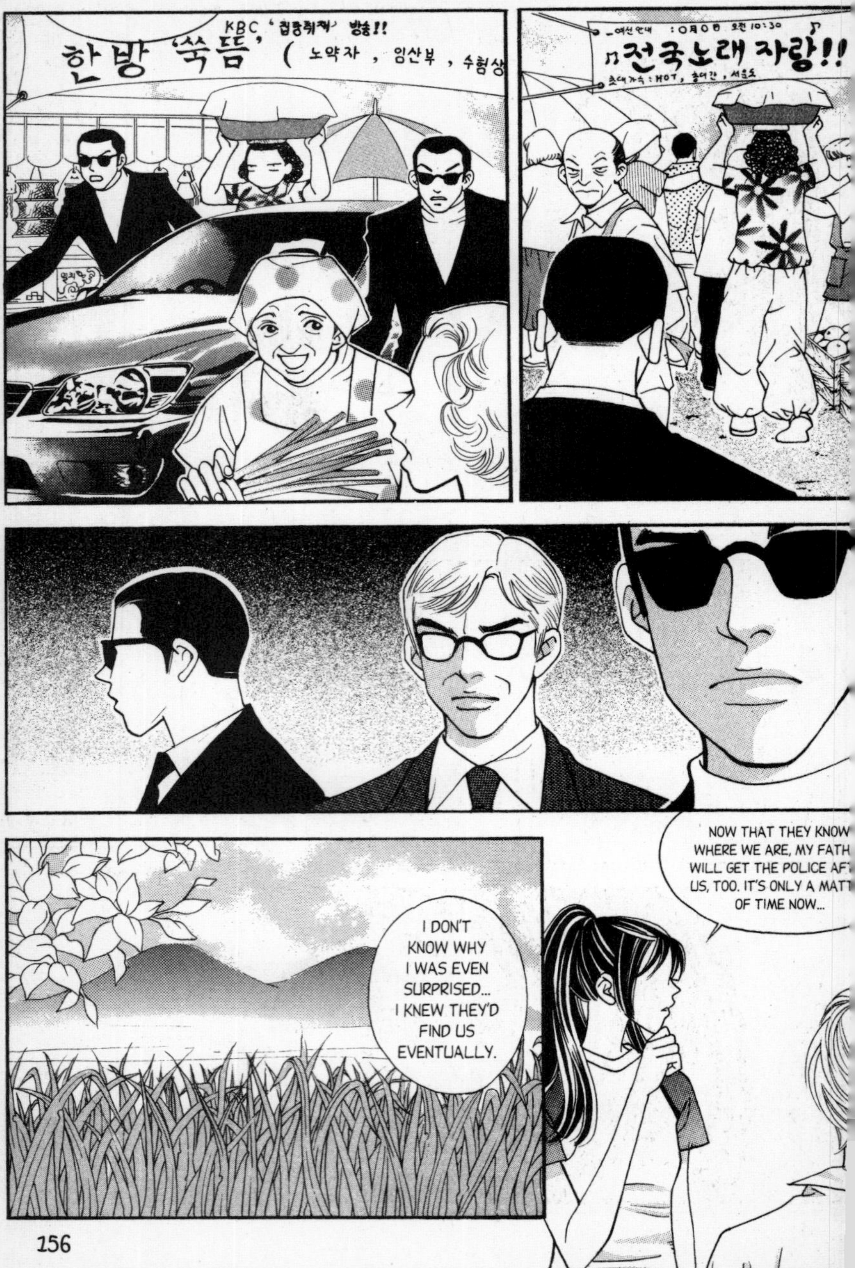

한방 '쑥뜸' (노약자 , 임산부 , 수험생
전국노래 자랑!!
I DON'T KNOW WHY I WAS EVEN SURPRISED... I KNEW THEY'D FIND US EVENTUALLY.
NOW THAT THEY KNOW WHERE WE ARE, MY FATH WILL GET THE POLICE AFT US, TOO. IT'S ONLY A MATT OF TIME NOW...

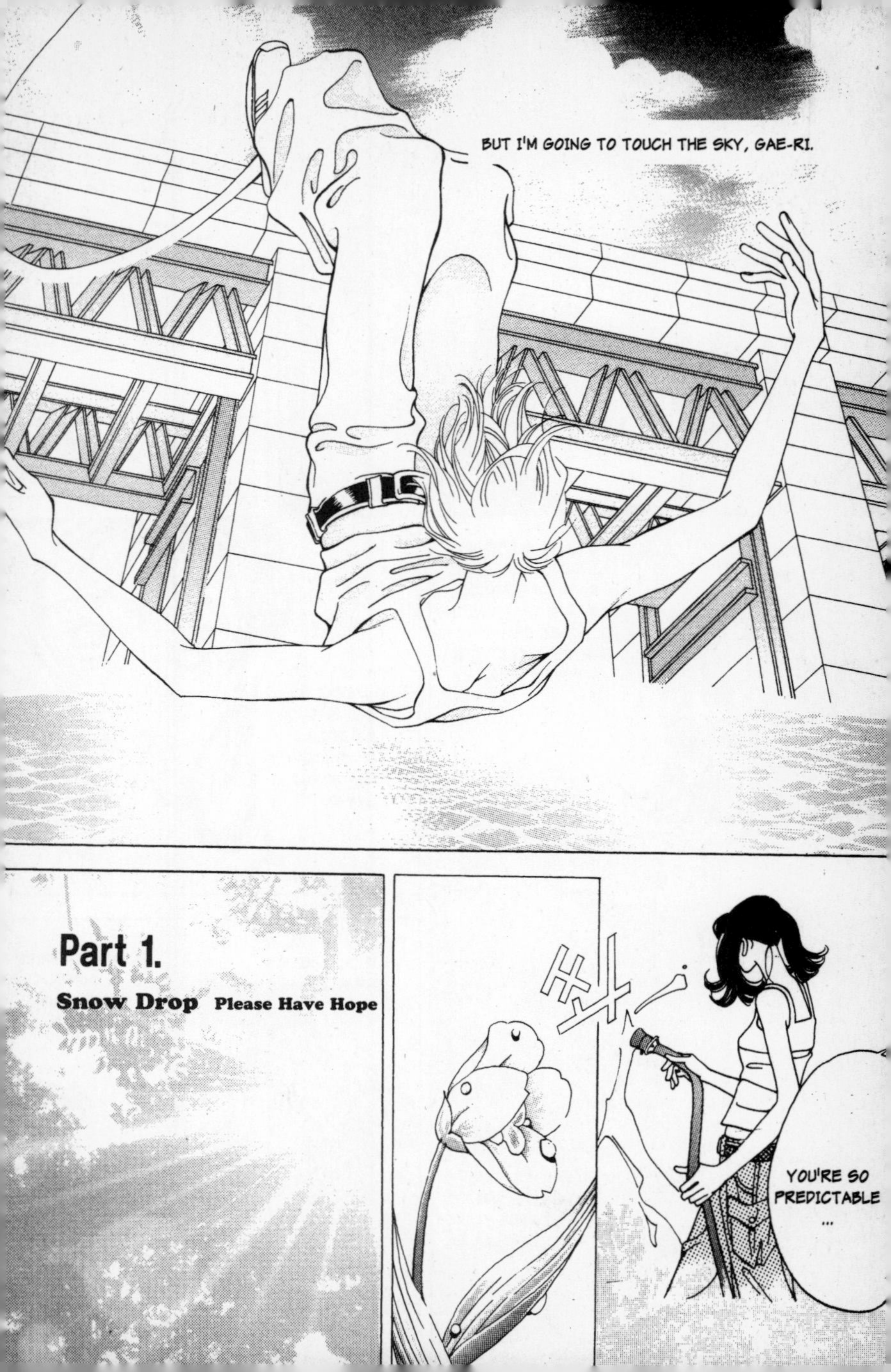
BUT I'M GOING TO TOUCH THE SKY, GAE-RI.
Part 1.
Snow Drop Please Have Hope
YOU'RE SO PREDICTABLE ...

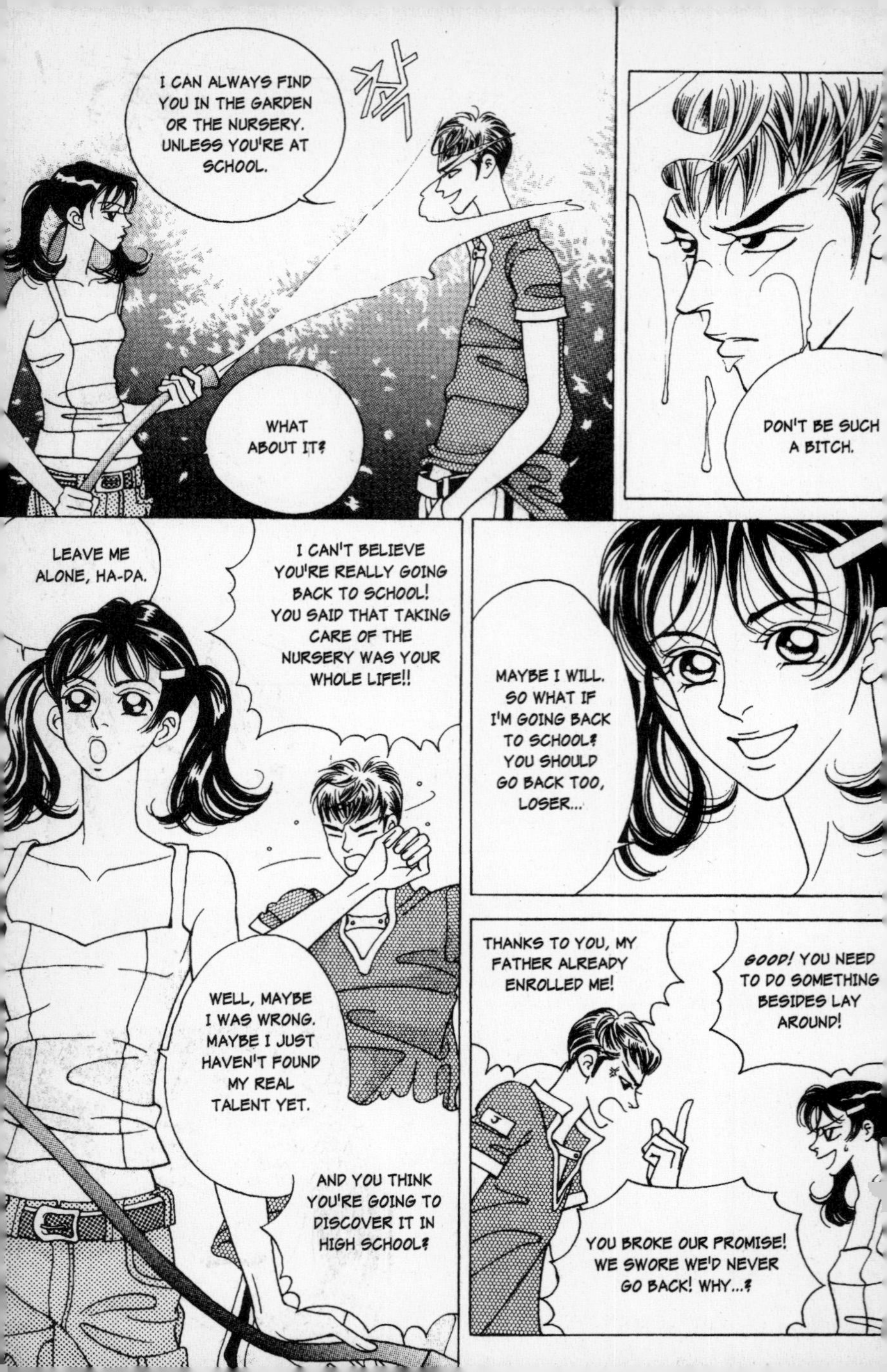
I CAN ALWAYS FIND YOU IN THE GARDEN OR THE NURSERY. UNLESS YOU'RE AT SCHOOL.
WHAT ABOUT IT?
DON'T BE SUCH A BITCH.
LEAVE ME ALONE, HA-DA.
I CAN'T BELIEVE YOU'RE REALLY GOING BACK TO SCHOOL! YOU SAID THAT TAKING CARE OF THE NURSERY WAS YOUR WHOLE LIFE!!
WELL, MAYBE I WAS WRONG. MAYBE I JUST HAVEN'T FOUND MY REAL TALENT YET.
AND YOU THINK YOU'RE GOING TO DISCOVER IT IN HIGH SCHOOL?
MAYBE I WILL. SO WHAT IF I'M GOING BACK TO SCHOOL? YOU SHOULD GO BACK TOO, LOSER...
THANKS TO YOU, MY FATHER ALREADY ENROLLED ME!
GOOD! YOU NEED TO DO SOMETHING BESIDES LAY AROUND!
YOU BROKE OUR PROMISE! WE SWORE WE'D NEVER GO BACK! WHY...?

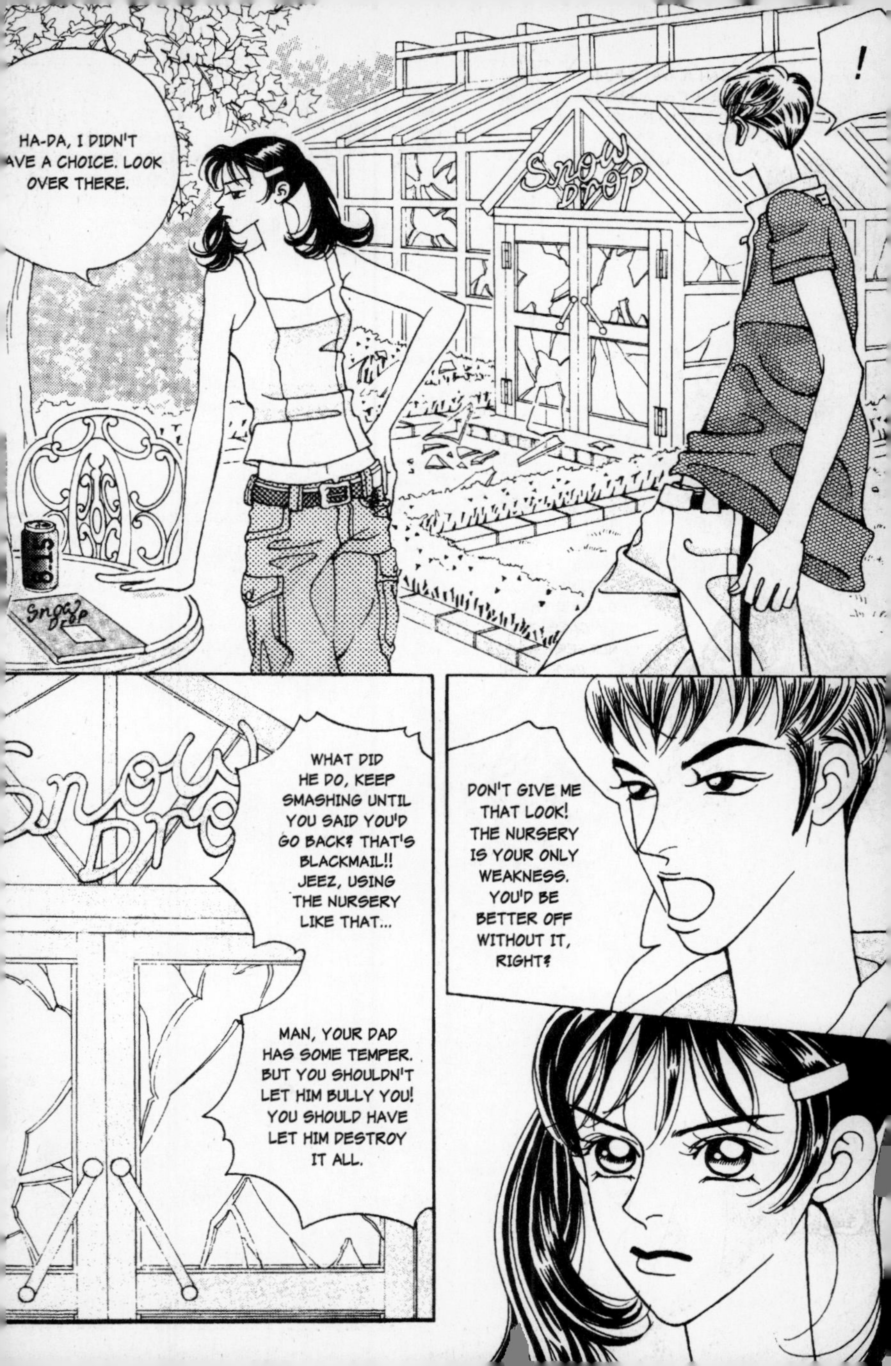
HA-DA, I DIDN'T AVE A CHOICE. LOOK OVER THERE.
!
Snow Drop
WHAT DID HE DO, KEEP SMASHING UNTIL YOU SAID YOU'D GO BACK? THAT'S BLACKMAIL!! JEEZ, USING THE NURSERY LIKE THAT...
MAN, YOUR DAD HAS SOME TEMPER. BUT YOU SHOULDN'T LET HIM BULLY YOU! YOU SHOULD HAVE LET HIM DESTROY IT ALL.
DON'T GIVE ME THAT LOOK! THE NURSERY IS YOUR ONLY WEAKNESS. YOU'D BE BETTER OFF WITHOUT IT, RIGHT?

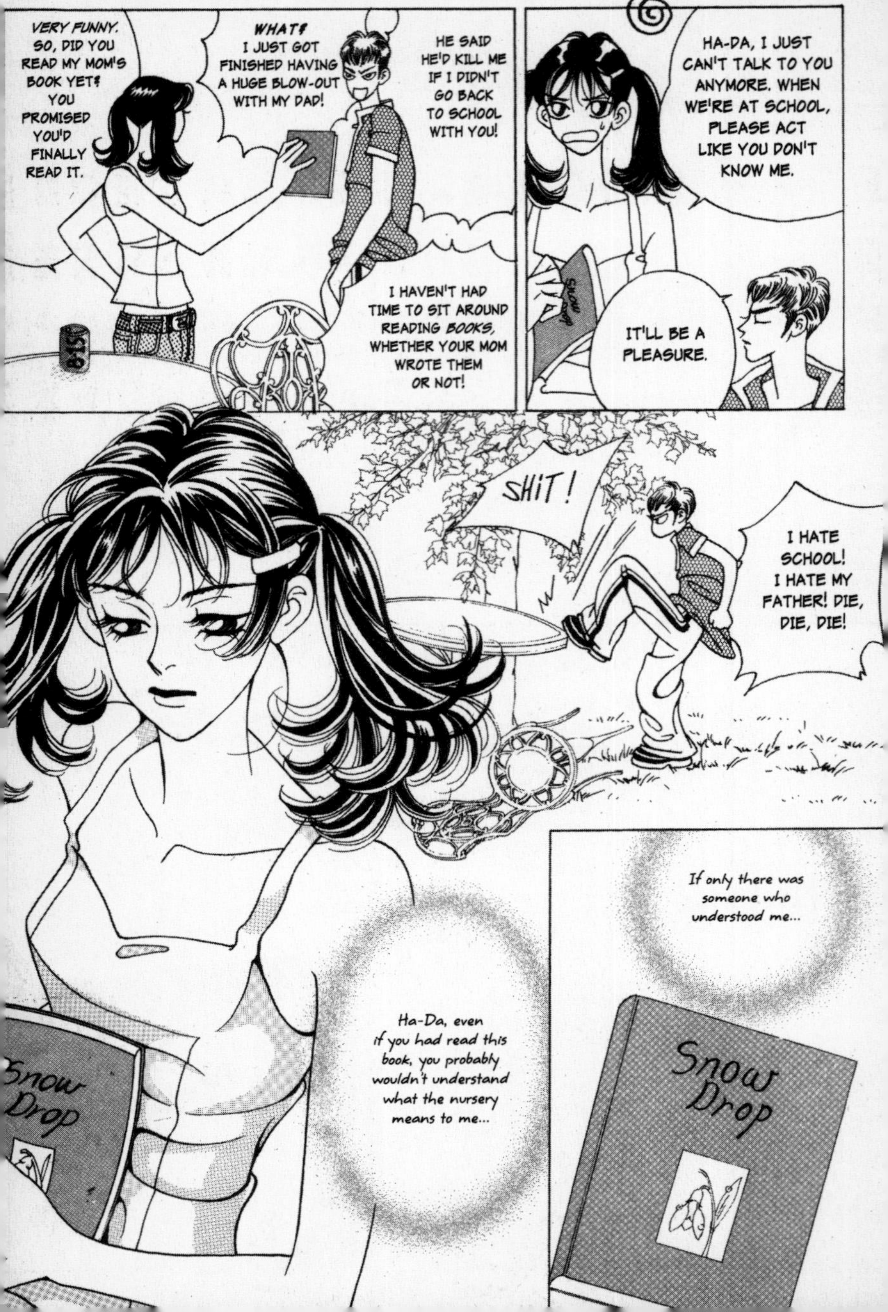
VERY FUNNY. SO, DID YOU READ MY MOM'S BOOK YET? YOU PROMISED YOU'D FINALLY READ IT.
WHAT? I JUST GOT FINISHED HAVING A HUGE BLOW-OUT WITH MY DAD!
HE SAID HE'D KILL ME IF I DIDN'T GO BACK TO SCHOOL WITH YOU!
I HAVEN'T HAD TIME TO SIT AROUND READING BOOKS, WHETHER YOUR MOM WROTE THEM OR NOT!
HA-DA, I JUST CAN'T TALK TO YOU ANYMORE. WHEN WE'RE AT SCHOOL, PLEASE ACT LIKE YOU DON'T KNOW ME.
IT'LL BE A PLEASURE.
SHIT!
I HATE SCHOOL! I HATE MY FATHER! DIE, DIE, DIE!
Ha-Da, even if you had read this book, you probably wouldn't understand what the nursery means to me...
If only there was someone who understood me...
Snow Drop

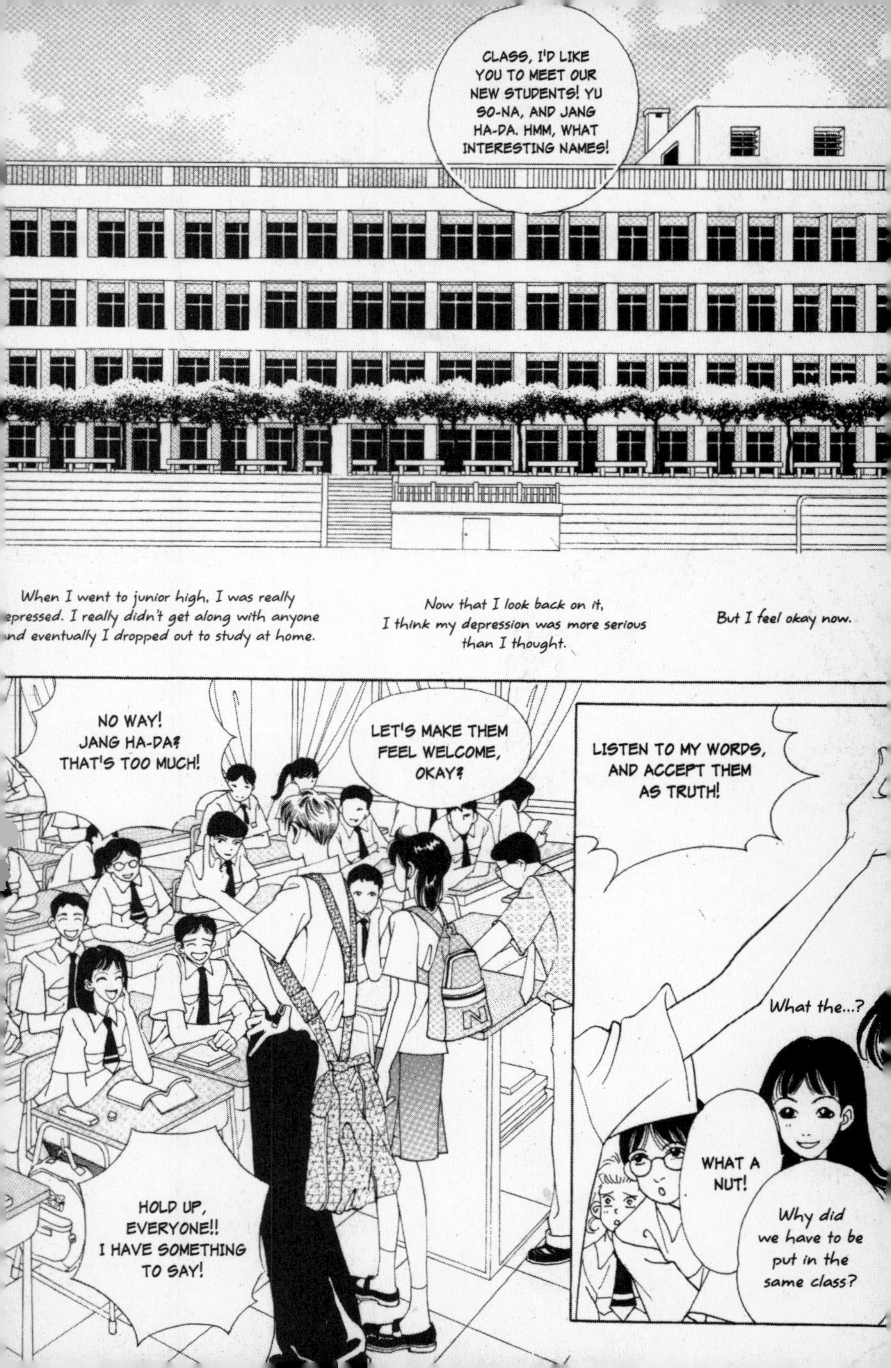
CLASS, I'D LIKE YOU TO MEET OUR NEW STUDENTS! YU SO-NA, AND JANG HA-DA. HMM, WHAT INTERESTING NAMES!
When I went to junior high, I was really depressed. I really didn't get along with anyone and eventually I dropped out to study at home.
Now that I look back on it, I think my depression was more serious than I thought.
But I feel okay now.
NO WAY! JANG HA-DA? THAT'S TOO MUCH!
LET'S MAKE THEM FEEL WELCOME, OKAY?
HOLD UP, EVERYONE!! I HAVE SOMETHING TO SAY!
LISTEN TO MY WORDS, AND ACCEPT THEM AS TRUTH!
What the...?
WHAT A NUT!
Why did we have to be put in the same class?

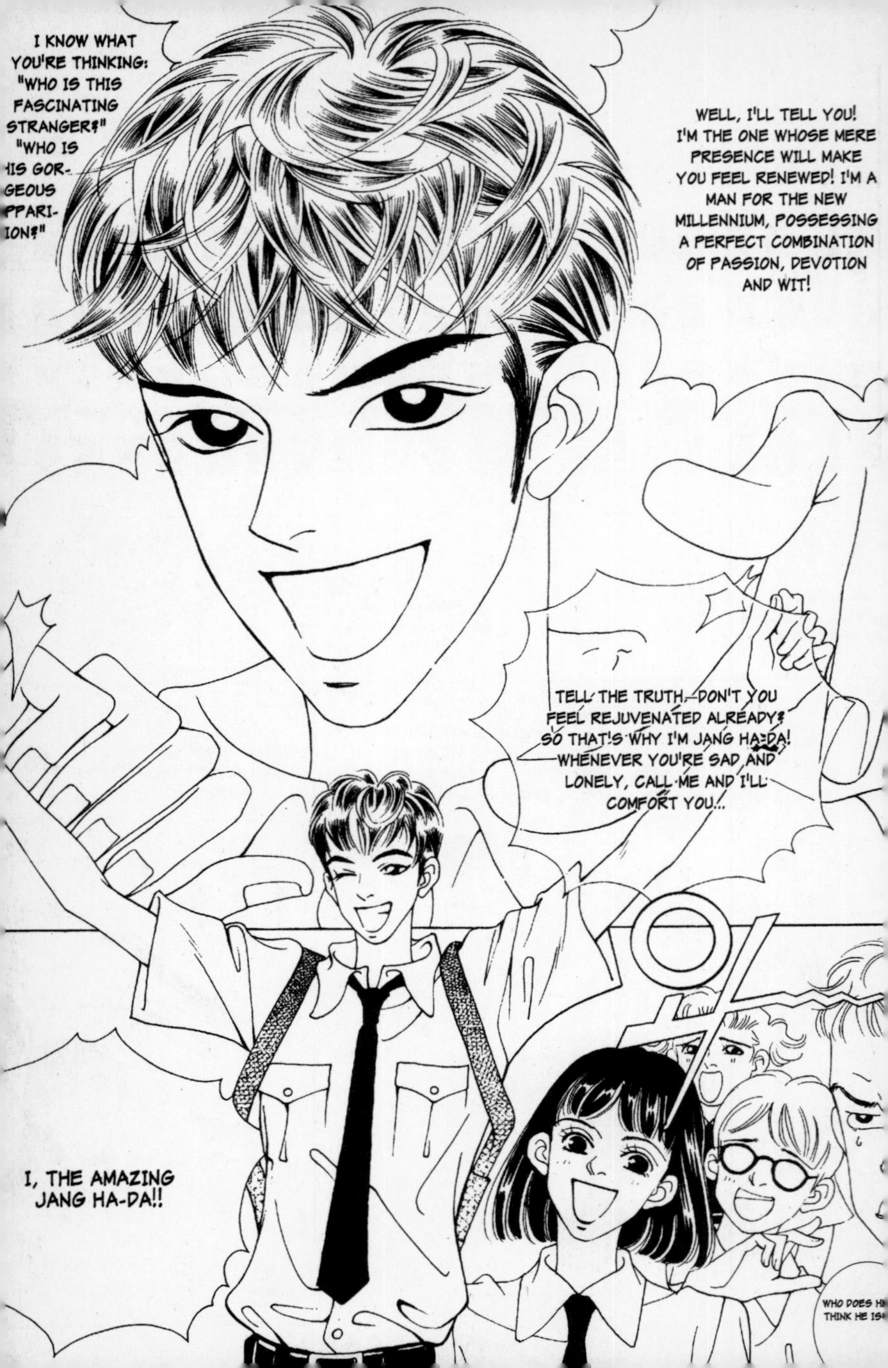
I KNOW WHAT YOU'RE THINKING: "WHO IS THIS FASCINATING STRANGER?" "WHO IS HIS GOR-GEOUS PPARI-ION?"
WELL, I'LL TELL YOU! I'M THE ONE WHOSE MERE PRESENCE WILL MAKE YOU FEEL RENEWED! I'M A MAN FOR THE NEW MILLENNIUM, POSSESSING A PERFECT COMBINATION OF PASSION, DEVOTION AND WIT!
TELL THE TRUTH, DON'T YOU FEEL REJUVENATED ALREADY? SO THAT'S WHY I'M JANG HA-DA! WHENEVER YOU'RE SAD AND LONELY, CALL ME AND I'LL COMFORT YOU...
I, THE AMAZING JANG HA-DA!!
WHO DOES HI THINK HE IS

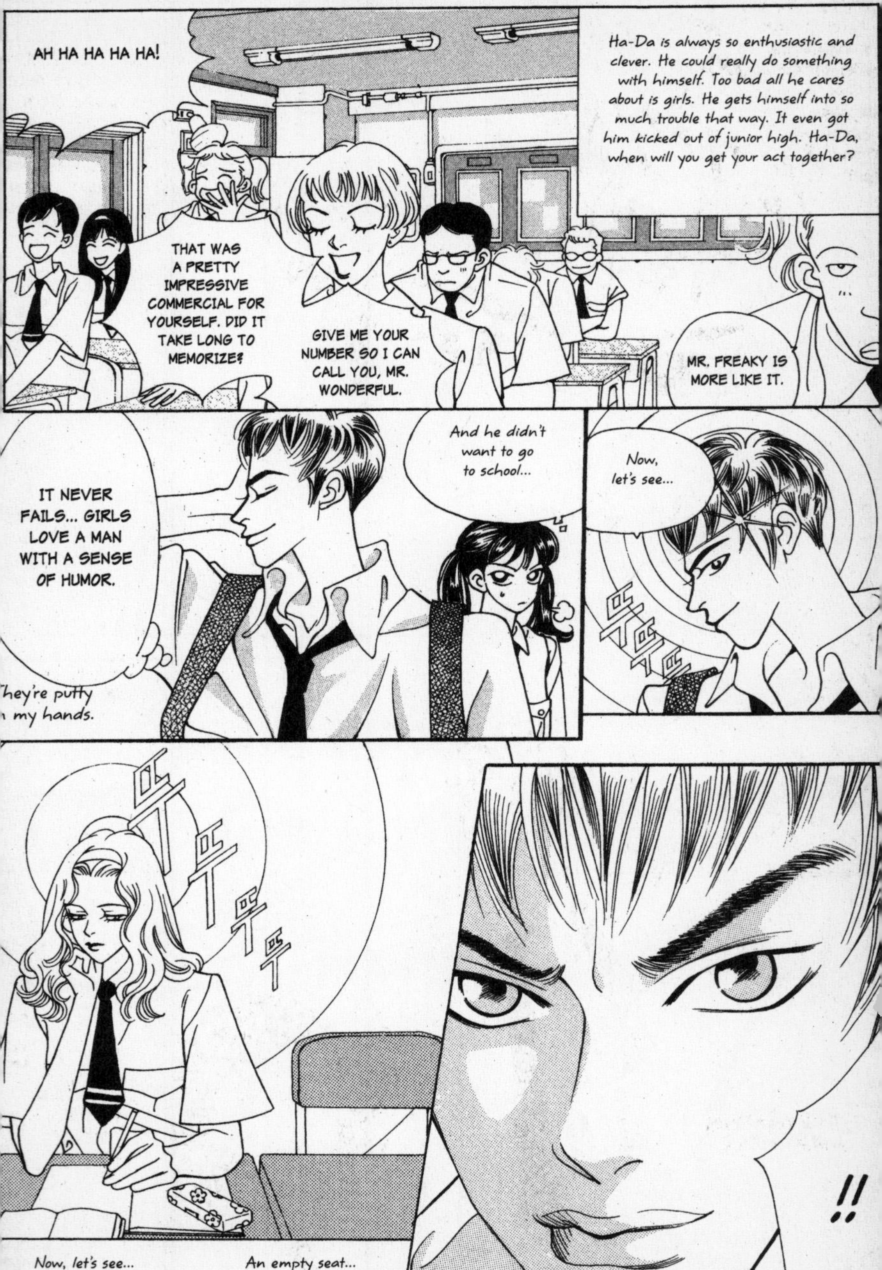
AH HA HA HA HA!
THAT WAS A PRETTY IMPRESSIVE COMMERCIAL FOR YOURSELF. DID IT TAKE LONG TO MEMORIZE?
GIVE ME YOUR NUMBER SO I CAN CALL YOU, MR. WONDERFUL.
Ha-Da is always so enthusiastic and clever. He could really do something with himself. Too bad all he cares about is girls. He gets himself into so much trouble that way. It even got him kicked out of junior high. Ha-Da, when will you get your act together?
...
MR. FREAKY IS MORE LIKE IT.
IT NEVER FAILS... GIRLS LOVE A MAN WITH A SENSE OF HUMOR.
hey're putty
n my hands.
And he didn't want to go to school...
Now, let's see...
!!
Now, let's see...
An empty seat...

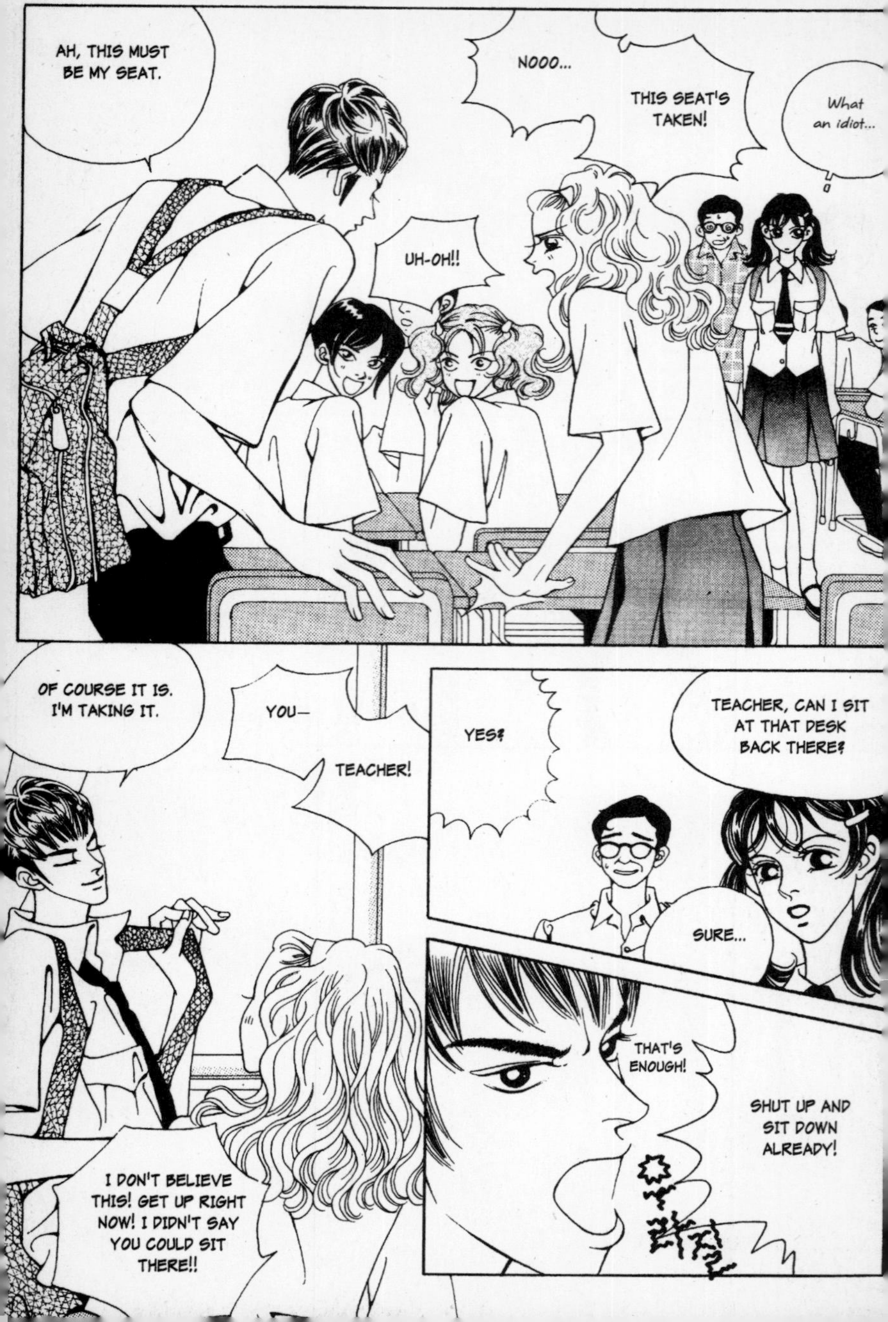
AH, THIS MUST BE MY SEAT.
UH-OH!!
NOOO...
THIS SEAT'S TAKEN!
What an idiot...
OF COURSE IT IS. I'M TAKING IT.
YOU—
TEACHER!
I DON'T BELIEVE THIS! GET UP RIGHT NOW! I DIDN'T SAY YOU COULD SIT THERE!!
YES?
TEACHER, CAN I SIT AT THAT DESK BACK THERE?
SURE...
THAT'S ENOUGH!
SHUT UP AND SIT DOWN ALREADY!

1

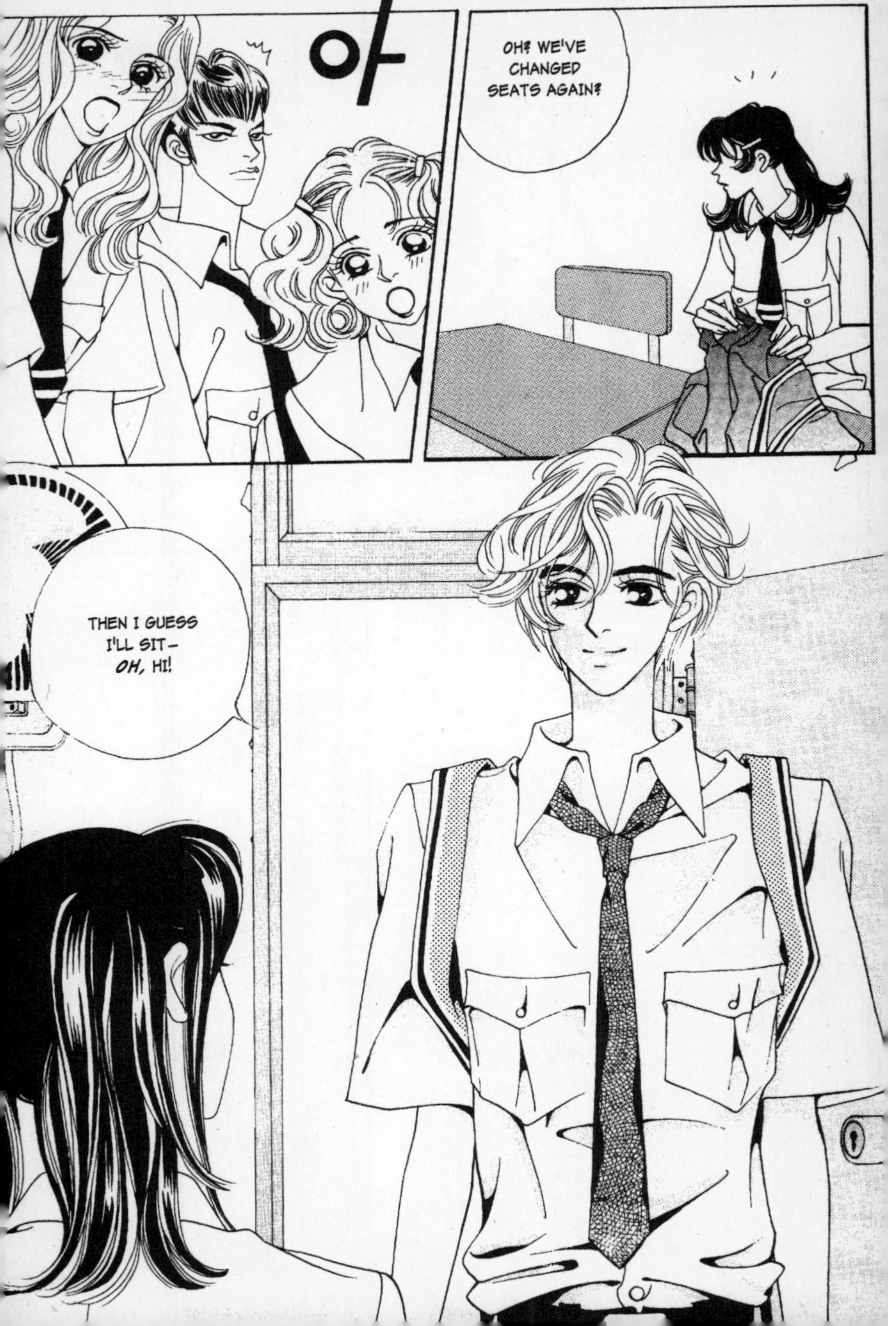
아
OH? WE'VE CHANGED SEATS AGAIN?
THEN I GUESS I'LL SIT— *OH,* HI!

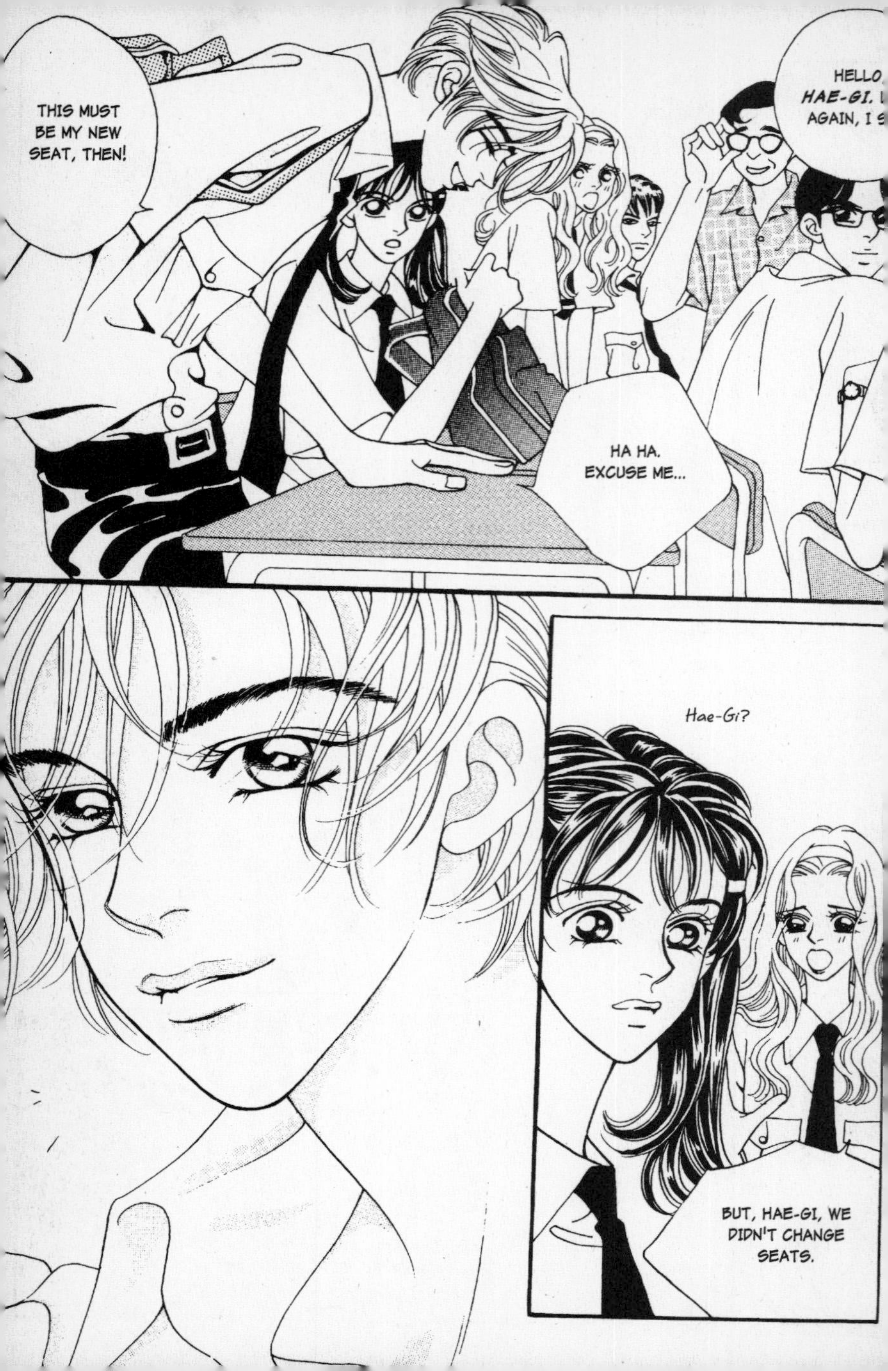
THIS MUST BE MY NEW SEAT, THEN!
HA HA. EXCUSE ME...
HELLO, HAE-GI.
AGAIN, I
Hae-Gi?
BUT, HAE-GI, WE DIDN'T CHANGE SEATS.

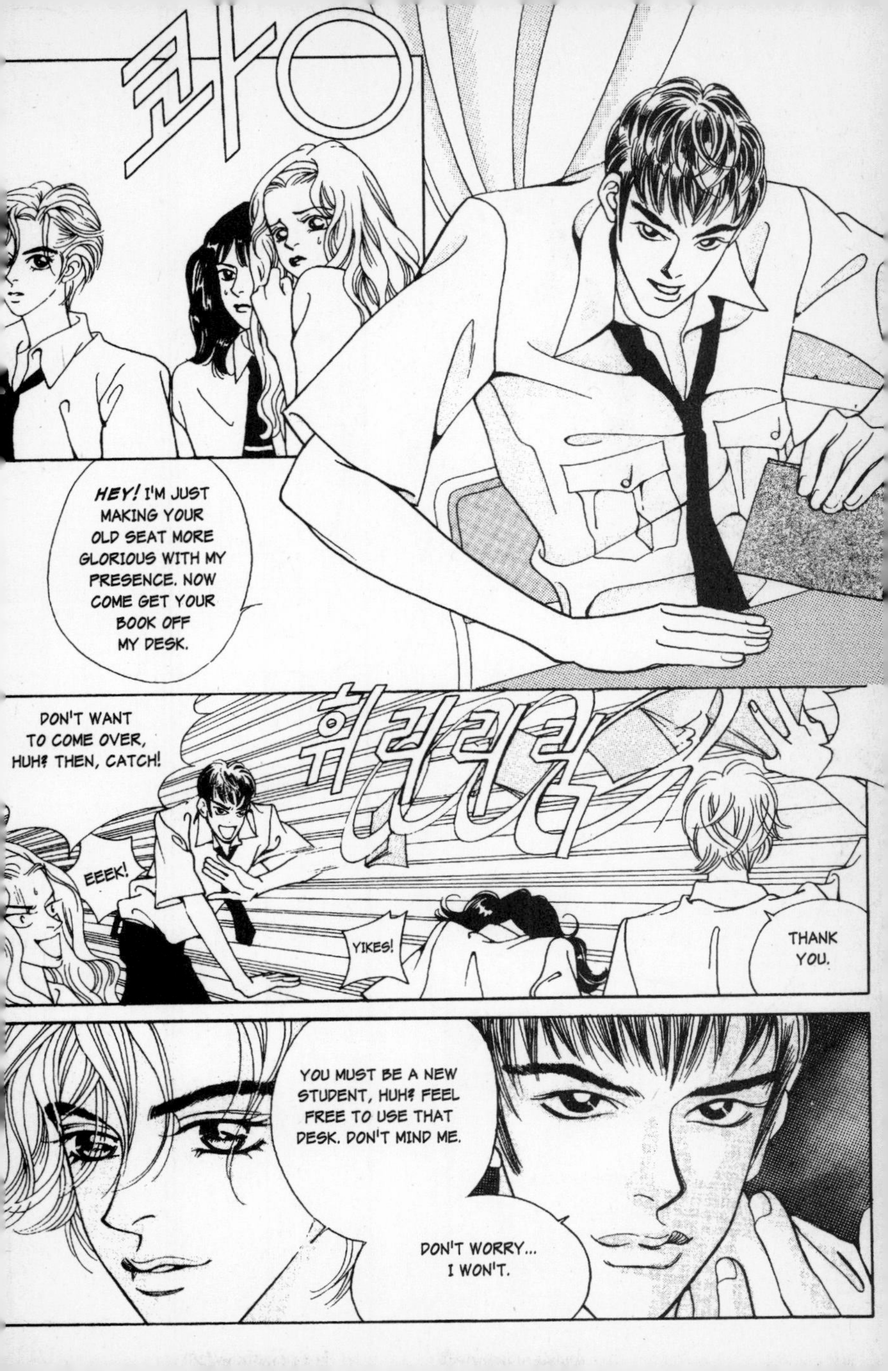
HEY! I'M JUST MAKING YOUR OLD SEAT MORE GLORIOUS WITH MY PRESENCE. NOW COME GET YOUR BOOK OFF MY DESK.
DON'T WANT TO COME OVER, HUH? THEN, CATCH!
휘리리릭
EEEK!
YIKES!
THANK YOU.
YOU MUST BE A NEW STUDENT, HUH? FEEL FREE TO USE THAT DESK. DON'T MIND ME.
DON'T WORRY... I WON'T.

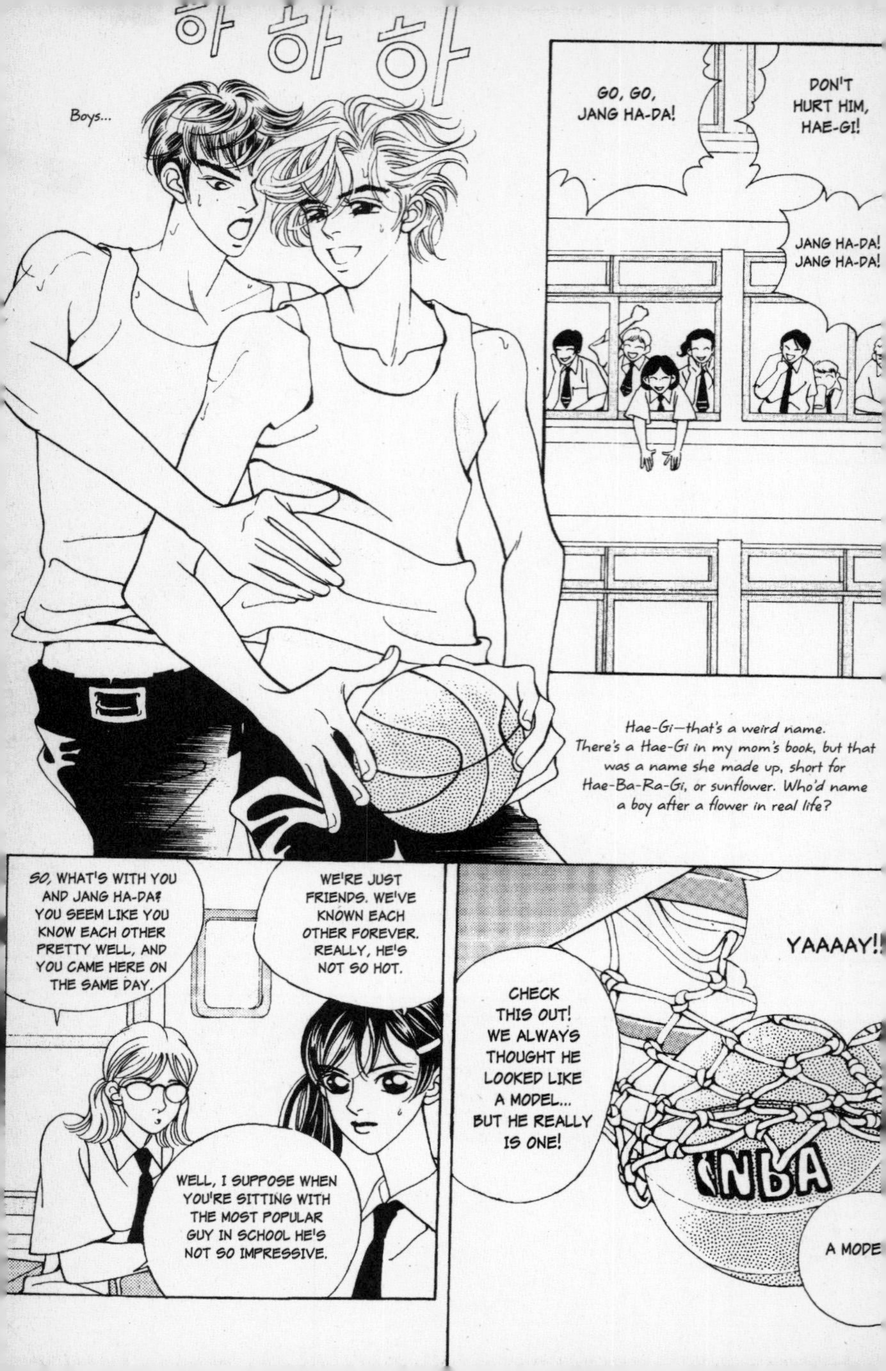
하 하 하
Boys...
GO, GO, JANG HA-DA!
DON'T HURT HIM, HAE-GI!
JANG HA-DA! JANG HA-DA!
Hae-Gi—that's a weird name. There's a Hae-Gi in my mom's book, but that was a name she made up, short for Hae-Ba-Ra-Gi, or sunflower. Who'd name a boy after a flower in real life?
SO, WHAT'S WITH YOU AND JANG HA-DA? YOU SEEM LIKE YOU KNOW EACH OTHER PRETTY WELL, AND YOU CAME HERE ON THE SAME DAY.
WE'RE JUST FRIENDS. WE'VE KNOWN EACH OTHER FOREVER. REALLY, HE'S NOT SO HOT.
WELL, I SUPPOSE WHEN YOU'RE SITTING WITH THE MOST POPULAR GUY IN SCHOOL HE'S NOT SO IMPRESSIVE.
YAAAAY!!
CHECK THIS OUT! WE ALWAYS THOUGHT HE LOOKED LIKE A MODEL... BUT HE REALLY IS ONE!
NBA
A MODE

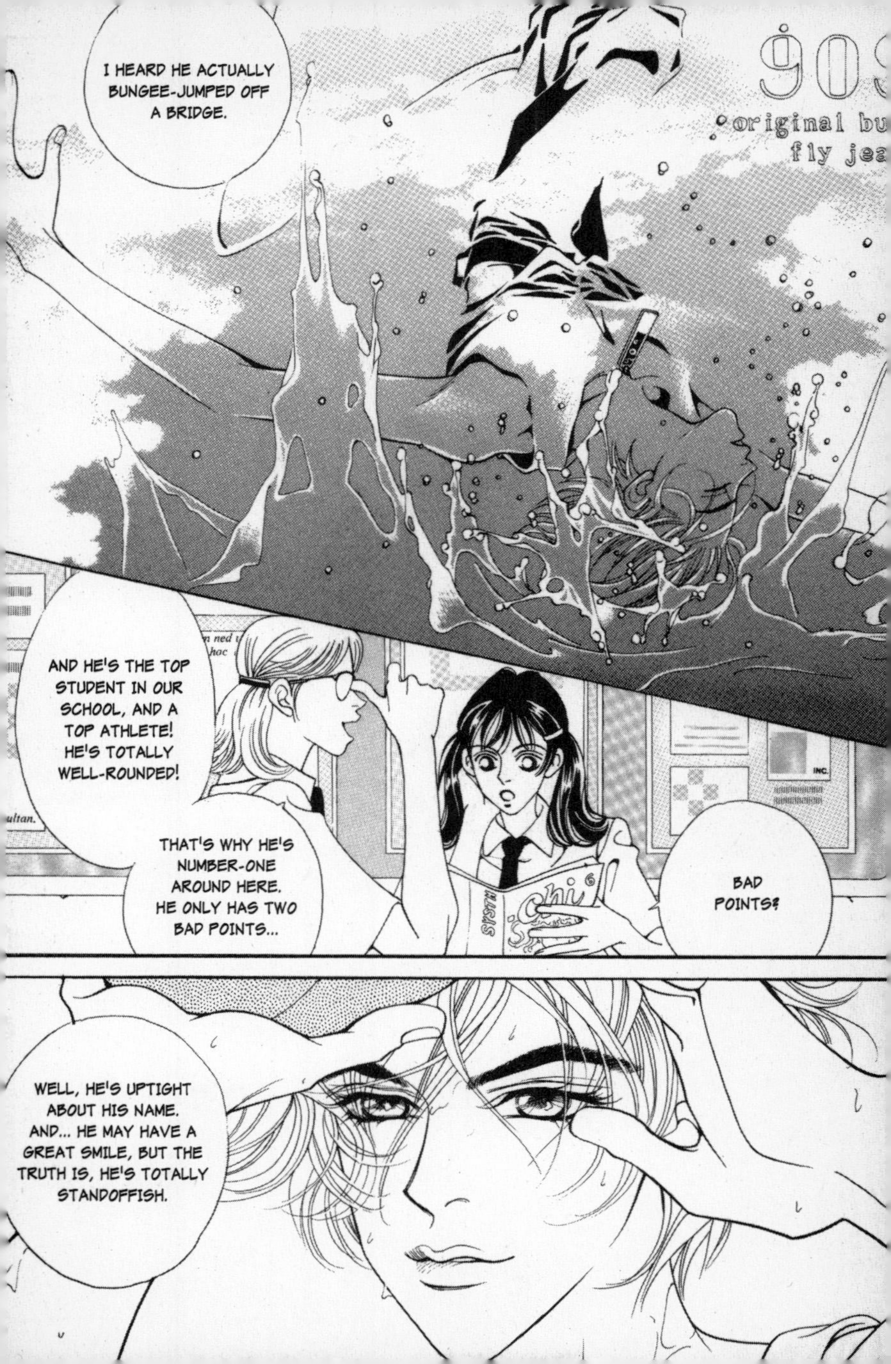
I HEARD HE ACTUALLY BUNGEE-JUMPED OFF A BRIDGE.
909
original bu
fly jea
AND HE'S THE TOP STUDENT IN OUR SCHOOL, AND A TOP ATHLETE! HE'S TOTALLY WELL-ROUNDED!
THAT'S WHY HE'S NUMBER-ONE AROUND HERE. HE ONLY HAS TWO BAD POINTS...
BAD POINTS?
WELL, HE'S UPTIGHT ABOUT HIS NAME. AND... HE MAY HAVE A GREAT SMILE, BUT THE TRUTH IS, HE'S TOTALLY STANDOFFISH.

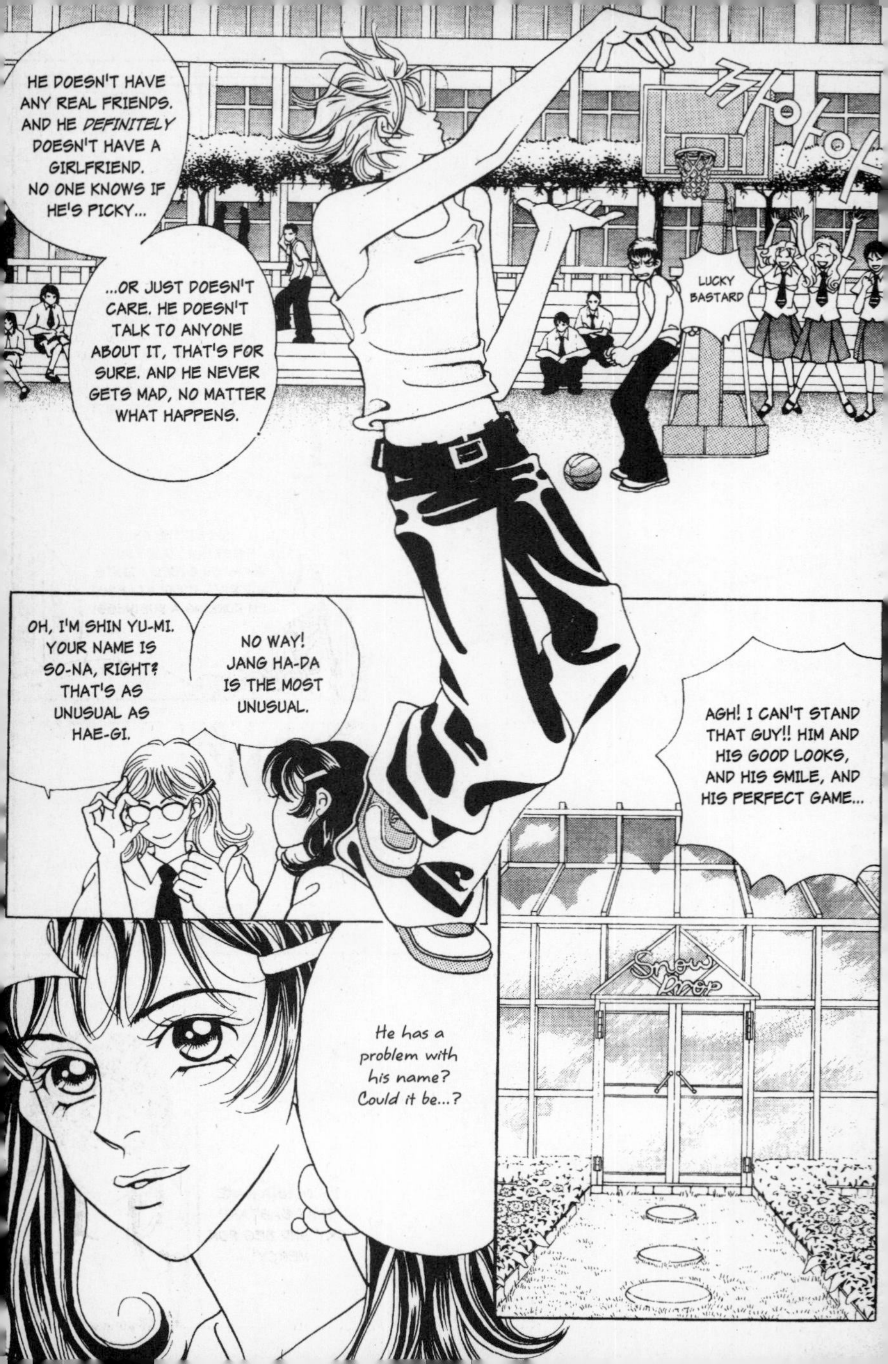
HE DOESN'T HAVE ANY REAL FRIENDS. AND HE *DEFINITELY* DOESN'T HAVE A GIRLFRIEND. NO ONE KNOWS IF HE'S PICKY...
...OR JUST DOESN'T CARE. HE DOESN'T TALK TO ANYONE ABOUT IT, THAT'S FOR SURE. AND HE NEVER GETS MAD, NO MATTER WHAT HAPPENS.
꺄아아아
LUCKY BASTARD
OH, I'M SHIN YU-MI. YOUR NAME IS SO-NA, RIGHT? THAT'S AS UNUSUAL AS HAE-GI.
NO WAY! JANG HA-DA IS THE MOST UNUSUAL.
AGH! I CAN'T STAND THAT GUY!! HIM AND HIS GOOD LOOKS, AND HIS SMILE, AND HIS PERFECT GAME...
He has a problem with his name? Could it be...?
Snow Drop

1

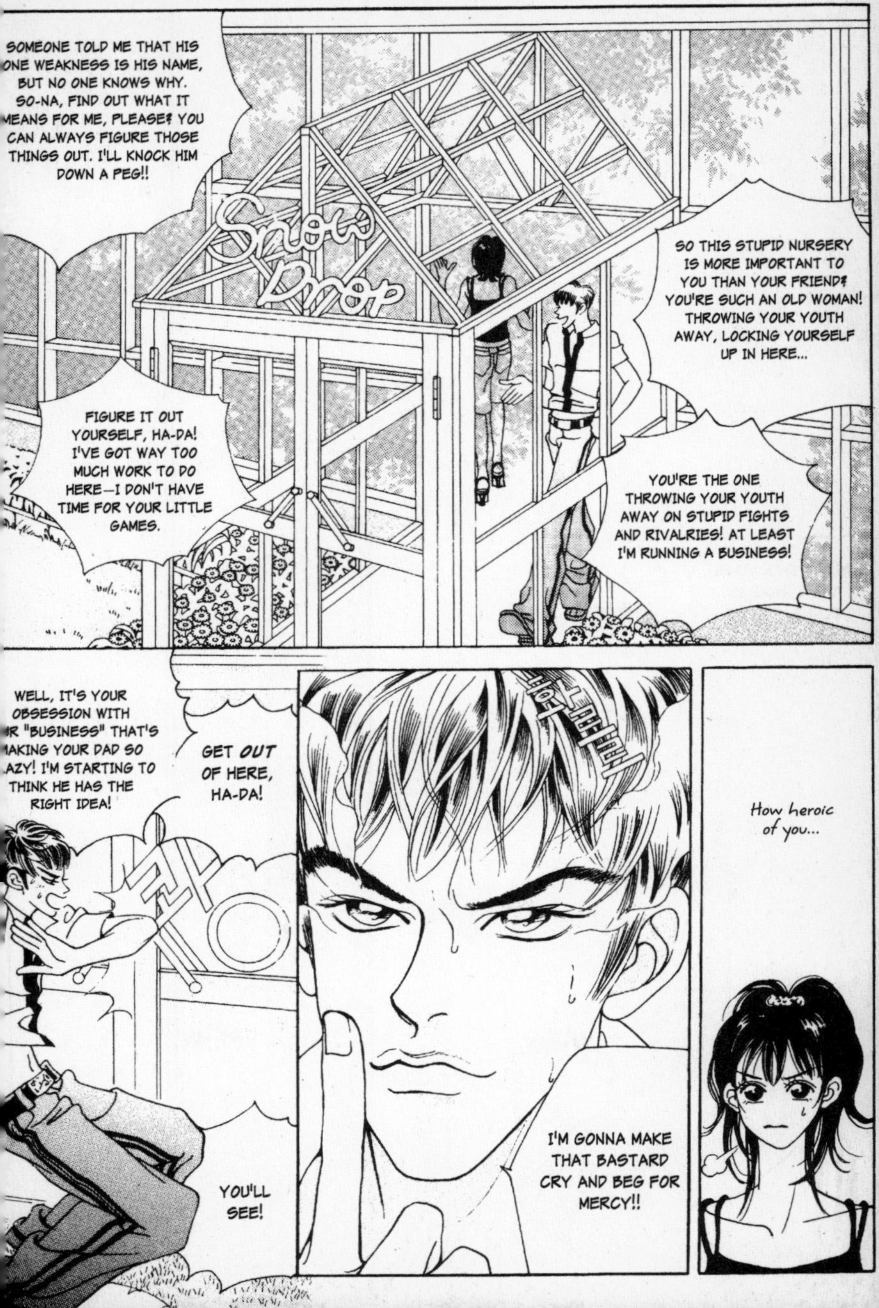
SOMEONE TOLD ME THAT HIS ONE WEAKNESS IS HIS NAME, BUT NO ONE KNOWS WHY. SO-NA, FIND OUT WHAT IT MEANS FOR ME, PLEASE? YOU CAN ALWAYS FIGURE THOSE THINGS OUT. I'LL KNOCK HIM DOWN A PEG!!
SO THIS STUPID NURSERY IS MORE IMPORTANT TO YOU THAN YOUR FRIEND? YOU'RE SUCH AN OLD WOMAN! THROWING YOUR YOUTH AWAY, LOCKING YOURSELF UP IN HERE...
Snow Drop
FIGURE IT OUT YOURSELF, HA-DA! I'VE GOT WAY TOO MUCH WORK TO DO HERE—I DON'T HAVE TIME FOR YOUR LITTLE GAMES.
YOU'RE THE ONE THROWING YOUR YOUTH AWAY ON STUPID FIGHTS AND RIVALRIES! AT LEAST I'M RUNNING A BUSINESS!
WELL, IT'S YOUR OBSESSION WITH R "BUSINESS" THAT'S AKING YOUR DAD SO AZY! I'M STARTING TO THINK HE HAS THE RIGHT IDEA!
GET OUT OF HERE, HA-DA!
YOU'LL SEE!
I'M GONNA MAKE THAT BASTARD CRY AND BEG FOR MERCY!!
How heroic of you...

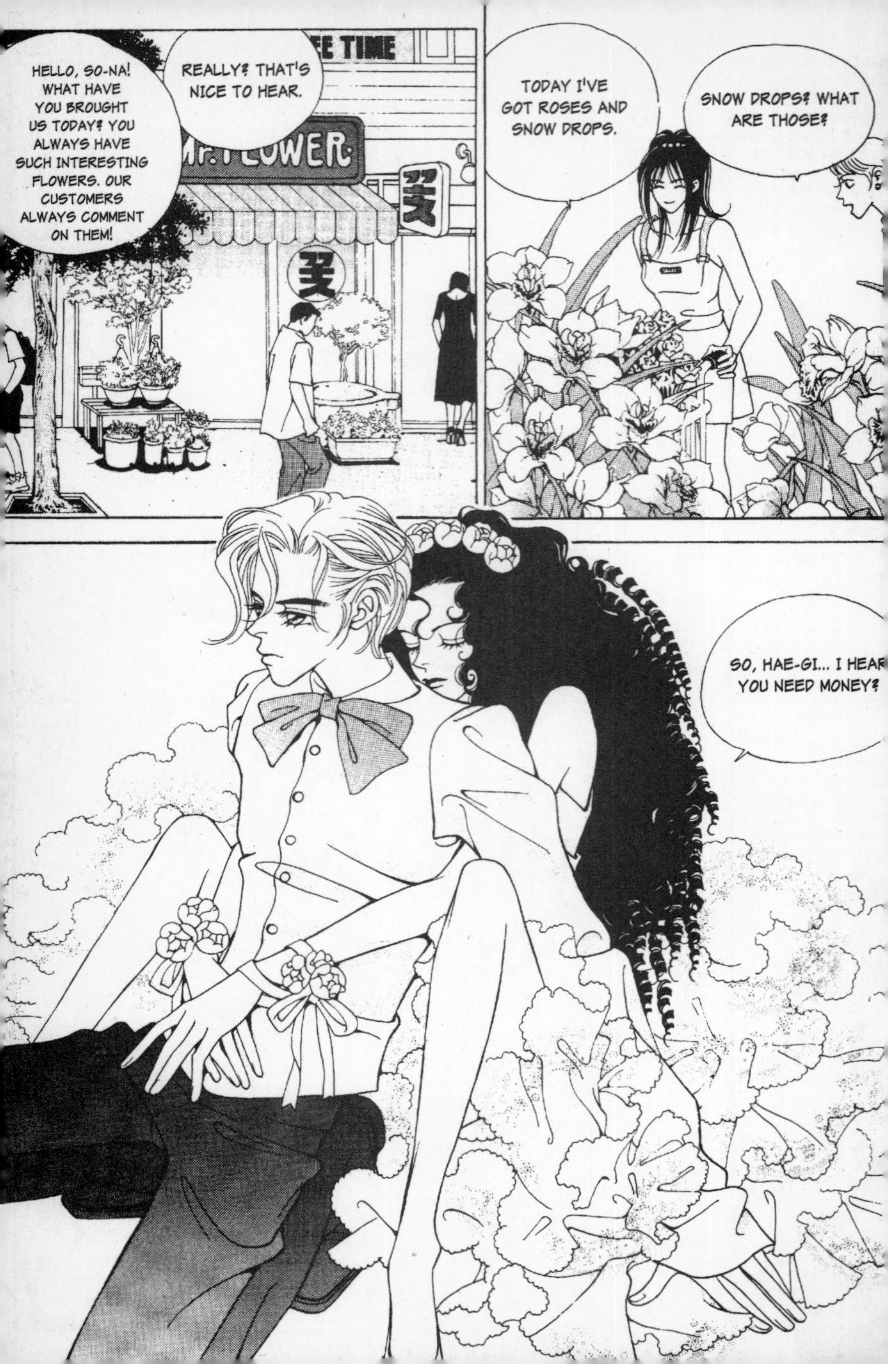
HELLO, SO-NA! WHAT HAVE YOU BROUGHT US TODAY? YOU ALWAYS HAVE SUCH INTERESTING FLOWERS. OUR CUSTOMERS ALWAYS COMMENT ON THEM!
REALLY? THAT'S NICE TO HEAR.
TODAY I'VE GOT ROSES AND SNOW DROPS.
SNOW DROPS? WHAT ARE THOSE?
SO, HAE-GI... I HEAR YOU NEED MONEY?

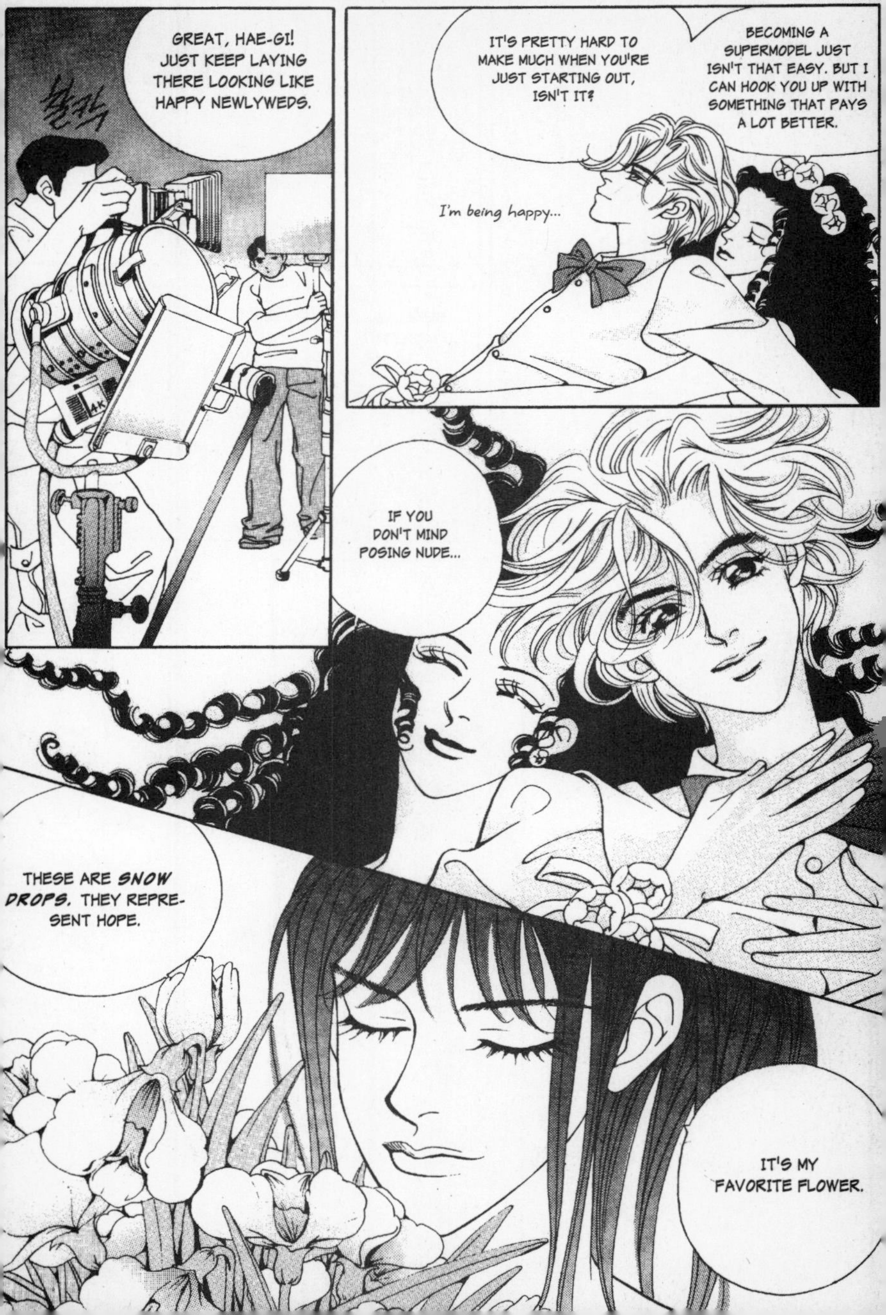
GREAT, HAE-GI! JUST KEEP LAYING THERE LOOKING LIKE HAPPY NEWLYWEDS.
IT'S PRETTY HARD TO MAKE MUCH WHEN YOU'RE JUST STARTING OUT, ISN'T IT?
BECOMING A SUPERMODEL JUST ISN'T THAT EASY. BUT I CAN HOOK YOU UP WITH SOMETHING THAT PAYS A LOT BETTER.
I'm being happy...
IF YOU DON'T MIND POSING NUDE...
THESE ARE *SNOW DROPS.* THEY REPRESENT HOPE.
IT'S MY FAVORITE FLOWER.

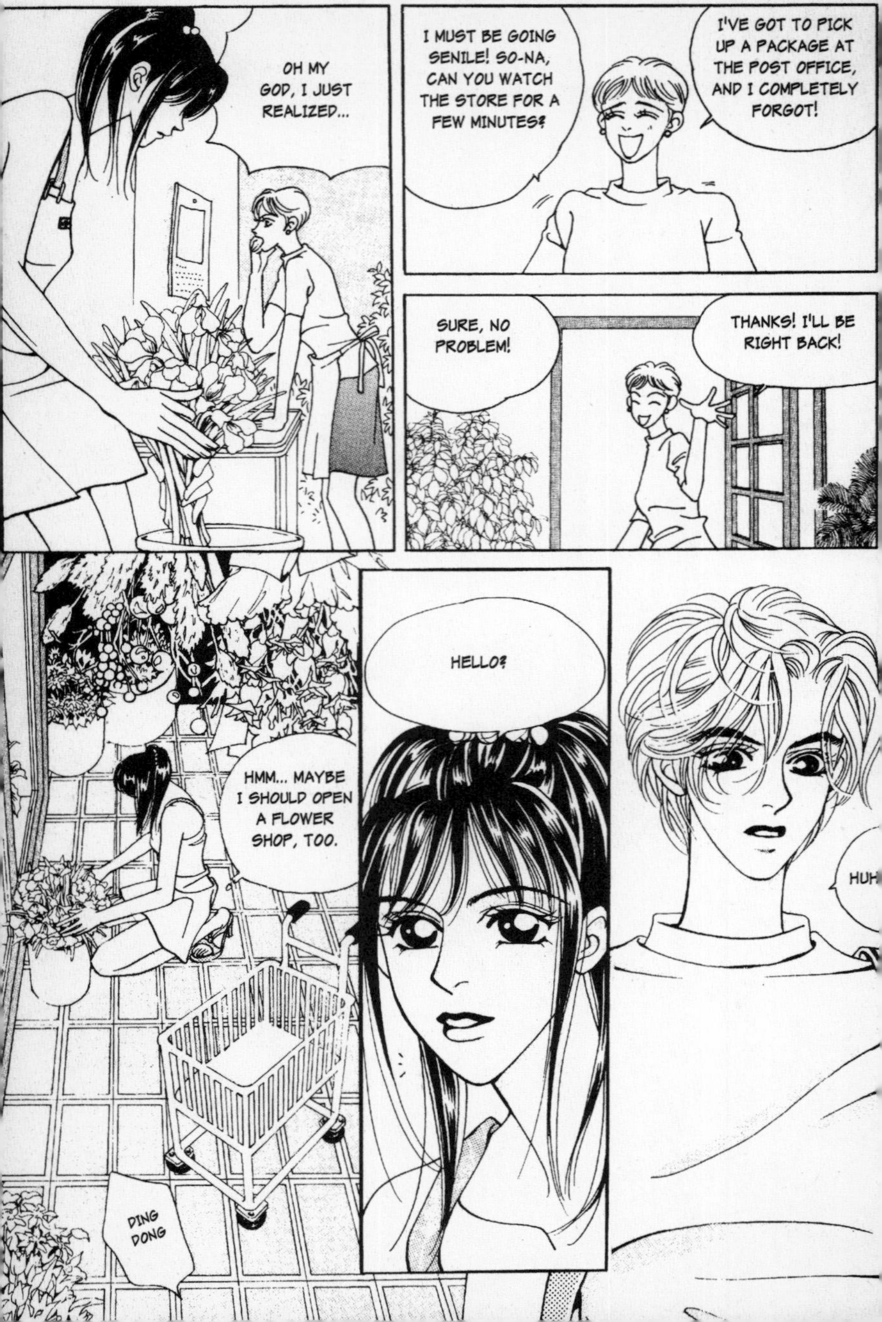
OH MY GOD, I JUST REALIZED...
I MUST BE GOING SENILE! SO-NA, CAN YOU WATCH THE STORE FOR A FEW MINUTES?
I'VE GOT TO PICK UP A PACKAGE AT THE POST OFFICE, AND I COMPLETELY FORGOT!
SURE, NO PROBLEM!
THANKS! I'LL BE RIGHT BACK!
HMM... MAYBE I SHOULD OPEN A FLOWER SHOP, TOO.
DING DONG
HELLO?
HUH

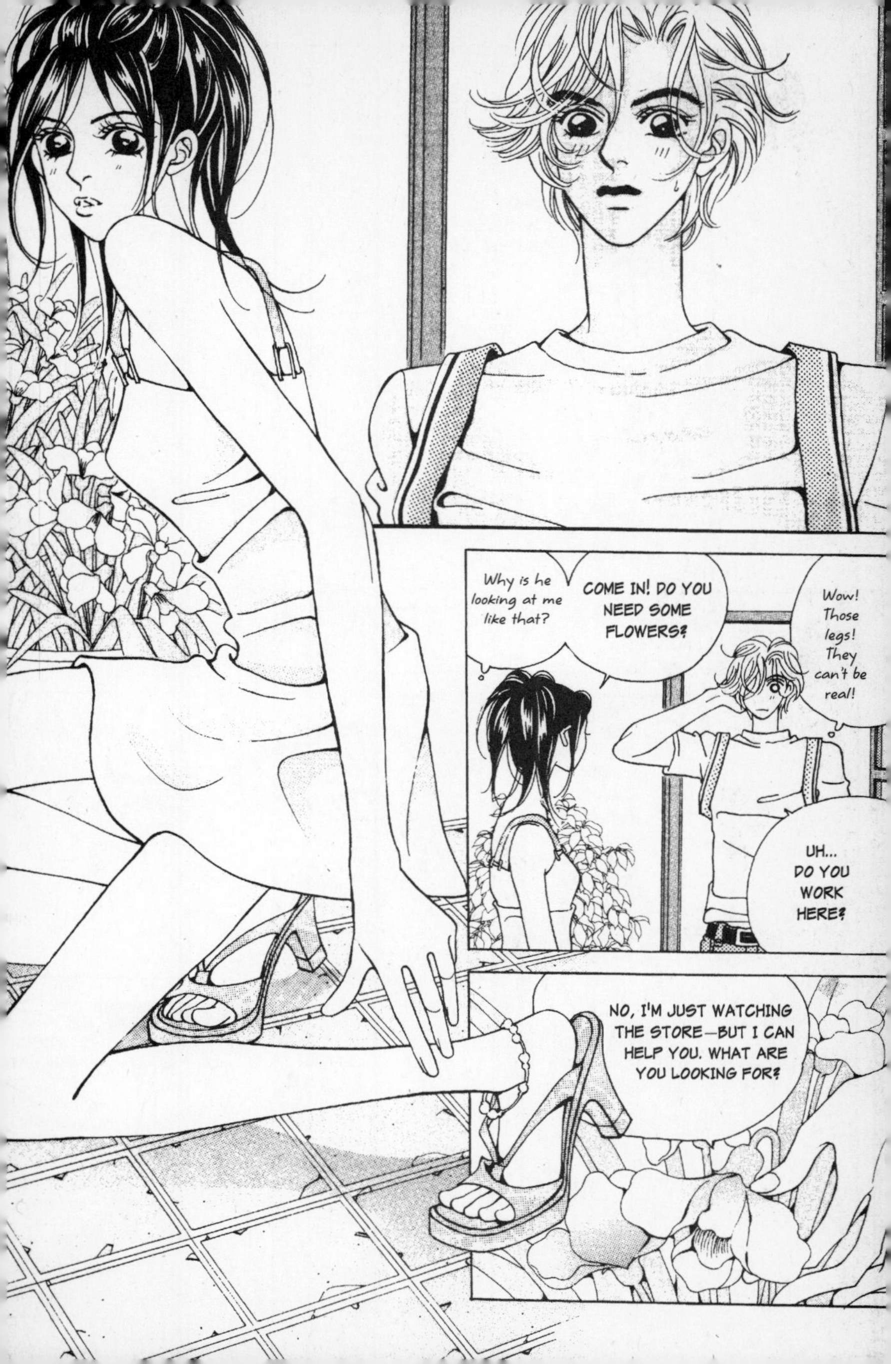
Wow! Those legs! They can't be real!
COME IN! DO YOU NEED SOME FLOWERS?
Why is he looking at me like that?
UH... DO YOU WORK HERE?
NO, I'M JUST WATCHING THE STORE—BUT I CAN HELP YOU. WHAT ARE YOU LOOKING FOR?

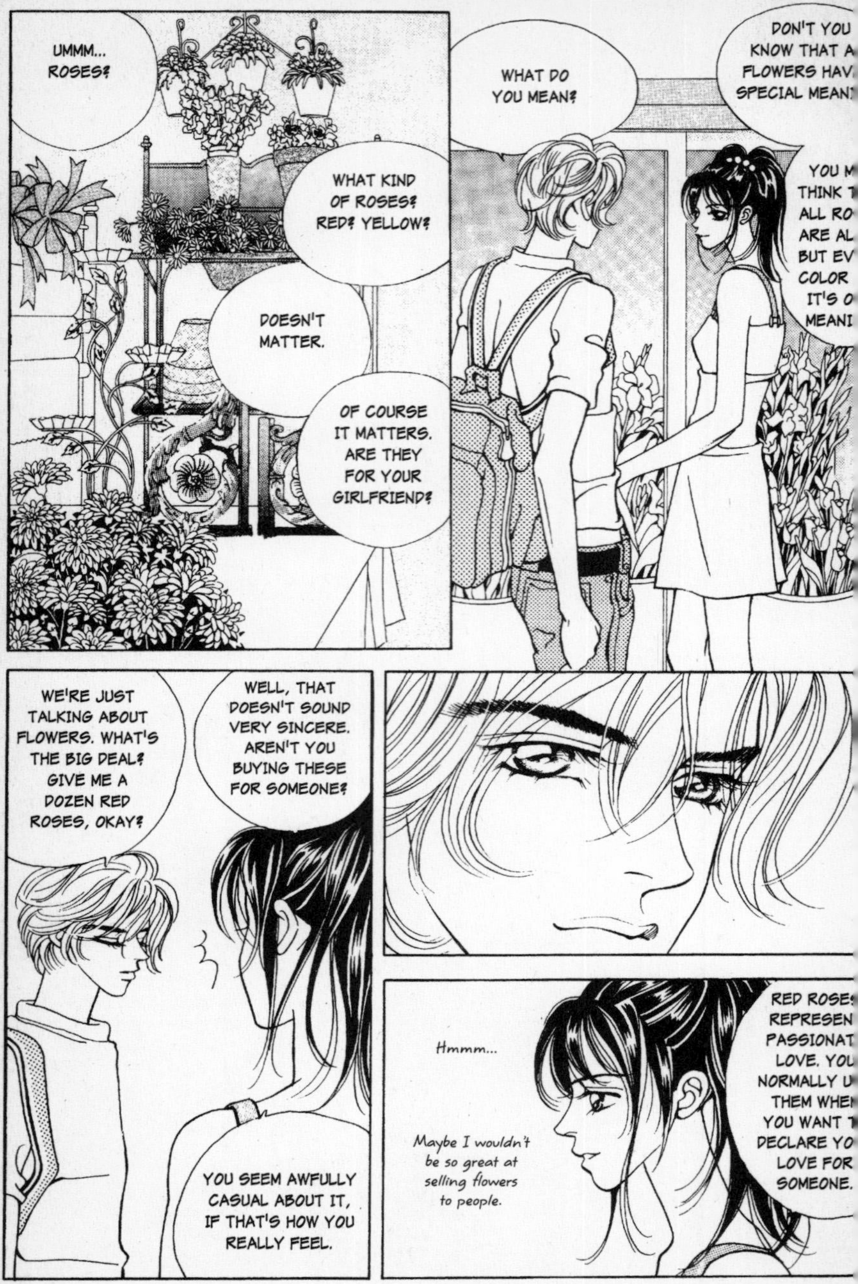
UMMM... ROSES?
WHAT KIND OF ROSES? RED? YELLOW?
DOESN'T MATTER.
OF COURSE IT MATTERS. ARE THEY FOR YOUR GIRLFRIEND?
WHAT DO YOU MEAN?
DON'T YOU KNOW THAT A FLOWERS HAV SPECIAL MEAN
YOU M THINK T ALL RO ARE AL BUT EV COLOR IT'S O MEANI
WE'RE JUST TALKING ABOUT FLOWERS. WHAT'S THE BIG DEAL? GIVE ME A DOZEN RED ROSES, OKAY?
WELL, THAT DOESN'T SOUND VERY SINCERE. AREN'T YOU BUYING THESE FOR SOMEONE?
YOU SEEM AWFULLY CASUAL ABOUT IT, IF THAT'S HOW YOU REALLY FEEL.
Hmmm...
Maybe I wouldn't be so great at selling flowers to people.
RED ROSE REPRESEN PASSIONAT LOVE. YOU NORMALLY U THEM WHE YOU WANT T DECLARE YO LOVE FOR SOMEONE.

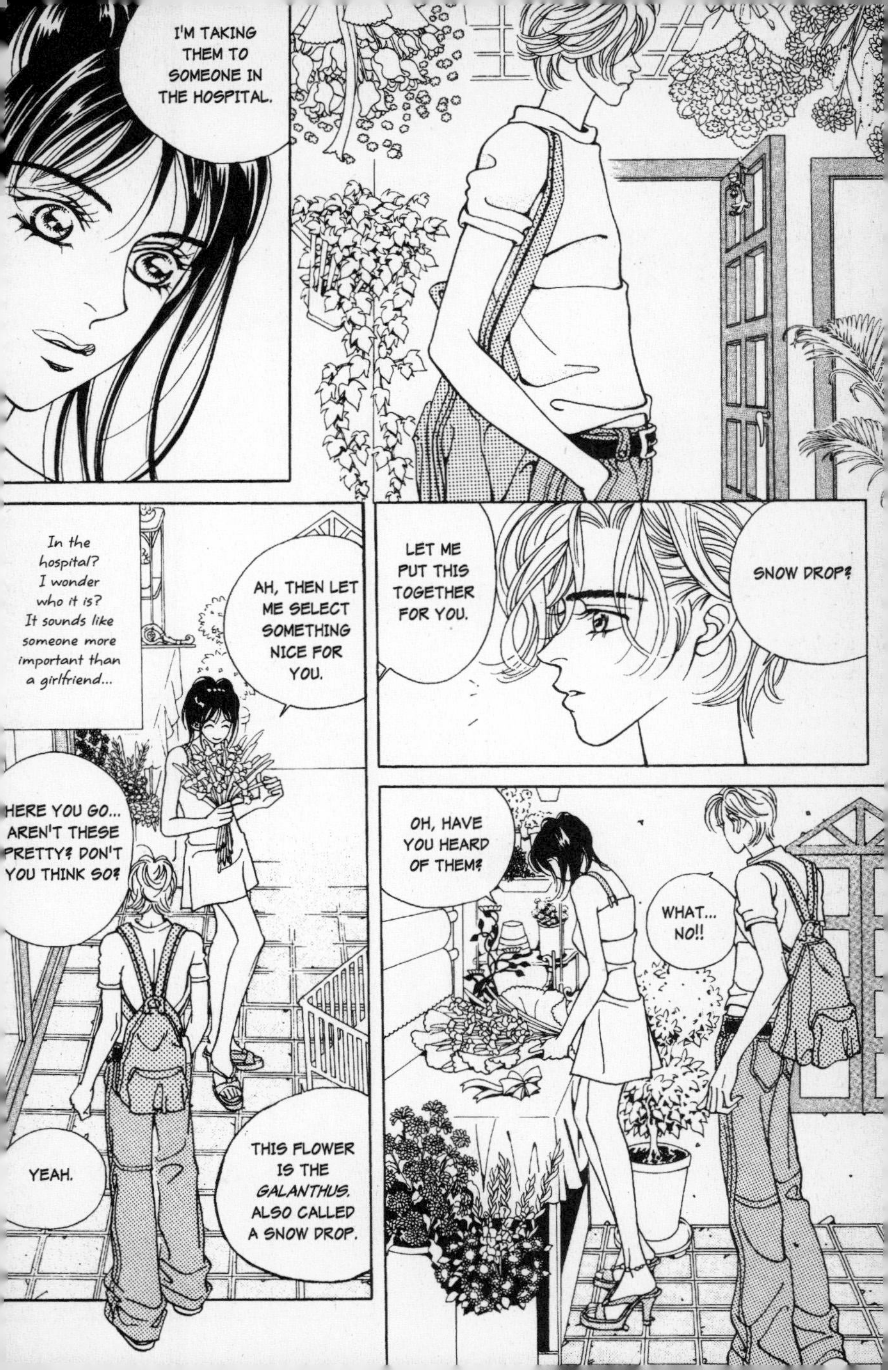
I'M TAKING THEM TO SOMEONE IN THE HOSPITAL.
In the hospital? I wonder who it is? It sounds like someone more important than a girlfriend...
AH, THEN LET ME SELECT SOMETHING NICE FOR YOU.
HERE YOU GO... AREN'T THESE PRETTY? DON'T YOU THINK SO?
THIS FLOWER IS THE GALANTHUS. ALSO CALLED A SNOW DROP.
YEAH.
LET ME PUT THIS TOGETHER FOR YOU.
SNOW DROP?
OH, HAVE YOU HEARD OF THEM?
WHAT... NO!!

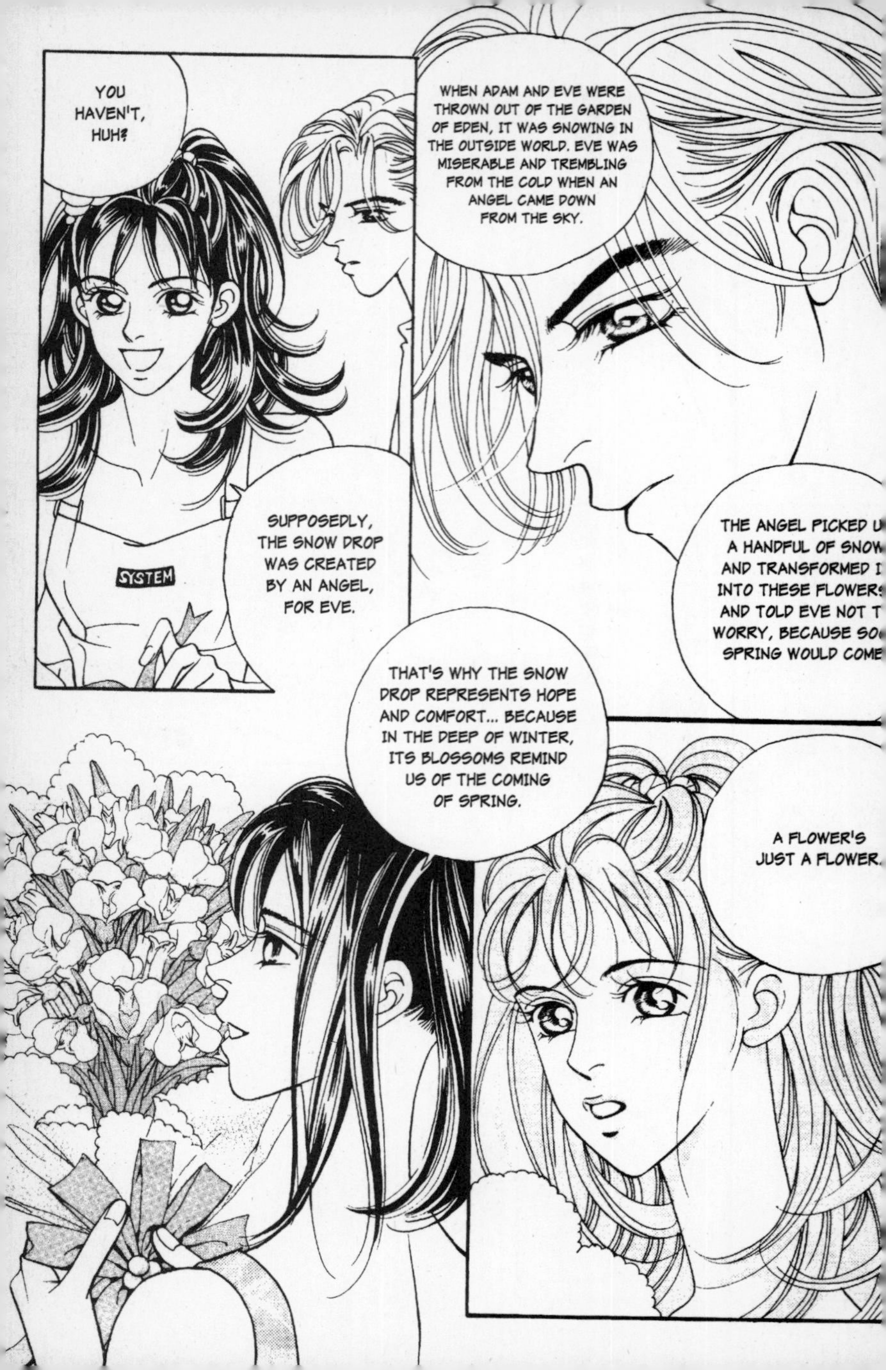
YOU HAVEN'T, HUH?
SUPPOSEDLY, THE SNOW DROP WAS CREATED BY AN ANGEL, FOR EVE.
SYSTEM
WHEN ADAM AND EVE WERE THROWN OUT OF THE GARDEN OF EDEN, IT WAS SNOWING IN THE OUTSIDE WORLD. EVE WAS MISERABLE AND TREMBLING FROM THE COLD WHEN AN ANGEL CAME DOWN FROM THE SKY.
THE ANGEL PICKED U A HANDFUL OF SNOW AND TRANSFORMED I INTO THESE FLOWERS AND TOLD EVE NOT T WORRY, BECAUSE SO SPRING WOULD COME
THAT'S WHY THE SNOW DROP REPRESENTS HOPE AND COMFORT... BECAUSE IN THE DEEP OF WINTER, ITS BLOSSOMS REMIND US OF THE COMING OF SPRING.
A FLOWER'S JUST A FLOWER.

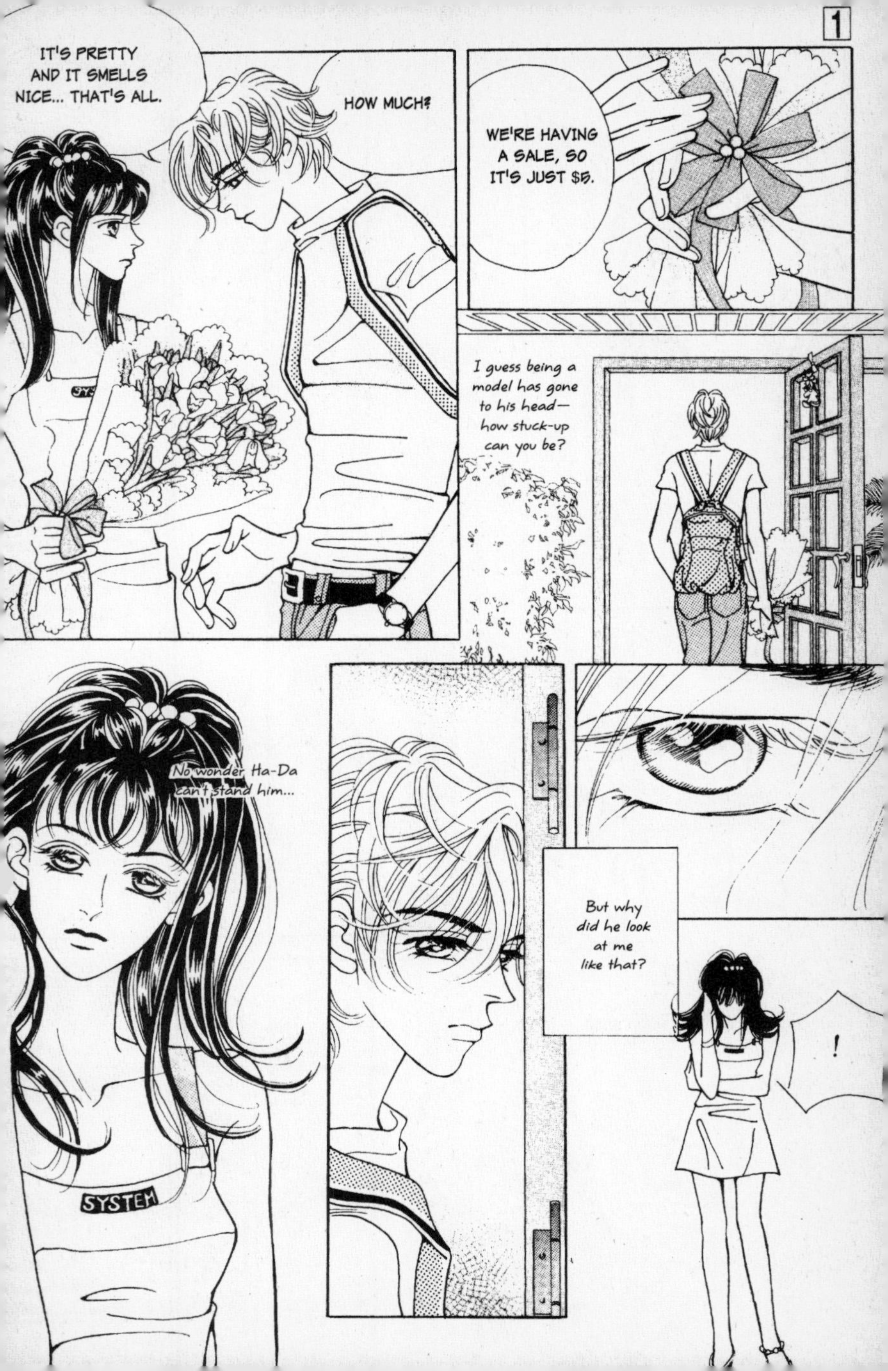
1
IT'S PRETTY AND IT SMELLS NICE... THAT'S ALL.
HOW MUCH?
WE'RE HAVING A SALE, SO IT'S JUST $5.
I guess being a model has gone to his head— how stuck-up can you be?
No wonder Ha-Da can't stand him...
But why did he look at me like that?
!

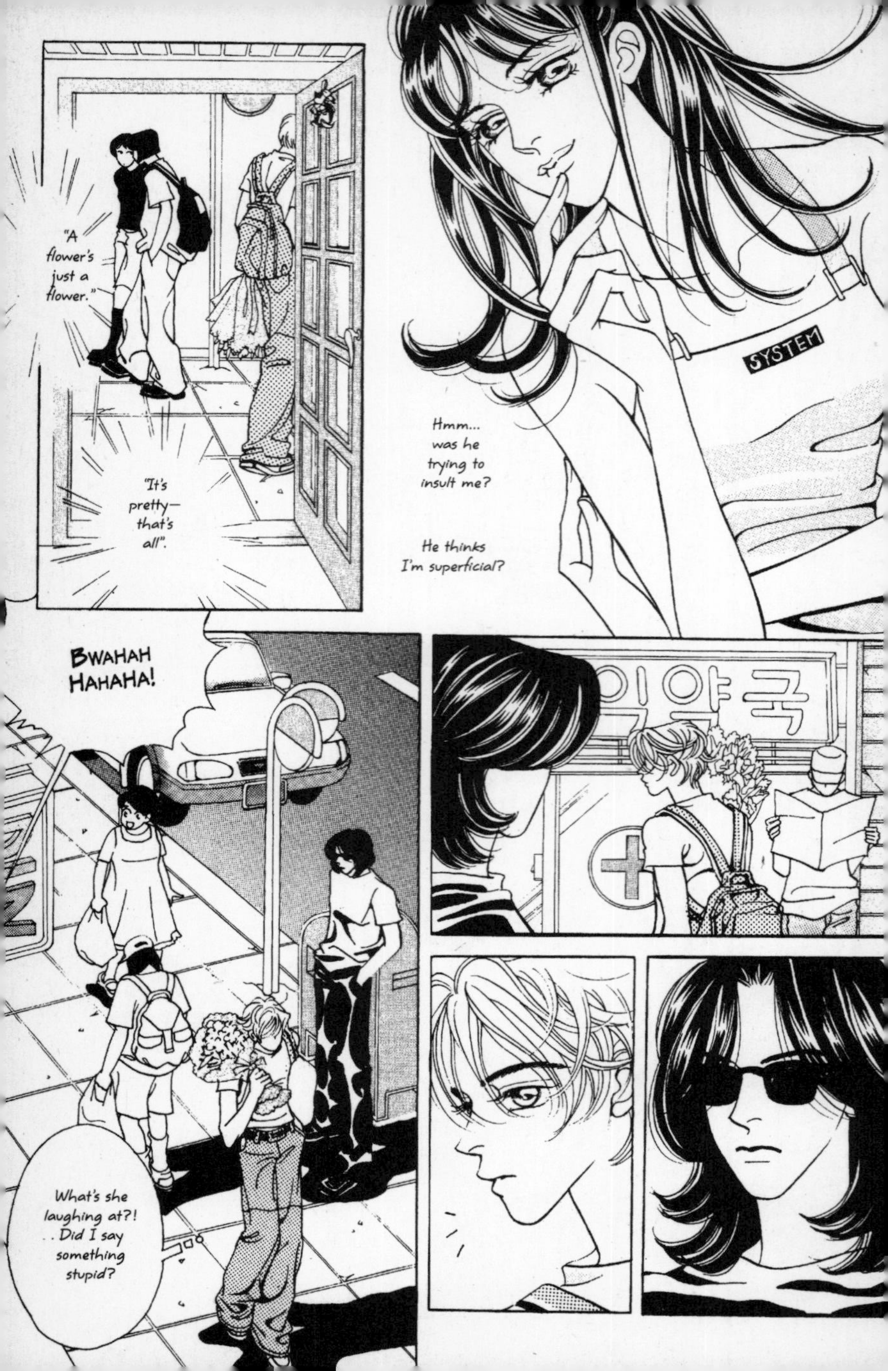
"A flower's just a flower."
"It's pretty— that's all".
Hmm... was he trying to insult me?
He thinks I'm superficial?
SYSTEM
BWAHAH HAHAHA!
What's she laughing at?! . . Did I say something stupid?
약국

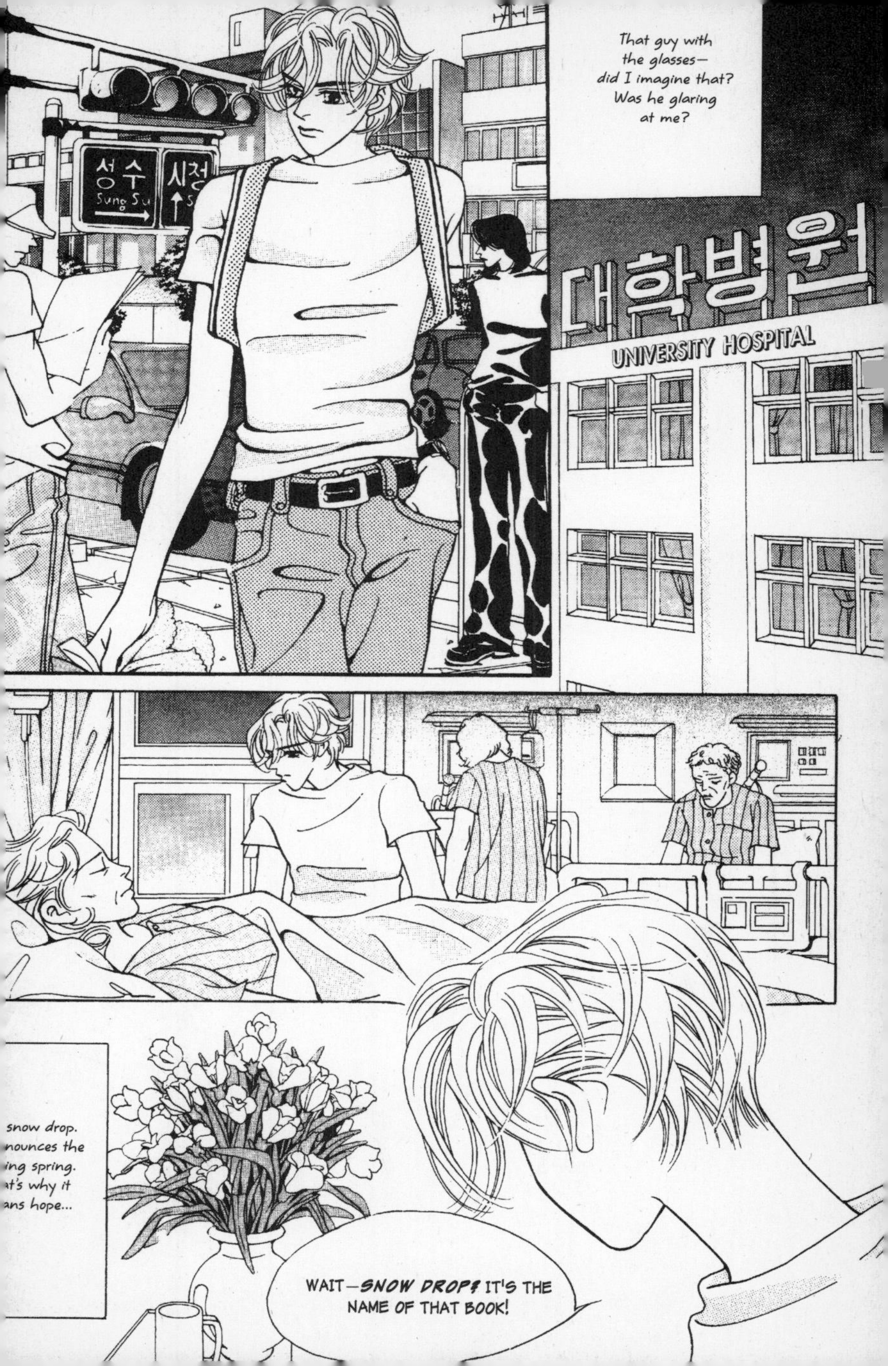
성수
Sung Su
시청
That guy with the glasses— did I imagine that? Was he glaring at me?
대학병원
UNIVERSITY HOSPITAL
snow drop. nounces the ing spring. at's why it ans hope...
WAIT—SNOW DROP? IT'S THE NAME OF THAT BOOK!

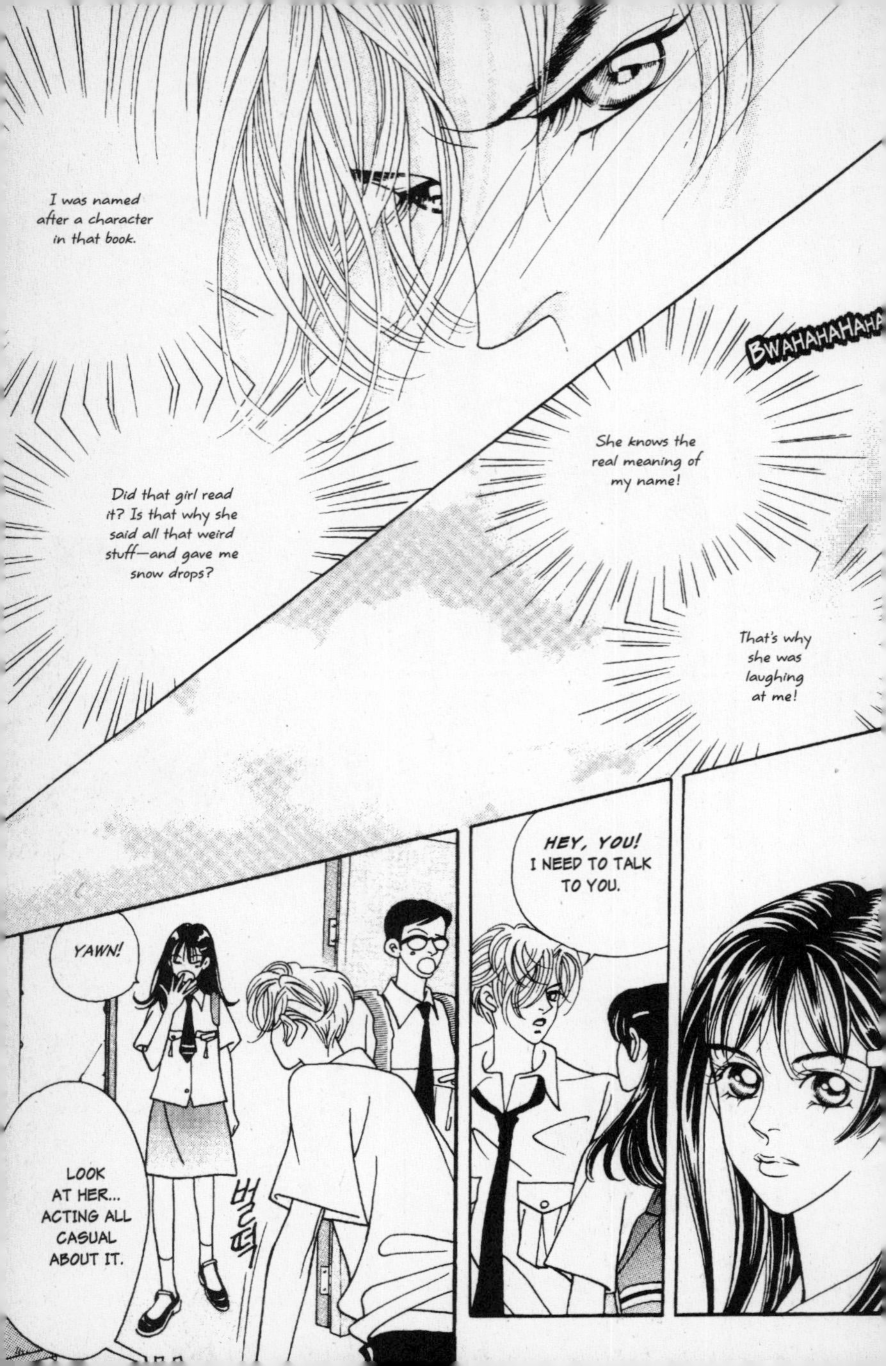
I was named after a character in that book.
Did that girl read it? Is that why she said all that weird stuff—and gave me snow drops?
BWAHAHAHAHA
She knows the real meaning of my name!
That's why she was laughing at me!
YAWN!
LOOK AT HER... ACTING ALL CASUAL ABOUT IT.
벌떡
HEY, YOU! I NEED TO TALK TO YOU.

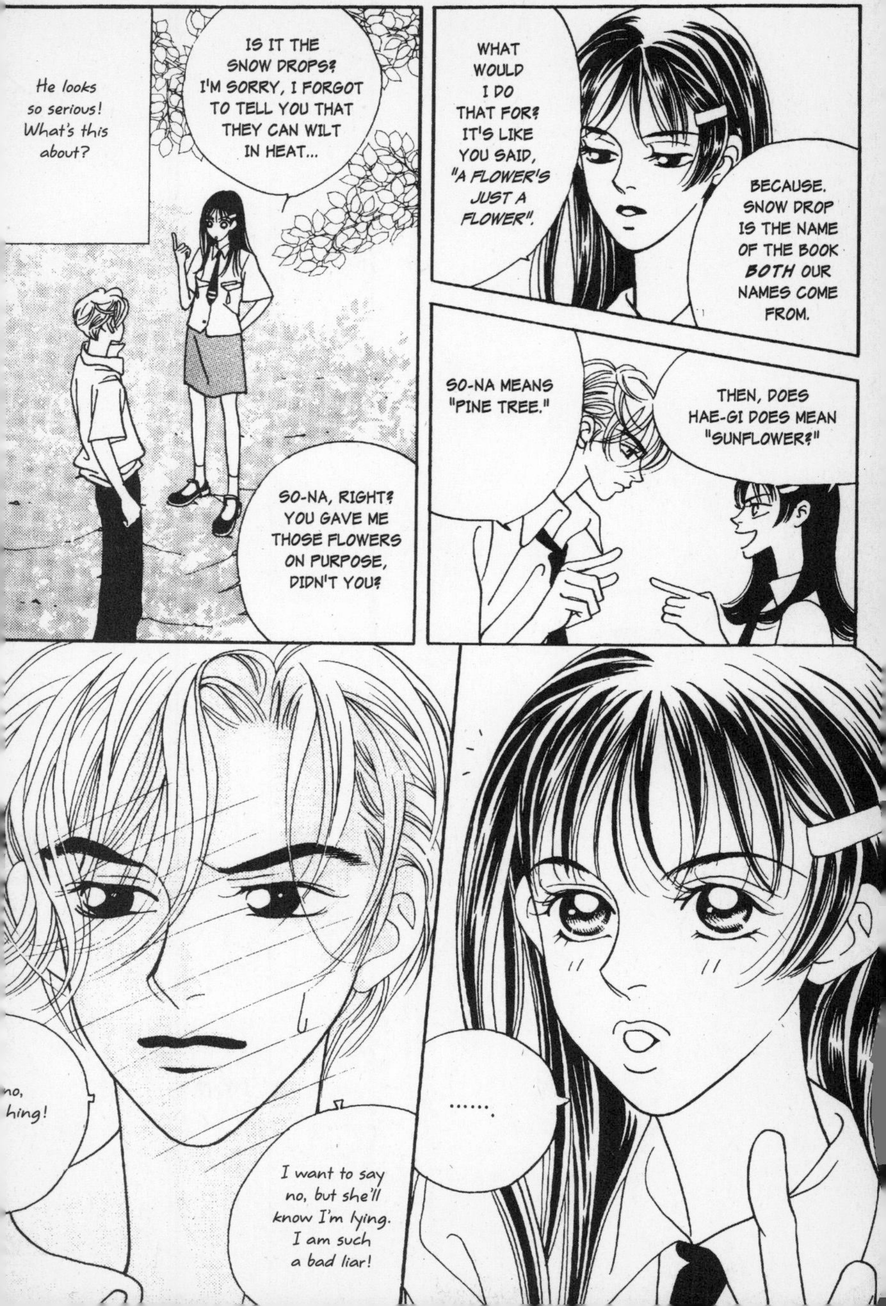
He looks so serious! What's this about?
IS IT THE SNOW DROPS? I'M SORRY, I FORGOT TO TELL YOU THAT THEY CAN WILT IN HEAT...
SO-NA, RIGHT? YOU GAVE ME THOSE FLOWERS ON PURPOSE, DIDN'T YOU?
WHAT WOULD I DO THAT FOR? IT'S LIKE YOU SAID, "A FLOWER'S JUST A FLOWER".
BECAUSE. SNOW DROP IS THE NAME OF THE BOOK BOTH OUR NAMES COME FROM.
SO-NA MEANS "PINE TREE."
THEN, DOES HAE-GI DOES MEAN "SUNFLOWER?"
I want to say no, but she'll know I'm lying. I am such a bad liar!
......

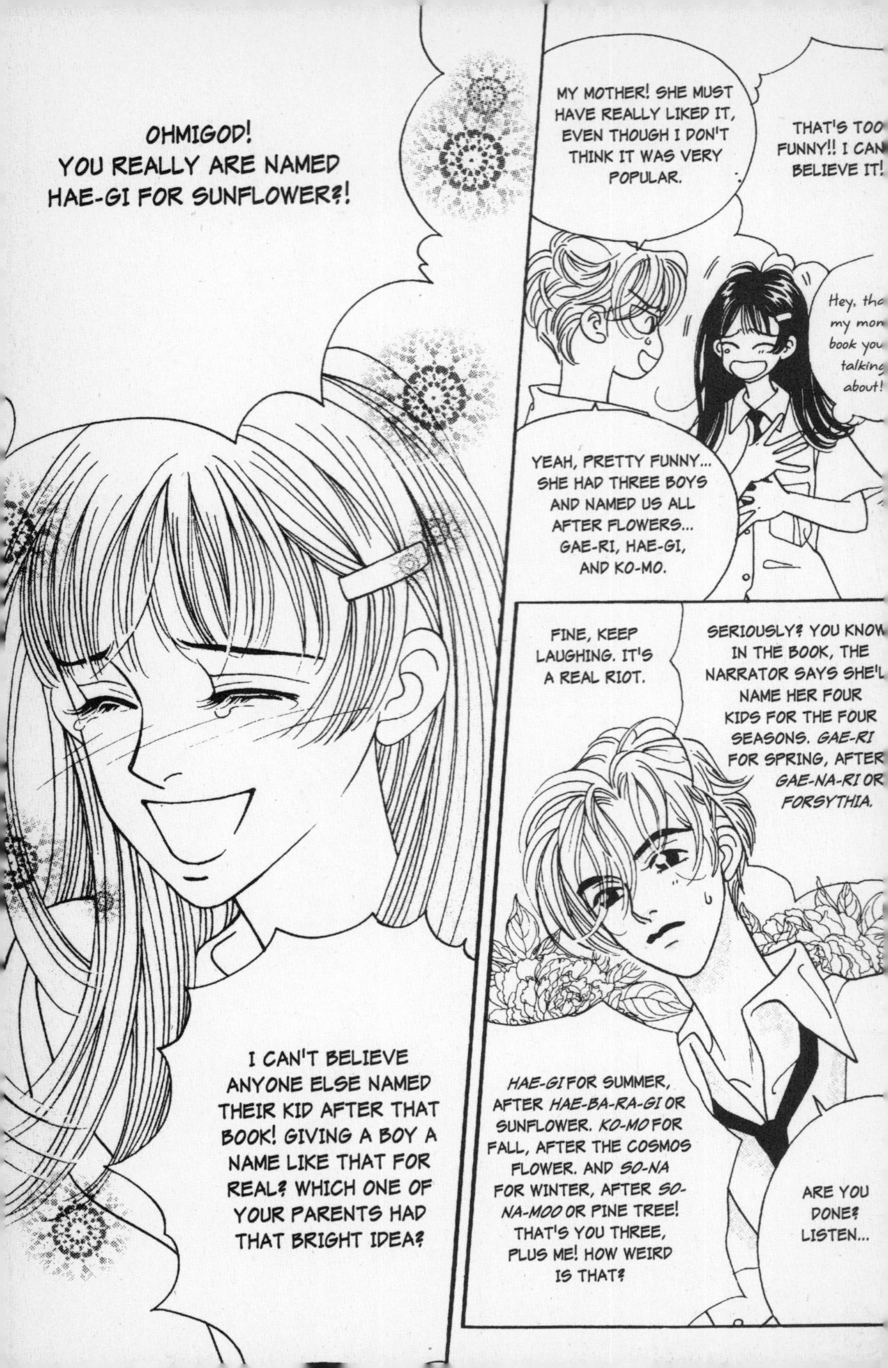
OHMIGOD! YOU REALLY ARE NAMED HAE-GI FOR SUNFLOWER?!
I CAN'T BELIEVE ANYONE ELSE NAMED THEIR KID AFTER THAT BOOK! GIVING A BOY A NAME LIKE THAT FOR REAL? WHICH ONE OF YOUR PARENTS HAD THAT BRIGHT IDEA?
MY MOTHER! SHE MUST HAVE REALLY LIKED IT, EVEN THOUGH I DON'T THINK IT WAS VERY POPULAR.
THAT'S TOO FUNNY!! I CAN BELIEVE IT!
Hey, tha my mom book you talking about!
YEAH, PRETTY FUNNY... SHE HAD THREE BOYS AND NAMED US ALL AFTER FLOWERS... GAE-RI, HAE-GI, AND KO-MO.
FINE, KEEP LAUGHING. IT'S A REAL RIOT.
SERIOUSLY? YOU KNOW IN THE BOOK, THE NARRATOR SAYS SHE'L NAME HER FOUR KIDS FOR THE FOUR SEASONS. *GAE-RI* FOR SPRING, AFTER *GAE-NA-RI* OR *FORSYTHIA.*
HAE-GI FOR SUMMER, AFTER *HAE-BA-RA-GI* OR SUNFLOWER. *KO-MO* FOR FALL, AFTER THE COSMOS FLOWER. AND *SO-NA* FOR WINTER, AFTER *SO-NA-MOO* OR PINE TREE! THAT'S YOU THREE, PLUS ME! HOW WEIRD IS THAT?
ARE YOU DONE? LISTEN...

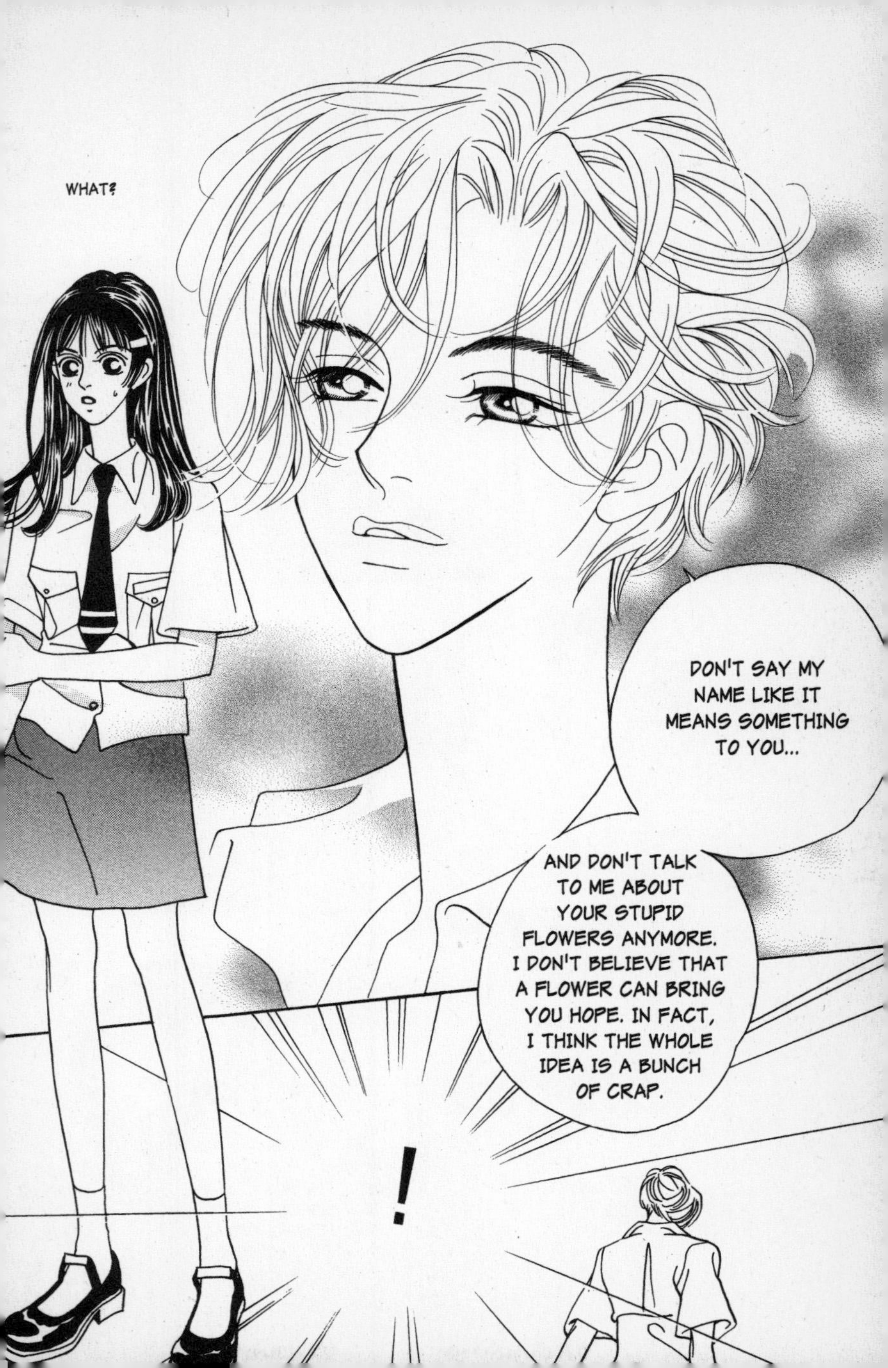
WHAT?
DON'T SAY MY NAME LIKE IT MEANS SOMETHING TO YOU...
AND DON'T TALK TO ME ABOUT YOUR STUPID FLOWERS ANYMORE. I DON'T BELIEVE THAT A FLOWER CAN BRING YOU HOPE. IN FACT, I THINK THE WHOLE IDEA IS A BUNCH OF CRAP.
!

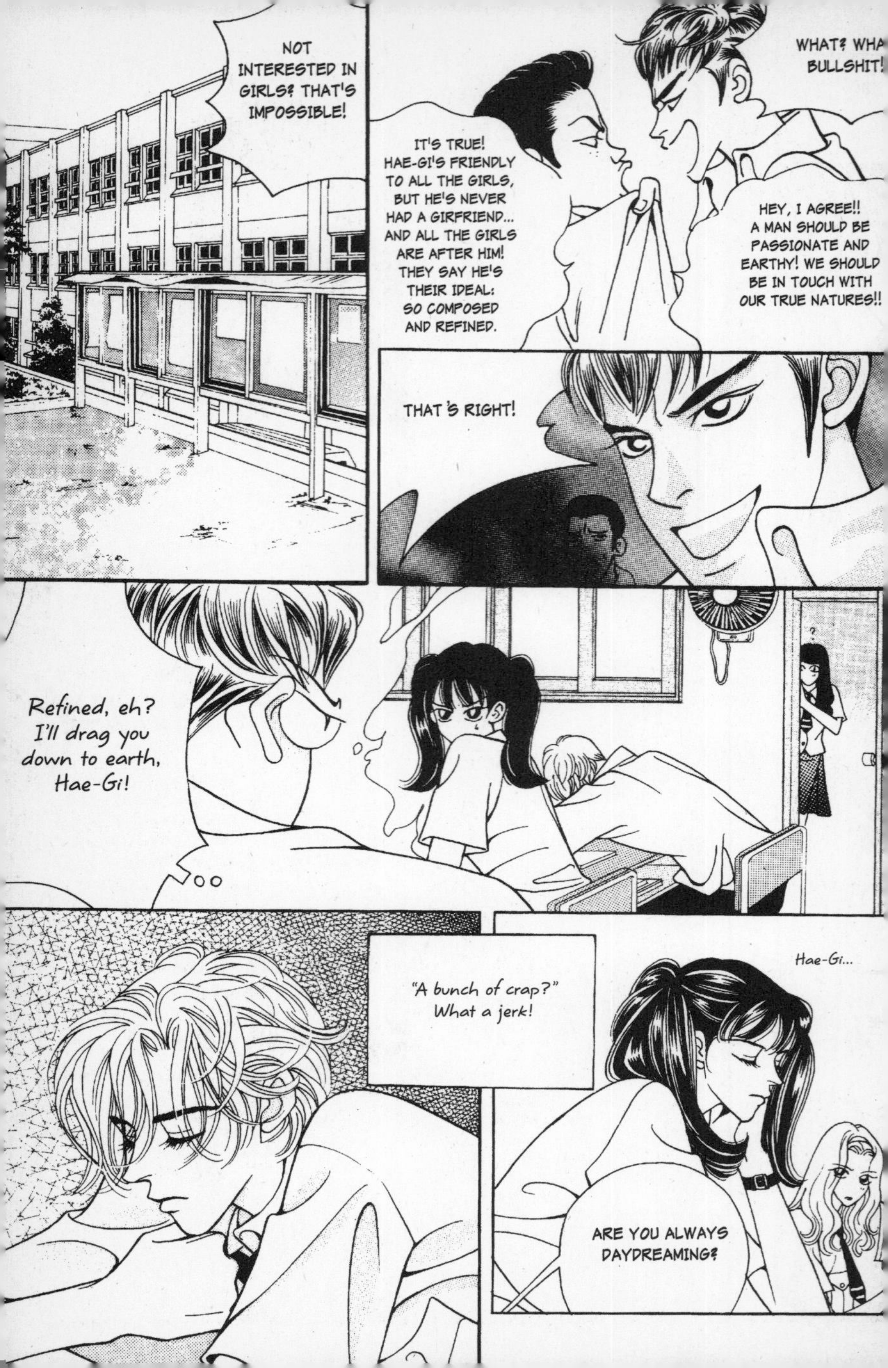
NOT INTERESTED IN GIRLS? THAT'S IMPOSSIBLE!
IT'S TRUE! HAE-GI'S FRIENDLY TO ALL THE GIRLS, BUT HE'S NEVER HAD A GIRFRIEND... AND ALL THE GIRLS ARE AFTER HIM! THEY SAY HE'S THEIR IDEAL: SO COMPOSED AND REFINED.
WHAT? WHA BULLSHIT!
HEY, I AGREE!! A MAN SHOULD BE PASSIONATE AND EARTHY! WE SHOULD BE IN TOUCH WITH OUR TRUE NATURES!!
THAT'S RIGHT!
Refined, eh? I'll drag you down to earth, Hae-Gi!
"A bunch of crap?" What a jerk!
Hae-Gi...
ARE YOU ALWAYS DAYDREAMING?

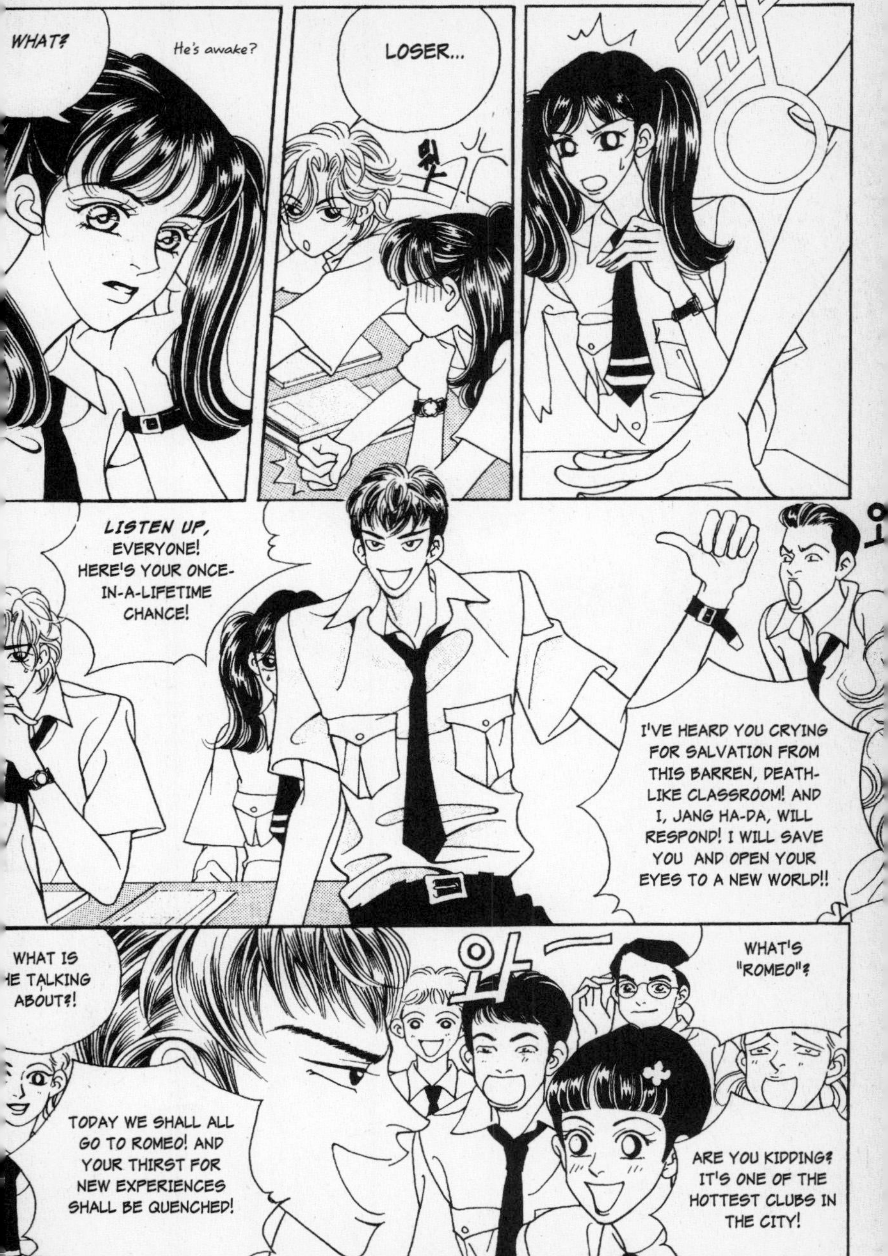
WHAT?
He's awake?
LOSER...
LISTEN UP, EVERYONE! HERE'S YOUR ONCE-IN-A-LIFETIME CHANCE!
I'VE HEARD YOU CRYING FOR SALVATION FROM THIS BARREN, DEATH-LIKE CLASSROOM! AND I, JANG HA-DA, WILL RESPOND! I WILL SAVE YOU AND OPEN YOUR EYES TO A NEW WORLD!!
WHAT IS HE TALKING ABOUT?!
TODAY WE SHALL ALL GO TO ROMEO! AND YOUR THIRST FOR NEW EXPERIENCES SHALL BE QUENCHED!
WHAT'S "ROMEO"?
ARE YOU KIDDING? IT'S ONE OF THE HOTTEST CLUBS IN THE CITY!

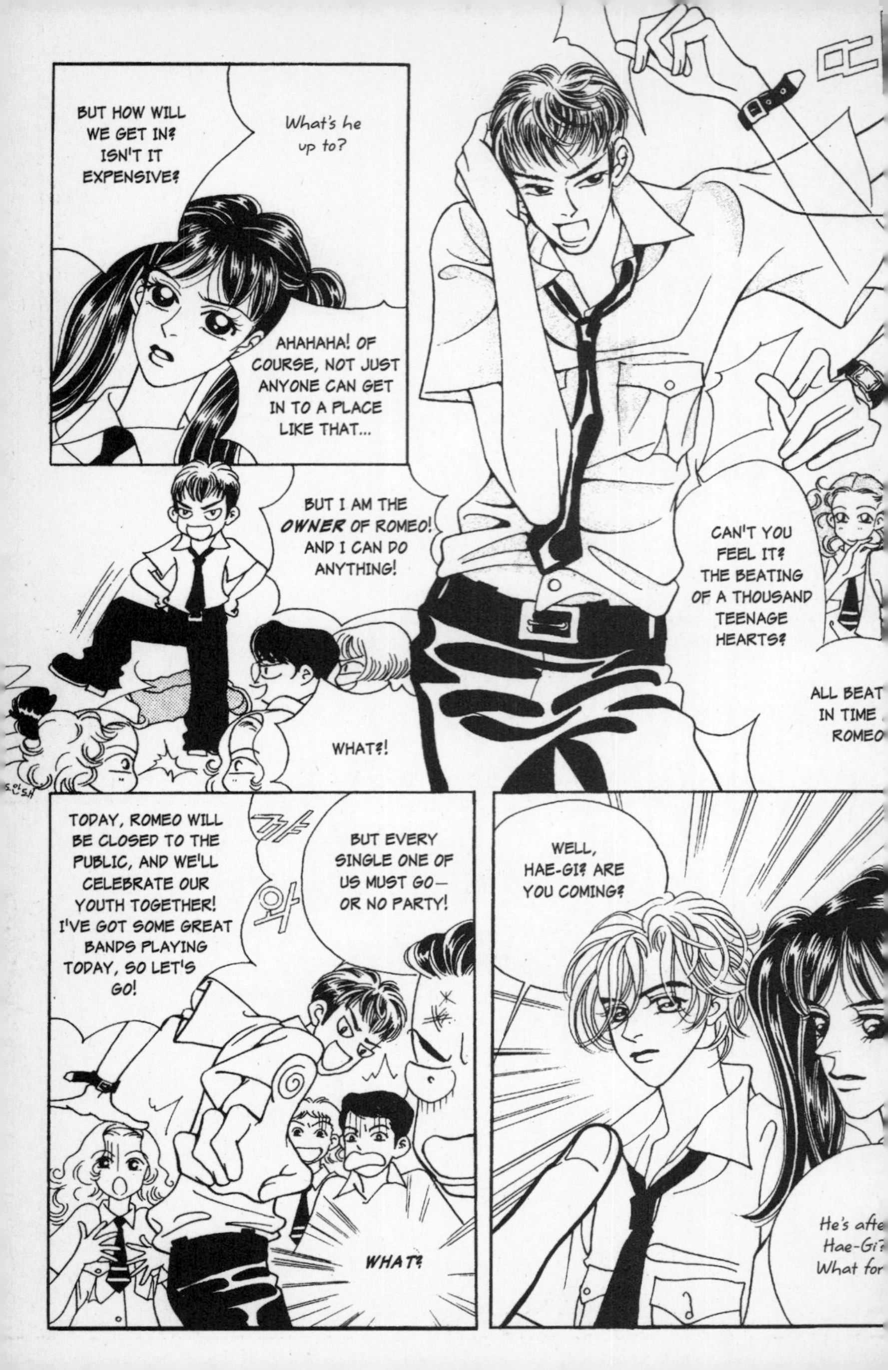
BUT HOW WILL WE GET IN? ISN'T IT EXPENSIVE?
What's he up to?
AHAHAHA! OF COURSE, NOT JUST ANYONE CAN GET IN TO A PLACE LIKE THAT...
BUT I AM THE ***OWNER*** OF ROMEO! AND I CAN DO ANYTHING!
WHAT?!
CAN'T YOU FEEL IT? THE BEATING OF A THOUSAND TEENAGE HEARTS?
ALL BEAT IN TIME ROMEO
TODAY, ROMEO WILL BE CLOSED TO THE PUBLIC, AND WE'LL CELEBRATE OUR YOUTH TOGETHER! I'VE GOT SOME GREAT BANDS PLAYING TODAY, SO LET'S GO!
BUT EVERY SINGLE ONE OF US MUST GO— OR NO PARTY!
WHAT?
WELL, HAE-GI? ARE YOU COMING?
He's afte Hae-Gi? What for

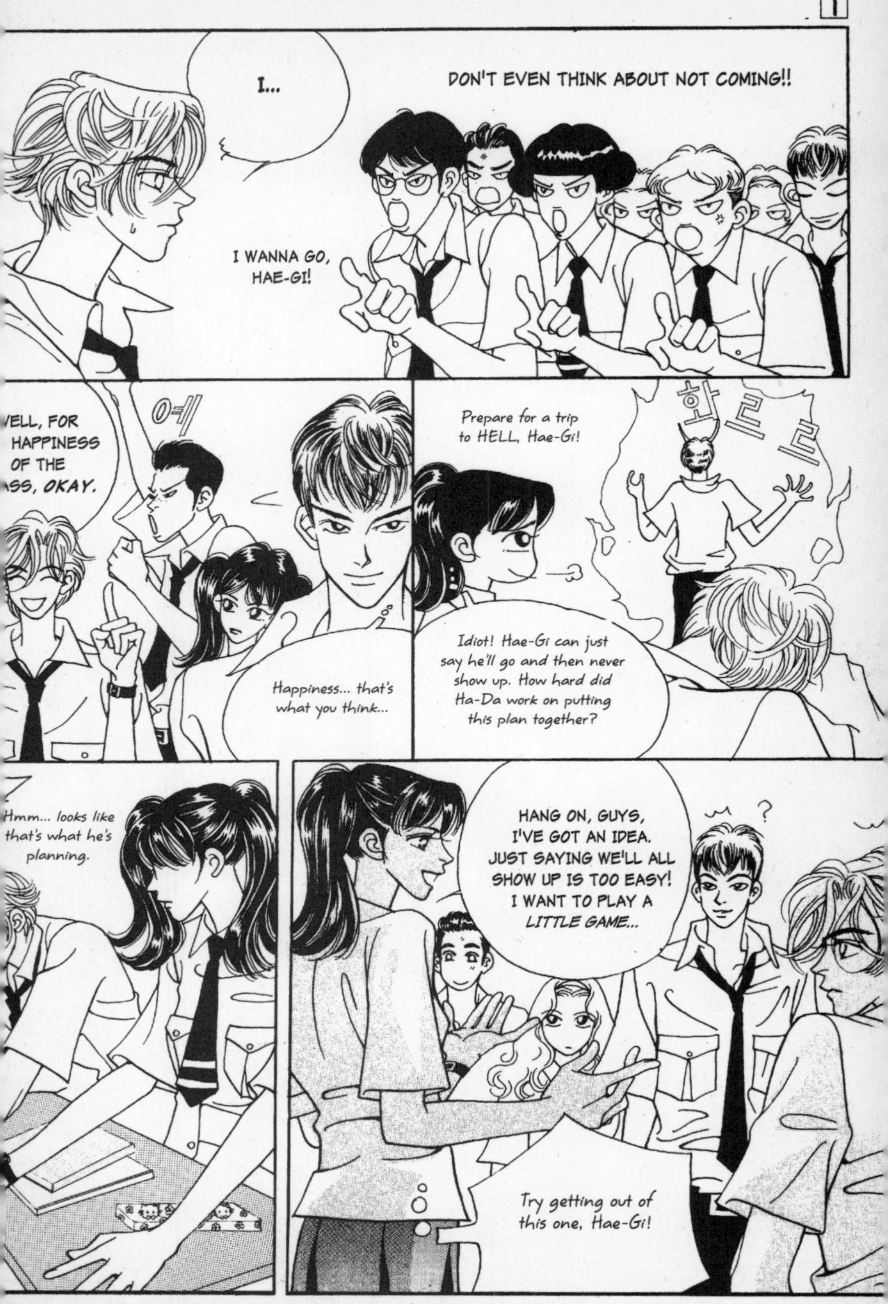
1
I...
DON'T EVEN THINK ABOUT NOT COMING!!
I WANNA GO, HAE-GI!
VELL, FOR HAPPINESS OF THE ASS, OKAY.
에
Happiness... that's what you think...
Prepare for a trip to HELL, Hae-Gi!
화르르
Idiot! Hae-Gi can just say he'll go and then never show up. How hard did Ha-Da work on putting this plan together?
Hmm... looks like that's what he's planning.
HANG ON, GUYS, I'VE GOT AN IDEA. JUST SAYING WE'LL ALL SHOW UP IS TOO EASY! I WANT TO PLAY A LITTLE GAME...
?
Try getting out of this one, Hae-Gi!

Snow Drop

Oh • Hae- • Gi

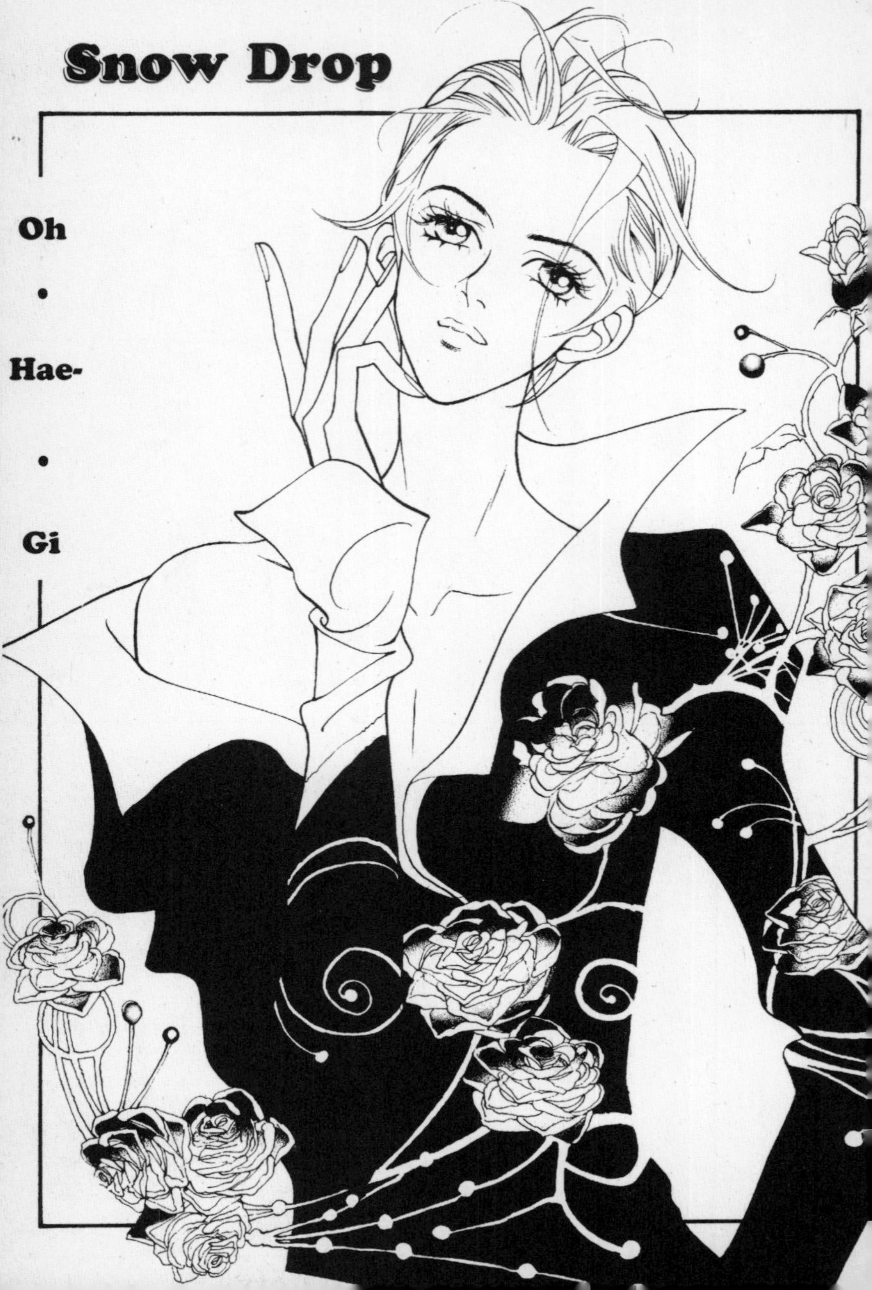

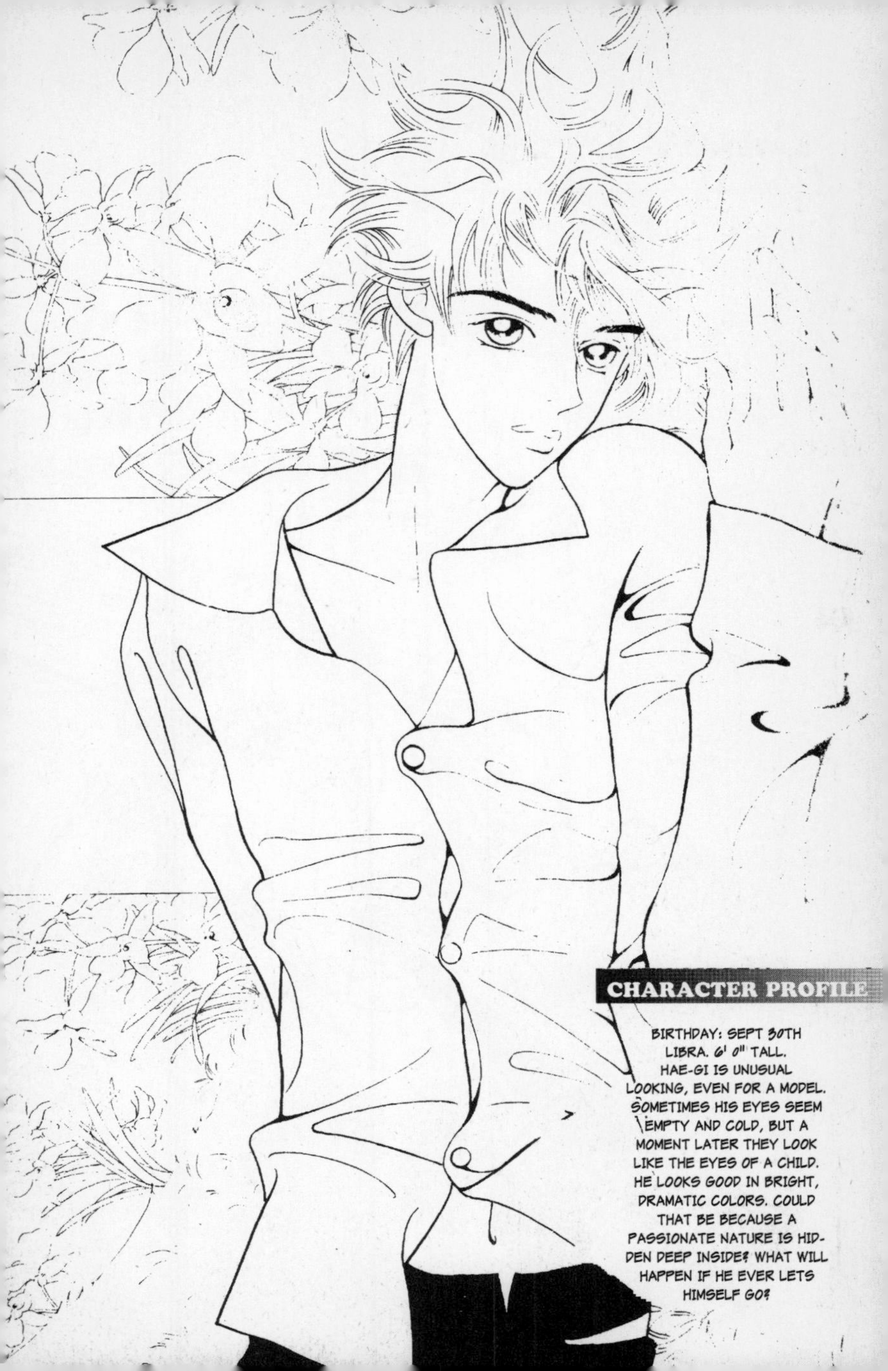
CHARACTER PROFILE
BIRTHDAY: SEPT 30TH
LIBRA. 6' 0" TALL.
HAE-GI IS UNUSUAL LOOKING, EVEN FOR A MODEL. SOMETIMES HIS EYES SEEM EMPTY AND COLD, BUT A MOMENT LATER THEY LOOK LIKE THE EYES OF A CHILD. HE LOOKS GOOD IN BRIGHT, DRAMATIC COLORS. COULD THAT BE BECAUSE A PASSIONATE NATURE IS HIDDEN DEEP INSIDE? WHAT WILL HAPPEN IF HE EVER LETS HIMSELF GO?

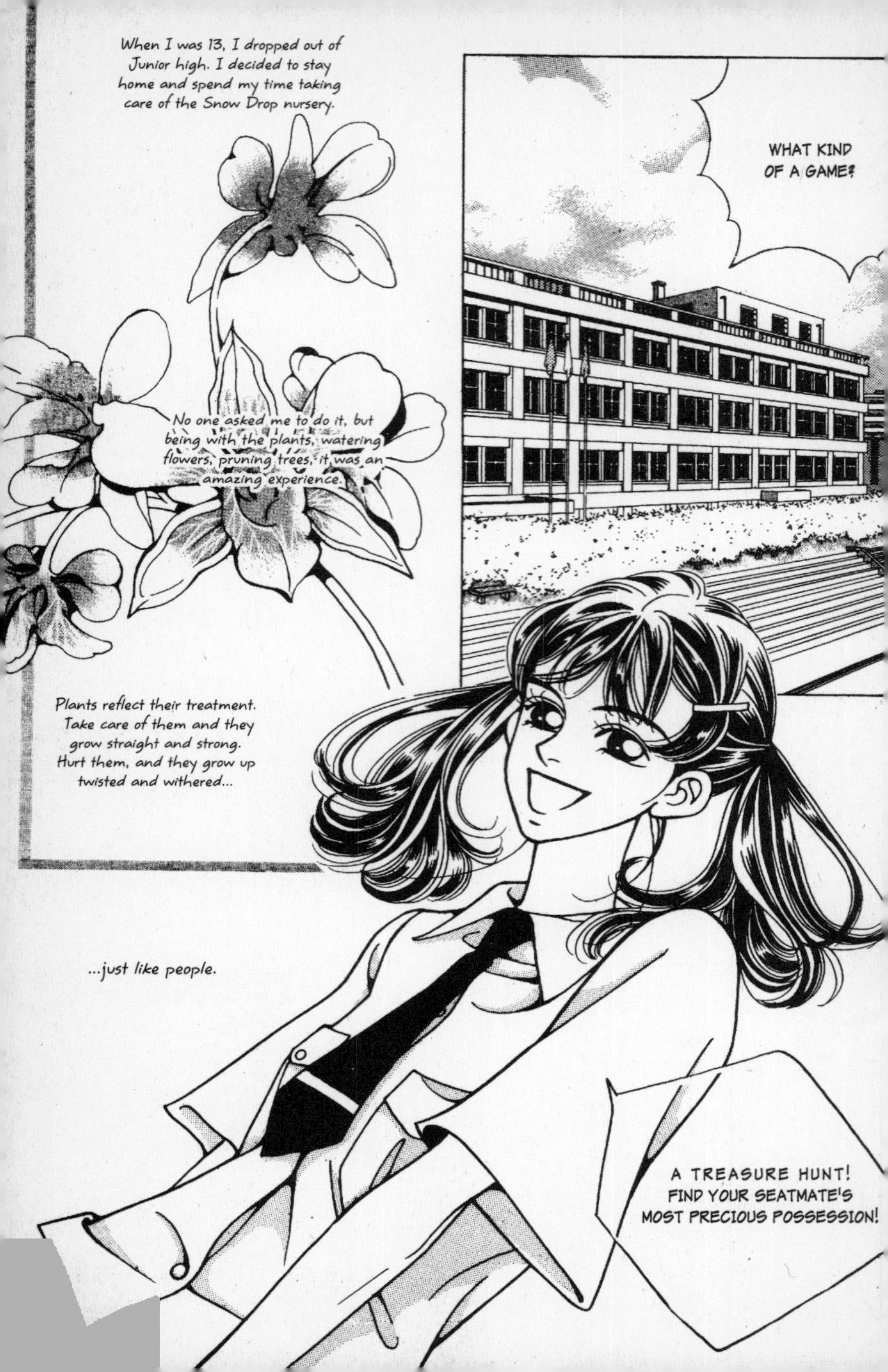
When I was 13, I dropped out of Junior high. I decided to stay home and spend my time taking care of the Snow Drop nursery.
No one asked me to do it, but being with the plants, watering flowers, pruning trees, it was an amazing experience.
Plants reflect their treatment. Take care of them and they grow straight and strong. Hurt them, and they grow up twisted and withered...
...just like people.
WHAT KIND OF A GAME?
A TREASURE HUNT! FIND YOUR SEATMATE'S MOST PRECIOUS POSSESSION!

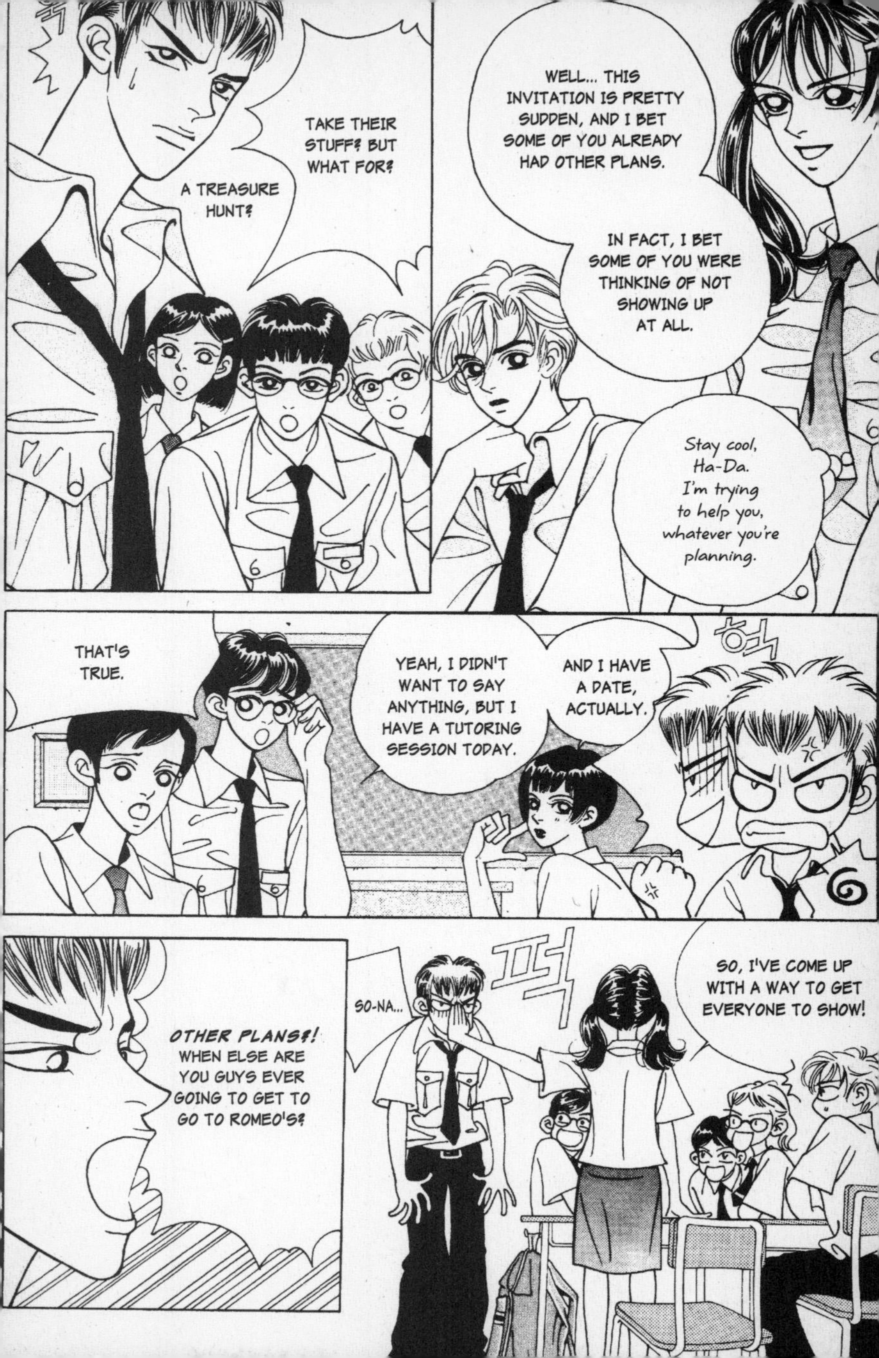
TAKE THEIR STUFF? BUT WHAT FOR?
A TREASURE HUNT?
WELL... THIS INVITATION IS PRETTY SUDDEN, AND I BET SOME OF YOU ALREADY HAD OTHER PLANS.
IN FACT, I BET SOME OF YOU WERE THINKING OF NOT SHOWING UP AT ALL.
Stay cool, Ha-Da. I'm trying to help you, whatever you're planning.
THAT'S TRUE.
YEAH, I DIDN'T WANT TO SAY ANYTHING, BUT I HAVE A TUTORING SESSION TODAY.
AND I HAVE A DATE, ACTUALLY.
OTHER PLANS?! WHEN ELSE ARE YOU GUYS EVER GOING TO GET TO GO TO ROMEO'S?
SO-NA...
SO, I'VE COME UP WITH A WAY TO GET EVERYONE TO SHOW!

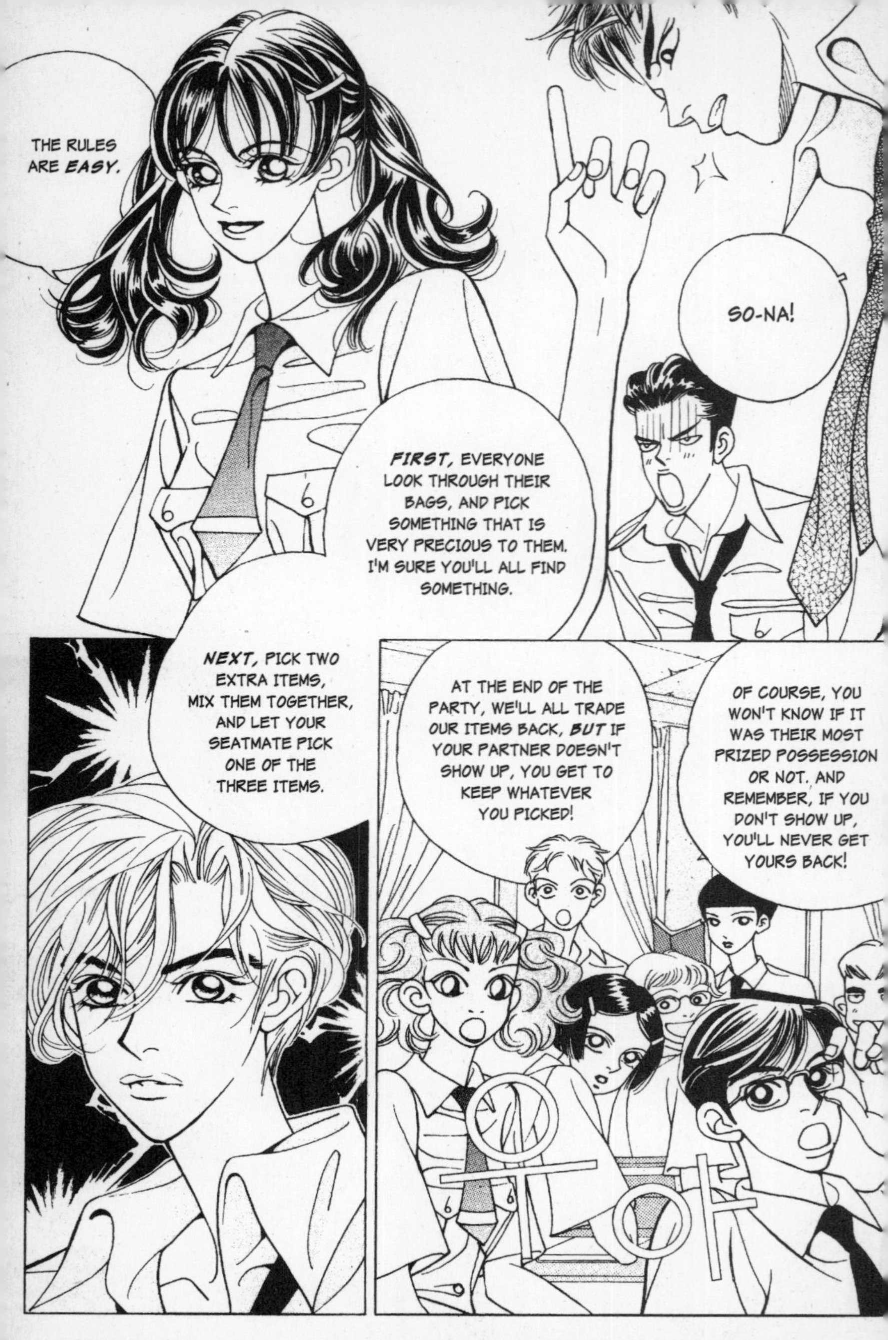
THE RULES ARE *EASY.*
FIRST, EVERYONE LOOK THROUGH THEIR BAGS, AND PICK SOMETHING THAT IS VERY PRECIOUS TO THEM. I'M SURE YOU'LL ALL FIND SOMETHING.
SO-NA!
NEXT, PICK TWO EXTRA ITEMS, MIX THEM TOGETHER, AND LET YOUR SEATMATE PICK ONE OF THE THREE ITEMS.
AT THE END OF THE PARTY, WE'LL ALL TRADE OUR ITEMS BACK, *BUT* IF YOUR PARTNER DOESN'T SHOW UP, YOU GET TO KEEP WHATEVER YOU PICKED!
OF COURSE, YOU WON'T KNOW IF IT WAS THEIR MOST PRIZED POSSESSION OR NOT. AND REMEMBER, IF YOU DON'T SHOW UP, YOU'LL NEVER GET YOURS BACK!

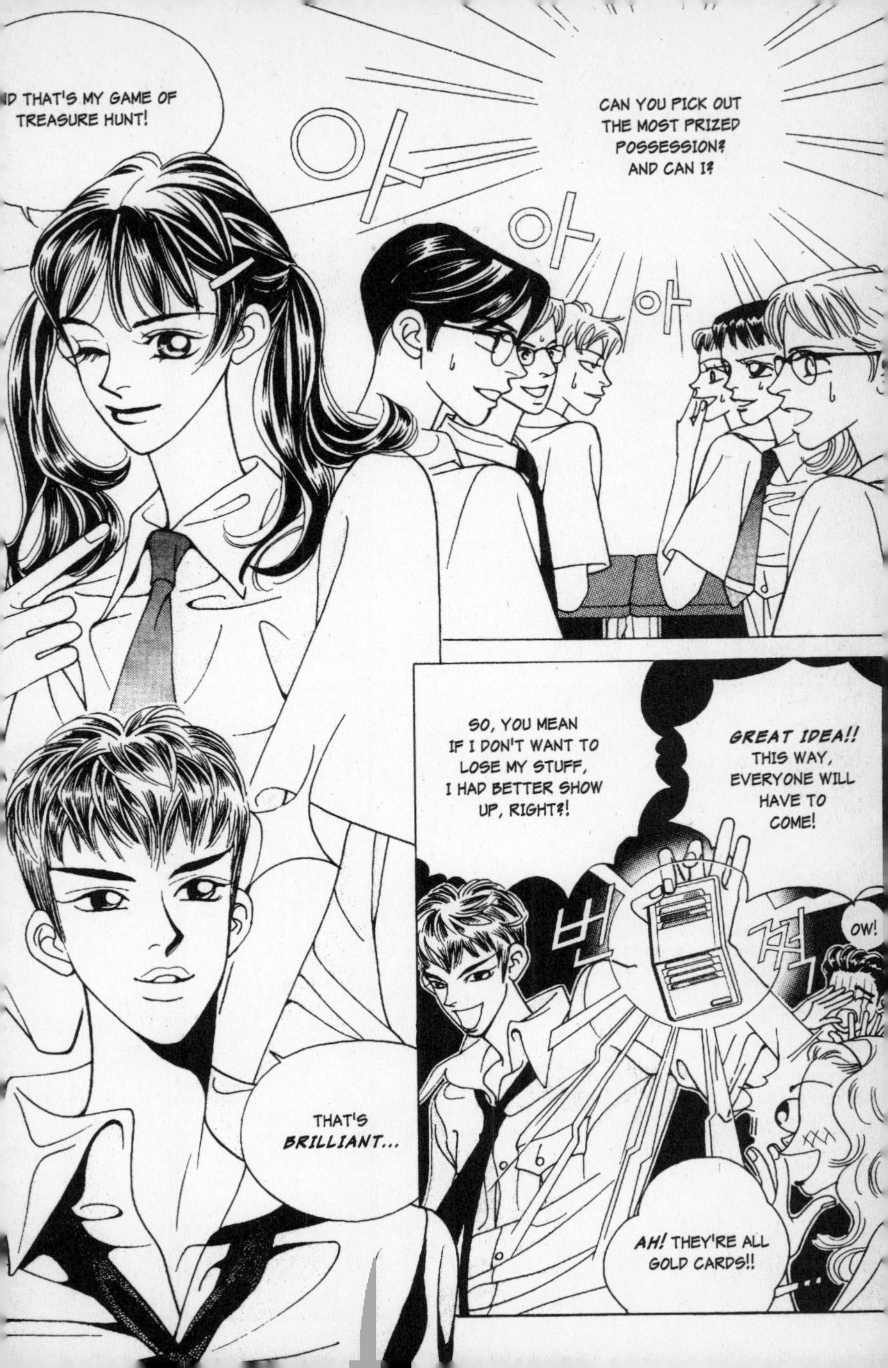
ND THAT'S MY GAME OF TREASURE HUNT!
CAN YOU PICK OUT THE MOST PRIZED POSSESSION? AND CAN I?
아 아 아
SO, YOU MEAN IF I DON'T WANT TO LOSE MY STUFF, I HAD BETTER SHOW UP, RIGHT?!
GREAT IDEA!! THIS WAY, EVERYONE WILL HAVE TO COME!
번 쩍
OW!
AH! THEY'RE ALL GOLD CARDS!!
THAT'S BRILLIANT...

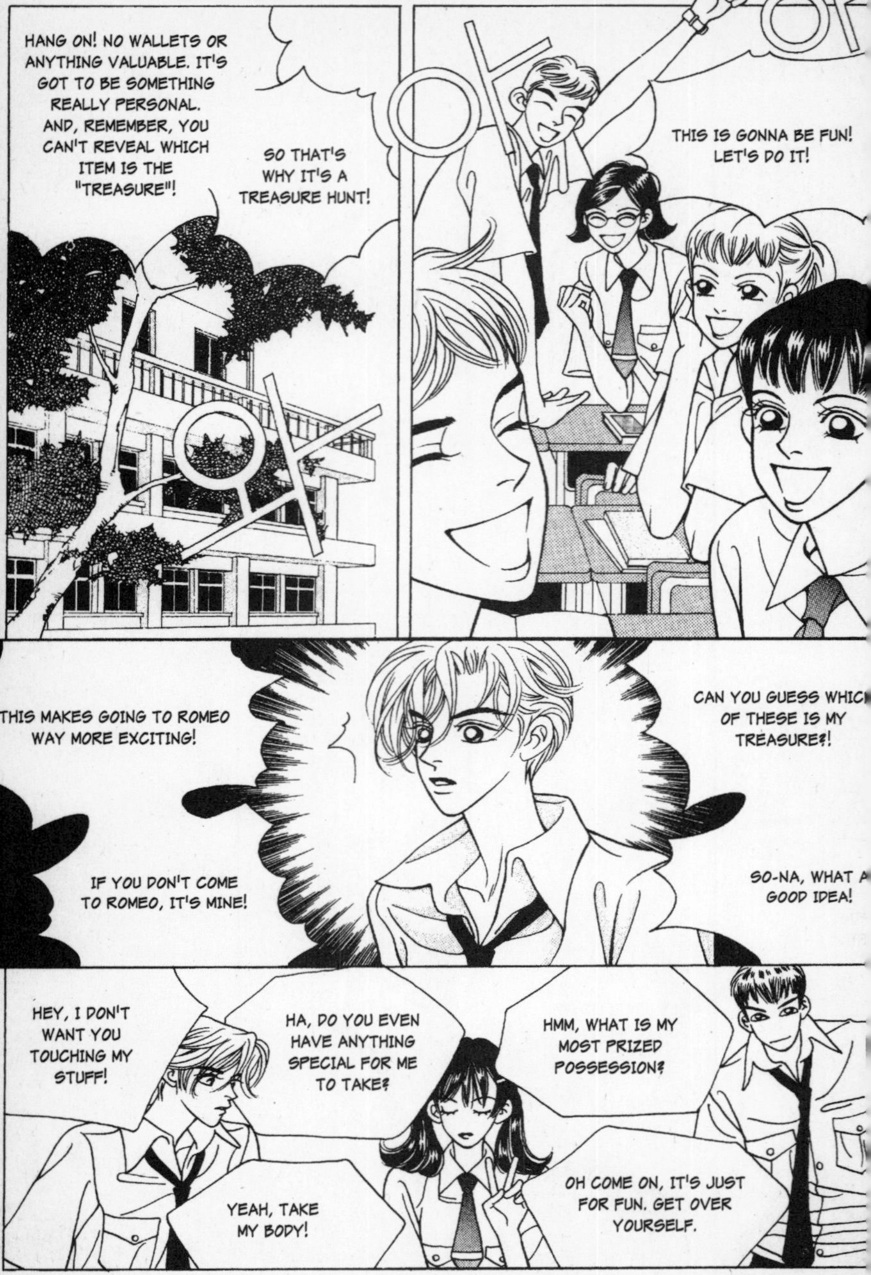
HANG ON! NO WALLETS OR ANYTHING VALUABLE. IT'S GOT TO BE SOMETHING REALLY PERSONAL. AND, REMEMBER, YOU CAN'T REVEAL WHICH ITEM IS THE "TREASURE"!
SO THAT'S WHY IT'S A TREASURE HUNT!
OK
OK
OK
THIS IS GONNA BE FUN! LET'S DO IT!
THIS MAKES GOING TO ROMEO WAY MORE EXCITING!
IF YOU DON'T COME TO ROMEO, IT'S MINE!
CAN YOU GUESS WHIC OF THESE IS MY TREASURE?!
SO-NA, WHAT A GOOD IDEA!
HEY, I DON'T WANT YOU TOUCHING MY STUFF!
YEAH, TAKE MY BODY!
HA, DO YOU EVEN HAVE ANYTHING SPECIAL FOR ME TO TAKE?
HMM, WHAT IS MY MOST PRIZED POSSESSION?
OH COME ON, IT'S JUST FOR FUN. GET OVER YOURSELF.

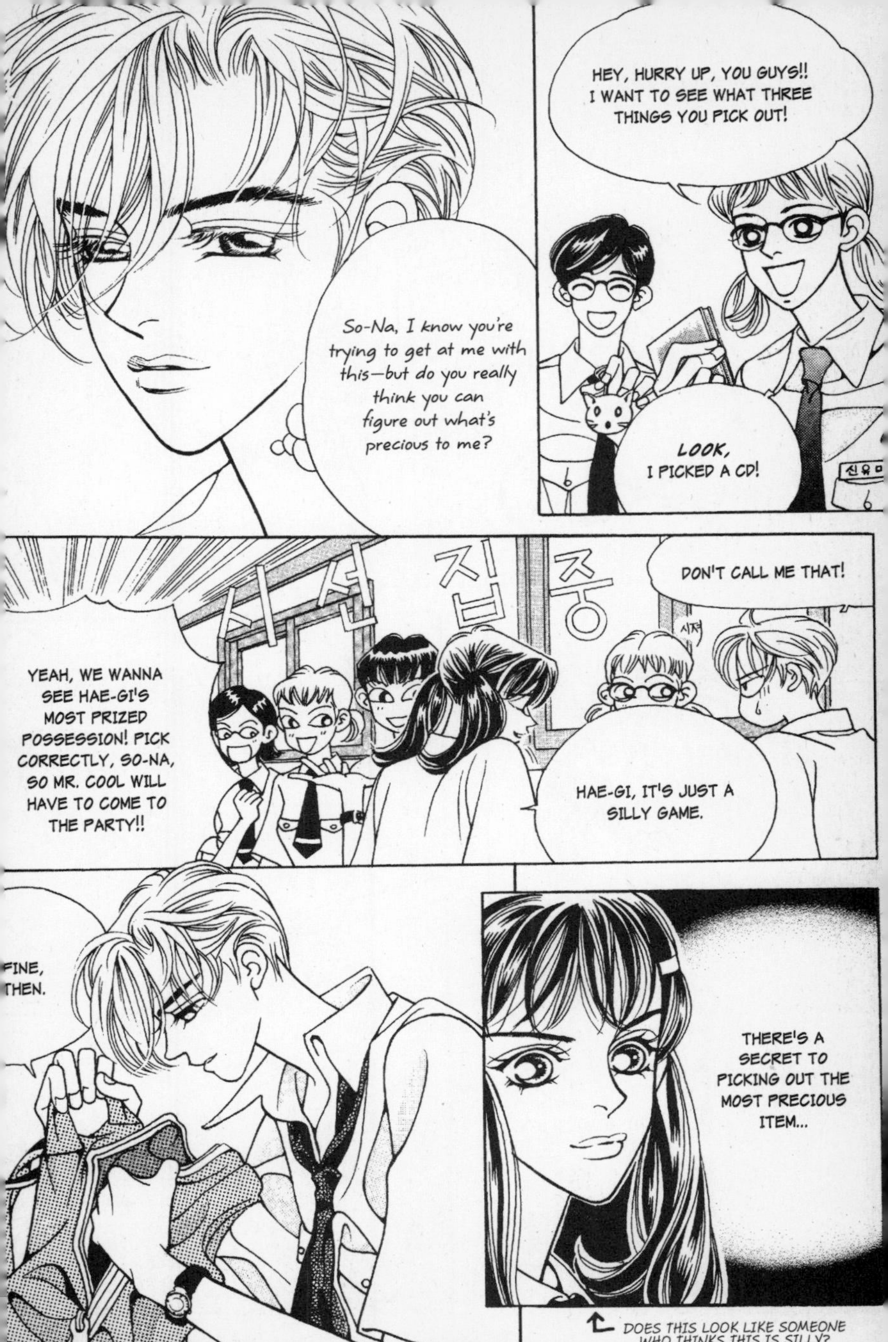
So-Na, I know you're trying to get at me with this—but do you really think you can figure out what's precious to me?
HEY, HURRY UP, YOU GUYS!! I WANT TO SEE WHAT THREE THINGS YOU PICK OUT!
LOOK, I PICKED A CD!
시선 집중
YEAH, WE WANNA SEE HAE-GI'S MOST PRIZED POSSESSION! PICK CORRECTLY, SO-NA, SO MR. COOL WILL HAVE TO COME TO THE PARTY!!
HAE-GI, IT'S JUST A SILLY GAME.
DON'T CALL ME THAT!
FINE, THEN.
THERE'S A SECRET TO PICKING OUT THE MOST PRECIOUS ITEM...

DOES THIS LOOK LIKE SOMEONE WHO THINKS THIS IS SILLY?

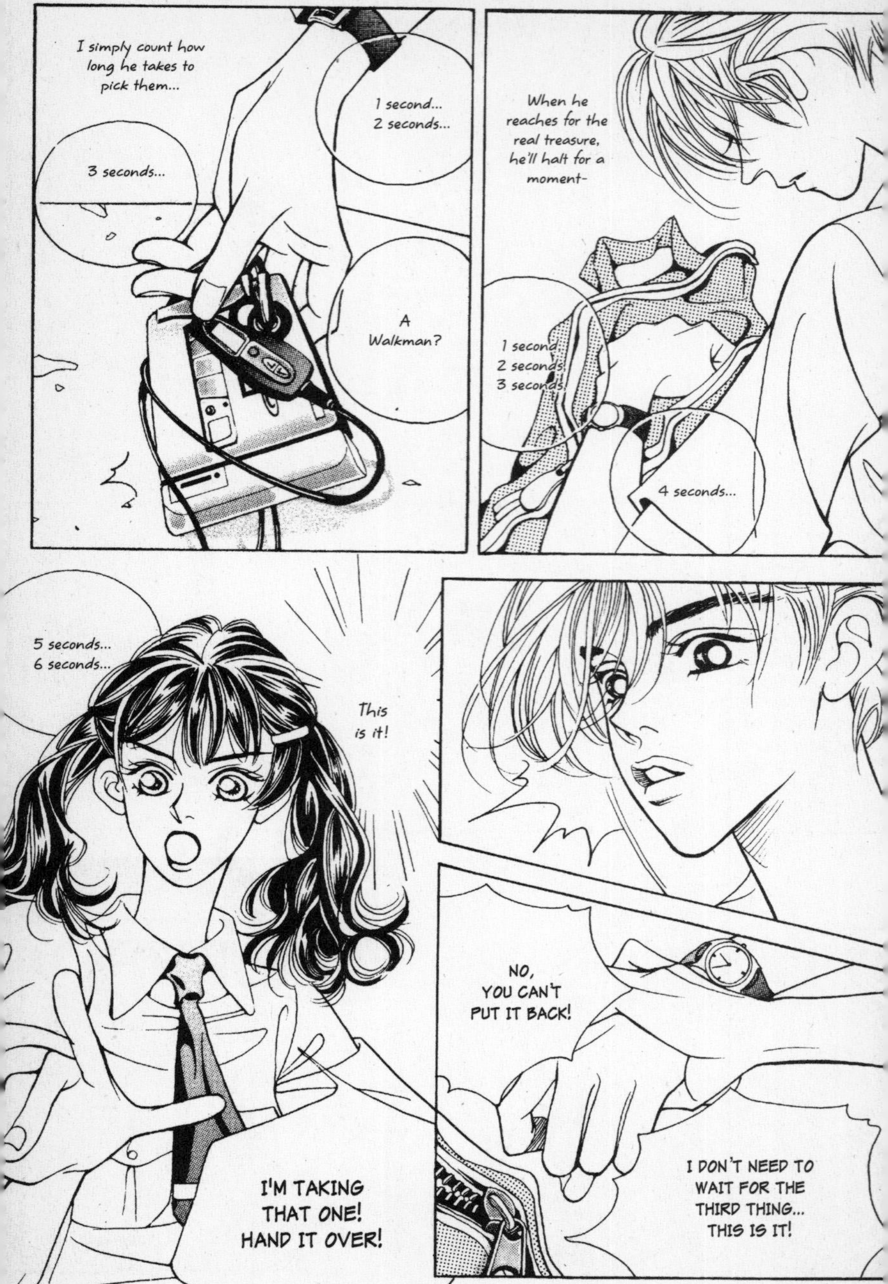
I simply count how long he takes to pick them...
1 second... 2 seconds...
3 seconds...
A Walkman?
When he reaches for the real treasure, he'll halt for a moment-
1 second 2 seconds 3 seconds
4 seconds...
5 seconds... 6 seconds...
This is it!
I'M TAKING THAT ONE! HAND IT OVER!
NO, YOU CAN'T PUT IT BACK!
I DON'T NEED TO WAIT FOR THE THIRD THING... THIS IS IT!

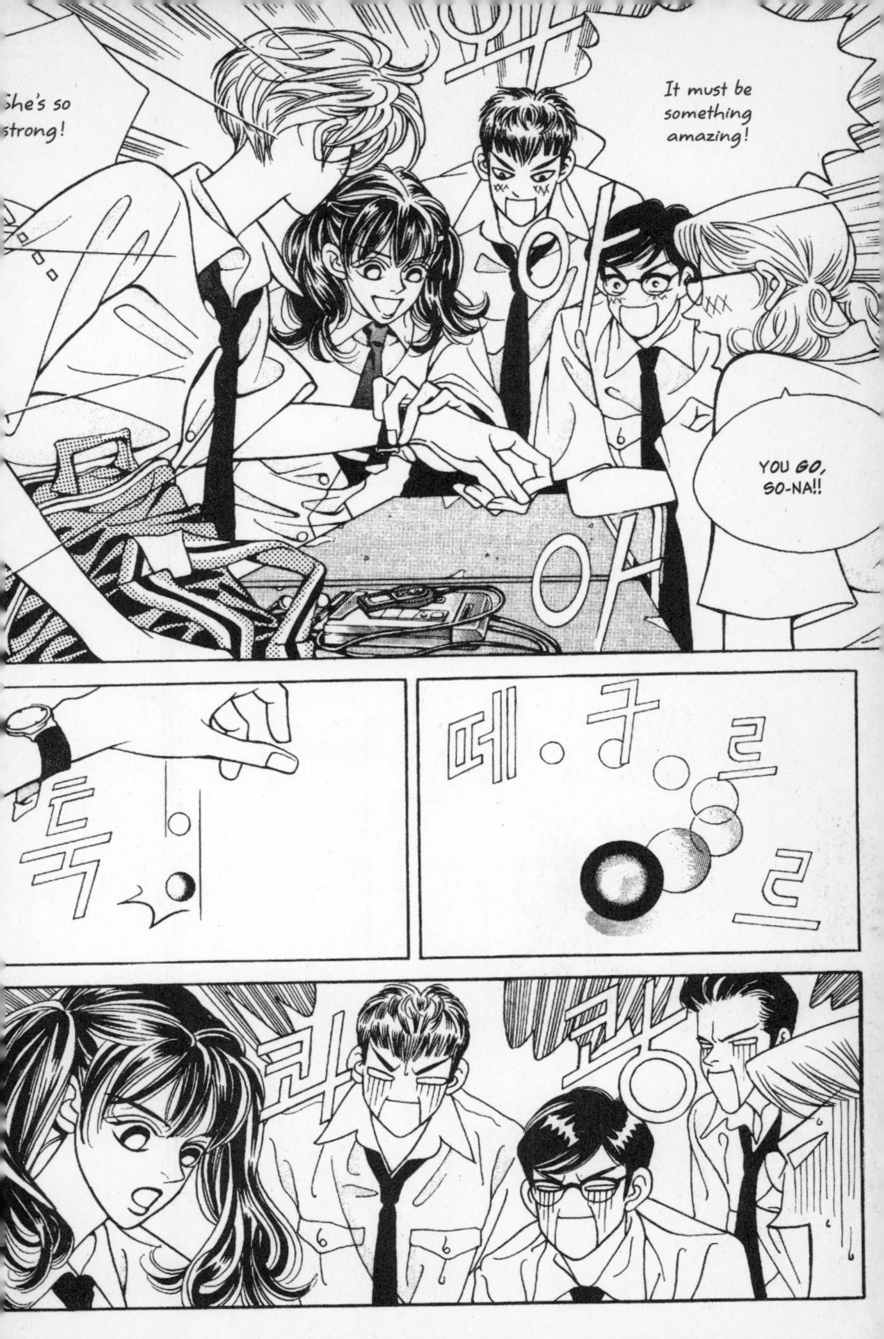
와
She's so strong!
It must be something amazing!
아
YOU GO, SO-NA!!
아
툭
데·구·르르

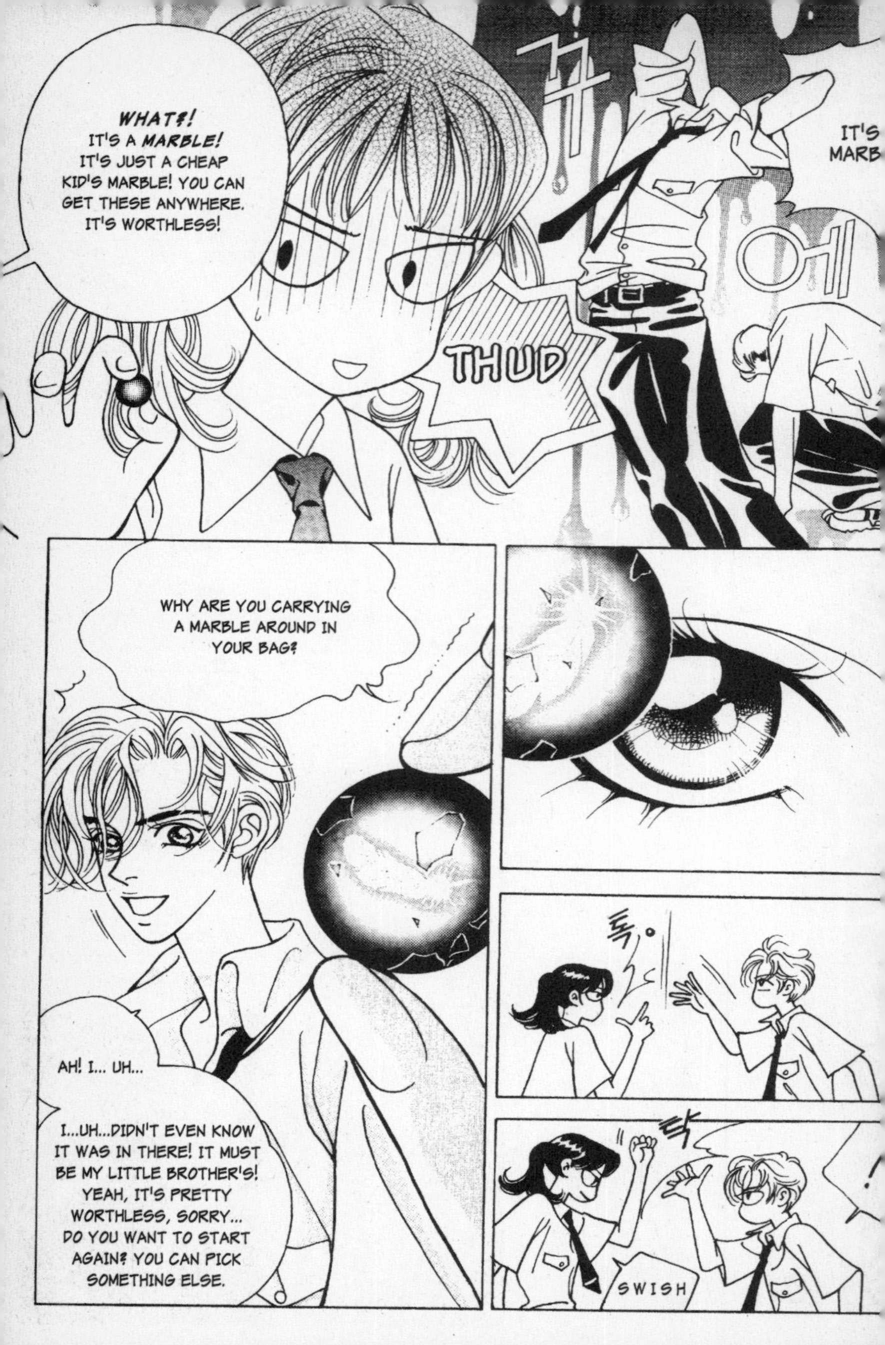
WHAT?! IT'S A MARBLE! IT'S JUST A CHEAP KID'S MARBLE! YOU CAN GET THESE ANYWHERE. IT'S WORTHLESS!
THUD
OH
IT'S MARB
WHY ARE YOU CARRYING A MARBLE AROUND IN YOUR BAG?
AH! I... UH...
I...UH...DIDN'T EVEN KNOW IT WAS IN THERE! IT MUST BE MY LITTLE BROTHER'S! YEAH, IT'S PRETTY WORTHLESS, SORRY... DO YOU WANT TO START AGAIN? YOU CAN PICK SOMETHING ELSE.
SWISH

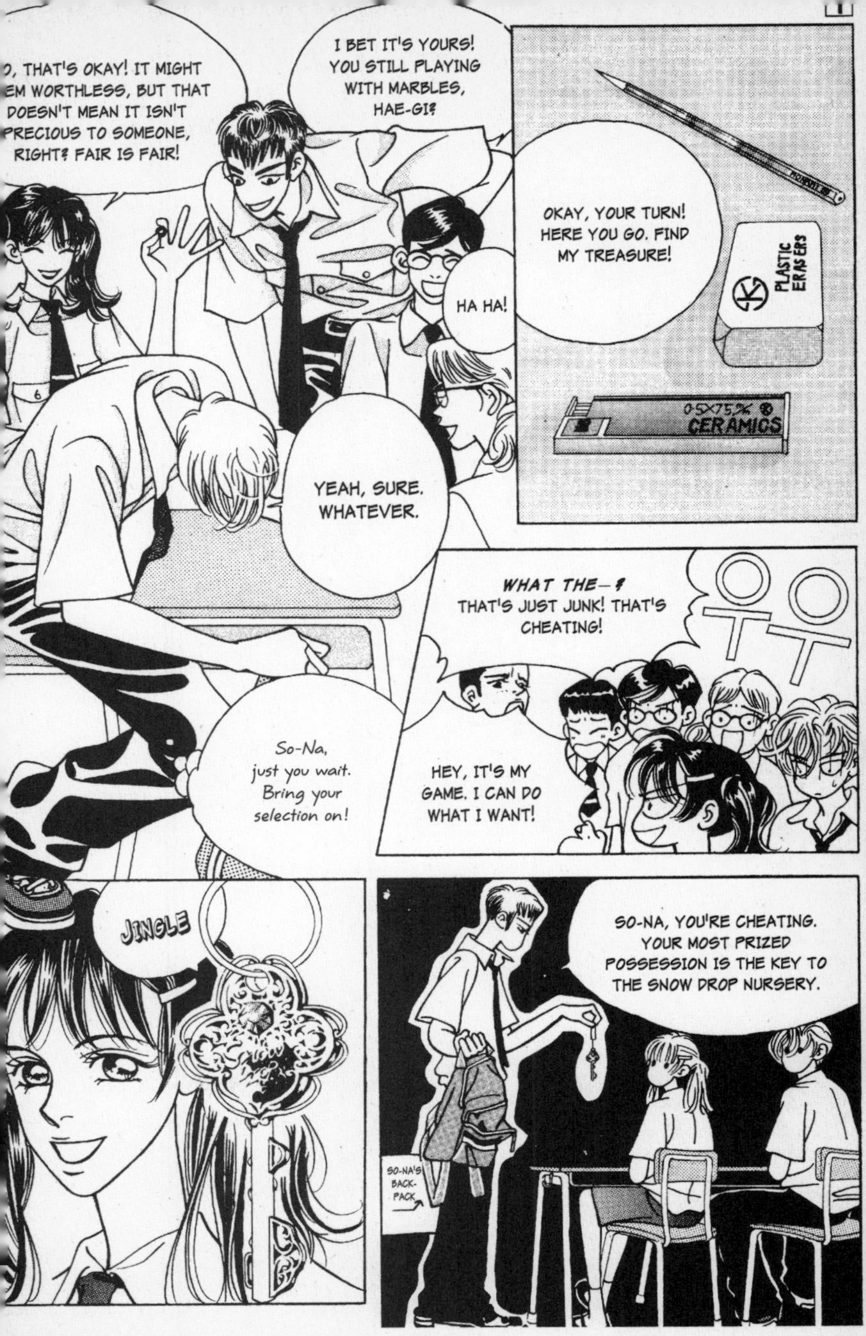

O, THAT'S OKAY! IT MIGHT EM WORTHLESS, BUT THAT DOESN'T MEAN IT ISN'T PRECIOUS TO SOMEONE, RIGHT? FAIR IS FAIR!
I BET IT'S YOURS! YOU STILL PLAYING WITH MARBLES, HAE-GI?
HA HA!
YEAH, SURE. WHATEVER.
OKAY, YOUR TURN! HERE YOU GO. FIND MY TREASURE!
PLASTIC ERASERS
0.5X75.% CERAMICS
So-Na, just you wait. Bring your selection on!
WHAT THE—? THAT'S JUST JUNK! THAT'S CHEATING!
HEY, IT'S MY GAME. I CAN DO WHAT I WANT!
JINGLE
SO-NA, YOU'RE CHEATING. YOUR MOST PRIZED POSSESSION IS THE KEY TO THE SNOW DROP NURSERY.
SO-NA'S BACK-PACK

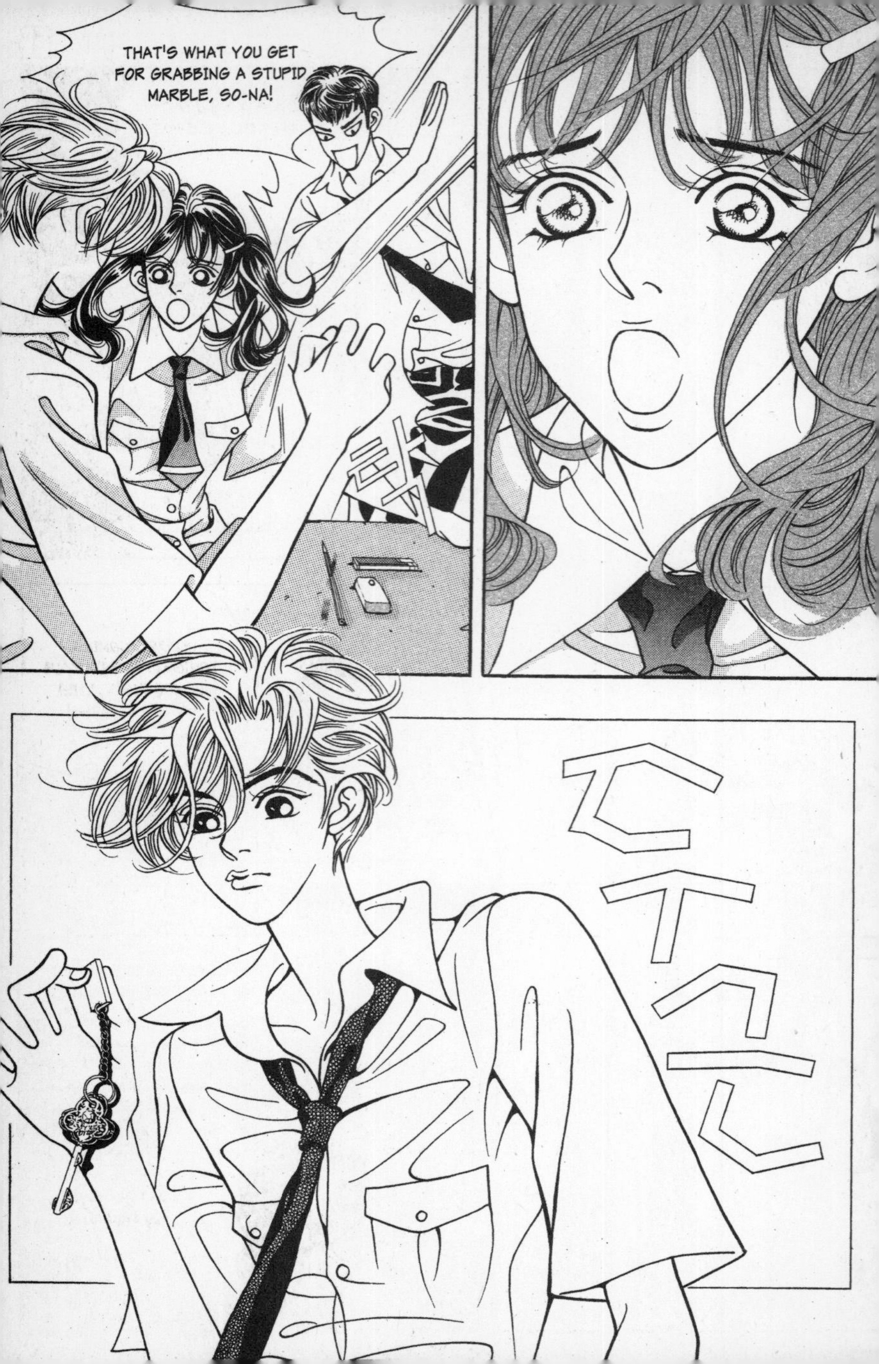
THAT'S WHAT YOU GET FOR GRABBING A STUPID MARBLE, SO-NA!

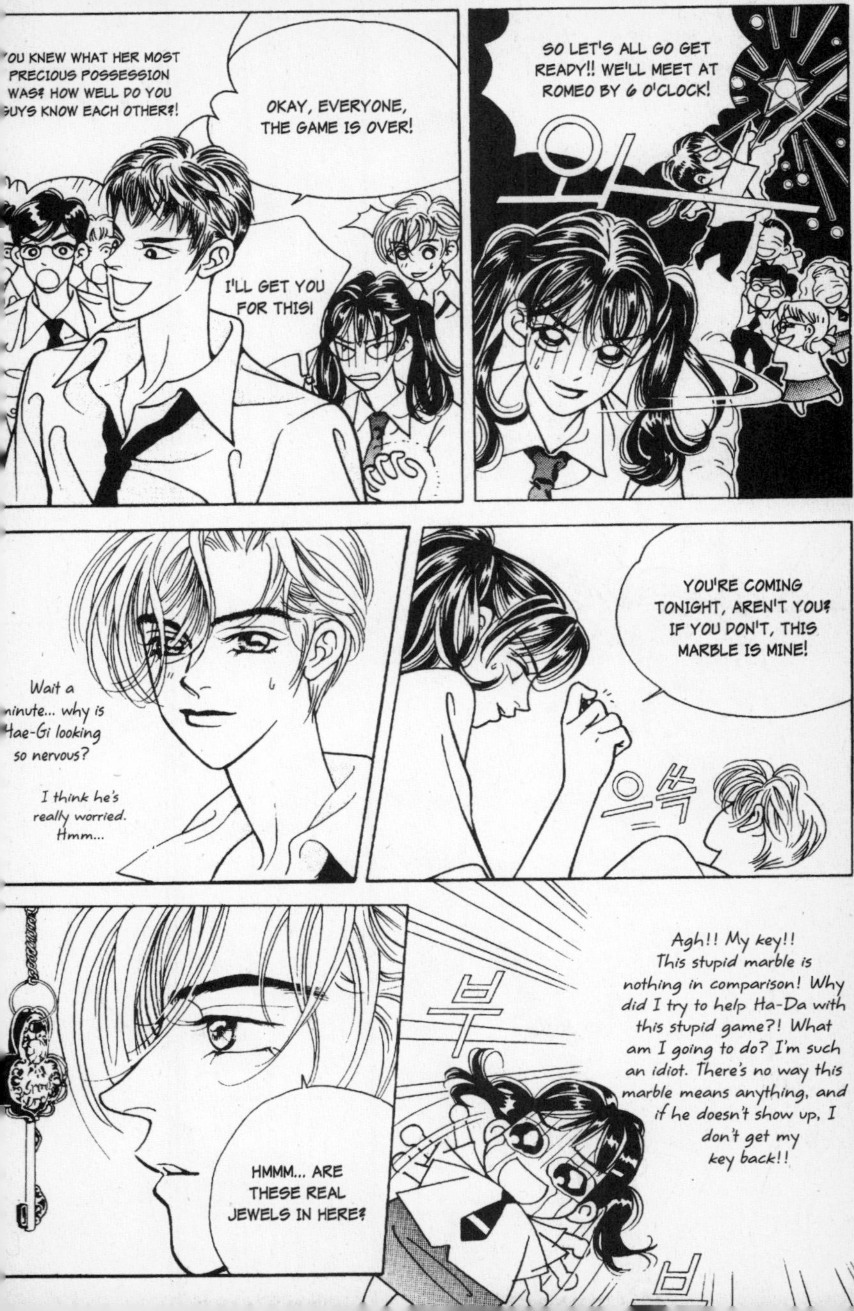
OU KNEW WHAT HER MOST PRECIOUS POSSESSION WAS? HOW WELL DO YOU GUYS KNOW EACH OTHER?!
OKAY, EVERYONE, THE GAME IS OVER!
I'LL GET YOU FOR THIS!
SO LET'S ALL GO GET READY!! WE'LL MEET AT ROMEO BY 6 O'CLOCK!
Wait a minute... why is Hae-Gi looking so nervous?
I think he's really worried. Hmm...
YOU'RE COMING TONIGHT, AREN'T YOU? IF YOU DON'T, THIS MARBLE IS MINE!
HMMM... ARE THESE REAL JEWELS IN HERE?
Agh!! My key!! This stupid marble is nothing in comparison! Why did I try to help Ha-Da with this stupid game?! What am I going to do? I'm such an idiot. There's no way this marble means anything, and if he doesn't show up, I don't get my key back!!

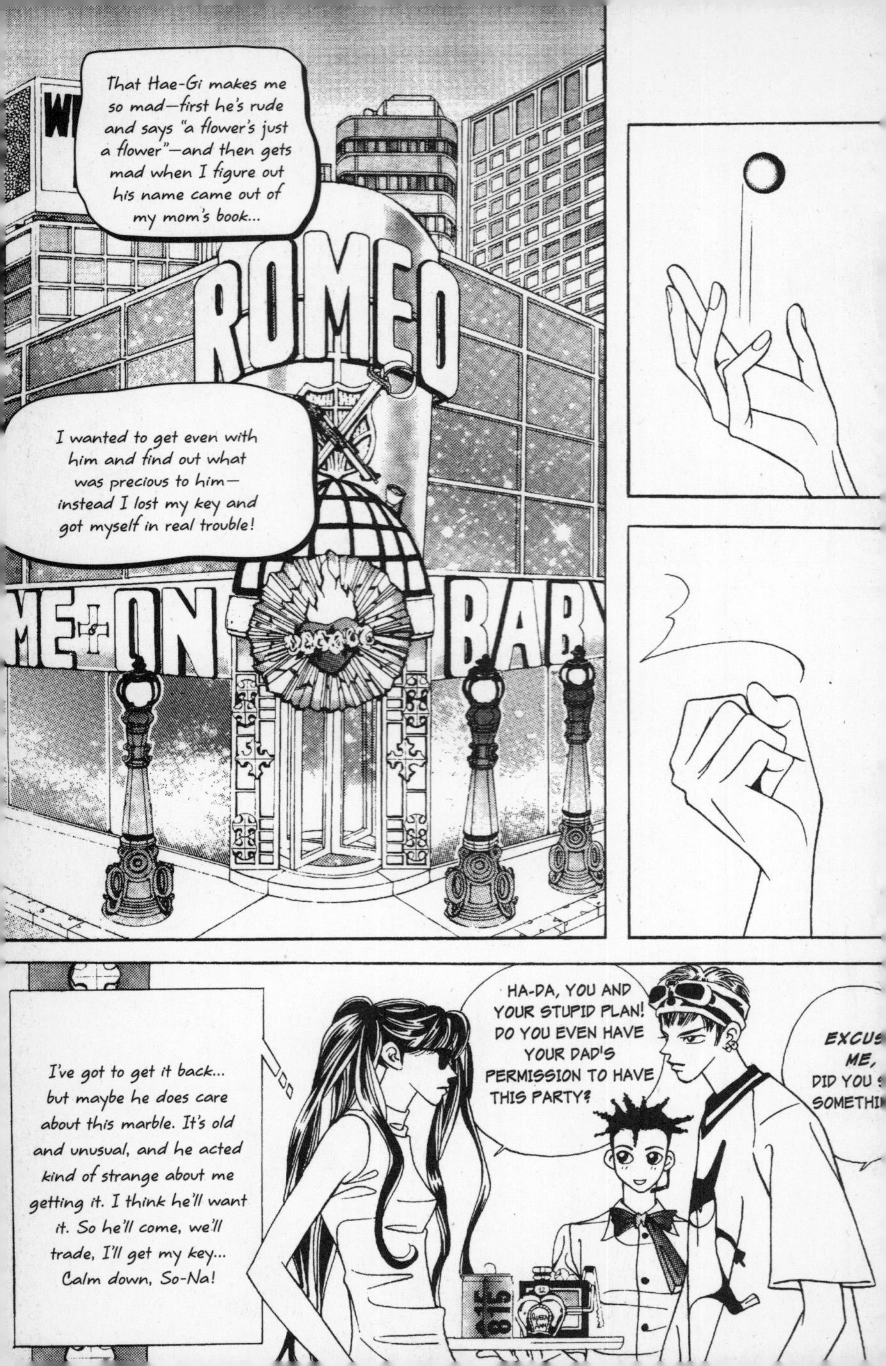
That Hae-Gi makes me so mad—first he's rude and says "a flower's just a flower"—and then gets mad when I figure out his name came out of my mom's book...
ROMEO
I wanted to get even with him and find out what was precious to him—instead I lost my key and got myself in real trouble!
ME+ON
BABY
I've got to get it back... but maybe he does care about this marble. It's old and unusual, and he acted kind of strange about me getting it. I think he'll want it. So he'll come, we'll trade, I'll get my key... Calm down, So-Na!
HA-DA, YOU AND YOUR STUPID PLAN! DO YOU EVEN HAVE YOUR DAD'S PERMISSION TO HAVE THIS PARTY?
EXCUS ME, DID YOU SOMETHI

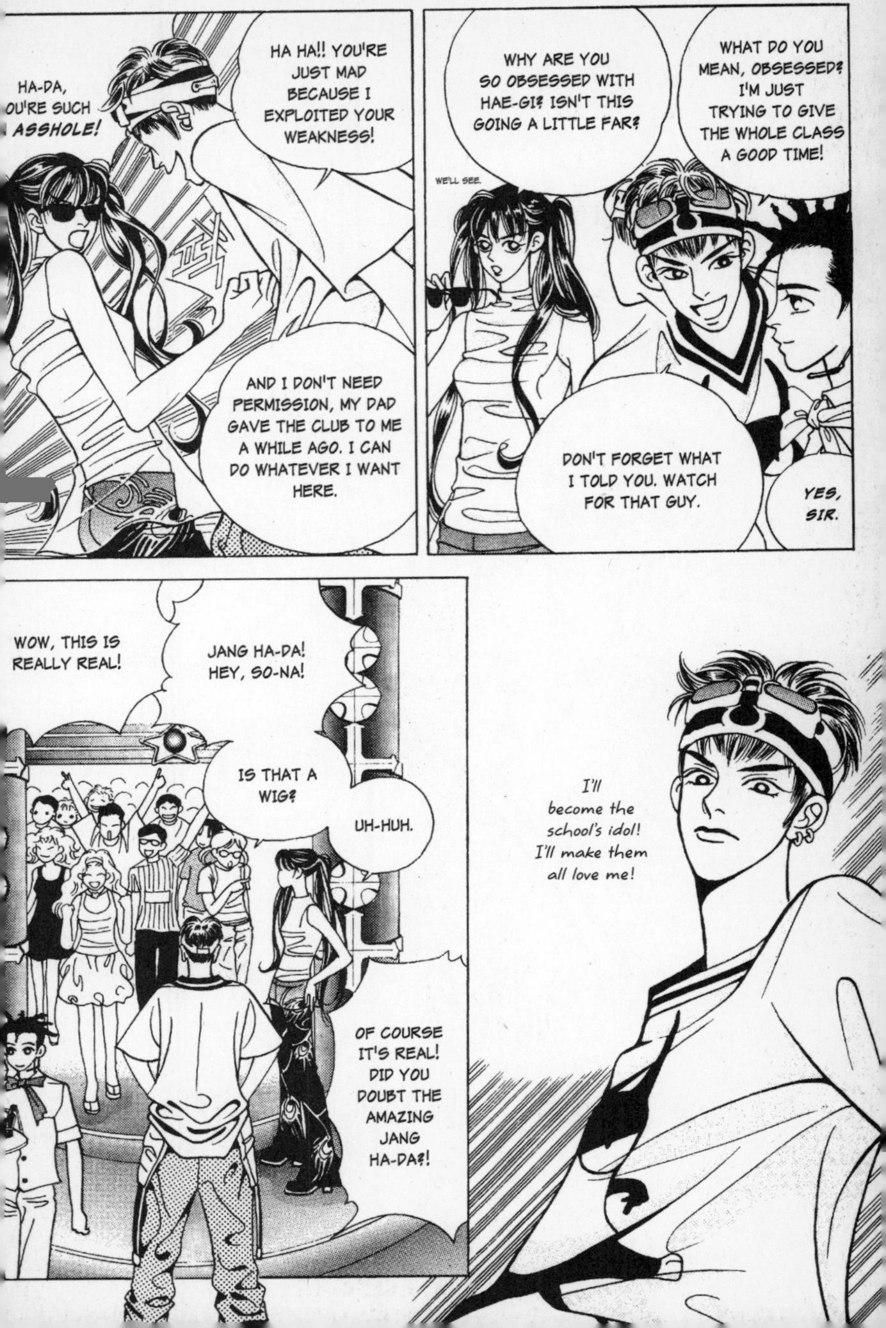
HA-DA, OU'RE SUCH ASSHOLE!
HA HA!! YOU'RE JUST MAD BECAUSE I EXPLOITED YOUR WEAKNESS!
AND I DON'T NEED PERMISSION, MY DAD GAVE THE CLUB TO ME A WHILE AGO. I CAN DO WHATEVER I WANT HERE.
WHY ARE YOU SO OBSESSED WITH HAE-GI? ISN'T THIS GOING A LITTLE FAR?
WE'LL SEE.
WHAT DO YOU MEAN, OBSESSED? I'M JUST TRYING TO GIVE THE WHOLE CLASS A GOOD TIME!
DON'T FORGET WHAT I TOLD YOU. WATCH FOR THAT GUY.
YES, SIR.
WOW, THIS IS REALLY REAL!
JANG HA-DA! HEY, SO-NA!
IS THAT A WIG?
UH-HUH.
OF COURSE IT'S REAL! DID YOU DOUBT THE AMAZING JANG HA-DA?!
I'll become the school's idol! I'll make them all love me!

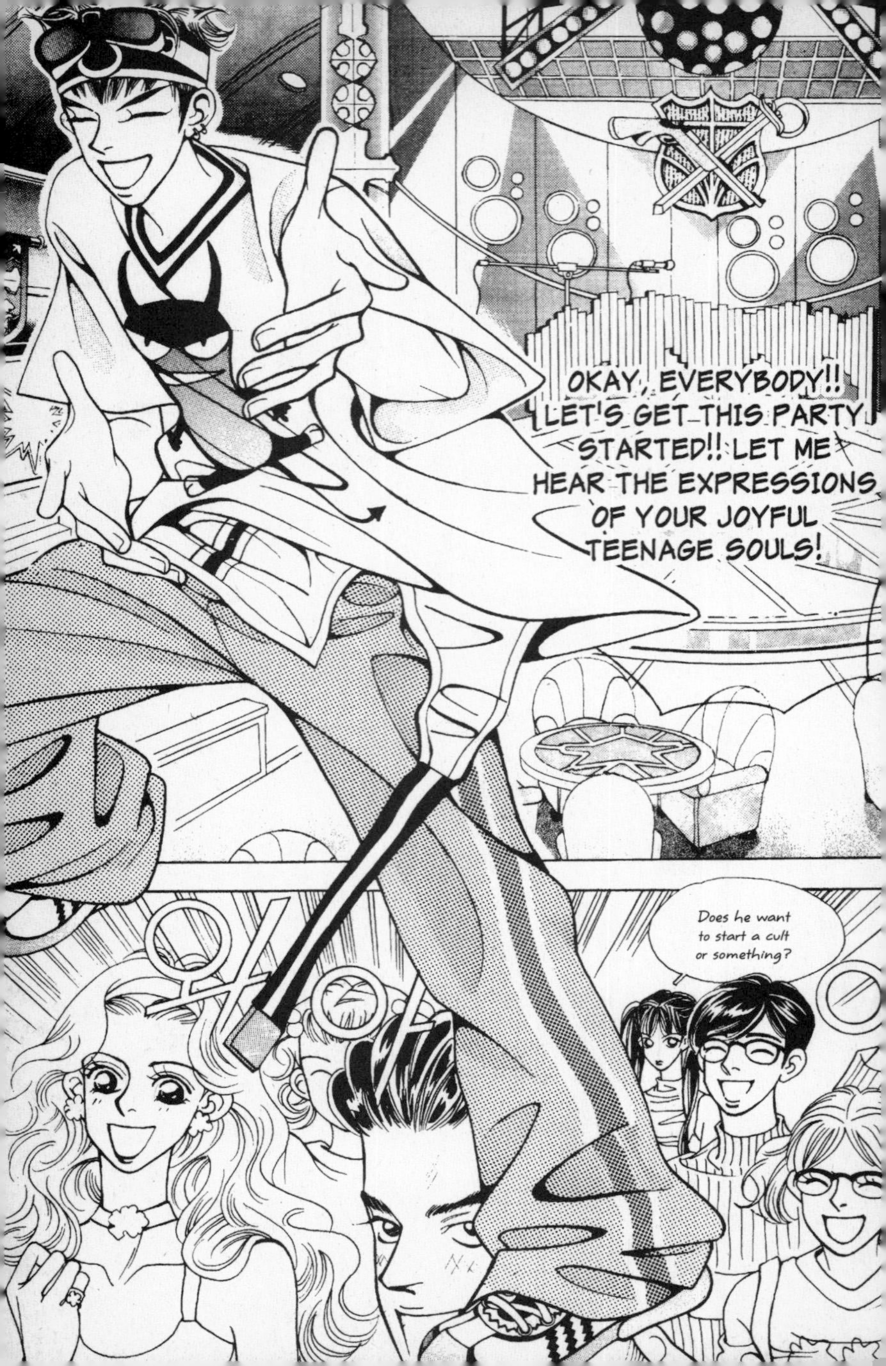
OKAY, EVERYBODY!! LET'S GET THIS PARTY STARTED!! LET ME HEAR THE EXPRESSIONS OF YOUR JOYFUL TEENAGE SOULS!
Does he want to start a cult or something?

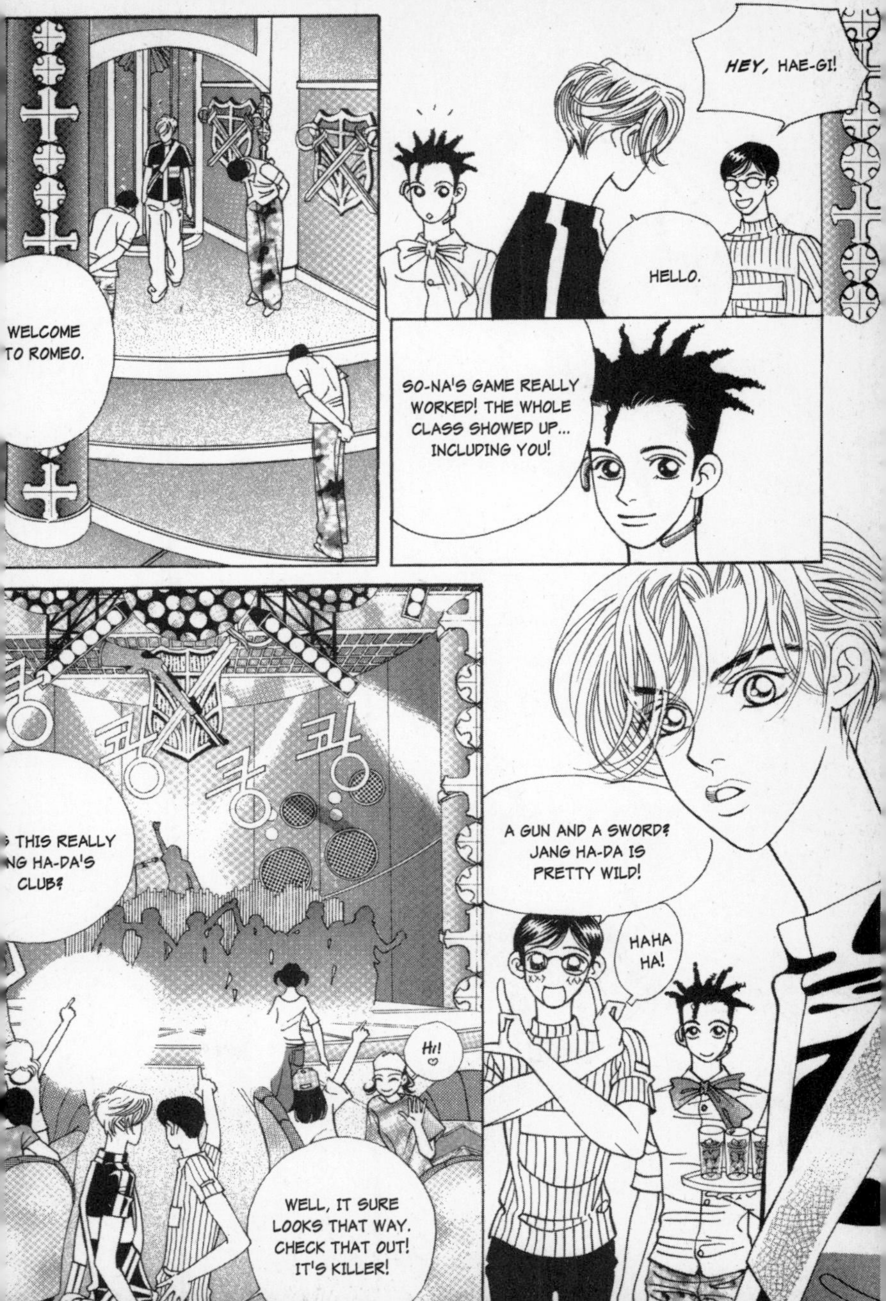
WELCOME
TO ROMEO.
HEY, HAE-GI!
HELLO.
SO-NA'S GAME REALLY WORKED! THE WHOLE CLASS SHOWED UP... INCLUDING YOU!
S THIS REALLY
NG HA-DA'S
CLUB?
HI!
WELL, IT SURE LOOKS THAT WAY. CHECK THAT OUT! IT'S KILLER!
A GUN AND A SWORD? JANG HA-DA IS PRETTY WILD!
HAHA HA!

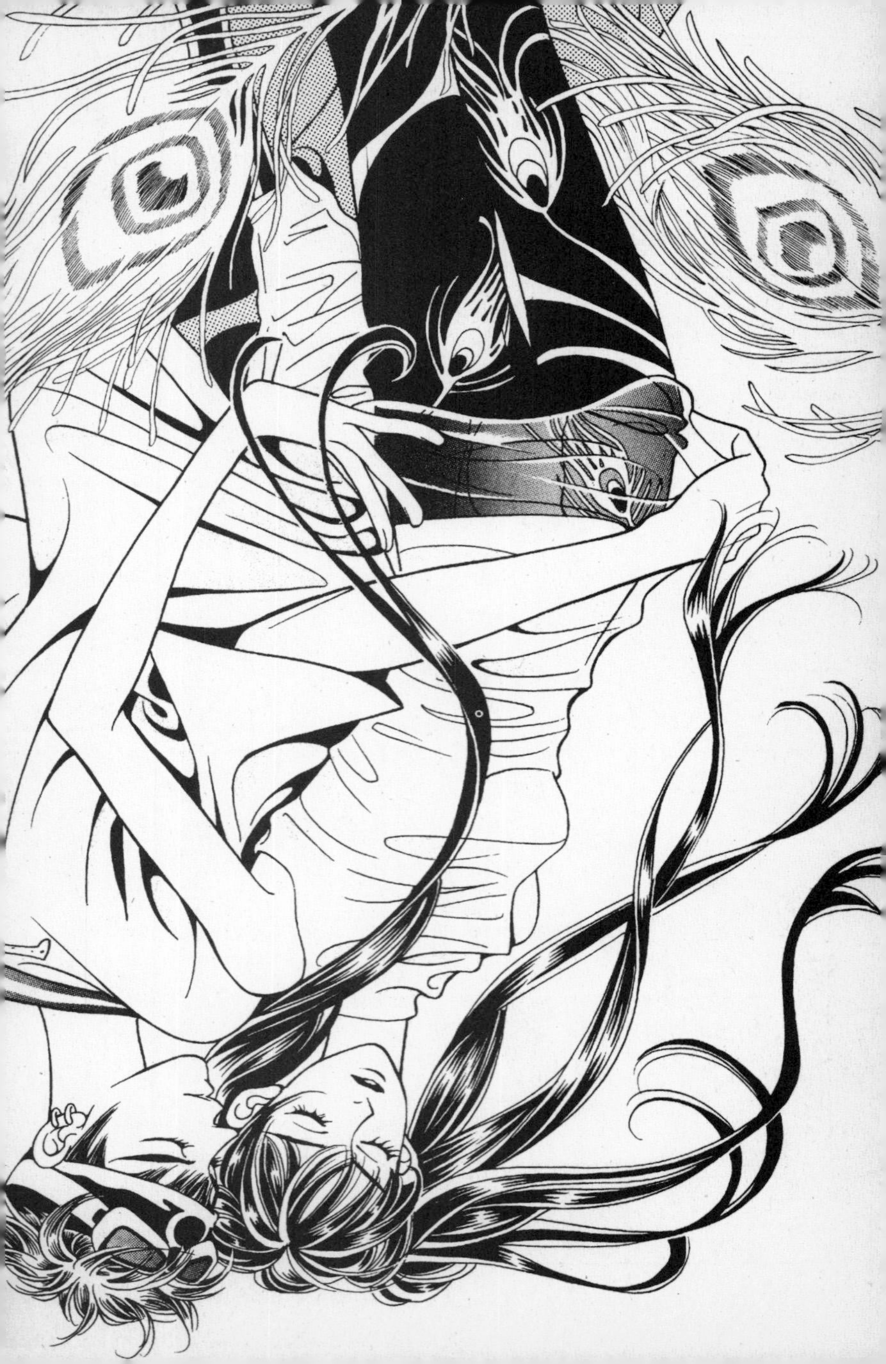

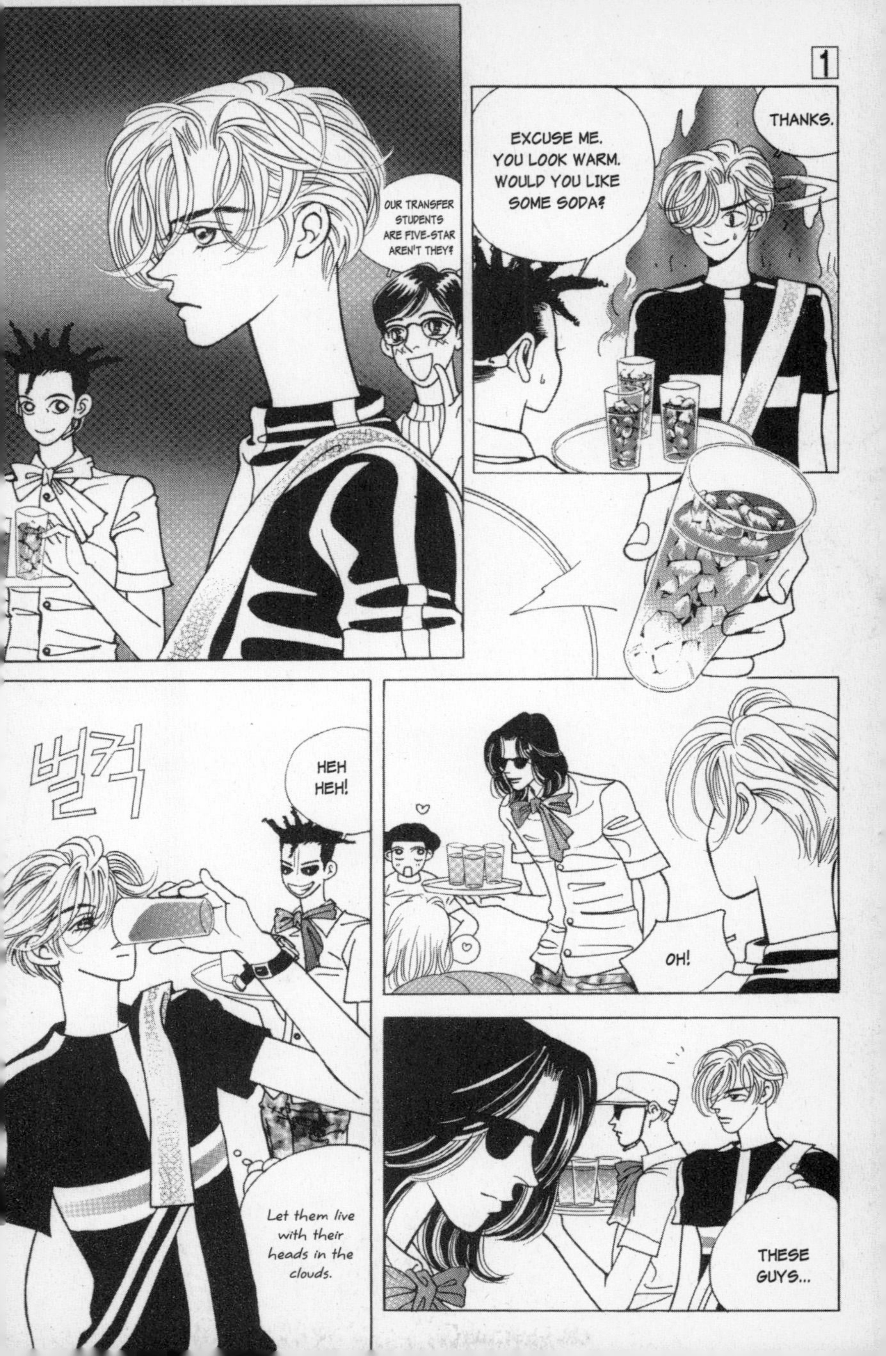
1
OUR TRANSFER STUDENTS ARE FIVE-STAR AREN'T THEY?
EXCUSE ME. YOU LOOK WARM. WOULD YOU LIKE SOME SODA?
THANKS.
벌컥
HEH HEH!
Let them live with their heads in the clouds.
OH!
THESE GUYS...

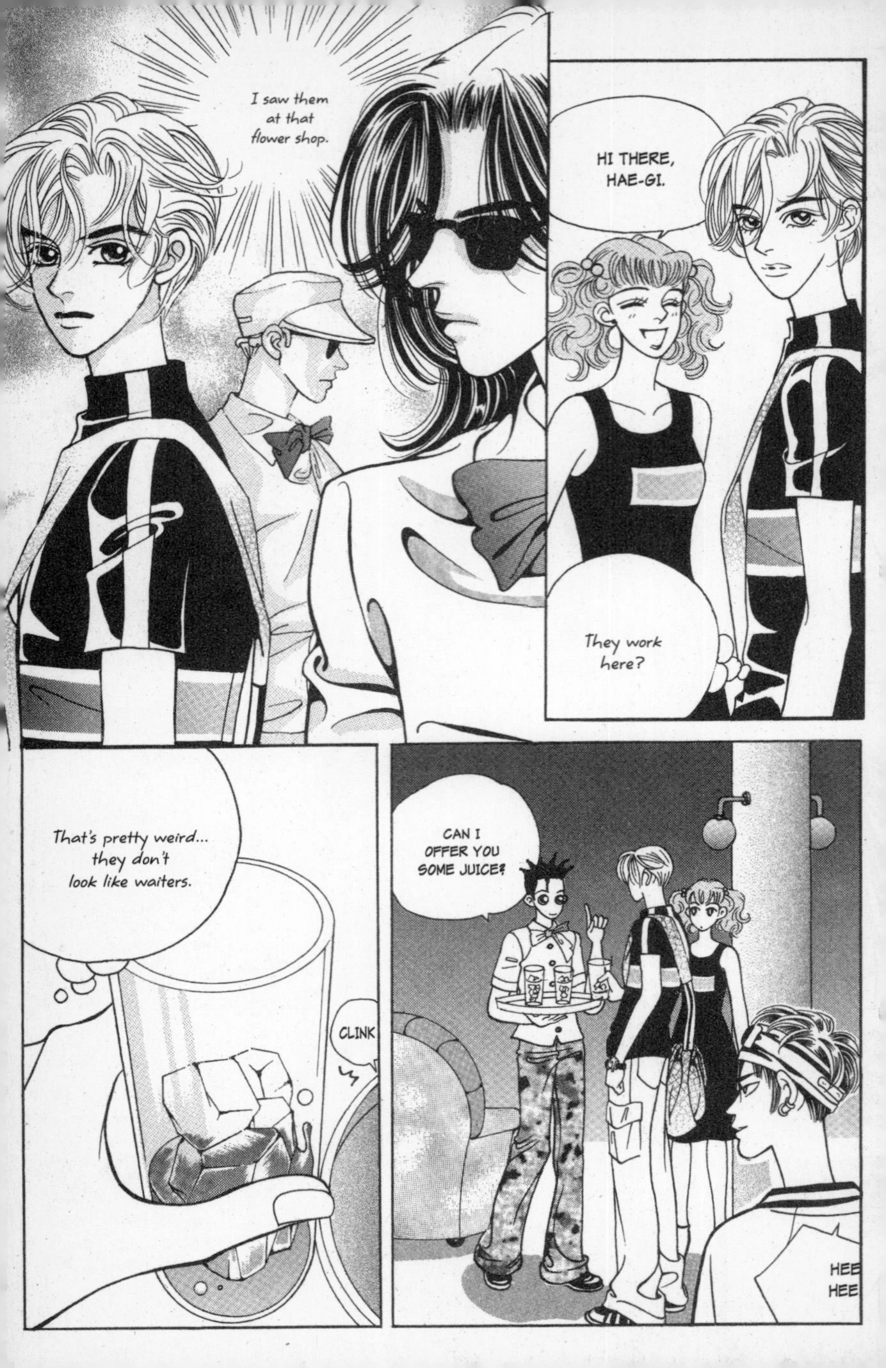
I saw them at that flower shop.
HI THERE, HAE-GI.
They work here?
That's pretty weird... they don't look like waiters.
CLINK
CAN I OFFER YOU SOME JUICE?
HEE HEE

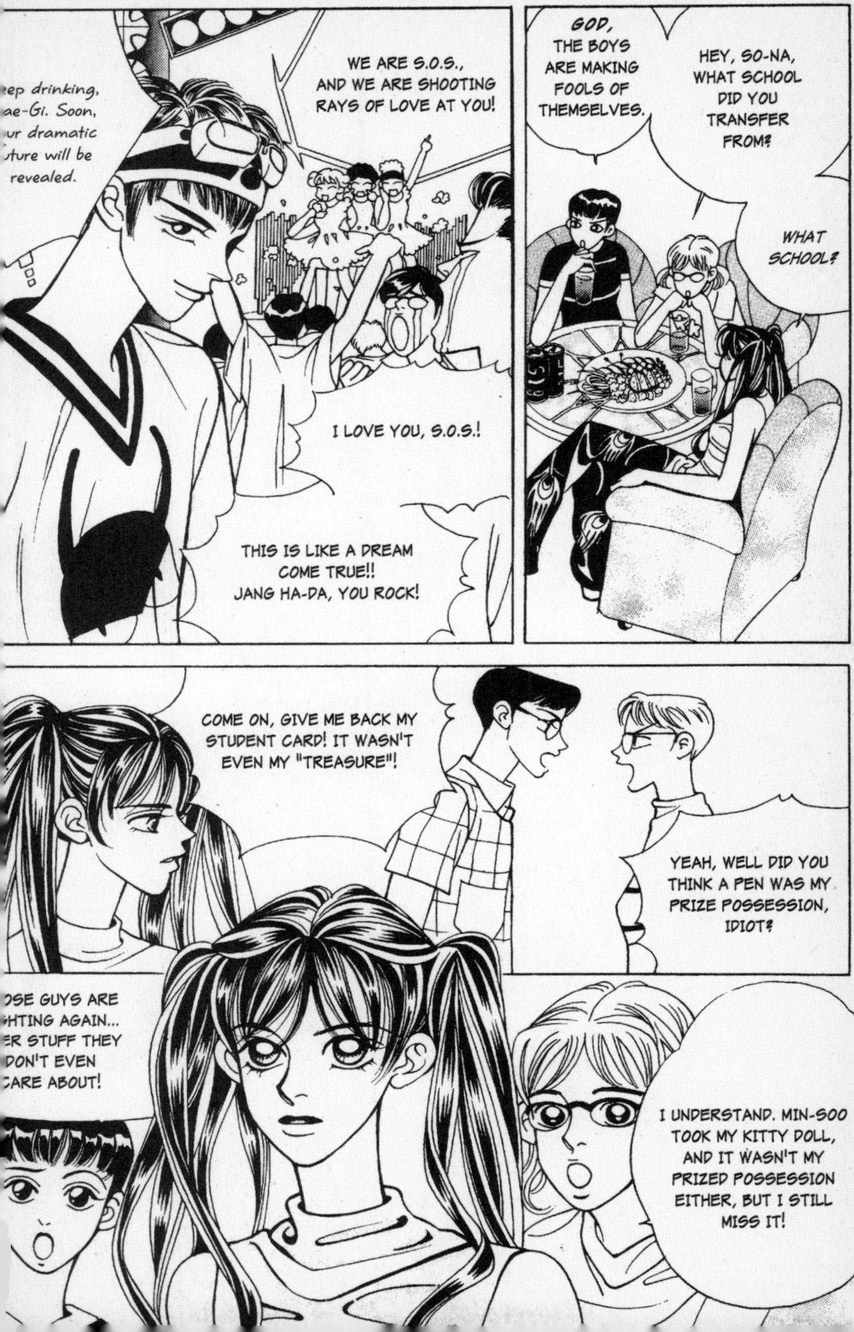

ep drinking, ae-Gi. Soon, ur dramatic uture will be revealed.
WE ARE S.O.S., AND WE ARE SHOOTING RAYS OF LOVE AT YOU!
I LOVE YOU, S.O.S.!
THIS IS LIKE A DREAM COME TRUE!! JANG HA-DA, YOU ROCK!
GOD, THE BOYS ARE MAKING FOOLS OF THEMSELVES.
HEY, SO-NA, WHAT SCHOOL DID YOU TRANSFER FROM?
WHAT SCHOOL?
COME ON, GIVE ME BACK MY STUDENT CARD! IT WASN'T EVEN MY "TREASURE"!
YEAH, WELL DID YOU THINK A PEN WAS MY PRIZE POSSESSION, IDIOT?
OSE GUYS ARE HTING AGAIN... ER STUFF THEY DON'T EVEN CARE ABOUT!
I UNDERSTAND. MIN-SOO TOOK MY KITTY DOLL, AND IT WASN'T MY PRIZED POSSESSION EITHER, BUT I STILL MISS IT!

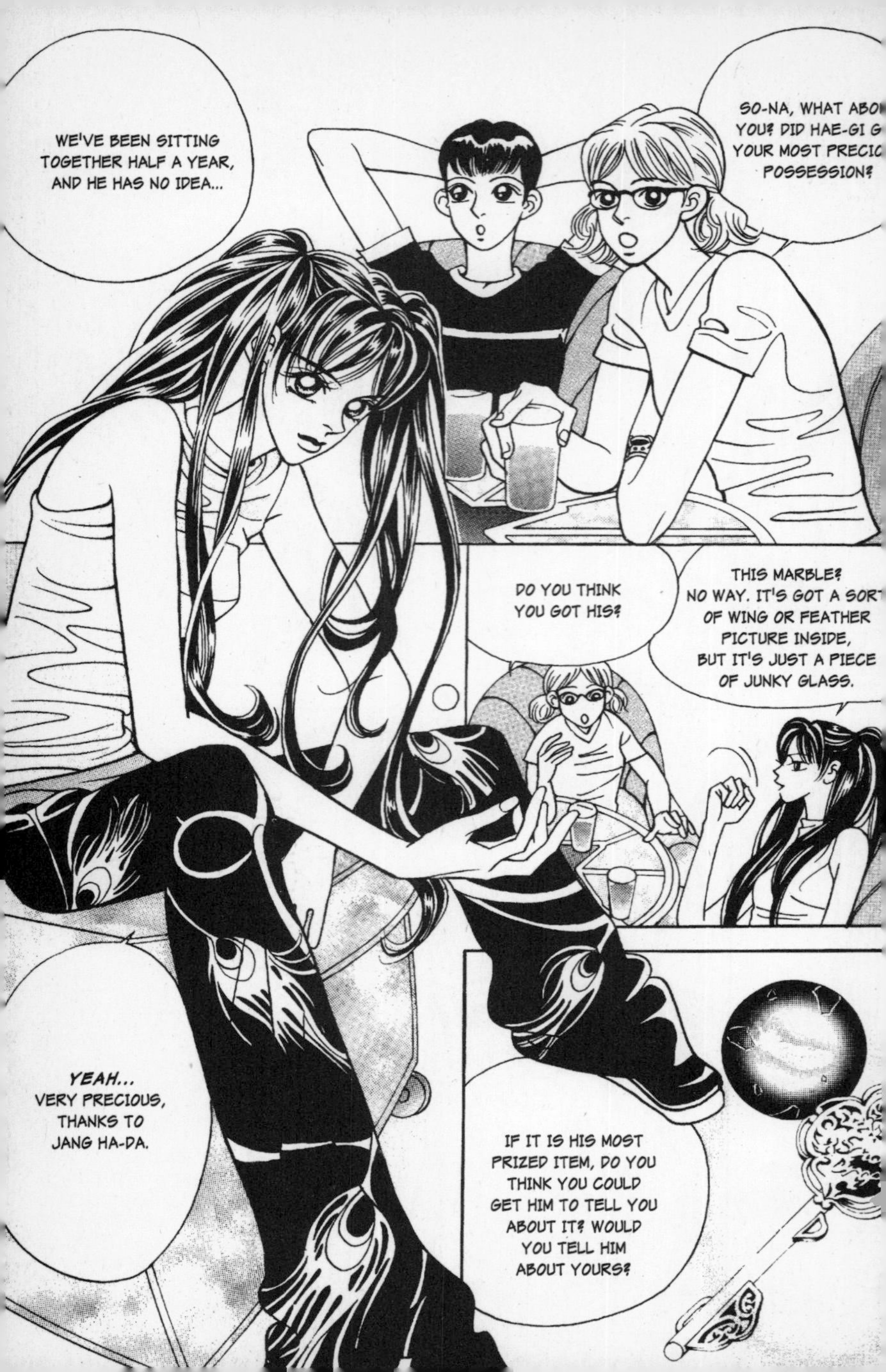
WE'VE BEEN SITTING TOGETHER HALF A YEAR, AND HE HAS NO IDEA...
SO-NA, WHAT ABO YOU? DID HAE-GI G YOUR MOST PRECIC POSSESSION?
DO YOU THINK YOU GOT HIS?
THIS MARBLE? NO WAY. IT'S GOT A SOR OF WING OR FEATHER PICTURE INSIDE, BUT IT'S JUST A PIECE OF JUNKY GLASS.
YEAH... VERY PRECIOUS, THANKS TO JANG HA-DA.
IF IT IS HIS MOST PRIZED ITEM, DO YOU THINK YOU COULD GET HIM TO TELL YOU ABOUT IT? WOULD YOU TELL HIM ABOUT YOURS?

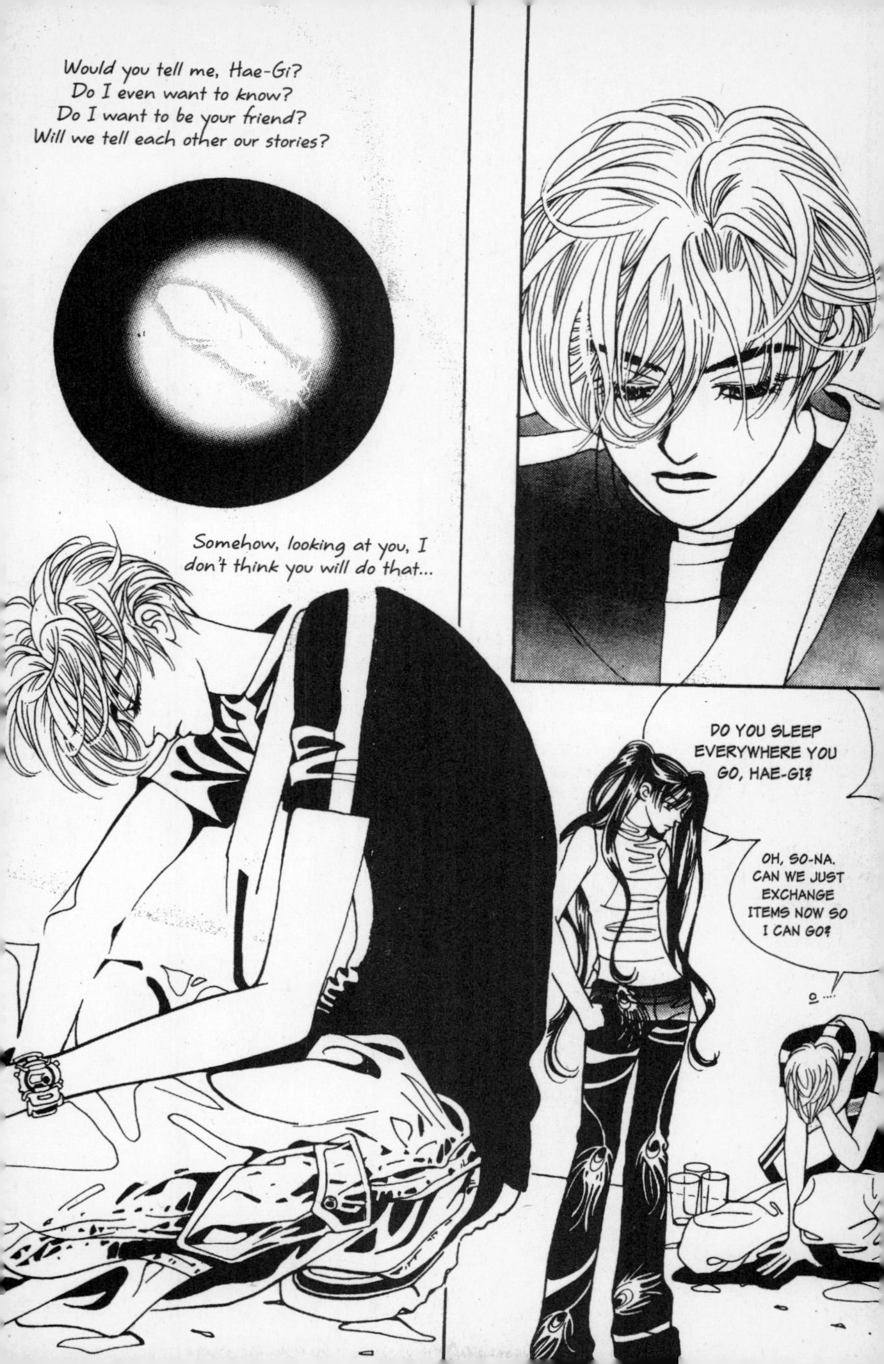
Would you tell me, Hae-Gi?
Do I even want to know?
Do I want to be your friend?
Will we tell each other our stories?
Somehow, looking at you, I don't think you will do that...
DO YOU SLEEP EVERYWHERE YOU GO, HAE-GI?
OH, SO-NA. CAN WE JUST EXCHANGE ITEMS NOW SO I CAN GO?
o....

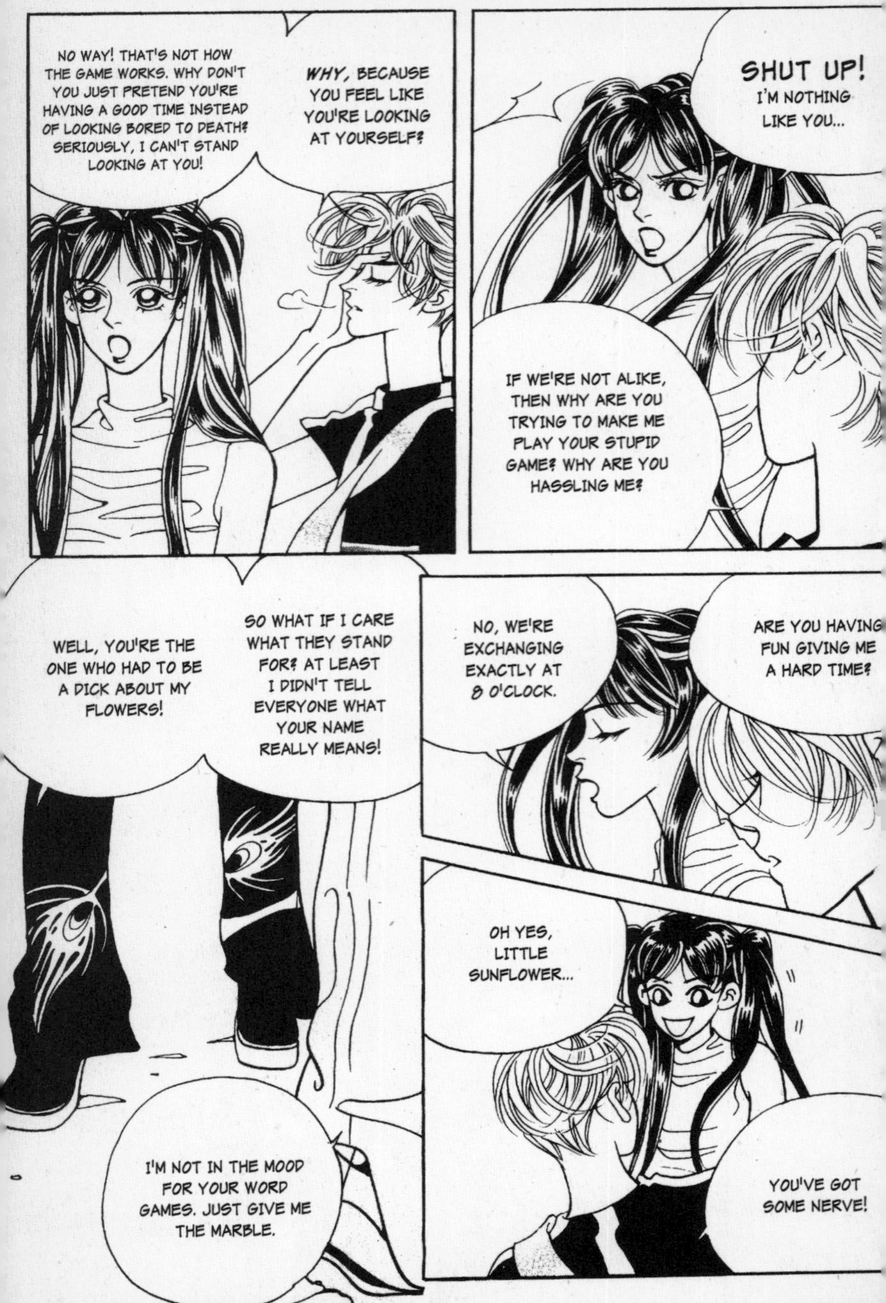
NO WAY! THAT'S NOT HOW THE GAME WORKS. WHY DON'T YOU JUST PRETEND YOU'RE HAVING A GOOD TIME INSTEAD OF LOOKING BORED TO DEATH? SERIOUSLY, I CAN'T STAND LOOKING AT YOU!
WHY, BECAUSE YOU FEEL LIKE YOU'RE LOOKING AT YOURSELF?
SHUT UP! I'M NOTHING LIKE YOU...
IF WE'RE NOT ALIKE, THEN WHY ARE YOU TRYING TO MAKE ME PLAY YOUR STUPID GAME? WHY ARE YOU HASSLING ME?
WELL, YOU'RE THE ONE WHO HAD TO BE A DICK ABOUT MY FLOWERS!
SO WHAT IF I CARE WHAT THEY STAND FOR? AT LEAST I DIDN'T TELL EVERYONE WHAT YOUR NAME REALLY MEANS!
I'M NOT IN THE MOOD FOR YOUR WORD GAMES. JUST GIVE ME THE MARBLE.
NO, WE'RE EXCHANGING EXACTLY AT 8 O'CLOCK.
ARE YOU HAVING FUN GIVING ME A HARD TIME?
OH YES, LITTLE SUNFLOWER...
YOU'VE GOT SOME NERVE!

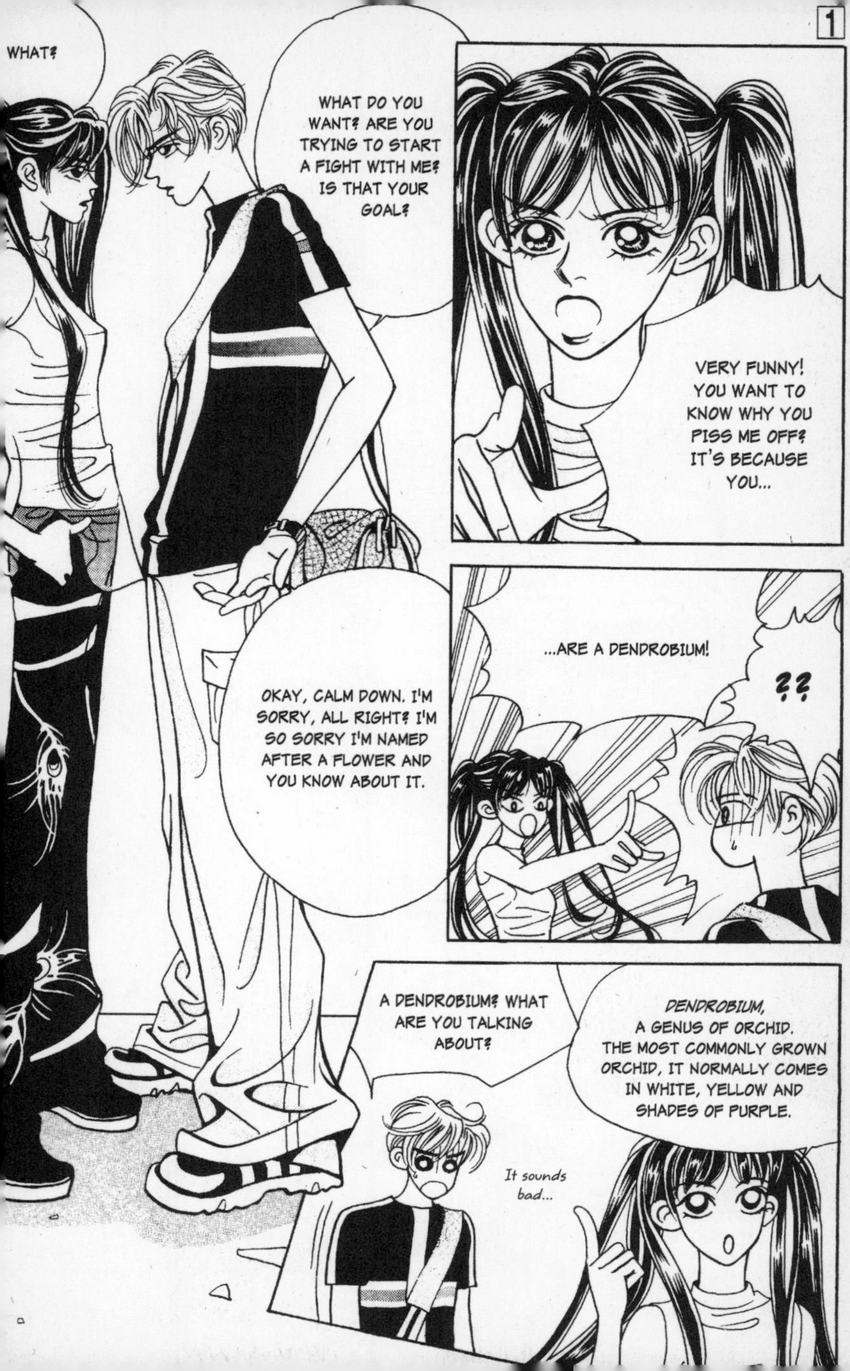
WHAT?
WHAT DO YOU WANT? ARE YOU TRYING TO START A FIGHT WITH ME? IS THAT YOUR GOAL?
OKAY, CALM DOWN. I'M SORRY, ALL RIGHT? I'M SO SORRY I'M NAMED AFTER A FLOWER AND YOU KNOW ABOUT IT.
VERY FUNNY! YOU WANT TO KNOW WHY YOU PISS ME OFF? IT'S BECAUSE YOU...
...ARE A DENDROBIUM!
??
A DENDROBIUM? WHAT ARE YOU TALKING ABOUT?
DENDROBIUM, A GENUS OF ORCHID. THE MOST COMMONLY GROWN ORCHID, IT NORMALLY COMES IN WHITE, YELLOW AND SHADES OF PURPLE.
It sounds bad...

Part 2. Dendrobium
A Haughty Beauty

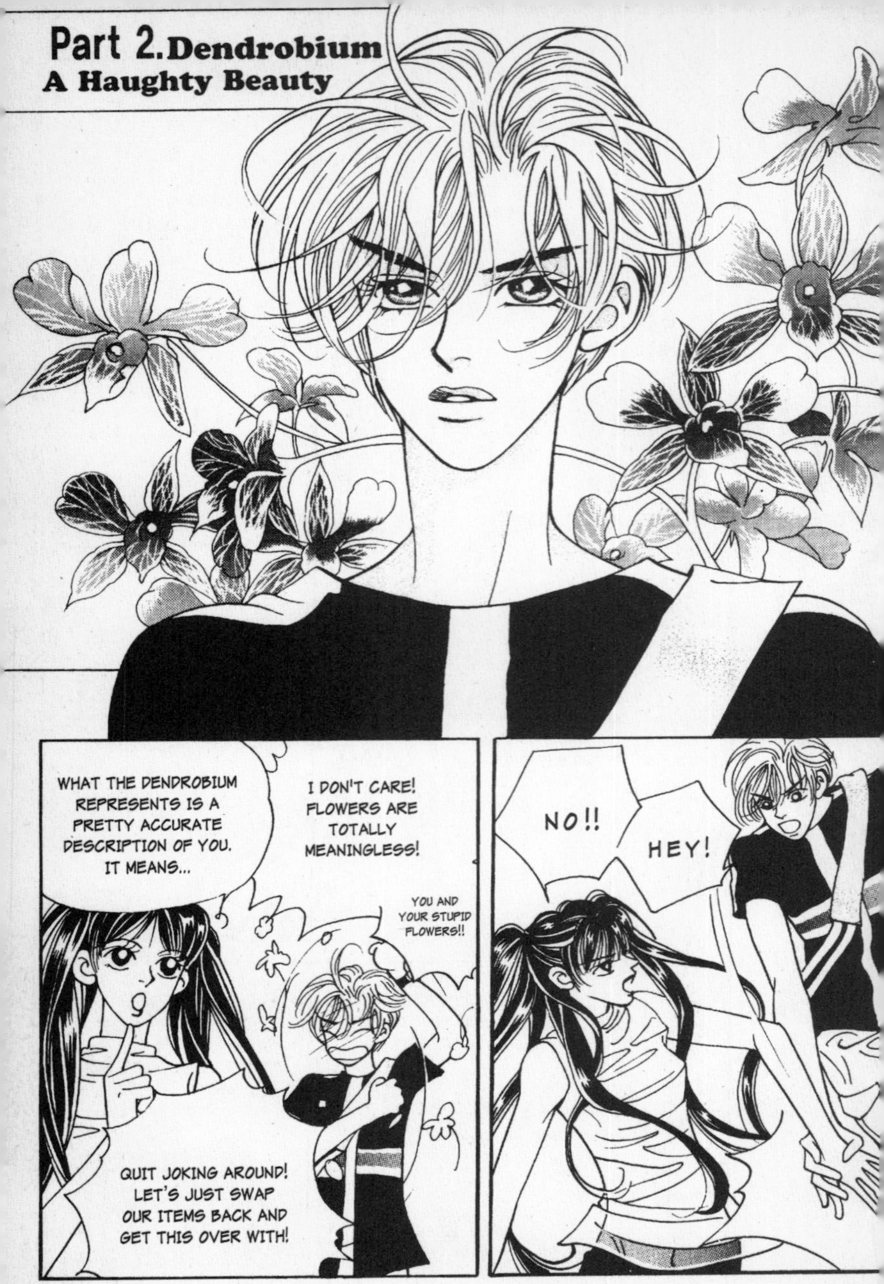
WHAT THE DENDROBIUM REPRESENTS IS A PRETTY ACCURATE DESCRIPTION OF YOU. IT MEANS...
I DON'T CARE! FLOWERS ARE TOTALLY MEANINGLESS!
YOU AND YOUR STUPID FLOWERS!!
QUIT JOKING AROUND! LET'S JUST SWAP OUR ITEMS BACK AND GET THIS OVER WITH!
NO!!
HEY!

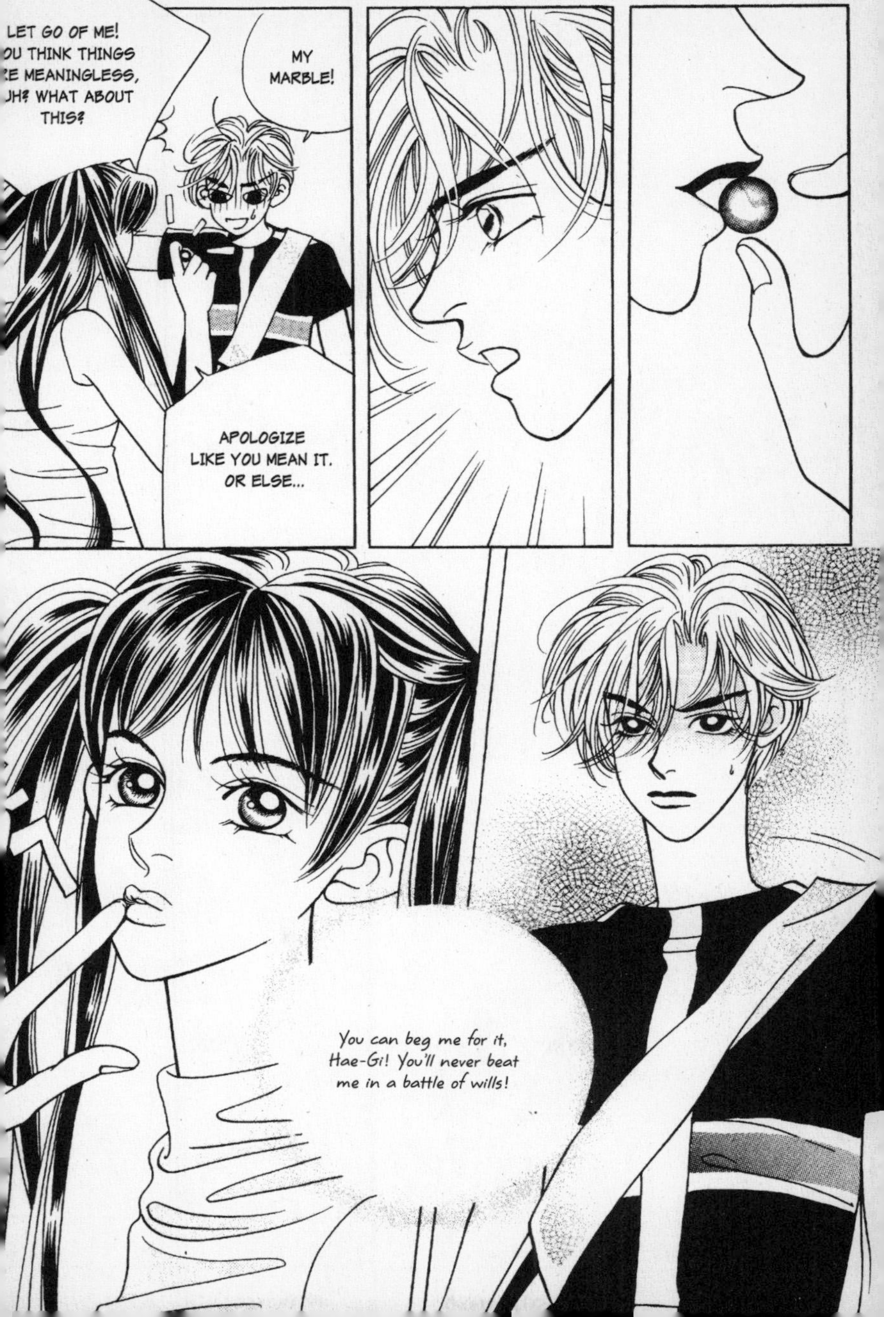
LET GO OF ME! OU THINK THINGS E MEANINGLESS, JH? WHAT ABOUT THIS?
MY MARBLE!
APOLOGIZE LIKE YOU MEAN IT. OR ELSE...
You can beg me for it, Hae-Gi! You'll never beat me in a battle of wills!

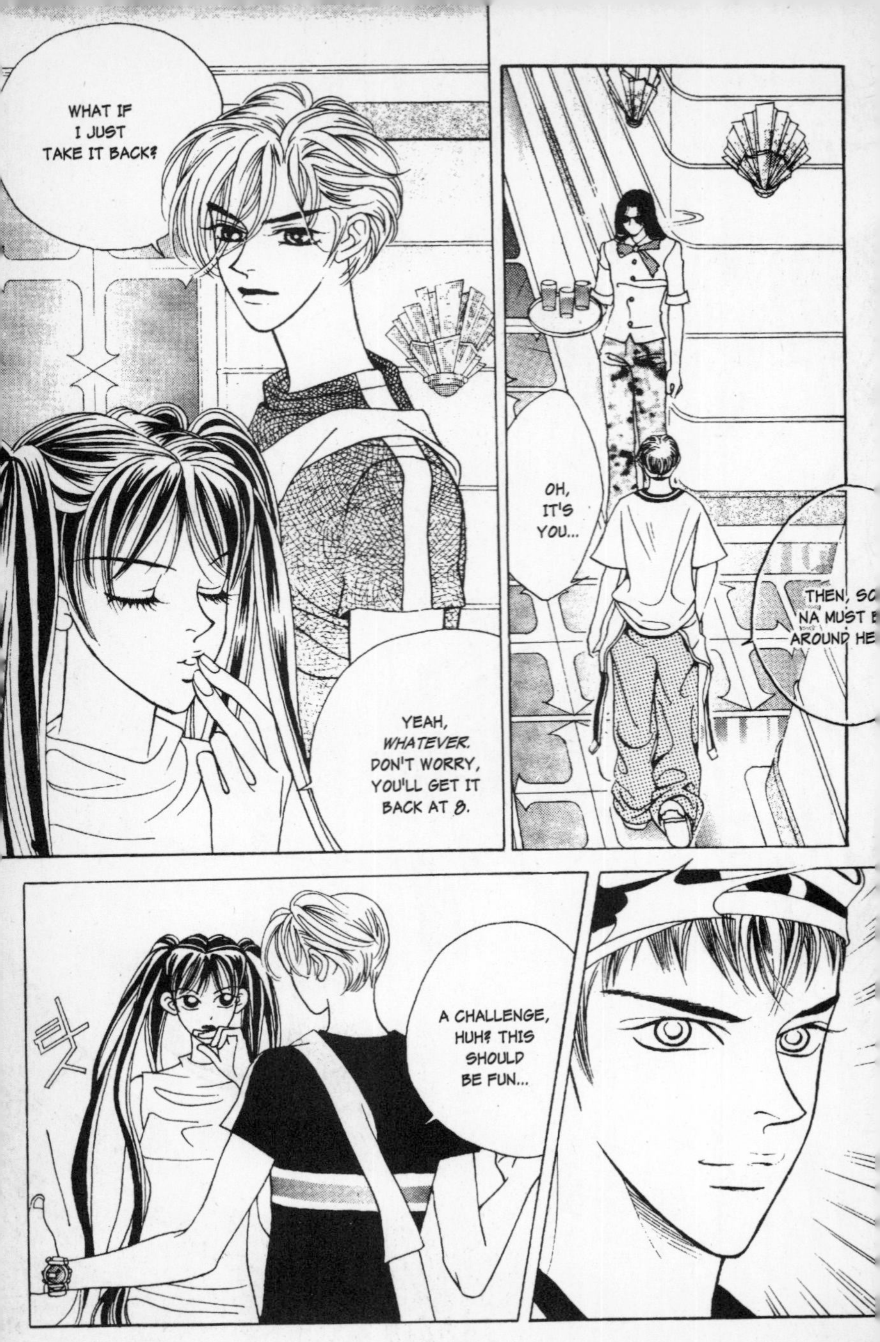
WHAT IF I JUST TAKE IT BACK?
YEAH, *WHATEVER.* DON'T WORRY, YOU'LL GET IT BACK AT 8.
OH, IT'S YOU...
THEN, SO NA MUST B AROUND HE
A CHALLENGE, HUH? THIS SHOULD BE FUN...

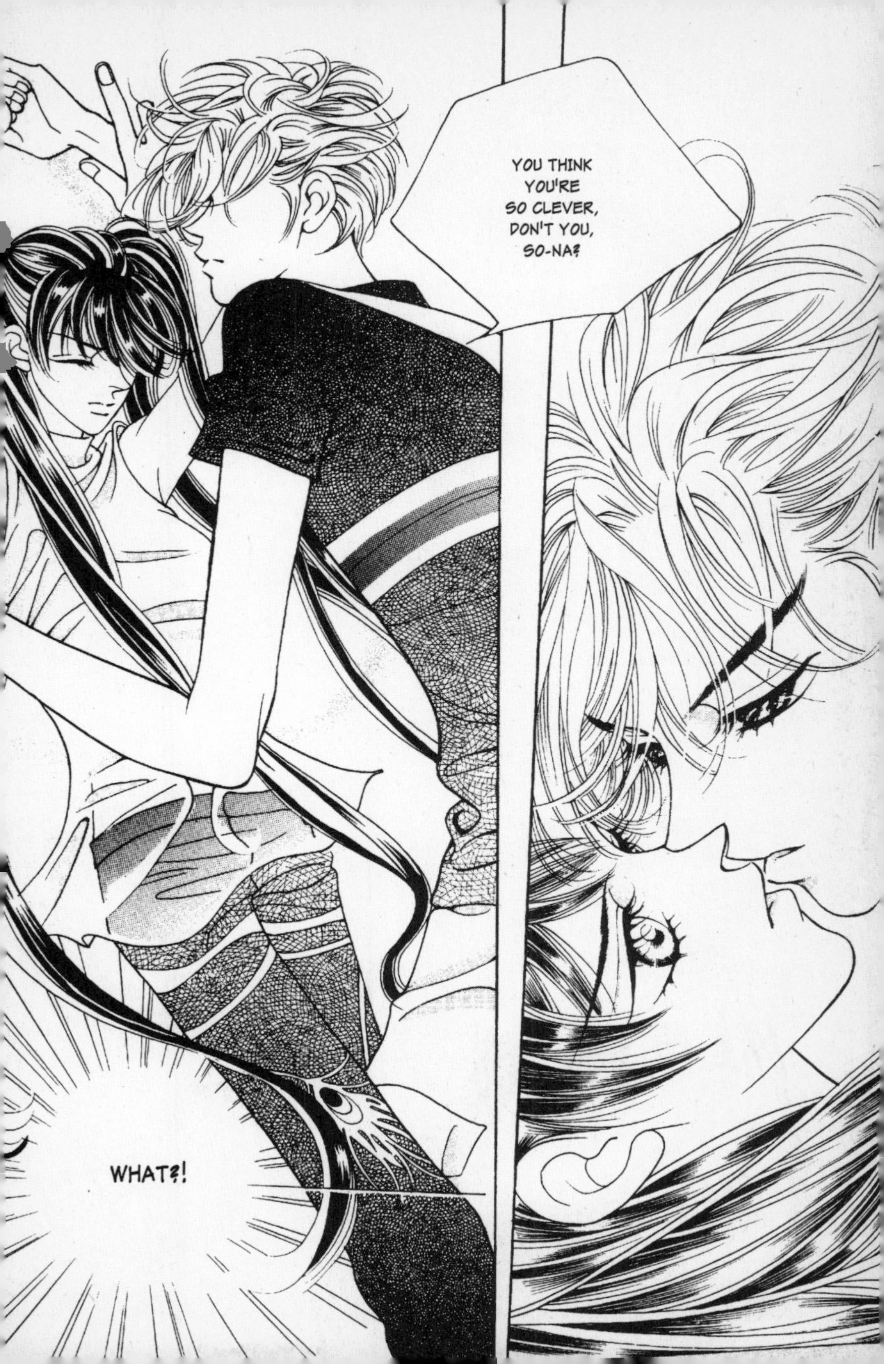
WHAT?!
YOU THINK YOU'RE SO CLEVER, DON'T YOU, SO-NA?

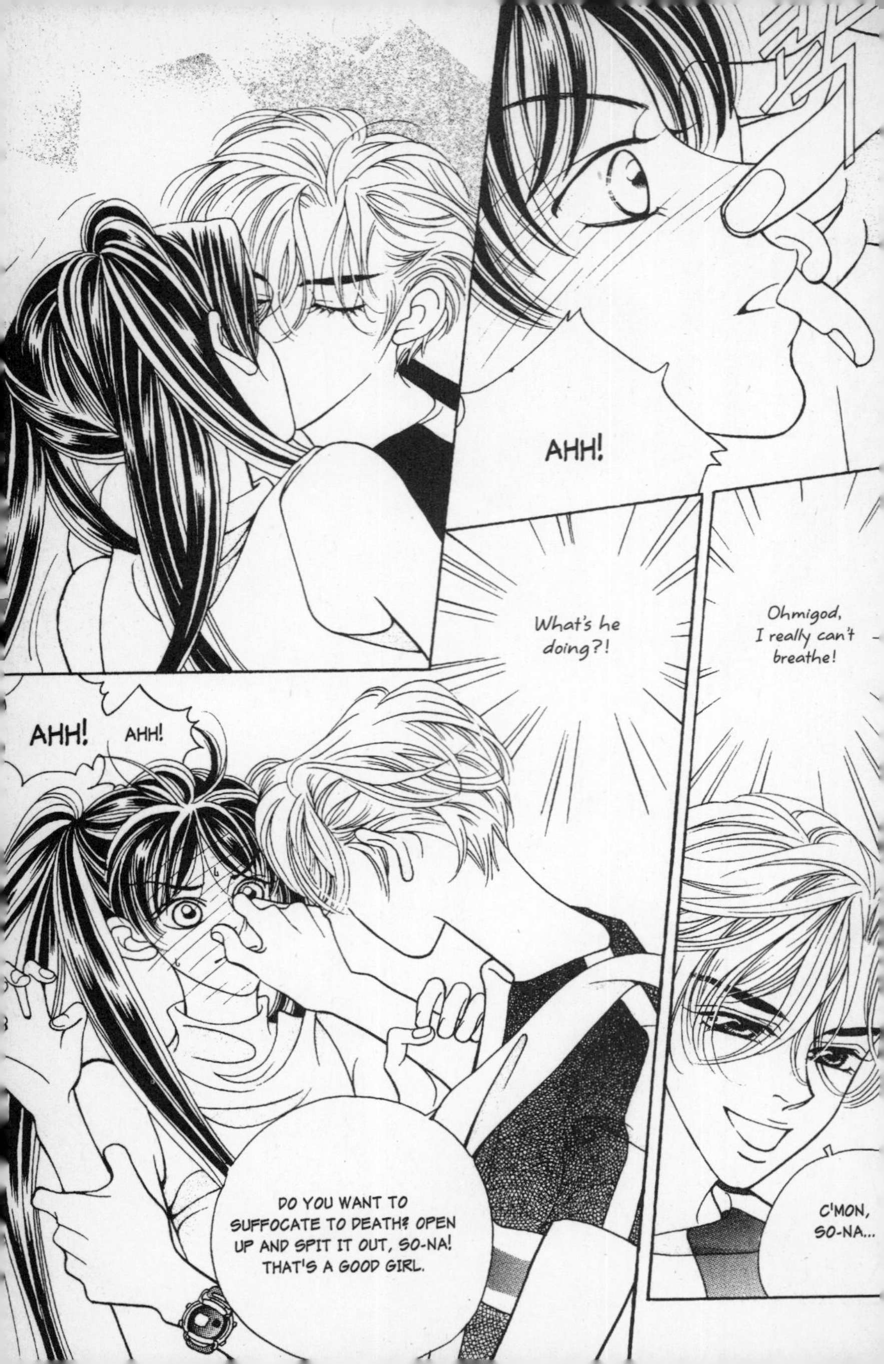
AHH!
What's he doing?!
Ohmigod, I really can't breathe!
AHH!
AHH!
DO YOU WANT TO SUFFOCATE TO DEATH? OPEN UP AND SPIT IT OUT, SO-NA! THAT'S A GOOD GIRL.
C'MON, SO-NA...

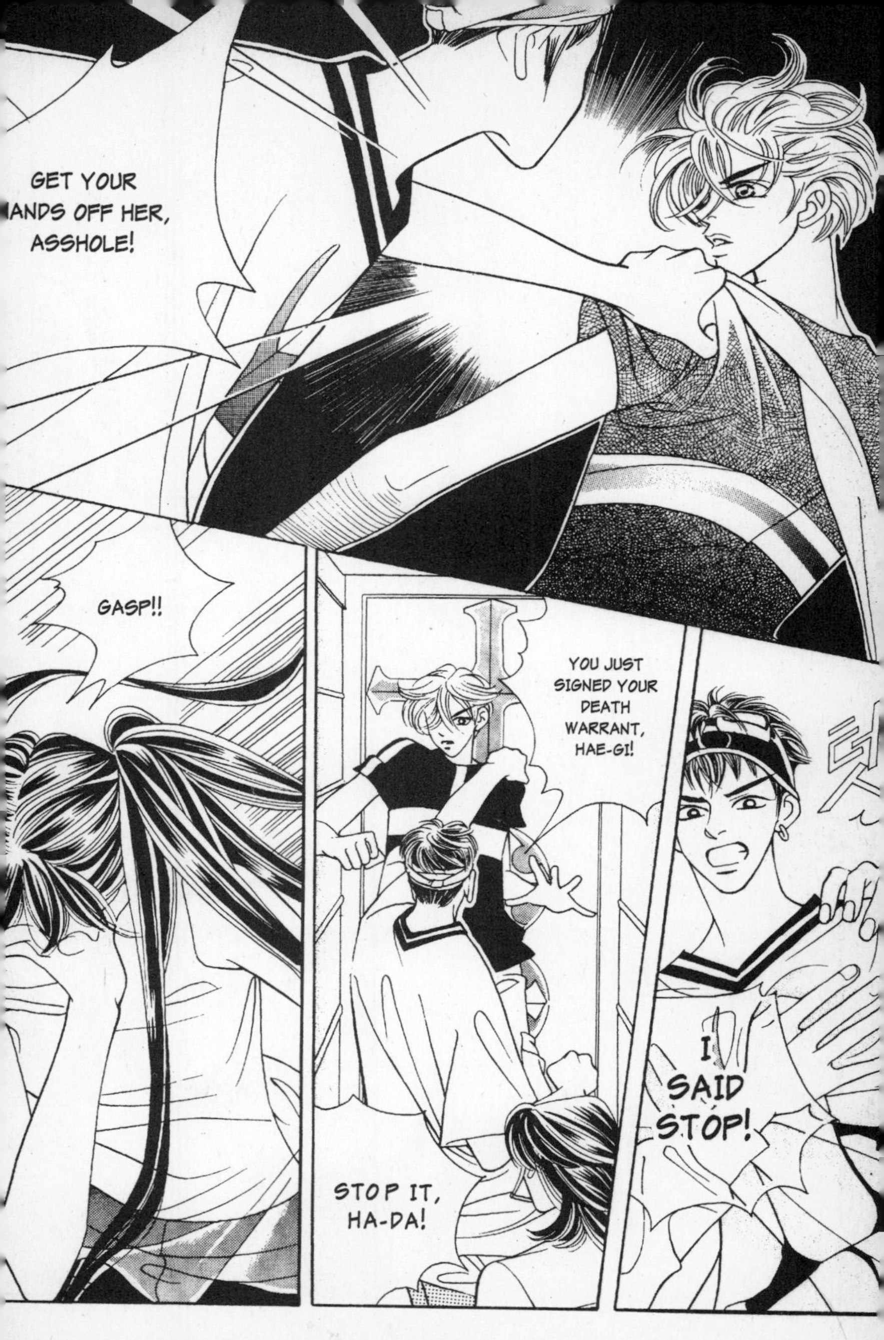
GET YOUR
HANDS OFF HER,
ASSHOLE!
GASP!!
YOU JUST SIGNED YOUR DEATH WARRANT, HAE-GI!
STOP IT, HA-DA!
I SAID STOP!

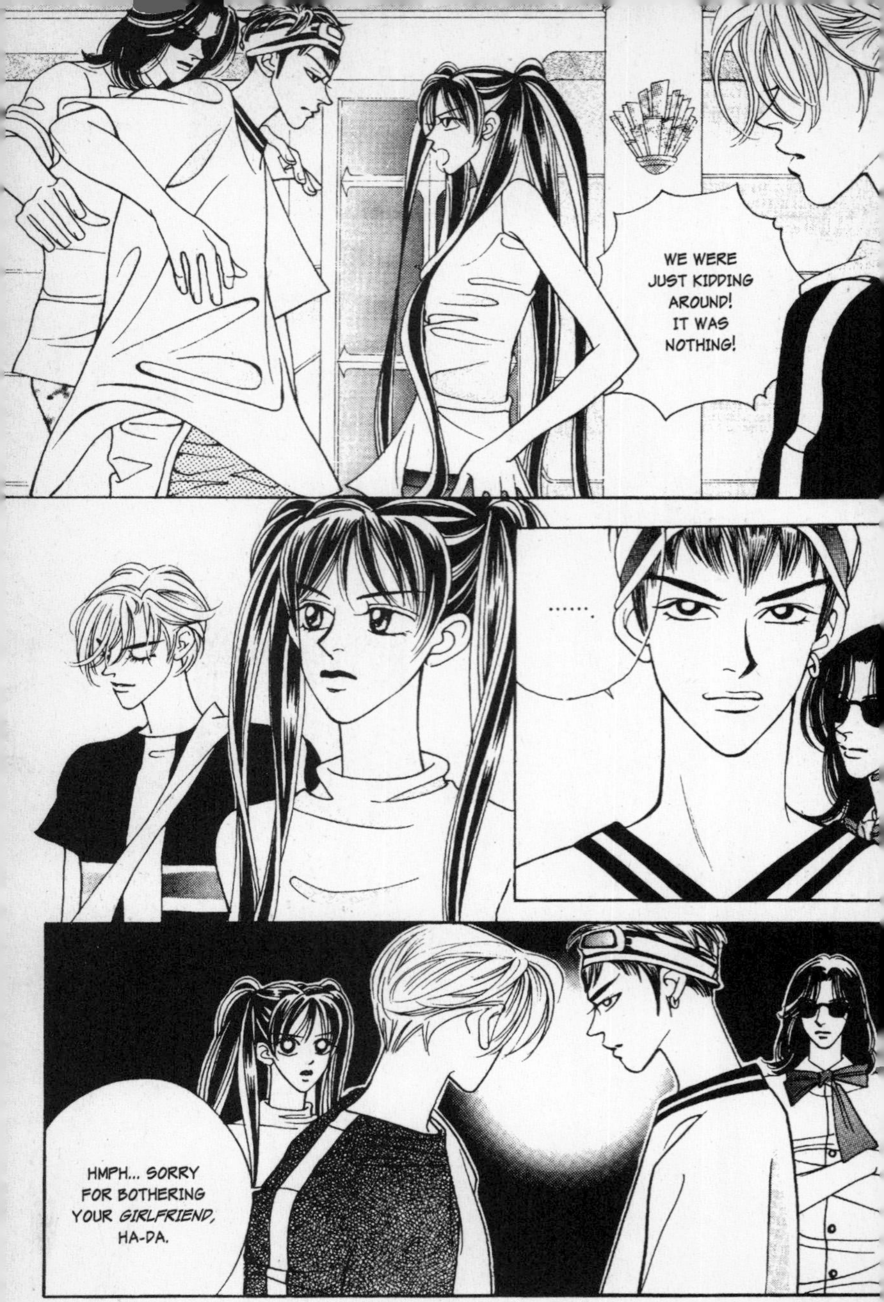
WE WERE JUST KIDDING AROUND! IT WAS NOTHING!
......
HMPH... SORRY FOR BOTHERING YOUR *GIRLFRIEND*, HA-DA.

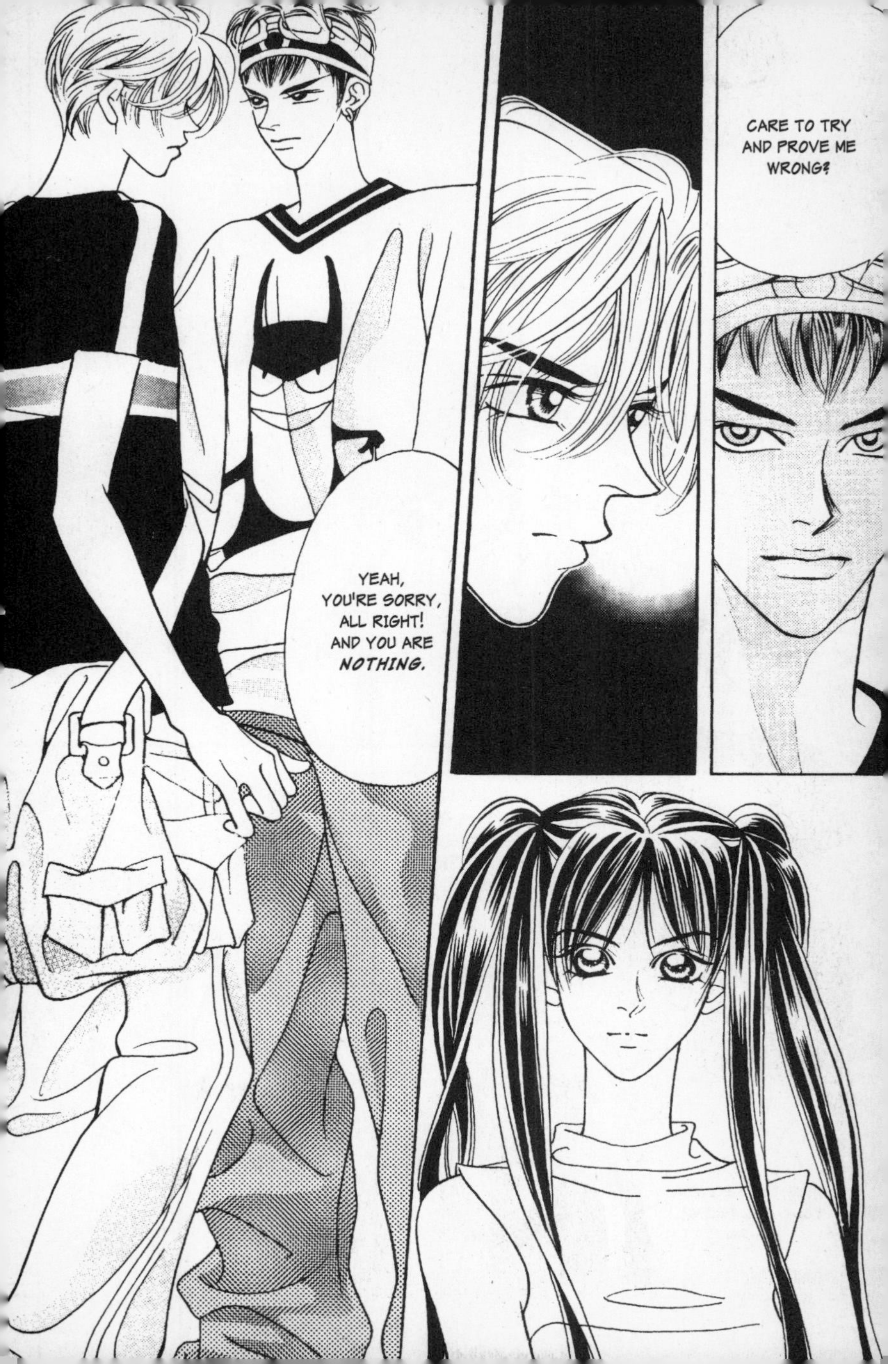
YEAH, YOU'RE SORRY, ALL RIGHT! AND YOU ARE *NOTHING.*
CARE TO TRY AND PROVE ME WRONG?

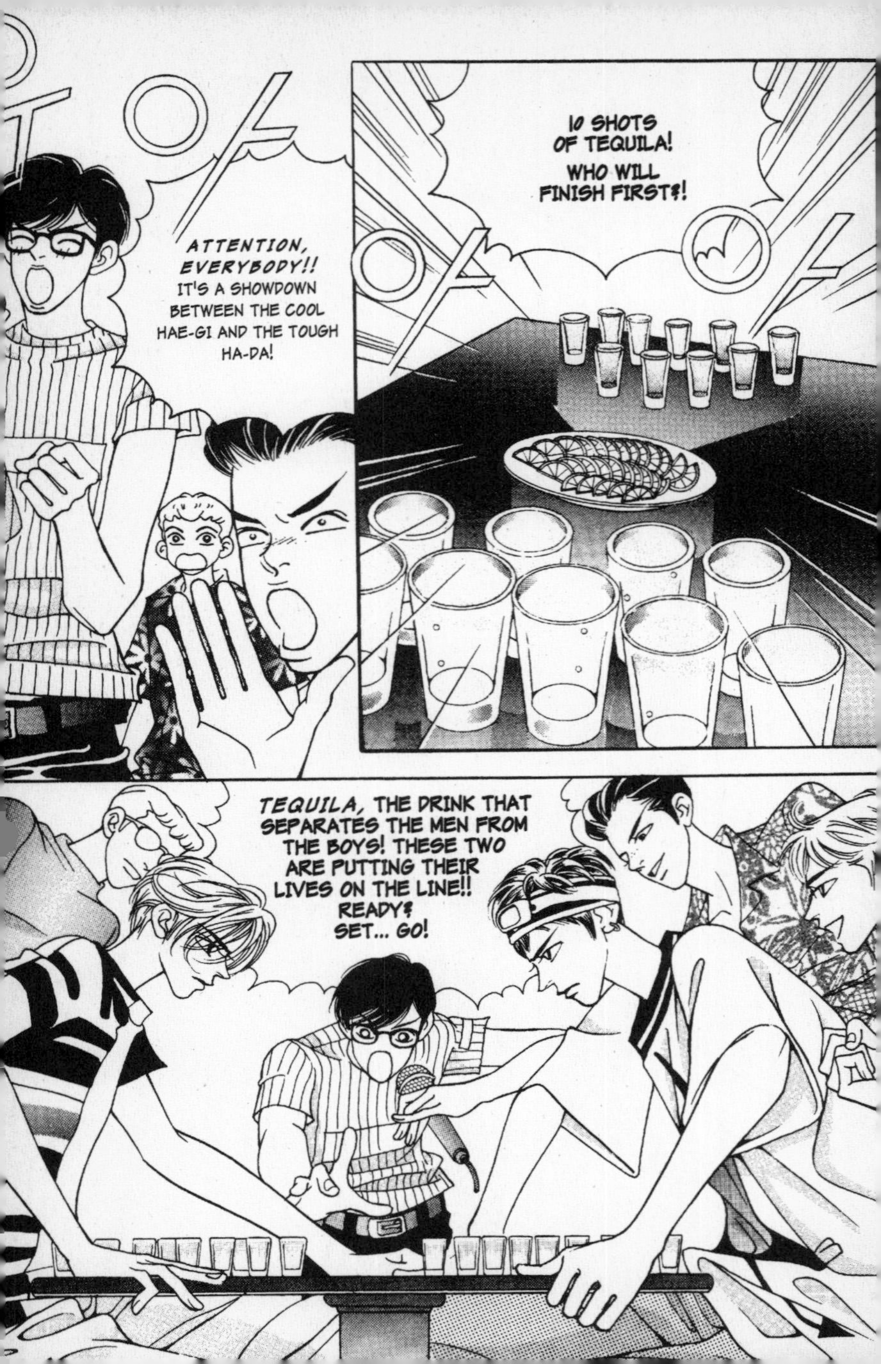
ATTENTION, EVERYBODY!! IT'S A SHOWDOWN BETWEEN THE COOL HAE-GI AND THE TOUGH HA-DA!
10 SHOTS OF TEQUILA! WHO WILL FINISH FIRST?!
TEQUILA, THE DRINK THAT SEPARATES THE MEN FROM THE BOYS! THESE TWO ARE PUTTING THEIR LIVES ON THE LINE!! READY? SET... GO!

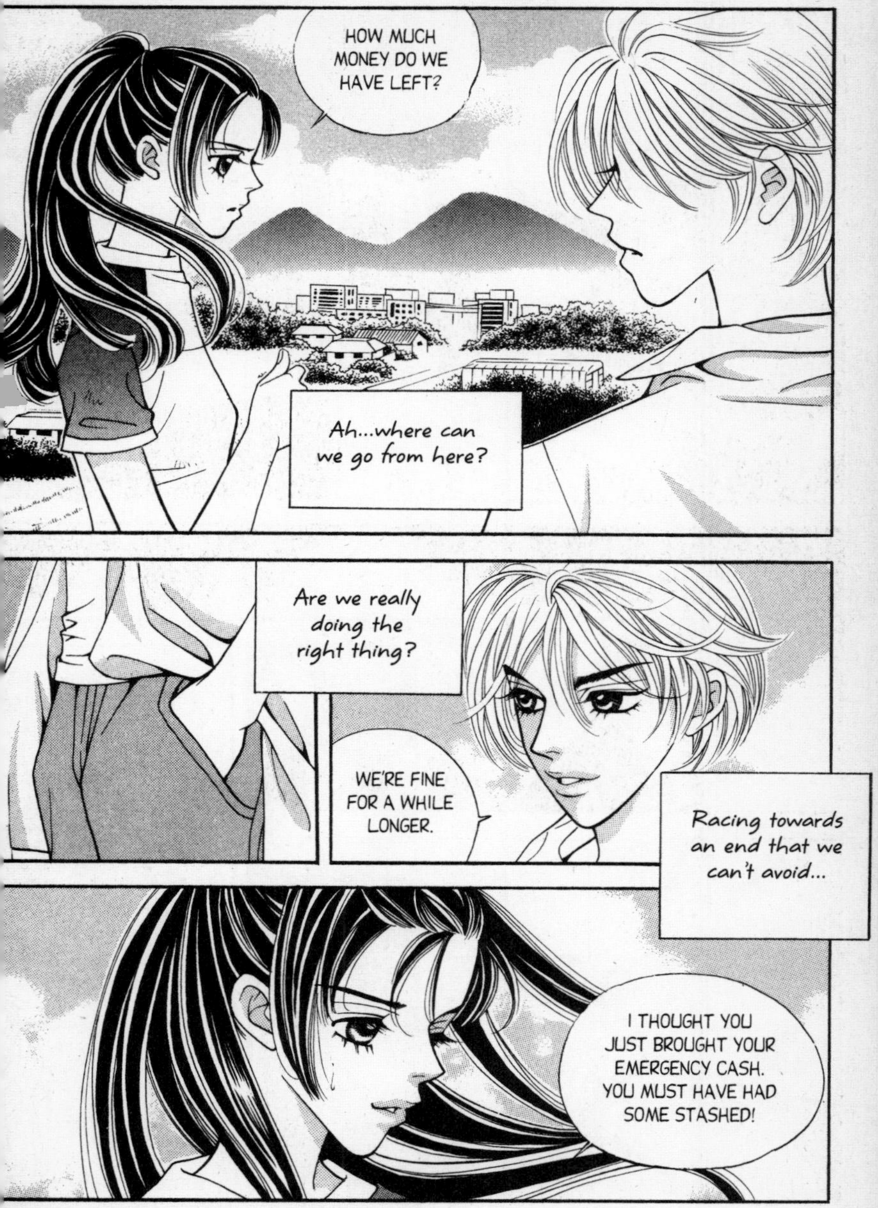
HOW MUCH MONEY DO WE HAVE LEFT?
Ah...where can we go from here?
Are we really doing the right thing?
WE'RE FINE FOR A WHILE LONGER.
Racing towards an end that we can't avoid...
I THOUGHT YOU JUST BROUGHT YOUR EMERGENCY CASH. YOU MUST HAVE HAD SOME STASHED!

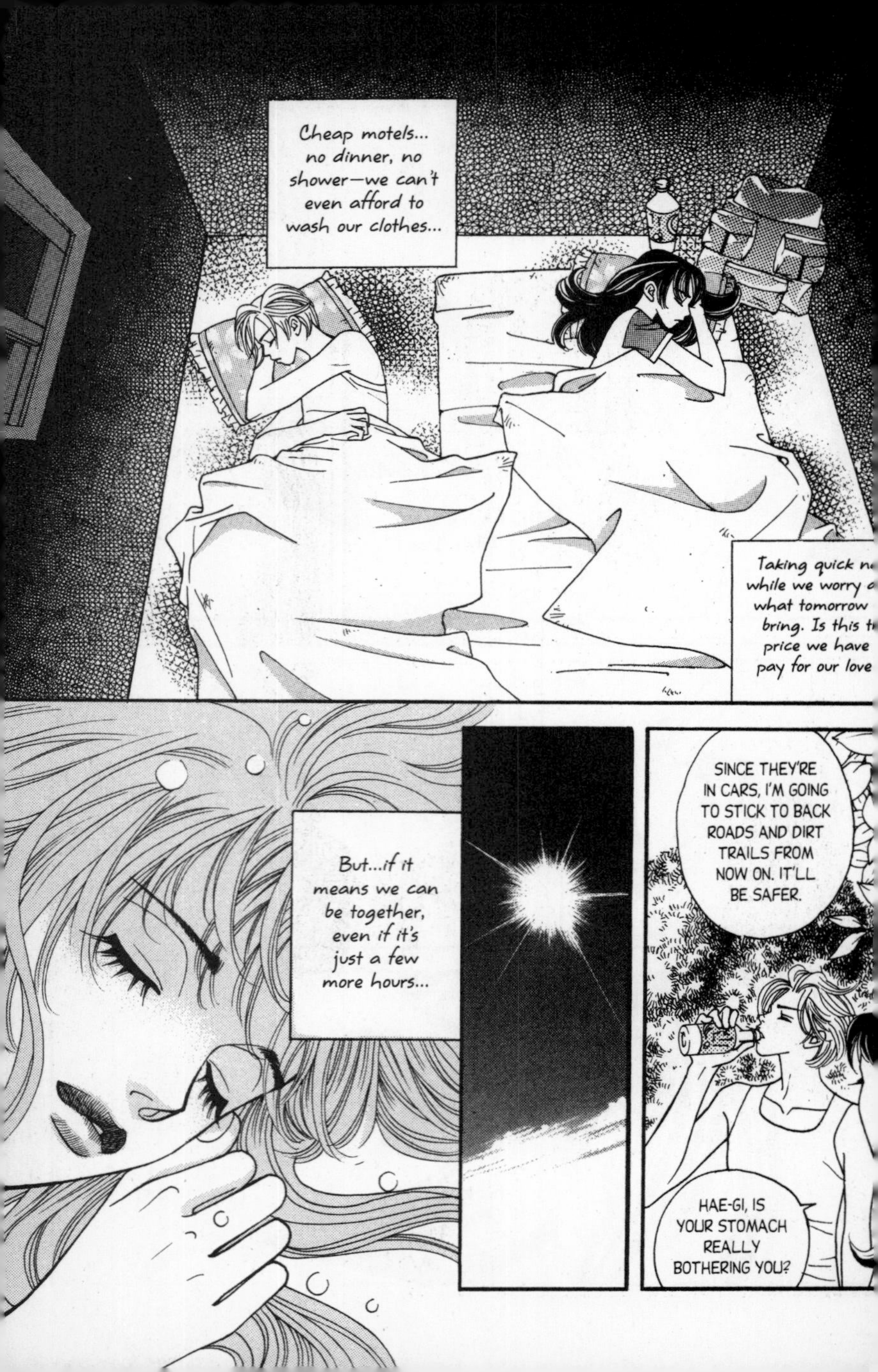
Cheap motels... no dinner, no shower—we can't even afford to wash our clothes...
Taking quick n while we worry a what tomorrow bring. Is this t price we have pay for our love
But...if it means we can be together, even if it's just a few more hours...
SINCE THEY'RE IN CARS, I'M GOING TO STICK TO BACK ROADS AND DIRT TRAILS FROM NOW ON. IT'LL BE SAFER.
HAE-GI, IS YOUR STOMACH REALLY BOTHERING YOU?

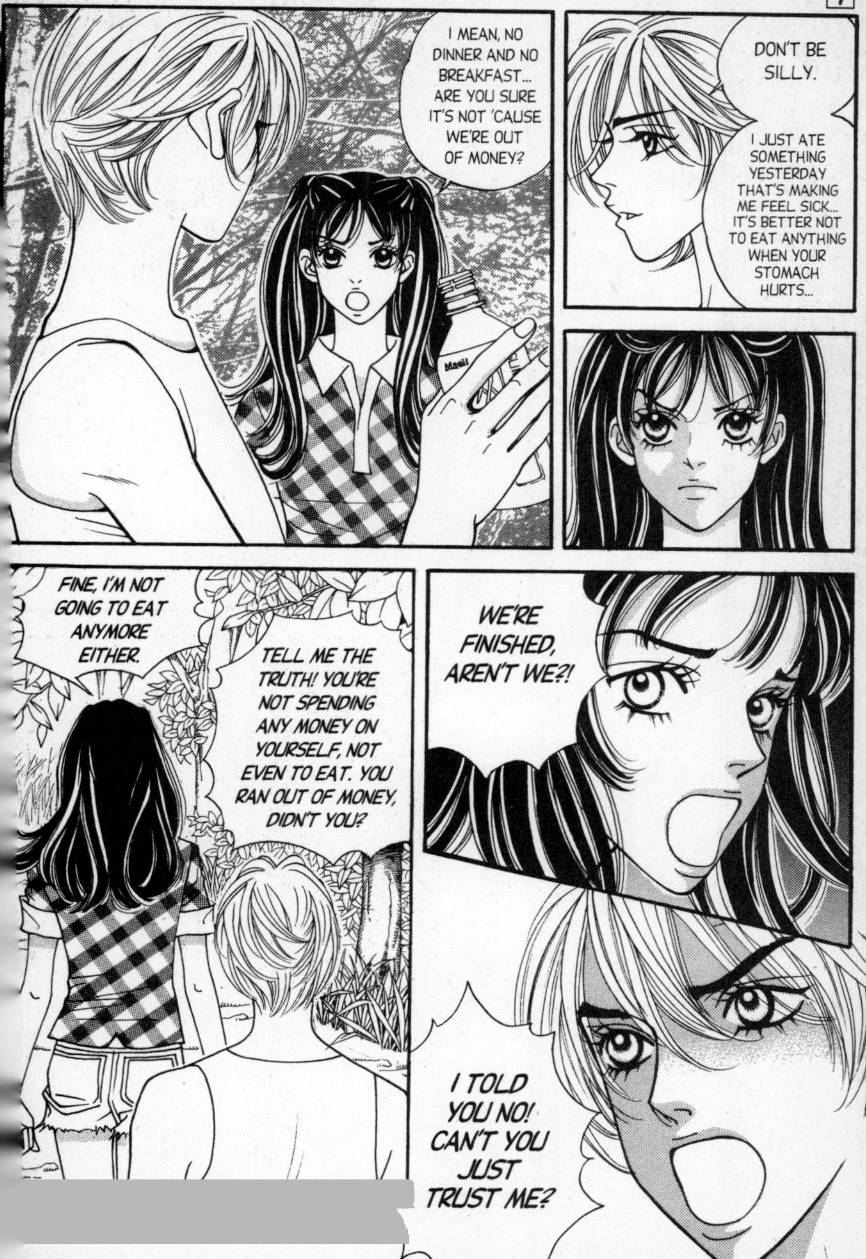
I MEAN, NO DINNER AND NO BREAKFAST... ARE YOU SURE IT'S NOT 'CAUSE WE'RE OUT OF MONEY?
DON'T BE SILLY.
I JUST ATE SOMETHING YESTERDAY THAT'S MAKING ME FEEL SICK... IT'S BETTER NOT TO EAT ANYTHING WHEN YOUR STOMACH HURTS...
FINE, I'M NOT GOING TO EAT ANYMORE EITHER.
TELL ME THE TRUTH! YOU'RE NOT SPENDING ANY MONEY ON YOURSELF, NOT EVEN TO EAT. YOU RAN OUT OF MONEY, DIDN'T YOU?
WE'RE FINISHED, AREN'T WE?!
I TOLD YOU NO! CAN'T YOU JUST TRUST ME?

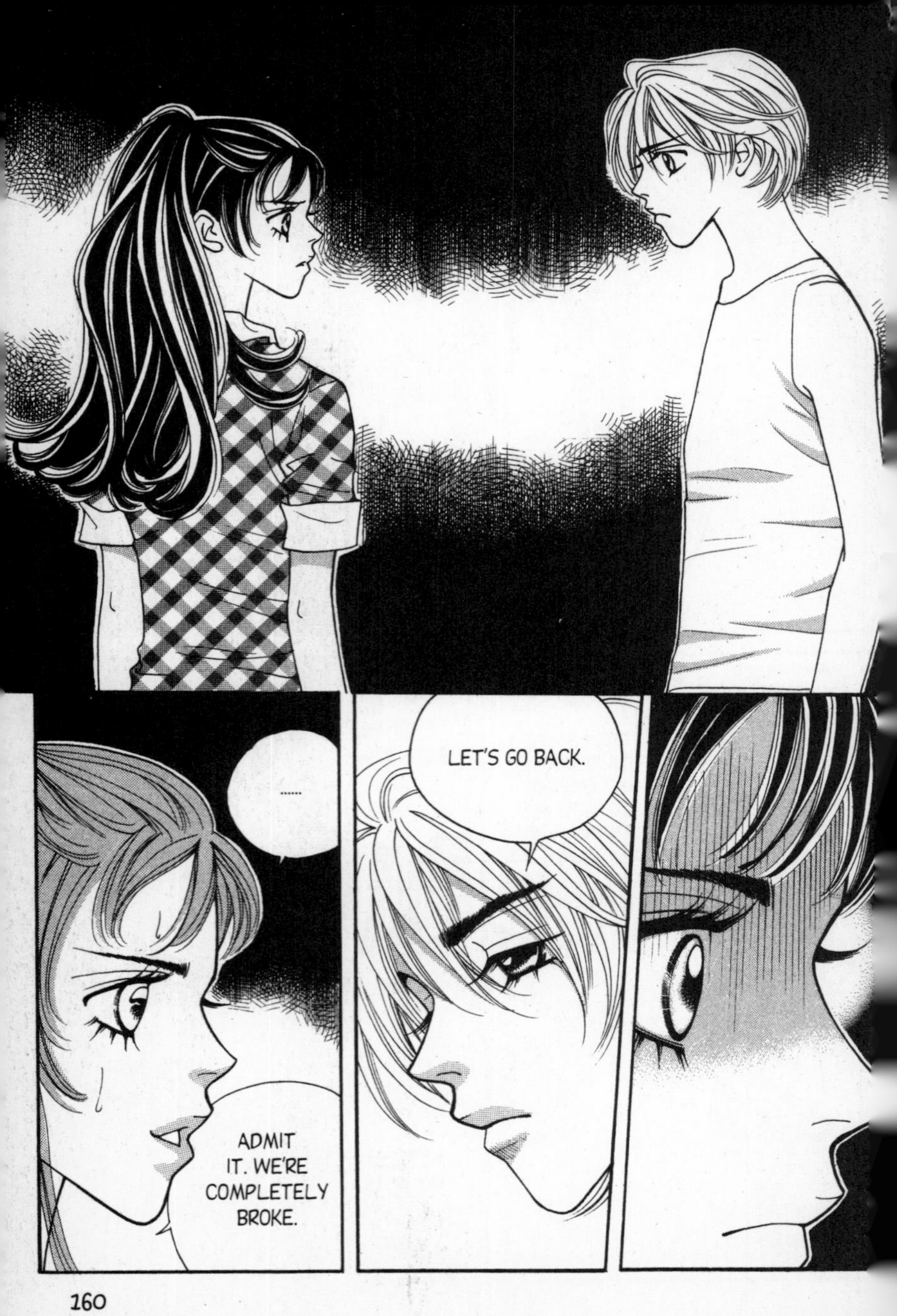
......
ADMIT IT. WE'RE COMPLETELY BROKE.
LET'S GO BACK.

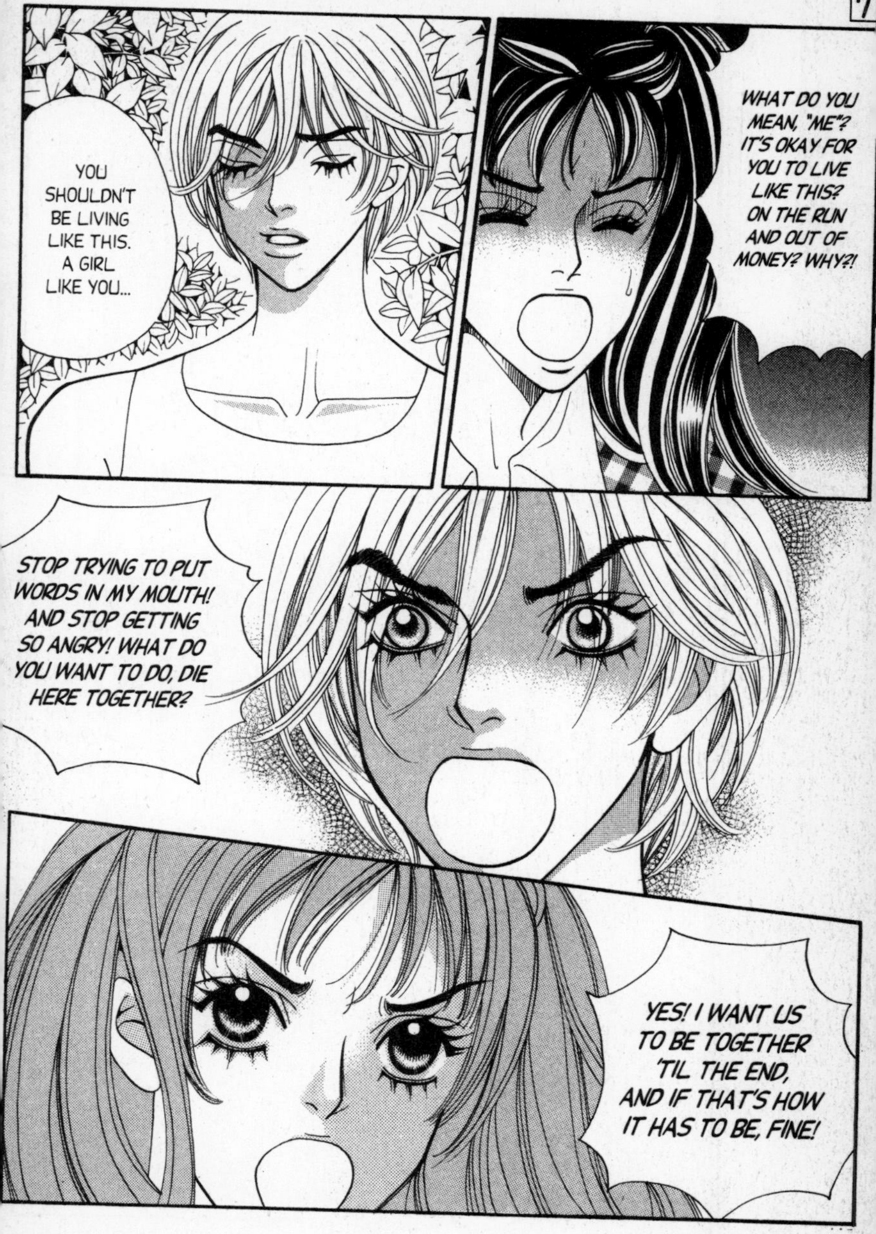
YOU SHOULDN'T BE LIVING LIKE THIS. A GIRL LIKE YOU...
WHAT DO YOU MEAN, "ME"? IT'S OKAY FOR YOU TO LIVE LIKE THIS? ON THE RUN AND OUT OF MONEY? WHY?!
STOP TRYING TO PUT WORDS IN MY MOUTH! AND STOP GETTING SO ANGRY! WHAT DO YOU WANT TO DO, DIE HERE TOGETHER?
YES! I WANT US TO BE TOGETHER 'TIL THE END, AND IF THAT'S HOW IT HAS TO BE, FINE!

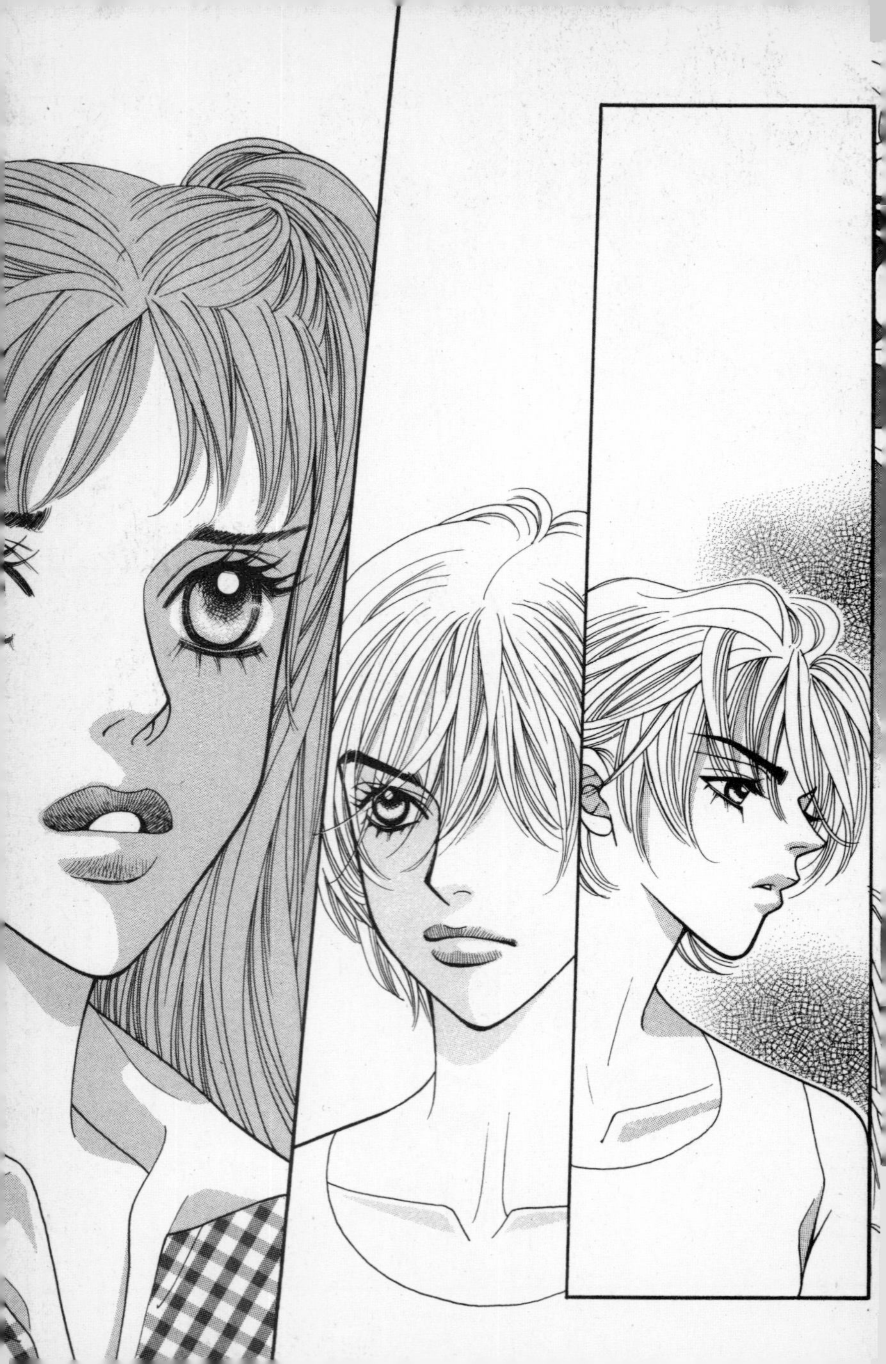

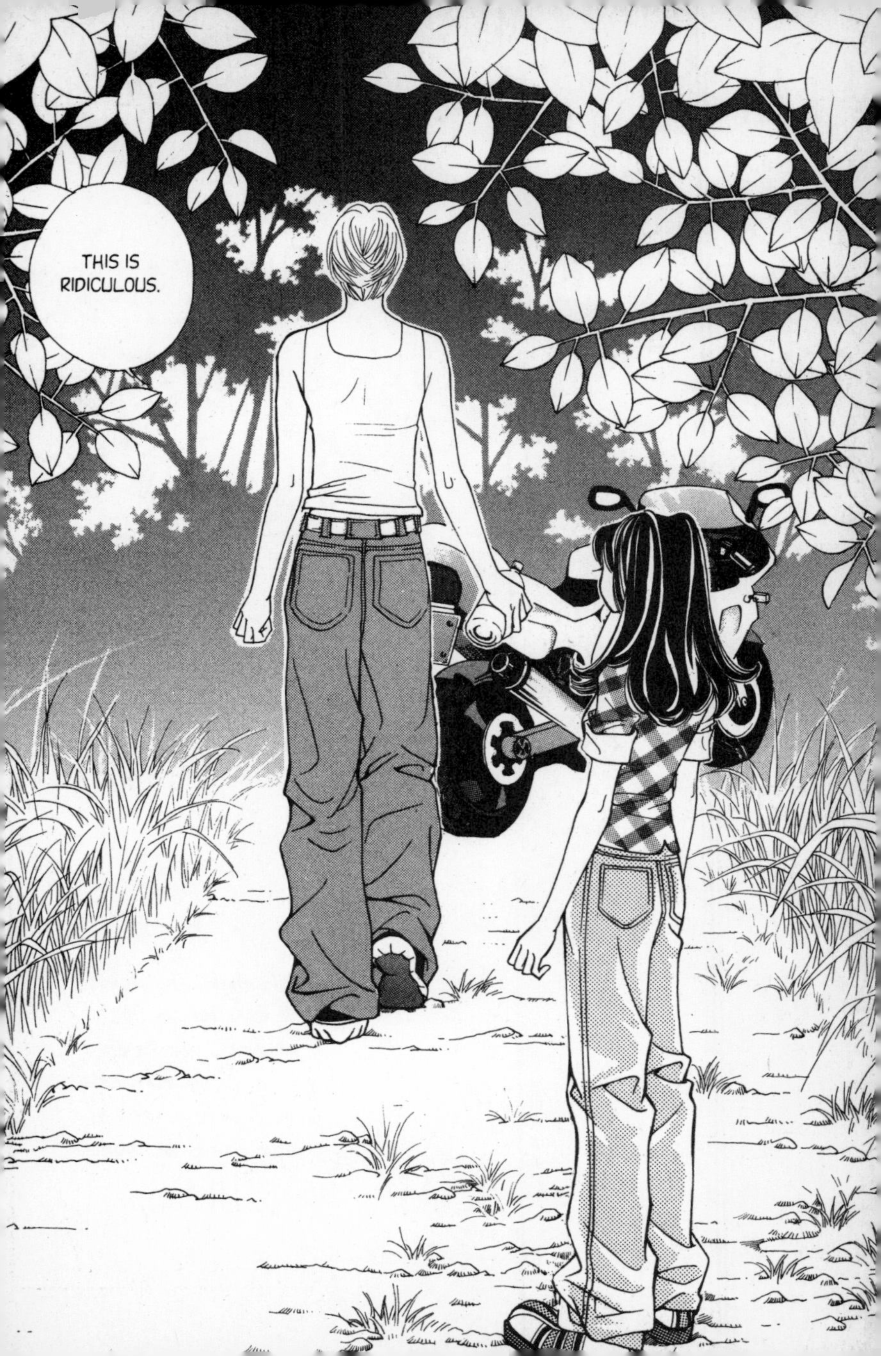
THIS IS RIDICULOUS.

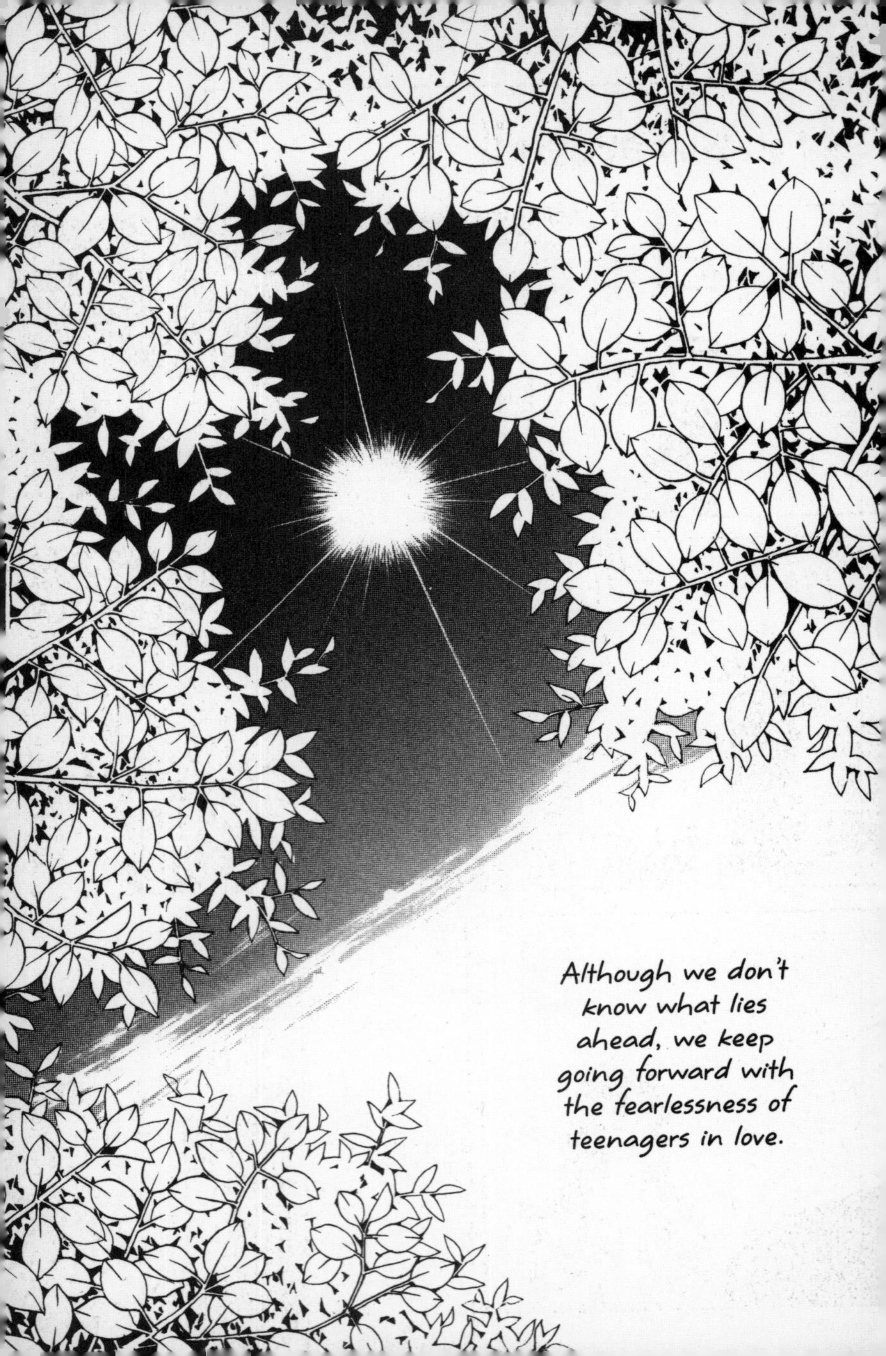
Although we don't know what lies ahead, we keep going forward with the fearlessness of teenagers in love.

Part 28: Farewell

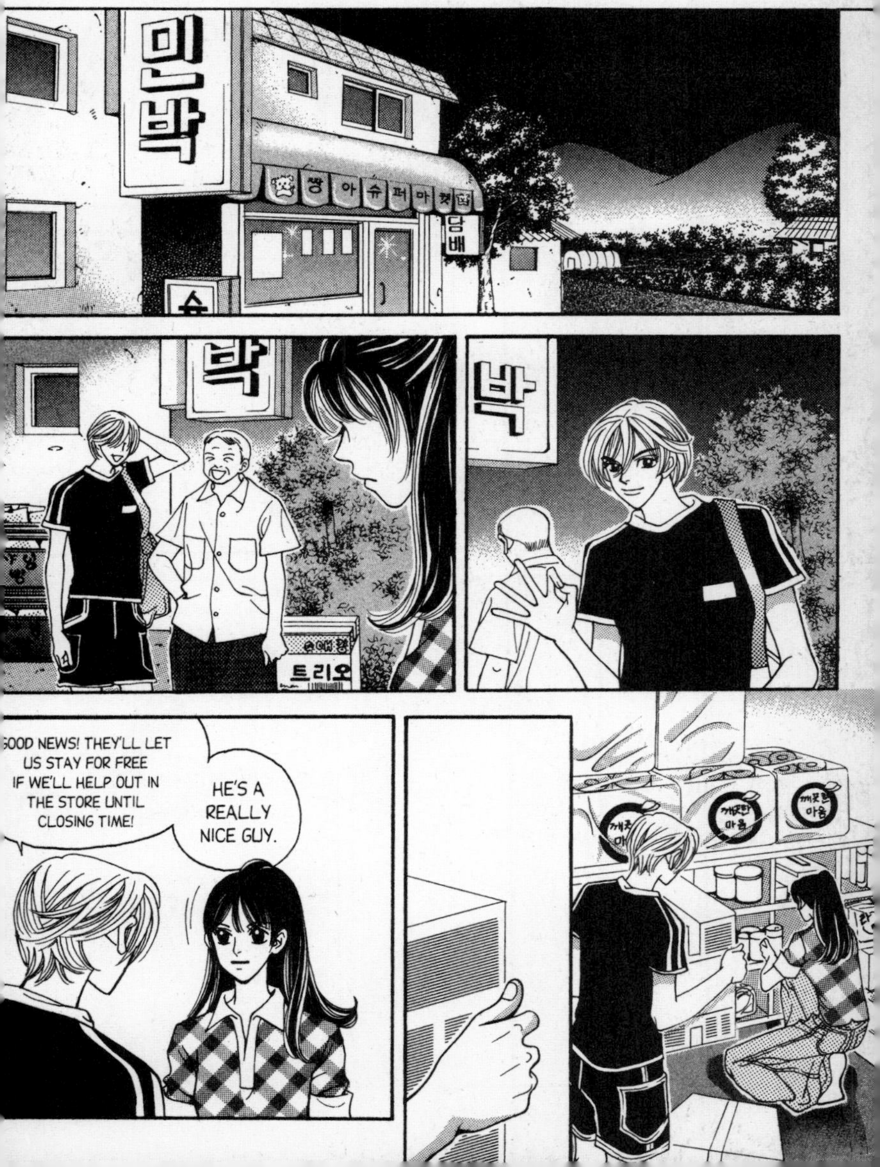
민
박
담
배
트리오
GOOD NEWS! THEY'LL LET US STAY FOR FREE IF WE'LL HELP OUT IN THE STORE UNTIL CLOSING TIME!
HE'S A REALLY NICE GUY.
깨끗한
마음

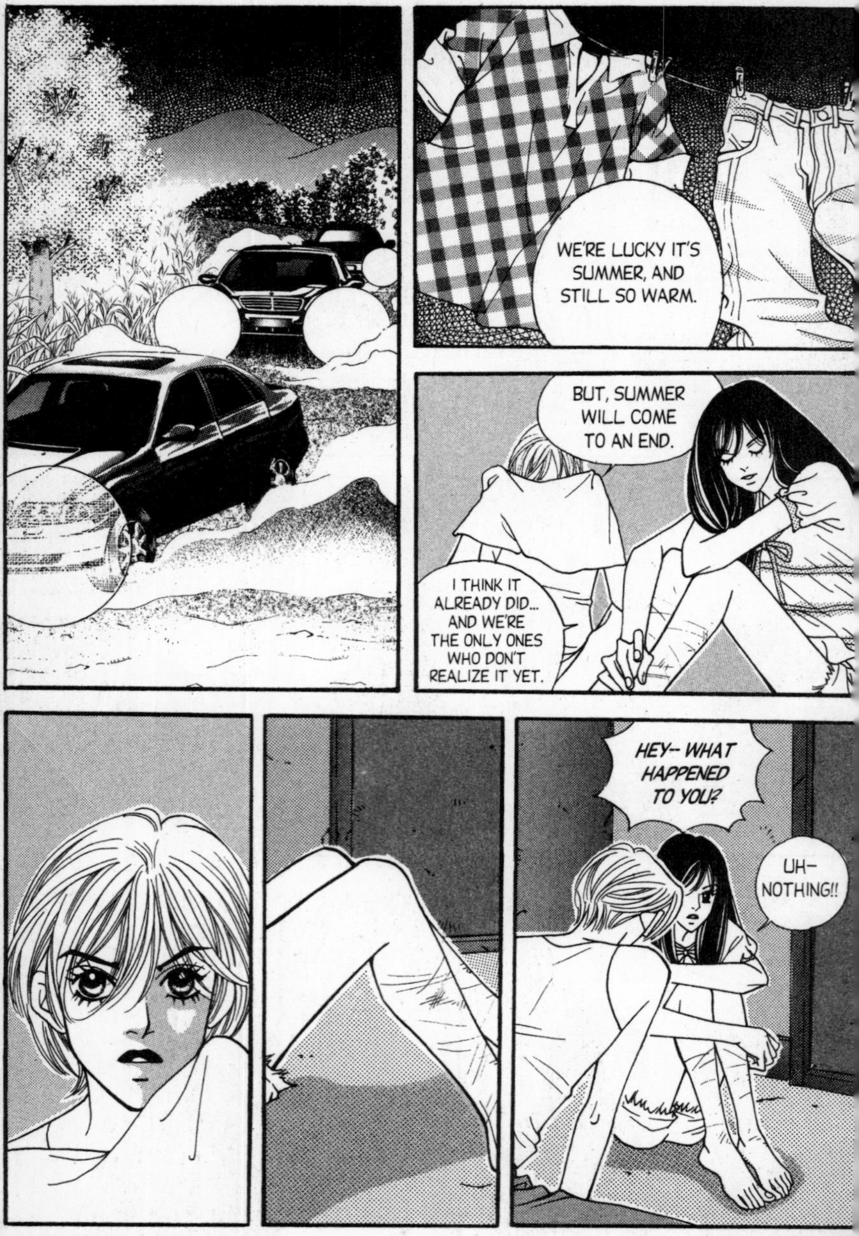
WE'RE LUCKY IT'S SUMMER, AND STILL SO WARM.
BUT, SUMMER WILL COME TO AN END.
I THINK IT ALREADY DID... AND WE'RE THE ONLY ONES WHO DON'T REALIZE IT YET.
HEY-- WHAT HAPPENED TO YOU?
UH-NOTHING!!

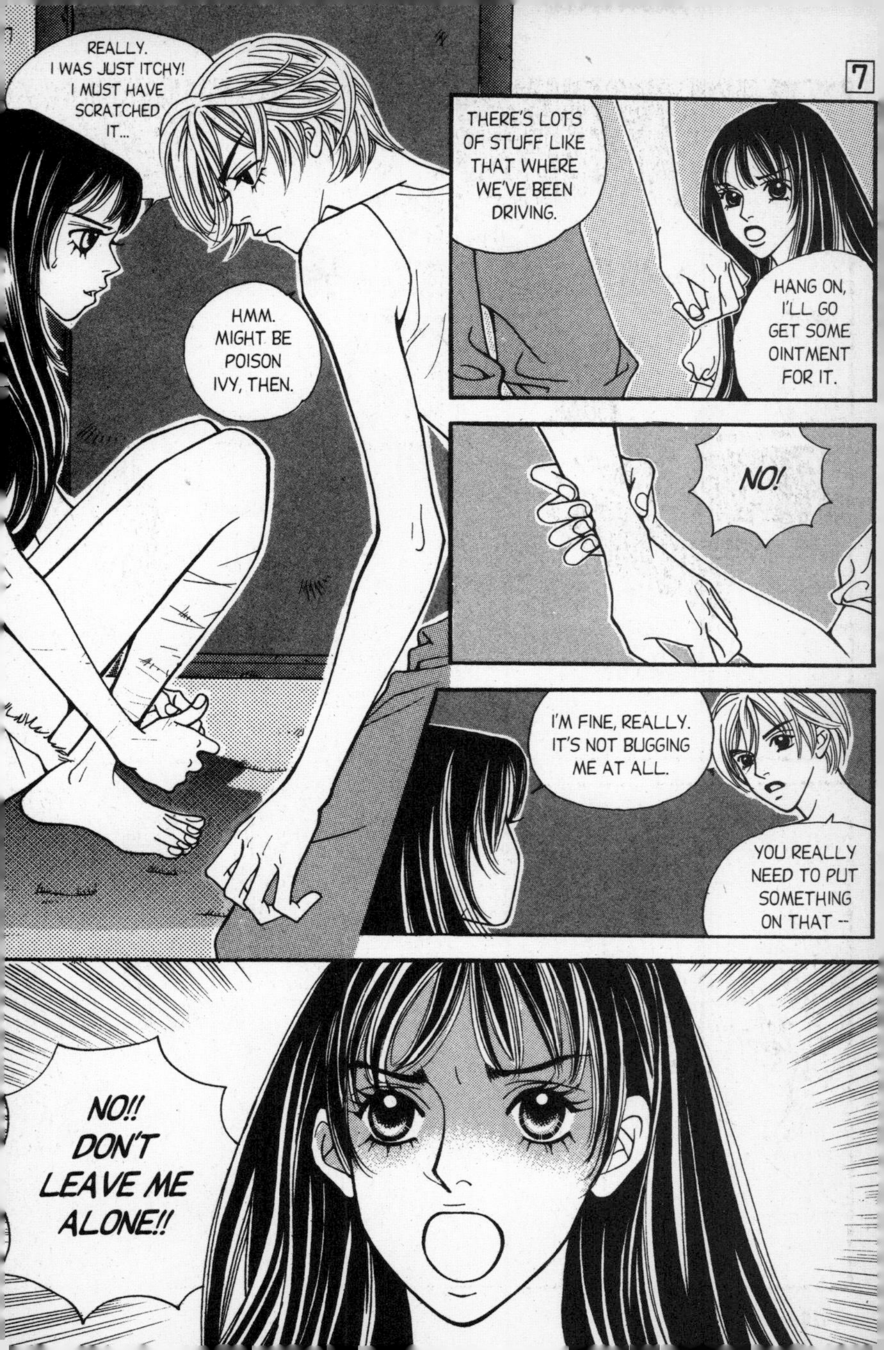
REALLY. I WAS JUST ITCHY! I MUST HAVE SCRATCHED IT...
HMM. MIGHT BE POISON IVY, THEN.
THERE'S LOTS OF STUFF LIKE THAT WHERE WE'VE BEEN DRIVING.
HANG ON, I'LL GO GET SOME OINTMENT FOR IT.
NO!
I'M FINE, REALLY. IT'S NOT BUGGING ME AT ALL.
YOU REALLY NEED TO PUT SOMETHING ON THAT --
NO!! DON'T LEAVE ME ALONE!!

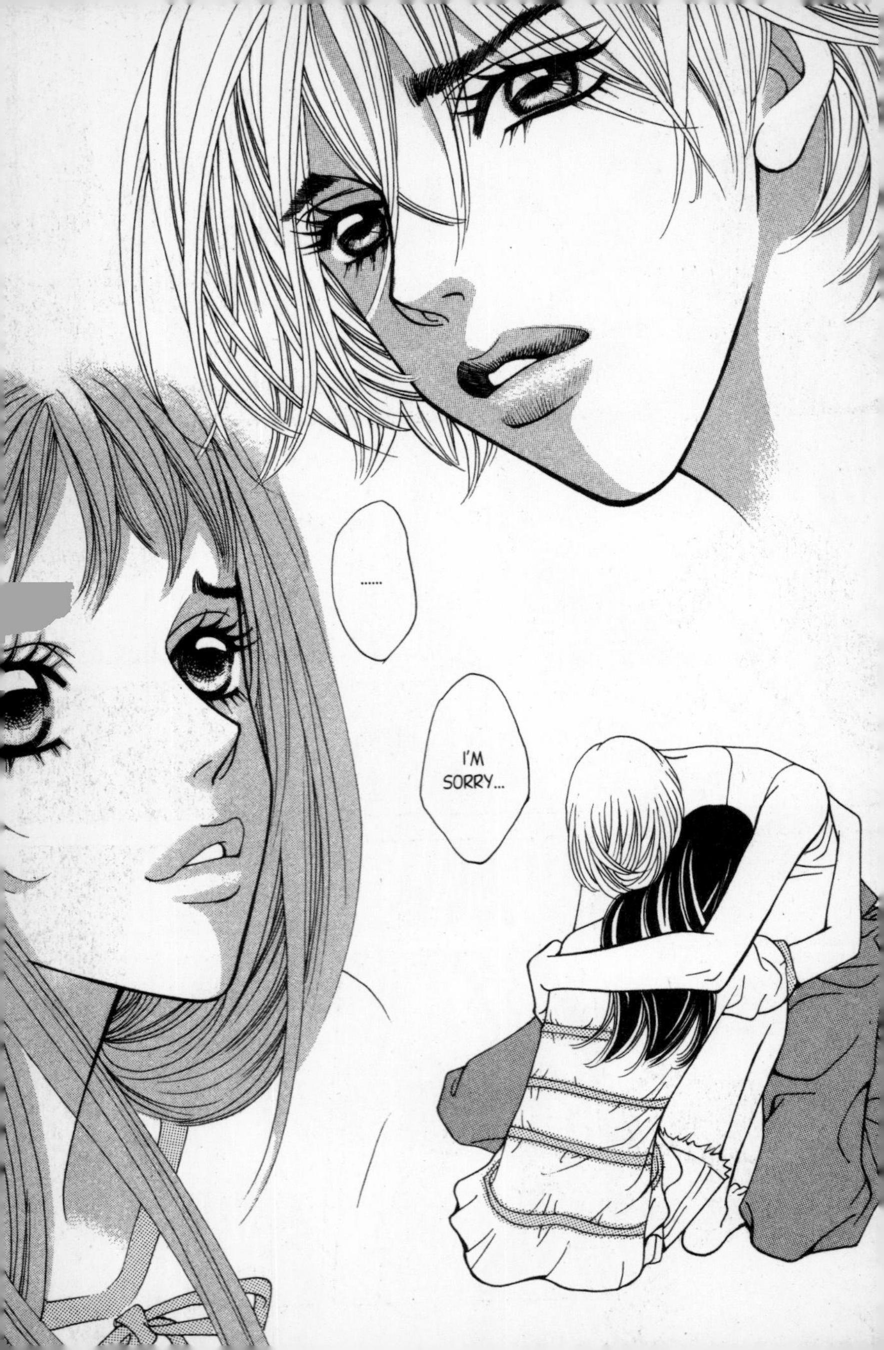
......
I'M SORRY...

HAE-GI... IF WE DO SPLIT UP. WHAT WILL YOU DO? HOW WILL YOU LIVE?

WHY ARE YOU ASKING ME THAT?

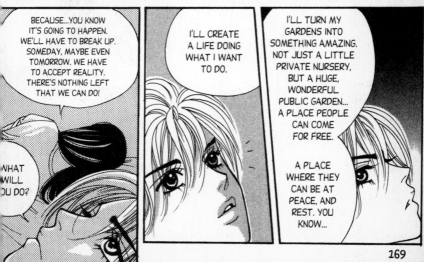

BECAUSE...YOU KNOW IT'S GOING TO HAPPEN. WE'LL HAVE TO BREAK UP. SOMEDAY, MAYBE EVEN TOMORROW. WE HAVE TO ACCEPT REALITY. THERE'S NOTHING LEFT THAT WE CAN DO!

WHAT WILL OU DO?

I'LL CREATE A LIFE DOING WHAT I WANT TO DO.

I'LL TURN MY GARDENS INTO SOMETHING AMAZING. NOT JUST A LITTLE PRIVATE NURSERY, BUT A HUGE, WONDERFUL PUBLIC GARDEN... A PLACE PEOPLE CAN COME FOR FREE.

A PLACE WHERE THEY CAN BE AT PEACE, AND REST. YOU KNOW...

169

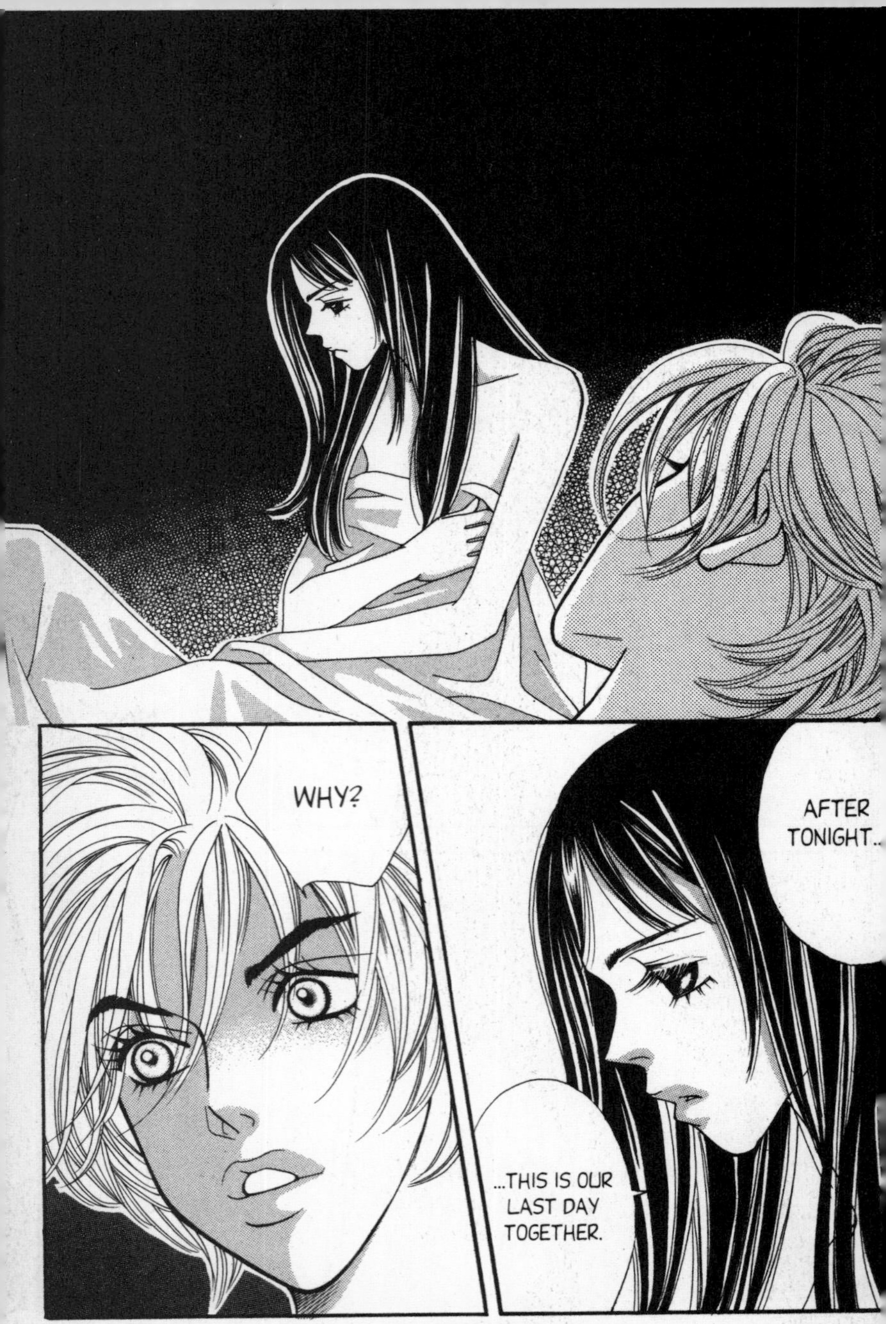
WHY?
AFTER TONIGHT...
...THIS IS OUR LAST DAY TOGETHER.

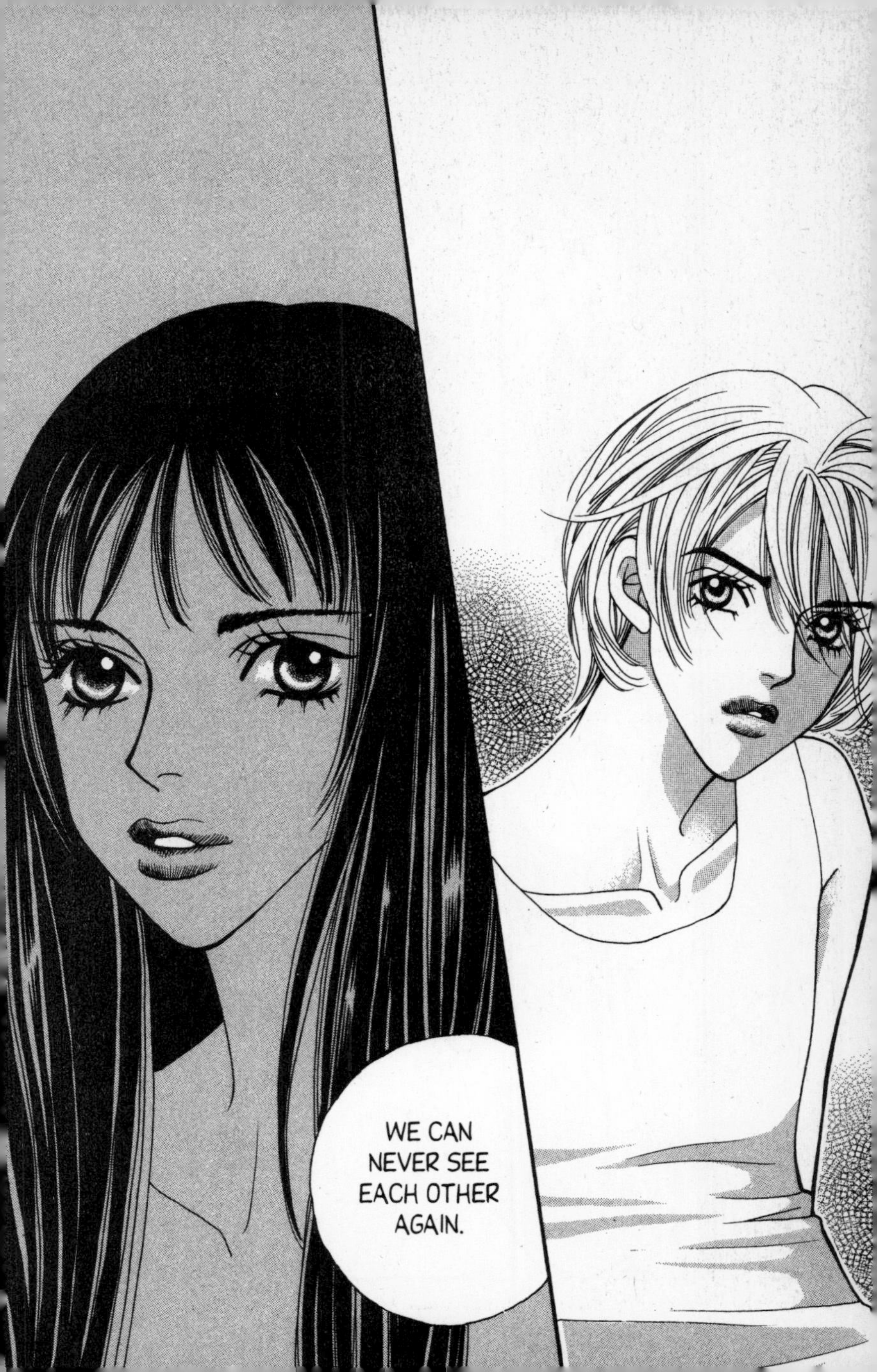
WE CAN NEVER SEE EACH OTHER AGAIN.

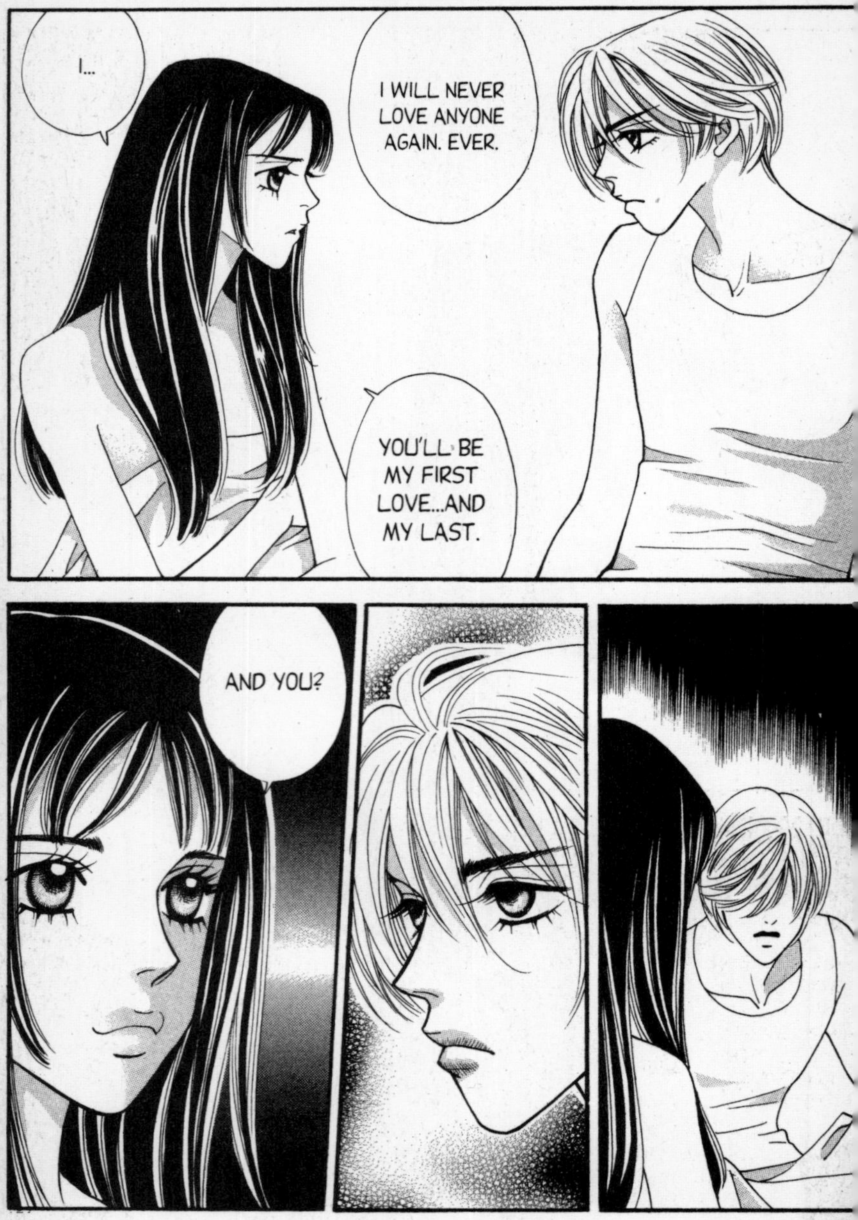
I...
I WILL NEVER LOVE ANYONE AGAIN. EVER.
YOU'LL BE MY FIRST LOVE...AND MY LAST.
AND YOU?

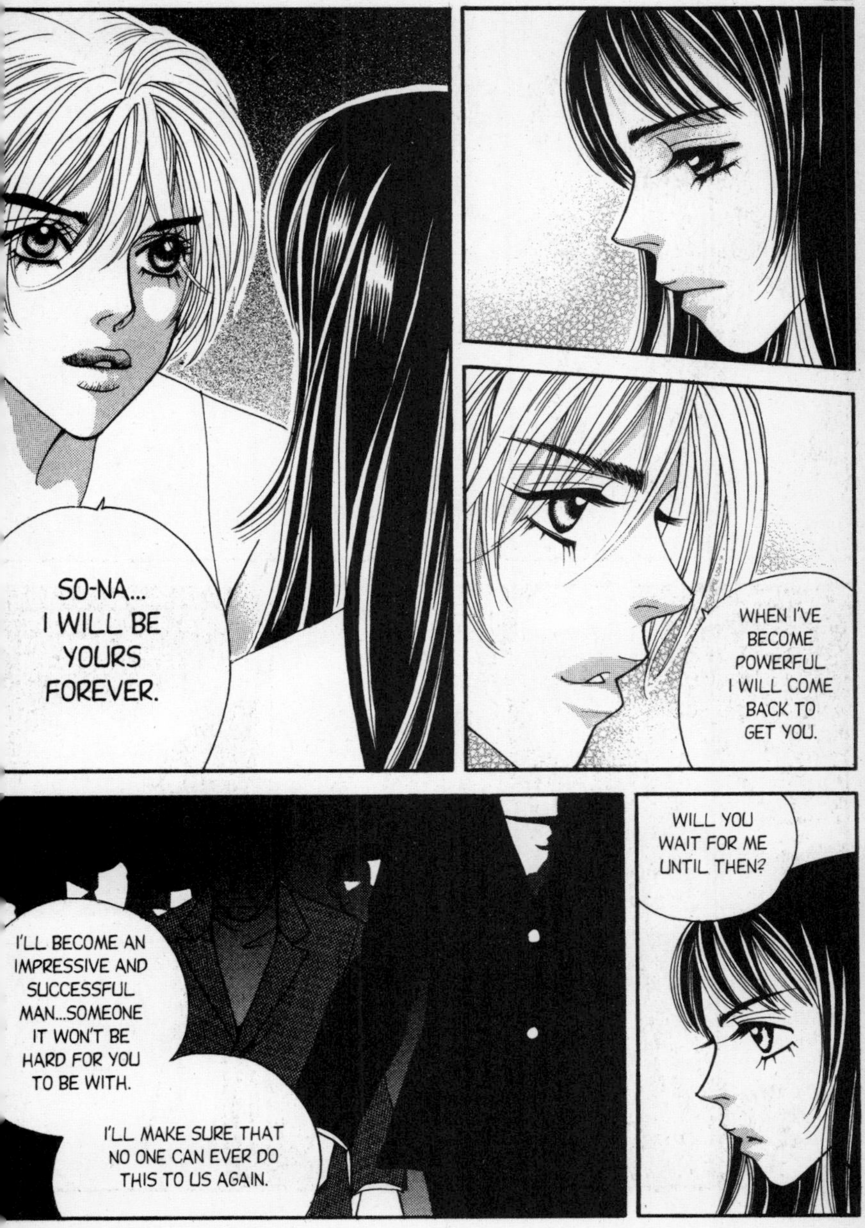
SO-NA... I WILL BE YOURS FOREVER.
WHEN I'VE BECOME POWERFUL I WILL COME BACK TO GET YOU.
I'LL BECOME AN IMPRESSIVE AND SUCCESSFUL MAN...SOMEONE IT WON'T BE HARD FOR YOU TO BE WITH.
I'LL MAKE SURE THAT NO ONE CAN EVER DO THIS TO US AGAIN.
WILL YOU WAIT FOR ME UNTIL THEN?

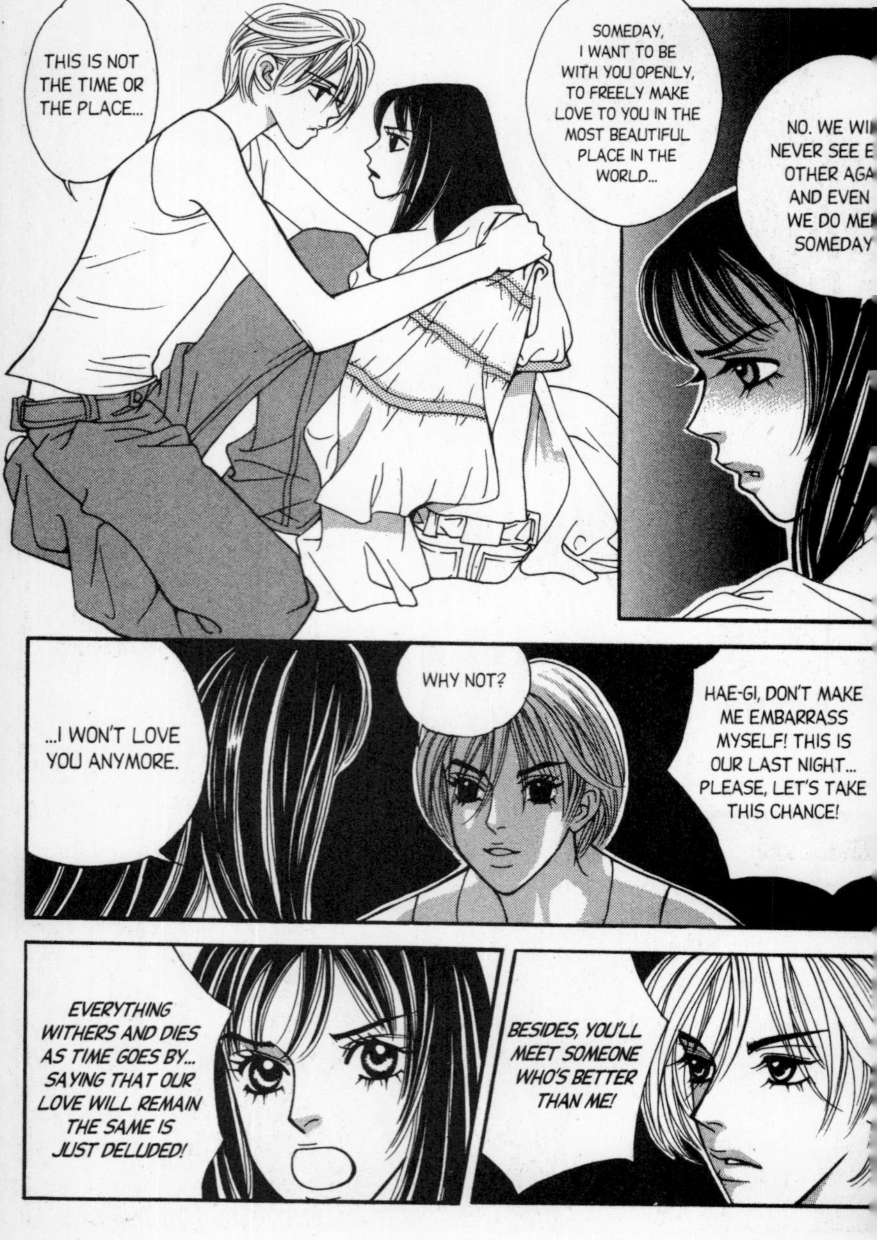
THIS IS NOT THE TIME OR THE PLACE...
SOMEDAY, I WANT TO BE WITH YOU OPENLY, TO FREELY MAKE LOVE TO YOU IN THE MOST BEAUTIFUL PLACE IN THE WORLD...
NO. WE WI NEVER SEE E OTHER AGA AND EVEN WE DO ME SOMEDAY
...I WON'T LOVE YOU ANYMORE.
WHY NOT?
HAE-GI, DON'T MAKE ME EMBARRASS MYSELF! THIS IS OUR LAST NIGHT... PLEASE, LET'S TAKE THIS CHANCE!
EVERYTHING WITHERS AND DIES AS TIME GOES BY... SAYING THAT OUR LOVE WILL REMAIN THE SAME IS JUST DELUDED!
BESIDES, YOU'LL MEET SOMEONE WHO'S BETTER THAN ME!

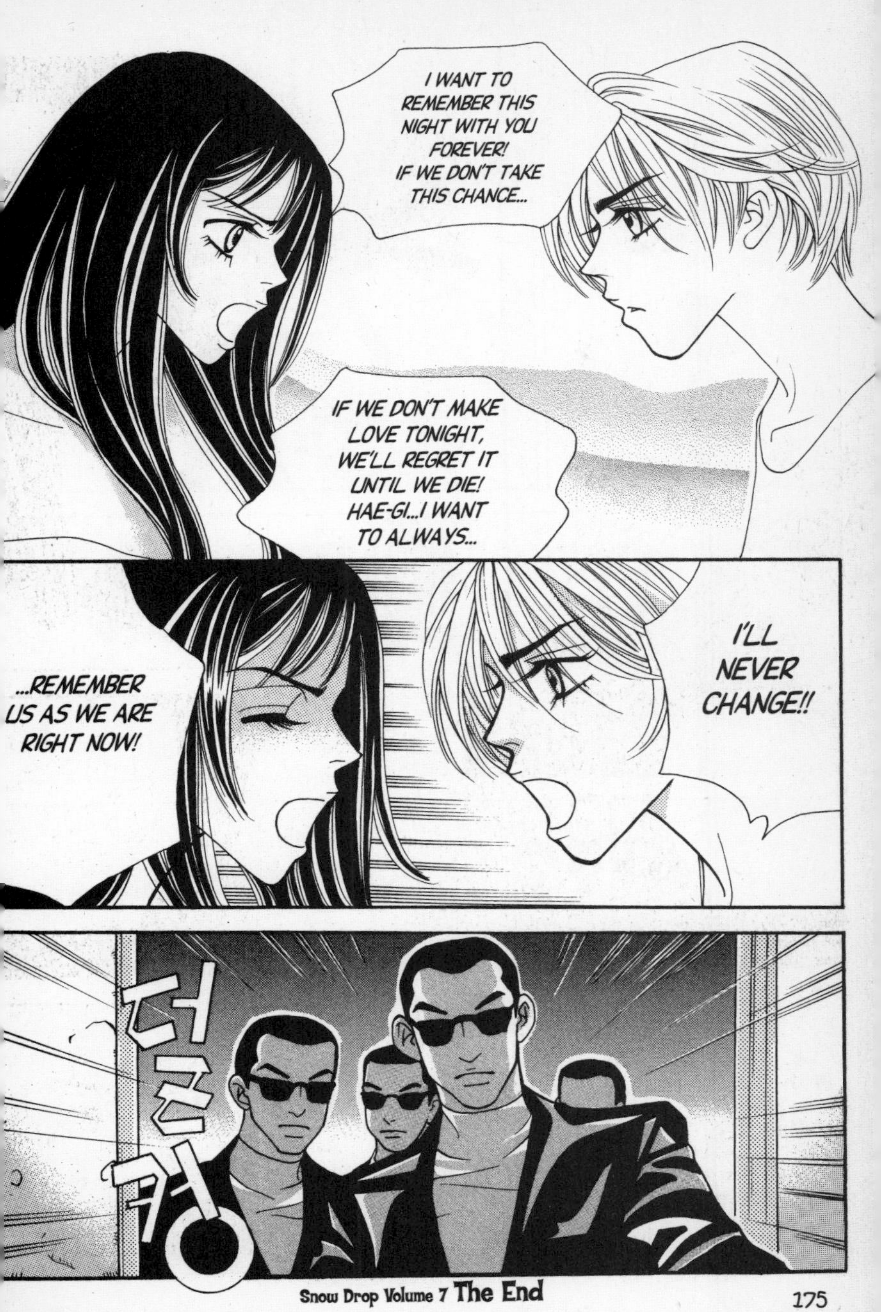
I WANT TO REMEMBER THIS NIGHT WITH YOU FOREVER! IF WE DON'T TAKE THIS CHANCE...
IF WE DON'T MAKE LOVE TONIGHT, WE'LL REGRET IT UNTIL WE DIE! HAE-GI...I WANT TO ALWAYS...
...REMEMBER US AS WE ARE RIGHT NOW!
I'LL NEVER CHANGE!!
덜컹

Snow Drop Volume 7 **The End**

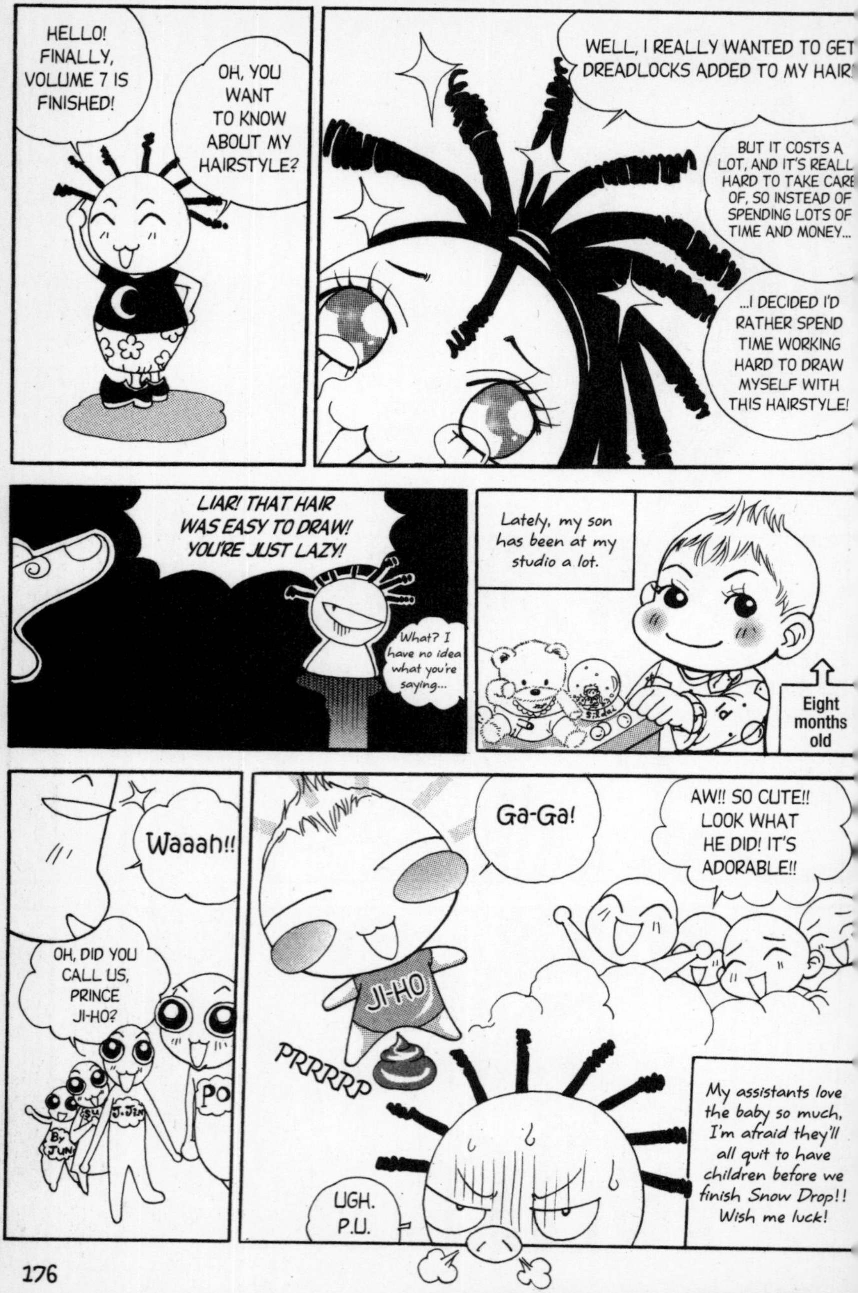
HELLO! FINALLY, VOLUME 7 IS FINISHED!
OH, YOU WANT TO KNOW ABOUT MY HAIRSTYLE?
WELL, I REALLY WANTED TO GET DREADLOCKS ADDED TO MY HAIR!
BUT IT COSTS A LOT, AND IT'S REALL HARD TO TAKE CARE OF, SO INSTEAD OF SPENDING LOTS OF TIME AND MONEY...
...I DECIDED I'D RATHER SPEND TIME WORKING HARD TO DRAW MYSELF WITH THIS HAIRSTYLE!
LIAR! THAT HAIR WAS EASY TO DRAW! YOU'RE JUST LAZY!
What? I have no idea what you're saying...
Lately, my son has been at my studio a lot.
Eight months old
Waaah!!
OH, DID YOU CALL US, PRINCE JI-HO?
BY JUN
SU
J. JIN
PO
Ga-Ga!
AW!! SO CUTE!! LOOK WHAT HE DID! IT'S ADORABLE!!
JI-HO
PRRRRRP
UGH. P.U.
My assistants love the baby so much, I'm afraid they'll all quit to have children before we finish Snow Drop!! Wish me luck!

Snow Drop Volume 7 THE END

Coming Soon

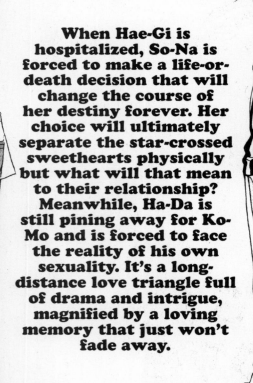

Snow Drop

Volume Eight

When Hae-Gi is hospitalized, So-Na is forced to make a life-or-death decision that will change the course of her destiny forever. Her choice will ultimately separate the star-crossed sweethearts physically but what will that mean to their relationship? Meanwhile, Ha-Da is still pining away for Ko-Mo and is forced to face the reality of his own sexuality. It's a long-distance love triangle full of drama and intrigue, magnified by a loving memory that just won't fade away.

**Drop in for
SNOW DROP Volume 8**

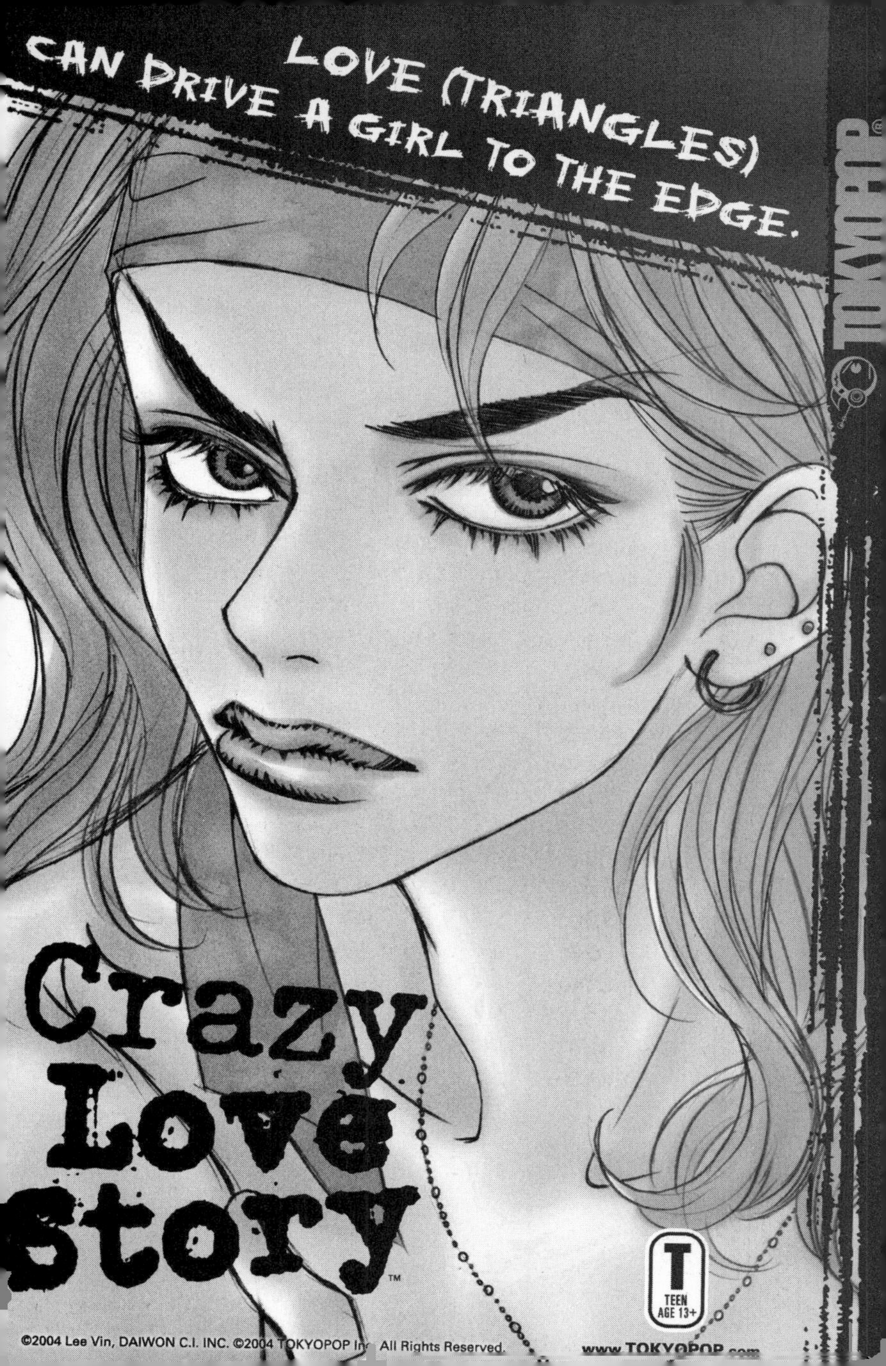
LOVE (TRIANGLES)
CAN DRIVE A GIRL TO THE EDGE.
TOKYOPOP®
Crazy Love Story™
T
TEEN
AGE 13+
©2004 Lee Vin, DAIWON C.I. INC. ©2004 TOKYOPOP In All Rights Reserved.
www.TOKYOPOP.com

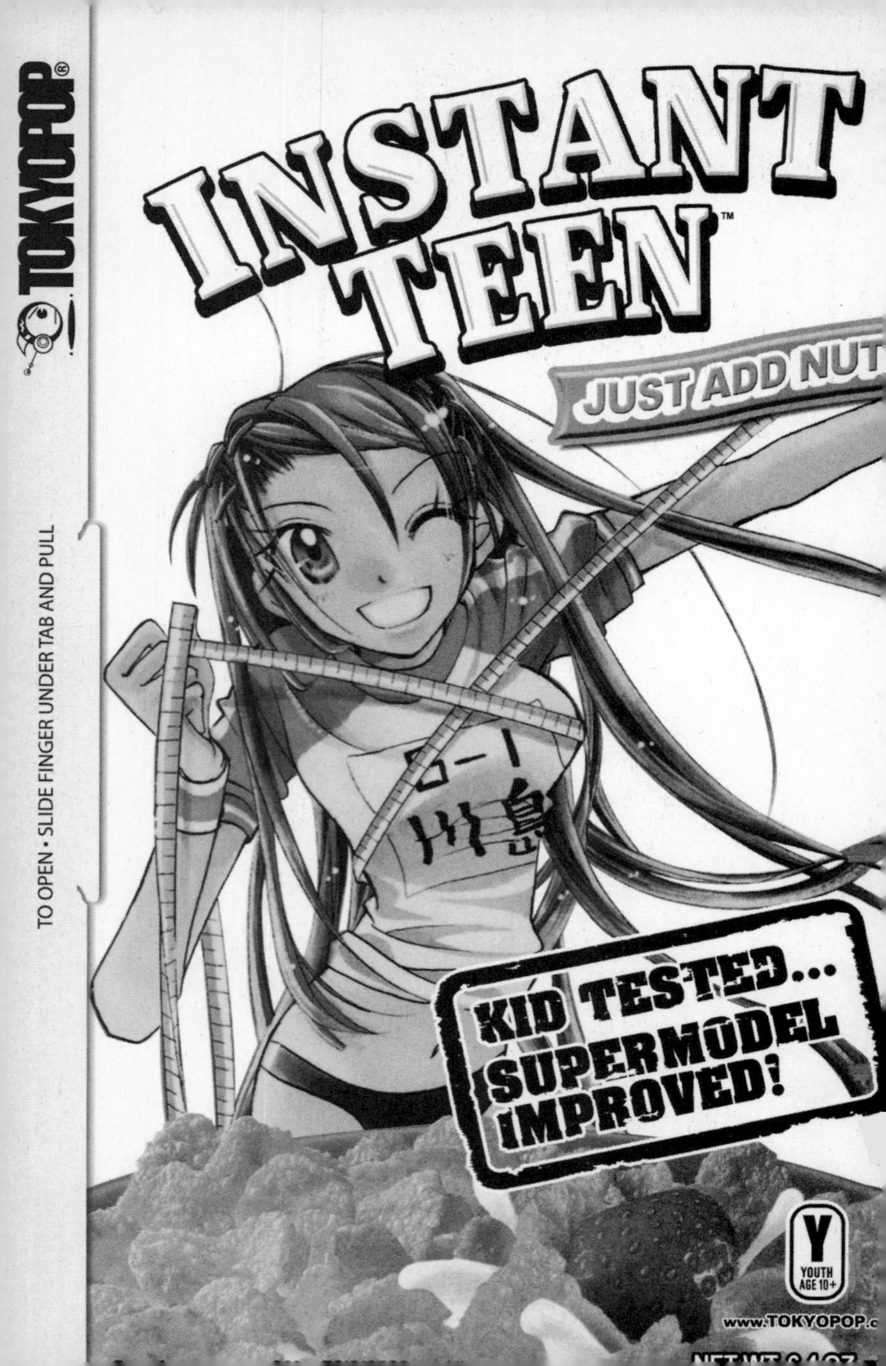
TOKYOPOP®
TO OPEN • SLIDE FINGER UNDER TAB AND PULL
INSTANT TEEN™
JUST ADD NUT
KID TESTED...
SUPERMODEL
IMPROVED!
Y
YOUTH
AGE 10+
www.TOKYOPOP.c

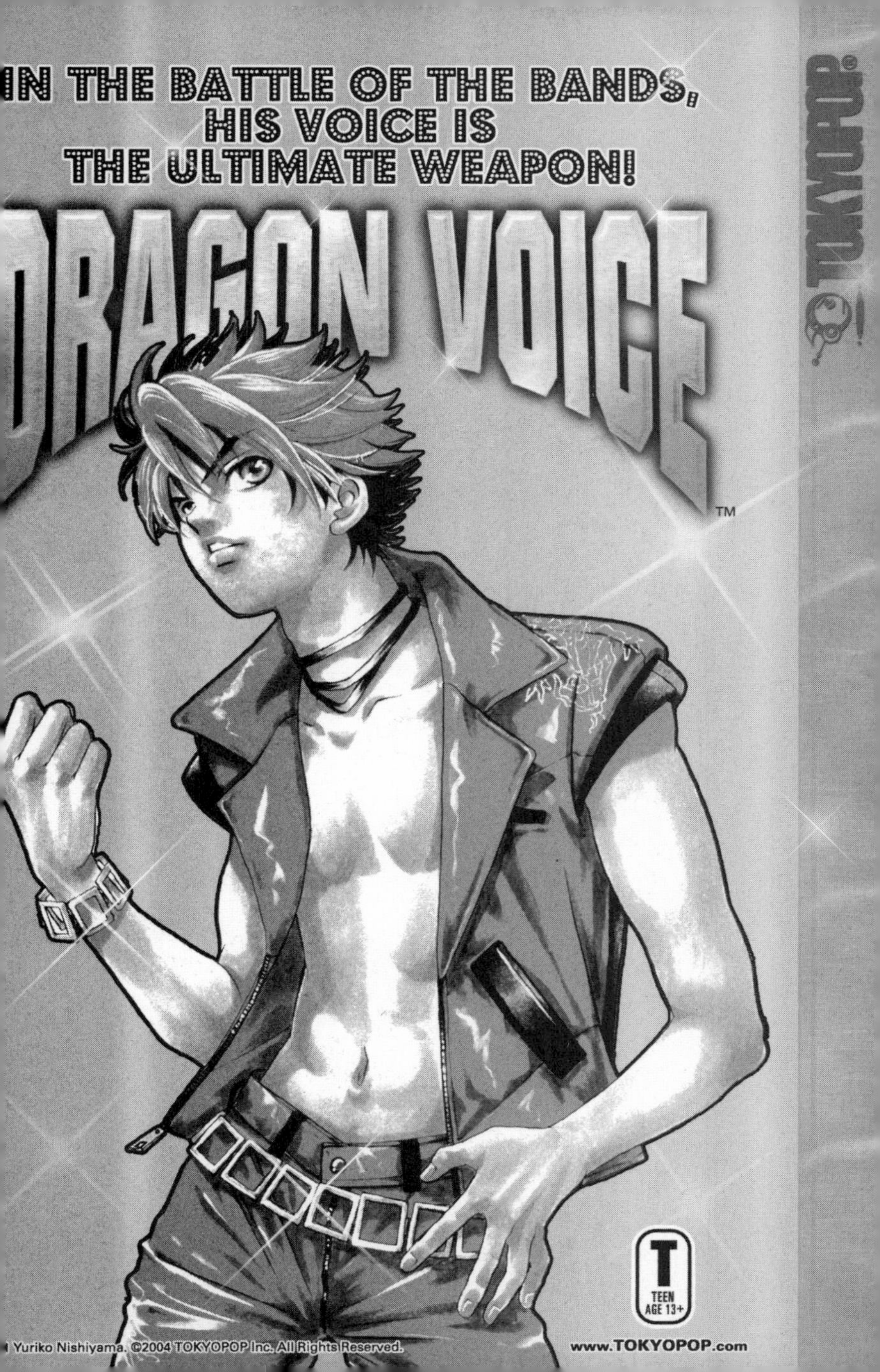
IN THE BATTLE OF THE BANDS,
HIS VOICE IS
THE ULTIMATE WEAPON!
DRAGON VOICE™
TOKYOPOP®
T
TEEN
AGE 13+
Yuriko Nishiyama. ©2004 TOKYOPOP Inc. All Rights Reserved.
www.TOKYOPOP.com

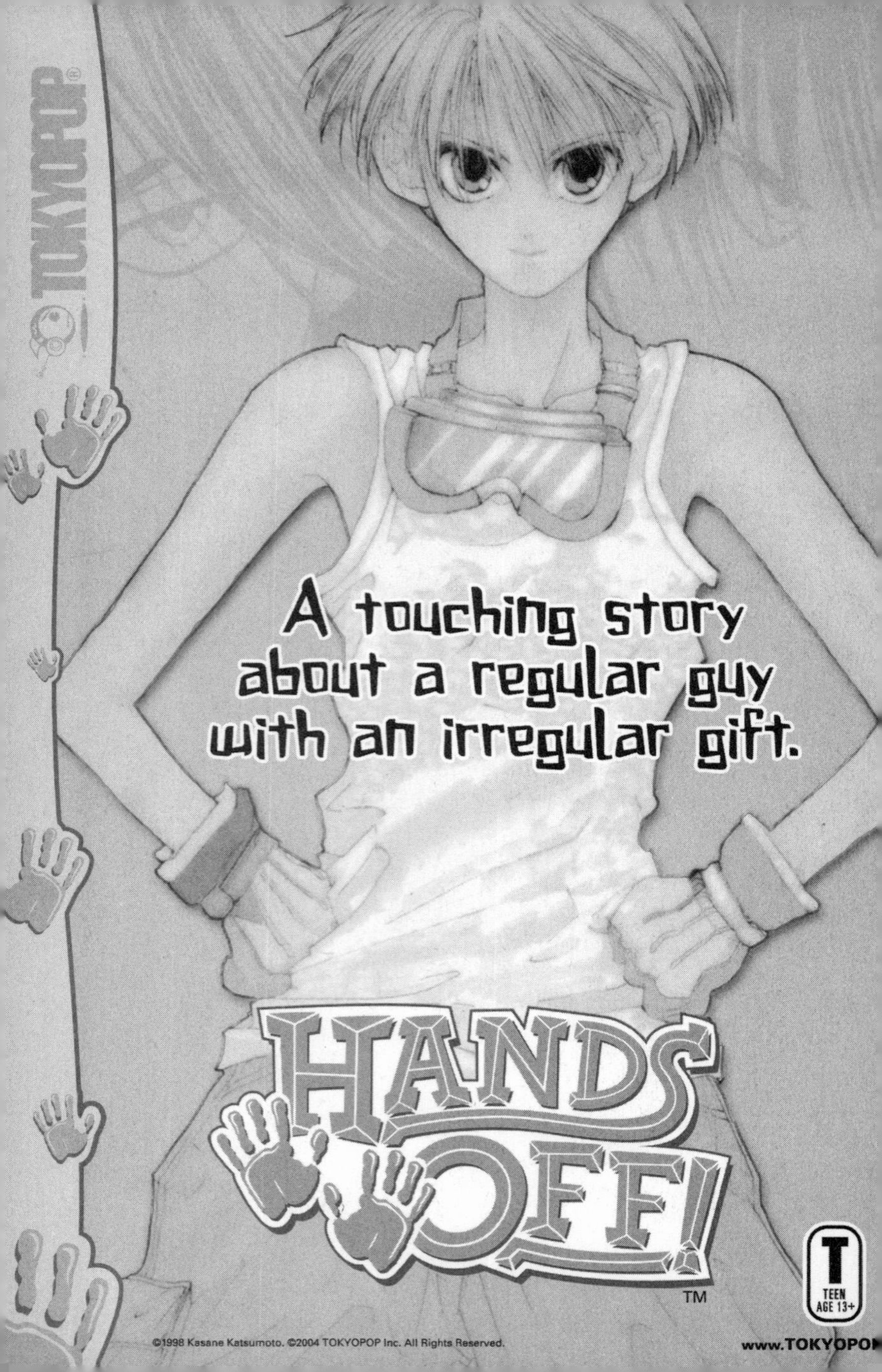
TOKYOPOP®
A touching story
about a regular guy
with an irregular gift.
HANDS OFF!
TM
T
TEEN
AGE 13+
©1998 Kasane Katsumoto. ©2004 TOKYOPOP Inc. All Rights Reserved.
www.TOKYOPOP

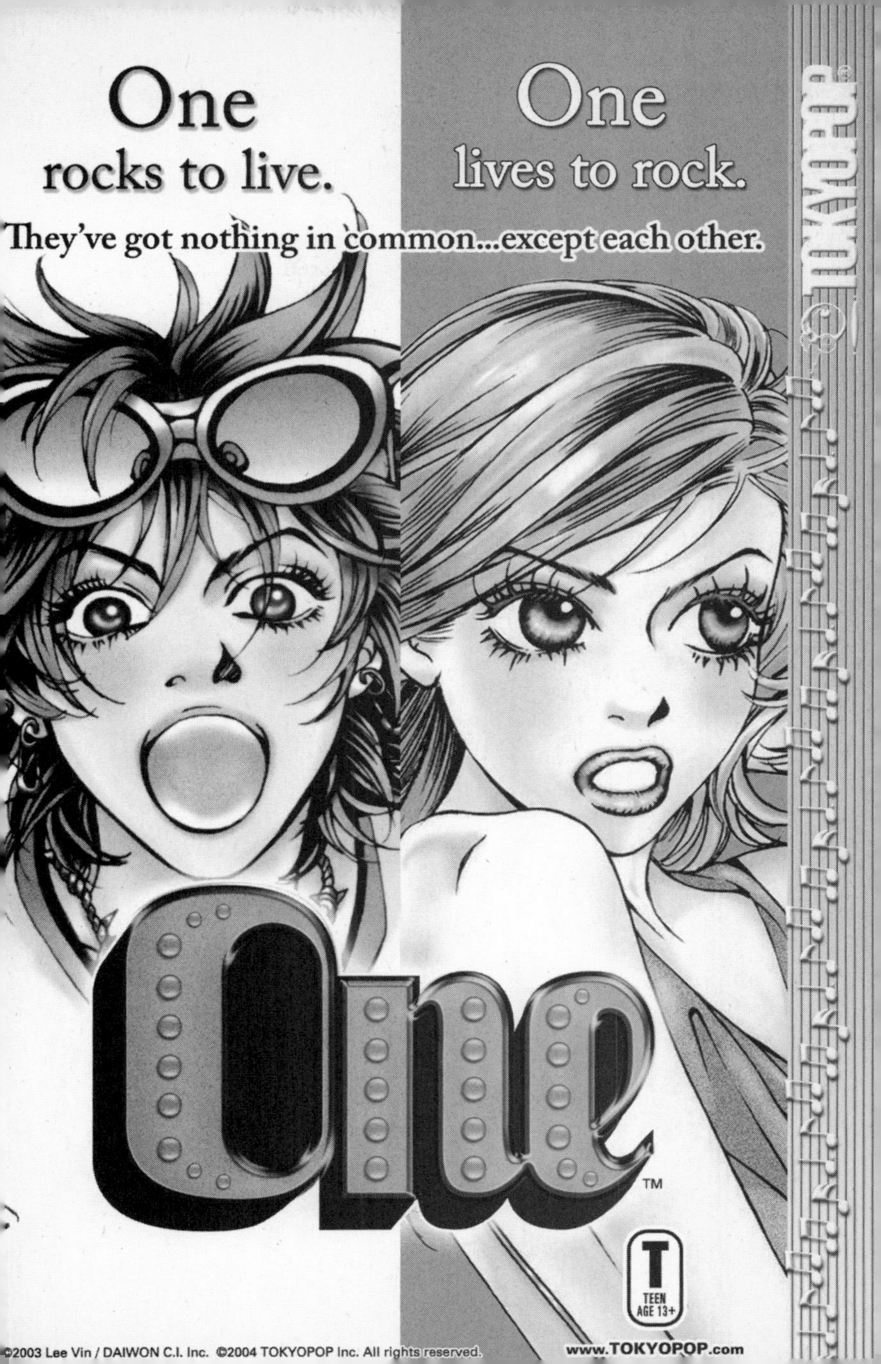
One
rocks to live.
One
lives to rock.
They've got nothing in common...except each other.
TOKYOPOP
One™
T TEEN AGE 13+
©2003 Lee Vin / DAIWON C.I. Inc. ©2004 TOKYOPOP Inc. All rights reserved.
www.TOKYOPOP.com

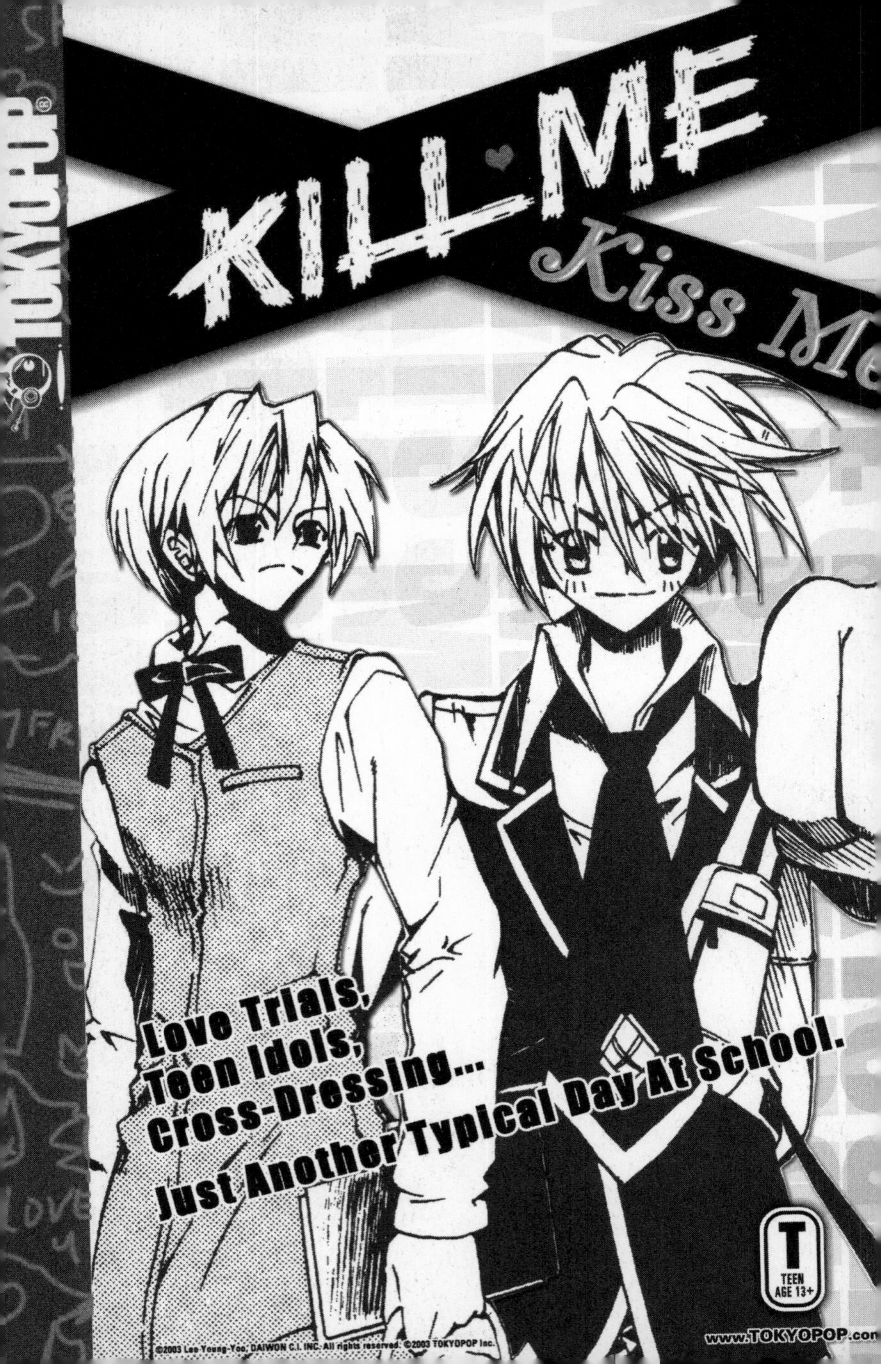
TOKYOPOP
KILL ME
Kiss Me
Love Trials,
Teen Idols,
Cross-Dressing...
Just Another Typical Day At School.
T
TEEN
AGE 13+
©2003 Lee-Young-Yoo, DAIWON C.I. INC. All rights reserved. ©2003 TOKYOPOP Inc.
www.TOKYOPOP.com

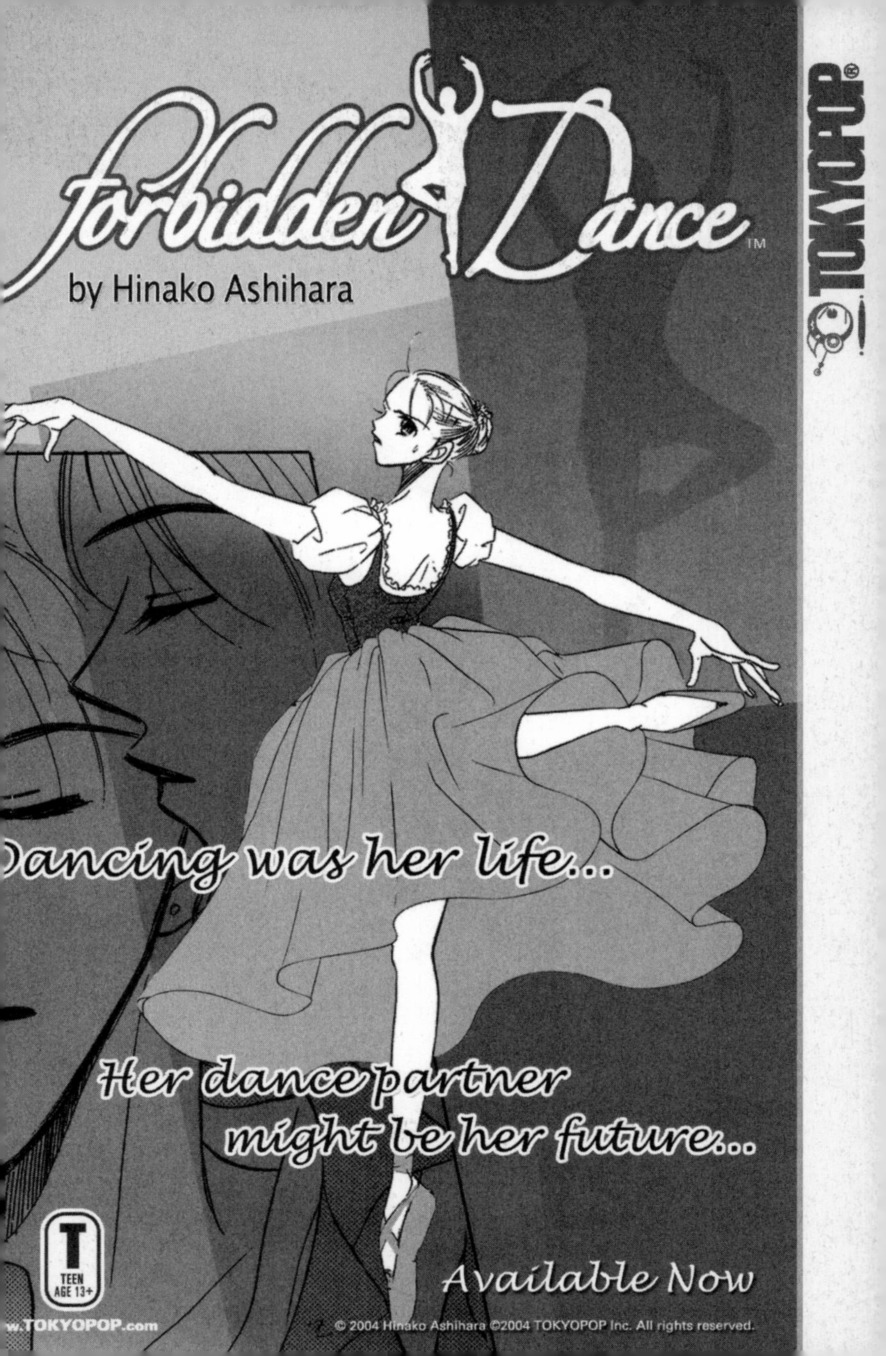

forbidden Dance

by Hinako Ashihara

Dancing was her life...

Her dance partner might be her future...

Available Now

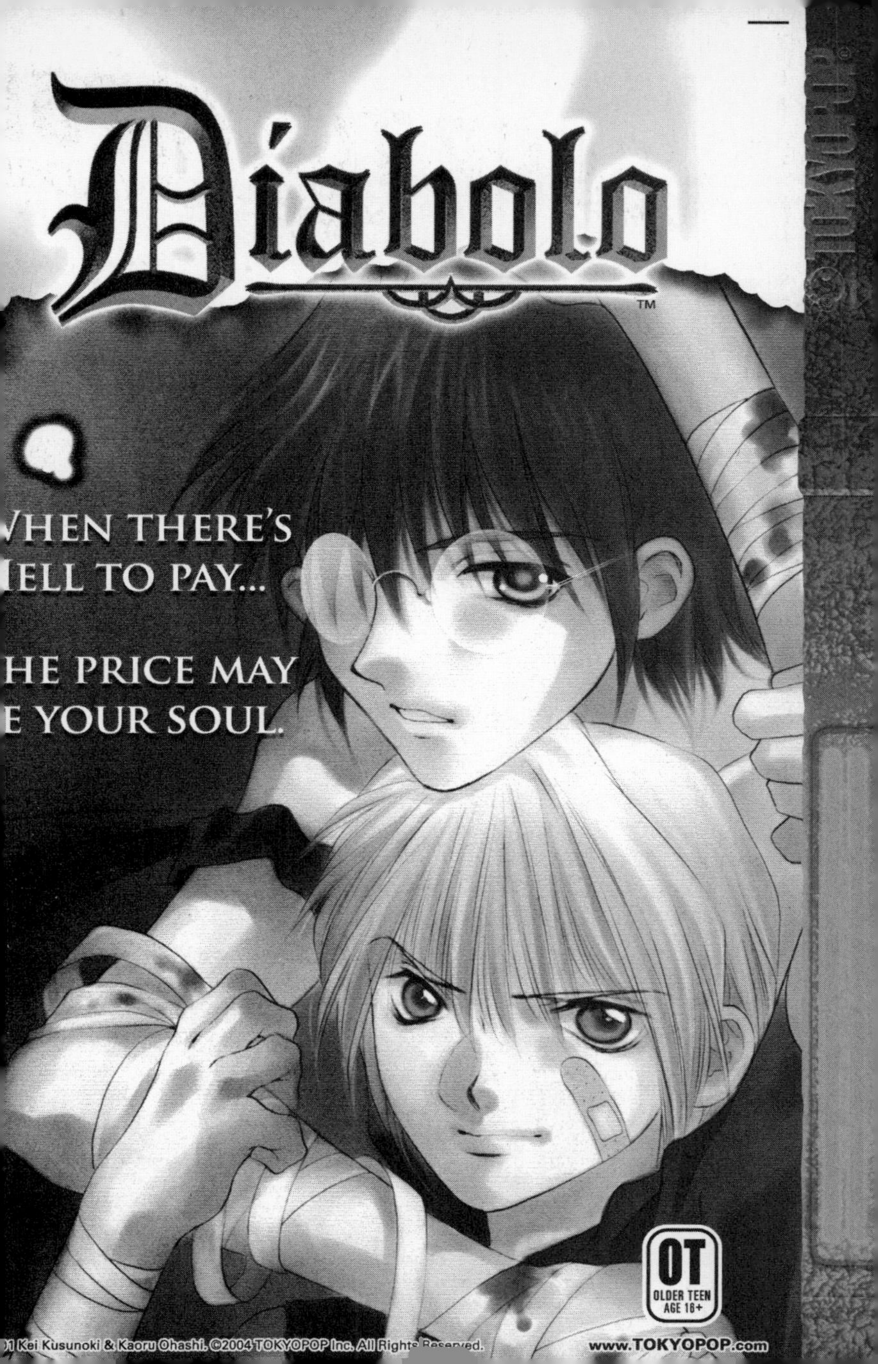
Diabolo™
VHEN THERE'S
IELL TO PAY...
HE PRICE MAY
E YOUR SOUL.
TOKYOPOP
OT
OLDER TEEN
AGE 16+
01 Kei Kusunoki & Kaoru Ohashi. ©2004 TOKYOPOP Inc. All Rights Reserved.
www.TOKYOPOP.com

ALSO AVAILABLE FROM TOKYOPOP

MANGA

ALSO AVAILABLE FROM TOKYOPOP

PLANETES
PRESIDENT DAD
PRIEST
PRINCESS AI
PSYCHIC ACADEMY
QUEEN'S KNIGHT, THE
RAGNAROK
RAVE MASTER
REALITY CHECK
REBIRTH
REBOUND
REMOTE
RISING STARS OF MANGA™, THE
SABER MARIONETTE J
SAILOR MOON
SAINT TAIL
SAIYUKI
SAMURAI DEEPER KYO
SAMURAI GIRL™ REAL BOUT HIGH SCHOOL
SCRYED
SEIKAI TRILOGY, THE
SGT. FROG
SHAOLIN SISTERS
SHIRAHIME-SYO: SNOW GODDESS TALES
SHUTTERBOX
SKULL MAN, THE
SNOW DROP
SORCERER HUNTERS
SOUL TO SEOUL
STONE
SUIKODEN III
SUKI
TAROT CAFÉ, THE
THREADS OF TIME
TOKYO BABYLON
TOKYO MEW MEW
TOKYO TRIBES
TRAMPS LIKE US
UNDER THE GLASS MOON
VAMPIRE GAME
VISION OF ESCAFLOWNE, THE
WARCRAFT
WARRIORS OF TAO
WILD ACT
WISH
WORLD OF HARTZ
X-DAY
ZODIAC P.I.

NOVELS

CLAMP SCHOOL PARANORMAL INVESTIGATORS
SAILOR MOON
SLAYERS

ART BOOKS

ART OF CARDCAPTOR SAKURA
ART OF MAGIC KNIGHT RAYEARTH, THE
PEACH: MIWA UEDA ILLUSTRATIONS
CLAMP NORTH SIDE
CLAMP SOUTH SIDE

ANIME GUIDES

COWBOY BEBOP
GUNDAM TECHNICAL MANUALS
SAILOR MOON SCOUT GUIDES

TOKYOPOP KIDS

STRAY SHEEP

CINE-MANGA®

ALADDIN
CARDCAPTORS
DUEL MASTERS
FAIRLY ODDPARENTS, THE
FAMILY GUY
FINDING NEMO
G.I. JOE SPY TROOPS
GREATEST STARS OF THE NBA
JACKIE CHAN ADVENTURES
JIMMY NEUTRON: BOY GENIUS, THE ADVENTURES OF
KIM POSSIBLE
LILO & STITCH: THE SERIES
LIZZIE MCGUIRE
LIZZIE MCGUIRE MOVIE, THE
MALCOLM IN THE MIDDLE
POWER RANGERS: DINO THUNDER
POWER RANGERS: NINJA STORM
PRINCESS DIARIES 2, THE
RAVE MASTER
SHREK 2
SIMPLE LIFE, THE
SPONGEBOB SQUAREPANTS
SPY KIDS 2
SPY KIDS 3-D: GAME OVER
TEENAGE MUTANT NINJA TURTLES
THAT'S SO RAVEN
TOTALLY SPIES
TRANSFORMERS: ARMADA
TRANSFORMERS: ENERGON

You want it? We got it!
A full range of TOKYOPOP
products are available **now** at:
www.TOKYOPOP.com/shop

10.19.04T

LEGAL DRUG ™

When no ordinary prescription will do...

FROM CLAMP CREATORS OF CHOBITS & TOKYO BABYLON

OT
OLDER TEEN
AGE 16+

www.TOKYOPOP.com

TOKYOPOP ®